Systems Approach to

Computer-Integrated Design and Manufacturing

In memory of my parents
Chaudhary Ram Chandra and Shrimati Bhagwati Devi

Systems Approach to Computer-Integrated Design and Manufacturing

Nanua Singh
Department of Industrial and Manufacturing Engineering
Wayne State University

John Wiley & Sons, Inc.
New York • Chichester • Brisbane • Toronto • Singapore

ACQUISITIONS EDITOR Charity Robey
MARKETING MANAGER Susan Elbe
PRODUCTION EDITOR Christopher Curioli/Ken Santor
DESIGNER Harry Nolan
MANUFACTURING MANAGER Mark Cirillo
ILLUSTRATION Jamie Perea
COVER ILLUSTRATION BY: © Marjory Dressler Photographics

Recognizing the importance of preserving what has been written, it is a policy of John Wiley & Sons, Inc. to have books of enduring value published in the United States printed on acid-free paper, and we exert our best efforts to that end.

The paper in this book was manufactured by a mill whose forest management programs include sustained yield harvesting of its timberlands. Sustained yield harvesting principles ensure that the number of trees cut each year does not exceed the amount of new growth.

Library of Congress Cataloging in Publication Data:
Singh, Nanua.
Systems approach to computer-integrated design and manufacturing/Nanua Singh.

p. cm.
Includes bibliographical references.
ISBN 0-471-58517-3 (cloth)
1. Computer integrated manufacturing systems. 2. CAD/CAM systems.
I. Title.

TS155.63.S56 1996
670'.285--dc20

94-40012
CIP

10 9 8 7 6 5 4

PREFACE

The twenty-first century business environment will be characterized by expanding global competition and an increasing variety of products with low demand. In the coming years, we are going to witness an era of mass customization of products. To survive in such a competitive environment, not only do we have to evolve efficient manufacturing processes and technologies, we also have to bring people into the picture. People have to be trained in the latest technologies and processes in the areas of design, manufacturing, and, most important, the tools of integration.

The objective of this book is to provide up-to-date coverage of topics in computer-integrated design and manufacturing. In this book, a systems approach to computer-integrated design and manufacturing is followed. This requires a thorough understanding of its various elements and their interactions for developing integrated systems. Accordingly, we discuss computer-aided design (Chapters 2 and 3), concurrent engineering (Chapter 4), computer-aided process planning (Chapter 5), control of manufacturing systems (Chapter 6), automated material-handling and storage systems (Chapter 7), robotics (Chapter 8), quality engineering, statistical process control, and automated inspection systems (Chapter 9), manufacturing planning and control (Chapter 10), just-in-time manufacturing systems (Chapter 11), group technology and cellular manufacturing systems (Chapter 12), and flexible manufacturing systems (Chapter 13). Integration tools such as computer communications, database management systems, and groupware are discussed in Chapter 14. This final chapter provides a framework for enterprise-wide integration, which requires understanding of all the technologies and processes discussed in Chapters 2 through 13.

The text is directed toward senior undergraduate and first-year graduate students from the departments of industrial, manufacturing, and mechanical engineering, as well as corresponding graduate programs in Engineering Technology. Given the coverage of topics in the book, two courses can easily be carved out. One could be a CAD/CAM course with an emphasis on CAD and CAM. The other course could be in computer-integrated manufacturing with an emphasis on advanced manufacturing systems and enterprise integration, such as JIT manufacturing, cellular manufacturing, flexible manufacturing, and enterprise-wide integration. Given the coverage of topics, instructors will have enough flexibility with this text to develop a course that meets the undergraduate or graduate requirements in computer-integrated design and manufacturing.

This book has a number of unique features. Besides traditional topics in CAD/CAM, detailed discussions of current topics such as concurrent engineering, just-in-time manufacturing, cellular manufacturing, flexible manufacturing, automated guided vehicles, automated storage and retrieval systems, and enterprise-wide integration are provided. The book provides a quantitative analysis of computer-integrated design and manufacturing systems. Accordingly, a large number of solved examples are included to illustrate the concepts presented. The latest references and a good number of problems are included at the end of each chapter. A solution manual is available to instructors and can be obtained from the publisher.

This book will also be useful to practicing engineers and managers from a variety of fields who wish to understand modern engineering design and manufacturing concepts through solved examples and illustrations. The book has gone through thorough classroom testing in several courses. During this process, a large number of students have contributed to the book in many ways. Yuan Li, Pramodh Narayan, and Parveen S. Goel deserve special mention. The book has gone through an exhaustive review process by colleagues. I am grateful to a number of professors whose comments and suggestions at various stages of this project were very helpful in reshaping the final version of the text. They include Gary L. Kinzel (Ohio State University), Behrokh Khoshnevis (University of Southern California), Andrew Kusiak (University of Iowa), Stanley B. Hopkins (New England Institute of Technology), S. Balakrishnan and D. Rajamani (University of Manitoba), Winston Knight (University of Rhode Island), C. Srikandarajah (University of Toronto), Donald R. Falkenburg, O.O. Mejabi and M.E. Ssemakula (Wayne State University), Michael P. Deisenroth (Virginia Polytechnic Institute and State University), and R. Du (University of Windsor). I express my sincere thanks to Jack C. H. Chung (Structural Dynamics Research Corporation) for constructive comments.

A number of companies and societies have contributed by providing updated information and photographs of their products and technologies. These include Giddings & Lewis, Ford Motor Company, Rapistan Demag Corporation, ABB Robotics, Hewlett Packard, Cincinnati Milacron, ASME, ASE Industries, ACCU-SORT Systems, Intergraph Corporation, IBM Corporation, and Burson-Marsteller.

I am also indebted to Charity Robey and Sean M. Culhane of John Wiley & Sons for requesting me to write this book. I appreciate their patience and tolerance during the preparation of the manuscript.

Finally, I would like to express my appreciation to my wife Bati, son Ravi, and daughter Sheenoo for their understanding and encouragement during many days and years that I spent on this book.

Nanua Singh

August 1995

CONTENTS

CHAPTER 1 / INTRODUCTION TO COMPUTER-INTEGRATED DESIGN AND MANUFACTURING SYSTEMS 1

1.1 An Overview of a Manufacturing Enterprise 1
1.2 Design and Manufacturing: A Historical Perspective 3
1.2.1 Design 3
1.2.2 Manufacturing 5
1.3 Systems Approach to Computer-Integrated Design and Manufacturing 8
1.4 Organization of the Book 10
1.5 Summary 14
References and Suggested Readings 14

CHAPTER 2 / COMPUTER-AIDED DESIGN: Design Process, CAD Hardware, Computer Graphics, and Transformations 17

2.1 The Product Design Process 17
2.1.1 Problem Identification 18
2.1.2 Preliminary Ideas 19
2.1.3 Refinement Process 19
2.1.4 Analysis Process 19
2.1.5 Decision Process 19
2.1.6 Implementation Process 19
2.2 Computer-Aided Design 19
2.3 A Brief History of CAD 20
2.4 CAD/CAM Systems 20
2.1.4 Mainframe-Based Systems 21

2.4.2 Minicomputer-Based Systems 23
2.4.3 Workstation-Based Systems 23
2.4.4 Microcomputer-Based Systems 23
2.5 CAD System Input–Output Devices 24
2.5.1 Input Devices 24
2.5.2 Output Devices 27
2.6 Selection of CAD/CAM Systems 28
2.6.1 System-Related Issues 28
2.6.2 Geometric Modeling–Related Issues 29
2.6.3 Design Documentation and Applications 29
2.7 Computer Graphics and Transformations 29
2.7.1 Introduction to Geometric Transformations 30
2.7.2 Geometric Transformations 30
2.7.3 Homogeneous Representation 36
2.7.4 Composition of Transformations 37
2.8 Summary 40
Problems 40
References and Suggested Reading 42

CHAPTER 3 / GEOMETRIC MODELING 43

3.1 Introduction to Geometric Modeling 43
3.2 Why is Knowledge of Geometric Modeling Necessary? 44
3.3 Geometric Modeling Approaches 45
3.4 Wireframe Modeling 46
3.4.1 Limitations of Wireframe Modeling 46
3.4.2 Wireframe Entities 47
3.4.3 Analytic Curves 49
3.4.4 Representation of Curves 52
3.4.5 Nonparametric Representation of Curves 52
3.4.6 Parametric Representation of Curves 54
3.4.7 Synthetic Curves 56
3.4.8 Parametric Representation of Synthetic Curves 57
3.4.9 Hermite Cubic Spline 59
3.4.10 Bezier Curves 63
3.4.11 B-Spline, Rational B-Spline, and Nonuniform Rational B-Spline Curves 66
3.4.12 Curve Manipulations 66
3.5 Surface Modeling 67

3.5.1 Surface Entities 68
3.5.2 Surface Representations 69
3.6 Solid Modeling 74
3.6.1 Boundary Representation 75
3.6.2 Basic Entities for BREP 75
3.6.3 Validation of BREP Model Using Euler's Law 76
3.6.4 Constructive Solid Geometry 78
3.6.5 Sweep Representation 81
3.6.6 Primitive Instancing Method 81
3.6.7 Cell Decomposition Scheme 81
3.6.8 Analytical Solid Modeling 83
3.6.9 Comparison of Various Solid Modeling Schemes 84
3.7 Parametric and Variational Design 84
3.7.1 Parametric Design 84
3.7.2 Variational Design 86
3.7.3 Comparison of Parametric and Variational Design 87
3.8 Computer-Aided Engineering Analysis 89
3.8.1 Finite-Element Analysis 89
3.8.2 Static, Dynamic, and Natural Frequency Analysis 90
3.8.3 Heat Transfer Analysis 90
3.8.4 Plastic Analysis 90
3.8.5 Fluid Flow Analysis 91
3.8.6 Motion Analysis 92
3.8.7 Tolerance Analysis 92
3.8.8 Design Optimization 93
3.8.9 Commercial Packages to Support Product Modeling and Analysis 93
3.9 CAD/CAM Data Exchange 93
3.9.1 IGES 94
3.9.2 PDES 94
3.9.3 DXF 96
3.10 Summary 96
Problems 96
References and Suggested Reading 100

CHAPTER 4 / CONCURRENT ENGINEERING 103

4.1 What Is Concurrent Engineering? 103
4.2 Sequential Engineering versus Concurrent Engineering 104

4.3 Why Concurrent Engineering? 106
4.4 Mathematical Model for Understanding Interactions Between Design and Manufacturing 108
4.4.1 Material Balance Equations 110
4.4.2 Cost Equation 110
4.4.3 Unit Cost 110
4.4.4 Average Manufacturing Lead Time 111
4.4.5 Pseudomeasure of Product Quality 111
4.5 Serial Engineering versus Concurrent Engineering: An Example 111
4.6 Understanding Benefits of Concurrent Engineering 114
4.6.1 Serial Engineering Approach 115
4.6.2 Concurrent Engineering Approach 115
4.6.3 Improvements in Unit Cost, Quality, and Manufacturing Lead Time 116
4.6.4 Other Benefits 116
4.7 Characterization of the Concurrent Engineering Environment 116
4.7.1 How to Design a Concurrent Engineering Program 117
4.7.2 Concurrent Engineering Environment Influencing Dimensions 117
4.7.3 Major Elements of the Concurrent Engineering Environment 119
4.8 Difficulties Associated with Performing Concurrent Engineering 130
4.8.1 Characteristics of the Design Process 130
4.8.2 Volume and Variety of Life-Cycle Knowledge 130
4.8.3 Separation of Life-Cycle Functions 130
4.9 A Framework for Integration of Life-Cycle Phases in a Concurrent Engineering Environment 130
4.10 Concurrent Engineering Techniques 132
4.10.1 Quality Function Deployment 133
4.11 Summary 142
Problems 143
References and Suggested Reading 145
Appendix: Framework for the Application of CE: A Journal Bearing Assembly Example 147

CHAPTER 5 / COMPUTER-AIDED PROCESS PLANNING 153

5.1 Overview of Manufacturing Processes 153
5.1.1 Turning Operations 153
5.1.2 Drilling Operations 154
5.1.3 Milling Operations 156
5.1.4 Grinding Operations 156

5.2 What Is Process Planning? 158
5.3 Basic Steps in Developing a Process Plan 159
5.3.1 Analysis of Part Requirements 159
5.3.2 Selection of Raw Workpiece 159
5.3.3 Determining Manufacturing Operations and Their Sequences 159
5.3.4 Selection of Machine Tools 161
5.3.5 Selection of Tools, Workholding Devices, and Inspection Equipment 163
5.3.6 Determining Machining Conditions and Manufacturing Times 164
5.4 The Principal Process Planning Approaches 168
5.4.1 The Manual Experience-Based Planning Method 168
5.4.2 The Computer-Aided Process Planning Method 169
5.5 Variant and Generative Process Planning Systems 178
5.6 Feature Recognition in Computer-Aided Process Planning 178
5.6.1 A Brief Review of Part Feature Recognition Approaches 179
5.6.2 Graph-Based Approach 179
5.7 Future Trends in Computer-Aided Process Planning 185
5.8 Summary 186
Problems 186
References and Suggested Reading 189

CHAPTER 6 / COMPUTER CONTROL OF MANUFACTURING SYSTEMS 193

6.1 Metal-Cutting Machines 193
6.1.1 Numerically Controlled Machines 194
6.1.2 Programming for NC Machines 196
6.1.3 Motion and Coordinate System Nomenclature for NC Machines 197
6.2 Basics of NC Part Programming 199
6.2.1 Structure of an NC Part Program 200
6.3 Fundamentals of NC Part Programming 204
6.3.1 Preparatory Functions 204
6.3.2 Axis Motion Commands 208
6.3.3 Feed and Speed Commands 209
6.3.4 Identification Commands 209
6.3.5 Miscellaneous Commands 210
6.3.6 Special Characters 211
6.3.7 Advanced Features 216
6.4 Loading the Program 216

6.4.1 Conventional Numerical Control 217
6.4.2 Direct Numerical Control 220
6.4.3 Computer Numerical Control 220
6.4.4 Distributed Numerical Control 221
6.5 Computer-Aided Part Programming 221
6.5.1 APT Language Basics 223
6.5.2 Initialization and Termination 224
6.5.3 Geometry Definition 224
6.5.4 APT Tool Definition and Motion 225
6.5.5 Postprocessor Commands 229
6.5.6 Advanced APT Programming Features 231
6.5.7 Other Part Programming System 232
6.6 CAD/CAM-Based Part Programming 232
6.7 Beyond Postprocessors 234
6.8 Programmable Logic Controllers 235
6.8.1 Logical Control 238
6.8.2 Programming the PLC 240
6.8.3 Counters and Timers 241
6.9 Generalized Process Control 246
6.9.1 Process Interface 246
6.9.2 Data Communication 247
6.9.3 Local Area Networks 249
6.10 Summary 249
Problems 249
References and Suggested Reading 252

CHAPTER 7 / AUTOMATED MATERIAL-HANDLING AND STORAGE SYSTEMS 257

7.1 What Is a Material-Handling System? 257
7.2 Principles of Material Handling 258
7.3 Material-Handling Equipment 259
7.4 Automated Guided Vehicle Systems 259
7.4.1 The Components of an AGVS 260
7.4.2 The Types of AGVSs 260
7.4.3 AGVS Guidance Systems 266
7.4.4 AGVS Steering Control 267
7.4.5 AGVS Routing 267

7.4.6 AGVS Control Systems 269
7.4.7 Interface with Other Subsystems 270
7.4.8 AGVS Load Transfer 270
7.4.9 AGVS Design Features 271
7.4.10 System Design of Automated Guided Vehicle Systems 271
7.4.11 Advantages of AGVSs Over Other Material-Handling Systems 275
7.4.12 Applications of AGVSs 277
7.5 Automated Storage and Retrieval Systems 277
7.5.1 Functions of Storage Systems and Definition of AS/RS 277
7.5.2 AS/RS Components and Terminology Used 278
7.5.3 Why an AS/RS? 279
7.5.4 Types of AS/RS 280
7.5.5 Design of an AS/RS 282
7.6 A Distributed Computer Control Architecture for AGVSs and AS/RSs 291
7.7 Conveyors 292
7.8 Summary 297
Problems 297
References and Suggested Reading 299

CHAPTER 8 / ROBOTIC SYSTEMS 303

8.1 What is an Industrial Robot? 303
8.2 Fundamentals of Robotics and Robotics Technology 305
8.2.1 Power Sources for Robots 305
8.2.2 Robotic Sensors 306
8.2.3 The Hand of a Robot: End-Effector 307
8.2.4 Robot Movement and Precision 307
8.3 The Robotic Joints 310
8.3.1 The Joint Notation 311
8.4 Robot Classification and Robot Reach 314
8.4.1 Classification Based on Physical Configuration 314
8.4.2 Classification Based on Control Systems 315
8.4.3 Robot Reach 317
8.5 Robot Motion Analysis: Forward and Backward Kinematic Transformation 317
8.5.1 Forward Kinetic Transformation 318
8.5.2 Backward Kinematic Transformation 321
8.5.3 Basic Homogeneous Transformations 325
8.6 Robot Programming and Languages 329

8.6.1 Programming Languages 330
8.7 Robot Selection 335
8.8 Robot Applications 338
8.8.1 A Single-Machine Robotic Cell Application 338
8.8.2 A Single-Machine Cell with a Double-Gripper Robot 339
8.8.3 Multimachine Robotic Cell Applications 340
8.8.4 Welding 340
8.8.5 Spray Painting 341
8.8.6 Assembly 341
8.8.7 Other Applications 342
8.9 Economic Justification of Robots 344
8.9.1 Payback Period Model 344
8.10 Summary 345
Problems 345
References and Suggested Reading 348

CHAPTER 9 / QUALITY ENGINEERING, STATISTICAL PROCESS CONTROL, AND AUTOMATED INSPECTION SYSTEMS 349

9.1 Understanding the Meaning of Quality 349
9.2 The Dimensions of Quality 350
9.3 Quality Costs 350
9.3.1 Prevention Costs 351
9.3.2 Appraisal Costs 351
9.3.3 Internal Failure Costs 351
9.3.4 External Failure Costs 351
9.4 A Framework for Quality Improvement 352
9.4.1 Designing Quality into Products and Processes 353
9.4.2 Robust Design of Products and Processes 358
9.4.3 A Case Study to Illustrate the Taguchi Approach to Parameter Design 363
9.5 Failure Mode and Effect Analysis 368
9.6 Improving Product Quality During the Production Phase 372
9.6.1 Histogram 373
9.6.2 Check Sheet 373
9.6.3 Pareto Chart 374
9.6.4 Cause-and-Effect Diagram 374
9.6.5 Defect Concentration Diagram 375

9.6.6 Scatter Diagram 375
9.6.7 Control Chart 375
9.7 Automated Inspection 379
9.7.1 On-Line/In-Process and On-Line/Postprocess Inspection Methods 379
9.7.2 Off-Line Inspection Methods 379
9.8 Summary 383
Problems 384
References and Suggested Readings 391
Appendix A 392
Appendix B 394

CHAPTER 10 / MANUFACTURING PLANNING AND CONTROL SYSTEMS 397

10.1 A Basic Framework for a Manufacturing Planning and Control System 397
10.2 Demand Management 400
10.2.1 Demand Forecasting 400
10.3 Aggregate Production Planning 403
10.3.1 A Mathematical Programming Model 405
10.4 Master Production Schedule 407
10.5 Rough-Cut Capacity Planning 407
10.6 Material Requirements Planning 408
10.6.1 Product Structure and Bill of Materials 408
10.6.2 Independent versus Dependent Demand 409
10.6.3 Parts Explosion 409
10.6.4 Gross Requirements of Component Items 409
10.6.5 Common-Use Items 410
10.6.6 On-Hand Inventory, Scheduled Receipts, and Net Requirements 410
10.6.7 Planned Order Reseases 410
10.6.8 Lead Time and Lead Time Offsetting 411
10.7 MRP Lot-Sizing Problem 412
10.7.1 Solution Algorithms 413
10.8 Capacity Planning 417
10.9 Order Release 417
10.10 Shop-Floor Control 418
10.10.1 Bar Code Systems for Shop-Floor Control 418
10.10.2 Operations Scheduling 423
10.10.3 Job Sequencing and Priority Rules 425

10.10.4 Comparison of Various Scheduling Rules 427
10.11 Summary 429
Problems 430
References and Suggested Reading 432
Appendix A 433

CHAPTER 11 / JUST-IN-TIME MANUFACTURING SYSTEMS 435

11.1 Toyota Production System: An Overview 435
11.1.1 Components of the Toyota Production System 436
11.1.2 Three Ms: Muda (Waste), Mura (Unevenness), and Muri (Overburden) 436
11.2 Pull versus Push System 438
11.3 Types of Kanbans 440
11.3.1 Withdrawal (or Conveyance) Kanban 440
11.3.2 Production Kanban 441
11.3.3 Flow of Withdrawal and Production Kanbans and Their Interactions 441
11.3.4 Preconditions (Rules) for Operating Kanban 442
11.4 Kanban Planning and Control Models 443
11.4.1 Determining the Number of Kanbans: A Deterministic Model 443
11.4.2 A Probabilistic Cost Model for Determining Optimal Number of Kanbans 447
11.4.3 Relationship between JIT Manufacturing, Setup Time, and Cost 449
11.5 Signal Kanban 450
11.5.1 Integer Programming Model for Determining Signal Kanbans 453
11.6 Other Types of Kanbans 455
11.6.1 Express Kanban 455
11.6.2 Emergency Kanban 456
11.6.3 Through Kanban 456
11.7 Level Schedules for Mixed-Model Assembly Lines 456
11.7.1 A Mathematical Model to Obtain Level Schedules 456
11.8 Alternative JIT systems 460
11.8.1 Periodic Pull System 460
11.8.2 Constant Work-in-Process System 460
11.8.3 Long Pull System 460
11.9 Just-in-Time Purchasing 461
11.9.1 Major Purchasing Activities 461

11.10 Total Quality Control and JIT 463
11.10.1 TQC Responsibilities 463
11.10.2 Principles of Quality 464
11.10.3 Quality Culture 464
11.11 Barriers to JIT Implementation 465
11.12 Potential Benefits of JIT Implementation 465
11.13 Summary 466
Problems 466
References and Suggested Reading 468
Appendix A Procedure for Determining the pmf for Number of Kanbans 471
Appendix B The Set of Constraints and Objective Function for Example 11.5 475

CHAPTER 12 / GROUP TECHNOLOGY AND CELLULAR MANUFACTURING SYSTEMS 477

12.1 What is Group Technology 477
12.2 Design Attributes and Manufacturing Features 478
12.3 GT Implementation 478
12.3.1 Visual Inspection Method 478
12.3.2 Coding Methods 480
12.3.3 The OPITZ Classification System 482
12.4 Part Family Formation: Classification and Coding System 486
12.5 Selection of Classification and Coding Systems 486
12.6 Benefits of Group Technology 487
12.7 What Is Cellular Manufacturing? 488
12.7.1 Design of Cellular Manufacturing Systems 488
12.8 Cell Formation Approaches 490
12.8.1 Machine–Component Group Analysis 490
12.8.2 Similarity Coefficient–Based Approaches 493
12.8.3 Exceptional Parts and Bottleneck Machines 496
12.8.4 Evaluation of Cell Designs 496
12.8.5 An Alternative Approach to Evaluating Goodness of Heuristic Solutions 498
12.8.6 Mathematical Programming Models 500
12.9 Economics of Group Tooling in Cellular Manufacturing 506
12.9.1 Conventional Tooling Method 506
12.9.2 Group Tooling Method 506

12.10 Production Planning and Control in Cellular Manufacturing Systems 506

12.10.1 An Integrated GT and MRP framework 507

12.10.2 Operations Allocation in a Cell with Negligible Setup Time 511

12.11 Summary 514

Problems 515

References and Suggested Reading 519

Appendix A: The Integer Programming Formulation for Example 13.7 in LINDO Format 522

Appendix B: Linear Programming Formulation of Example 12.12 524

Appendix C: Syntactic Pattern Recognition Approach to Allocation of New Parts to Existing Part Families and Cells 525

CHAPTER 13 / FLEXIBLE MANUFACTURING SYSTEMS 529

13.1 Flexibility 529

13.1.1 Machine Flexibility 530

13.1.2 Routing Flexibility 530

13.1.3 Process Flexibility 531

13.1.4 Product Flexibility 531

13.1.5 Production Flexibility 531

13.1.6 Expansion Flexibility 531

13.2 Volume–Variety Relationships for Understanding Production Systems 532

13.2.1 High-Volume, Low-Variety (H–L) Production System 532

13.2.2 Low-Volume, High-Variety (L–H) Production System 533

13.2.3 Mid-Volume, Mid-Variety (M–M) Production Systems 533

13.3 Key Characteristics of Various Manufacturing Systems 534

13.4 What Is an FMS? 535

13.5 Basic Features of Physical Components of an FMS 538

13.5.1 Numerical Control Machine Tools 538

13.5.2 Workholding and Tooling Considerations 540

13.5.3 Material-Handling Equipment 541

13.5.4 Inspection Equipment 542

13.5.5 Other Components 542

13.6 Basic Features of Control Components of an FMS 542

13.6.1 Work-Order Processing and Part Control System 543

13.6.2 Machine-Tool Control System 543

13.6.3 Tool Management and Control System 544

13.6.4 Traffic Management Control System 544

13.6.5 Quality Control Management System 544

13.6.6 Maintenance Control System 544
13.6.7 Management Control System 544
13.6.8 Interfacing of These Subsystems with the Central Computer 544
13.7 Operational Problems in FMS 545
13.7.1 Part Type Selection and Tool Management Problems 545
13.7.2 Fixture and Pallet Selection Problem 551
13.7.3 Machine Grouping and Loading Problems 552
13.8 Layout Considerations 552
13.8.1 Linear Single- and Double-Row Machine Layout 553
13.8.2 Circular Machine Layout 553
13.8.3 Cluster Machine Layout 553
13.8.4 Loop Layout 553
13.8.5 A Model for the Single-Row Machine Layout Problem 553
13.8.6 Heuristic Algorithm for Circular and Linear Single-Row Machine Layouts 555
13.9 Sequencing of Robot Moves in Robotic Cells 558
13.9.1 Sequencing of Robot Moves in a Two-Machine Robotic Cell 558
13.9.2 Algorithm 560
13.10 Simulation Modeling 560
13.10.1 The Elements of Discrete Simulation 562
13.10.2 Basic Steps in Developing and Using a Simulation Model 563
13.10.3 A Simulation Case Study of an FMS Cell 564
13.11 FMS Benefits 566
13.11.1 Responsiveness to Short-Term Problems 566
13.11.2 Responsiveness to Long-Term Problems 567
13.12 Summary 567
Problems 568
References and Suggested Reading 570
Appendix A: Problem Formulation for Examples 13.1 and 13.2 572
Appendix B: Sequencing of Robot Moves in a Three-Machine Robotic Cell 573

CHAPTER 14 / ENTERPRISE INTEGRATION, CIM, AND FUTURE TRENDS 577

14.1 Introduction to CIM and Enterprise-Wide Integration 577
14.2 Network Communications 580
14.2.1 Selection of Network Technology 581
14.2.2 Network Architectures and Protocols 586

14.2.3 Network Interconnection and Devices 589
14.2.4 Network Performance 593
14.3 Database Management Systems 597
14.3.1 Data Models 598
14.3.2 Designing a System Using the Object-Oriented Paradigm 608
14.3.3 Database Size Calculation 609
14.4 Database Linkages 611
14.4.1 Level 0: Isolation 612
14.4.2 Level 1: Converters 612
14.4.3 Level 2: Neutral File Formal 612
14.4.4 Level 3: A Centralized Database 615
14.4.5 Level 4: Integration of Stand-Alone Components 615
14.5 Group Work in Enterprises 615
14.5.1 A Case Study of Groupware Systems 617
14.6 Framework for Enterprise-Wide Integration 620
14.6.1 Integration Concepts 620
14.6.2 Integration Architectures 622
14.7 Realizing CIM 623
14.7.1 An Illustration of Integration Concepts 624
14.7.2 A Case Study of CIM 625
14.8 Future Trends in Manufacturing Systems: Agile Manufacturing 630
14.8.1 Unlearning of Currently Held Truths 631
14.9 Summary 631
Problems 631
References and Suggested Reading 633

Appendix/Cumulative Standard Normal Distribution 635

CHAPTER 1

INTRODUCTION TO COMPUTER-INTEGRATED DESIGN AND MANUFACTURING SYSTEMS

1.1 AN OVERVIEW OF A MANUFACTURING ENTERPRISE

For most enterprises, the long-term goal is to stay in business, grow, and make a profit. This is particularly true of manufacturing enterprises, which must understand the dynamic changes that are taking place in the business environment. The twenty-first century business environment can be characterized by expanding global competition and products of increasing variety and lower demand. The globalization of economic activity has brought about a sea change in the attitudes of customers. Customer individualism is certain to become the central theme of business. What we are going to witness is an era of mass customization. This means manufacturing products for the mass market in such a way that products are customized for each individual in that market. Recall that in the 1970s, the cost of products was the main lever for obtaining competitive advantage. Later in the 1980s, quality superseded cost and became an important competitive dimension. Now low unit cost and high quality of products no longer solely define competitive advantage. Today, the customer takes both minimum cost and high quality for granted. Factors such as delivery performance and customization and environmental issues such as waste generation are assuming a predominant role in defining the success of organizations in terms of increased market share and profitability. The question is, what can we do under these changing circumstances to stay in business and retain competitive advantages?

As a first step what is needed is the development of the right business strategy to meet the challenges of present and future markets. In doing so, a manufacturing organization has not only to understand what customers want but also to develop internal mechanisms to respond instantly to the changes demanded by customers. This requires a paradigm shift in everything our factories do. They must not only make use of state-of-the-art technologies and concepts but also think in the reverse direction (Davidow and Malone, 1992). ''Reverse direction'' means building products that realize customer expectations. That is, when an organization is deciding about business plans, it has to address several questions. Will the customer find any change in what one does as a result of using this? Will the customer be able to define any benefit? From the customer's point of view, a company has to respond to smaller and smaller market niches quickly with standardized products that will be built in lower and lower volume. In other words, we can say that a future successful manufacturing organization will be a virtual corporation that is instantaneously responsive to customer needs. This view has been shared by an industry-led consortium on twenty-first century manufacturing enterprise strategy (Goldman and Preiss, 1991).

The next step is to determine the right kind of resources to support the business strategy. This requires the right choice of people, technology, and business processes. What is further needed is a marriage of corporate strategies, technology, people, and business processes with a view to evolving policies so that all the functional organs of an organization (finance, sales and marketing, product engineering, manufacturing, and human resources) work in a synchronized manner to achieve corporate objectives. The obvious question then is, how should a manufacturing enterprise work?

We know that all the functional organs of a manufacturing enterprise, such as finance, sales and marketing, design and manufacturing, and human resources, continually receive feedback about products, product attributes, and market segments. Figure 1.1 shows how customers play a pivotal role in defining the manufacturing enterprise. Corporate objectives such as growth in market share, profitability, work force stability, and other financial measures essentially emanate from the understanding of the marketplace. For example, marketing identifies a range of products, product market segments, and new product ideas to satisfy customer needs. Can a company deliver the kinds of products needed to satisfy order-winning criteria such as cost, quality, lead time, and so on? The answer to this question lies with design and manufacturing, which explore various product design and manufacturing process options as well as assess infrastructure to see if they can satisfy the order-winning criteria. Obviously, the human resources, technology, finance, and business processes in the company play a

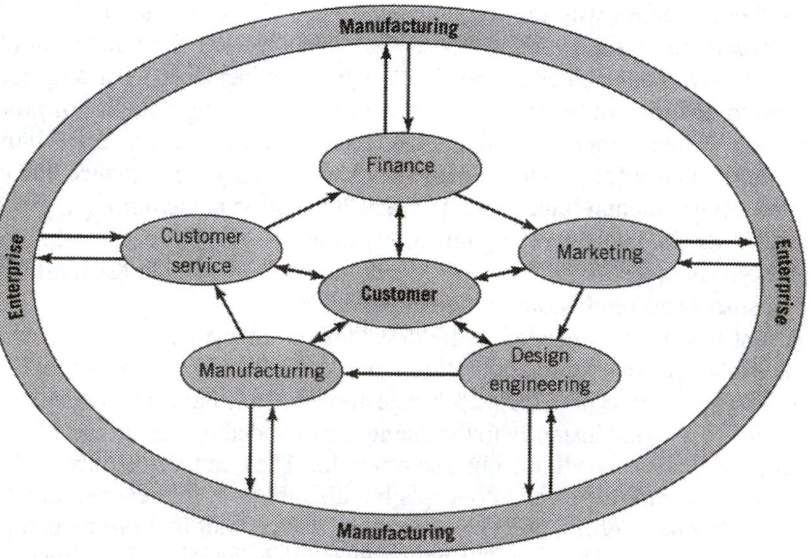

FIGURE 1.1 Customer and manufacturing enterprise.

major role in answering this question and their interaction with manufacturing is very important. Accordingly, the manufacturing strategy should evolve from collaborative decision making that satisfies the requirements of finance, sales and marketing, design and manufacturing, and human resources. Collaborative decision making is a way to achieve congruence between the corporate objectives, marketing goals, and manufacturing capabilities of a manufacturing enterprise. This process may lead to revised corporate objectives and marketing goals. What eventually emerges from this process will be an implementable product design and manufacturing plan. This plan will satisfy order-winning criteria considering the requirements of business segments represented by marketing, finance, strategic planning, human resources, and manufacturing management. A design and manufacturing plan is built considering such aspects as product and process definition, manufacturing planning and control, and factory automation. Integration of a complete enterprise would facilitate successful implementation of these plans in realizing the corporate goals. Information resource management, communications, and a common database are required for the integration of a complete enterprise.

As discussed earlier in this section, mass customization with high delivery performance, high quality, low cost, and environmentally conscious products is required for a manufacturing organization to remain successful in the twenty-first century. To support such a virtual organization for discrete products manufacturing, a thorough understanding of the concepts and technologies for the design and manufacturing of products is necessary. Although the understanding of functional areas such as marketing, finance, and personnel is also important for the successful operation of a manufacturing enterprise, the scope of this book is limited to two major functional areas: design and manufacturing. Accordingly, this book provides a systems approach to understanding the concepts and technologies in computer-integrated design and manufacturing systems. In later chapters we will discuss computer-aided design (CAD), concurrent engineering (CE), computer-aided process planning (CAPP), computer-aided manufacturing (CAM), quality engineering, automated material handling, robotics, manufacturing planning and control, cellular manufacturing, just-in-time manufacturing (JIT), flexible manufacturing systems (FMSs), and enterprise integration. Before starting our journey of understanding of these concepts and technologies, let us have a look at the recent past; it will be beneficial in placing and judging things in the right perspective.

1.2 DESIGN AND MANUFACTURING: A HISTORICAL PERSPECTIVE

1.2.1 Design

Design and manufacturing are the core activities for realizing a marketable and profitable product. A number of evolutionary changes have taken place over the past couple of decades in the areas of both design and manufacturing. First we explore the developments in what is called CAD. The major focus in CAD technology development has been on advancing representation completeness. Figure 1.2 shows the evolution of mechanical CAD/CAM systems over the past three decades (Saxena and Irani, 1994). First there was the development of a two-dimensional (2D) drafting system in the 1960s. Then the extension of 2D drafting systems to three-dimensional (3D) models led to the development of wireframe-based modeling systems. However, it was not

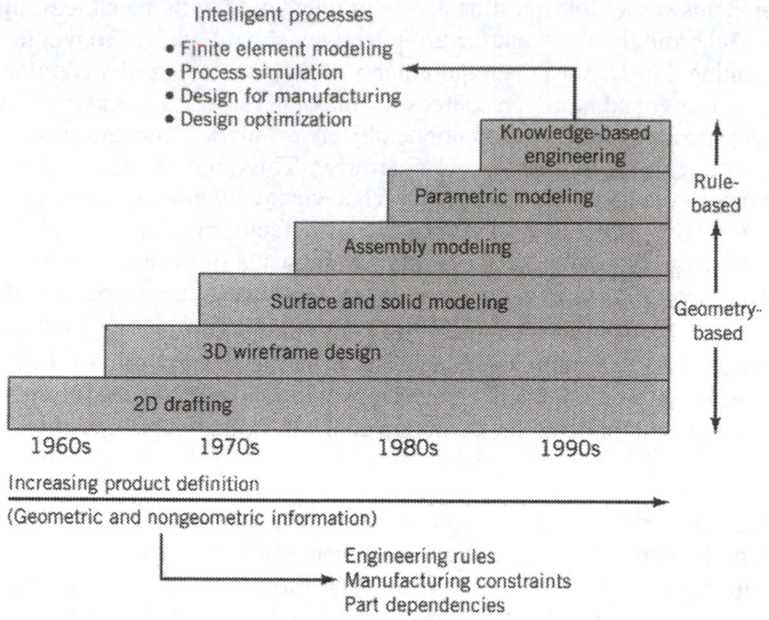

FIGURE 1.2 The evolution of mechanical CAD/CAM systems. (Reproduced from Saxena and Irani (1994) with permission from Academic Press, U.K.)

possible to represent higher-order geometry data such as surface data. To bridge this gap, surface-based models were developed in the early 1970s. Even though the surface models provided some higher-level information, such as surface data for boundary representation, this was still not sufficient to represent solid or volume enclosure information. The need for solid modeling intensified with the development of application programs such as numerical control (NC) verification codes and automation mesh generation. A volume representation of the part is needed for performing topological validity checks. The solid modeling technology has evolved only since the mid-1970s. A large number of comprehensive software products are now available that enable integration of geometric modeling with design analysis and computer-aided manufacturing. These software products include Pro/Engineer from Parametric Technology Corporation, IDEAS from SDRC, Unigraphics from Electronic Data Systems, and MES from Intergraph Corporation, among many others.

The solid modeling schemes provide mechanisms for defining informationally complete models. However, these schemes have an inherent weakness because they provide a low-level representation of parts. That means that to model a part, the designer has to provide model description in terms of geometric and topological entities that constitute the model. For example, for a boundary representation of a part model, the designer has to specify curves and surfaces and their corresponding edges and faces or a Boolean combination of primitives for a constructive solid geometry (CSG)–based representation. For example, a solid model of a rotating shaft with one key stores information in terms of only edges and faces. Further developments in parametric modeling (Chung and Schussi, 1990) provide scope for a higher level of representation of model. Details of parametric and variational design are given in Chapter 3. These models provide only a higher level of abstraction of the underlying geometry and fail to capture the methodology used to design, configure, and assemble products (Saxena and Irani, 1994).

The latest evolutionary development in the CAD/CAM industry has been knowledge-based engineering systems that can capture both geometric and nongeometric product information, such as engineering rules, part dependences, and manufacturing constraints, resulting in more informationally complete product definitions (Nielsen et al., 1987; Irani and Saxena, 1993; Saxena and Irani, 1993, 1994). The commercial knowledge-based system known as Intelligent-CAD (ICAD) is available from ICAD, Cambridge, Massachusetts. Because ICAD is based on the principles of object-oriented modeling technology, it provides a development environment with powerful geometric and artificial intelligence (AI)–based tools.

1.2.2 Manufacturing

Manufacturing is not just the transformation of raw materials into value-added outputs meeting specifications. It has a much broader meaning. The CAM-I definition of manufacturing essentially captures this broad meaning:

> *Manufacturing is a series of interrelated activities and operations involving design, material selection, planning, production, quality assurance, management, and marketing of discrete consumer and durable goods.*

This definition of manufacturing lays a foundation for the need for systems thinking. That means that, given the complexities involved in manufacturing because of the large number of interrelated activities, there is need for coordinated efforts from every organ of an organization. Furthermore, for a manufacturing organization to remain competitive, it must deliver products to customers at the minimum possible cost, the best possible quality, and the minimum lead time starting from the product conception stage to final delivery, service, and disposal. This implies the notion of the product life-cycle approach to design and manufacturing. To accomplish these objectives, a high level of integration is required among all these activities.

Present-day manufacturing activities may be classified in two broad categories: continuous-process and discrete-product production. The focus of this book is on discrete-product manufacturing systems. To satisfy the order-winning criteria of low cost, high quality, and quick delivery response in a discrete-product manufacturing environment requires the combination of the attributes of mass production with those of a job shop. It is important to realize that systems based on the job-shop concept have high product flexibility. That is, these systems are capable of making a variety of parts with ease but overall productivity tends to be low. On the other hand, mass production systems are dedicated to one type of product, which makes them much less flexible, but their level of productivity is much higher than that of comparable job shops. To address the problem of low productivity while retaining high levels of flexibility, new types of systems have been developed. These are called flexible manufacturing systems. FMSs rely heavily on computer-controlled equipment such as computer numerical control (CNC) equipment, automated guided vehicles (AGVs), and robots. They are developed on the basis of group technology concepts making use of similarities in design attributes and manufacturing features. We will introduce some of these concepts later in this chapter, and they are discussed in detail in later chapters. Before that, let us quickly review the stages of developments in the field of manufacturing technology.

For all the advances in manufacturing we are indebted to our ancestors who developed the steam engine, water mills, wind mills, iron furnaces, and other innovations. The concept of division of labor, introduced by Adam Smith in 1776, had a profound influence on the creation of the factory system and on productivity improvement. Development of flow line assembly systems for engines by Henry Ford in 1913 was a giant step toward integrated manufacturing. This led to the realization of reduced labor and increased production rate. Frederick Taylor introduced the scientific approach to many such ideas. Other production specialists in the scientific management movement, such as Frank B. Gilbreth and Henry L. Gantt, made especially significant contributions. Gilbreth's primary contribution was the identification, analysis, and measurement of fundamental motions involved in performing work. Gantt devised the so-called *Gantt chart,* which provides a systematic graphical procedure for preplanning and scheduling work activities, reviewing progress, and schedule updating. The Great Depression of 1929 forced everyone to think in a new direction requiring employee motivation and satisfaction, which led to the development of the idea of job enrichment and enlargement.

In the area of machines, G. C. Devol developed a controller device in 1946 that could record electrical signals magnetically and play them back to operate a mechanical machine (U.S. patent issued in 1952). A number of interesting developments since then in the areas of numerically controlled machine tools, robotics, material-handling systems, and computer control systems have led to the current state of automated manufacturing technology, such as flexible manufacturing systems. We provide a brief historical perspective on each of these.

1.2.2.1 Numerically Controlled Machines

The first successful numerically controlled machine was demonstrated at the Massachusetts Institute of Technology (MIT) under a subcontract from Parsons Corporation of Traverse City, Michigan, funded by the U.S. Air Force in the 1950s. Automatic tool changers and indexing worktables were added in the 1960s. During this period the concept of direct numerically controlled (DNC) systems, in which several NC machines are linked to a main computer, was developed. Control system development in 1971 was the next milestone and led to the introduction of microcomputer-controlled NC machines, also called CNC machines. The major advantage of CNC was the ability to store many part programs in memory, in addition to communicating with other controllers or a central computer. The advantages of CNC and DNC were combined in other systems that are also known as DNC, but here DNC stands for distributed numerically controlled. In such DNC systems several CNC machines are linked to a main host computer. In the 1980s CNC machines were further developed by making them capable of carrying hundreds of tools, having multiple spindles, and controlling movements in up to six axes. These capabilities, coupled with developments in computer communications technology, have led to advances in automated manufacturing systems such as computer-integrated manufacturing systems. In a separate chapter we discuss not only NC, CNC, and NC part programming but also programmable logic controllers and computer control.

1.2.2.2 Material-Handling Systems

Material handling is an integral part of any manufacturing system. Manufacturing system performance can be significantly improved by using computer-controlled material flow, which reduces waiting time and work-in-process inventory compared with manual loading and unloading and manual material handling systems. To this end, developments in floor-mounted and overhead roller conveyors, stacker cranes, and automated guided vehicles have contributed substantially to smooth material flow on the factory floor. Through a system of programmable logic controllers, computers, and computer networks, the material handling systems, material storage systems, and machine tools can be integrated to configure an automated manufacturing system to meet customer requirements. This book provides good coverage of automated guided vehicle systems, automated storage and retrieval systems, and conveyor systems.

1.2.2.3 Robotics

The word "ROBOT" was first used to mean "forced labor" in a satirical fantasy play, "Rossum's Universal Robots," written by Karel Capek in 1921. Robotics, along with the technological developments in the areas of microprocessor and numerical control, have advanced the frontiers of automation. The technology for the present generation of robots was developed by Cyril Walter Kenward in 1954 in Britain and G. C. Devol in the United States. The first computer-type robot programming language was developed at Stanford Research Institute (SRI) in 1973 for research called WAVE, followed by the language AL in 1974. The two languages were subsequently developed into the commercial VAL language for Unimation by Victor Scheinman and Bruce Simano. In the 1980s several off-line programming systems were developed. Since then, several types of robots have been built and several robot programming languages have been developed. Robots are being used in industry for applications including painting, welding, material handling, and assembly. Chapter 8 of this volume discusses robotics.

1.2.2.4 Computer Control Systems

Computer control systems have provided a major impetus to automation. The use of mainframe computers in the 1950s and 1960s for planning, scheduling, and controlling batch production became quite commonplace. A number of management information systems and database management systems were developed and used for a variety of functions in companies. Accounting, payroll, shop floor control, and maintenance information systems are a few examples. Factory automation also resulted from advances in local area and wide area networks (LANs and WANs), bar codes, programmable logic controllers (PLCs), and computer controls. Automatic identification technology such as bar code systems, automatic data collection and analysis systems, and real-time transfer of information provided a stimulus to the growth of factory automation. We discuss the bar code systems for shop floor control in Chapter 10 and PLCs and computer control in Chapter 6.

1.2.2.5 Flexible Manufacturing Systems

The technological developments in CNC, DNC, PLC, robotics, AGVs, automated storage and retrieval systems (AS/RSs), automatic tool changers, tool magazines, modular fixturing, local area networks, and associated technologies such as group technology laid foundations for automated manufacturing of a high to medium variety of parts having low to medium levels of demand. This led to the evolution of FMSs in the early 1960s. The Sunstrand Corporation was one of the first to develop such systems to manufacture a variety of aircraft gearbox casings. The system had eight NC machine centers and two multispindle drills linked by a computer-controlled roller conveyor system. Although it did not have the flexibility of current-day FMSs, it was the first system with built-in automated material flow integration. Current systems provide higher levels of flexibility and a high degree of automation. We provide a detailed discussion of FMS technology as well as design, planning, and control issues in FMS in Chapter 13.

1.2.2.6 Other Significant Supporting Technologies

Besides developments in the areas already mentioned, the need for reduced cost and lead time and high quality led to the introduction of quality engineering approaches to product design. Notable among these is the Taguchi method of product design, which introduced the concept of loss function and signal-to-noise ratio for product design. Material requirements planning and manufacturing resource planning, just-in-time manufacturing philosophy, group technology, and cellular manufacturing led to significant changes in the way production is now planned and controlled at the shop floor.

1.3 SYSTEMS APPROACH TO COMPUTER-INTEGRATED DESIGN AND MANUFACTURING

A system can be defined as a collection of components in which individual components are constrained by connecting interrelationships such that the system as a whole fulfills some specific functions in response to varying demands. This suggests a well-known input–output framework for defining systems. In the case of manufacturing systems, the inputs include related strategies, technology, business processes, and people. The outputs are the products or services that help realize the goals of a manufacturing enterprise. A product has to be understood in a much broader context. What matters is the overall performance of the product during its life cycle. Therefore, the product life-cycle approach provides a logical framework for understanding and analysis.

Opportunities for reduction in cost and lead time and improvements in product quality must be sought from all the areas of a product life cycle. The product life cycle includes the following phases:

- Design phase
- Manufacturing phase
- Product usage phase
- Disposal phase

During the product life cycle, design and manufacturing have major effects on the subsequent phases. Consequently, they are responsible for the lion's share of life-cycle cost as shown in Figure 1.3. The issues of product quality and overall lead time are intimately tied to these phases. Looking exclusively at a single phase of the life cycle will miss the dependences that exist between them. Obviously, what is needed is a systems approach to understand each of the phases and the linkages between them.

The primary objective of the present book is to provide a systems approach to understanding some of the design, planning, and control issues in computer-integrated design and manufacturing. Accordingly, we provide a basic understanding of major subsystems in a product life cycle in Chapters 2 to 13. Finally, in Chapter 14 we discuss issues of enterprise integration to determine how subsystems can be integrated

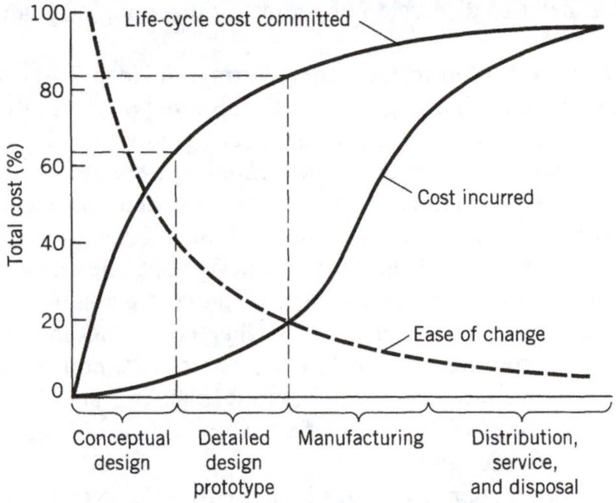

FIGURE 1.3 Characteristic curve representing cost incurred and committed during product life cycle

into a computer-integrated manufacturing system. Throughout the book we provide a quantitative basis for understanding major activities that occur during the design and manufacturing phases of a product life cycle. Let us elaborate on some of these activities.

Product design sets the stage for product success or failure in the marketplace. The reason is that product design has a direct impact on product cost, quality, and reliability; introduction intervals; manufacturing process yields; future maintenance costs; and cost to dispose of the product. Typically, 80% of the cost of a product is fixed at the design stage (Dransfield, 1994), as shown in Figure 1.3. We need a concurrent engineering approach to consider the interaction between various phases of the product life cycle.

The product design process starts with the identification of customer needs and goes through a sequence of activities. These include:

- Identifying the attributes of the need for which the product is being designed and defining the problem domain.
- Generation of preliminary ideas with respect to technical choices, materials, design complexities, and so on.
- Refinement of the product ideas using geometric modeling.
- Analysis of best designs from the point of view of cost, functional requirements, and marketability using such tools as finite-element methods, assembly analysis, and so on.
- Selection of a design that has all the desirable characteristics including manufacturability, serviceability, maintainability, et cetera.
- Creation of a detailed design providing detailed specifications with respect to materials, tolerances, surface roughness, and so on.

We provide a discussion of the design process, CAD/CAM tools, and computer graphics in Chapter 2. A detailed discussion of geometric modeling of products is provided in Chapter 3.

From the point of view of efficient manufacturing, the idea is to capture manufacturing information at the design stage so that the required product information can be used to manufacture the parts. Concurrent engineering provides a broader perspective that relates design and manufacturing with technology, business processes, and the people in a manufacturing enterprise. Basic issues in concurrent engineering are discussed in Chapter 4. The link between design and manufacturing is provided by process planning. Process planning helps translate design specifications into process details. A detailed discussion of various aspects of process planning, process planning approaches, and feature recognition is given in Chapter 5. Other manufacturing issues such as numerical control, programmable logic controllers, computer control, automated material handling, robotics, manufacturing planning and shop floor control, just-in-time manufacturing, cellular manufacturing, and flexible manufacturing are discussed in Chapters 6 through 13.

We follow the systems approach in this book by focusing on a basic understanding of the elements of computer-integrated design and manufacturing in Chapters 2 through 13. Then, a conceptual framework for enterprise integration is provided for the integration of all these elements in the last chapter.

1.4 ORGANIZATION OF THE BOOK

The material in this book is organized in logical order following the product life-cycle stages and systems approach as shown in Figure 1.4. Accordingly, we proceed from design to manufacturing, covering associated subsystems and elements, followed by the last chapter on enterprise integration. A brief outline of each chapter is given next.

Chapter 2: Computer-Aided Design: Design Process, CAD Hardware, Computer Graphics, and Transformations

In this chapter we provide an understanding of the design process. The basic architecture of a computer-aided design system is presented. This provides links among the

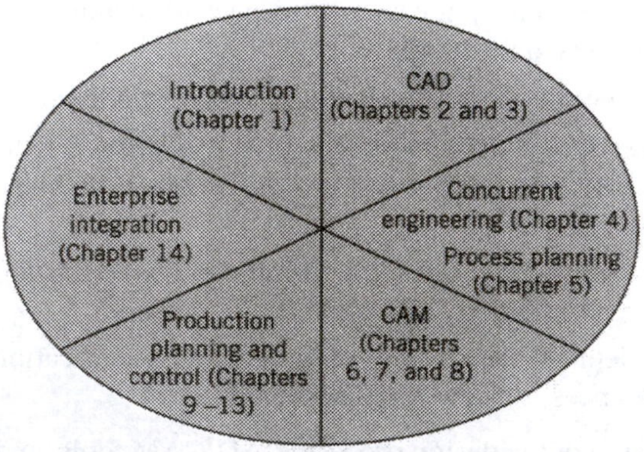

FIGURE 1.4 Logical ordering of chapters in this book.

CAD model database, input–output devices, device drivers, graphics utilities, application software, and the user interface. Various types of CAD/CAM systems, such as mainframe-, minicomputer-, workstation-, and microcomputer-based systems are described. Criteria for the selection of CAD/CAM systems related to system, geometric modeling, and design documentation and applications are elaborated upon. Finally, geometric transformations such as translation, rotation, and scaling, which are important design manipulation tools, are treated in detail.

Chapter 3: Geometric Modeling

We use geometric models to translate conceptual ideas into real products. In this chapter we provide a comprehensive coverage of various geometric modeling approaches: wireframe, surface, and solid modeling. Solid modeling is effectively used in process planning, assembly planning, and computer-aided engineering analysis using such tools as finite-element analysis (FEA). A number of solved examples are used to illustrate the concepts in wireframe modeling. Synthetic curves such as the Hermite cubic spline, Bezier, and B-spline are characterized. A parametric representation of synthetic surfaces is given. Solid modeling is becoming an effective tool for the integration of computer-aided design and manufacturing. For example, solid models are being used for analysis in conjunction with FEA. Also, solid models are used for feature recognition and feature-based design. Computer-aided process planning systems based on feature recognition systems are examples of CAD/CAM integration. We provide a good coverage of solid modeling and illustrate the concepts with solved examples. Parametric and variational design concepts and computer-aided engineering analysis are also discussed.

Chapter 4: Concurrent Engineering

The twenty-first century's response to competitive conditions of the world market will be concurrent engineering. Often, CE refers to the process of considering simultaneously the requirements of assembly and manufacturing with design requirements in order to reduce unit cost of production, improve quality, and reduce total lead time. A broader view of CE involves managing the mutual dependences between all phases of the product life cycle, whether in design, manufacturing, distribution, support, or service. In that case, the aim is to minimize life-cycle costs, maximize customer satisfaction, maximize flexibility, and minimize lead times from product conception to delivery to the customer. In this chapter we provide a basic understanding of CE principles and tools. A simple mathematical modeling framework is also presented to estimate quantitatively the cost, quality, and lead time as a consequence of different decision strategies and interactions of functional areas. A design methodology for developing a concurrent engineering program is given. The quality function deployment methodology is also discussed in detail. An architecture for integration of life-cycle phases in a concurrent engineering environment is then provided.

Chapter 5: Computer-Aided Process Planning

Process planning refers to a set of instructions that are used to make a component so that the design specifications are met. Process planning translates design specifications into manufacturing process details. Therefore, it acts as a bridge between design and manufacturing. The use of computers in process planning results in a number of benefits: producing accurate and consistent process plans; reducing the cost and lead time of process planning, resulting in increased productivity of process planners; and easy interfacing of other tools such as work standards, cost, and lead time estimation. In this chapter we provide a basic understanding of principles of process planning. A detailed account of process planning activities is given. Various computer-aided process planning approaches are described. A section on feature recognition is also provided.

Chapter 6: Computer Control of Manufacturing Systems

The productivity and efficiency of manufacturing systems can be improved by automatic control of machine tools, equipment, and systems. The technologies used include numerical control of machine tools, programmable logic controllers, and computers. In this chapter we provide a detailed discussion of NC and CNC machines and NC part programming, as well as the use of programmable logic controllers and computers for automatic control of manufacturing equipment and systems.

Chapter 7: Automated Material-Handling and Storage Systems

In manufacturing, efficient execution of operations is important because that is where the value is added to the product. However, real-life products often consist of a number of components that have to be transported from one manufacturing or assembly center to another. The transportation of raw, semifinished, and finished parts and products increases the unit cost and contributes significantly to the manufacturing lead time of final products. Reduced cost and lead time are necessary for increased market share and profitability. It is therefore important to have efficient material-handling systems and to interface them with manufacturing systems to make profitable products. In this chapter we discuss the latest concepts in automated guided vehicle systems and automated storage and retrieval systems. Design, planning, and control issues are discussed. We also provide a brief discussion of conveyor systems.

Chapter 8: Robotic Systems

Robots and robotic technology together have permeated all facets of manufacturing. Robotics is now becoming an integral part of automated discrete-parts manufacturing systems such as flexible manufacturing and assembly systems. In fact, the driving force for the purchase of robotic technology is the applications of robots in hostile, strenuous, and repetitive environments as well as highly competitive situations in which the economic pressure to reduce costs is extremely high. Such robotic applications include welding, painting, and pick-and-place material handling. In this chapter we provide a basic understanding of robotics and robot technology. A detailed discussion and analysis of robot motion, robot programming languages, and economic justification are included. A number of solved examples are included in this chapter to illustrate these concepts.

Chapter 9: Quality Engineering, Statistical Process Control, and Automated Inspection Systems

Quality is an important and valued attribute of any product. Therefore, various quality improvement strategies have been adopted by product manufacturers. An important quality improvement strategy will be to build quality right at the design stage. Such a strategy is called quality engineering. We provide a detailed discussion of Taguchi's approach to quality engineering. The concepts are explained by a case study. During the production stage, a common strategy would be to apply statistical process control procedures to improve the output quality. Automated inspection techniques are also discussed.

Chapter 10: Manufacturing Planning and Control Systems

The primary objective of a manufacturing planning and control system (MPCS) in any organization is to ensure that the desired products are manufactured at the right time, in the right quantities, meeting quality specifications, and at minimum cost. The MPCS encompasses a number of activities in an integrated manner. These activities include determining end-item demand, translating end-item demand into feasible manufacturing plans, establishing detailed plans of material flows and capacity to support the overall manufacturing plans, and finally helping execute these plans by such actions as detailed cell scheduling and purchasing. We discuss in detail all the issues involved, including demand management, aggregate production planning, material requirements planning, capacity planning, shop floor scheduling, and control. A number of examples are solved to illustrate the concepts.

Chapter 11: Just-in-Time Manufacturing Systems

Just-in-time philosophy is based on the pull strategy, in which only the necessary products, at the necessary time, in necessary quantities are manufactured and the stock on hand is held down to a minimum. This philosophy emerged as a result of the manufacturing planning and control system at the Toyota Motor Company. In this chapter we provide an overview of the Toyota production system. The principles and design of JIT systems are discussed in detail. A strategy for obtaining level schedules for mixed model assembly lines is given.

Chapter 12: Group Technology and Cellular Manufacturing Systems

Group technology provides a means of identifying and exploiting similarities of parts and processes. Processing together groups of similar parts reduces unnecessary duplication of effort by standardizing and simplifying related activities. In product design, the focus is on geometric similarities. However, the focus in manufacturing engineering is on similar machining operations, similar tooling and machine setup procedures, and similar methods of transporting and sorting materials. In this chapter we provide a good understanding of various types of coding and classification systems, cell formation methodologies, planning, and control in a cellular manufacturing environment.

Chapter 13: Flexible Manufacturing Systems

The scenario for the twenty-first century has highly demanding requirements: increased product variety, low unit costs and lead times, and high levels of product quality. The multitude of product variations and the complexity and exacting nature of these products, coupled with increased international competition, the need to reduce manufacturing cycle time, and the pressure to cut the production cost, all require the development of manufacturing technologies and methods that permit small-batch production to gain economic advantages similar to those of mass production while retaining the flexibility of discrete-product manufacturing. The development of flexible manufacturing systems for midvolume, midvariety parts addresses some of these problems. In this chapter, we provide a basic understanding of flexibility, volume variety relationships, and their characteristics that distinguish among various CIM Systems. The physical and control subsystems of FMS are discussed. We also provide discussion on layout problems, various part type selection, and tool management strategies.

Chapter 14: Enterprise Integration, CIM, and Future Trends

The key to the success of organizations in a highly competitive environment is enterprise integration. The traditional computer-integrated manufacturing (CIM) strategy for automation may not work in the twenty-first century's highly dynamic business environment. Enterprise-wide integration strategies are required for making group decisions in real time to cope effectively with such dynamic changes. In this chapter we provide a framework for enterprise integration. Network communications, database management systems and groupware are also discussed because they are vital for realizing enterprise integration.

1.5 SUMMARY

The twenty-first century marketplace will be characterized by increasing product varieties demanding increasing technical complexity, decreasing levels of demand, and expanding global competition. To survive in such a dynamic business environment, mass customization of products is required. Such a complex discrete-product manufacturing environment makes the understanding of various elements of a manufacturing system imperative. Design and manufacturing are the major elements of such an enterprise. The primary objective of this book is to provide a comprehensive understanding of various aspects of design and manufacturing. For this purpose, a systems approach is followed to present the design and manufacturing knowledge. A quantitative approach is used in all chapters. Several solved examples are used to illustrate the design and manufacturing concepts. Interesting features of the book include detailed coverage of such topics as concurrent engineering, automated guided vehicle systems, automated storage and retrieval systems, quality engineering, just-in-time manufacturing, cellular manufacturing, flexible manufacturing, and enterprise integration. With such coverage of basic as well as advanced topics in design and manufacturing, the book will be suitable not only as a text for senior undergraduate and junior graduate engineering students but also as a useful reference for practicing engineers and managers from a wide range of industries.

REFERENCES AND SUGGESTED READING

Chorafus, D. N. (1993). *Manufacturing Databases and Computer Integrated Systems.* CRC Press, Ann Arbor, Michigan.

Chung, J. C. H., and Schussi, M. D. (1990). Technical evaluation of variational and parametric design. *Proceedings of the 1990 ASME Computers in Engineering Conference,* Vol. 1, pp. 289–298, American Society of Mechanical Engineers, New York.

Davidow, W. H., and Malone, M. S. (1992). *The Virtual Corporation: Structuring and Revitalizing the Corporation of the 21st Century.* Harper Business, New York.

Dransfield, J. (1994). Design for manufacturability at nothern telecom. In *Successful Implementation of Concurrent Engineering Products and Processes* (S. G. Shina, ed.). Van Nostrand Reinhold, New York.

Goldman, S., and Preiss, K. (eds.) (1991). 21st century manufacturing enterprise strategy: An industry-led view. Harold S. Mohler Laboratory No. 200, Iacocca Institute, Lehigh University, Bethlehem, Pennsylvania.

Harrington, J. H. (1984). *Understanding the Manufacturing Process: Key to CAD/CAM Implementation.* Marcel Dekker, New York.

Irani, R. K., and Saxena, M. (1993). An integrated NMT-based CAE environment: Part I: Boundary-based features modelling utility, *Engineering with Computers,* 9:210–219.

Mize, J. H. (1994). *Guide to Systems Integration.* Institute of Industrial Engineers, Norcross, Georgia.

Nielsen, E. H., Dixon, J. R., and Simmons, M. K. (1987). How shall we represent the geometry of designed products? Technical Report 6-87, Mechanical Design Automation Laboratory, University of Massachusetts, Amherst.

Ranky, P. G. (1986). *Computer Integrated Manufacturing: An Introduction with Case Studies.* Prentice Hall, Englewood Cliffs, New Jersey.

Saxena, M., and Irani, R. K. (1993). An integrated NMT-based CAE environment: Part II: Application to automated gating plan syntheses for injection molding. *Engineering with Computers,* 9:220–230.

Saxena, M., and Irani, R. K. (1994). A knowledge-based engineering environment for automated analysis of nozzles. *Concurrent Engineering: Research and Applications,* 2(1):45–57.

Sheridan, J. H. (1992). The CIM evolution: Bringing people back into the equation. *Industry Week,* April 20, pp 29–51.

Umar, A. (1993). *Distributed Computing: A Practical Synthesis.* Prentice-Hall, Englewood Cliffs, New Jersey.

Viswanadham, N. and Narahari, Y. (1992). *Performance Modeling of Automated Manufacturing Systems,* Prentice-Hall, Englewood Cliffs, New Jersey.

CHAPTER 2

COMPUTER-AIDED DESIGN

Design Process, CAD Hardware, Computer Graphics, and Transformations

A large number of factors are responsible for the success of any engineering organization. Engineering design of products and processes is one of the most critical factors for success. Understanding of the design process and the computer-aided design (CAD) tools is required to realize a producible product design. In this chapter we provide a brief discussion of the design process. Various types of CAD systems used in the design process are covered. A brief discussion of input–output devices used in CAD systems is also included.

Computer graphics plays an important role in the product development process by generating, presenting, and manipulating geometric models of the objects. During the product development process, for proper understanding of the designs, it is necessary not only to generate geometric models of objects but also to perform such manipulations on these models as rotation, translation, and scaling. In this chapter we provide basic understanding of two- and three-dimensional transformations such as scaling, translation, and rotation.

2.1 THE PRODUCT DESIGN PROCESS

Contemporary design is a highly sophisticated process. It requires the involvement of not only design engineers but also personnel from the departments of manufacturing, finance, marketing, and so on. The primary input to the design process is the recognition of the fact that a need for a product or service exists. Therefore, the product design usually begins with the motive that a new product is needed to meet the market or customers' demands. The design process is not unique because it is viewed differently by different people. For example, the emphasis is now on concurrent design of products and processes, and the traditional approach is now referred to as sequential or serial engineering. It is clear that certain basic steps such as problem identification, development of preliminary ideas and alternatives, refinement of these ideas, engineering evaluation of the best designs, selection of a compromise design, and finally implementation are required to realize a producible design for a product. In the engineering design community, these steps have been identified in various forms: feasibility studies, preliminary design and detailed design, design synthesis, design analysis, and so forth. In this chapter we adopt the design process approach followed by Earle (1992), which involves the following six steps:

- Problem identification
- Preliminary ideas
- Refinement process
- Analysis process
- Decision process
- Implementation

The design process is essentially an iterative process. The relationship of these steps is illustrated in Figure 2.1.

2.1.1 Problem Identification

The key to designing a successful product lies in properly identifying the need and the attributes of that need for which the product is to be designed. The product is the final outcome of the need identification process. There is an old adage: garbage in, garbage out. If the need and its characteristics are not properly identified, the final product design will not reflect reality. Therefore, the problem identification process should involve collection of field data; conducting field surveys and experiments; use of intuition, judgment, and personal observation; and physical measurements. For example, consider the problem of developing a line of high-quality notebook-sized computers that will eventually beat the competition. There is a need to identify the characteristics of the product that will be successful in a highly competitive market. For example, the designed product should be light in weight, highly portable, self-con-

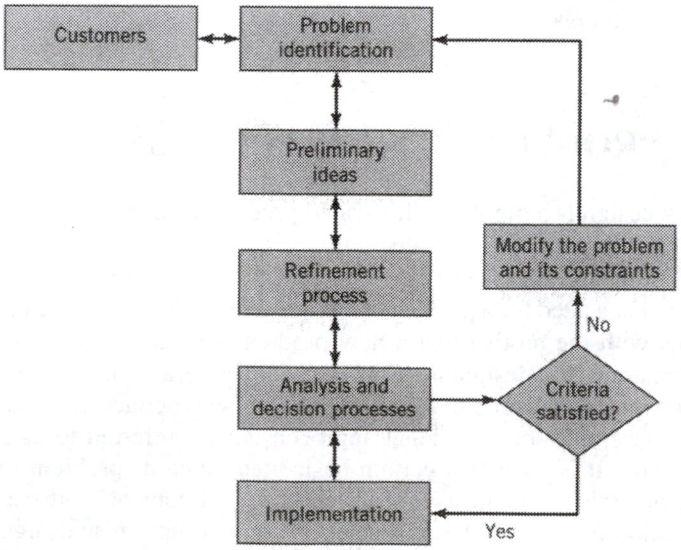

FIGURE 2.1 The design process.

tained, and sized to fit in a briefcase, have a standard keyboard layout feel, and have a compatible operating system, among many other features.

2.1.2 Preliminary Ideas

Once the problem domain has been identified, the second phase is to generate as many ideas as possible. Brainstorming sessions should be used to develop solutions to the present problem that may revolutionize present methods. For example, in the case of notebook-sized computers, consider the possibility of technological choices in very large scale integrated (VLSI) circuits; material choices and design complexities for price competitiveness; and choices for making the product reliable, testable, and producible.

2.1.3 Refinement Process

During the refinement process, several good ideas are pursued, using scale drawings to determine their merits in terms of space requirements, critical measurements, dimensions of structural members, and interactions of surfaces and planes. The use of geometrical modeling will help in determining the identity of the product.

2.1.4 Analysis Process

The analysis phase is concerned with the evaluation of best designs from the point of view of a number of criteria such as cost, functional requirements, and marketability. Other engineering tools such as finite-element methods and assembly analysis tools should be used to evaluate alternative designs from the functionality point of view.

2.1.5 Decision Process

Most often, a product is manufactured using a single design. Therefore, in the decision phase of the design process, the idea is to select a design that has all the desirable characteristics: the design that is manufacturable at minimum possible cost; the design in which the quality has been built in at the design stage, the design that can be quickly manufactured to make the product available to the customers faster. A decision matrix approach can be employed to make a best trade-off solution by using proper weighting schemes for various attributes in the candidate solutions.

2.1.6 Implementation Process

This step is essentially a detailed design phase. The detailed specifications of materials, dimensions, tolerances, and surface roughness should be provided. The idea is to make the drawings to be used directly for developing process plans so that the product can be manufactured.

2.2 COMPUTER-AIDED DESIGN

As the name suggests, computer-aided design refers to the design process with the aid of computers. At this point, it is important to emphasize that the computer does not change the basic nature of the design process. That is, the design engineer essentially provides knowledge and creativity and controls the design process from the stage of problem identification to the implementation phase. However, what the computer does is equally important. It helps improve the efficiency and productivity of the design process by accurately generating easily modifiable graphics, performing complex design analysis at amazingly high speeds, and storing and recalling information with consistency and speed. Therefore, a CAD system is essentially a blend of the best characteristics of human designer and computers to achieve the best possible design and manufacture of products.

Computer-aided design drafting (CADD) is used to generate working drawings and other engineering documents using computers. It is therefore proper to say that the computer-aided design system should be viewed as a partner in the engineering design team. Today, with the trend of integrating CAD and computer-aided manufacturing (CAM), computer-aided design may be found both in CAD and CAM systems. A number of CAD/CAM tools, both hardware and software, are required during both the design and the manufacturing process. In the following sections, we provide a brief history of CAD followed by a brief discussion of various types of CAD/CAM tools.

2.3 A BRIEF HISTORY OF CAD

Automotive and aerospace industries have been at the forefront of development of CAD technology. However, its origin can be traced back to the development of interactive computer graphics, and graphical representation on computers can in turn, be, traced back to the beginning of digital computers. The theoretical basis for computer graphics software was laid in the pioneering work of Ivan Sutherland (1963) in his Ph.D. thesis describing a system called the ''sketch pad.'' The system based on the sketch pad is now known as interactive graphics. The sketch pad was developed under the Semi-Automatic Ground Environment (SAGE) project; it helped change radar information into computer-integrated pictures and allowed the flexibility of choosing the information by pointing a light pen at the desired location on the cathode-ray tube (CRT) display.

Since then, there has been a stream of new developments in the areas of hardware and software. The development of three-dimensional solid modeling in the 1970s dramatically changed the scenario, because the same CAD could now be used for both engineering drawing and engineering analysis. Systems with attributes such as higher processing speeds, larger memory, and smaller size are available at affordable prices. The future trends will be to integrate artificial intelligence with the CAD system with the objective of achieving design automation.

2.4 CAD/CAM SYSTEMS

A wide variety of CAD/CAM systems are currently available. Each system comes with various configurations and options to satisfy users' requirements. Essentially, a CAD consists of three major components: hardware, which incudes the computer and input–output devices, application software, and the operating system software. The operating system software acts as the interface between the hardware and the CAD application software system. The basic CAD system architecture is shown in Figure 2.2. The classification scheme we use in this section is based on hardware of the

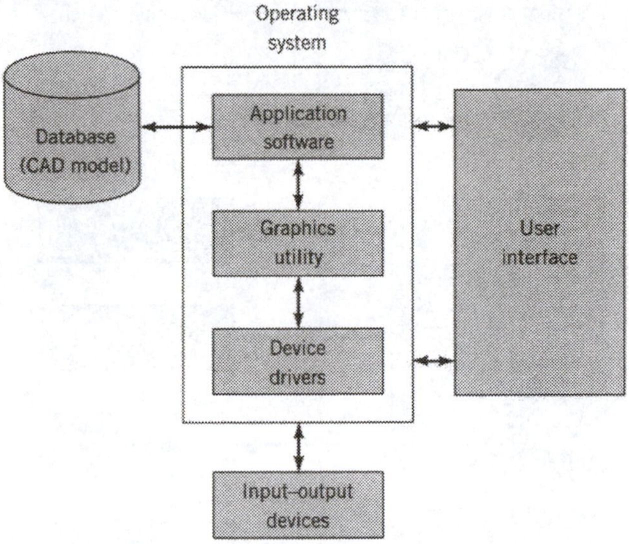

FIGURE 2.2 Basic architecture of a CAD system.

system. More specifically, we classify systems by the host computer that drives the system.

Generally, CAD/CAM systems are classified into four types:

- Mainframe-based systems
- Minicomputer-based systems
- Workstation-based systems
- Microcomputer-based systems

However, CAD systems can be classified in a number of other ways. For example, we can classify CAD systems according to applications area, such as mechanical engineering, architectural design and construction engineering, circuit design, and board layout. Other classifications could be based on modeling methods, such as two- and three-dimensional drawing, sculptured surface, and three-dimensional solid modeling.

2.4.1 Mainframe-Based Systems

Mainframe-based systems are being used in many companies, especially when large engineering projects are involved. These systems have advantages in modeling, in running large-scale modeling software, and in networking and communication with other stations such as accounting, planning, and management information databases. The organization of the system is shown in Figure 2.3 *a* and *b*. Two major computer system environments are the user and the system environment. The user environment includes workstations and peripherals such as printers and plotters. The number of workstations is limited by the capacity of the host computer so as to permit a desired level of system response time. The main segments of a workstation are the input and output devices. Input devices include cursor control devices for graphics input and a keyboard, which may have programmed function keys, for text input. The light pen, joystick, mouse, and electronic pen (stylus) with a digitizing tablet are commonly used

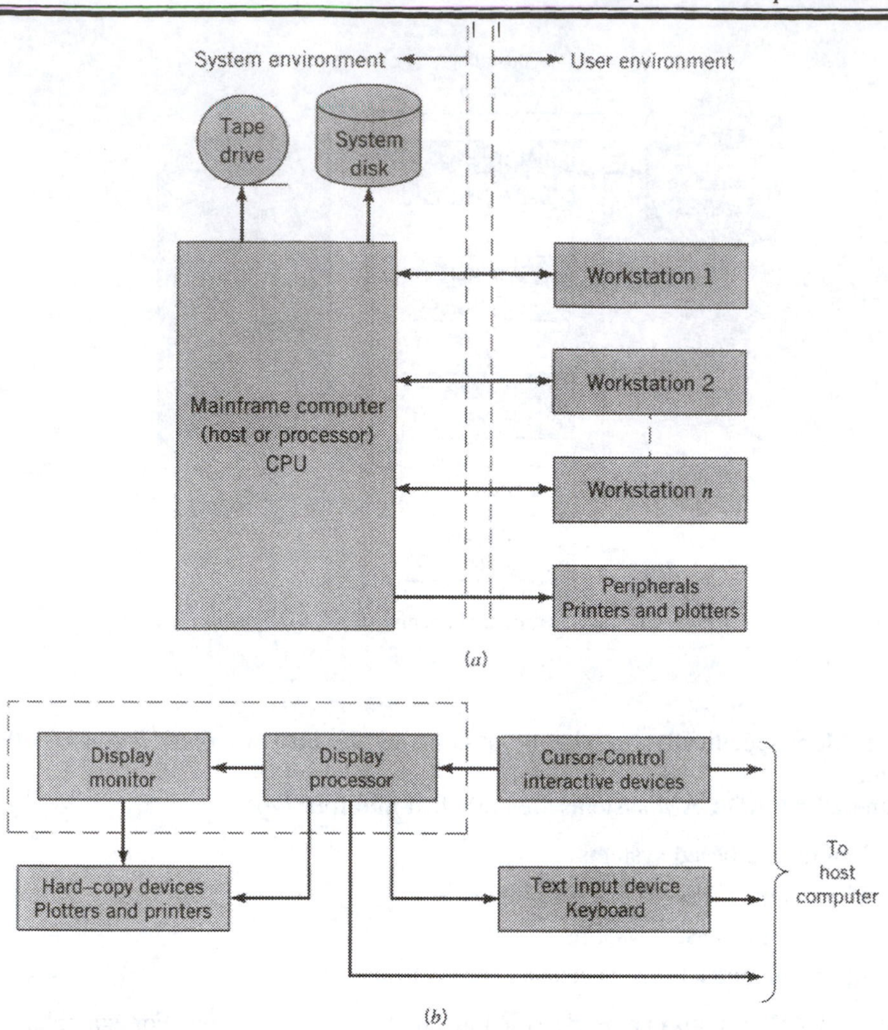

FIGURE 2.3 Mainframe-based CAD system organization: (*a*) the basic elements; (*b*) the workstation elements.

devices for controlling the cursor. Output devices consist of graphics display with a printer. Laser jet and color printers are commonly used. Input and output devices are discussed in Section 2.5.

Input and output devices are usually well equipped and organized on a sharing basis. However, the sharing strategy causes some problems. One is unpredictable response time, because mainframes process jobs in batches, especially when input–output access occurs. Some research results show that when the response time is longer than 1 s the brain activity rate decreases. Keeping a reasonable response time is an important factor when mainframe-based systems are organized. For example, we keep CAD/CAM stations in a relatively higher probity level in order to have fewer interruptions and faster responses to satisfy users. The number of end users should also be considered. For example, having too many CAD/CAM stations linked to the mainframe will cause the same problems.

2.4.2 Minicomputer-Based Systems

With great advances in the field of electronics, especially large-scale integrated (LSI) and now VLSI circuits, minicomputers can now perform almost all the functions of the early mainframes at less cost and with greater speed. Super-minicomputers, such as the VAX 11/780 with 32-bit word and virtual memory operating systems, have appeared during the past two decades. They extend this advantage further and provide a more adequate environment for contemporary sophisticated CAD/CAM.

The structure and organization of minicomputers are similar to those of mainframe-based systems, except that the host computer is a minicomputer instead of a mainframe. Usually, a minicomputer-based system is smaller than a mainframe system. There are fewer workstations in a minicomputer system than in a mainframe system.

Because the cost of a minicomputer is much less than that of a mainframe, minicomputers can be purchased for particular applications such as running CAD/CAM application software only. This makes it easier to configure a trouble-free system with less maintenance. Today, suppliers of minicomputer systems offer the computer hardware, software, and postsale support such as maintenance, technical training, documentation, and consultation. Popular minicomputer suppliers include SUN, HP, DEC and IBM.

2.4.3 Workstation-Based Systems

Workstation-based systems represent the downward evolution of well-established super-minicomputer–based system technologies into a single-user or office environment. The workstation-based systems have several advantages over mainframe or minicomputer-based systems. For example, the problem of having a time-sharing, central computing facility accessed through graphics display terminals, which exists in mainframe- or super-mini–based systems, is eliminated in these systems. The dedication to single tasks without affecting other users offers consistency of time responses. This is one of the major attractive features of workstation-based systems. The workstation-based systems have their own computing power, an advantage similar to that of personal computer (PC)–based systems. Furthermore, they also have the well-established features of mainframe- and minicomputer-based systems. Considering the present trends in CAD/CAM system technologies, it appears that workstation-based systems will form the backbone of the next generation of CAD/CAM systems. Figure 2.4 shows a typical workstation-based CAD/CAM system configuration. The output device, which is discussed in Section 2.5, is not shown.

2.4.4 Microcomputer-Based Systems

Today, microcomputers dominate both computer markets and applications worldwide. The most popular systems that run the CAD/CAM application software we encounter are microcomputer-based systems. The popular microcomputer-based CAD/CAM systems include IBM PS/2 and Macintosh IICx and generally utilize one computer per terminal. There are several reasons for the popularity of microcomputers, in addition to low cost. First, speed, size, and accuracy problems have been overcome in the past 10 years. For example, a 32-bit word length central processing unit (CPU) is enough to run CAD/CAM application software. Second, various independent PC application

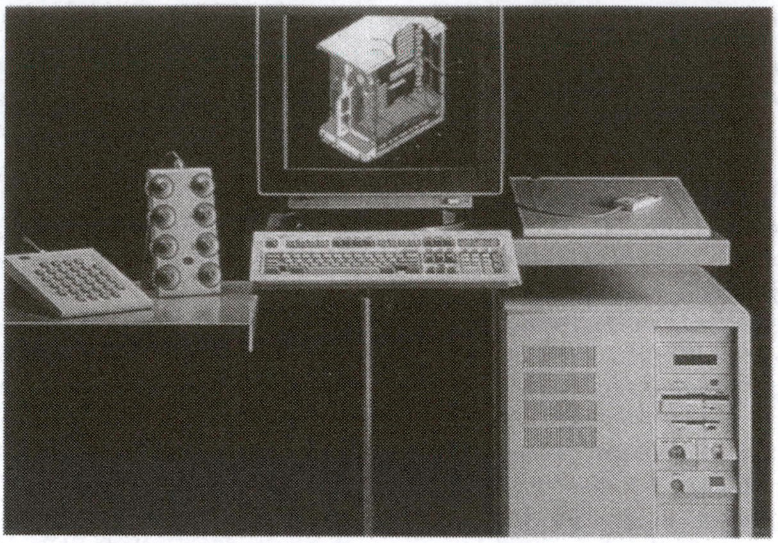

FIGURE 2.4 IBM's RISC/6000 workstation (Photo courtesy of IBM).

programs have matured and now cover a wide range of applications. The CPU speed and enhanced graphics adaptor can support EGA, VGA, and Super-VGA monitors. This makes the interactive job more pleasant. The new trends in PC window software have also greatly facilitated the maturing of microcomputer-based systems. Remember, for a period of time the window systems were available only in mainframes or minicomputer-based systems.

2.5 CAD SYSTEM INPUT-OUTPUT DEVICES

The CAD system accessories and peripherals are divided into input and output devices (Figure 2.5).

2.5.1 Input Devices

Input devices are tools that users employ to communicate with computer systems. Input technology has improved greatly over the years, and a variety of input devices are currently available. The input device used depends on the type of information that is to be input. The possible types of information include text, graphics, and sound.

Text and graphics provide the essential data needed in CAD/CAM applications. We can therefore classify input devices according to these data types. Devices used to input text are called text-input devices. A typical example of this type of device is the alphanumeric (character-oriented) keyboard. Sound-input devices are mainly microphones. Devices used for graphics input are further divided into three categories: locating devices, digitizers, and image-input devices.

Locating devices are used to input a particular position on the screen, for example, to pick the position of a point on screen. The most popular devices include light pen, mouse, joystick, trackball, and thumbwheel, which can usually provide a relatively

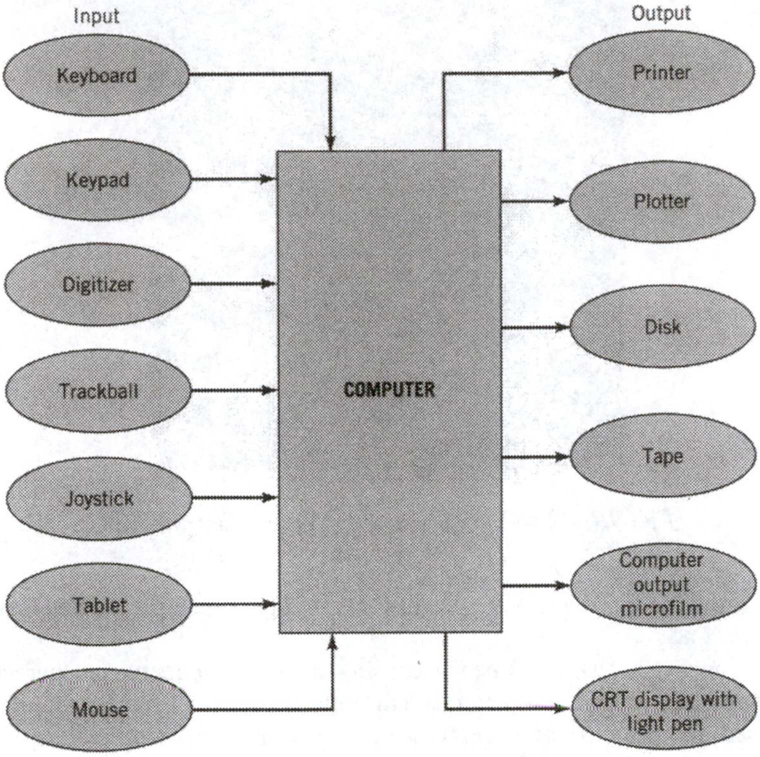

FIGURE 2.5 Input–output devices.

accurate position on the screen. Among these devices, the mouse (developed by office automation pioneer Doug Engelbant in the mid-1960s) is the most widely used input device other than the keyboard. A mouse can have one button, two buttons, or three buttons. Usually the mouse is considered as basic an element of a computer system as the keyboard. Other devices include digitizing tablets and styluses, touch screens, and touch pads, which are often used to input low-resolution information and most probably input information via the window's menu button or icon-oriented user interfaces. Generally, they are inadequate for graphics design.

The digitizer is another type of graphics-input device. A digitizer consists of an electronic board with a stylus, which is similar to traditional drafting tools such as paper and pencils. It is therefore quite popular as a graphic-input tool. Usually, the electronic board contains a blank area with a menu from which selections can be made by using a stylus.

Image-input devices are those that can automatically input the image of a frame of graphics or picture. Typical devices include video frame grabbers and scanners. Figure 2.6 shows a typical scanner. A scanner can directly input a graphical image into a computer. Also, a video frame grabber can store a frame of video image in a computer. This type of input device is much used in the area of image processing. Robot vision is a potential application of this technique. When information about the shape and dimensions of an object can be extracted from a frame of a video image, the problems of robot movements in the presence of obstacles are largely solved. Another major revolutionary application is in the area of text processing. Software is already available that

FIGURE 2.6 A typical scanner (Photo courtesy of IBM).

can convert the image of a text document to a text file, which greatly reduces tedious typing work.

Input devices are also classified according to three independent characteristics: absolute or relative, direct or indirect, and discrete or continuous. For example, a tablet or touch pad that has a frame of reference can input position with respect to devices such as a mouse or joystick. Trackballs can input only changes from their previous position.

With a direct input device, such as a light pen or touch screen, the user points directly at the screen with a finger or surrogate finger. Figure 2.7 shows a typical direct input device, a light pen. With an indirect input device, such as a tablet or mouse, the user moves the device in a separate place and the movement is translated to the cursor

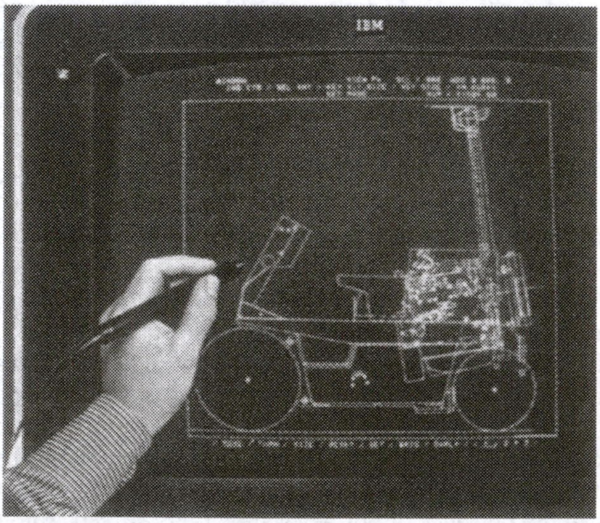

FIGURE 2.7 The light pen input device (Photo courtesy of IBM).

movement that is shown on the screen. A continuous input device can create a smooth cursor motion; a discrete input device usually cannot. Tablet, mouse, and joystick all belong to the former category and cursor-control keys belong to the latter.

2.5.2 Output devices

Generally, output devices are classified into the *soft-type* and *hard-type* devices.

2.5.2.1 Soft-Type Output Devices

Soft-type devices are those that display graphics or text on the monitor screen. However, usually we cannot keep them permanently. Nonetheless, the graphics display is an important component of a workstation because the quality of the displayed image affects the perception of generated designs. A number of graphics display technologies are now available. They include the cathode ray tube, the liquid crystal display (LCD), the light-emitting diode (LED), and plasma displays. The CRT remains the dominant graphics display device. The basic concept used in most of these technologies is to convert the computer's electrical signals, controlled by the corresponding digital information, into visible images at high speeds.

2.5.2.2 Hard-Type Output Devices

In contrast, hard-type devices are those used to produce hard copies that can be stored permanently, such as a paper printout. The output devices are often shared by many users and sometimes placed in a separate room, often called a hard-copy room. Plotters and printers belong to this category.

Plotters A plotter can be defined as a machine directed by the computer to make a drawing. Plotters can be categorized into two types: flatbed and drum or roll-feed plotters. In the case of a flatbed plotter, the pen is moved in either a raised or lowered position on the paper, which is attached to the bed to make the drawing. With a drum plotter, the pen is suspended over the paper, which is held in a spool and rolled over a rotating drum. As the drum rotates, the pen moves left or right along the drum to complete a drawing. A plotter is shown in Figure 2.8.

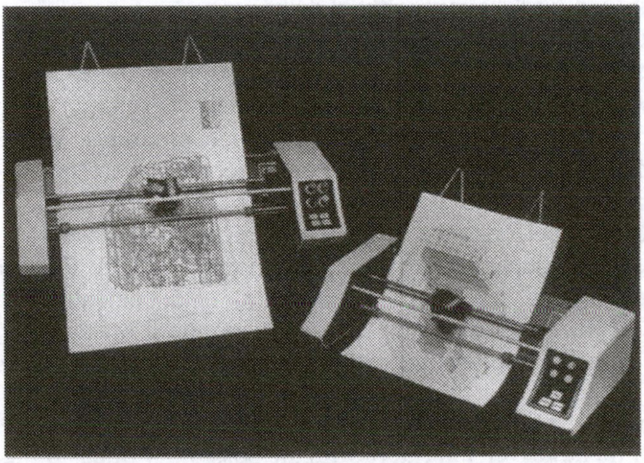

FIGURE 2.8 A plotter (Photo courtesy of IBM).

Printers Printers are common devices operated by computers to make images or print text on paper. There are two types of printers: impact and nonimpact printers. Impact printers are just like typewriters, forming characters by forcing typefaces to strike an inked ribbon and paper. A dot matrix printer is a popular example of an impact printer. In contrast, ink sprays or laser beams are used to form characters from a distance. For example, ink-jet printers form a pattern of dots. Multicolor graphics can be generated by using multiple jet nozzles. Laser jet printers and color printers are now commonly used.

2.6 SELECTION OF CAD/CAM SYSTEMS

We have discussed broad categories of CAD/CAM systems in the previous sections. There are, however, many variations on these systems on the market today. The variety is a result of implementation of these systems by various software developers and hardware manufacturers. The diversity is increased by the fact that there are vendors who are more than willing to provide all kinds of features in these systems to survive in a very competitive industry. This makes the CAD/CAM system selection process difficult. In this section we provide a brief characterization of various elements of CAD/CAM systems. This will help in evaluating the systems by assigning some kind of weighting scheme representing the aspirations of the company or individuals planning to acquire these systems. Often, the cost and the quality of after-sale service are given high priority. These system characteristics can be broadly classified into the following:

- System-related issues
- Geometric modeling–related issues
- Design documentation and applications

2.6.1 System-Related Issues

System-related issues essentially concern hardware, software, maintenance, and service support. The hardware and software issues are critical for any CAD/CAM system. Normally, there are two popular hardware configurations of workstations: workstations with disks and workstations without disks.

Systems with disks are stand-alone systems that have enough disk space and memory, whereas systems without disks are essentially connected to a central computer, which is often referred to as a server. Servers normally have large disks and sufficient memory to store user files and execute application programs. What a CAD/CAM customer needs from a system is flexibility and good response time. Having enough swapping disks in each workstation when they are connected to the server will help avoid degradation in performance in terms of response time.

Software selection depends predominantly on three factors: the type of operating system, the type of user interface, and the quality of documentation. From the customer's point of view, software that runs on a standard operating system is often recommended. Interface options depend on the type of working environment, that is, whether it is pure application oriented or development oriented or both. For a development environment, it might be nice to have an interface system that offers both menu-driven and non-menu-driven interfaces with the possibility of customized menus. The quality of documentation is easy to evaluate from the system manuals.

When selecting a system, it is important to examine critically the issues of repair and maintenance of hardware systems and upgrades of the software. The availability of system support is crucial for smooth functioning of CAD/CAM systems.

2.6.2 Geometric Modeling–Related Issues

One cannot imagine a CAD/CAM system without a geometric modeling module. The question is what types of modeling representations are adequate to meet customers' needs. Although most commercial systems support wireframes, surfaces, and solid modeling, the issues to be looked into are the integration between various representations and the applications they support. Furthermore, it is important to know various entities supported by each representation, as well as the effectiveness of the system in generating, verifying, and editing these entities.

Another important issue is that of having various coordinate systems that give the designer flexibility in generating geometric models. For example, the working coordinate system provides the opportunity to define planes of construction that may not be parallel to the standard orthogonal planes representing front, top, and right-hand-side views. Similarly, the input coordinates can be Cartesian, cylindrical, or spherical.

Geometric databases are normally used for numerically controlled (NC) part programming, robot movement control, and design of tools, jigs, and fixtures for many applications. It is therefore important to consider the compatibility of data exchange standards among such systems.

2.6.3 Design Documentation and Applications

The utility of any CAD/CAM system is judged on the basis of its ability to generate quality engineering drawings quickly and support a number of applications. For example, design packages are available for performing a variety of applications. These include mass property calculations, finite-element modeling and analysis, tolerance analysis, mechanism analysis, injection moulding analysis, and simulation. Manufacturing applications include NC part programming, computer-aided process planning, computer-integrated manufacturing (CIM), and robot applications. Integration and interfacing issues with the CAD/CAM system geometric databases together with the capability of such software should be carefully examined.

2.7 COMPUTER GRAPHICS AND TRANSFORMATIONS

Global competition has changed the dimensions of corporate success. Product development time has now become one of the most dominating dimensions. Computer graphics plays an important role in the product development process by generating, presenting, and manipulating geometric models of objects. During the product development process, for proper understanding of the designs, it is necessary not only to generate geometric models of objects but also to perform such manipulations on these models as rotation, translation, and scaling. In this chapter we provide basic understanding of two-dimensional (2D) and three-dimensional (3D) transformations such as scaling, translation, and rotation.

2.7.1 Introduction to Geometric Transformations

Computer graphics plays a pivotal role in geometric representation of objects on CAD workstations. Essentially, computer graphics is concerned with generating, presenting, and manipulating models of an object and its different views using computer hardware, software, and graphic devices. The question is why the presentation and manipulation of geometric models are important. Can you imagine modifying the design of a product without knowing what it looks like? A computer is a machine that is capable of generating data in numerical form at amazingly high speed. These data may be difficult to comprehend and interpret. However, if the data can be presented in graphic form and if the graphic can be manipulated to be viewed from different sides, enlarged, or reduced in size, it will provide good communication between the computer and the designers, making it possible to modify the product designs. Computer graphics is now becoming pervasive in our daily lives in applications ranging from weather forecasting and traffic management to the development of sophisticated products and their manufacture. In this chapter we study some of the basic functions of graphics, such as changing the scale of an image, translating it to another location, or rotating it by a certain angle to get a better view of it. The geometric transformation techniques can be used to accomplish these computer graphic functions. Geometric transformation is one of the basic routines in many applications such as graphics, robotics, and finite-element analysis. In animation, geometric transformation is utilized to create animated files. We provide a mathematical basis for these transformation techniques in the following sections.

2.7.2 Geometric Transformations

In this section we present basic 2D and 3D geometric transformations such as translation, scaling, and rotation of objects.

2.7.2.1 Two-Dimensional Transformations

Translation In 2D translation, we can determine the new position of points in the $x-y$ plane by adding the translation amount to the initial coordinates of the points. Mathematically, we can write for each point $V(x, y)$ to be moved to the new point $V'(x', y')$ by d_x and d_y units parallel to the x- and y-axes, respectively, as follows:

$$x' = x + d_x \qquad \text{and} \qquad y' = y + d_y \tag{2.1}$$

If we define the points and the distance in column vector form

$$\mathbf{V}' = \begin{bmatrix} x' \\ y' \end{bmatrix}, \qquad \mathbf{V} = \begin{bmatrix} x \\ y \end{bmatrix}, \qquad \mathbf{D} = \begin{bmatrix} d_x \\ d_y \end{bmatrix}$$

we will have

$$\mathbf{V}' = \mathbf{V} + \mathbf{D} \tag{2.2}$$

where $\mathbf{V}'$ = new (translated) variable point vector of the object

$\mathbf{V}$ = original (before translation) variable point vector of the object

$\mathbf{D}$ = distance vector

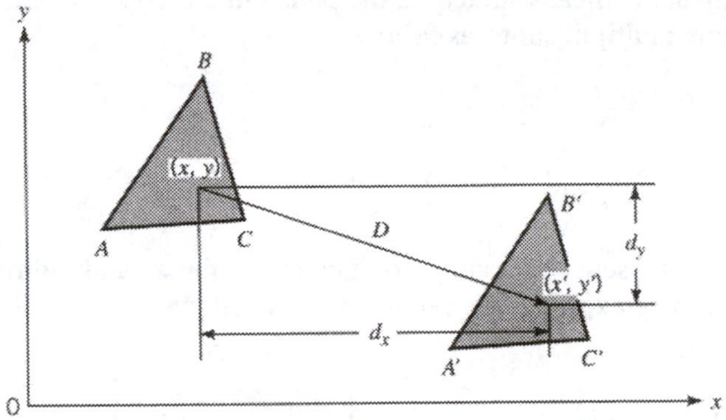

FIGURE 2.9 Illustration of translation.

For example, in Figure 2.9 an object in the shape of the shaded triangle ABC is translated by distance vector $\mathbf{D} = [d_x, d_y]^T$, and the new coordinates of each point of the triangle $A'B'C'$ can be represented by Equation (2.2). It is important to point out that the size and shape of the object(s) do not change after translation.

EXAMPLE 2.1

In Figure 2.9, suppose the initial coordinates of vertices A, B, C are (1, 3), (4, 5), and (5, 3.5), respectively. Determine the coordinates of new vertices A', B', C' after translating the triangle by a distance vector $\mathbf{D} = [7, -2]^T$ (where T represents transpose). Verify that the lengths of the edges of the triangle are unchanged.

Solution

Using Equation (2.2), we can easily obtain:

$$\begin{bmatrix} x'_A \\ y'_A \end{bmatrix} = \begin{bmatrix} 1 \\ 3 \end{bmatrix} + \begin{bmatrix} 7 \\ -2 \end{bmatrix} = \begin{bmatrix} 8 \\ 1 \end{bmatrix} \tag{2.3}$$

$$\begin{bmatrix} x'_B \\ y'_B \end{bmatrix} = \begin{bmatrix} 4 \\ 5 \end{bmatrix} + \begin{bmatrix} 7 \\ -2 \end{bmatrix} = \begin{bmatrix} 11 \\ 3 \end{bmatrix} \tag{2.4}$$

$$\begin{bmatrix} x'_C \\ y'_C \end{bmatrix} = \begin{bmatrix} 5 \\ 3.5 \end{bmatrix} + \begin{bmatrix} 7 \\ -2 \end{bmatrix} = \begin{bmatrix} 12 \\ 1.5 \end{bmatrix} \tag{2.5}$$

Therefore, the coordinates of A', B', C' are (8, 1), (11, 3), (12, 1.5), respectively. Next, we verify the lengths of the edges of triangular objects before and after translation. We have

$$\begin{aligned} AB &= \sqrt{(1-4)^2 + (3-5)^2} = \sqrt{13} \\ A'B' &= \sqrt{(8-11)^2 + (1-3)^2} = \sqrt{13} \end{aligned} \tag{2.6}$$

$$\begin{aligned} BC &= \sqrt{(5-4)^2 + (3.5-5)^2} = \sqrt{3.25} \\ B'C' &= \sqrt{(12-11)^2 + (1.5-3)^2} = \sqrt{3.25} \end{aligned} \tag{2.7}$$

$$\begin{aligned} CA &= \sqrt{(5-1)^2 + (3.5-3)^2} = \sqrt{16.25} \\ C'A' &= \sqrt{(12-8)^2 + (1.5-1)^2} = \sqrt{16.25} \end{aligned} \tag{2.8}$$

Thus means that the size and shape of the triangle are unchanged.

Scaling Scaling in 2D means stretching the points in the $x-y$ plane. It can be accomplished by simple multiplications as follows:

$$x' = s_x \cdot x$$
$$y' = s_y \cdot y \tag{2.9}$$

where s_x and s_y represent the scaling coefficients in the x- and y-directions, respectively. Scaling can be expressed in vector form as follows:

$$\mathbf{V}' = [S]\,\mathbf{V} \quad \text{or} \quad \begin{bmatrix} x' \\ y' \end{bmatrix} = \begin{bmatrix} s_x & 0 \\ 0 & s_y \end{bmatrix} \begin{bmatrix} x \\ y \end{bmatrix} \tag{2.10}$$

where $\mathbf{V}'$ = new (after scaling) variable point vector of the object

$\mathbf{V}$ = original variable point vector (before scaled) of the object

$[S]$ = scaling coefficient matrix

Notice that the object changes in both size and position in general cases. When $s_x = s_y$, it is called uniform scaling; otherwise, it is differential (or nonuniform) scaling.

Example 2.2

From Figure 2.10, show that the length of edge $A'B'$ is equal to three times that of AB after scaling the object uniformly by factor 3.

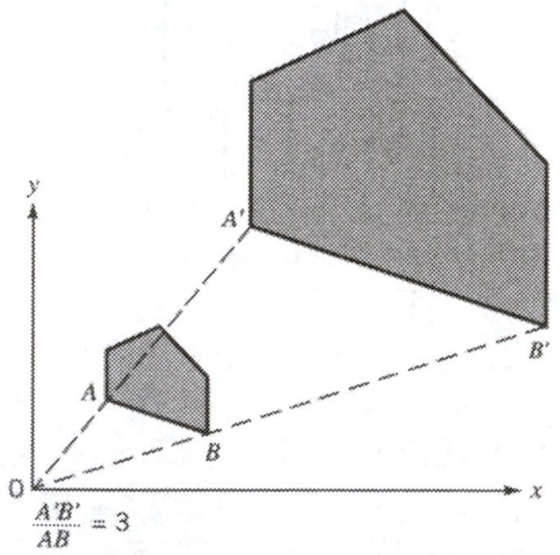

FIGURE 2.10 Scaling of an object.

Solution

Let $A = (a_1, b_1)$, $B = (a_2, b_2)$. Then, from Equation (2.10) we have

$$A' = 3 \cdot [a_1, b_1]^T = [3a_1, 3b_1]^T$$
$$B' = 3 \cdot [a_2, b_2]^T = [3a_2, 3b_2]^T$$

Calculating the dimensions of the edges AB and $A'B'$, we have

$$\begin{aligned} A'B' &= \sqrt{(3a_1 - 3a_2)^2 + (3b_1 - 3b_2)^2} \\ &= 3\sqrt{(a_1 - a_2)^2 + (b_1 - b_2)^2} \\ &= 3AB \end{aligned}$$

Rotation Rotation in 2D space is defined as moving any point (x, y) of an object to a new position by rotating it through a given angle θ about some reference point. Positive angles are measured counterclockwise from x toward y. The mathematical expression for the rotation transformation is not as obvious as the formulas for translation and scaling. In order to have a clear understanding we provide a derivation here.

From Figure 2.11, in which a point $V(x, y)$ is rotated to $V'(x', y')$ through angle θ about the origin, by simple trigonometry we have

$$\begin{aligned} x &= r \cos \phi \\ y &= r \sin \phi \end{aligned} \tag{2.11}$$

and

$$\begin{aligned} x' &= r \cos(\theta + \phi) = r \cos \phi \cos \theta - r \sin \phi \sin \theta \\ y' &= r \sin(\theta + \phi) = r \cos \phi \sin \theta + r \sin \phi \cos \theta \end{aligned}$$

On simplification, we get

$$\begin{aligned} x' &= x \cos \theta - y \sin \theta \\ y' &= x \sin \theta + y \cos \theta \end{aligned}$$

which is the forward transformation equation.

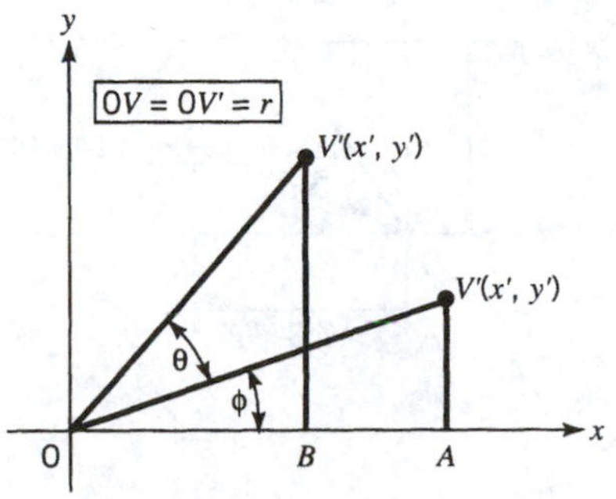

FIGURE 2.11 Rotation of an object.

In matrix form, this expression can be represented as follows:

$$\begin{bmatrix} x' \\ y' \end{bmatrix} = \begin{bmatrix} \cos\theta & -\sin\theta \\ \sin\theta & \cos\theta \end{bmatrix} \begin{bmatrix} x \\ y \end{bmatrix} \tag{2.12}$$

This can be written more concisely in matrix form as

$$V' = [R]\,V$$

where $[R]$ is the rotational matrix for rotating the initial point V to its final position V'. It is easy to prove that the size of the object remains the same. It is worth mentioning that we consider the rotation in the counterclockwise direction and the measured angle from the x-axis toward the y-axis as positive.

EXAMPLE 2.3

Determine the new position of object A placed on a round holding table after the table has been rotated by 35° (see Figure 2.12).

Solution

By substituting for θ, x, and y in Equation (2.12) the values 35°, 347.3792, and 149.0298 cm, respectively, we have

$$\begin{bmatrix} x' \\ y' \end{bmatrix} = \begin{bmatrix} \cos 35 & -\sin 35 \\ \sin 35 & \cos 35 \end{bmatrix} \begin{bmatrix} 347.3792 \\ 149.0298 \end{bmatrix}$$

Further simplification gives

$$\begin{bmatrix} x' \\ y' \end{bmatrix} = \begin{bmatrix} 199.0764 \\ 321.3266 \end{bmatrix} \tag{2.13}$$

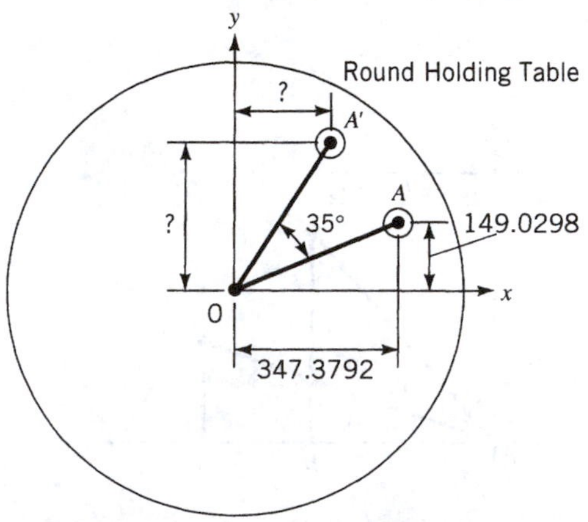

FIGURE 2.12 Example of rotation.

2.7.2.2 Three-Dimensional Transformations

3D transformations are similar to 2D transformations in both definition and derivation. We provide 3D translation, scaling, and rotation transformations in matrix form as follows:

Translation In this case we translate a point $V(x, y, z)$ by (dx, dy, dz) to point $V'(x', y', z')$. This can be expressed in matrix form as

$$\begin{bmatrix} x' \\ y' \\ z' \end{bmatrix} = \begin{bmatrix} x \\ y \\ z \end{bmatrix} + \begin{bmatrix} d_x \\ d_y \\ d_z \end{bmatrix} \tag{2.14}$$

Scaling If S is the scaling coefficient matrix, then the scaling transformation in 3D is

$$\begin{bmatrix} x' \\ y' \\ z' \end{bmatrix} = \begin{bmatrix} s_x & 0 & 0 \\ 0 & s_y & 0 \\ 0 & 0 & s_z \end{bmatrix} \begin{bmatrix} x \\ y \\ z \end{bmatrix} \tag{2.15}$$

Rotation The rotation of an object could be about any of the axes. We provide rotational transformations about all of the three axes as follows:

1. *About z.* When we want to rotate about the z-axis, the z-coordinate of a point $V(x, y, z)$ after rotation will not change because the rotation takes place in the $x-y$ plane. Therefore, the new (x, y) coordinates will be the same as those obtained in the case of 2D rotation [see Equation (2.12)]. Suppose the location of the initial point is $V(x, y, z)$; then we have the location of new point $V'(x', y', z')$ as follows:

$$\begin{aligned} z' &= z \\ x' &= x \cos\theta - y \sin\theta \\ y' &= x \sin\theta + y \cos\theta \end{aligned} \tag{2.16}$$

In matrix form we have

$$\begin{bmatrix} x' \\ y' \\ z' \end{bmatrix} = \begin{bmatrix} \cos\theta & -\sin\theta & 0 \\ \sin\theta & \cos\theta & 0 \\ 0 & 0 & 1 \end{bmatrix} \begin{bmatrix} x \\ y \\ z \end{bmatrix} \tag{2.17}$$

Similarly, we obtain the equations for rotations about x- and y-axes: Accordingly,

2. *About x:*

$$\begin{bmatrix} x' \\ y' \\ z' \end{bmatrix} = \begin{bmatrix} 1 & 0 & 0 \\ 0 & \cos\theta & -\sin\theta \\ 0 & \sin\theta & \cos\theta \end{bmatrix} \begin{bmatrix} x \\ y \\ z \end{bmatrix} \tag{2.18}$$

3. *About y:*

$$\begin{bmatrix} x' \\ y' \\ z' \end{bmatrix} = \begin{bmatrix} \cos\theta & 0 & \sin\theta \\ 0 & 1 & 0 \\ -\sin\theta & 0 & \cos\theta \end{bmatrix} \begin{bmatrix} x \\ y \\ z \end{bmatrix} \tag{2.19}$$

In general, $V' = [R]V$, where $[R]$ is the rotational matrix in 3D.

2.7.3 Homogeneous Representation

Although the 2D and 3D transformations presented in the previous sections have obvious geometric meaning, it is not efficient or economical to implement them on a computer. This is because translation involves addition of matrices whereas scaling and rotations are performed by their multiplication. It is, however, possible to develop what is called a homogeneous transformation scheme, which requires only multiplications of matrices in all cases. This simplifies the transformation process. A homogeneous representation scheme is widely used in transformation computations.

In the geometric transformation methods discussed in previous sections, translation, scaling, and rotation have nonuniform equations as follows:

$$\mathbf{V}' = \mathbf{V} + \mathbf{D}$$
$$\mathbf{V}' = [S]\,\mathbf{V}$$
$$\mathbf{V}' = [R]\,\mathbf{V}$$

where $\mathbf{V}$ and $\mathbf{V}'$ are the positions of the original and new point vectors. Notice that the equation for translation is different from the others by its addition operation. In a homogeneous representation, however, all the transformations have the multiplicative form

$$\mathbf{V}' = [H]\,\mathbf{V}$$

where $[H]$ is the homogeneous transformation matrix. This is one of the main reasons why homogeneous transformations have been widely used in graphics subroutines and display processors.

2.7.3.1 What Is Homogeneous Transformation?

Homogeneous transformation is based on mapping an N-dimensional space into $(N + 1)$-dimensional space. That means that one more coordinate is added to represent the position of a point. For example, a three-dimensional space point that has coordinates (x, y, z) is represented by vector (x, y, z, w) in homogeneous transformation. In this case, w is a dummy that on normalization gives $(x/w, y/w, z/w, 1)$. This additional 1 serves as a tool to accomplish the addition of matrices required in translation by matrix multiplication. Because other transformations such as scaling and rotation are performed by matrix multiplication, in this way we homogenize the process of transformation. From the geometric point of view, the additional element 1 can be regarded as the $(n + 1)$th coordinate of the point. For more information on geometric interpretation of homogeneous transformations, refer to Foley et al. (1990). Next, we provide homogeneous transformation equations for translation, scaling, and rotation.

1. *For translation:*

$$[H] = \begin{bmatrix} 1 & 0 & 0 & d_x \\ 0 & 1 & 0 & d_y \\ 0 & 0 & 1 & d_z \\ 0 & 0 & 0 & 1 \end{bmatrix} \tag{2.20}$$

where $[H]$ is the translation transformation matrix with the translation values d_x, d_y, and d_z with respect to x-, y-, and z-axes, respectively.

2. *For scaling:*

$$[H] = \begin{bmatrix} s_x & 0 & 0 & 0 \\ 0 & s_y & 0 & 0 \\ 0 & 0 & s_z & 0 \\ 0 & 0 & 0 & 1 \end{bmatrix} \tag{2.21}$$

where $[H]$ is the scaling transformation matrix with the scale values s_x, s_y, and s_z with respect to the x-, y-, and z-axes, respectively.

3. *For rotation:*

$$[H_z] = \begin{bmatrix} \cos\theta & -\sin\theta & 0 & 0 \\ \sin\theta & \cos\theta & 0 & 0 \\ 0 & 0 & 1 & 0 \\ 0 & 0 & 0 & 1 \end{bmatrix}$$

$$[H_x] = \begin{bmatrix} 1 & 0 & 0 & 0 \\ 0 & \cos\theta & -\sin\theta & 0 \\ 0 & \sin\theta & \cos\theta & 0 \\ 0 & 0 & 0 & 1 \end{bmatrix}$$

$$[H_y] = \begin{bmatrix} \cos\theta & 0 & \sin\theta & 0 \\ 0 & 1 & 0 & 0 \\ -\sin\theta & 0 & \cos\theta & 0 \\ 0 & 0 & 0 & 1 \end{bmatrix} \tag{2.22}$$

where $[H_x]$, $[H_y]$, and $[H_z]$ are the rotational transformation matrix when the rotation angle is θ with respect to x-, y-, and z-axes, respectively.

2.7.4 Composition of Transformations

In the previous section, we presented one-step transformations of points. In practice, a series of transformations may have to be applied to an object. The techniques for combining series of transformations are very useful in such situations. The process of composition is accomplished by multiplying the $[H]$ matrix of various transformations. Composition is also referred to as compounding, or concatenation of $[H_1]$, $[H_2]$, . . . , $[H_n]$. In general, if the transformation is done with $[H_1]$, $[H_2]$, . . . , $[H_n]$, we have the composition of transformations:

$$V' = [H_n][H_{n-1}] \cdots [H_1]\, V \tag{2.23}$$

where n refers to the nth transformation in sequence. In the following example, we illustrate homogeneous transformations as well as concatenation of transformations.

EXAMPLE 2.4

Consider the 3D object shown in Figure 2.13*a*. The coordinates of the vertices are given as follows:

$$A = [3, 5, 3]$$
$$B = [7, 5, 3]$$
$$C = [7, 5, 5]$$
$$D = [3, 5, 5]$$
$$E = [3, 6, 5]$$
$$F = [3, 6, 3]$$

Rotate the 3D object by 30° in clockwise direction at point D about the y-axis.

Solution

Since we know how to rotate an object about the origin, we need a sequence of the following fundamental transformations:

- First we translate (T_1) the object at the reference point D to bring it to the origin.
- Then we rotate (R_1) about the y-axis.
- Finally, we translate (T_2) the point D from the origin back to its original position.

Accordingly, the final position of the object represented by V_{final} is given as

$$[V_{\text{final}}] = [T_2][R_1][T_1][V_{\text{initial}}] \tag{2.24}$$

where the old position of the object V_{initial}, the translation T_1, rotation R_1, and the translation T_2 are:

$$V_{\text{initial}} = \begin{bmatrix} 3 & 7 & 7 & 3 & 3 & 3 \\ 5 & 5 & 5 & 5 & 6 & 6 \\ 3 & 3 & 5 & 5 & 5 & 3 \\ 1 & 1 & 1 & 1 & 1 & 1 \end{bmatrix} \tag{2.25}$$

$$T_1 = \begin{bmatrix} 1 & 0 & 0 & -3 \\ 0 & 1 & 0 & -5 \\ 0 & 0 & 1 & -5 \\ 0 & 0 & 0 & 1 \end{bmatrix} \tag{2.26}$$

$$R_1 = \begin{bmatrix} \cos(-30) & 0 & \sin(-30) & 0 \\ 0 & 1 & 0 & 0 \\ -\sin(-30) & 0 & \cos(-30) & 0 \\ 0 & 0 & 0 & 1 \end{bmatrix} \tag{2.27}$$

$$T_2 = \begin{bmatrix} 1 & 0 & 0 & 3 \\ 0 & 1 & 0 & 5 \\ 0 & 0 & 1 & 5 \\ 0 & 0 & 0 & 1 \end{bmatrix} \tag{2.28}$$

Notice that the angle in equation (2.27) is $-30°$ because the object is rotated in a clockwise direction.

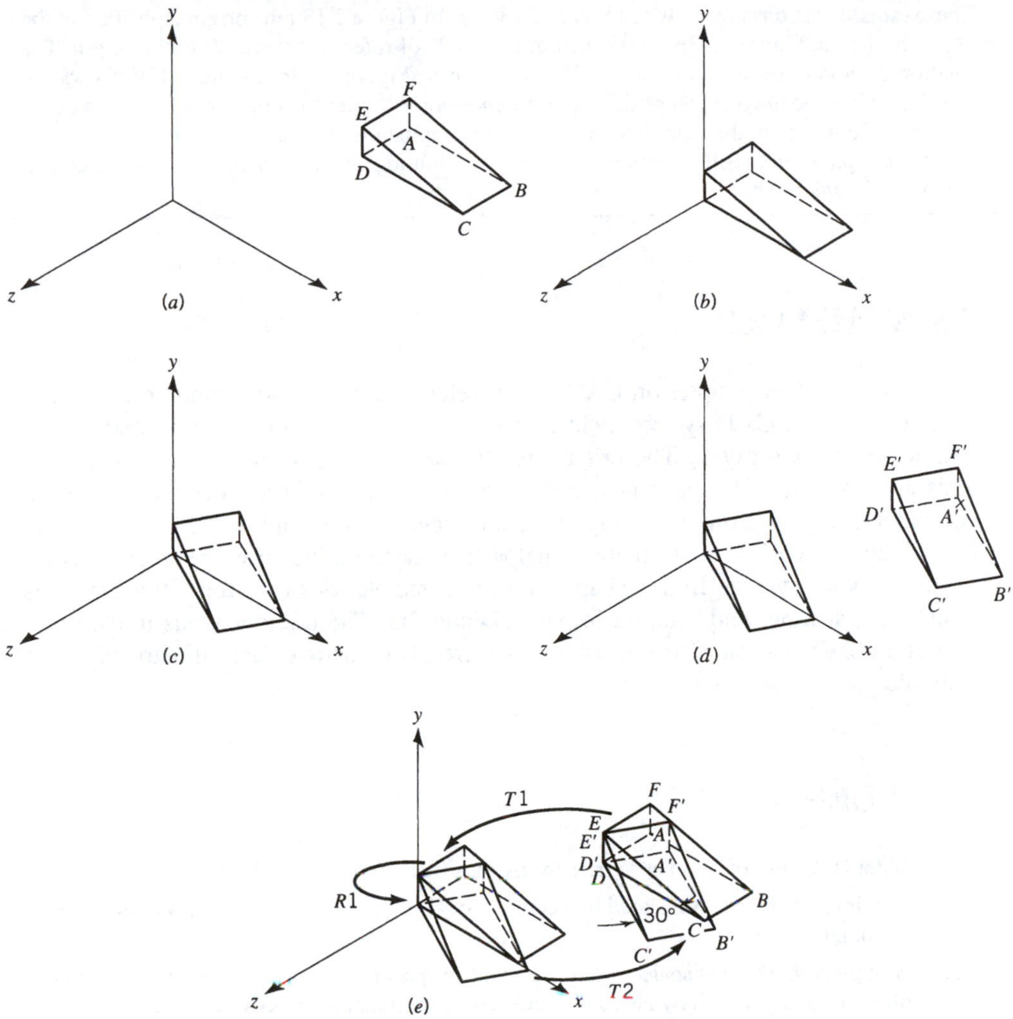

FIGURE 2.13 (*a*) Position of object in 3D space; (*b*) translation of point *D* to the origin; (*c*) rotation by an angle 30°; (*d*) translating the object back to the original position of point *D*; (*e*) the complete transformation process.

Upon concatenation using equation (2.24), we have

$$V_{\text{final}} = \begin{bmatrix} (3 + 2\sin 30) & (3 + 4\cos 30 + 2\sin 30) & (3 + 4\cos 30) & 3 & 3 & (3 + 2\sin 30) \\ 5 & 5 & 5 & 5 & 6 & 6 \\ (5 - 2\cos 30) & (5 - 2\cos 30 + 4\sin 30) & (5 + 4\sin 30) & 5 & 5 & (5 - 2\cos 30) \\ 1 & 1 & 1 & 1 & 1 & 1 \end{bmatrix} \tag{2.29}$$

Simplifying Equation (2.29), we have the new positions of all the vertices of the object after being rotated.

$$V_{\text{final}} = \begin{bmatrix} 4.00 & 7.46 & 6.46 & 3.00 & 3.00 & 4.00 \\ 5.00 & 5.00 & 5.00 & 5.00 & 6.00 & 6.00 \\ 3.27 & 5.27 & 7.00 & 5.00 & 5.00 & 3.27 \\ 1.00 & 1.00 & 1.00 & 1.00 & 1.00 & 1.00 \end{bmatrix} \tag{2.30}$$

These transformations are shown in Figure 2.13*a*–*e*. In Figure 2.13*a* the original position of the object is shown. Figure 2.13*b* shows the translation T_1 of reference vertex *D* to the origin. The rotation R_1 about the *y*-axis by angle 30° is shown in Figure 2.13*c*. Figure 2.13*d* shows the translation back to the original position of reference point *D* after the object has been rotated. In Figure 2.13*e* we show the complete process of accomplishing the transformations.

This simple example illustrates the usefulness of homogeneous transformations and concatenation of transformations.

2.8 SUMMARY

In this introductory chapter on CAD, we developed a basic understanding of the design process. The CAD system architecture, various CAD/CAM systems, and input–output devices are given. The criteria for the selection of various CAD/CAM systems are discussed. We have provided a brief discussion of transformations used in computer graphics. Computer graphics is an integral part of any CAD/CAM system. Knowledge of basic transformations helps in understanding how these are accomplished in your system. In this chapter we discussed various transformations such as translation, scaling, and rotation in both 2D and 3D. The homogeneous transformation and concatenation of transformations were also discussed and illustrated by an example.

PROBLEMS

2.1 What is the use of geometric transformations in computer graphics?

2.2 A point *A*(3, 4, 7) is translated by vector $\mathbf{V} = 4\mathbf{i} + 5\mathbf{j} + 3\mathbf{k}$. Find the new coordinate of the point.

2.3 A point *A*(4, 56, 3) is scaled by factor 5 with respect to origin. Find the new coordinates of the scaled point. Why is scaling different from translation? Give an example.

2.4 Give an example of nonuniform scaling.

2.5 Rotate a point *A*(1, 2) in 2D with respect to the origin by 36° counterclockwise, and find coordinates of the rotated point.

2.6 Rotate the point *A*(1,2) in Problem 2.5 with respect to point *B*(3, 4) for the same angle, and find the coordinates of the rotated point.

2.7 Rotate a point *V*(2, 3, 4) in 3D with respect to a point *W*(8, 5, 6) by 45° counterclockwise, about x-axis and find the coordinates of the rotated point.

2.8 Why is homogeneous transformation needed?

2.9 The two endpoints of a line are (3, 2, 6), and (1, 4, 7). First, the line is rotated by 47° counterclockwise with respect to a line defined by points (9, 3, 15) and (4, 3, 9). Then it is scaled by a factor of 3 with respect to the origin. Find the coordinates of the endpoints of the transformed line.

2.10 Consider the object shown in Figure P2.1. Perform the following transformations if the coordinates of the vertices of the object are *A*(1, 12), *B*(13, 2), *C*(19, 2), *D*(19, 8), and *E*(13, 12).

(a) Scale the object such that the edges are increased by a factor of 4.

(b) Rotate the object about point *A* by 45° in the counterclockwise direction.

2.11 Prove that two successive 2D transformations are additive: $T(d_1)T(d_2) = T(d_1 + d_2)$. Is this also valid in the 3D case?

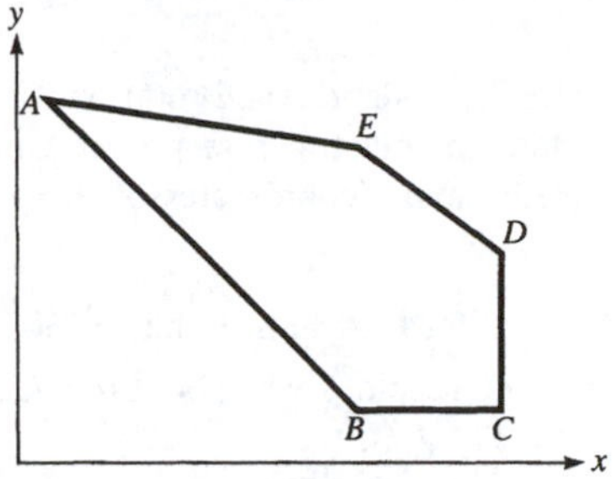

FIGURE P2.1 Object for Problem 2.10

2.12 Repeat Problem 2.11 for rotation.

2.13 Every transformation discussed in Chapter 2 is a special case of the general linear transformation given by:

$$x' = m_1x + n_1y + l_1$$
$$y' = m_2x + n_2y + l_2$$

Specify the range of parameters m_1, n_1, l_1, m_2, n_2, and l_2 that define the transformations discussed in Chapter 2.

2.14 The inverse transformation is also useful in practice. Given point $A(2, 3)$, after a rotation at a certain angle, the new coordinates are (3, 2). Find the rotation angle.

2.15 Consider a simple product and discuss various phases of the design process involved.

2.16 Discuss the architecture of the CAD system that you are using.

2.17 Enumerate various input–output devices used in CAD/CAM systems.

2.18 Discuss the various criteria used for the selection of CAD/CAM systems.

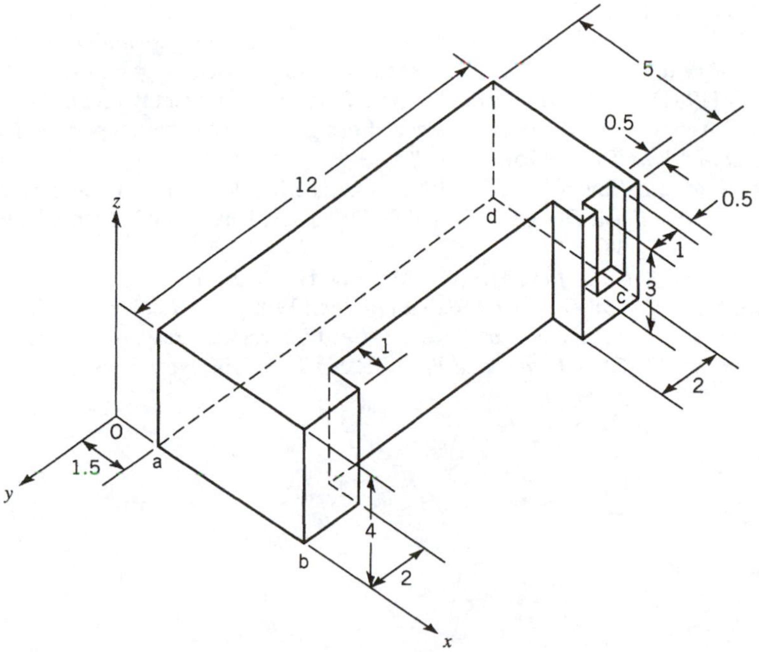

FIGURE P2.2 Object for lab project.

Laboratory Project

Write a program to perform scaling, translation, and rotation for an arbitrary object. The rotation routine should be able to rotate an object with respect to an arbitrary line in 3D. Consider the object as shown in Figure P2.2 having coordinates of the point O as (0, 0, 0) and do the following:

(a) Translate the object by a vector $\mathbf{D} = 3.4\mathbf{i} - 4.5\mathbf{j} + 6\mathbf{k}$.

(b) Rotate the object by 56° counterclockwise about the vector **D** in (a).

(c) Scale the object by a factor of 4.56.

(d) The transformations in (a), (b), and (c) were performed independently. Now perform their concatenation in the order (b), (c), and (a).

(e) Verify your results using other software such as Matlab, Mathematica, or AutoCAD.

REFERENCES AND SUGGESTED READING

Amirouche, F. M. L. (1993). *Computer Aided Design and Manufacturing.* Prentice Hall, Englewood Cliffs, New Jersey.

Ashimov, M. (1962). *Introduction to Design.* Prentice Hall, Englewood Cliffs, New Jersey.

Bedworth, D. D., Henderson, M. R., and Wolfe, P. M. (1991). *Computer-Integrated Design and Manufacturing.* McGraw-Hill, New York.

Chang, T. C., Wysk, R. A., and Wang, H. P. (1991). *Computer-Aided Manufacturing,* Prentice Hall, Englewood Cliffs, New Jersey.

Critchlow, A. J. (1985). *Introduction to Robotics.* Macmillan, New York.

Cutkosky, M. R., and Tenenbaum, J. M. (1990). A methodology and computational framework for concurrent product and process design. *Mechanism and Machine Theory,* 25(3):365–381.

Demel, J. T., and Miller, M. J. (1984). *Introduction to Computer Graphics.* Brooks/Cole Engineering Division, Monterey, California.

Earle, J. H. (1992). *Graphics for Engineers: AutoCAD Release 11,* Addison-Wesley, Reading, Massachusetts.

Foley, J. D., Dam, A. V., Feiner, S. K., and Hughes, J. F. (1990). *Computer Graphics: Principles and Practice.* Addison-Wesley, Reading, Massachusetts.

Glegg, G. L. (1981). *The Development of Design.* Cambridge University Press, Cambridge, UK.

Jain, P., and Agogino, A. M. (1990). Theory of design: An optimization perspective. *Mechanism and Machine Theory,* 25(3):287–303.

Kannapan, S. M. and Marshek, N. M. (1992). Engineering design methodologies: A new perspective. In *Intelligent Design and Manufacturing,* (A. Kusiak, ed.). John Wiley & Sons, New York, pp. 3–38.

Koren, Y. (1985). *Robotics for Engineers.* McGraw-Hill, New York.

Mortenson, M. E. (1985). *Geometric Modelling.* John Wiley & Sons, New York.

Suh, N. P. (1990). *The Principles of Design.* Oxford University Press, New York.

Zeid, I. (1991). *CAD/CAM Theory and Practice.* McGraw-Hill, New York.

CHAPTER 3

GEOMETRIC MODELING

The ultimate objective of any economic activity is to translate the customer's needs into a salable and profitable product(s). One of the major activities in this process is developing a geometric model of the product from the conceptual ideas. Geometric modeling is concerned with defining geometric objects using computational geometry. The product may be defined with the help of either a simple wireframe model, a surface model, or a solid model for proper representation. Therefore, geometric modeling is an integral part of any computer-aided design (CAD) system. In this chapter we discuss various geometric modeling approaches, such as wireframe, surface, and solid modeling. Basic computational geometric methods for defining simple entities such as curves, surfaces, and solids are given. We provide a brief discussion of CAD data transfer schemes such as Initial Graphics Exchange Specification (IGES), Product Data Exchange Standard (PDES), and Drawing Exchange File format (DXF). Concepts of parametric and variational design and their differences are explained. We also provide a brief discussion of computer-aided engineering analysis approaches such as finite-element analysis, tolerance analysis, and plastics analysis.

3.1 INTRODUCTION TO GEOMETRIC MODELING

Two major activities in physically realizing a product are design and manufacturing. The geometry of the product is one of the primary inputs to the design and manufacturing process. The geometric information about an object essentially includes types of surfaces and edges and their dimensions and tolerances. Traditionally, the geometric information about a part(s) has been provided on blueprints by a draftsperson. Today, in an era of agile manufacturing, the emphasis is on paperless manufacturing. That is, the geometric information should be directly transferred from the CAD databases to the computer-aided manufacturing (CAM) databases to enable subsequent manufacture of the part. This would significantly reduce product development and manufacturing lead time. Therefore, what is needed is an efficient representation of the complete information about a design that can easily be used by subsequent applications without ambiguity. Geometric modeling refers to a set of techniques concerned mainly with developing efficient representations of geometric aspects of a design. Therefore, geometric modeling is a fundamental part of virtually all CAD tools. It is the basis of many applications such as mass property calculations, mechanism analysis, finite-element modeling, and numerical control (NC) programming. Under these circumstances, geometric modeling has a tremendous influence in the process of development and manufacturing of a product(s).

Usually, there are a number of requirements for geometric modeling. The first requirement is completeness of the part representation. It means that the representation should provide enough data for users for the purpose of queries and analysis. In terms of the completeness of part representation, both topological and geometric data are required. Informally speaking, topological data represent the relationships between entities, whereas geometric data describe the geometry of the entities. For example, for a line segment, we want to know geometric data such as the length and the orientation. We also want to know topological data such as to which line it is connected. This type of information is important in many applications such as computer-aided process planning (CAPP), computer-aided assembly planning, and NC part programming. The second requirement is that the modeling method be easy to use by designers. For example, some methods are powerful but are difficult to manipulate. The third requirement concerns the rendering capability, which means how fast the entities can be accessed and displayed by the computer. This is especially important when we model a large and complex object or in situations involving some animation.

In the early years of CAD, improving the productivity of a draftsperson was the major concern. Methods for representing and storing curves and surfaces were developed for various purposes. More recently, the existing geometric modeling methods have been challenged by new engineering applications. This is due to the fact that sometimes useful information is not adequately represented by early geometric modeling methods. Some modeling techniques are application oriented. Moreover, the three requirements of a modeling method mentioned in the preceding paragraph are sometimes conflicting. For example, there is a need to consider a trade-off between concise storage and fast access. To overcome these problems, some new methods have been developed and more developments are expected.

3.2 WHY IS KNOWLEDGE OF GEOMETRIC MODELING NECESSARY?

Over the years, CAD tools have proved very successful in improving the productivity of the draftsperson and in other applications. Generally, most of the CAD software is well designed and tested. It is true that a designer who does not know much about the "inside" of the software may still be able to use it. However, a large portion of most software is usually object oriented and the computer database is limited. It is therefore natural that some extension of the commercial software or package will be needed for special applications. Moreover, knowledge of the structure and technique of the software is very helpful in understanding fully and avoiding misunderstanding the software manual. It is, therefore, necessary to study existing geometric models to utilize fully the attributes of these models or to create new systems for special applications. The study of geometric models will also help CAD/CAM users to finish the training process efficiently and reach a higher level of understanding of the computer-aided design process. In the following sections we provide a detailed discussion of various geometric modeling approaches.

3.3 GEOMETRIC MODELING APPROACHES

In traditional drawing practices, an object is represented by a number of views in two dimensions. To represent a part completely, three views are often needed: plan view, front view, and side elevations. In these views, the geometric and topological information is captured by viewing an object from different directions. Multiple views of a part are shown in Figure 3.1. To master this drawing technique, much training is necessary. Mistakes in the drawing often occur. In computer-aided design, two-dimensional multi-view drawing is still widely used, in which the computer screen serves as sketch paper and the keyboard and mouse serve as a pencil. Many functions such as erasing, reproducing, and copying, traditionally considered as tedious and time-consuming, are now effectively supported in CAD systems. This obviously increases the draftsperson's productivity. However, some basic mental functions in developing these multi-view drawings are still performed by the designer or draftsperson. Another major problem associated with this approach is that it does not support subsequent applications such as finite-element analysis (FEA) or NC part programming.

To try to overcome these problems, a number of methods have been developed over the past two decades. In these methods, a 3D model of the part is created directly. Then 2D view drawing can be generated by computer, if required. Moreover, these models support many engineering applications such as FEA, mass property calculation, and

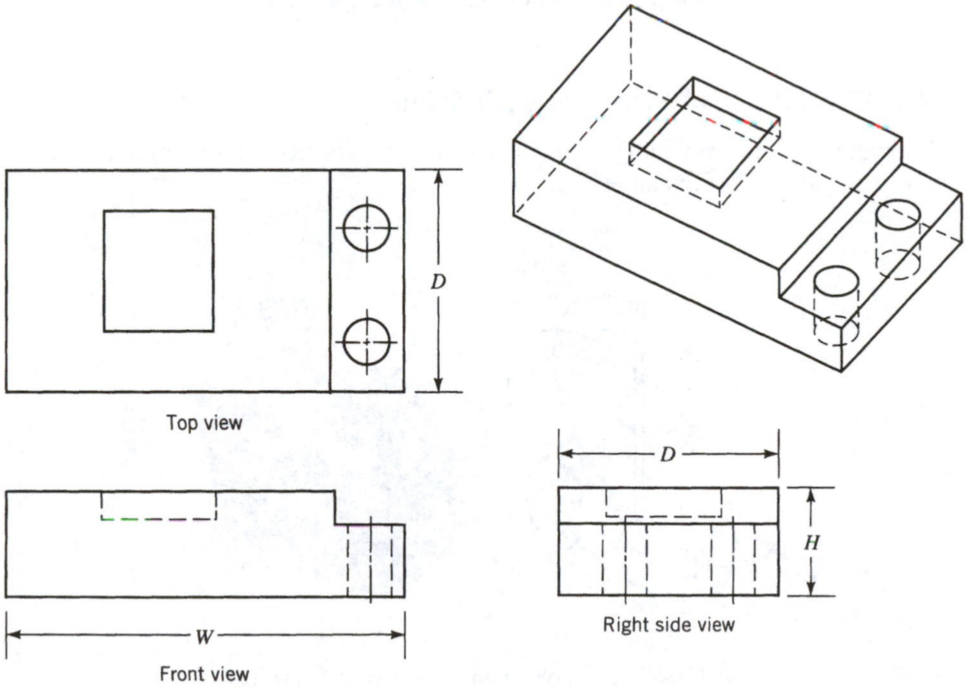

FIGURE 3.1 Multiview of a part.

process planning. This leads us one step closer to full engineering automation. In this category, the basic geometric modeling approaches available to designers on CAD/CAM systems are *wireframe, surface,* and *solid* modeling.

Normally, solid modeling requires extensive computations to produce and render a solid. It is therefore mainly confined to mainframes, minicomputers, and workstations. However, with the upgrading of microcomputers and improvements in solid modeling algorithms, this scenario has changed to some degree. Many microcomputer-based systems are now capable of running new versions of solid modeling. However, serious professional designers still prefer to have at least one workstation around. Wireframe modeling requires much less hardware support and its use is widespread on microcomputer-based systems. In the following sections, we provide a basic understanding of these approaches to geometric modeling.

3.4 WIREFRAME MODELING

Wireframe is one of the most basic methods of geometric modeling. Informally, it can be defined as the computer version of the traditional methods of drafting. In traditional drafting, the draftsperson represents entities by drawing lines on paper using pencils. In a wireframe model, we represent entities by points, lines, arcs and circles, conics, and other type of curves utilizing light pen, keyboard, mouse, and so on interactively via the cathode-ray tube (CRT). A hard copy of the drawing is obtained by sending the drawing to a printer or plotter.

Wireframe modeling uses points, curves (i.e., lines, circles, arcs), and so forth to define objects. For example, a user may, with three-dimensional (3D) wireframe models, enter 3D vertices, say (x, y, z), and then join the vertices to form a 3D object. An example of a 3D wireframe model is shown in Figure 3.2.

3.4.1 Limitations of Wireframe Modeling

Although wireframe modeling is simple and straightforward in concept, it has a number of limitations. For example,

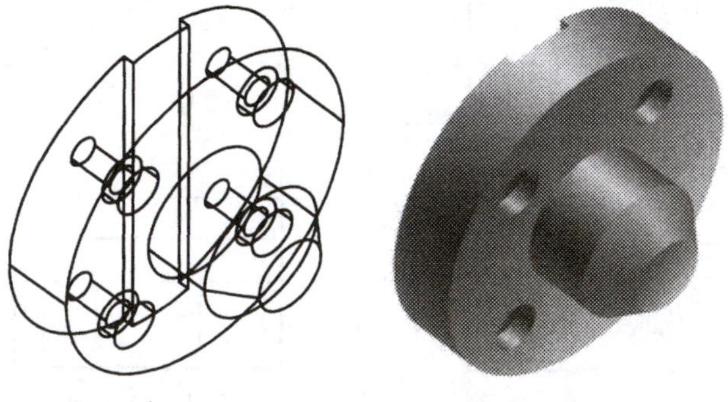

(a) (b)

FIGURE 3.2 Wireframe model (a) of a part (b).

- From the point of view of engineering applications, it is not possible to calculate volume and mass properties of a design. Other applications, such as NC path generation, cross-sectioning, and interference detection, also encounter problems when wireframe modeling is used.Because the wireframe model database contains only low-level information such as points and lines, the wireframe methods are limited in scope when high-level information is required by particular applications such as process planning.
- In the wireframe representation, the virtual edges (profile or silhouette) are not usually provided. For example, a cylinder is represented by three edges, that is, two circles and one straight line. But the straight line is not enough to represent the profile or silhouette of a cylinder (see Figure 3.3*b*).
- There are many wireframe representation schemes. However, ambiguous representations of real objects may be created. For example, the wireframe model shown in Figure 3.3*a* may be recognized as either a block or an inward corner. Figure 3.3*b* may be considered as either a boss or a hole. Figure 3.3*c* is just a nonsense object.
- The creation of wireframe models usually involves more user effort to input necessary information than that of solid models, especially for large and complex parts. For example, consider the creation of a 3D model of a simple cube. In the wireframe model we need to draw 12 lines, whereas with solid modeling methods a cube may be created by providing the positions of three corner points. Furthermore, the latter model provides more information, such as the inside or outside of the part.

3.4.2 Wireframe Entities

Wireframe models consist of only points and lines, which are the basic entities of these models. Basic knowledge of how to represent these entities in a computer database is provided in the following section, which may help CAD users increase their productivity. It is not uncommon to ask how to draw an ellipse, how to create a circle that is tangent to a line, or what a Bezier curve is and how to draw it. Furthermore, this will

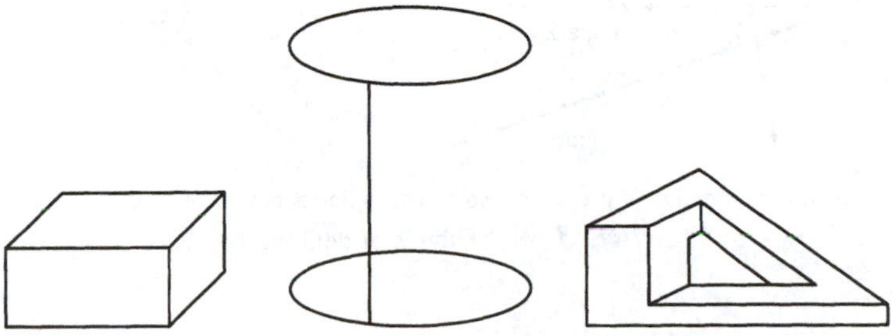

(*a*) (*b*) (*c*)

FIGURE 3.3 Examples of ambiguous representation.

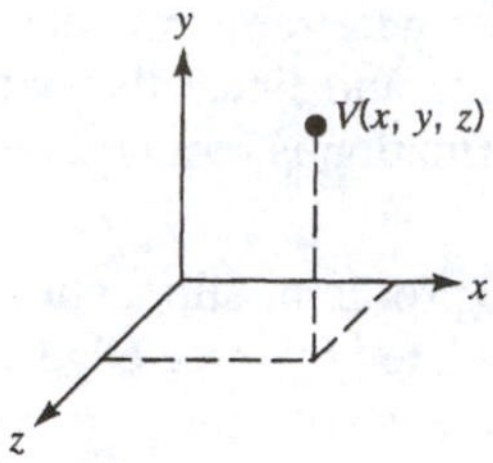

1. Absolute Cartesian coordinates (straightforward method).

   Select existing points, such as the center of a circle or the end points of a line.

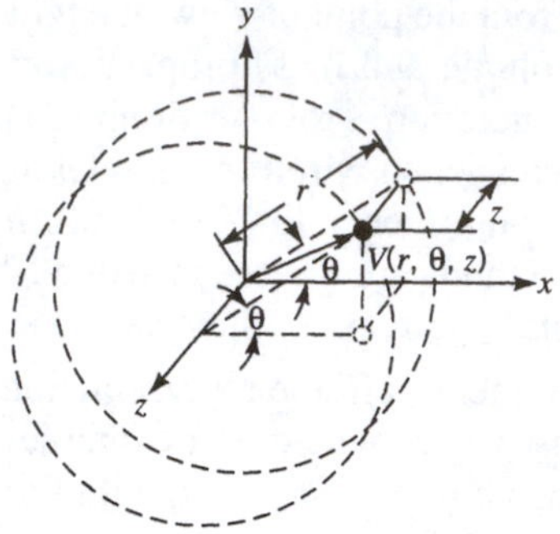

2. Absolute cylindrical coordinates.

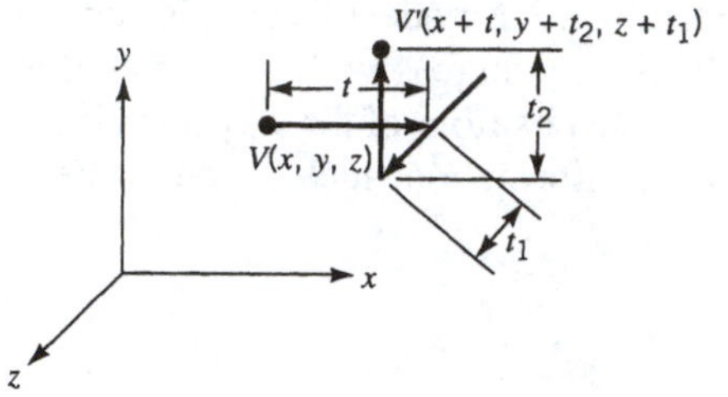

3. Incremental Cartesian coordinates (quite convenient for continuous moving points).

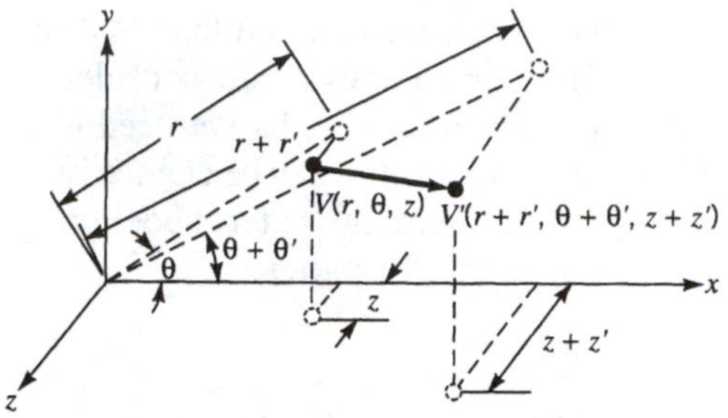

4. Incremental cylindrical coordinates. (Note: In some CAD/CAM systems, the above methods are combined to create new defining methods, For example, methods 3 and 4 are combined in AutoCAD to define a point).

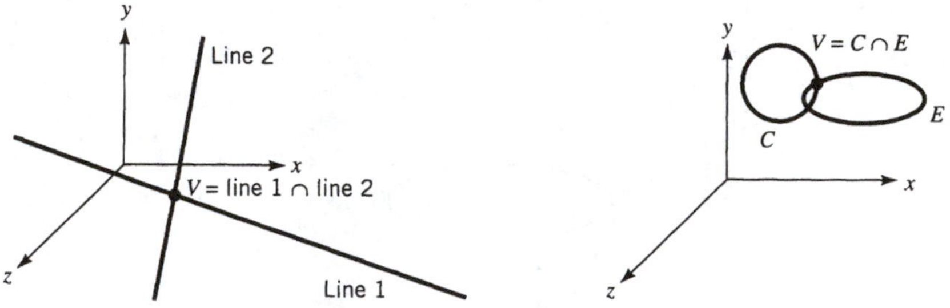

5. The intersection of two lines, two circles, a line and a circle, and so forth.

FIGURE 3.4 Methods of defining points.

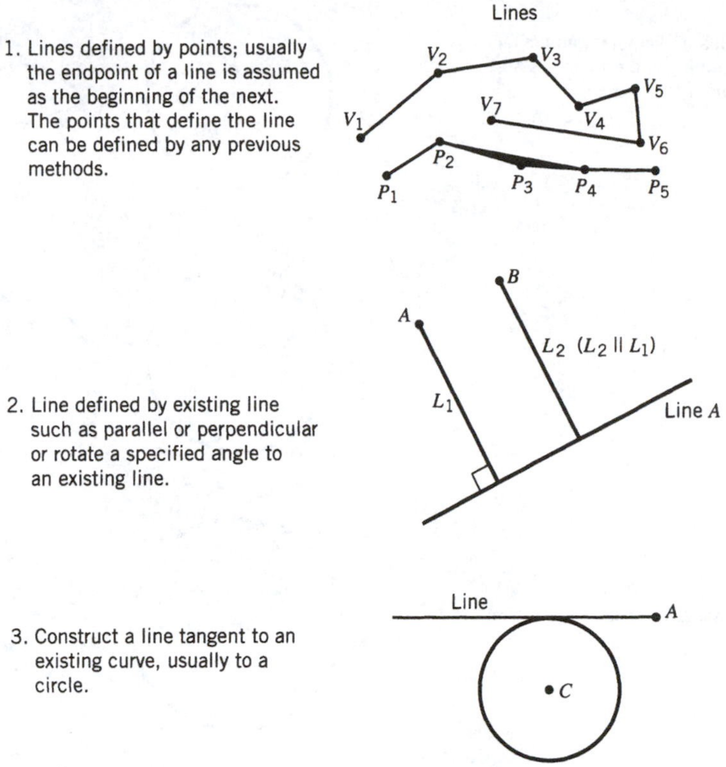
Lines
1. Lines defined by points; usually the endpoint of a line is assumed as the beginning of the next. The points that define the line can be defined by any previous methods.
V_1
V_2
V_3
V_4
V_5
V_6
V_7
P_1
P_2
P_3
P_4
P_5
2. Line defined by existing line such as parallel or perpendicular or rotate a specified angle to an existing line.
B
A
L_2 ($L_2 \parallel L_1$)
L_1
Line A
3. Construct a line tangent to an existing curve, usually to a circle.
Line
A
C

FIGURE 3.5 Methods of defining lines.

serve as the basis for further discussion. Normally, wireframe entities are divided into two categories: analytic and synthetic entities.

3.4.3 Analytic Curves

Analytic entities include points, straight lines, arcs, circles, ellipses, parabolas, and hyperbolas. The properties of these entities and the techniques for manipulating them are well studied and usually taught in high school mathematics courses. The methods for defining these entities in a computer are easy to understand. The most common methods used by CAD/CAM systems to create wireframe entities are shown in Figures 3.4 to 3.7, and synthetic entities are shown in Figure 3.14. Different CAD/CAM systems provide different methods, but they are mostly extensions or subsets of the above. It is, therefore, recommended that the user's manual be looked into carefully. For example, AutoCAD covers all of the preceding methods, whereas some of the packages provide only a few of these defining methods for particular applications. In the following example, we try to illustrate the use of analytical entities to create a wireframe model of a part. Although it is a simple part, it clearly illustrates how to define 3D points, lines, and circles in a computer aided design system.

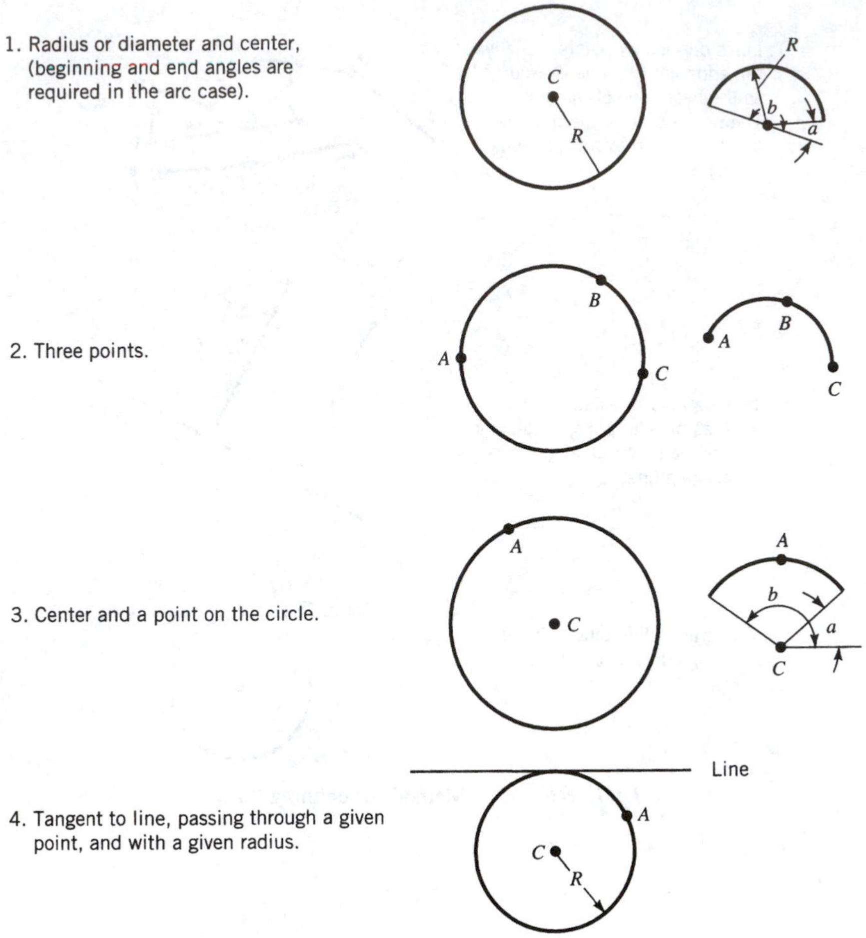

FIGURE 3.6 Methods of defining arcs and circles.

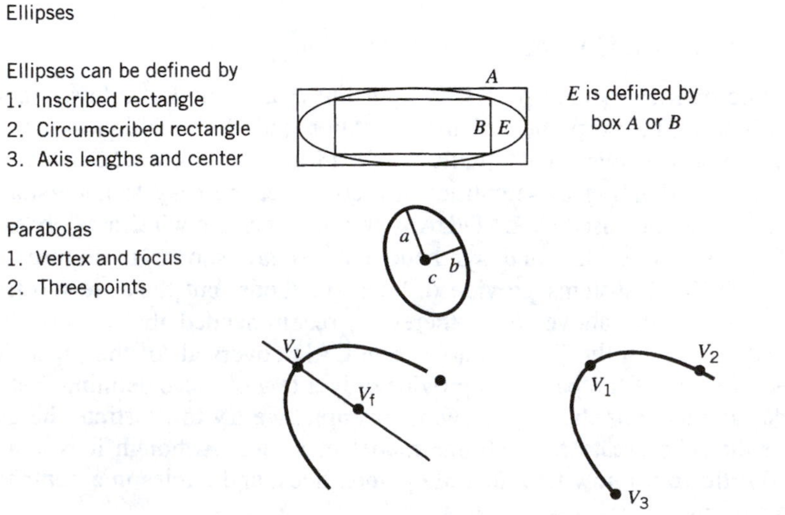

FIGURE 3.7 Methods of defining ellipses and parabolas.

EXAMPLE 3.1

For the object shown in Figure 3.8, create the following:

1. The model database utilizing a CAD/CAM system.
2. Orthographic views of the model.

Solution

1. The model database is created as follows.

(a) To create the wireframe of this part, we have to use the line command to draw all the lines. There are, however, many ways in which we can draw this object. The most effective way (software dependent) is to make the 2D profile of the part and then sweep it across a space distance in the direction perpendicular to the profile plane to create the outline of the 3D model.

To create the profile we may try different points and define a method that, in turn, defines the line segments of the profile. For example, it is easier to define every point separately by inputting the coordinates of the ending points of the line segments, if the points' coordinates are available. If the coordinates of the points are not available, it is more convenient to define each point by incremental methods using the dimension of the part directly.

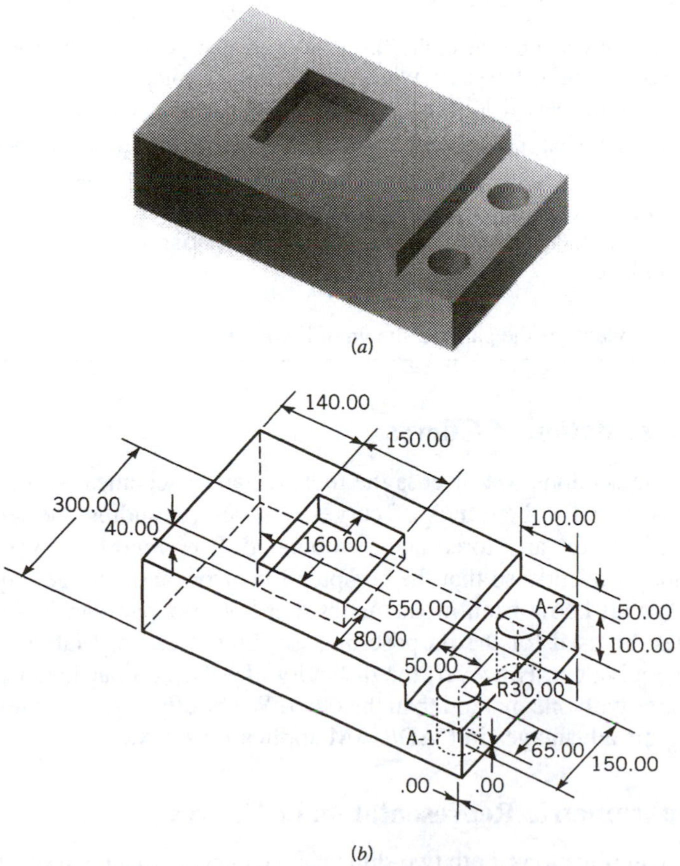

FIGURE 3.8 Part model for Example 3.1.

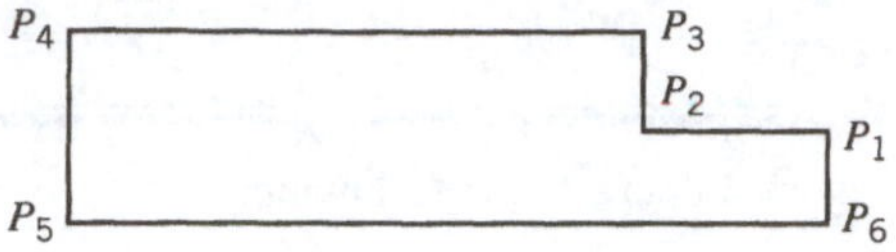

FIGURE 3.9 Outline profile of the part.

TABLE 3.1 **Coordinates of Each Point**

	Coordinates of Points		
Point	*x*	*y*	*z*
P_1	0	100.00	0
P_2	100.00	100.00	0
P_3	100.00	150.00	0
P_4	550.00	150.00	0
P_5	550.00	0	0
P_6	0	0	0

Here, we create the profile by inputting the coordinates of the points as given in Table 3.1. The 2D profile is shown in Figure 3.9.

(b) After the sweeping profile of the 3D model is created, we define the sweeping distance, which is the width of the part. When this is done, the computer creates the 3D model of the base of the part, that is, the part without the pocket and holes.

(c) The procedure outlined in steps (a) and (b) can be used to create the pocket of the part.

(d) The final step is to create the two holes. Use of some edit commands such as array, rotate, or mirror is an efficient way to duplicate holes. In this example, one hole is created first, then the other hole is created by rotating (with copy function on) the existing hole.

2. Orthographic views of the part are shown in Figure 3.1.

3.4.4 Representation of Curves

In the following sections, we discuss the representation schemes of curves. In CAD/CAM systems, usually thousands of curves or lines (including the straight line, a special case of curves) are stored and manipulated. It is important to represent them effectively and efficiently so that the computation effort and storage requirement are minimized. We all know from mathematics that both nonparametric and parametric equations may be used for the purpose of describing a curve. Mathematically, both methods are equivalent. However, the difficulty of solving a particular problem may be much greater with one method than the other. We briefly review these two methods and discuss their advantages in CAD/CAM applications next.

3.4.5 Nonparametric Representation of Curves

In engineering applications, both two-dimensional curves (plane curves, which means that the curves lie in a plane) and three-dimensional space curves are used. These curves can be defined by nonparametric equations, which we call the nonparametric representation of the curves. For example, a 2D straight line can be defined as $y = x + 1$. This equation defines the x and y coordinates of each point without the assistance of extra parameters. Thus, it is called the nonparametric equation of a line. The same line may be described by defining the coordinates of each point using the equation $V = [x, y]^T = [x = t,\ y = t + 1]^T$, where T represents transpose. In this equation, the coordinates of each point are defined with the help of the "extra" parameter t, and it is called the parametric equation of the line. These two methods have their advantages and disadvantages. They are discussed in detail next.

Nonparametric equations of curves can be further divided into explicit and implicit nonparametric equations. The explicit nonparametric representation of general two-dimensional and three-dimensional curves takes the form:

$$\mathbf{V}_1 = [x, y]^T = [x, f(x)]^T \tag{3.1}$$

$$\mathbf{V}_2 = [x, y, z]^T = [x, f(x), g(x)]^T \tag{3.2}$$

where $\mathbf{V}_1$ and $\mathbf{V}_2$ are the position vectors of the points V_1 and V_2 in two-dimensional and three-dimensional space, respectively. The graphic representation of these equations is shown in Figure 3.10. Equation (3.1) enables us to obtain the y-coordinates of points on the curves by direct substitution of values of x. Equation (3.2) gives the y- and z-coordinates directly. The implicit nonparametric representation of a general n-dimensional space curve takes the form

$$\begin{cases} F_1(x_1, x_2, \ldots x_n) = 0 \\ F_2(x_1, x_2, \ldots x_n) = 0 \\ \vdots \\ F_{n-1}(x_1, x_2, \ldots x_n) = 0 \end{cases} \tag{3.3}$$

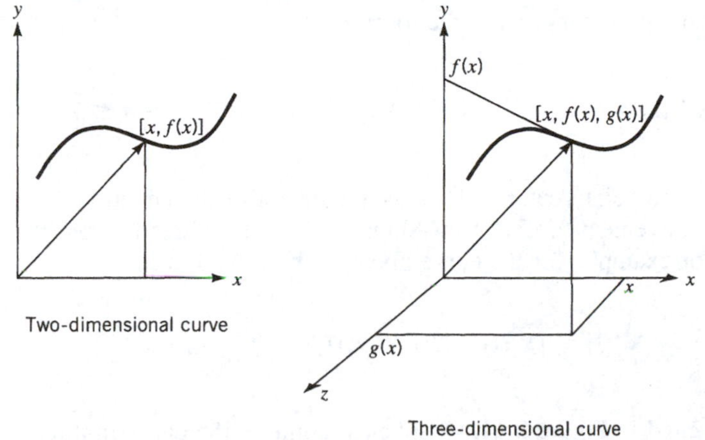

FIGURE 3.10 Explicit nonparametric representation of curves.

For example, for two-dimensional curves Equation (3.3) assumes the following form:

$$F(x, y) = 0 \tag{3.4}$$

Equation (3.4) expresses a relationship between the coordinates x and y of each point in two-dimensional space.

Similarly, for three-dimensional curves the equations would be

$$\begin{cases} F(x, y, z) = 0 \\ G(x, y, z) = 0 \end{cases} \tag{3.5}$$

Equation (3.5) expresses the relationship between the coordinates x and y, x and z of each point in three-dimensional space; the relationship between y and z is implicit. This equation, however, must be solved analytically to obtain the explicit form, which is not easily done by computer, or one can resort to a numerical procedure to obtain approximate points on the curve. It is often the case that the curve is displayed as a series of points or straight-line segments and the computations involved can be extensive. This limits its use in CAD/CAM systems.

3.4.6 Parametric Representation of Curves

Parametric representation of curves, on the other hand, has properties well suited for its use in CAD/CAM systems. In parametric form, each point on a curve is expressed as a function of a parameter t by equations of the form $x = X(t)$, $y = Y(t)$, and $z = Z(t)$. The value of the parameter t can be either bounded by the minimum (T_{min}) and maximum (T_{max}) range or the normalized range between 0 and 1.

The parametrization enables us to obtain the x, y, z coordinates of points on the curves by directly substituting the values of the parameter t. Equations in this form are known as parametric or freedom equations for x, y, and z. The parameter t acts as a local coordinate for points on the curves. The parametric equation for a three-dimensional or space curve takes the form

$$\mathbf{V}(t) = [x, y, z]^{\mathrm{T}} = [X(t), Y(t), Z(t)]^{\mathrm{T}}, \qquad T_{min} \leq t \leq T_{max} \tag{3.6}$$

where $\mathbf{V}(t)$ is the point vector and t is the parameter of the equation.

It is also convenient to obtain the slope of the curve directly from the parametric equations. For example, for the curve given by $\mathbf{V}(t)$, we have

$$\mathbf{V}'(t) = [X'(t), Y'(t), Z'(t)]^{\mathrm{T}}, \qquad T_{min} \leq t \leq T_{max}$$

This is illustrated in Figure 3.11, where each point on the curve in three-dimensional space is represented in one-dimensional space as a function of parameter t. Next, we illustrate the parametric equation concept by a few examples:

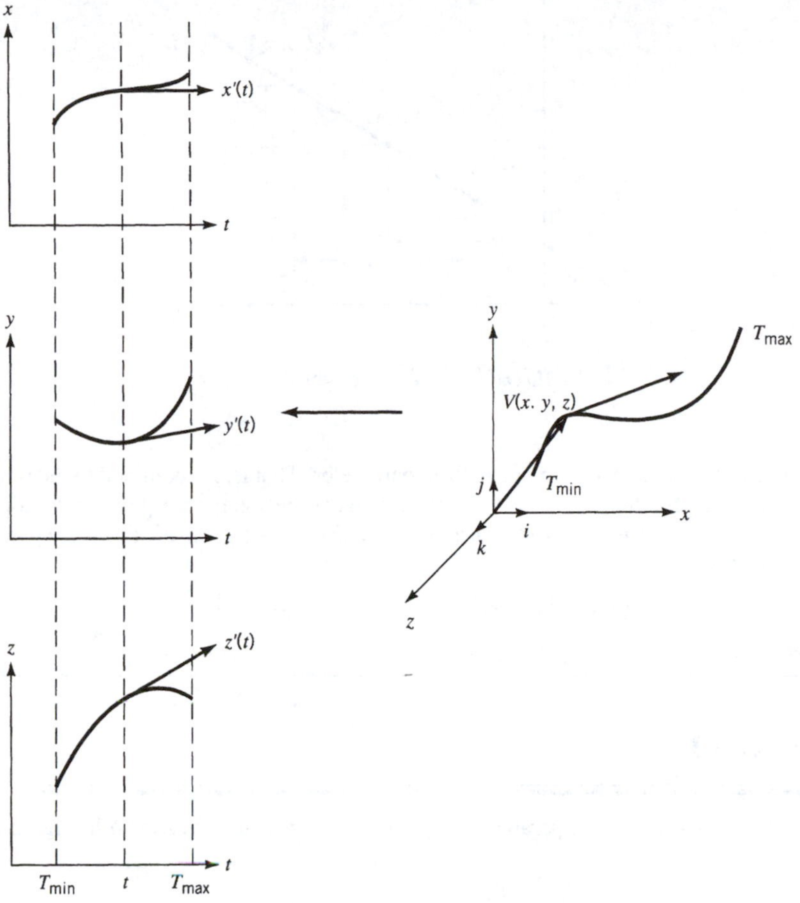

FIGURE 3.11 Illustration of parametric representation of curves.

EXAMPLE 3.2

Develop the parametric line equations from nonparametric equation of a line. Using the resulting equations, find the slopes.

Solution

A familiar form of nonparametric representation of a line is

$$(x_2 - x_1)(y - y_1) = (y_2 - y_1)(x - x_1)$$

This equation is used to describe a straight line as the locus of points collinear with two given points V_1 and V_2 with coordinates (x_1, y_1), and (x_2, y_2), respectively, as illustrated in Figure 3.12. This equation is an implicit form of a line. A simple way to get the parametric equation is to define a parameter t equal to the ratio VV_1/V_2V_1, that is,

$$t = \frac{VV_1}{V_2V_1} = \frac{x - x_1}{x_2 - x_1} = \frac{y - y_1}{y_2 - y_1}$$

By rearranging this equation, we get the following parametric equation:

$$\begin{cases} x = (1 - t)x_1 + tx_2 \\ y = (1 - t)y_1 + ty_2 \end{cases}$$

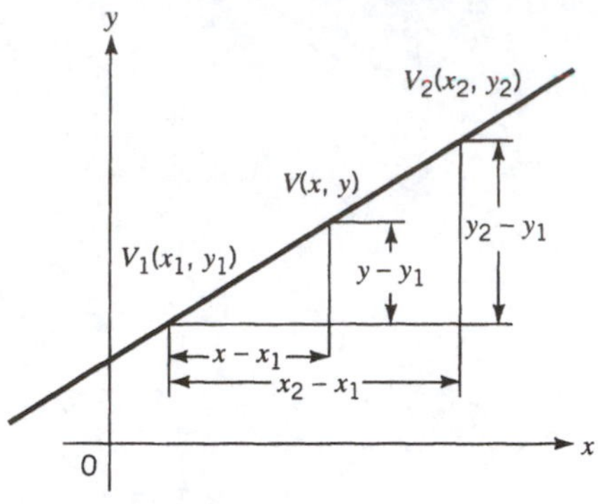

FIGURE 3.12 Straight line.

In these parametric equations, t is a normalized parameter. That is, t is confined to the range 0 to 1, which is defined by the ratio VV_1/V_2V_1. The distance between start point and endpoint is V_2V_1, and VV_1 is the distance between variable point V and start point V_1. From the parametric equations, we have

$$x'(t) = x_2 - x_1 \qquad \text{and} \qquad y'(t) = y_2 - y_1$$

Therefore, slope $= (y_2 - y_1)/(x_2 - x_1)$.

EXAMPLE 3.3

Develop the nonparametric and parametric equations for an ellipse as shown in Figure 3.13.

Solution

From Figure 3.13, we know that the major and minor radii of the ellipse are A and B, respectively, and the center of the ellipse is at the point $C(a, b)$. Therefore, the implicit nonparametric equation of the ellipse can be expressed as

$$\frac{(x - a)^2}{A^2} + \frac{(y - b)^2}{B^2} = 1$$

The parametric equation for an ellipse can be developed by using trigonometric functions. For this purpose, we need to know the coordinates of a variable point $V(x, y)$ as a function of an angle α.

Accordingly, we have the following parametric equation of the ellipse:

$$x = a + CW = a + A\cos\alpha$$

$$y = b + VW = b + B\sin\alpha$$

Also, note the difference between parameter α and angle VCW. At this point, we have developed the parametric equation of the ellipse. By varying the parameter α, we may define any point on the ellipse. It is, however, worth mentioning that the use of trigonometric functions may increase the computational effort.

3.4.7 Synthetic Curves

In addition to simple analytic entities that we discussed in the previous section, some more general methods for representing curves are needed to meet geometric design requirements of mechanical parts and various engineering applications. Much research

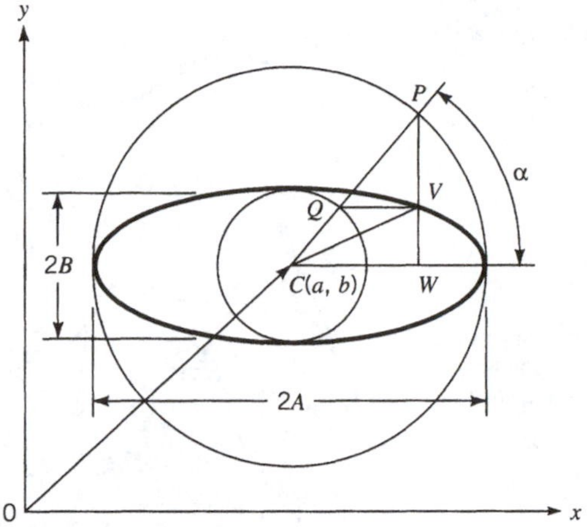

FIGURE 3.13 Ellipse for Example 3.3.

has been done during the past couple of decades on developing better methods for representing general curves and shapes and easier ways to manipulate them by computer. Generally speaking, a good representation of engineering objects has to have the following properties:

- Easy to control the continuity of the curves to be designed
- Requires less storage to represent a curve
- Less computation time and no computational problems
- Easy to input by user

The methods used to define these curves in CAD/CAM are shown in Figure 3.14. The mathematical representations of these curves are discussed in the following sections, which may help in further understanding how synthetic curves are represented in CAD/CAM systems.

3.4.8 Parametric Representation of Synthetic Curves

Analytic curves, as described in the previous section, are usually well defined and well studied. However, in the geometric design of mechanical parts, some other curves are required. They do not belong to any analytic curves we presented in the previous section. One familiar example is the car body. The curves of the car body not only have to envelop inside the mechanical parts but also help reduce air resistance. It is unusual for a well-designed car body to consist only of analytic curves or surfaces such as circles or cylinders. Other examples include the fuselage, wings, and propeller blades of airplanes, whose shape is based on aerodynamic and fluid flow simulations. How are those curves or surfaces created in CAD/CAM systems? What are their mathematical representations? To answer these questions, we provide a detailed discussion of various types of synthetic curves and surfaces in the following sections.

First we introduce the concept of continuity. Intuitively, continuity means the smoothness of the connection of two curves or surfaces at the connection points or edges. Normally, three types of continuity, called C^0, C^1, and C^2, are defined to characterize the smoothness of connection of two curves. C^0 continuity implies simply

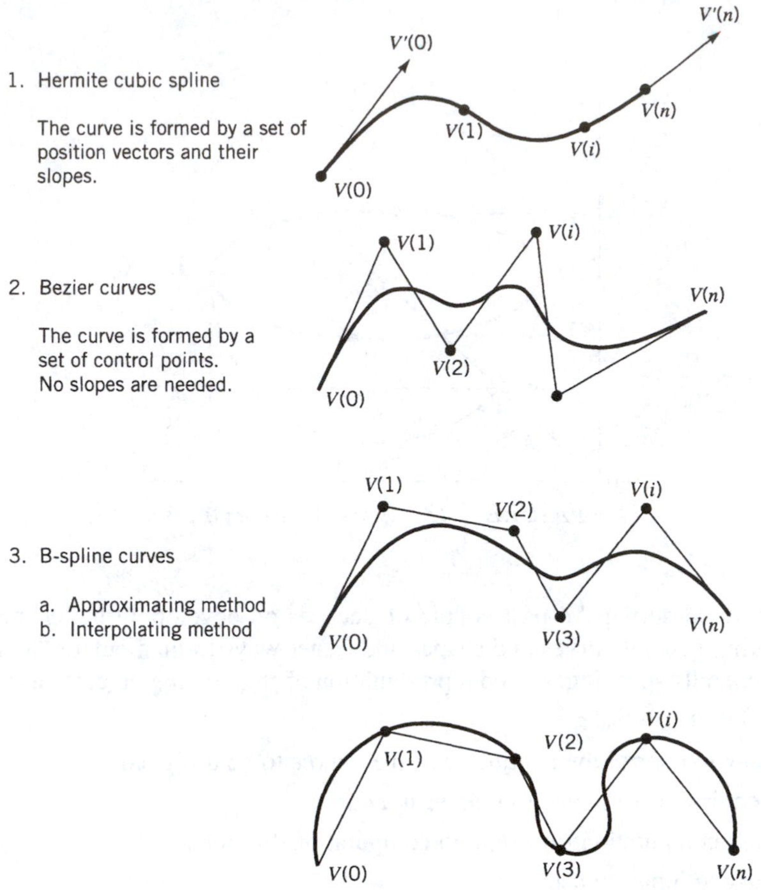
1. Hermite cubic spline
The curve is formed by a set of position vectors and their slopes.
V'(0)
V'(n)
V(0)
V(1)
V(i)
V(n)
2. Bezier curves
The curve is formed by a set of control points. No slopes are needed.
V(1)
V(i)
V(2)
V(n)
V(0)
3. B-spline curves
a. Approximating method
b. Interpolating method
V(1)
V(2)
V(i)
V(0)
V(3)
V(n)
V(i)
V(2)
V(1)
V(0)
V(3)
V(n)

FIGURE 3.14 Methods of defining synthetic curves.

connecting two curves. That means that the gradients of these curves at the point of joining as well as their curvatures may be different (Figure 3.15*a*). In C^1 continuity, the gradients at the point of joining must be same (Figure 3.15*b*). However, C^2 implies curvature continuity; that is, not only the gradient but also the center of curvature is the same, as shown in Figure 3.15*c*.

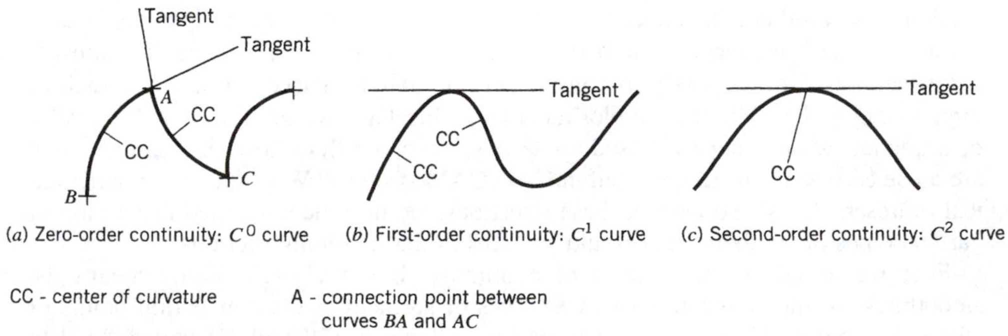
Tangent
Tangent
A
CC
CC
B
C
Tangent
CC
CC
Tangent
CC
(a) Zero-order continuity: C⁰ curve
(b) First-order continuity: C¹ curve
(c) Second-order continuity: C² curve
CC - center of curvature
A - connection point between curves BA and AC

FIGURE 3.15 Types of continuities.

Curves that are constructed by many curve segments are called synthetic curves. Different types of curve segments can be used to construct synthetic curves, with certain continuity requirements. Synthetic curves usually have some good properties; for example, it is easy to control the continuity of the curve to be designed and computation requirements are low. The types of synthetic curves normally provided by major CAD/CAM systems include:

- Hermite cubic spline
- Bezier curves
- B-spline curves
- Rational B-splines
- Nonuniform rational B-splines

In the following sections, these curves are briefly discussed.

3.4.9 Hermite Cubic Spline

The main idea of the Hermite cubic spline is that a curve is divided into segments. Each segment is approximated by an expression, namely a parametric cubic function. The reasons for using cubic functions to approximate the segments are:

- A cubic polynomial is the minimum-order polynomial function that generates C^0, C^1, and C^2 continuity curves.
- A cubic polynomial is the lowest-degree polynomial that permits inflection within a curve segment and allows representation of nonplanar (twisted) space curves.
- Higher-order polynomials have some drawbacks, such as oscillation about control points, and are uneconomical in terms of storing information and computation.

The general form of a cubic function can be written as

$$\mathbf{r} = \mathbf{V}(t) = \mathbf{a}_0 + \mathbf{a}_1 t + \mathbf{a}_2 t^2 + \mathbf{a}_3 t^3 \tag{3.7}$$

where the point vector $\mathbf{r}$ of the cubic curve is defined by the parametric equation $\mathbf{V}(t)$. The segment defined by the equation has highest-degree polynomial t^3. The parameter t is traditionally bounded by the parameter interval $0 \le t \le 1$.

This general form represents the whole family of cubic curves. We can define any particular curves by specifying the four coefficient vectors (that is, $\mathbf{a}_0$, $\mathbf{a}_1$, $\mathbf{a}_2$, $\mathbf{a}_3$). However, the coefficients do not all have direct physical significance and are not convenient "handles" for adjusting the segment shape or incorporating it into a composite curve (Rooney and Steadman, 1987).

The Hermite cubic spline presents a way to define the coefficients more meaningfully. That is, we want to define a curve by $\mathbf{V}(0)$ and $\mathbf{V}(1)$, $\mathbf{V}'(0)$ and $\mathbf{V}'(1)$, where $\mathbf{V}(0)$ and $\mathbf{V}(1)$ are the position vectors at the ends of the segment and $\mathbf{V}'(0)$ and $\mathbf{V}'(1)$ are the derivative values or the tangent vectors of the endpoints. The geometric meaning is that the two endpoints of the Hermite cubic curve are at $\mathbf{V}(0)$ and $\mathbf{V}(1)$ and the two tangent vectors at the two endpoints are $\mathbf{V}'(0)$ and $\mathbf{V}'(1)$. This gives users a way to connect two curves and assure a certain degree of continuity. An example of a Hermite cubic spline is shown in Figure 3.16. We next derive the parameter equation, given that $\mathbf{V}(0)$, $\mathbf{V}(1)$, $\mathbf{V}'(0)$, and $\mathbf{V}'(1)$ are known.

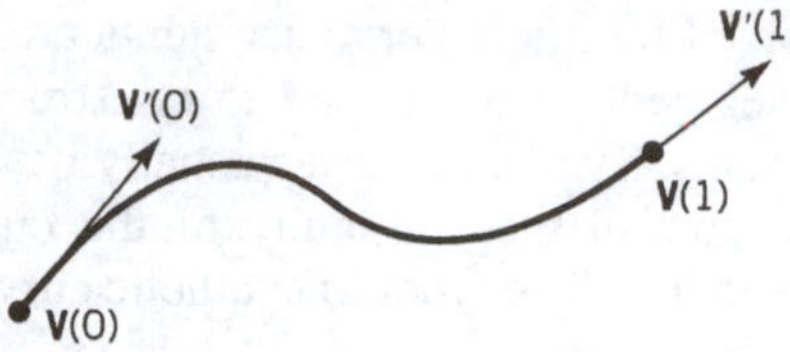

FIGURE 3.16 A Hermite cubic spline.

Upon differentiation of Equation (3.7), we have

$$\mathbf{V}'(t) = \mathbf{a}_1 + 2\mathbf{a}_2 t + 3\mathbf{a}_3 t^2 \tag{3.7a}$$

Applying the boundary conditions to Equations (3.7) and (3.7a) yields

$$\begin{aligned} &\text{At } t = 0: \quad \mathbf{V}(0) = \mathbf{a}_0, && \mathbf{V}'(0) = \mathbf{a}_1 \\ &\text{At } t = 1: \quad \mathbf{V}(1) = \mathbf{a}_0 + \mathbf{a}_1 + \mathbf{a}_2 + \mathbf{a}_3, && \mathbf{V}'(1) = \mathbf{a}_1 + 2\mathbf{a}_2 + 3\mathbf{a}_3 \end{aligned} \tag{3.7b}$$

On solving these four equations simultaneously for the coefficients, we get

$$\begin{aligned} \mathbf{a}_0 &= \mathbf{V}(0) \\ \mathbf{a}_1 &= \mathbf{V}'(0) \\ \mathbf{a}_2 &= 3[\mathbf{V}(1) - \mathbf{V}(0)] - 2\mathbf{V}'(0) - \mathbf{V}'(1) \\ \mathbf{a}_3 &= 2[\mathbf{V}(0) - \mathbf{V}(1)] + \mathbf{V}'(0) + \mathbf{V}'(1) \end{aligned} \tag{3.7c}$$

Substituting Equations (3.7c) into Equations (3.7) and (3.7a) and rearranging gives

$$\begin{aligned} \mathbf{V}(t) = {} & \mathbf{V}(0)(1 - 3t^2 + 2t^3) + \mathbf{V}(1)(3t^2 - 2t^3) \\ & + \mathbf{V}'(0)(t - 2t^2 + t^3) + \mathbf{V}'(1)(-t^2 + t^3) \end{aligned} \tag{3.7d}$$

$$\begin{aligned} \mathbf{V}'(t) = {} & \mathbf{V}(0)(-6t + 6t^2) + \mathbf{V}(1)(6t - 6t^2) \\ & + \mathbf{V}'(0)(3t^2 - 4t + 1) + \mathbf{V}'(1)(3t^2 - 2t) \end{aligned} \tag{3.7e}$$

The equation (3.7d) can be represented as

$$\mathbf{r} = \mathbf{VMA} = [1 \quad t \quad t^2 \quad t^3] \begin{bmatrix} 1 & 0 & 0 & 0 \\ 0 & 0 & 1 & 0 \\ -3 & 3 & -2 & -1 \\ 2 & -2 & 1 & 1 \end{bmatrix} \begin{bmatrix} \mathbf{V}(0) \\ \mathbf{V}(1) \\ \mathbf{V}'(0) \\ \mathbf{V}'(1) \end{bmatrix} \tag{3.7f}$$

This form can be conveniently adjusted to yield various shapes of curve segment by altering one or more of $\mathbf{V}(0)$, $\mathbf{V}(1)$, $\mathbf{V}'(0)$, and $\mathbf{V}'(1)$ appropriately. The Hermite form of a cubic spline is determined by defining positions and tangent vectors at the data points, and this is shown in Figure 3.16.

There are some disadvantages of this method. For example,

- First-order derivatives are needed; it is not convenient for a designer to provide first-order derivatives.
- There is no local control support.
- The order of the curve is constant regardless of the number of data points.

EXAMPLE 3.4

Determine and plot the equation of Hermite form of a cubic spline from given position vectors and slopes at the data points with vector magnitude equal to 1.

Point 1: $A = [1, 2]^T$, slope$(A) = 60°$

Point 2: $B = [3, 1]^T$, slope$(B) = 30°$

Solution

In this example, we illustrate how to obtain the cubic spline in Hermite form. For simplicity, only one segment is considered.

From Equation (3.7d), we have

$$\begin{aligned} V_x = V_x(t) &= V_x(0)(1 - 3t^2 + 2t^3) + V_x(1)(3t^2 - 2t^3) \\ &+ V_x'(0)(t - 2t^2 + t^3) + V_x'(1)(-t^2 + t^3) \end{aligned} \tag{3.7g}$$

From the given data, we have

$$V_x(0) = 1, \qquad V_x(1) = 3$$

Because the magnitude of the tangent vector is 1,

$$V_x'(0) = 1 \cdot \cos 60, \qquad V_x'(1) = 1 \cdot \cos 30$$

Upon substitution of these values in Equation (3.7d), we obtain

$$\begin{aligned} V_x &= 1(1 - 3t^2 + 2t^3) + 3(3t^2 - 2t^3) + \cos 60(t - 2t^2 + t^3) + \cos 30(-t^2 + t^3) \\ &= 1 + \frac{1}{2}t + \left(5 - \frac{\sqrt{3}}{2}\right)t^2 + \left(\frac{\sqrt{3}}{2} - \frac{7}{2}\right)t^3 \end{aligned}$$

Similarly, from Equation (3.7d),

$$\begin{aligned} V_y = V_y(t) &= V_y(0)(1 - 3t^2 + 2t^3) + V_y(1)(3t^2 - 2t^3) \\ &+ V_y'(0)(t - 2t^2 + t^3) + V_y'(1)(-t^2 + t^3) \end{aligned} \tag{3.7h}$$

Again, from the given data,

$$V_y(0) = 2, \qquad V_y(1) = 1$$

$$V_y'(0) = 1 \cdot \sin 60, \qquad V_y'(1) = 1 \cdot \sin 30$$

Upon substitution of these values in Equation (3.7d), we obtain

$$\begin{aligned} V_y &= 2(1 - 3t^2 + 2t^3) + 1(3t^2 - 2t^3) + \sin 60(t - 2t^2 + t^3) + \sin 30(-t^2 + t^3) \\ &= 2 + \frac{\sqrt{3}}{2}t + \left(-\frac{7}{2} - \sqrt{3}\right)t^2 + \left(\frac{5}{2} + \frac{\sqrt{3}}{2}\right)t^3 \end{aligned}$$

To verify it, we substitute $t = 0, 1$ into the previous equations; then $V(t = 0) = [1, 2]$, $V(t = 1) = [3, 1]$,

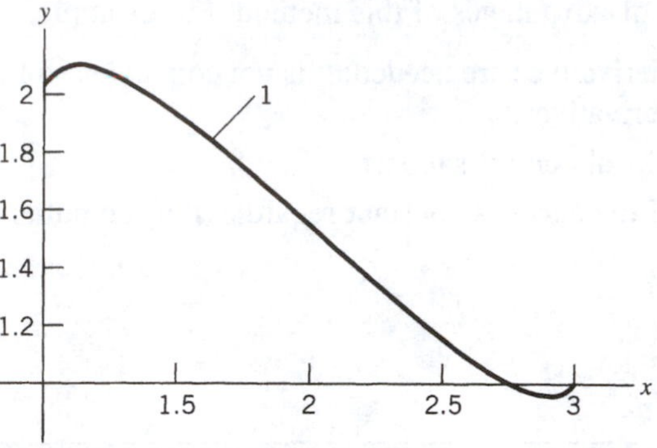

FIGURE 3.17 Hermite curve of Example 3.4.

$$\text{Slope }(A) = \left.\frac{V'_y}{V'_x}\right|_{(t=0)} = \sqrt{3}$$

$$\text{Slope }(B) = \left.\frac{V'_y}{V'_x}\right|_{(t=1)} = \frac{\sqrt{3}}{3} = \frac{1}{\sqrt{3}}$$

which is what we expect. This can be seen from the plot of the curve shown in Figure 3.17.

EXAMPLE 3.5

On changing the tangent vector of the curve, the shape of the curve changes accordingly. Using the data given in Example 3.4, plot the curves given that the magnitude of the tangent vector equals 1, 2, 3, 6, and 12 respectively.

Solution

Following the procedure of Example 3.4, we can find the Hermite curve family equations with different magnitude of tangent vectors. These curves are plotted in Figure 3.18.

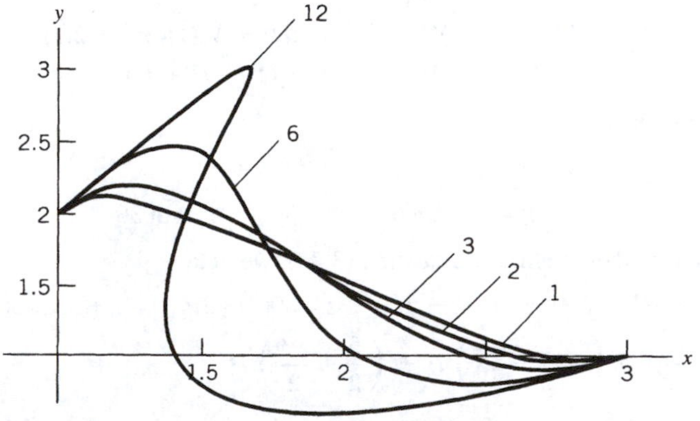

FIGURE 3.18 Hermite curve family for Example 3.5.

3.4.10 Bezier Curves

The Hermite curve discussed in the previous section is based on interpolation techniques. On the contrary, Bezier curves are based on approximation techniques that produce curves that do not pass through all the given data points except the first and the last control point. A Bezier curve does not require first-order derivative; the shape of the curve is controlled by control points.

As in the previous section, we consider one segment of the curve. For $n + 1$ control points, the Bezier curve is defined by a polynomial of degree n as follows:

$$\mathbf{V}(t) = \sum_{i=0}^{n} \mathbf{V}_i B_{i,n}(t), \qquad 0 \leq t \leq 1 \tag{3.8}$$

where $\mathbf{V}(t)$ is the position vector of a point on the curve segment and $B_{i,n}$ are the Bernstein polynomials, which serve as the blending or basis function for the Bezier curve.

The Bernstein polynomial is defined as

$$B_{i,n}(t) = C(n, i)t^i(1 - t)^{n-i} \tag{3.8a}$$

where $C(n, i)$ is the binomial coefficient given by

$$C(n, i) = \frac{n!}{i!(n - i)!} \tag{3.8b}$$

Combining Equations (3.8) and (3.8a), we get

$$\mathbf{V}(t) = \sum_{i=0}^{n} C(n, i)t^i(1 - t)^{n-i}\mathbf{V}_i \tag{3.8c}$$

Here $\mathbf{V}_0, \mathbf{V}_1, \ldots, \mathbf{V}_n$ are the position vectors of $n + 1$ points ($\mathbf{V}_0, \mathbf{V}_1, \ldots, \mathbf{V}_n$ in Figure 3.19) that form the so-called characteristic polygon of the curve segment. The Bezier curve has the following properties:

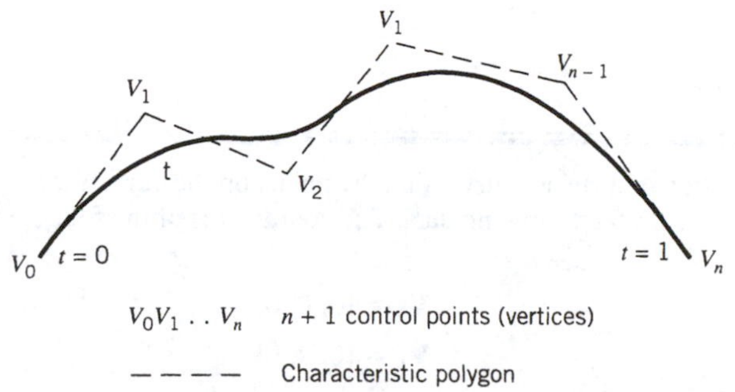

FIGURE 3.19 Bezier curve and its characteristic polygon.

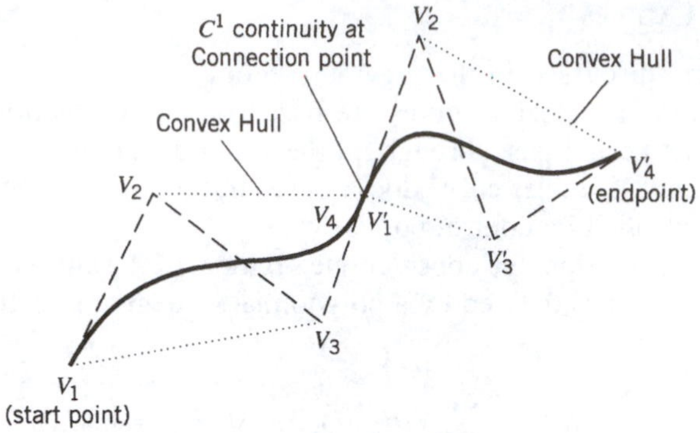

FIGURE 3.20 Properties of the Bezier curve.

1. The curves pass through the first and last control points ($\mathbf{V}_0$ and $\mathbf{V}_n$ from the preceding function) at parameter values 0 and 1 (refer to Figure 3.19). In Figure 3.20, the starting point V_1' of the second line and the endpoint V_4 of the first line have the same position.

2. The tangents at the first and last points are in the directions of the first and last segments of the characteristic polygon. This can easily be seen:

$$\begin{aligned} \mathbf{V}'(0) &= n[\mathbf{V}(1) - \mathbf{V}(0)] \\ \mathbf{V}'(1) &= n[\mathbf{V}(n) - \mathbf{V}(n-1)] \end{aligned} \tag{3.8d}$$

where $[\mathbf{V}(1) - \mathbf{V}(0)]$ and $[\mathbf{V}(n) - \mathbf{V}(n-1)]$ define the first and last segments of the curve polygon. This implies that by aligning the last control point of the first Bezier curve segment, the connection point, and the first control point of the next curve segment will result in C^1 continuity between the two curve segments (see Figure 3.20). In general, the rth derivative at an endpoint is determined by the r neighboring vertices. Furthermore, the length of each tangent vector is proportional to the length of the corresponding line segments V_0V_1, or $V_{n-1}V_n$.

3. The Bezier curve has the convex hull property. By convex hull property we mean that the entire curve lies within the characteristic polygon. This property is useful when curve intersection and spatial bounds on the curve segments are calculated (see Figure 3.20).

EXAMPLE 3.6

Develop the equation of a Bezier curve, find the points on the curve for $t = 0, 1/4, 1/2, 3/4$, and 1, and plot the curve for the following data. The coordinates of the four control points are given by

$$\mathbf{V}_0 = [0, 0, 0]$$
$$\mathbf{V}_1 = [0, 2, 0]$$
$$\mathbf{V}_2 = [4, 2, 0]$$
$$\mathbf{V}_3 = [4, 0, 0]$$

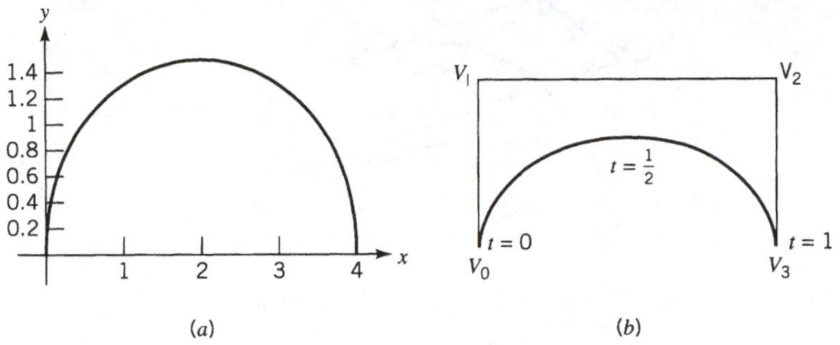

FIGURE 3.21 (*a*) Bezier curve for Example 3.6; (*b*) Bezier curve obtained using CAD software.

Solution

From Equation (3.8c), because the number of control points is 4 (that is, $4 = n + 1$), we set $n = 3$. Then we have the Bezier curve function as follows:

$$\mathbf{V}(t) = \sum_{i=0}^{3} \frac{3!}{i!(3-i)!} t^i(1-t)^{3-i}\,\mathbf{V}_i \tag{3.9}$$

$$\mathbf{V}(t) = \mathbf{V}_0(1-t)^3 + 3\mathbf{V}_1 t(1-t)^2 + 3\mathbf{V}_2 t^2(1-t) + \mathbf{V}_3 t^3 \qquad 0 \le t \le 1$$

Substituting the values $t = 0, 1/4, 1/2, 3/4, 1$ into this equation, we get

$$\mathbf{V}(0) = \mathbf{V}_0 = [0, 0, 0]^{\mathrm{T}}$$

$$\mathbf{V}\left(\frac{1}{4}\right) = \frac{27}{64}\mathbf{V}_0 + \frac{27}{64}\mathbf{V}_1 + \frac{9}{64}\mathbf{V}_2 + \frac{1}{64}\mathbf{V}_3 = \left[\frac{5}{8}, \frac{9}{8}, 0\right]^{\mathrm{T}}$$

$$\mathbf{V}\left(\frac{1}{2}\right) = \frac{1}{8}\mathbf{V}_0 + \frac{3}{8}\mathbf{V}_1 + \frac{3}{8}\mathbf{V}_2 + \frac{1}{8}\mathbf{V}_3 = \left[2, \frac{3}{2}, 0\right]^{\mathrm{T}}$$

$$\mathbf{V}\left(\frac{3}{4}\right) = \frac{1}{64}\mathbf{V}_0 + \frac{9}{64}\mathbf{V}_1 + \frac{27}{64}\mathbf{V}_2 + \frac{27}{64}\mathbf{V}_3 = \left[\frac{27}{8}, \frac{9}{8}, 0\right]^{\mathrm{T}}$$

$$\mathbf{V}(1) = [4, 0, 0]^{\mathrm{T}}$$

Plotting these points, we get the curve shown in Figure 3.21*a*. By directly plotting these points using CAD software, we get the Bezier curve shown in Figure 3.21*b*.

EXAMPLE 3.7

Repeat Example 3.6 for the following 3D control points.

$$\mathbf{V}_0 = [0, 0, 0]$$
$$\mathbf{V}_1 = [0, 2, 2]$$
$$\mathbf{V}_2 = [4, 2, 2]$$
$$\mathbf{V}_3 = [4, 0, 0]$$

Solution

We get the same parametric equation as in Example 3.6. However, the curve is a 3D curve in this problem. The 3D curve is shown in Figure 3.22.

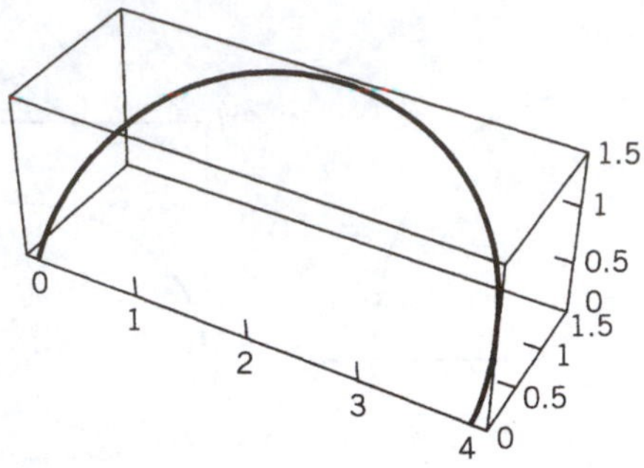

FIGURE 3.22 Bezier curve in 3D.

3.4.11 B-Spline, Rational B-Spline, and Nonuniform Rational B-Spline Curves

The B-spline is considered a generalization of the Bezier curve. Local control is an interesting feature of B-spline curves. Local control implies that changing the local control point affects only part of the curve, as shown in Figure 3.23. With Hermite and Bezier curves, changing one control point (or slope) affects the whole curve, which may cause some inconvenience for designers when they want to modify only part of the curve.

Rational B-splines (RBSs) are generalizations of B-splines. Interestingly, an RBS has an added parameter (also called weight) associated with each control point to control the behavior of the curve. An RBS can be used to define a variety of curves and surfaces. The most widely used class of RBS is the nonuniform rational B-spline (NURBS). The NURBS is used on a scale similar to that of an industrial standard. Using a NURBS, a designer can model free-form surfaces by defining a mesh of control points. NURBS technology is now used in many software packages, for example, IDEAS software from Structural Dynamics Research Corporation.

3.4.12 Curve Manipulations

Various types of analytical and synthetic curves were presented in the previous sections. For these curves to be useful in design and manufacturing applications, it is

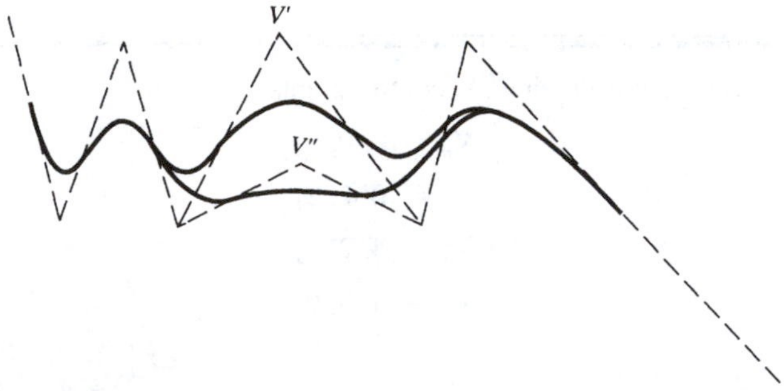

FIGURE 3.23 B-spline curve demonstrating local control.

important to understand the curve manipulation opportunities available in CAD/CAM systems. These include displaying curves, blending different segments of curves into one curve by ensuring various continuities, segmenting a curve, trimming, intersection, and transformation (for a comprehensive analysis of these topics, refer to Zeid, 1991).

3.5 SURFACE MODELING

In wireframe modeling, we take advantage of the simplicity of certain surfaces. For example, a plane is represented by its boundaries. We say nothing about the middle of the plane, which is fine because we know the middle of a plane is still a plane. However, this assumption is not applicable to general cases. It is common knowledge that the shapes of cars, airplanes, ships, and so forth do not simply consist of standard geometry such as planes and cylinders. Therefore, it is not easy to represent them by wireframe models. To overcome the problems inherent in wireframe modeling, a different geometric modeling scheme called surface modeling is available to engineers.

Surface modeling is a widely used modeling technique in which objects are defined by their bounding faces. Surface modeling systems contain definitions of surfaces, edges, and vertices. Surface modeling goes one step farther than wireframe modeling. For example, it contains not only the information of a wireframe model but also other information such as the connection of two surfaces. A surface model of an object can be used to determine the cutter path, whereas a wireframe usually cannot. In such surface modeling systems, a user may input the vertices and edges of a workpiece in a manner that outlines or bounds one face at a time. Surface modeling systems offer better graphic interaction, although the models are more difficult to create than wireframe models. Sometimes, an intermediate model must be created. For example, the generic surface in Figure 3.24 is created by first creating a cube block. With the references of the cube, it is easier to input the space control points that are used to define the generic surface.

Although a surface modeling scheme is better than a wireframe modeling scheme, it still has some drawbacks. It does not provide information about the topology of the entities, such as the concept of the component's inside and outside. As a result, with surface models, a user may still not be able to distinguish the interior and exterior of an

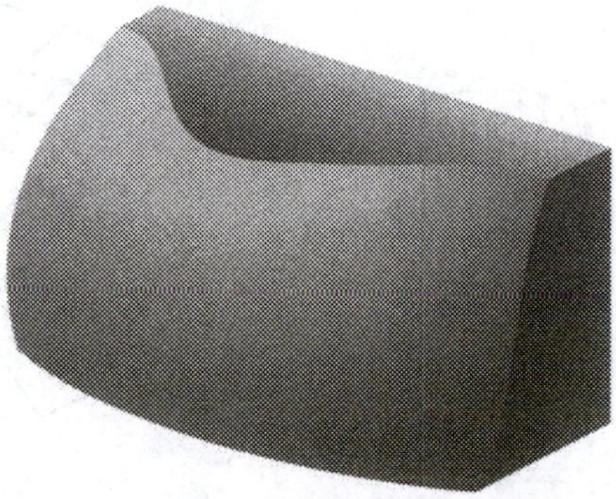

FIGURE 3.24 Example of a surface model.

object on the monitor. As a matter of fact, a surface modeling system may not guarantee that the user has designed a realizable object; that is, the collection of surfaces may not define a physical part.

3.5.1 Surface Entities

We provide a brief discussion of various surface entities that are needed to construct a surface model.

3.5.1.1 Plane Surface

A plane surface is the simplest surface that is defined by three noncoincident points or its variation. It is the most basic surface in engineering design. Two plane surfaces are shown in Figure 3.25*a*.

3.5.1.2 Ruled (Lofted) Surface

A ruled (lofted) surface can be defined as a linear interpolation between two general curves. Informally speaking, the straight lines connecting the two rails (general curves) form the surface. This is a special case of using interpolation between two general curves. Figure 3.25*b* shows two space curves ''connected'' by straight lines that form a surface.

3.5.1.3 Surface of Revolution

This surface is generated by rotating a planar curve in space about an axis at a certain angle. In Figure 3.25*c* a straight line revolves about an axis and forms a revolution surface.

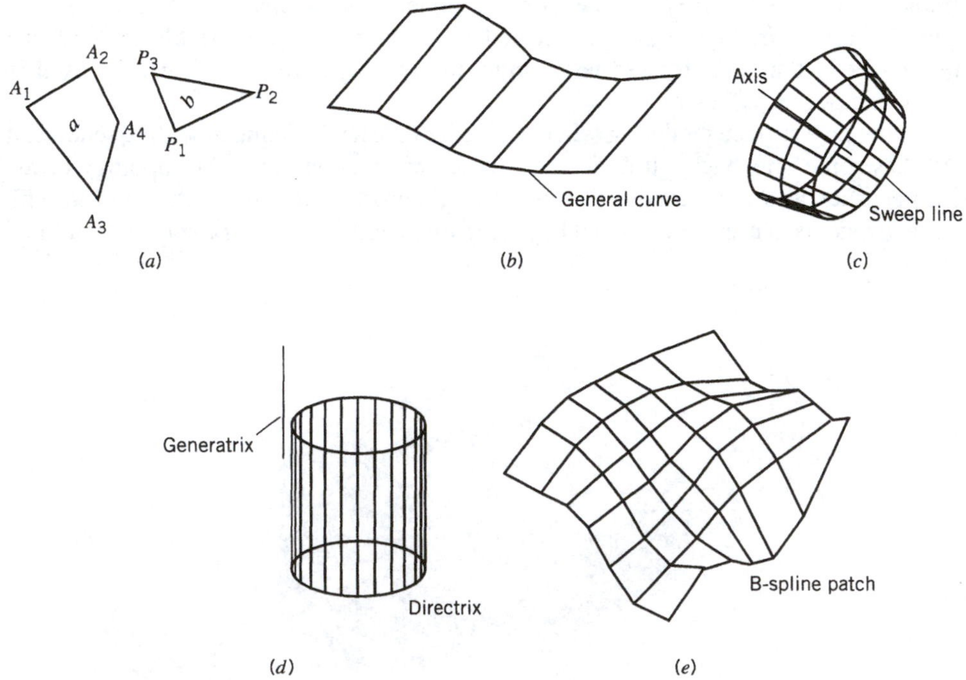

FIGURE 3.25 Surface entities: (*a*) plane surface; (*b*) ruled (lofted) surface; (*c*) surface of revolution; (*d*) tabulated cylinder; (*e*) B-spline surface.

3.5.1.4 Tabulated Cylinder

This surface is generated by sweeping a planar curve in space in a certain direction at a certain distance. In Figure 3.25*d* a straight line sweeps along a path that is a circle and forms a surface. The straight line is called a generatrix and the circle a directrix.

3.5.1.5 Bezier Surface and B-Spline Surface

Bezier and B-spline surfaces are both synthetic surfaces. Like synthetic curves, a synthetic surface approximates given input data (an array of given points in 3D space). Bezier and B-spline surfaces are general surfaces that permit twists and kinks. The difference between them, also similar to the case of curves, is that local control is possible for the B-spline surface but not for the Bezier surface. Figure 3.25*e* shows a B-spline surface.

3.5.2 Surface Representations

As with the discussion of curves, we start our discussion of surfaces with their representation equation. Recall that a general curve can be defined by either an implicit or an explicit equation. A general surface can also be defined by implicit and explicit equations as follows.

3.5.2.1 Implicit Equation

$$F(x, y, z) = 0 \tag{3.10}$$

Its geometric meaning is that the locus of the points that satisfy the constraint equation defines the surface.

3.5.2.2 Explicit Equation

$$\mathbf{V} = [x, y, z]^{\mathrm{T}} = [x, y, f(x, y)]^{\mathrm{T}} \tag{3.11}$$

where $\mathbf{V}$ is the position vector of a variable point on the surface. In this equation, we directly define the variable point coordinates x, y, z. The z coordinates of the position vector of the variable points are defined by x, y through a suitable function $f(x, y)$, as shown in Figure 3.26.

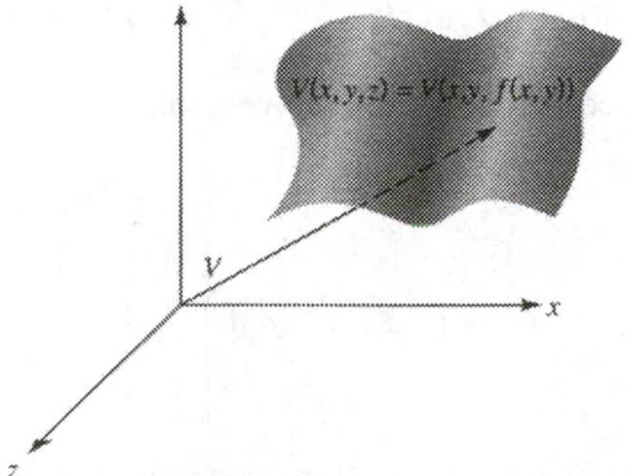

FIGURE 3.26 Explicit equation in surface representation.

Comparing Equations (3.10) and (3.11) with those for the curves, we can see the difference between a space curve and a surface mathematically. The points on a space curve have one degree of freedom; the points on a surface have two.

The general form of the function $f(x, y)$ for a surface to pass through all the given data points is a polynomial with respect to x and y. Usually, an arbitrary surface is defined by an $x-y$ grid of size $(p + 1) \cdot (q + 1)$ points.

3.5.2.3 Parametric Equation of a Surface

There are no extra parameters in Equations (3.10) and (3.11), and the surface representation equations of this form were called nonparametric equations. Equations that utilize parameters are called parametric equations. Because the points on the surface have two degrees of freedom, it is natural to write the parametric representation of a surface as

$$\mathbf{V}(s, t) = [x, y, z]^{\mathrm{T}} = [X(s, t), Y(s, t), Z(s, t)]^{\mathrm{T}}, \qquad s_{\min} \leq s \leq s_{\max}, t_{\min} \leq t \leq t_{\max} \tag{3.12}$$

where X, Y, and Z are functions of the two parameters s and t.

3.5.2.4 Parametric Representation of Synthetic Surfaces

Hermite Bicubic Surface Surfaces are normally defined in patches; each patch corresponds to a rectangular domain in $s-t$ *space,* just as we discussed space curves in the s domain in the previous section. Remember, a curve is defined in segments. Surface patches are dealt with in the same way; however, patches are much more complicated than curve segments.

We have given a general polynomial parametric equation [see Equation (3.12)], but generally in computer design systems, polynomial parameter equations of third order are used. Here we discuss mainly the cubic parametric equation.

The cubic parametric equation is a 16-term third-power series as follows:

$$\begin{aligned}
\mathbf{r} &= \mathbf{V}(s, t) \\
&= \sum_{i=1}^{4} \sum_{j=1}^{4} a_{ij} s^{i-1} t^{j-1} \\
&= (a_{11} + a_{12}t + a_{13}t^2 + a_{14}t^3) \\
&\quad + (a_{21} + a_{22}t + a_{23}t^2 + a_{24}t^3)s \\
&\quad + (a_{31} + a_{32}t + a_{33}t^2 + a_{34}t^3)s^2 \\
&\quad + (a_{41} + a_{42}t + a_{43}t^2 + a_{44}t^3)s^3, \qquad 0 \leq s \leq 1, 0 \leq t \leq 1
\end{aligned} \tag{3.13}$$

The matrix form of this equation is more convenient:

$$\begin{aligned}
\mathbf{r} &= \mathbf{V}(s, t) \\
&= [1\ s\ s^2\ s^3][a_{ij}] \begin{bmatrix} 1 \\ t \\ t^2 \\ t^3 \end{bmatrix}
\end{aligned} \tag{3.14}$$

where $[a_{ij}](i, j = 1, 2, 3, 4)$ is the (4×4) matrix form of the vector coefficients.

Remember the transformation we did on the parametric cubic curve, where an appropriate basis matrix **M** was applied to transform the old basis function to a new basis function. We use the same method on a surface patch. This transformation may be expressed in matrix form as follows:

$$\mathbf{r} = \mathbf{V}(s, t) = \mathbf{UMAM}^{\mathrm{T}}\ \mathbf{V}^{\mathrm{T}} \tag{3.15}$$

where $\mathbf{M}$ = basis matrix

$\mathbf{U} = [1\ s\ s^2\ s^3]$

$\mathbf{V} = [1\ t\ t^2\ t^3]$

$\mathbf{A}$ = the (4×4) matrix of the given vector

A is defined as follows:

$$\mathbf{A} = \begin{bmatrix} \mathbf{V}(0,0) & \mathbf{V}(0,1) & \mathbf{V}_t(0,0) & \mathbf{V}_t(0,1) \\ \mathbf{V}(1,0) & \mathbf{V}(1,1) & \mathbf{V}_t(1,0) & \mathbf{V}_t(1,1) \\ \mathbf{V}_s(0,0) & \mathbf{V}_s(0,1) & \mathbf{V}_{st}(0,0) & \mathbf{V}_{st}(0,1) \\ \mathbf{V}_s(1,0) & \mathbf{V}_s(1,1) & \mathbf{V}_{st}(1,0) & \mathbf{V}_{st}(1,1) \end{bmatrix} \tag{3.16}$$

where $\mathbf{V}(0, 0)$, $\mathbf{V}(0, 1)$, $\mathbf{V}(1, 0)$, and $\mathbf{V}(1, 1)$ are the four corner points; $\mathbf{V}_t(0, 0)$, $\mathbf{V}_t(0, 1)$, $\mathbf{V}_t(1, 0)$, and $\mathbf{V}_t(1, 1)$ are the derivatives at the four corners in the t direction; $\mathbf{V}_s(0, 0)$, $\mathbf{V}_s(0, 1)$, $\mathbf{V}_s(1, 0)$, and $\mathbf{V}_s(1, 1)$ are the derivatives at the four corners in the s direction; and $\mathbf{V}_{st}(0, 0)$, $\mathbf{V}_{st}(0, 1)$, $\mathbf{V}_{st}(1, 0)$, and $\mathbf{V}_{st}(1, 1)$ are the cross-slope derivatives at the four corners with respect to s and t. By giving (without derivation) the values of the **M** matrix, we get the Hermite bicubic parametric equation. Here, we call **M** matrix the transformation matrix that transfers the data for the four corner points to the coefficients of the parametric equation of the Hermite surface patch. Although the derivation is rather more complicated than that for a Hermite curve, the procedure is basically the same. **M** is the same as given by equation (3.7f) in section 3.4.9.

$$\mathbf{M} = \begin{bmatrix} 1 & 0 & 0 & 0 \\ 0 & 0 & 1 & 0 \\ -3 & 3 & -2 & -1 \\ 2 & -2 & 1 & 1 \end{bmatrix} \tag{3.17}$$

The labeling scheme and the tangent vector for the equation are illustrated in Figure 3.27.

The main property of the Hermite surface patch is that the position and derivative data for four corners (say, $\mathbf{V}_{00}$, $\mathbf{V}_{01}$, $\mathbf{V}_{02}$, and $\mathbf{V}_{03}$ in Figure 3.27) can define (1) the boundary edge curve of the surface patch and (2) the cross-slope derivatives at each point on the edge. The practical meaning of this property is that two or more Hermite bicubic surface patches can be combined with continuity of position and slope. We need only ensure that the common corners share the same position and derivative data. Like Hermite bicubic curves, a Hermite surface also requires the values of the tangent vectors at the corners of the surface.

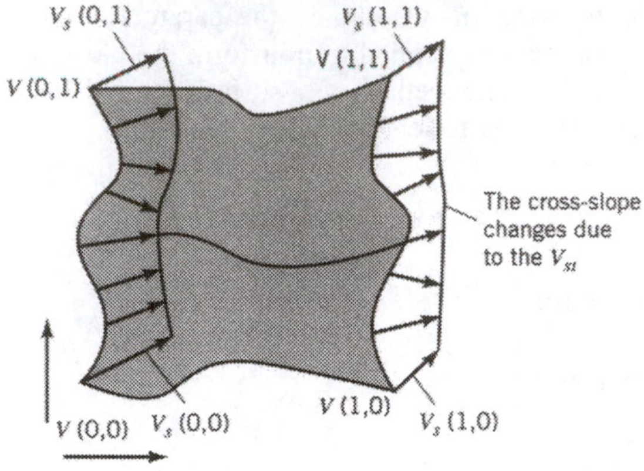

FIGURE 3.27 Notation for a bicubic surface.

EXAMPLE 3.8

Given a set of four space points and the tangent vectors at those points, find the equation of the Hermite surface patch. The four corner points are $A(0, 0, 1)$, $B(0, 2, 2)$, $C(4, 2, 3)$, $D(4, 0, 4)$. The tangent vectors of the corner points are 1 with magnitude 1. The cross-slope vectors are assumed to be 0.

Solution

In this problem, the position vectors are **A, B, C,** and **D**. The slopes and cross-slope are 1. Therefore, we have the following **A** matrix:

$$\mathbf{A} = \begin{bmatrix} \mathbf{A}(0,0,1) & \mathbf{B}(0,2,2) & 1 & 1 \\ \mathbf{D}(4,0,4) & \mathbf{C}(4,2,3) & 1 & 1 \\ 1 & 1 & 0 & 0 \\ 1 & 1 & 0 & 0 \end{bmatrix}$$

From Equation (3.15), we have

$$\mathbf{V}(s, t) = \mathbf{UMAM^TV^T}$$

where **M** is given by Equation (3.17). The plotted equation is shown in Figure 3.28.

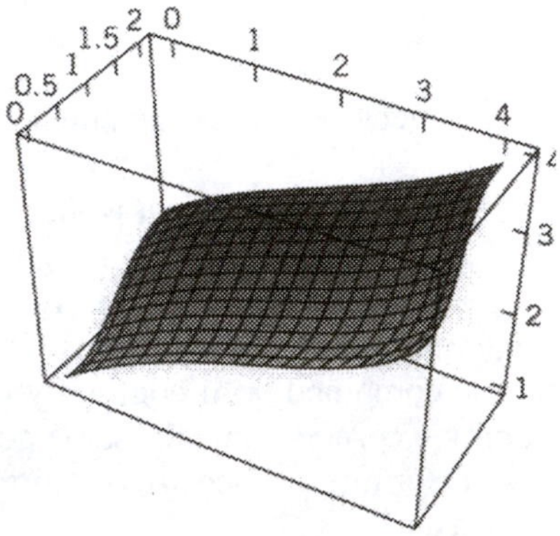

FIGURE 3.28 The Hermite bicubic patch in Example 3.9.

Bezier Surface Patches Mathematically, the only difference between a Hermite surface patch and a Bezier surface patch is that different basis functions are used. As with the Bezier curve, the Bernstein basis function is used for the Bezier surface patch.

The transformation matrix **M** (without derivation) is as follows:

$$\mathbf{M} = \begin{bmatrix} 1 & 0 & 0 & 0 \\ -3 & 3 & 0 & 0 \\ 3 & -6 & 3 & 0 \\ -1 & 3 & -3 & 1 \end{bmatrix} \tag{3.18}$$

Substituting the value of **M** into Equation (3.15), we get the Bezier surface patch parametric equation. $\mathbf{A} = [\mathbf{r}_{ij}]$ is a 4×4 matrix of the position vectors for 16 points forming a characteristic polyhedron (or net). It is useful to know that $\mathbf{V}_{00}$, $\mathbf{V}_{03}$, $\mathbf{V}_{30}$, and $\mathbf{V}_{33}$ lie at the corners of the surface patch itself, whereas the remaining points do not.

Uniform Cubic B-Spline Surfaces When we change the basis function to

$$\mathbf{M} = \frac{1}{6}\begin{bmatrix} 1 & 4 & 1 & 0 \\ -3 & 0 & 3 & 0 \\ 3 & -6 & 3 & 0 \\ -1 & 3 & -3 & 1 \end{bmatrix} \tag{3.19}$$

and substitute it into Equation (3.15), we obtain an equation of a cubic B-spline surface. Here, the vector coefficients form a net of control points that define the surface but none of which interpolate the patch, as in the case of the *B*-spline curve.

An advantage of B-spline surface is that it supports local control of the surface. Some other techniques also widely used include (for details, refer to Rooney and Steadman, 1988):

- Hermitian interpolation of two curves
- Bilinear interpolation of four boundary curves
- Hermite interpolation of four boundary curves and slope functions
- Composite surfaces

3.5.2.5 Other Types of Parametric Equations

Generally, the domain of the parameters is rectangular. However, in some particular cases (see Figure 3.29) the domain of the parameters may be triangular or pentagonal. A pentagonal domain may be divided into a triangular and a rectangular domain. The triangular domain is the key issue, and this resulted in the triangulation techniques. Briefly, a triangle domain is a symmetric triangle. Three dependent parameters are defined on this domain, as illustrated in Figure 3.29.

3.5.2.6 Surface Manipulation

Various surface manipulation techniques are available in CAD/CAM systems, and these are described briefly next.

Displaying The simplest and most widely used method is to display a surface by a mesh of curves. This is usually called a *mesh* in the CAD software. By holding one parameter constant at a time, a mesh of curves is generated to represent the surface,

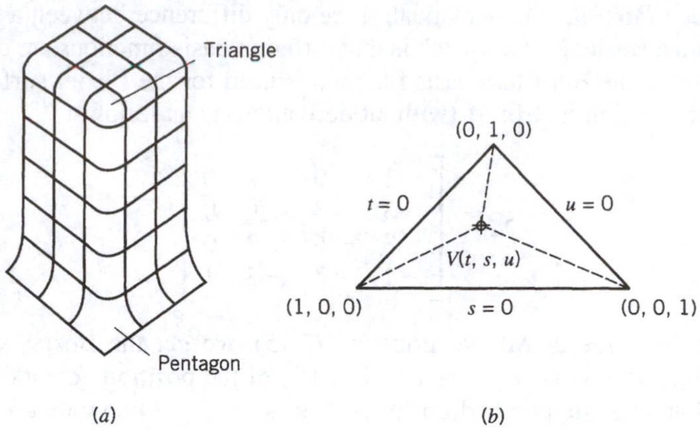

FIGURE 3.29 (*a*) Triangular and pentagonal patches; (*b*) triangular domain.

and these curves are displayed by the methods we mentioned in the previous section. Shading of a surface is also available in many CAD/CAM systems, which gives the displayed objects a realistic image.

Trimming and Segmentation Segmentation and trimming is essentially a problem of representing an entity by its particular partition as required. For example, if we want to show a particular partition of a surface on a screen or get a portrait on a printer or for editing purposes, the surface is split first and then the required part is displayed and the rest is blanked.

Intersection This function is usually provided in CAD/CAM systems. Various curves may result when two general surfaces intersect. This also serves as a way to define a curve.

Projection Projecting an entity onto a plane or surface is basically the problem of projecting a point to plane or surface. When a curve or surface is projected, the point projections are performed repeatedly. This function is used in determining shadows of entities.

Transformation As with the curve transformation, we can translate, rotate, mirror, and scale a surface in most CAD/CAM systems. To transform a surface, the control points of the surface are evaluated and then transformed to a new position and/or orientation. The new surface is then created according to the newly transformed control points. A detailed treatment of transformations is given in Chapter 2.

3.6 SOLID MODELING

The wireframe and surface modeling approaches, as mentioned earlier, have limited engineering applications. Solid modeling finds wide applications that cut across functional boundaries, such as the use of solid models with finite-element analysis and fluid flow analysis in the conceptual design of products, NC part programming for computer-aided manufacturing, and generation of CAPP. Furthermore, solid models can be used to evaluate the size, shape, and weight of products early during the conceptual design phase.

In a solid modeling system, objects are defined directly by primitive shapes called building blocks, instead of the surfaces, lines, and points used in wireframe and surface modeling. This means that an independent surface, line, or point does not have any meaning in solid modeling. An interesting feature of solid modeling is its complete and unambiguous representation of objects.

There are a number of representation schemes for solid modeling, including:

- Boundary representation (BREP)
- Constructive solid geometry (CSG)
- Sweep representation
- Primitive instancing
- Cell decomposition
- Analytical solid modeling

BREP and CSG are the most widely used representation schemes for solid modeling. However, for different applications, one may be more suitable than the other. For example, BREP is more suitable for representing complex designs, whereas with CSG, models are easy to create but are usually used in representing relatively simple objects. In some modelers, a hybrid scheme employing both BREP and CSG is used. These representation schemes are discussed in more detail in the following sections.

3.6.1 Boundary Representation

Boundary representation is essentially a scheme that, as the name implies, describes the geometry of an object in terms of its boundaries, namely vertices, edges, and surfaces. An example of BREP is shown in Figure 3.30. In order to represent a solid object by its surfaces, we require the orientation of each surface that defines the inside or outside of the object. Usually, the inside is the material part and the outside is the void space. The direction of the face normal is usually used as the orientation of the face, and the face that carries the orientation information is called orientable surface. A solid is bounded by orientable surfaces, and we can define a solid by a set of faces. A face is generally bounded by edges and edges are bounded by vertices (with the exception of spheres and circles). Although any complex solid can be represented by faces, the system of equations known as Euler's equations (which appear as syntax of CAD/CAM systems) is used to ensure the validity of BREP models, that is, to ensure that a real object is formed or bounded. For example, three planes will not form a solid object. Similarly, a face is bounded by edges, and a face will not be bounded by two straight lines. We illustrate the use of Euler's equations through examples in later sections.

Theoretically, BREPs can be used to describe any object. However, some BREPs are restricted to planar and polygonal boundaries. It is worth mentioning that curved surfaces are difficult to represent and, in general, are approximated by polygons.

3.6.2 Basic Entities for BREP

To create a model of a part using the boundary representation scheme, designers try to define the part faces explicitly. In turn, the faces are defined by edges and the edges are

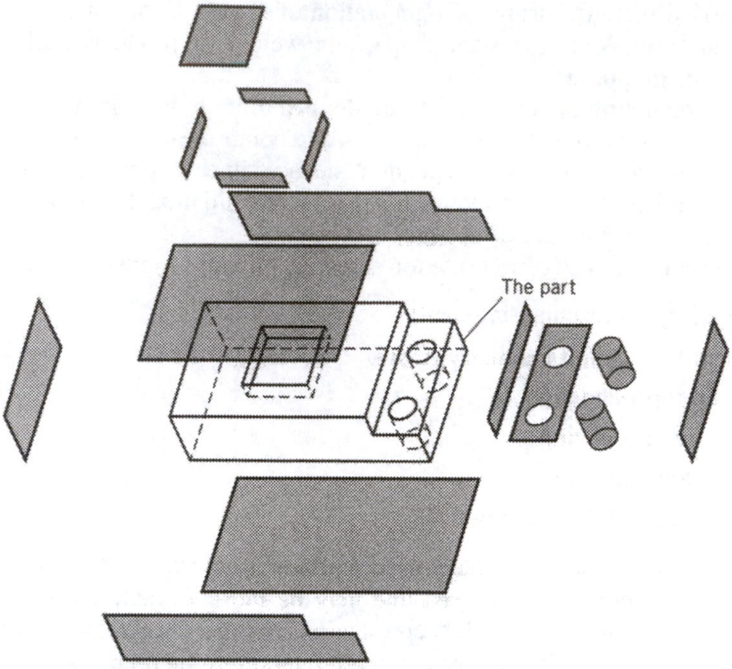

FIGURE 3.30 Example of boundary representation.

defined by vertices. Face, edge, and vertex are usually regarded as the basic elements of BREP. The methods of defining a vertex (point), an edge (line), and a face are similar to those discussed in previous sections.

3.6.3 Validation of BREP Model Using Euler's Law

Euler's law states that a polyhedron is topologically valid if the following equation is satisfied:

$$F - E + V = 2 \tag{3.20}$$

which means that to construct a valid polyhedron, the number of faces (F), edges (E), and vertices (V) must satisfy this equation. For example, the simplest polyhedron, a tetrahedron, consists of 4 faces, 6 edges, and 4 vertices. Similarly, a cube has 6 faces, 12 edges, and 8 vertices.

The generalized version of Euler's law is

$$F - E + V - L = 2(B - G) \tag{3.21}$$

where F, E, V, L, B, and G are the numbers of faces, edges, vertices, faces' inner loops, bodies, and genera (such as torus, through-hole), respectively. This law is used for the purpose of validation of polyhedral objects with passageways and holes. It may not ensure the validity of such solids with passageways in all cases. For example, for objects with curved surfaces such as cylinders, spheres, and cones, it is not so easy to apply Euler's law. In such cases we have to define the structure of the curved objects.

From this discussion we know that the validity of a polyhedral object is ensured via Euler's law. In order to create a valid BREP model, we have to follow the construction syntax of the software, which is mainly based on Equation (3.21).

Both topological and geometric information is necessary to define a solid. While we provide the connectivity of entities, the related geometric information is also attached, such as the equations of curves and surfaces and the coordinates of points. The information is stored in an ordered structure, the object-body-genus-face-loop-edge-vertex structure. This means that when we look closely at the database of a model of an object, we will find that the data on vertices are related to edges, edges to loops, loops to faces by a pointer, and so on. Usually, the entities are manipulated by Euler operators that are based on Euler's law. However, the operators of various systems may have different meaning. Usually, operators such as "make vertex, make face, kill vertex, kill face" are provided. One of the major disadvantages of BREP modeling is the large information requirement imposed by explicit storage for model boundaries.

EXAMPLE 3.9

Verify Euler's law for the two parts shown in Figure 3.31.

Solution

(a) We see Figure 3.31*a* that the part has nine edges, five faces, and six points. Accordingly, from Euler's law we have

$$F - E + V = 5 - 9 + 6 = 2$$

which satisfies Euler's rule.

(b) We assume that two cylinders are approximated by two cubic holes. Accordingly, the part in Figure 3.31*b* has 54 edges (12 edges for the pocket, 12 for each cubic hole corresponding to a cylinder, 18 in the outside boundary of the object), 21 faces, and 36 vertices (three or more than three intersecting lines define a vertex), 5 inner loops (that is, four end loops of the two holes and one loop of the bracket), 1 body, and 2 genuses (the two holes). Therefore, from Euler's rule we have

$$F - E + V - L = 21 - 54 + 36 - 5 = -2$$

$$2(B - G) = 2(1 - 2) = -2$$

which satisfies Euler's rule.

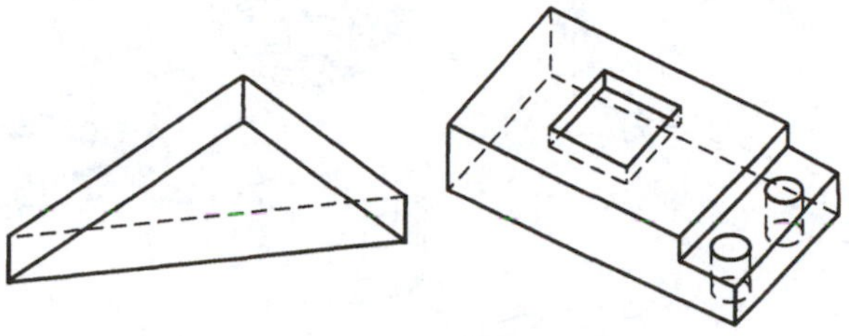

(*a*) (*b*)

FIGURE 3.31 Example parts to verify Euler's law: (*a*) simple part; (*b*) complex part.

3.6.4 Constructive Solid Geometry

Constructive solid geometry is another popular approach in solid modeling. In CSG, a solid object is constructed by simple solid objects. The simplest solid objects are called primitives, entities, or bounded solid primitives. These primitives are arranged in a tree structure using Boolean operators to construct a solid model (to be more precise, regularized set operators, which are discussed in Section 3.6.4.3). The primitives are the leaves of the tree. To construct CSG models with primitives and Boolean operations is relatively easy. The structure is concise and relatively less storage is required for the CSG model. However, there are some disadvantages too. For example, CSG is slow in displaying the objects. It is usually converted internally into a BREP to display the model or generate the wireframe drawing. This is why many systems provide both BREP and CSG: CSG provides easier input and BREP provides faster display and line drawing.

3.6.4.1 Solid Entities (Primitives)

We construct a wireframe model by inputting data consisting of points and lines. A solid model of an object is constructed by inputting data consisting of simple basic shapes that are considered as the solid modeling entities, such as block, cylinder, cone, and sphere, as shown in Figure 3.32. These entities are not simply objects represented by a few lines as in wireframe modeling. For example, a block entity is not a simple object consisting of 12 lines and 8 vertices; it is an object that occupies space. The consequence is that when two blocks intersect, a more complex combined object is created due to intersection of lines, whereas the wireframe model creates only 24 lines and a 16-vertex set, which represents nothing.

Various entities are provided to users by various CAD/CAM systems. The entities provided also depend on the application orientation of the system. Some CAD/CAM systems give users some degree of freedom to define entities that are not predefined in the system.

Generally, the four entities most commonly available to users of most systems are block, cylinder, cone, and sphere. They can be used to construct complex objects or user-defined entities. These entities usually represent certain machining operations. For example, a block of material may be removed by milling, which may result in a step, a pocket, or a slot. A cylinder of material may be removed by drilling, which may be used to construct a hole in an object.

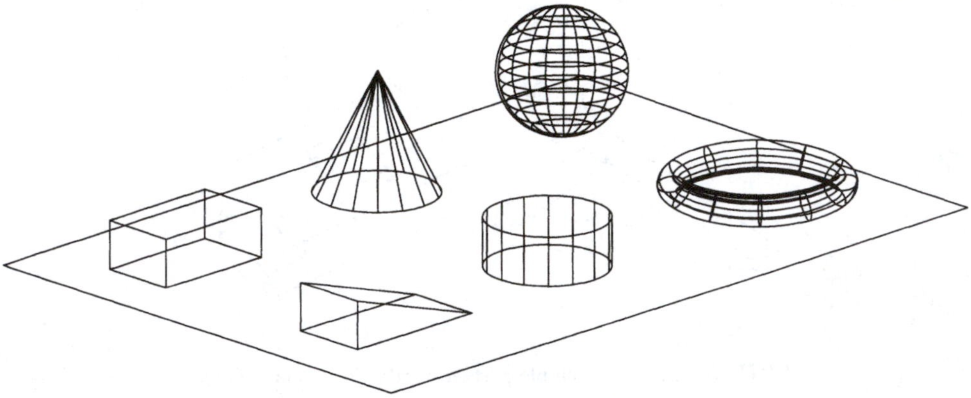

FIGURE 3.32 Solid modeling entities.

3.6.4.2 Half-Spaces

In fact, the primitives themselves may be viewed as combinations of even simpler entities termed unbounded half-spaces, which provide a basis for mathematical understanding. In this section, we present this concept and how half-spaces are used in CSG.

In general, a half-space is considered the basic element of primitives. By applying set operations to combine half-spaces, various primitives (theoretically, any complex solid) may be constructed. Mathematically, a half-space is defined as a regular point set in E^3 space as follows:

$$H = \{V: f(V) < 0, V \in E^3\} \tag{3.22}$$

where V is a point set in E^3 (3D space) and $f(V) = 0$ defines the surface equation of the half-space boundaries. The point set V that satisfies $f(V) < 0$ is considered a solid part, whereas the point set V that validates the $f(V) > 0$ equation is considered empty.

Although $f(V) < 0$ may represent any surface boundaries, the most commonly used half-spaces are planar, cylindrical, spherical, conical, and toroidal. Using these half-spaces, we may form many primitives by set operations. For example, a block can be formed by six planar half-spaces using AND operators.

The basic element of entities is the half-space. However, the block, cylinder, cone, and sphere are usually considered the basic entities of CSG without further concern about half-spaces. This is analogous to another situation: when we program using high-level languages, we are not concerned that the high-level languages are supported by some lower-level languages.

3.6.4.3 Regularized Set Operations and Their Geometric Meaning

Boolean set operations are utilized in CSG to combine various primitives. We know that set operations include UNION, INTERSECTION, and DIFFERENCE. The geometric meaning of these operators is shown in Figure 3.33. A binary tree is formed to represent the complete object data structure.

First, let us understand that there are problems with set operations when they are used in geometric modeling. It is normal to define a point by the intersection of two straight lines. This can be represented using set operations as: point A = line L1 ∩ line L2. Extending this concept to solid modeling and using two solid cubes, we have the following situation: with set operation intersection, we may generate a null set, a point, a line, a surface, or a cube. However, points, lines, and surfaces are not objects or parts in the real world. Furthermore, their presence leads to problems in solid modeling. Because we need set operations, a modification of the set operations is necessary. The modified set operation is called regularized set operation (for more information on regularized set operations, see Zeid, 1991).

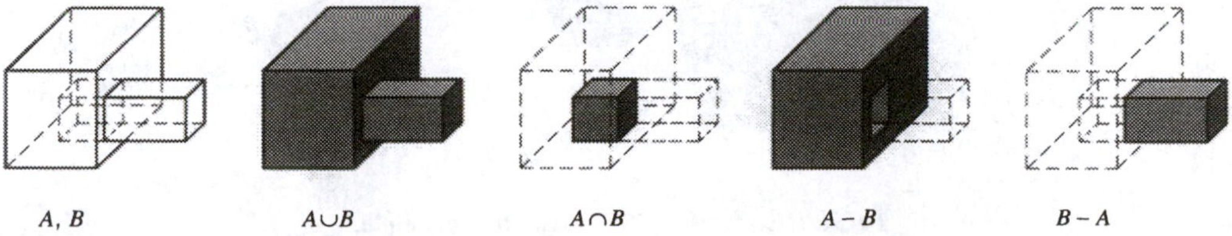

FIGURE 3.33 The geometric meaning of set operators.

EXAMPLE 3.10

Create a CSG model of the solid shown in Figure 3.34.

Solution

Before creating a CSG model of the solid, we have to know the available primitives in a particular CAD/CAM system. For example, if we have a primitive that has the exact shape of the solid object we want (which may happen in some systems in which users can define primitives), then we do not have to create the shape by set operations or provide the topology of the object. Instead, we need only give the dimensions that define the size of the object. In fact, such a modeling technique is called *pure primitive instancing*. In this scheme, one predefined object may represent a family of objects having the same topology. However, the applicability of this modeling technique is limited by the storage size of the system, and the variety of real-life objects may be prohibitively large.

In this example, we assume that the primitives available are block and cylinder. It is obvious that a combination of these primitives is needed to create a solid model for this object. Also, we have to provide the dimensions as well as the location of the primitives and the Boolean operations needed. We illustrate the use of set operations for constructing the solid (without dimensions).

The solid in the example can be constructed using the following set operations:

1. $A \cup B$
2. $C \cup (A \cup B)$
3. $D - E$
4. $(D - E) - (C \cup (A \cup B))$

This is shown in Figure 3.34.

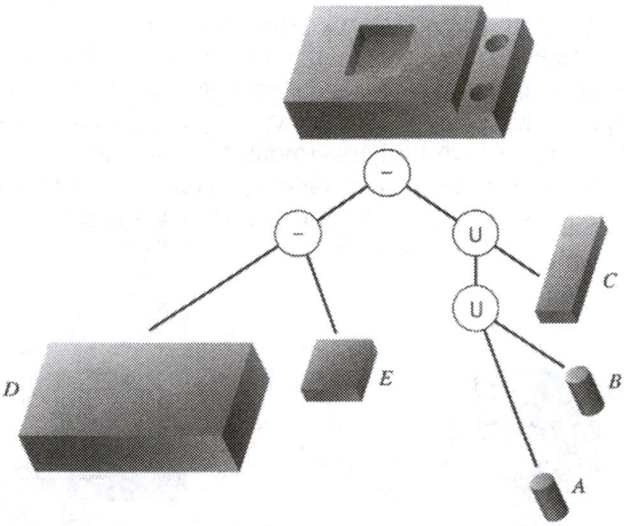

FIGURE 3.34 CSG illustrative example.

The set operations used to construct a solid are not unique. For example, you can use other sequences of set operations to construct a solid.

3.6.5 Sweep Representation

In sweep representation, a solid is defined in terms of volumes swept out by two- or three-dimensional laminae as they move along a curve, which is usually called a path. The path types may be classified in three categories: linear, nonlinear, and hybrid. A linear path is described by a linear equation; a nonlinear path is a curve described by a higher-order equation (quadratic, cubic, or higher). The hybrid sweep is a way of combining the previous two methods via set operations. In translational sweep, a planar two-dimensional lamina is moved a distance in space in a perpendicular direction (called the directrix) to the plane of the laminae. A rotational sweep is created by rotating the laminae about an axis of rotation (which forms the axis of symmetry of the object to be created) at a given angle.

3.6.6 Primitive Instancing Method

The pure primitive instancing technique is based on considering an object that has the same topology as a potential primitive (also called generic primitive) but different geometry. By predefining the topology of the primitives, the user is required to provide only the geometry of an object and the family to which the object belongs. For example, a bolt can be defined by Bolt (number of sides, length, pitch, diameter); the other dimensions are generated automatically and the topology is predefined. This scheme is basically the philosophy of group technology. It is easier to use and creates unambiguous and unique solids. The main disadvantage is clearly the limited domain of objects that can be handled. The method is restricted to the primitives predefined in the system, and they are quite limited. Another problem is lack of generality to develop any algorithm to infer the properties of the represented solid.

3.6.7 Cell Decomposition Scheme

In cell decomposition, we represent a solid object by dividing or decomposing its volume into smaller volumes or cells that are mutually contiguous and do not interpenetrate. Although the cells may be any shape and do not have to be identical, we often choose the cells to be cuboid and all cells to be identical. Usually, cell decomposition is an approximate representation of an object. When an object is decomposed, three types of cells are created. They are empty, full, or partial depending on whether they are entirely outside, entirely inside, or partially inside the object. The partial cells may be further decomposed into empty, full, or partial. Clearly, the partial cell size determines the resolution (Figure 3.35*a*). Because the information about cells does not tell how the cell is filled or how much the cell is filled, the computer will consider two partially full cells identical unless a further decomposition is made.

A number of decomposition schemes have been developed. We discuss two decomposition schemes next.

3.6.7.1 Simple Regular Grid

In this scheme, the domain of three-dimensional space is divided into an array of cells. The cells are mutually contiguous cuboidal volumes of the same size. This decompo-

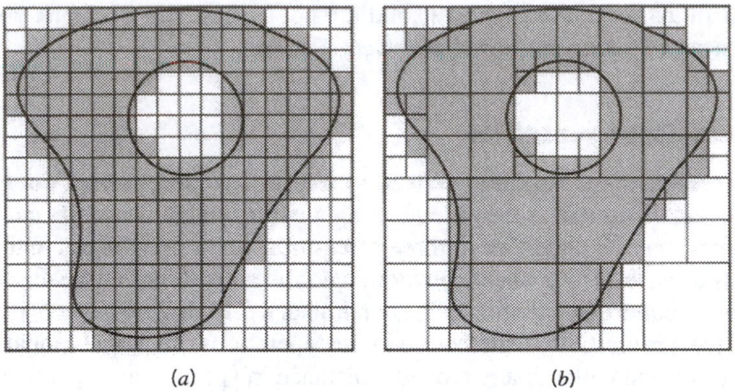

FIGURE 3.35 (*a*) Simple regular grid decomposition; (*b*) quadtree adaptive grid decomposition.

sition scheme is also known as a spatial occupancy enumeration. We have the following equation:

$$V_{\text{full}} \leq V_{\text{object}} \leq V_{\text{full}} + V_{\text{partial}}$$

where V_{object} is the volume of the object, V_{full} is the sum of all full cell volumes, and V_{partial} is the sum of the volumes of all partial cells. Because the decomposition is three-dimensional, the number of cells is directly proportional to the third power of the linear resolution of the grid. Therefore, to double the resolution of the grid, each cell is divided into eight smaller identical cells, leading to an eightfold increase in the number of cells and hence in the amount of storage space required, not to mention the computational time. For simplicity, we show the decomposition scheme in two dimension in Figure 3.35*a*, where the total number of cells is proportional to the second power of the linear resolution of the grid.

3.6.7.2 Octree Adaptive Grid

In this scheme, instead of slicing the three-dimensional space into an array of equal-sized and regularly spaced cells, a hierarchical subdivision scheme is used. At the initial level a simple regular grid is formed, and at each subsequent level further subdivision may be performed on the partial cells. This gives rise to smaller and smaller cell sizes, leading to higher and higher spatial resolution. The 3D space decomposition results in eight subdivisions, hence the name octree. In this scheme, the number of cells at the boundary of the object increases rapidly, so the amount of computer storage is proportional to the surface area of the object. This is, however, more economical than the simple grid decomposition scheme, in which the computer storage is proportional to the volume of the object. Figure 3.35*b* shows a quadtree, which is the 2D version of an octree. It is evident from Figure 3.35*a* and *b* that the quadtree requires fewer cells than the simple regular grid decomposition scheme for the same resolution.

3.6.8 Analytical Solid Modeling

In analytical solid modeling (ASM), the tensor product method that is used to represent surfaces is extended to three-dimensional parametric space with parameters, say, s, t, and u. This is similar to representing a curve by one-dimensional parametric space with one parameter (say t) and a surface by two-dimensional parametric space with two parameters (say s and t). The techniques for creating spline or patch curve segments or surface patches are valid in ASM. As in surface representation, a general solid described by x, y, and z in Cartesian space is mapped into three-dimensional parametric space via the tensor product formulation. This solid is called a parametric solid or a hyperpatch because it is similar to a surface patch in surface representation. The variable point of the solid is given by

$$\mathbf{V}(s, t, u) = [x, y, z] = [x(s, t, u), y(s, t, u), z(s, t, u)],$$
$$s_{\min} \leq s \leq s_{\max}, t_{\min} \leq t \leq t_{\max}, \leq u_{\min} \leq u \leq u_{\max} \quad (3.23)$$

TABLE 3.2 **Comparison of Various Solid Modeling Schemes**

	BREP	*CSG*	*Sweep*	*ASM*	*Cell Decomposition*	*Primitives Instancing*
Accuracy	Curved surface support is needed to reach high accuracy	Nonpolyhedral primitives are needed to reach high accuracy	High accuracy	Good in accuracy	Usually used in low-accuracy applications	Similar to sweep
Domain	Theoretically, it can support any object	Similar to BREP	Limited to certain domain	With computational effort, it is fairly good	Almost any object	Similar to sweep
Uniqueness	No	No	Need careful definition	No	Simple grid and octree generally generate unique object	Similar to sweep
Validity	Hard to check	Easy to check	Easy to check	Easy to check	Easy to check	Easy to check
Closure	Fairly good	Fairly good	Hard to achieve	Fairly good	Fairly good	Hard to achieve
Compactness and efficiency	Good at internal process	Good for user interface	Good for interface	Good for internal use	Good for interface	Good for interface

A general solid can be represented by the following polynomial:

$$\mathbf{V}(s, t, u) = \sum_{i=1}^{4} \sum_{j=1}^{4} \sum_{k=1}^{4} C_{ijk} s^{i-1} t^{j-1} u^{k-1}, \qquad 0 \le s \le 1, 0 \le t \le 1, 0 \le u \le 1 \quad (3.24)$$

Now compare Equation (3.24) with the surface patch equation (3.13), and from the discussion of surface properties we can get similar properties of the hyperpatch. Although this polynomial can essentially represent any complex solid, we prefer to combine simple hyperpatches and manipulate them to create complex objects. ASM originated from finite-element analysis applications, so it is natural that this method of modeling is appealing in design and analysis applications.

3.6.9 Comparison of Various Solid Modeling Schemes

We have presented a number of solid modeling schemes. There are similarities as well as dissimilarities among these schemes. These modeling schemes are compared in Table 3.2 on the basis of such attributes as accuracy, domain, uniqueness, validity, closure, compactness, and accuracy.

3.7 PARAMETRIC AND VARIATIONAL DESIGN

At the preliminary design stage, design engineers are often not sure what configurations will satisfy the design requirements. This leads to various modifications in product configurations and inevitably leads to changes in the geometric models and dimensions. It is therefore important for CAD/CAM systems to provide automation tools to support such modifications. However, traditional CAD/CAM tools are based on building geometry with specific dimensions and creating geometry with specific initial relationships to existing geometry. To overcome this inflexibility of traditional CAD/CAM systems in supporting these changes, two new approaches, known as parametric and variational design, have emerged. In this section, we provide a discussion of these approaches and their differences based on Chung and Schussel (1990).

3.7.1 Parametric Design

Parametric design is a methodology that utilizes special case searching and solution techniques to provide dimension-driven capability that is applied primarily to uncoupled geometric constraints and simple equations. Let us first understand the meaning of dimension-driven capability, uncoupled geometric constraints, and simple equations.

By dimension-driven capability we mean that an object defined by a set of dimensions can vary in size according to the dimensions associated with it at any time during the design process. This is big leap from the traditional CAD/CAM systems. In traditional CAD/CAM, for example, when a line is drawn, it cannot be changed except to redraw it. That is, neither its position nor its length can be changed by changing the values associated with it. Generally, the traditional CAD/CAM systems lack dimension-driven capability.

Geometric constraints are constraints that specify certain relationships between geometric entities, such as parallelism, tangency, and linear and angular dimensions.

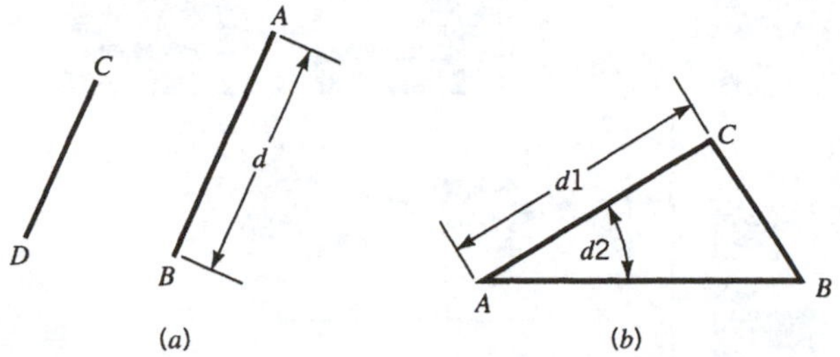

FIGURE 3.36 (*a*) Lines *CD* and *AB* are constrained by parallelism and the length of *AB* is constrained by dimension *d*. (*b*) A triangle defined by the position of points *A*, *B*, and *C*. (From Chung and Schussel, 1990. Reproduced with permission from ASME.)

For example, in Figure 3.36*a* we show that line *AB* is parallel to *CD* and line *AB* is constrained by dimension *d* in terms of length. Uncoupled geometric constraints mean that it is unnecessary to solve a set of simultaneous equations to obtain the solution and completely define the geometry. For example, if we know that the coordinate of point *A*, (x, y), and the coordinates of point B, (x_1, y_1), are defined by two equations, $x_1 = x + r_1$, $y_1 = y + r_2$, we say that *B* is defined by uncoupled geometric constraints. This is because we obtain the values of (x_1, y_1) by solving these two equations independently.

On the other hand, coupled geometric constraints are those that must be considered simultaneously to get a solution. For example, in Figure 3.36*b*, the triangle *ABC* can be defined by the positions or the coordinates of points *A*, *B*, *C* in a CAD/CAM database. However, users may want to define it by providing the coordinates of *A* and *B*, the linear dimension d_1, and the angular dimension d_2. To obtain the coordinates of *C*, we have to solve simultaneous equations that represent constraints d_1 and d_2.

The simple equations here mean the equations that govern the relationships between constraints. They can be used to define the relationship between the current dimensions or geometric and engineering constraints. Geometric constraints and engineering relations essentially define constraints in engineering design. Engineering relations represent the underlying physical principles in the form of mathematical and logical expressions. Such expressions could be in the form of equality, inequality, or conditional relations. For example,

Equality relation:

$$\text{Stress} = \frac{\text{force}}{\text{area}} = \frac{\text{force}}{3.14 \cdot R^2}$$

where *R* is the dimension of the radius. Therefore, the *R* is bounded by this equation.

Inequality relation:

In the case of a journal bearing system we have

$$\text{Bearing hole diameter} > \text{journal diameter}$$

Conditional relations:

$$\text{If } (B_1/B_2 < A_1) \text{ then } (B_3 = 10)\text{; otherwise } (B_3 = 5)$$

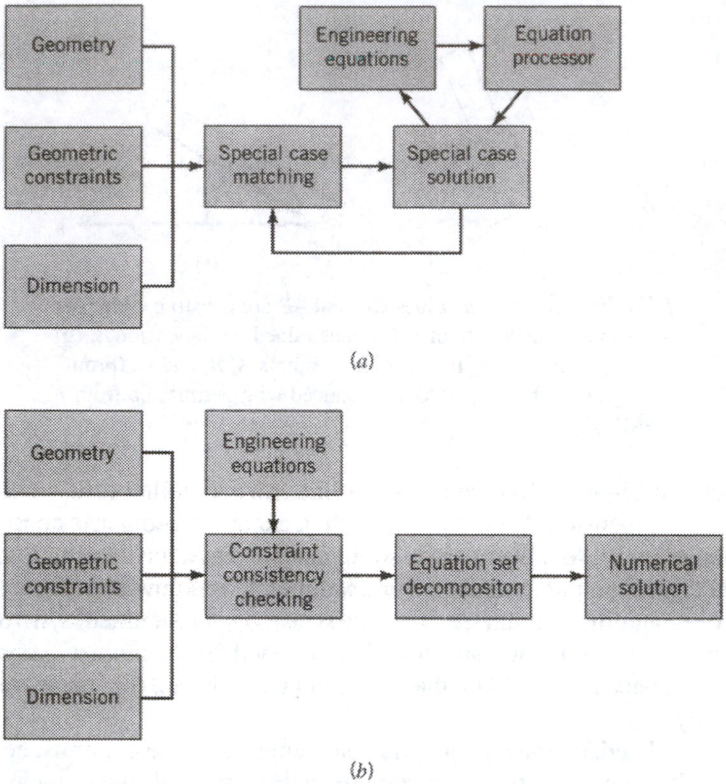

FIGURE 3.37 Schematic frameworks of (*a*) a parametric design system and (*b*) a variational design system. (From Chung and Schussel, 1990: Reproduced with permission from ASME).

The framework suggested by Chung and Schussel (1990) for use of parametric design to solve problems is shown in Figure 3.37*a*.

3.7.2 Variational Design

Variational design is a design methodology that utilizes fundamental graph theory and robust constraint-solving techniques to provide constraint-driven capability that is applied to a coupled combination of geometric constraints and engineering equations (Chung and Schussel, 1990). As this definition indicates, although parametric design and variational design have much in common, the differences are also significant. In variational design, geometry, engineering equations, and dimensions of the design are all regarded as constraints. Therefore, it provides constraint-driven capability. It is unique in the sense that the constraints can be arbitrarily coupled and solved simultaneously if needed to arrive at a design configuration that satisfies all the design criteria specified by the engineer. In fact, variational design is a superset of parametric design. Therefore, it is more general than parametric design.

All the constraints and engineering equations in variational design are represented in the form of constraint networks. Techniques from graph theory are utilized in variational design. By using graph theory, a large constraint network may be decomposed into smaller simultaneous equation sets so that the networks can be solved efficiently. A framework for how variational design solves a problem is shown in Figure 3.37*b*.

3.7.3 Comparison of Parametric and Variational Design

Both parametric and variational designs provide methods for representing geometric constraints and engineering relationships. Although the user input required by the CAD/CAM system and geometric output may be the same for some design problems, the systems may be based on different design methods. Because the solution procedures are totally transparent to the users, it is sometimes difficult to distinguish whether a parametric or variational design system has been used. However, there are some fundamental differences between these two methods.

We next explain these differences using a triangle example from Chung and Schussel (1990). The triangle is shown in Figure 3.38*a*. A variational design system automatically creates all the necessary symbolic variables to define the geometry fully. All these variables are defined in terms of engineering equations and geometric constraints and the constraints set defines the design. When a constraint or equation is specified, the system internally creates mathematical equations relating these symbolic variables. For the triangle in Figure 3.38*a*, the full set of constraint equations is given below:

$$\text{THETA\_L3} = \text{THETA\_L1} + \text{D3} + 180 \tag{3.25}$$

$$\text{SQRT((X\_P1} - \text{X\_P3)**2} + \text{(Y\_P1} - \text{Y\_P3)**2)} = \text{D2} \tag{3.26}$$

$$\text{SQRT((X\_P1} - \text{X\_P2)**2} + \text{(Y\_P1} - \text{Y\_P2)**2)} = \text{D1} \tag{3.27}$$

$$\text{Y\_P1*COS(THETA\_L3)} - \text{X\_P1*SIN(THETA\_L3)} + \text{DO\_L3} = 0.0 \tag{3.28}$$

$$\text{Y\_P3*COS(THETA\_L3)} - \text{X\_P3*SIN(THETA\_L3)} + \text{DO\_L3} = 0.0 \tag{3.29}$$

$$\text{Y\_P3*COS(THETA\_L2)} - \text{X\_P3*SIN(THETA\_L2)} + \text{DO\_L2} = 0.0 \tag{3.30}$$

$$\text{Y\_P2*COS(THETA\_L2)} - \text{X\_P2*SIN(THETA\_L2)} + \text{DO\_L2} = 0.0 \tag{3.31}$$

$$\text{THETA\_L1} = 0.0 \tag{3.32}$$

$$\text{Y\_P2*COS(THETA\_L1)} - \text{X\_P2*SIN(THETA\_L1)} + \text{DO\_L1} = 0.0 \tag{3.33}$$

$$\text{Y\_P1*COS(THETA\_L1)} - \text{X\_P1*SIN(THETA\_L1)} + \text{DO\_L1} = 0.0 \tag{3.34}$$

where THETA_L1, THETA_L2, and THETA_L3 are the angles between GRD and L1, L2, and L3, respectively. Similarly, DO_L1, DO_L2, and DO_L3 are the offsets of L1, L2, and L3, respectively.

These constraints are generated automatically based on the input or the intent of the designer. For example, Equation (3.32) is a self-generated equation in which THETA_L1 = 0.0 is an interpretation of the horizontal line L1.

There is a generic nonlinear simultaneous equation solver in variational design–based CAD/CAM systems. After the generation of the constraint equations, the solutions for all the variables are obtained by solving the equation sets via the solver. Decomposition techniques are used to increase the efficiency of the solution process.

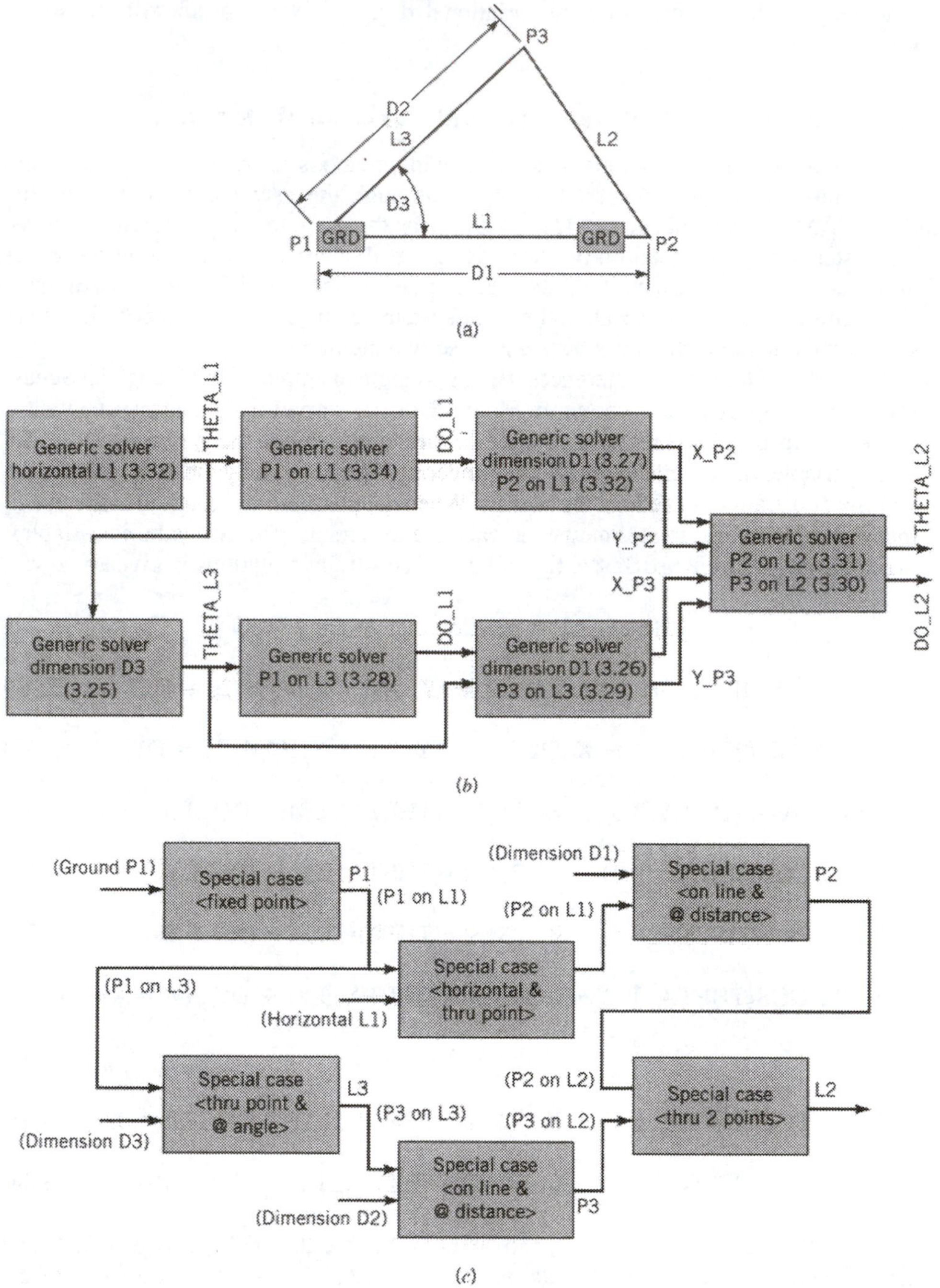

FIGURE 3.38 (*a*) A simple triangle example in which D1, D2, and D3 and the ground point P1 (X–P1 and Y–P1) are user specified. (*b*) Variational solution sequence for the triangle example. (*c*) Parametric solution sequence for the triangle example. (From Chung and Schussel, 1990: Reproduced with permission from ASME).

The solution sequence is shown in Figure 3.38*b*. In this figure, THETA_L1 is solved first by Equation (3.32). Then, either THETA_L3 or DO_L1 is solved. Finally, DO_L2 and THETA_L2 are obtained.

Parametric design, however, handles this problem differently. In parametric design, the whole design geometry is viewed as a combination of special cases. For example, GRD point P1 is regarded as a special case of geometry and may be called a fixed point. L2 is another special case, namely through two points P1 and P2. By solving a sequence of special combinations, the solutions for all the variables can be obtained. The solution process is shown in Figure 3.38*c*.

From this example, we see that parametric design solves the constraints set by way of special cases. However, there are many special cases and the combinations of the special cases increase in factorial order. Therefore, one may encounter problems of growing combinations in some situations (for more information on this subject see Chung and Schussel, 1990). From our discussion in this section, we can say that parametric design is based on special cases from analytic geometry. Its use is limited primarily to noncoupled dimension-driven design. On the other hand, variational design is based on graph theory and numerical analysis. It is a generic approach for dimension-driven design as well as for advanced applications such as tolerance analysis, mechanisms analysis, and design optimization.

3.8 COMPUTER-AIDED ENGINEERING ANALYSIS

Engineering analysis is concerned with analysis and evaluation of engineering product designs. For this purpose, a number of computer-based techniques are used to calculate the product's operational, functional, and manufacturing parameters. Finite-element analysis is one of the most frequently used engineering analysis techniques. Besides FEA, tolerance analysis, design optimization, mechanism analysis, and mass property analysis are some of the computer-aided techniques available to engineers for the purposes of analysis and evaluation of the engineering product designs. We provide brief discussions of some of them in the following sections.

3.8.1 Finite-Element Analysis

Finite-element analysis is a powerful numerical analysis process widely used in engineering applications. FEA is used to analyze and study the functional performance of an object by dividing it into a number of small building blocks, called finite elements. For example, functional performances of an object or continuum, such as a structure's stresses and deflections, are predicted using FEA. The core of the FEA method is an idealization of the object or continuum by a finite number of discrete variables. For this purpose, the object is first divided into a grid of *elements* that forms a model of the real object. This process is also called *meshing*. Each element is a simple shape such as a square, triangle, or cube or other standard shape for which the finite-element program has information to write the governing equations in the form of a stiffness matrix. The unknowns for each element are the displacements at the node points, which are the points at which the elements are connected. The finite-element program assembles the stiffness matrices for these simple elements to form the global stiffness matrix for the entire model. This stiffness matrix is solved for the unknown displacements, given the known forces and boundary conditions. From the displacement at the nodes, the stresses in each element can then be calculated. The following steps are usually followed in applying FEA:

1. Discretization of the given continuum
2. Selection of the solution approximation
3. Development of element matrices and equations
4. Assembly of the element equations
5. Solution for the unknown at the nodes
6. Interpretation of the result

A number of software packages for engineering analysis have been developed that are capable of covering a wide range of applications. These applications include:

- Static analysis
- Transient dynamic analysis
- Natural frequency analysis
- Heat transfer analysis
- Plastic analysis
- Fluid flow analysis
- Motion analysis
- Tolerance analysis

3.8.2 Static, Dynamic, and Natural Frequency Analysis

In static analysis, the deflections, strains, and stresses in a structure under a fixed load are determined, whereas in a transient dynamic analysis the objective is to determine the deflections and stresses under changing load conditions using the natural frequency response time of the structure. However, our aim in natural frequency analysis is to compute the stress on a structure caused by vibrations at the natural frequency of the structure. These analyses help in designing robust products and structures.

3.8.3 Heat Transfer Analysis

In heat transfer analysis, the objective is to determine the temperature distribution. For example, in metal-cutting operations, the temperature distribution of the workpiece helps determine optimal machining conditions that do not alter the metallurgical properties of the workpiece. Other applications include evaluating automotive cooling system designs for heat removal from engine components, plastic injection mold design, and casting operations in general. Separate software has been developed for injection mold design, often referred to as plastic analysis. Next, we provide a brief discussion on plastic analysis applied to injection mold design.

3.8.4 Plastic Analysis

Plastic injection molding is a plastic-forming process that is normally performed on large plastic injection molding machines. Usually, plastic injection molding is for high-volume production. At the beginning, the plastic pellets or granules are fed into a heated chamber to be melted. Then the melted plastic is injected into split-die molds under pressure by a hydraulic piston or ram. After a short period of cooling, the mold is opened and the formed plastic part is ejected. Elements of the plastic injection molding process include the plastic part, runner geometry, material properties, mold gate and vent locations, cooling system, and molding temperatures and pressures. All these factors are especially important for plastics and the analysis results help users identify potential problems and obtain optimum part, mold, and process design early in the development process.

A critical parameter is the cooling speed or the cooling time. To increase the production rate, we want the plastic part cooled as rapidly as possible. On the other hand, if the plastic is cooled too rapidly, it may not completely fill the mold or it may warp when it is taken out of the mold because of locked-in thermal stresses. Therefore, in order to design a good injection-molded part and optimize the injection-molding cycle time, it is necessary to analyze the filling and cooling process. To model the molding process we usually have to model and analyze the components that may influence the molding process most. Generally, these components include the plastic part, the runner and gates, the mold, and the cooling system. A number of computer modeling and analysis tools are now available for plastics analysis. Examples are the I-DEAS and EMS plastic analysis modules (see Table 3.3). Figure 3.39 shows the results of plastic injection analysis using EMS software.

3.8.5 Fluid Flow Analysis

It is interesting to note that flow of fluids through pipes satisfies many needs, such as for water and petroleum products. In many applications, the fluid flows at high flow rates, temperature, and pressure. Failure of a piping system may lead to severe damage in terms of property and loss of life. It is therefore important to determine optimum piping system design. Fluid flow analysis software helps analyze various characteristics of fluid flow such as flow rate, diffusion, dispersion, and consolidation for the purpose of piping system design.

TABLE 3.3 **Some of the Commercial CAD/CAM Systems**

Name of System	*Vendor*	*Capabilities**
AutoCAD	Autodesk Inc, Sausalito, California	WF, SF, SM (with ASM)
PDGS	Ford Motor Company, Dearborn, Michigan	WF, SF
CATIA	IBM	WF, SF, SM, Mfg, AT
Pro/Engineer	Parametric Technology Corporation, Waltham, Massachusetts	WF, SF, SM, Mfg, AT
I-DEAS	SDRC-Structural Dynamics Research Corporation, Milford, Ohio	WF, SF, SM, Mfg, AT
Unigraphics	EDS, Troy, Michigan	WF, SF, SM, Mfg
EMS	Intergraph Corporation, Huntsville, Alabama	WF, SF, SM, AT
ICEM CFD/CAE	Control Data Systems, Arden Hills, Minnesota	WF, SF, SM, Mfg, AT
ICAD	ICAD, Cambridge, Massachusetts	WF, SF, SM, Mfg, AT, IMC

* WF, wireframe modeling; SF, surface modeling; SM, solid modeling; AT, analysis tool such as plastic, dynamic, fluid flow analysis; Mfg, manufacturing modules; IMC, intelligent modeling capabilities.

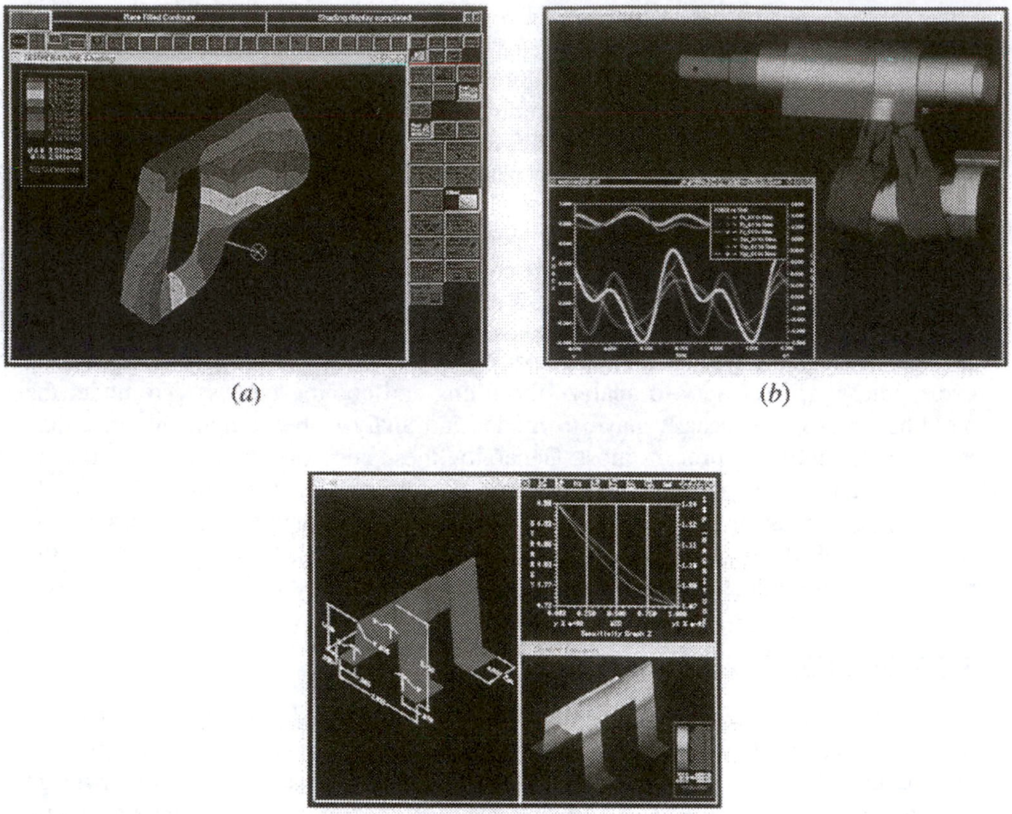

(a) (b) (c)

FIGURE 3.39 (*a*) Plastic injection analysis software analyzes the effects of time, temperature, and pressure on the flow of molten plastic and displays the results graphically for efficient interpretation. (Courtesy of Intergraph Corporation.) (*b*) Output from mechanical system analysis software. (Courtesy of Intergraph Corporation.) (*c*) Output from design optimization software. (Courtesy of Intergraph Corporation.)

3.8.6 Motion Analysis

Motion analysis, often referred to as kinematic analysis, is the analysis of geometric properties of a mechanism to produce a desired motion. By geometric properties we mean the displacement, velocity, and acceleration. The objective in motion analysis is to determine limits of motion, interference, and optimum geometric conditions by simulating the solid model or the 3D model of an object in motion. This helps users to identify problems of interference and changing forces during system operation before they are passed on to production. Figure 3.39*b* shows an output from Intergraph's mechanical systems analysis software.

3.8.7 Tolerance Analysis

In engineering design, tolerances are usually assigned to the dimensions. Properly assigning the tolerances is important, especially for the situations in which tolerance stack-up occurs or tight tolerances are required. From a functional point of view, tight tolerances may result in good performance. However, when tolerances are overly stringent, parts are rejected unnecessarily and production costs increase rapidly.

Tolerance analysis is the process of determining the proper assignment of tolerances. For this purpose, various analysis methods such analytical, statistical, and simulation methods are used. Note that in the area of tolerancing, tolerance analysis and tolerance synthesis have different implications. Here we refer to the whole tolerancing process as tolerance analysis. A number of systems have been developed that help allocate tolerances on components of an assembled product.

3.8.8 Design Optimization

The product design process has a number of steps. After the completion of the preliminary design, we want to optimize the design further to some specific objectives such as a minimum weight or reduced vibration. The analysis process for achieving these objectives is called design optimization. Design optimization is based on the design variables, constraints, and goals that are provided by the designers. Alternatives are explored to find the optimal solutions. This analysis is different from the preliminary design or other conceptual design in which the design variables and some constraints are determined. Various software packages support such an analysis. Figure 3.39*c* shows an analysis based on design optimization software of Intergraph.

3.8.9 Commercial Packages to Support Product Modeling and Analysis

Because of the importance of product modeling and analysis, a number of commercial software packages have emerged to support product development and analysis. In Table 3.3 we provide brief information on the capabilities of some of the commercial systems. It is important to point out that more and more systems are being developed and more capabilities are being added to existing systems. The details provided in the table by no means fully characterize the capabilities of these systems.

3.9 CAD/CAM DATA EXCHANGE

It is common knowledge that the primary cause of data-sharing problems between two or more systems is software incompatibility. This is due to the fact that vendors of computer applications design different proprietary formats to store the data required and produced by their systems. For example, to realize a product physically, we first have to design the product. The design information is stored in data files, some of which may be in the form of shape and size of the product. This information should be available to the manufacturer planning to develop process plans and manufacture the product. However, this will not be possible if the manufacturing planning system cannot read the CAD file. There are two ways to solve this problem. The first and desirable solution is to develop these systems so that they are compatible with each other, in which case we can say that two commercial products are integrated. The other solution is to have what is called a neutral data exchange format for the purposes of data sharing. By neutral file, we mean that the file has a format that can be utilized by various systems. If the model of an object can be transferred between systems, the design cycle time and the mistakes that may happen during the redesign phase will be greatly reduced. It is therefore natural that we require systems that are capable of translating models created by other systems. This is essentially a database translation problem, because every model is stored in or created in a database. This function is achieved by a translator, and the translation strategy may be direct or indirect.

In a direct translation strategy, one translator is capable only of translating the information of one pair of systems. If we have N systems, every system has to have $N - 1$ translators installed in order to input the database of any other systems created. The total number of translators needed would then be $N(N - 1)$. Moreover, the strategy is so complicated that it is almost impossible for a system to transfer data to all other systems.

In the indirect strategy, a neutral database structure is predefined. ''Neutral'' means that the file format is independent of different formats utilized by the various CAD/CAM system vendors. With this strategy each system needs only to have a preprocessor and a postprocessor to transfer the database universally. The function of a preprocessor is to translate the neutral file format database to the system's own database format when the system is reading the database. The function of a postprocessor is to translate the given database format to neutral file format when output is made. In this strategy, N CAD/CAM systems will need only $2N$ translators. However, indirect translating is usually slower than direct translating.

A successful data exchange format or standard or neutral file must meet a minimum set of requirements. The standard must cover the common entities, such as wireframe entities and surface entities, used in various modeling systems. The standard format has to be compact, which may help achieve faster storage and retrieval; that is, higher speed in converting data to and from the neutral format and smaller size of the resulting neutral file. The compatibility of a format is also crucial; that is, the future versions of the format must be downward compatible with the old and/or existing versions.

These guidelines are not easy to achieve, and because of the development of the standard itself, various translation problems may occur. However, a neutral file is still the best solution to establishing communication between dissimilar CAD/CAM systems. Among many standards available today, the IGES and PDES standards are the most widely used. Next, we briefly discuss IGES and PDES. Also, we provide a brief introduction to DXF.

3.9.1 IGES

The Initial Graphics Exchange Specification was first published in 1980 and subsequently updated in 1983, 1986, 1988, and 1990. It is the first widely accepted standard exchange format used to communicate a modeling database among dissimilar CAD/CAM systems. In fact, IGES has also been utilized for transfer of data between the company and its suppliers and customers. We can consider IGES as a means of creating a model of an object. Because the entities of the IGES are a superset of common entities of all systems, all systems can communicate with it. Thus, IGES helps develop a communication link among systems.

The basic elements of IGES are entities we have discussed in previous sections. Therefore, the format of the data is basically a description of entities. In IGES, each entity is assigned a number. Numbers 1 through 599 and 700 through 5000 are allocated for specific assignments, and 600 through 699 and 10,000 through 99,999 are for user-defined entities. Entities are classified as geometric entities (such as shape, curve, surface) and nongeometric entities (such as relation between various entities).

The geometric entities are described via two distinct but related Cartesian coordinate systems, namely, the model space coordinate system (MCS) or world coordinate system and the working coordinate system (WCS) or local coordinate system. Because entities described in MCS may have to be transformed to MCS, a transformation matrix is attached to the coordinate system. When the transformation matrix is a null matrix, the two coordinate systems are identical.

IGES reserves numbers 100 through 199 to define geometric entities. Each entity has two main types of data: directory data and parameter data. The directory data define entity type and parameter data describe the parameters of entities. In addition, some other related data are provided, such as file structure and entity attributes. For example, the IGES circular arc has type number 100. The parameters include center (X_c, Y_c), a starting point (X_s, Y_s), and an ending point (X_e, Y_e), where starting point and ending point simply imply an arc with a counterclockwise direction and the displacement of the arc from the $x-y$ plane of the WCS.

Although IGES covers common entities that occur in general CAD/CAM systems, some entities are not included in the IGES standard. In such cases, approximate conversions are made to replace the target entities by the closest available entities. For example, a native B-spline entity that could be of degree 1 to 7 must be replaced by two IGES entities. That is, a native B-spline of degree 1 to 3 can be represented by IGES entity 112 and one of degree 4 to 7 by 126, where 112 is a parametric spline curve and 126 a rational B-spline curve. In IGES, annotation entities are used to represent drafting data. For example, entity 202 is angular dimension and 206 is diameter dimension. IGES contains structure entities that are used to represent other information such as associativity, drawing, view, and external reference.

Like many other standard formats, the IGES file structure is formed in this fashion: flag section, start section, global section, directory entry section, parameter data section, and terminate section. The flag section is used to share information such as the standard's name, version, and error message (conversion). This tells the user directly whether the conversion is successful. The start section stores information such as the name of the sending (source) and receiving (target) CAD/CAM systems. The global section describes global information that will affect all entities that are stored in the next two sections; that is, the directory entry section and the parameter data section. The directory entry section is the body of the IGES file, which contains the entities' names as discussed before. The parametric data in the parameter data section define the entities. The terminate section contains a single record for checking purposes.

3.9.2 PDES

The International Organization for Standardization (ISO) is currently involved in developing an international standard called STEP (standard for transfer and exchange of product model data). STEP is a step for global standardization of exchange of information related to automated manufacturing. PDES stands for Product Data Exchange Standard or Product Data Exchange using STEP. It is a more comprehensive and complex standard and designed to support various applications in industry. The fundamental difference between IGES and PDES is that PDES data exchange is done in terms of *applications,* whereas IGES utilizes entities as basic elements. This philosophy is also called *discipline models* or *mental models* and is reflected in the PDES three-layer architecture: application layer, logical layer, and physical layer.

The application layer is the interface between the user and PDES. In this layer, the application model is explicitly expressed and the description and information are expressed formally via information modelling techniques. The next layer, logical layer, is used to provide a consistent, and computer independent description. This is used to ensure that there is no redundancy but sufficient information is available to support the wide range of applications. The physical layer takes care of structure and format of the exchange file itself to keep efficiency in file size.

3.9.3 Drawing Exchange File Format

DXF (AutoCAD, 1990) stands for Drawing Exchange File format. It has been developed by AutoDesk Inc. to assist in interchange of drawings between AutoCAD and other programs. All implementations of AutoCAD accept this format and are able to convert it to and from their internal drawing file representation. Moreover, with the spread of AutoCAD, DXF has become one of the standards for drawing exchange. Many software packages support the DXF format. DXF files are standard ASCII text files. They can easily be translated to the formats of other CAD systems or submitted to other programs for specialized analysis.

The overall organization of a DXF file is as follows:

1. *Header section:* general information about the drawing.
2. *Tables section:* definitions of named items.
3. *Blocks section:* block definition entities describing the entities constituting each block in the drawing.
4. *Entities section:* the drawing entities, including any block references.
5. END OF FILE

3.10 SUMMARY

In this chapter we presented a detailed but basic analysis of geometric modeling approaches such as wireframes, surfaces, and solids. Geometric modeling of products is the heart of the CAD process. Solid modeling systems, although powerful compared with wireframe and surface modeling techniques, require substantial computational resources. There has been a dramatic increase in the speed-to-cost ratio of computing hardware over the past decade. Industrial applications of solid modeling are now supported on various types of workstations that are affordable and effective. However, it is not easy to run a professional solid model on a microcomputer-based system. Despite steady progress, many of the problems identified over a decade ago still remain, such as efficient modeling of very large complex objects (over 10,000 primitives), better user interfaces, use of parallel and distributed system architectures, robustness, and numerical inaccuracies.

PROBLEMS

3.1 Derive the parametric equation for $(x - a)^2 + (y - b)^2 = r^2$.

3.2 For a particular CAD/CAM software package, name all the methods for defining a point.

3.3 Repeat Problem 3.2 for lines and circles. Does the software provide methods for defining ellipses and parabolas? If not, how will you resolve the problem?

3.4 Draw multiviews of the part shown in Figure 3.8 in your CAD/CAM system. Compare various methods with respect to drafting productivity.

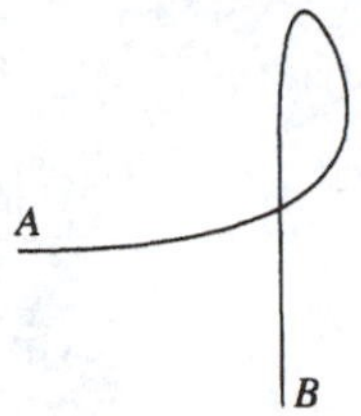

FIGURE P3.1 Hermite curve modeling.

3.5 Discuss why we need synthetic curves. Name at least three applications.

3.6 Two endpoints of a curve segment are $A(2, 3)$ and $B(4, 6)$ and the slopes at these two points are 45° and 75°, respectively, with magnitude 4. Develop the Hermite curve equation and draw the curve.

3.7 Suppose the endpoint of another curve segment is $A(7, 9)$ and the slope is 35°. Develop a curve that is connected to the curve in Problem 3.6 with C^1 continuity.

3.8 Is it possible that the curve shown in Fig. P3.1 is a Hermite curve? If yes, assume the necessary data and derive the equation.

3.9 Given four control points $A(4, 8)$, $B(7, 9)$, $C(8, 1)$, and $D(10, 4)$, develop the cubic Bezier curve equation and draw the curve.

3.10 Draw plane, ruled, tabulated, revolution, and B-spline surfaces in your CAD system.

3.11 Repeat Problem 3.10 with respect to a quadratic B-spline surface.

3.12 Draw a general B-spline surface in your CAD/CAM system.

3.13 Why is solid modeling necessary?

3.14 What do you mean by regularized Boolean set operations?

3.15 Why is Euler's formula used in solid modeling? Verify it for a tetrahedron and a cube. Draw an arbitrary solid object and verify its validity using Euler's generalized rule.

3.16 Develop the boundary representation model of the part shown in Figure P3.2. Verify its validity by Euler's rule.

3.17 Develop the CSG representation of the part shown in Figure P3.2. Can you develop the CSG model if the primitives are half-spaces?

3.18 Is the CSG representation unique? Show that by an example.

3.19 Compare various solid modeling approaches available in your system.

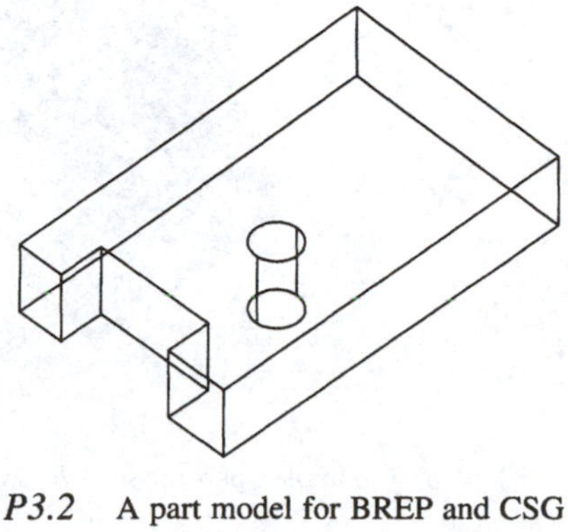

FIGURE P3.2 A part model for BREP and CSG model construction.

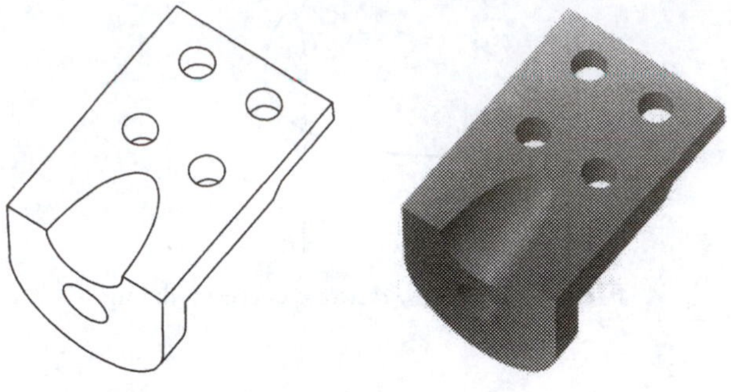

(a) (b)

FIGURE P3.3 (*a*) A simple part model; (*b*) Solid model of the part in (*a*).

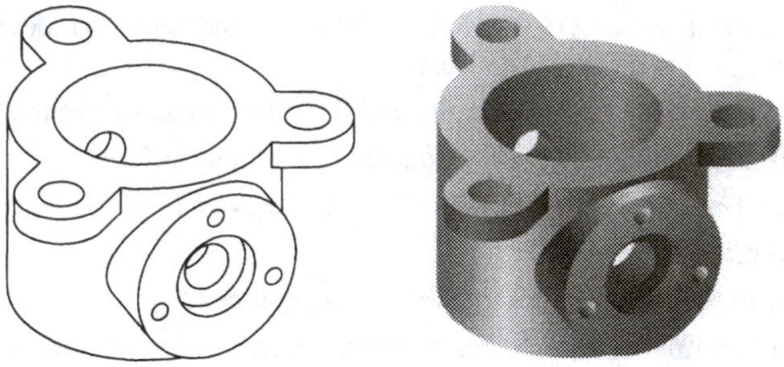

(a) (b)

FIGURE P3.4 (*a*) Valve housing; (*b*) solid model of valve housing.

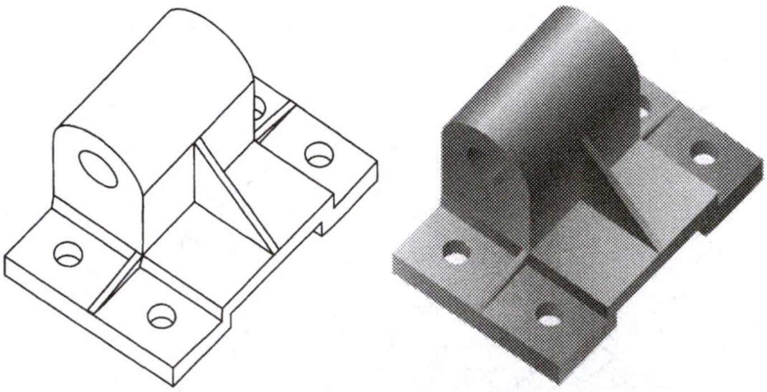

(a) (b)

FIGURE P3.5 (*a*) A complex part model; (*b*) solid model of the part in (*a*).

FIGURE P3.6 I-section surface model.

Laboratory Assignments

Laboratory assignments are given next with a view to developing hands-on experience with your CAD/CAM system. The objective is to learn various alternative ways of building a model of a part as well as to explore various features that are available on your CAD/CAM system.

3.20 Explore different solid modeling features that are available in your CAD software using the part shown in Figure P3.3*a* and *b*. The features included in this part are the extruded solid base feature, holes, patterning of a hole, angular slot, cut, round, chamfer, and protrusion from the base feature. The slot is angular, which requires an angular datum to create.

3.21 The part shown in Figure P3.4*a* and *b* is a valve housing that exemplifies the different types of holes that can be created, for example, coaxial and radial, blind, thorough-all, or counter-bore holes or holes through up to the next feature. There is also a boss created (opposite to a hole) radial to the cylindrical base feature. Additional features are the threaded holes on the boss. (*Hint:* Assume suitable dimensions. Start by creating a solid extruded cylinder, the base feature, and then create the other features in the following sequence: a coaxial through-all hole through the cylinder; the cylindrical boss radial to the base feature axis, blind up to the height; and a blind hole coaxial to the boss that digs radially into the opposite surface of the base cylinder. Make the counter-bore hole coaxial to the boss, create one of the threaded holes on the boss, and copy this hole at the other locations. Extrude a radial protrusion on the front surface of the base, and copy this feature at the other locations after creating the through-all hole through this protrusion. To finish, round off the necessary edges.)

3.23 This part shows that there is more than one way to create any part, and the choice depends on the modeler. While creating the model, one should be able to visualize the problems that might arise later during the course of building the whole model. Explore alternative ways of developing a model of the part shown in Figure P3.5*a* and *b*. Evaluate the speed and efficiency of the different approaches to modeling this part.

3.24 The part shown in Figure P3.6 is an I-section surface, swept along a B-spline curve. Note that this is an open-ended part, which is common in the sheet metal industry. To create this part, sketch a B-spline curve, and then sweep an I-section from a plane perpendicular to the plane of the sweep. This part is a ''surface'' feature and not a solid.

3.25 Develop and assemble Oldham's coupling (Figure P3.7*a* and *b*). Oldham's coupling consists of Oldham's disc (1 off; Figure P3.7*c*), Oldham's flange (2 off; Figure P3.7*d*), Oldham's shaft (2 off; Figure P3.7*e*), and keys (2 off; Figure P3.7*f*). The first three parts are all cylindrical surfaces, and can be created as revolved solids. The process of revolving a solid adds flexibility to the modeling process. (*Hint:* To assemble the disc and flange, align the axes of the two parts and mate the protrusion of the disc with that of the

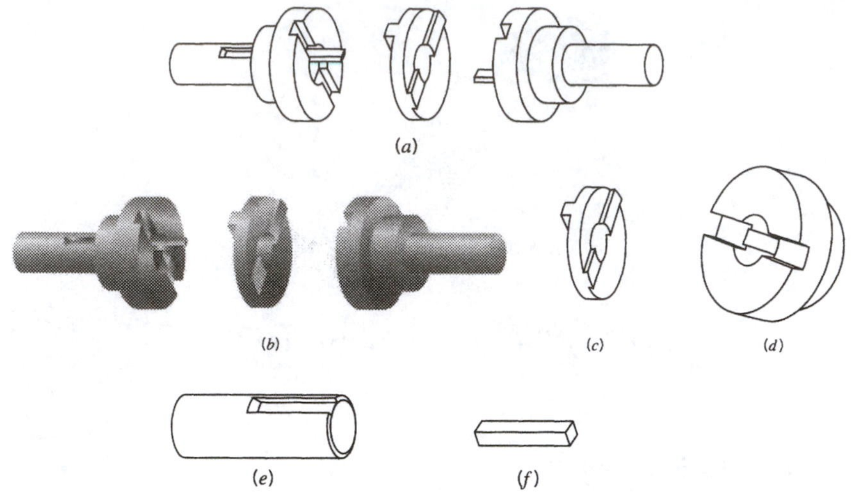

FIGURE P3.7 (*a*) Oldham coupling assembly; (*b*) solid model of Oldham's coupling; (*c*) disk; (*d*) flange; (*e*) Oldham shaft; (*f*) key. Figs. (*c*), (*d*), (*e*) and (*f*) are not in the same scale.

slot of the flange. To assemble the shaft into the above sub-assembly, again align the axes and insert the shaft into the flange in such a manner as to orient the keyways on the flange and shaft in the same direction. To place the key in the keyway, mate two surfaces of the key with two respective faces on the keyway. Also, be sure to mate the larger end of the key with the protrusion on the disc. Complete the assembly on the other half of the disc with the same parts.)

REFERENCES AND SUGGESTED READINGS

AutoCAD Reference Manual (1990). AutoDesk, Inc., Sausalito, California.

Chung, J. C. H., and Schussel, M. D. (1990). Technical evaluation of variational and parametric design. *Proceedings of the ASME Computers in Engineering Conference,* Vol. 1, pp. 289–298, The American Society of Mechanical Engineers, New York.

Foley, J. D., van Dam, A., Feiner, S. K., and Hughes, J. F. (1990). *Computer Graphics: Principles and Practice,* 2nd ed. Addison-Wesley Publishing Company, Reading, Massachusetts.

Lawry, M. H. (1991). I-DEAS: Integrated Design Engineering Analysis Software Student Guide. Structural Dynamics Research Corporation, Milford, Ohio.

Melkanoff, M. A. (1990). Design process for new products. In *Product Development and Production Engineering in Manufacturing Engineering* (C. Foulard, ed.). Hemisphere Publishing Corporation, New York.

Mortenson, M. E. (1985). *Geometric Modeling.* John Wiley & Sons, New York.

Rehg, J. A. (1994). *Computer-Integrated Manufacturing,* Prentice-Hall Career & Technology, Englewood Cliffs, New Jersey.

Rooney, J., and Steadman, P. (eds.) (1988). *Principles of Computer-Aided Design.* Prentice Hall, Englewood Cliffs, New Jersey.

Sharp, R. J., Thomas, P. J., and Thorne, R. W. (1982). Constructive geometry in three dimensions for computer-aided design. *Journal of Mechanical Design,* 104:813–816.

Su, BuQing, and Liu, DingYuan (1989). *Computational Geometry—Curve and Surface Modeling* (Translated by GengZhe Chang). Academic Press, San Diego.

Teicholz, E. (1985). *Computer-Aided Design and Manufacturing Handbook.* McGraw-Hill, New York.

Wolfe, R. N., Wesley, M. A., Kyle, J. C., Jr., Gracer, F., and Fitzgerald, W. J. (1987). Solid modeling for production design. *IBM Journal of Research and Development,* Vol. 31, no. 3, pp. 275–275.

Zeid, I. (1991). *CAD/CAM Theory and Practice.* McGraw-Hill, New York.

CHAPTER 4

CONCURRENT ENGINEERING

Market share and profitability are the major determinants of the success of any organization. The cornerstone of increased market share and profitability is the edge an organization has over its competitors. The factors that influence and improve the competitive edge of a company are unit cost of products, quality, and lead time. Concurrent engineering (CE) has emerged as a discipline to help achieve the objectives of reduced cost, better quality, and improved delivery performance. Concurrent engineering is being implemented in many organizations. CE is perceived as a vehicle for change in the way the products and processes are designed, manufactured, and distributed. In this chapter we discuss the basics of concurrent engineering, that is, what CE is and why it is important. We explore relationships between design and manufacturing. The CE influencing dimensions and CE elements are defined. Quality function deployment, an important tool used in concurrent engineering, is discussed. Some simple models are developed to illustrate the interactions between design and manufacturing.

4.1 WHAT IS CONCURRENT ENGINEERING?

The U.S. Institute of Defense has defined concurrent engineering as follows:

> *Concurrent Engineering is a systematic approach to the integrated, concurrent design of products and their related processes, including manufacture and support. This approach is intended to cause the developers, from the outset, to consider all elements of the product life cycle from conception to disposal, including quality, cost, schedule, and user requirements. (Pennell and Winner, 1989)*

Concurrent engineering is a management and engineering philosophy for improving quality and reducing costs and lead time from product conception to product development for new products and product modifications (Creese and Moore, 1990). CE means that the design and development of the product, the associated manufacturing equipment and processes, and the repair tools and processes are handled concurrently.

The evolution of the product and the associated manufacturing and repair capabilities are treated as a single integrated activity. The concurrent engineering idea contrasts sharply with current industry sequential practices, where the product is first designed and developed, the manufacturing approach is then established, and finally the approach to repair is determined (Meth, 1991).

4.2 SEQUENTIAL ENGINEERING VERSUS CONCURRENT ENGINEERING

Sequential engineering, also known as *serial engineering,* is characterized by departments supplying information to design only after a product has been designed, verified, and prototyped (Turino, 1991). A flow diagram of the serial engineering organization is shown in Figure 4.1*a*. In serial engineering the various functions such as design, manufacturing, and customer service are separated. The information in serial engineering flows in succession from phase to phase. For example, the prototype model, verified by either simulation or hardware prototyping or both, is reviewed for manufacturing, quality, and service. Usually, some changes are suggested after the review. If the suggested changes in the design are made, there are increases in the cost and time to develop the product, resulting in delays in marketing the product. If the changes cannot be made because of market pressure to launch the product quickly or the fact that the design is already behind schedule, then specialists in other functional areas or managers from manufacturing, quality, and service, among others, are informed of impending problems.

What distinguishes concurrent engineering from sequential engineering? In concurrent engineering all the functional areas are integrated with the design process. During the design process, concurrent engineering draws on various disciplines to

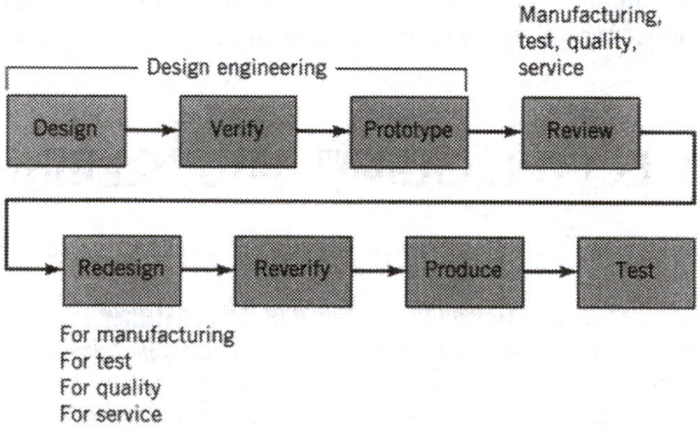

(*a*)

FIGURE 4.1 (*a*) Flow diagram of the serial engineering organization (From Turino, 1991; Reproduced with permission from *IEEE Spectrum*). (*b*) Flow diagram of the concurrent engineering organization (From Turino, 1991; Reproduced with permission from *IEEE Spectrum*). (*c*) Multidisciplinary, cross-functional team for design in a concurrent engineering environment.

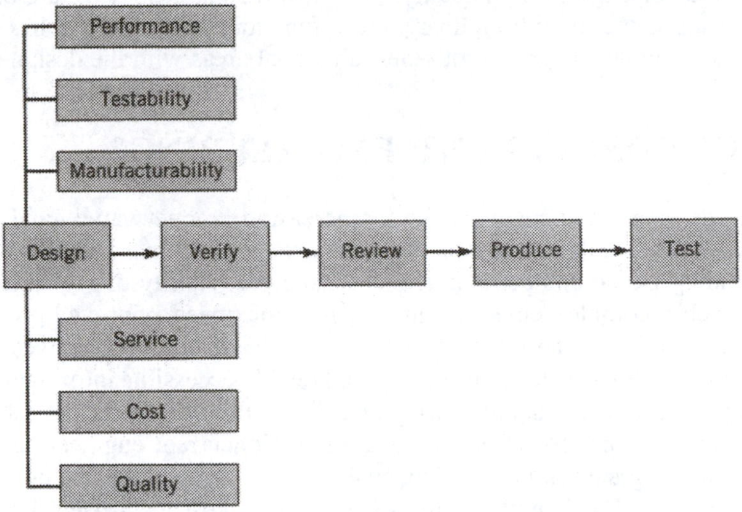

(b)

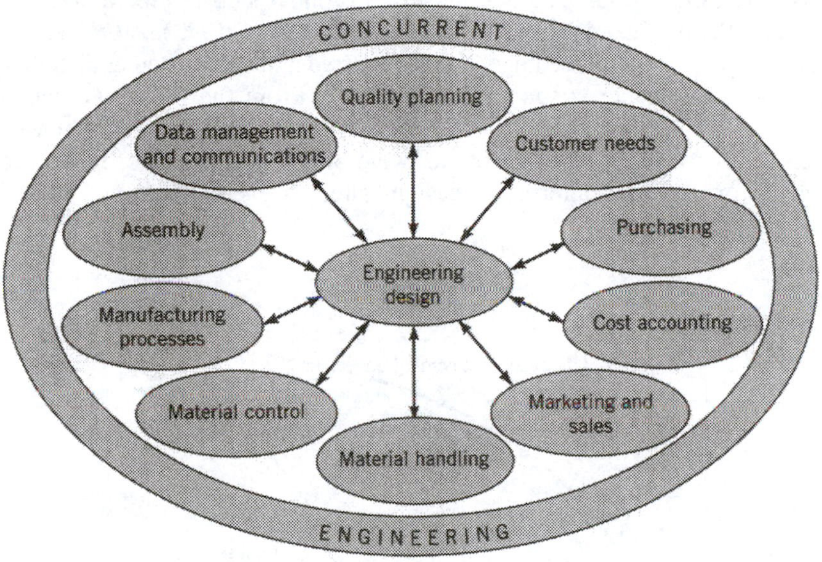

(c)

FIGURE 4.1 (continued)

trade off parameters such as manufacturability, testability, and serviceability, along with customer performance, size, weight, and cost (Turino, 1991). A flow diagram of the concurrent engineering organization is shown in Figure 4.1*b*. The information flow in concurrent engineering is interlinked with various phases. There is multidirectional exchange of information between all functional areas, such as design, manufacturing, and service. The decision-making process in the concurrent engineering environment differs from that in sequential engineering in that decisions are taken considering the constraints of all the stages of the product life cycle at every stage. The integration of other functional areas with the design process helps discover hard-to-solve problems at the design stage. Thus, when the final design is verified, it is already manufacturable, testable, serviceable, and of high quality. The most distinguishing feature of concurrent engineering is the multidisciplinary, cross-functional team approach. For example, Figure 4.1*c* shows integration of other functional areas with the design process.

4.3 WHY CONCURRENT ENGINEERING?

The present-day market is characterized by increasing product variety and technical complexity, decreasing levels of demand, a discrete product manufacturing environment, expanding global competition, and declining profitability of organizations. To survive in such a complex environment, organizations need improved productivity, quality, and flexibility. The question is how to achieve these objectives. What is required is comprehensive, accurate, timely, and readily accessible information related to the design of products, manufacturing and distribution of products, customer requirements, and so forth for effective integration. Concurrent engineering is a concerted effort to integrate fully the design, analysis, and engineering functions of products and processes. The integration results in reduced cost, decreased development time, and improved quality.

Many studies have indicated that most of a product's cost is fixed early in its life cycle, before the original design cycle is complete (Miller, 1993). A typical characteristic curve depicting the percentage of cost incurred and committed at different stages of a product's life cycle is shown in Figure 4.2. From the figure we can see that significant cost is committed during the design stage. This implies that we should consider various aspects of product life cycle at the design stage. If we provide a mechanism for exploring alternative designs and, for each alternative, assessing the

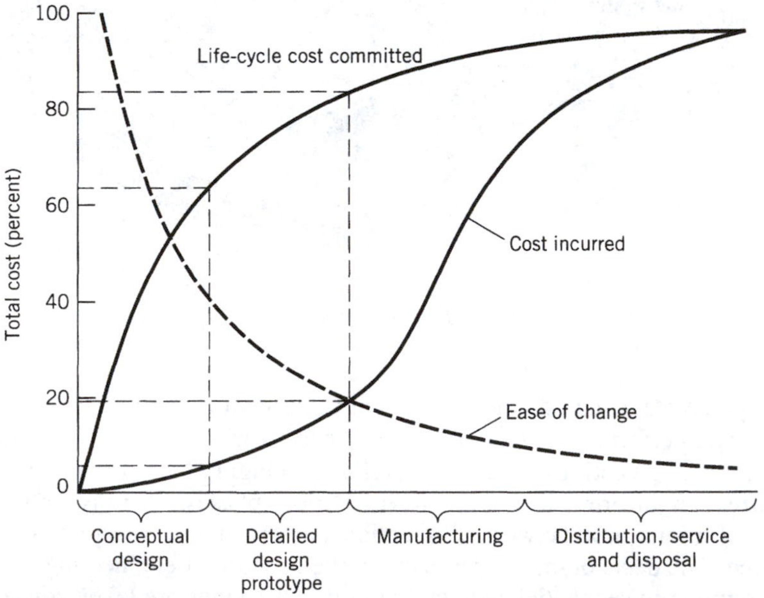

FIGURE 4.2 A characteristic curve representing cost incurred and com mitted during the product life cycle.

implications for subsequent stages from manufacturing through disposal, we can then decide on a design that not only is X-able (i.e., manufacturable, reliable, maintainable, disposable) but also leads to a low-cost, high-quality product deliverable in the least possible time. The concurrent engineering framework provides an opportunity to integrate all aspects of the product life cycle starting from the conceptualization of the design.

Linton et al. (1992) have summarized the results of a survey that include the following improvements to specific product lines by the applications of concurrent engineering. Also, significant benefits from the application of concurrent engineering have been reported in a survey conducted by the Institute of Defense Analysis for the U.S. Undersecretary of Defense for Acquisition (Pennell and Winner, 1989) in the areas of quality improvement, cost reduction, and reduced development time. Kohli and Forgionne (1992) have briefly summarized these reported benefits of concurrent engineering by some of the leading U.S. companies as follows:

1. *Development and production lead times*
   - Product development time reduced up to 60%.
   - Production spans reduced 10%.
   - AT&T reduced the total process time for the ESS programmed digital switch by 46% in 3 years.
   - Deere reduced product development time for construction equipment by 60%.
   - ITT reduced the design cycle for an electronic countermeasures system by 33% and its transition-to-production time by 22%.
2. *Measurable quality improvements*
   - Yield improvements of up to four times.
   - Field failure rates reduced up to 83%.
   - AT&T achieved a fourfold reduction in variability in a polysilicon deposition process for very large scale integrated circuits and achieved nearly two orders of magnitude reduction in surface defects.
   - AT&T reduced defects in the ESS programmed digital switch up to 87% through a coordinated quality improvement program that included product and process design.
   - Deere reduced the number of inspectors by two-thirds through emphasis on process control and linking the design and manufacturing processes.
3. *Engineering process improvements*
   - Engineering changes per drawing reduced up to 15 times.
   - Early production engineering changes reduced by 15%.
   - Inventory items stocked reduced up to 60%.
   - Engineering prototype builds reduced up to three times.
   - Scrap and rework reduced up to 87%.
4. *Cost reduction*
   - McDonnell Douglas had a 60% reduction in life-cycle cost and 40% reduction in production cost on a short-range missile proposal.

- Boeing reduced a bid on a mobile missile launcher and realized costs 30 to 40% below the bid.
- IBM reduced direct costs in system assembly by 50%.
- ITT saved 25% in ferrite core bonding production costs.

These concrete examples document the performance improvement potential of concurrent engineering. In large measure, these improvements have been accomplished through the formation of cross-functional product development teams. In the next section we explore underlying system behavior that enables this improvement.

4.4 MATHEMATICAL MODEL FOR UNDERSTANDING INTERACTIONS BETWEEN DESIGN AND MANUFACTURING

In this section we present a mathematical model based on our work (Singh and Sushil, 1990a; Singh and Falkenburg, 1994) on understanding the interactions between design and manufacturing. The mathematical model serves as a decision support system integrating issues related to design and manufacturing and helps address the following questions:

- How does design affect manufacturing cost, quality, and manufacturing lead time?
- What is the influence of manufacturing process design on these factors?
- How does the concurrent engineering approach help obtain a better solution compared with the serial engineering approach?

To answer these questions, we consider a simple product, a cylindrical part (shaft). The design stage is concerned with specifying tolerances on the shaft. The manufacturing stage is essentially a transformation process, changing a bar stock into a finished shaft meeting tolerance specifications. The process involves a turning operation that can be performed on a turret lathe, an engine lathe, an automatic screw machine, or a numerically controlled (NC) turning center. The transformation process indicating inputs and outputs is shown in Figure 4.3*a* and the unit normal curve indicating tolerances and the fraction rejects in Figure 4.3*b*.

Suppose the design department specifies the tolerance limits to meet certain functional requirements. Let t_k^u and t_k^l represent the upper and lower tolerance limits, respectively, for a component shaft for the *k*th alternative system of tolerances. Also, let σ_j and μ_j be the standard deviation and the process mean of the output dimension of the shaft, respectively, for the *j*th manufacturing option. Assuming that the dimensions are normally distributed, we have

$$\frac{t_k^u - \mu_j}{\sigma_j} = Z_{jk}^u \tag{4.1}$$

$$\frac{t_k^l - \mu_j}{\sigma_j} = Z_{jk}^l \tag{4.2}$$

where Z_{jk}^u and Z_{jk}^l designate the standard normal variates for the upper and lower tolerance limits, respectively, for the *k*th alternative system of tolerances using the *j*th

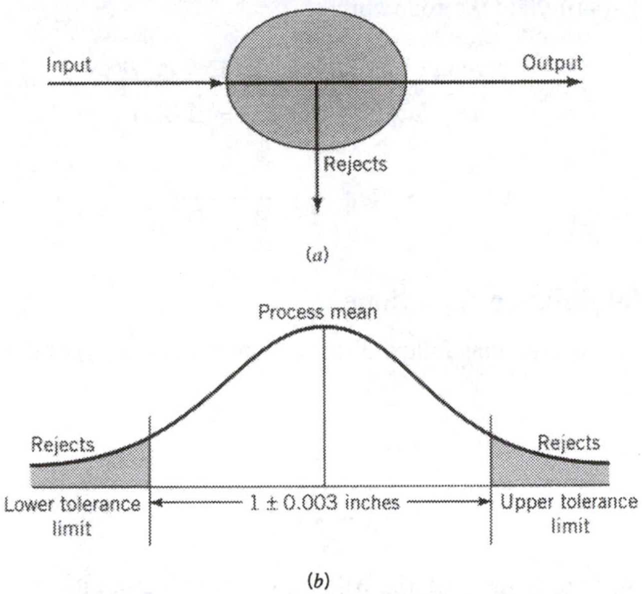

FIGURE 4.3 (*a*) The transformation process; (*b*) normal curve for shaft dimensions

manufacturing option. In the rest of this section j refers to manufacturing and k to tolerance options.

We present a simple analysis without rework. This means that the shafts below the lower tolerance limits and above the upper tolerance limits are scrapped. Let Y^{o}_{jk}, Y^{i}_{jk} and Y^{s}_{jk} represent the output, input, and scrap units, respectively. Then, at the transformation stage using the jth machining process, we have the fraction of scrap (SC_{jk}) as follows:

$$\mathrm{SC}_{jk} = \frac{Y^{\mathrm{s}}_{jk}}{Y^{\mathrm{i}}_{jk}} = \Phi(Z^{\mathrm{l}}_{jk}) + 1 - \Phi(Z^{\mathrm{u}}_{jk}) \tag{4.3}$$

where $\Phi(\ )$ represents the c.d.f. (cumulative density function) of the standard normal variate.

Furthermore, at the transformation stage we have the mass balance equation

$$Y^{\mathrm{i}}_{jk} = Y^{\mathrm{o}}_{jk} + Y^{\mathrm{s}}_{jk} \tag{4.4}$$

We define the following technological coefficients per unit output to represent the input requirements and scrap generated (units below the lower tolerance limit and units above the upper tolerance limit), respectively:

$$k^{\mathrm{i}}_{jk} = \frac{Y^{\mathrm{i}}_{jk}}{Y^{\mathrm{o}}_{jk}} \tag{4.5}$$

$$k^{\mathrm{s}}_{jk} = \frac{Y^{\mathrm{s}}_{jk}}{Y^{\mathrm{o}}_{jk}} \tag{4.6}$$

Equations (4.1)–(4.6) yield the following:

$$k^{s}_{jk} = \frac{SC_{jk}}{1 - SC_{jk}} = \frac{\Phi(Z^{l}_{jk}) + 1 - \Phi(Z^{u}_{jk})}{\Phi(Z^{u}_{jk}) - \Phi(Z^{l}_{jk})} \tag{4.7}$$

$$k^{i}_{jk} = 1 + k^{s}_{jk} = \frac{1}{\Phi(Z^{u}_{jk}) - \Phi(Z^{l}_{jk})} \tag{4.8}$$

4.4.1 Material Balance Equations

The material balance equations follow directly from the definition of the technological coefficients:

$$Y^{i}_{jk} = k^{i}_{jk} Y^{o}_{jk} \tag{4.9}$$

$$Y^{s}_{jk} = k^{s}_{jk} Y^{o}_{jk} \tag{4.10}$$

Also, equation (4.4) provides material balance between input, output and scrap.

4.4.2 Cost Equation

At a transformation process, the dollar inflow rate equals the dollar outflow rate. If X^{i}_{jk}, X^{o}_{jk}, and X^{s}_{jk} are the unit average cost of input, output, and scrap, respectively, and $f(Y^{i}_{jk})$ is the processing cost per unit, we obtain the following cost flow rate by appropriately multiplying the flow rates by their respective average unit costs:

$$X^{i}_{jk} Y^{i}_{jk} + Y^{i}_{jk} f(Y^{i}_{jk}) = X^{o}_{jk} Y^{o}_{jk} + X^{s}_{jk} Y^{s}_{jk} \tag{4.11}$$

Upon dividing Equation (4.11) by Y^{o}_{jk}, we get the unit output cost X^{o}_{jk} as follows:

$$X^{o}_{jk} = \left(\frac{Y^{i}_{jk}}{Y^{o}_{jk}}\right) X^{i}_{jk} - \left(\frac{Y^{s}_{jk}}{Y^{o}_{jk}}\right) X^{s}_{jk} + \left(\frac{Y^{i}_{jk}}{Y^{o}_{jk}}\right) f(Y^{i}_{jk})$$

or

$$X^{o}_{jk} = k^{i}_{jk} X^{i}_{jk} - k^{s}_{jk} X^{s}_{jk} + k^{i}_{jk} f(Y^{i}_{jk}) \tag{4.12}$$

The governing equations (4.9), (4.10), and (4.12) provide an analytical model for understanding the interaction between design and manufacturing from the point of view of unit cost of production, quality, and manufacturing lead time.

4.4.3 Unit Cost

Equation (4.12) provides the relation for unit cost as a function of design and manufacturing parameters. This analytical relationship is helpful in understanding the implications of changes in the design specifications as well as manufacturing technological options for unit cost.

4.4.4 Average Manufacturing Lead Time

We can determine the average manufacturing lead time by making use of Equation (4.9). If the average processing time per unit using the jth manufacturing technology is t_j and S_j is the setup time, then the average manufacturing lead time (T_j) to produce Y^{o}_{jk} finished units meeting specifications is given by

$$T_j = S_j + t_j k^{i}_{jk} Y^{o}_{jk} \tag{4.13}$$

4.4.5 Pseudomeasure of Product Quality

Equation (4.10) provides the expected number of defective units produced for a given combination of tolerances and manufacturing process parameters. The expected number of defective units produced is a pseudomeasure of product quality. Another interesting measure of quality is given by what is known as Taguchi's quality loss function (for details, see Chapter 9).

One of the objectives of concurrent engineering is to select the design and the manufacturing process simultaneously so as to ensure minimum possible cost, best possible quality, and minimum possible lead time. We now have a model that provides assessment criteria in terms of cost, quality, and lead time as a function of design parameters such as tolerances, manufacturing parameters such as manufacturing processes and their costs, raw material cost, and salvage value. In the following section we use this model as a decision support system to understand interaction between design and manufacturing as well as to illustrate serial and concurrent engineering approaches.

4.5 SERIAL ENGINEERING VERSUS CONCURRENT ENGINEERING: AN EXAMPLE

To illustrate the benefits of the concurrent engineering approach, we propose the following simple problem. ABC company requires 1000 units of a turned cylindrical part (shaft). The design department of ABC company defines a need for a cylindrical part to be finished to 1 ± 0.003 inch. A *serial engineering* approach and a *concurrent engineering* solution are presented in the two scenarios that follow. We compare two situations that emerge from these strategies.

EXAMPLE 4.1

Serial Engineering Approach

The design department of ABC recommends a shaft dimension and tolerance of 1 ± 0.003 inch; this information is transmitted to the manufacturing engineering department. In the serial engineering approach, manufacturing engineering accepts these specifications and attempts to find the best manufacturing technology to accommodate the request made by design. Manufacturing engineering will challenge the specification only if the design is not producible. Drawing on the preceding analysis, manufacturing engineering decides to produce the parts on a turret lathe because the desired tolerances can be obtained. The process average and the standard deviation are estimated to be 1.00 and 0.003 inch, respectively. Other relevant data are:

Unit cost of raw material = \$10.00

Unit salvage value = \$2.00

Unit processing cost = \$7.00

The process engineer determines the unit cost of output, number of units of scrap generated, and number of raw units required to produce 1000 finished units using the model developed in the previous section as follows:

Unit Cost and Scrap Calculations

As a turret lathe is the first manufacturing technology option, $j = 1$; assuming tolerance 1 ± 0.003 inch as the first design option, $k = 1$. All parts above and below the tolerance limits are scrapped. For the given data, we get, $Z^{u}_{11} = 1.00$ and $Z^{l}_{11} = -1.00$. Therefore, from the normal tables, the percentage of items above the upper limit = 15.87 and the percentage of items below the lower tolerance limit = 15.87. The total percentage of rejects is 15.87 + 15.87 = 31.74. Accordingly,

$$\text{Technological coefficient of scrap, } k^{s}_{11} = \frac{SC_{11}}{1 - SC_{11}} = \frac{0.3174}{1 - 0.3174} = 0.4649$$

$$\text{Technological coefficient of input, } k^{i}_{11} = 1 + k^{s}_{11} = 1 + 0.4649 = 1.4649$$

$$\text{Number of units scrapped, } Y^{s}_{11} = k^{s}_{11} Y^{o}_{11} = 0.4649 \times 1000 = 465 \text{ (approximately)}$$

$$\text{Number of raw units (input) required, } Y^{i}_{11} = k^{i}_{11} Y^{o}_{11} = 1.4649 \times 1000 = 1465 \text{ (unit)}$$

$$\begin{aligned}\text{Unit output cost, } X^{o}_{11} &= k^{i}_{11} X^{i}_{11} - k^{s}_{11} X^{s}_{11} + k^{i}_{11} f(Y^{i}_{11}) \\ &= 1.4649 \times 10.00 - 0.4649 \times 2.00 + 1.4649 \times 7.00 \\ &= 23.97\end{aligned}$$

It is important to emphasize that the serial engineering approach is driven by a design specification. The process engineer assumes that the tolerances are driven by performance requirements, and a manufacturing process is selected that will meet the design specification. In this example, the expected number of rejects is too high, which will eventually lead to reexamination of the process and design specifications. In the serial engineering approach there is no formal mechanism for considering these aspects simultaneously. Therefore, the process of change may take significant time. During that period, the system normally operates at significantly low performance levels, that is, higher rejects, unit costs, and lead time. On the contrary, in the concurrent engineering approach, design specifications are finalized after considering manufacturing and other implications.

Concurrent Engineering Approach

As mentioned before, concurrent engineering is based on cross-functional and multi-disciplinary teams representing various functional areas. Therefore, the concurrent engineering concept cuts across functional boundaries of an organization. This means that in the concurrent engineering approach, marketing, design, manufacturing engineering, and all stakeholders in the product development process are brought together to discuss integrating issues of functional design, manufacturing, quality control, customer service, and so forth. This multifunctional team is responsible for addressing various issues:

- The marketing services of ABC found that the tolerance range of 1 ± 0.003 inch may be too tight.
- The quality department did not like the number of rejections.
- The manufacturing planning department wants to use machine tools with better process capabilities.
- The purchasing department cannot buy so many raw shafts because of the restricted availability of such steel.

This process leads to a sequence of interactions that are documented in the following set of meetings of the concurrent engineering team.

Concurrent Engineering Team Meeting 1

The team begins by agreeing to hold the shaft dimensions to 1 ± 0.003 inch. The manufacturing department recommends an engine lathe, which has higher process capability resulting in a process standard deviation of 0.002 inch. However, the processing cost increases to $9.00 per unit from the previous $7.00. Other data are the same as before. The unit cost of output, number of units of scrap generated, and number of raw units required to produce 1000 finished units are determined as follows:

Because the engine lathe is the second manufacturing technological alternative, $j = 2$. Also, $k = 1$, because there is no change in the design specifications. $Z^{u}_{21} = 1.5$, $Z^{l}_{21} = -1.5$, percent rejection above the upper limit = 6.7, percent rejection below the lower limit = 6.7, total percent rejection = 13.4, $k^{s}_{21} = 0.1547$, $k^{i}_{21} = 1.1547$. Accordingly,

Number of units scrapped, $Y^{s}_{21} = k^{s}_{21}Y^{o}_{21} = 0.1547 \times 1000 = 154.7 = 155$ (approximate)

Number of raw units (input) required, $Y^{i}_{21} = k^{i}_{21}Y^{o}_{21} = 1.1547 \times 1000 = 1155$ (approximate)

Unit output cost,
$$\begin{aligned} X^{o}_{21} &= k^{i}_{21}X^{i}_{21} - k^{s}_{21}X^{s}_{21} + k^{i}_{21}f(Y^{i}_{21}) \\ &= 1.1547 \times 10.00 - 0.1547 \times 2.00 + 1.1547 \times 9.00 \\ &= 21.63 \end{aligned}$$

Concurrent Engineering Team Meeting 2

The quality and purchasing departments are still not satisfied with the amount of scrap generated, and the marketing department feels that the unit cost is still too high. As a consequence of this feedback from marketing, the design engineers believe that the customer requirements can be met with tolerance limits of 1 ± 0.004 inch. The team explores this scenario. They consider the component tolerances to be 1 ± 0.004 inch as recommended jointly by the marketing services and design engineers. An engine lathe is to be used to manufacture the component.

It is pertinent to point out that the design tolerances for individual components are allocated based on stacking of assembly tolerances. This aspect is illustrated in the journal bearing assembly example given in the Appendix. Other data are the same as those considered in meeting 1. The unit cost of output, number of units of scrap generated, and number of raw units required to produce 1000 finished units are determined as follows:

In this case $j = 2$ and $k = 2$. Using a procedure similar to that used in meeting 1, we obtain:

Number of units scrapped, $Y^{s}_{22} = k^{s}_{22}Y^{o}_{22} = 0.0456 \times 1000 = 46$ (approximately)

Number of raw units (input) required, $Y^{i}_{22} = k^{i}_{22}Y^{o}_{22} = 1.0456 \times 1000 = 1046$ units (approximately)

Unit output cost,
$$\begin{aligned} X^{o}_{22} &= k^{i}_{22}X^{i}_{22} - k^{s}_{22}X^{s}_{22} + k^{i}_{22}f(Y^{i}_{22}) \\ &= 1.0456 \times 10.00 - 0.0456 \times 2.00 + 1.0456 \times 9.00 \\ &= 19.78 \end{aligned}$$

Concurrent Engineering Team Meeting 3

Our cross-functional multi-disciplinary team compares the results of the two meetings and seeks reductions in the cost of manufacturing, the number of rejects, and consequently the number of pieces of raw shaft material required. Although the number of rejects has been reduced considerably, quality level is still not acceptable to the customer. The customer is, however, willing to pay more per unit. The team explores the possibility of using an automated screw machine (ASM), whose process capability is much better than that of an engine lathe. This would, however, increase the unit processing cost.

For the ASM the standard deviation is now 0.001 inch and the unit processing cost is $12.00. Other data are the same as in the previous meetings. In this meeting the team wants to know the unit cost of output, number of units of scrap generated, and number of raw units required to produce 1000 finished units considering both 1 ± 0.003 and 1 ± 0.004 inch as tolerance limits. The relevant calculations follow.

For the tolerance limit of 1 ± 0.003, and automated screw machine $k = 1$ and $j = 3$.

$$\text{Number of units scrapped, } Y_{31}^{s} = k_{31}^{s} Y_{31}^{o} = 0.0027 \times 1000 = 3 \text{ (approximately)}$$

$$\text{Number of raw units (input) required, } Y_{31}^{i} = k_{31}^{i} Y_{31}^{o} = 1.002 \times 1000 = 1003 \text{ units}$$

$$\begin{aligned}\text{Unit output cost, } X_{31}^{o} &= k_{31}^{i} X_{31}^{i} - k_{31}^{s} X_{31}^{s} + K_{31}^{i} f(Y_{31}^{i}) \\ &= 1.0027 \times 10.00 - 0.0027 \times 2.00 + 12.00 \times 1.0027 \\ &= 22.054\end{aligned}$$

For the tolerance limit of 1 ± 0.004, $j = 3$ and $k = 2$.

$$\begin{aligned}\text{Number of units scrapped, } Y_{32}^{s} &= k_{32}^{s} Y_{32}^{o} = 0.000 \times 1000 = 00 \\ K_{32}^{i} &= 1 + 0.00 = 1.00\end{aligned}$$

$$\text{Number of raw units (input) required, } Y_{32}^{i} = k_{32}^{i} Y_{32}^{o} = 1.00 \times 1000 = 1000 \text{ units}$$

$$\begin{aligned}\text{Unit output cost, } X_{32}^{o} &= k_{32}^{i} X_{32}^{i} - k_{32}^{s} X_{32}^{s} + K_{32}^{i} f(Y_{32}^{i}) \\ &= 1.00 \times 10.00 - 0.00 \times 2.00 + 1.00 \times 12.00 = 22.00\end{aligned}$$

Concurrent Engineering Meeting 4

There have been dramatic improvements in the product quality as well as manufacturing lead time as a result of the multi-disciplinary cross-functional team–based approach of concurrent engineering. The scrap has been reduced to zero, which addressed the concerns of the quality control and sales departments.

In its earlier deliberations, the team did not consider the influence of economies of scale of production. Consider the situation in which the tolerance specifications are 1 ± 0.004 inch. Suppose the processing cost function for the automatic screw machine option is

$$f(Y_{32}^{i}) = 12.00 - 0.003 Y_{32}^{i}$$

Then the processing cost per unit when manufacturing 1000 units is 9. Accordingly, the unit cost of output is

$$\begin{aligned}X_{32}^{o} &= k_{32}^{i} X_{32}^{i} - k_{32}^{s} X_{32}^{s} + K_{32}^{i} f(Y_{32}^{i}) \\ &= 1.00 \times 10.00 - 0.00 \times 2.00 + 1.00 \times 9.00 = 19.00\end{aligned}$$

The sequence of meetings of the concurrent engineering team has led to them to understand the interaction between design and manufacturing by simultaneously considering both design and manufacturing issues. These interactions are summarized in Table 4.2. Furthermore, these concepts can be extended to cases involving multistage production and rework at each stage.

4.6 UNDERSTANDING BENEFITS OF CONCURRENT ENGINEERING

We mentioned earlier that unit cost, quality, and manufacturing lead time are three major determinants of market share and profitability of an organization. In this section we explore how the use of concurrent engineering concepts results in reduced unit cost, improved quality, and reduced lead time compared with the serial engineering approach. The basic data used are summarized in Table 4.1. We use the results obtained in Sections 4.6.1 and 4.6.2 for the serial and concurrent engineering approaches as shown in Table 4.2.

TABLE 4.1 **The Basic Data Used in the Shaft Examples**

Manufacturing Options	*Unit Processing Costs*	*Setup Time*	*Unit Processing Time*	*Process Standard Deviation*
Turret lathe	7.00	20.00	1.00	0.003
Engine lathe	9.00	25.00	0.80	0.002
ASM	12.00	50.00	0.70	0.001

4.6.1 Serial Engineering Approach

From Section 4.5 we know the unit cost in the serial engineering approach. The number of rejects can be considered as a measure of quality. We are also interested in estimating the manufacturing lead time. Now suppose it takes one unit time to manufacture a unit on a turret lathe. We then have

Unit cost = \$23.97

Setup time = 20 time units

Number of rejects (a measure of quality) = 465

Manufacturing lead time = setup time + (number of units turned on turret lathe × time per unit)
= 20 + (1465 × 1.00)
= 1485 time units

4.6.2 Concurrent Engineering Approach

We consider the scenario in meeting 3 that reflects the concurrent engineering approach. Suppose it takes 0.70 unit of time to manufacture a unit on an automatic screw machine compared with 1 unit of time on a turret lathe. In the case of concurrent engineering we then have

Unit cost = \$22.00,

Setup time = 50 time units

Number of rejects (a measure of quality) = 00

Manufacturing lead time = setup time + number of units turned on ASM × time per unit
= 50 + 1000 × 0.70
= 750 time units

TABLE 4.2 **Interaction Between Design and Manufacturing**

Manufacturing Technological Options	*Tolerances (in.)* 1 ± 0.003 *Unit Cost*	*Scrap (Units)*	*Lead Time*	1 ± 0.004 *Unit Cost*	*Scrap (Units)*	*Lead Time*
Turret lathe	23.97	465	1485	20.37	184	1204
Engine lathe	21.63	155	949	19.78	46	862
Automatic screw machine	22.05	3	752	22.00	00	750

4.6.3 Improvements in Unit Cost, Quality, and Manufacturing Lead Time

We are now in a position to evaluate the improvements in all three areas, unit cost, quality, and manufacturing lead time, by using concurrent engineering as follows:

Percentage improvement in unit cost = [(23.97 − 22)/23.97] × 100 = 8.21%

Improvement in quality = zero scrap compared with 465 units scrapped in serial engineering

Percentage improvement in manufacturing lead time = [(1485 − 750)/1485] × 100
= 49.50%

4.6.4 Other Benefits

We have demonstrated that an integrated concurrent engineering team can produce a better quality part with less waste and at lower cost. One of the most important benefits of concurrent engineering is not explicitly addressed in this simple example. In many large development projects, especially product development, lack of communication among members of the product development team can lead to extensive engineering design changes. Each design change consumes time in the product development cycle. This increase in time to reach market can influence the acceptance of the product, market position, project cost, and quality. These issues alone are compelling reasons for a firm to adopt the concurrent engineering approach.

4.7 CHARACTERIZATION OF THE CONCURRENT ENGINEERING ENVIRONMENT

Concurrent engineering considers all the issues involved in product development, from conception to disposal (life cycle), in a concurrent and integrated manner. Techniques and systems that support CE by advising designers on aspects that reduce life-cycle problems (Jakiela et al., 1984; Young et al., 1992) include the use of:

- Design teams
- Handbooks
- Checklists and procedures
- Process planning and manufacturing simulation
- Rule-based expert systems

The techniques and systems, however, represent only some of the many dimensions of concurrent engineering. The CALS/CE (Computer-aided acquisition and logistic support/concurrent engineering) Electronic Systems Working Group Report by Linton et al. (1992) provides a comprehensive treatment of various elements of concurrent engineering environments based on the complexity of products and systems. In the following sections we provide a framework for designing a concurrent engineering program based on the report by Linton et al. (1992).

4.7.1 How to Design a Concurrent Engineering Program

Given the importance of concurrent engineering, the natural question is how to design a proper concurrent engineering program to produce products that meet the challenges of competition. To answer this question, a framework for designing a concurrent engineering program is presented next. Intuitively, it consists of three phases.

Phase I: Identification of Influencing Dimensions and their Levels

- Identify the dimensions of the products and the programs that influence the concurrent engineering approach, such as product complexity, product technology, competition, and resource tightness.
- Establish the levels of influencing dimensions on an individual basis using information on the product features, product requirements, and any other aspects. For example, levels of product complexity could be catalog items, mostly common parts (little state-of-the-art), state-of-the-art items (sensitive interfaces), and pushing the state-of-the-art envelope. These levels can be categorized as A, B, C, and D representing increasing order of complexity.
- Establish an aggregate level by considering the relative importance of the influencing dimensions. This establishes the "should be" concurrent engineering environment for the product development program.

Phase II: Identification of Concurrent Engineering Elements and Their Levels

- Identify the concurrent engineering elements and sub-elements as well as their levels to support the "should be" concurrent engineering environment. What levels of organizational requirements, communications, and product development methodology are required to support adequately the concurrent engineering environment envisioned in phase I? For example, to produce a product with complexity level "push the state of the art" (rated D), the major sub-element "team member" of the organization element of concurrent engineering should be more research-oriented members. Similar analyses for all other concurrent engineering elements should be carried out.

Phase III: Evaluation

- Determine the improvements that are needed to match the required levels of concurrent engineering elements starting from your present stage. These improvements will depend on the influencing dimensions of products and programs, as well as CE elements and their levels.

In the following sections we provide brief descriptions of various influencing dimensions of products and programs (phase I) as well as the concurrent engineering elements (phase II) to help identify the required levels of various dimensions.

4.7.2 Concurrent Engineering Environment Influencing Dimensions

The dimensions of the products and programs that influence the concurrent engineering environment include:

1. Product complexity
2. Product technology
3. Program structure
4. Program futures
5. Competition

6. Business relationships
7. Team scope
8. Resource tightness
9. Schedule tightness

Brief discussions of these dimensions follow.

4.7.2.1 Product Complexity

The complexity of the product is determined by the types of parts involved, such as catalog parts, state-of-the-art parts, and parts that push the state-of-the-art envelope. For example, a product design requiring readily available catalog parts is less complex than the one using mostly common parts with a limited number of items representing state-of-the-art parts. A highly complex product may push the state-of-the-art part envelope, for example, developing a lens or seal system for the camera installed in the Hubble space telescope.

Consider products such as a car, a refrigerator, and a computer. The design of such products requires expertise from a number of disciplines such as mechanical, electrical, electronics, metallurgical, and chemical engineering. One expert cannot understand the full spectrum of the product's functionality. Therefore, a formal committee approach is essential to consider different perspectives of such products.

4.7.2.2 Product Technology

The levels of technology to be used in the product design may vary from readily available technology to new applications of existing technologies, requiring new technological capabilities and new core technology. For example, consider designing and drafting using available computer software such as Autocad, Pro/Engineer, or Unigraphics. New capabilities can be added by using artificial intelligence techniques. Process design may require new core technology such as parallel processing computer hardware and software.

4.7.2.3 Program Structure

The program structure represents what is needed to execute the program. Essentially, it includes the number of people, layers of reporting hierarchy, role of formal and informal communication channels, and physical distribution of the program staff. The program structure may vary from a small staff with informal reporting hierarchies and communication channels to a large staff with deep reporting hierarchies, structured communication channels, and physical distribution across multiple companies.

4.7.2.4 Program Futures

The basic idea in program futures is to assess the long-term opportunities afforded by the product development program. That is, program futures refer to the follow-on opportunities for the program in the minds of all team members. Futures deal with how much incentive there is to invest in the current phase to optimize product success in later phases or future products or, in other words, requirements for long-range business decisions and investments. The levels for program futures may vary from a stand-alone program without any long-term investment requirements to a program that is strategically aligned with enterprise enabling significant future opportunities.

4.7.2.5 Competition

Competition is an important dimension. It refers to the level of activity in the relevant industry and the criticality of anticipating and reacting to competitors' moves. This dimension emphasizes the need for flexibility of the program and its ability to react quickly to competitive pressures. Competition may vary from a minimal level to significant pressures to anticipate and react to competitors' actions. The minimum may involve a few competitors or protected niche market positions. Active competition may mean few barriers to increasing market share. Lead time, unit cost, and quality of products are the major determinants of market share and profitability in a competitive market.

4.7.2.6 Business Relationships

The business relationship is just like any relationship and is characterized by its degree of formality. For example, the level of formality of the relationship between customers, vendors, suppliers, team partners, and prime developers may vary from an arms-length relationship in which buying and selling of preexisting goods are the primary forms of interaction to active collaboration between the suppliers and the customers establishing joint requirements and implementation approaches as in just-in-time manufacturing environments. Active collaboration is desirable.

4.7.2.7 Team Scope

The diversity of perspectives required for program execution defines the team scope. For example, a small core design team receiving advice from numerous sections such as assembly, testing, and packaging has a limited scope. A multifunctional team having members from a number of competing disciplines has a larger perspective and scope and forms the backbone of CE programs.

4.7.2.8 Resource Tightness

The level of available resources (e.g., staffing and funding) may vary from not severely constrained to very tightly constrained. Severely resource-constrained programs lead to creative changes in the development process.

4.7.2.9 Schedule Tightness

This refers to the limited schedule slack times to counteract deficiencies in the existing concurrent engineering methodology or environment. The levels of schedule tightness may vary from significant slack time on noncritical paths to severely constrained schedules. Severely constrained schedules may lead to cost overruns and negative business impacts due to schedule slippage.

A summary of all influencing dimensions is given in Table 4.3. It should be emphasized that each dimension deals with specific aspects of program complexity and influences the recommended approach to concurrent engineering. The most appropriate approach for a specific program should be determined on the basis of the aggregate of all influences (Linton et al., 1992).

4.7.3 Major Elements of the Concurrent Engineering Environment

In order to characterize the concurrent engineering environment and examine the relevant aspects in detail, the CALS/CE Electronic Systems Task Group (Linton et al., 1992) identified the following four major elements of the concurrent engineering environment:

- Organization
- Requirements

TABLE 4.3 **Program and Product Influencing Dimensions**

	Levels of Concurrent Engineering Influencing Dimensions			
	A	*B*	*C*	*D*
Product complexity	Catalog items	Mostly common parts, little state of the art	State-of-the-art items Sensitive interfaces	Pushing the state-of-the-art envelope
Product technology	Available technology	New applications/custom built	New capabilities from core technologies	New core technology
Program structure	Small staff/informal communications	Moderate size staff, layered structure	Multiple locations, formal communications	Large staff, deep reporting structure
Program futures	No follow-on planned	Investments made to minimize costs	Investment plan Contractual boundaries	Significant future opportunities
Competition	Minimal competition	Significant barriers to market entry exist	Competitive analysis, market expansion	Active competition, pressure to anticipate and react
Business relationships	Arms length	Contractual	Teaming	Enterprise-wide, common goals
Team scope	Dominant perspective	Competing dominant perspective	Competing perspectives Interrelated optimization	Aggressive optimization to meet requirements
Resource tightness	Not severely constrained	Limited in-process resolution	No in-process correction	Tightly constrained
Schedule tightness	Significant schedule slack time	Adequate for first success	Aggregative, requires first-pass success	Severely constrained

Source: CALS/CE Electronic Systems Working Group Report by Linton et al. (1992); Reproduced with permission from Larry R. Linton, Chairman, NSIA CALS/CE Working Group.

- Communications
- Product development methodology

These elements and their subelements provide a basis for assessing specific capabilities within individual programs to address the concurrent engineering approach to product and process development.

4.7.3.1 Organization

Organizational issues refer to aspects of team dynamics, strategic business issues, and management and corporate culture that affect product development. The organization and its culture must support a concurrent engineering methodology if it is to succeed. The major organizational elements and their themes are:

Organizational Elements	***Theme***
Team membership	Team integration
Team leadership	Effectiveness
Team member contribution	Synergism
Business interrelationships	Participation
Training and education	Awareness
Responsibility and authority	Empowerment
Management decisions	Perspective

Various levels of organizational elements are summarized in Table 4.4.

4.7.3.2 Requirements

Requirements refer to external and internal constraints and assertions that affect the development of products. The elements that characterize requirements are given below with their themes:

Requirement Elements	***Theme***
Product definition	Completeness
Schedule types	Parallelism
Planning style	Adaptability
Validation of specifications to requirements	Accuracy

Product definition refers to the process of capturing and translating customer demands into the specification of product and process features to satisfy complete life-cycle needs, including manufacturability, supportability, and upgradability. The tools used for this purpose include a requirements database and quality function deployment (QFD). Scheduling practices to help plan and implement projects may include Gantt charts, CPM/PERT (critical path method/program evaluation and review technique) programs, and real-time scheduling. The validation process ensures that the specification meets the total requirements.

A summary of requirement elements is given in Table 4.5.

4.7.3.3 Communication

Communication is one of the key elements of concurrent engineering. Concurrent engineering means providing horizontal communication among all functional areas of design, manufacturing, and support along with customers and suppliers. The objective is to optimize design decisions and improve development, manufacturing, and support

TABLE 4.4 **Concurrent Engineering Self-Assessment Criteria Considering Organizational Elements**

	Concurrent Engineering Environments			
Organizational Elements	*A*	*B*	*C*	*D*
Team membership (Critical members)	The theme of team membership is team integration. The higher level of team integration is required as the CE environment changes from A to D.			
	Members have task perspective	Members have multidisciplinary perspective	Members have product perspective	Members have strategic perspective
Team leadership	The theme of team leadership is effectiveness.			
	Management-appointed team leader	Management-selected team facilitator	Team-selected facilitator	Natural emergence of temporary, most knowledgeable leader
Team member contribution	The theme of team member contribution is synergism.			
	Segmented; discipline-specific functionality	Leveraged; interfaced tools and multidisciplinary advisors	Cooperative; unified data model, central master database	Collaboration; Computer-assisted cooperative product development
Business (key) relationships	The theme of business interrelationships is participation.			
	Transaction based	Contractual	Joint venture	Partnership
Training education	The theme of training and education is awareness.			
	Team concepts; computer-assisted instruction	Multidisciplinary understanding; computer-based training	Cooperative decision process; multimedia computer-based training	Synergistic knowledge discovery; interactive simulation
Responsibility/authority	The theme of responsibility/authority is empowerment.			
	Member responsibility and rewards	Multidisciplinary group responsibility, rewards	Team decision, responsibility	Team autonomy, reward
Management decisions	The theme of management decisions is perspective.			
	Profit based decisions/planning using product unit cost accounting models	Single-phase planning/investments using design to cost accounting with risk management	Multiphase planning/investments using value-based decision support systems	Life cycle–based decisions using life-cycle decision support systems

Source: CALS/CE Electronic Systems Working Group Report by Linton et al. (1992); Reproduced with permission from Larry R. Linton, Chairman, NSIA CALS/CE Working Group.

TABLE 4.5 **Concurrent Engineering Self-Assessment Criteria Considering Requirement Elements**

	Concurrent Engineering Environments			
Requirement Elements	*A*	*B*	*C*	*D*
Definition	The theme is thoroughness.			
	Itemized requirements definition; requirements database	Requirements traceability; traceability cross-referencing	Requirements weighting; multirequirement trade study capabilities	Unambiguous specification; executable specification environment
Schedule types	The theme is to schedule in parallel.			
	Task duration–based schedule; Gantt chart	Calendar-based schedule; PERT charts	Event-based schedule; event-driven program management tools	Continuous addition of value to the enterprise; new scheduling paradigm
Planning/methodology	The theme is adaptability.			
	Bottom-up collation of task definitions; task management planning tools	Top-down determination of task definitions; requirement satisfaction–driven work breakdown structure	Synchronization of concurrent interrelated tasks; interrelated process-driven planning tool	Iteratively refined abstract plans; environment-driven planning tools
Validation (specification to requirements)	The theme is accuracy.			
	Validation to itemized requirements	Validation of interrelated constraints	Validate to end-use requirements	Validation to end-use and product business strategy

Source: CALS/CE Electronic Systems Working Group Report by Linton et al. (1992); Reproduced with permission from Larry R. Linton, Chairman, NSIA CALS/CE Working Group.

processes. This overcomes the hierarchical barriers to the exchange of timely and accurate information. The elements of communication and their themes are as follows:

Communication Elements	***Theme***
Management of working data	Control
Data acquisition and sharing	Accessability
Lessons learned feedback	Experience
Decision traceability	Legacy
Interpersonal	Equality

A summary of various communication elements is given in Table 4.6.

4.7.3.4 Product Development Methodology

Product development is a complex process and involves a number of people from various functional areas. The product development methodology includes all the activities involved in customer requirements planning, the total product development process, the design of the manufacturing process, and the design of product support processes. It is therefore important that the product development methodology is predetermined, documented, and followed by all the people involved. The various elements of the product development methodology are:

Development Methodology Elements	***Theme***
Optimization	Customer satisfaction
Data libraries	Consistency
Development process	Controllability
Reviews	Noninterruptive
Process measurements	Information content
Analysis architecture	Hierarchical
Verification	Compliance

A summary of various elements is given in Table 4.7.

We present an example from Linton et al. (1992) to illustrate how to use the self-assessment technique to assess the current level of concurrent engineering dimensions as well as the "should be" environment. It will be helpful in understanding where improvements are needed and what resources are required.

EXAMPLE 4.2

Consider the following scenario: The program manager of XYZ company has been charged with the responsibility for developing a line of high-quality notebook-sized computers that will eventually beat the competition. The idea is to market with increased features and with highly competitive pricing resulting in a high market share. The product should have the following key features:

- Lightweight
- Highly portable
- Self-contained (keyboard, display, central processing unit, battery, data storage, and so on
- Sized to fit in a briefcase
- Standard keyboard layout feel
- Compatible operating system

TABLE 4.6 **Concurrent Engineering Self-Assessment Criteria Considering Communication Elements**

	Concurrent Engineering Environments			
Communication Elements	*A*	*B*	*C*	*D*
Working data management	The theme is control.			
	Local individual data management; workstation release control system	Data structured for project-wide sharing; configuration management	Program repository of working data; central program database	Enterprise repository of working data; extensible data base
Data acquisition/sharing	The theme is accessibility.			
	As-needed data extraction; networked workstations with file management	Data supplied by most knowledgeable source; network communication	Data available as generated; program sharing; central database storage on program network	Enterprise-wide availability of data; central database storage on enterprise network
Lessons learned from feedback	The theme is experience.			
	Design guides with rationale/intent; checking with structured query capability	Consolidated design guide with rationale; checking with structured query capability/increasingly integrated rules	Rationale and weighting for each product development rule; checking with unstructured query capability with impact weighting	Dynamic lessons learned feedback; checking with unstructured query capability and impact assessment
Decision traceability	The theme is legacy.			
	Individual decision rationale ownership; repository with structured keyword search	Project decision rationale ownership; repository with unstructured keyword search	Program decision rationale ownership; repository with unstructured keyword search	Enterprise decision rationale ownership; repository with unstructured keyword search
Interpersonal	The theme is equality.			
	Member specific terminology; electronic communication	''Common'' terminology; multiple view (jargon to jargon translator)	Equal input/impact; knowledge-based cross-discipline advisors	Knowledge-based perspective; knowledge-based generative tools

Source: CALS/CE Electronic Systems Working Group Report by Linton et al. (1992); Reproduced with permission from Larry R. Linton, Chairman, NSIA CALS/CE Working Group.

TABLE 4.7 **Concurrent Engineering Self-Assessment Criteria Considering Product Development Methodology Elements**

Product Development Methodology Elements	*Concurrent Engineering Environments* *A*	*B*	*C*	*D*
Optimization	The theme is customer satisfaction.			
	Review-based optimization; single requirement optimization	Limited interrelated requirement optimization; multiple requirement optimization	Program-wide requirement optimization; Multiple requirement optimization	Total weighted requirement optimization; weighted multirequirement optimization
Data libraries (single master library source)	The theme is consistency.			
	Control of preferred parts and process libraries; on-line libraries selection assistance	Controlled libraries of reusable module and intent; program accessible network library	Controlled technology-independent libraries; technology information external to tools	Controlled real-time library data from source; technology information external to tools
Development process	The theme is controllability.			
	Product-independent, repeatable, and consistent process; consistent methodology enforcement	Measurement standards definition; key parameter identification tools	Closed-loop control; integrated process methodology	Process improvement and optimization; integrated process optimization
Reviews	The theme is being noninterruptive.			
	Schedule-driven product and process critiques	Event-driven reviews	Immediate issue resolution	Status reporting
Measurements	The theme of measurements is information content.			
	Measurement using function-specific deterministic indices; information systems handle project requirements	Measurement using process-related deterministic indices; expanded information system to include process	Measurment using heuristic predictive indices; statistical process control	Measurement using relevant, analytical, interrelated predictive indices; integrated, enterprise-wide factual data
Analysis architecture	The theme of analysis architecture is hierarchical.			
	Single-level modeling; single-level simulation and analysis tools	Multilevel modeling; multilevel simulation and analysis tools	Mixed mode with multiple view; behavioral modeling with synthesis	Mixed signal/mode process modeling; total synthesis, simulation, and verification capture
Verification	The theme of verification is compliance.			
	Member-dependent verification; complete suite of analysis tools	Multidiscipline verification; multidisciplinary analysis tools	Team verification; compliance monitoring	Correct by construction; compliance assistance

Source: CALS/CE Electronic Systems Working Group Report by Linton et al. (1992); Reproduced with permission from Larry R. Linton, Chairman, NSIA CALS/CE Working Group.

The assignment also poses a number of requirements or needs that drive product attributes and constraints and therefore product requirements:

- A low-risk approach drives technology choices, design reuse, and so forth.
- Price competitiveness drives material choice, design complexity, and so forth.
- Market share drives the need for a reliable, testable, and producible product.

Aspects that affect the program include:

- Multiple products under way at various stages (concept through production phase-down)
- Short individual product life
- Long-term production capacity

Analysis

Using information on the product features, product requirements, and other aspects that affect the program, subjective decisions regarding the levels of influencing dimensions on an individual basis are established. Then the relative importance of the dimensions is considered. This establishes the ''should be'' concurrent engineering environment for the product development program. From this, the levels of various concurrent engineering elements and their sub-elements can be determined. Also, we can determine the ''where you are'' assessment of the concurrent engineering dimensions using the approach given in Section 4.7.2. Understanding the ''where you are'' and ''should be'' environments will help in the resource planning process.

Let us consider the influencing dimensions with their level of complexity one by one (on an individual basis) for the present case as follows:

Product Complexity

The design is highly producible because only common packaged devices that are autoinsertable into double-sided boards are utilized. Therefore, the order of complexity is B.

Product Technology

New application of existing technology is required for the product design. The level of complexity is now B but moving to C. This is because the design of newer products will require new capabilities from core technologies.

Program Structure

The size of the program staff including development and production is moderately large. Because multiple products are under way at various stages (concept through production phase-down), the program structure is fairly well established. Therefore the level of program structure is C.

Program Futures

Investment in manufacturing automation will be made. Therefore, the level of program futures is C.

Business Relationships

Relationships with suppliers are mostly commercial transactions; therefore the level is A. However, some key suppliers may be involved in just-in-time relationships involving joint developmental efforts. Thus, the level of business relationships may be B.

Team Scope

There is good team effort. However, manufacturing is the dominant activity given the level of product design and technology complexity. Therefore, the team scope category is B.

Resource Tightness

The level of resource tightness is of the order of A in the beginning and may be B later on because of price sensitivity of the product.

Schedule Tightness

The objective of introducing more products into the market and increasing market share will lead to constrained schedules. Remember, shorter throughput time is one of the dimensions (besides low cost and improved quality) for increasing market share and profitability. The level of tightness is C and is going to be D.

These levels of various dimensions are given in Table 4.8.

Now consider the relative importance of the dimensions. Suppose that the dimensions are equally important; then the present concurrent engineering environment should be at least of level B. As the concurrent engineering program becomes more established with product base, C may be the concurrent engineering approach needed now. It should, however, be emphasized that the program manager is the right person to make these subjective decisions. This establishes the "should be" concurrent engineering environment for the program.

Now, using the self-assessment concurrent engineering criteria given in Tables 4.4 to 4.7, evaluate where you are and compare it with the "should be" concurrent engineering environment. This will provide the basis for improvements. The process of self-assessment for each major element is discussed next:

Organization

The majority of team members are product oriented, the product manager being appointed by the management. The dominant members are the manufacturing engineers receiving advice from other design-influencing disciplines. The relationships with the suppliers is mostly based on purchasing. There are, however, some design and development exchanges with the key suppliers. Training is encouraged but mostly discipline oriented. Performance awards are given to key individuals. Long-term investments are being made to penetrate the market.

Requirements

Customer requirements are documented. The customer needs are recognized through market surveys and competitive benchmarking. Because the product reputation is critical, products will not be released until they are ready for production. Therefore, the schedules are program event driven. The product specifications are validated against the customer requirements.

TABLE 4.8 **Influencing Dimensions Matrix for Example 4.2**

	Concurrent Engineering Environment Level			
Influencing Dimensions	*A*	*B*	*C*	*D*
Product complexity		X		
Product technology		X	X	
Program structure			X	
Program futures			X	X
Competition				
Business relationships	X	X		
Team scope		X		
Resource tightness	X	X		
Schedule Tightness			X	X

Source: CALS/CE Electronic Systems Working Group Report by Linton et al. (1992); Reproduced with permission from Larry R. Linton, Chairman, NSIA CALS/CE Working Group.

Communications

The basic design data are stored at the program level. The product information is shared across product projects, which encourages part commonality and design reuse. The team members are focused on the product and their project goals.

Development Methodology

The objective is to consider all the interrelated customer requirements in the product design. Data libraries have been established across the program to provide application-independent data to all projects as well as complete product design data packages. The design methodology is documented and followed. The verification process is very thorough to ensure proper performance of the products delivered to the customers.

The self-assessment of the concurrent engineering program is now complete. Table 4.9 shows the evaluation of various concurrent engineering elements. There are 7A, 10B, and 7C checks marked in the table. Now suppose the "should be" concurrent engineering environment was rated as C; then a larger improvement plan in all the concurrent engineering elements would be needed.

TABLE 4.9 **Concurrent Engineering Environment Assessment Matrix**

	Concurrent Engineering Environments			
Elements of Concurrent Engineering	*A*	*B*	*C*	*D*
Organization				
Team membership	X			
Team leadership	X			
Team interaction		X		
Business relationships		X		
Training/education		X		
Responsibility/authority	X			
Management decisions			X	
Requirements				
Definition	X			
Schedule types			X	
Planning/methodology			X	
Validation		X		
Documentation	X			
Communication				
Data management/accessibility		X		
Data acquisition/sharing			X	
Lessons learned/feedback		X		
Design traceability			X	
Interpersonal			X	
Product development methodology				
Optimization		X		
Data libraries			X	
Development process		X		
Reviews		X		
Measurements	X			
Analysis architecture	X			
Verification		X		

Source: CALS/CE Electronic Systems Working Group Report by Linton et al. (1992); Reproduced with permission from Larry R. Linton, Chairman, NSIA CALS/CE Working Group.

4.8 DIFFICULTIES ASSOCIATED WITH PERFORMING CONCURRENT ENGINEERING

Concurrent engineering is most desirable from the point of view of reducing cost, improving quality, and decreasing development time. There are, however, many sources of difficulty (Baxter, 1984; Harfmann, 1987; Evans, 1988; Young et al., 1992) in implementing CE. They include:

- Characteristics of the design process
- Volume and variety of life-cycle knowledge
- Separation of life-cycle functions

4.8.1 Characteristics of the Design Process

The characteristics of the design process are one of the sources of difficulty in achieving integrated concurrent engineering. The design process involves a number of activities separated into stages, such as conceptual design, detailed design, analysis, and evaluation. Each stage is further divided into subproblems. Each subproblem is then solved iteratively to evolve an acceptable design. It is the separation of the design problem into stages and of each stage into subproblems that causes problems. The separation can result in suboptimization as the designer concentrates on narrow issues and ignores the overall concurrent engineering problem (Chieng and Hoeltzel, 1987; Young et al., 1992).

4.8.2 Volume and Variety of Life-Cycle Knowledge

The knowledge required to consider a number of life-cycle factors such as design, manufacturing, manufacturing control, testing, servicing, and redesign is voluminous. Furthermore, a large variety of knowledge including both qualitative and quantitative knowledge is required for all these functions. The variety and volume of knowledge may force the designers to concentrate on the optimization of single life-cycle factors rather than taking a holistic approach. Therefore, the volume and variety of knowledge are another source of difficulty in achieving integrated concurrent engineering.

4.8.3 Separation of Life-Cycle Functions

Life-cycle functions such as design, process planning, manufacturing, testing, maintenance, and service are often separated. Different departments are responsible for different functions. Therefore, there is a problem of communicating knowledge of all the life-cycle factors to the design department as and when needed. Separation of life-cycle functions is the third source of difficulty in achieving integrated concurrent engineering. To circumvent these problems, we provide a framework for integration of life-cycle phases in a concurrent engineering environment in the next section.

4.9 A FRAMEWORK FOR INTEGRATION OF LIFE-CYCLE PHASES IN A CONCURRENT ENGINEERING ENVIRONMENT

Often, concurrent engineering refers to considering simultaneously the requirements of assembly and manufacturing with design requirements in order to reduce unit cost of production, improve quality, and reduce total lead time. A broader view of CE involves managing mutual dependences between all phases of the product life cycle, whether in design, manufacturing, distribution, support, or disposal. In that case, the aim is to minimize life-cycle costs, maximize customer satisfaction, maximize flexibility, and minimize lead times from product conception to customer delivery. Simultaneous consideration of these issues requires the integration of decision making in the design process with decision making in manufacturing and all other phases of the product life cycle. The functions of life-cycle phases can be accomplished with the help of software modules such as computer-aided design (CAD), computer-aided process planning (CAPP), computer-aided manufacturing (CAM), and assembly analysis.

What distinguishes this concurrent engineering framework from the traditional approach is the need for active collaboration among all modules representing various aspects of product life-cycle phases. Collaboration is needed for decision making considering multiple perspectives, for forward and backward information flow, and for sharing common information. Support for collaboration involves human interaction, intelligent user interfaces, and interaction among various phases of the product life cycle. Collaboration and related issues can be addressed at different levels of integration applicable in different problem contexts. We provide an architecture in Figure 4.4 that shows different layers corresponding to collaborative decision-making support, information and work flow support, and shared context/information support.

The face-to-face team work sessions provide a first level of integration. Essentially, this represents what we call a cross-functional team approach for concurrent engineering. Membership of the cross-functional team may include design, manufacturing, distribution, customer service, and disposal. The committee is responsible for designing products from these aspects considering performance criteria such as product cost, quality, and lead time. Through a system of deliberations, discussions, and moderation, product and process designs can be finalized considering the impacts on product

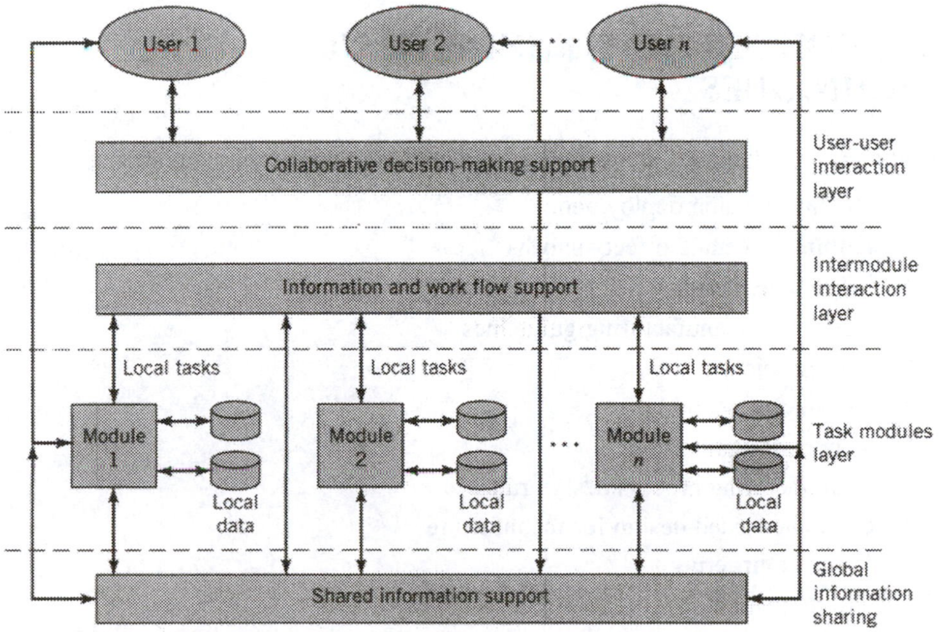

FIGURE 4.4 An architecture for integration of life-cycle phases in a concurrent engineering environment.

life-cycle components. Various decision-making techniques within the concurrent engineering framework can be employed to arrive at trade-off solutions.

The next level of integration could be to provide support for shared information through intelligent graphical user interfaces (IGUIs) to modules. Such tools help users to add rules and objects to applications. Rules can be selected or written dynamically to the IGUI to determine what files and information are needed by each module. This will increase both the productivity and efficiency of interactions between modules. For example, a member can access the relevant product design files and information while preparing a process plan. If there are inconsistencies, he or she can relay the information back to the design team. Similarly, other members of the product development team can have access to each other's work and communicate with each other through their workstations to suggest modifications.

Another level of integration could be what we call the seamless integration of modules to automate information and work flow. This can be accomplished by developing bridges through the use of object-oriented programming systems between the software modules, on a project-to-project basis to start with and on a more generic level later. The success of integration will depend on the establishment of proper communication channels. For the purposes of reducing user effort and increasing consistency, a knowledge-based evaluation shell in each module can be provided to help decide when and with which module to communicate and to obtain trade-off solutions.

The levels of integration we have described pertain to user-user interaction, user-module interaction, and module-module interaction. Figure 4.4 depicts an overall architecture for integration of life-cycle phases in a concurrent engineering environment. This architecture provides a basis for system design. To suit individual applications, system design can be modified depending on the level of support desired, the type of user interfaces, and the degree of collaboration required.

4.10 CONCURRENT ENGINEERING TECHNIQUES

A number of techniques are useful for implementing concurrent engineering:

- Quality function deployment
- Failure-mode and effect analysis
- Axiomatic design
- Design for manufacturing guidelines
- Design science
- Design for assembly
- Robust design
- Manufacturing process design rules
- Computer-aided design for manufacture
- Value engineering
- Group technology

Quality function deployment is a cross-functional planning tool that is used to ensure that the voice of the customer is heard throughout the product planning and design stages. Its use facilitates concurrent engineering, encouraging teamwork toward a common goal of ensuring customer satisfaction (Smith, 1991). In this chapter we provide a detailed discussion of QFD. Other techniques, such as robust design and failure-mode and effect analysis, are covered in Chapter 9; group technology is covered in Chapter 12. For a discussion of other techniques refer to Stoll (1988).

4.10.1 Quality Function Deployment

The main objective of a manufacturing company is to bring new (and carryover) products to market sooner than the competition with lower cost and improved quality. The mechanism for doing this is called quality function deployment. QFD provides a means of translating customer requirements into appropriate technical requirements for each stage of product development and production, that is, marketing strategy, planning, product design and engineering, prototype evaluation, production process development, production, and sales (Sullivan, 1986). QFD was introduced in Japan by Y. Akao in 1972 in conjunction with his work at the Mitsubishi Heavy Industries Kobe Shipyard. A detailed discussion of almost all aspects of QFD is given in Akao (1990).

There are four phases of QFD based on four key documents:

1. Product planning phase
2. Part deployment phase
3. Process deployment phase
4. Production deployment phase

We describe these phases and illustrate the steps involved in each phase in the following sections using illustrations from Sullivan (1986).

4.10.1.1 Product Planning Phase

In this phase, the overall customer requirements drawn from market evaluations, comparison with competitors, and market plans are converted into specified final product control characteristics. For this purpose, a document called the *product planning matrix* is used. Eight steps are involved in developing this matrix.

Step 1: State the product requirements in customer terms, that is, what the customer wants. The primary customer requirements (basic customer wants) are expanded into secondary and tertiary requirements to obtain a more definite list as shown in Figure 4.5. This information is obtained from a variety of sources, such as marketing research data, dealer input, sales department wants, and special customer surveys.

Step 2: List the final product control characteristics that should meet the customer-stated product requirements as shown in Figure 4.6. These characteristics are the product requirements that are related directly to the customer requirements and must be selectively deployed throughout the design, manufacturing, assembly, and service process to manifest themselves in the final product performance and customer acceptance (Sullivan, 1986).

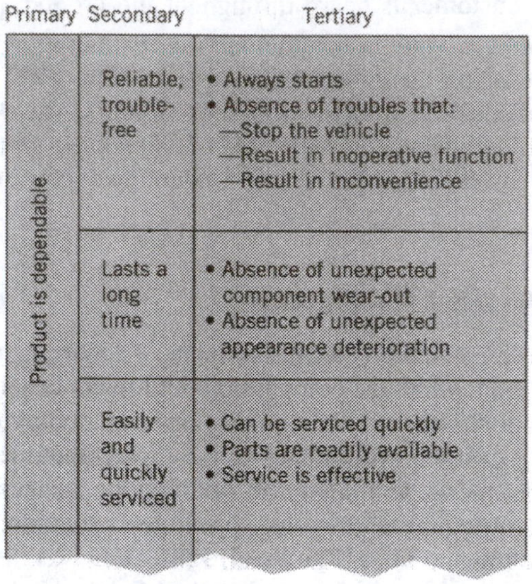
Primary
Secondary
Tertiary
Product is dependable
Reliable, trouble-free
• Always starts
• Absence of troubles that:
—Stop the vehicle
—Result in inoperative function
—Result in inconvenience
Lasts a long time
• Absence of unexpected component wear-out
• Absence of unexpected appearance deterioration
Easily and quickly serviced
• Can be serviced quickly
• Parts are readily available
• Service is effective

FIGURE 4.5 Step 1: state requirements in customer terms. (From Sullivan, 1986; Reproduced with permission from Quality Progress: Sullivan, 1986)

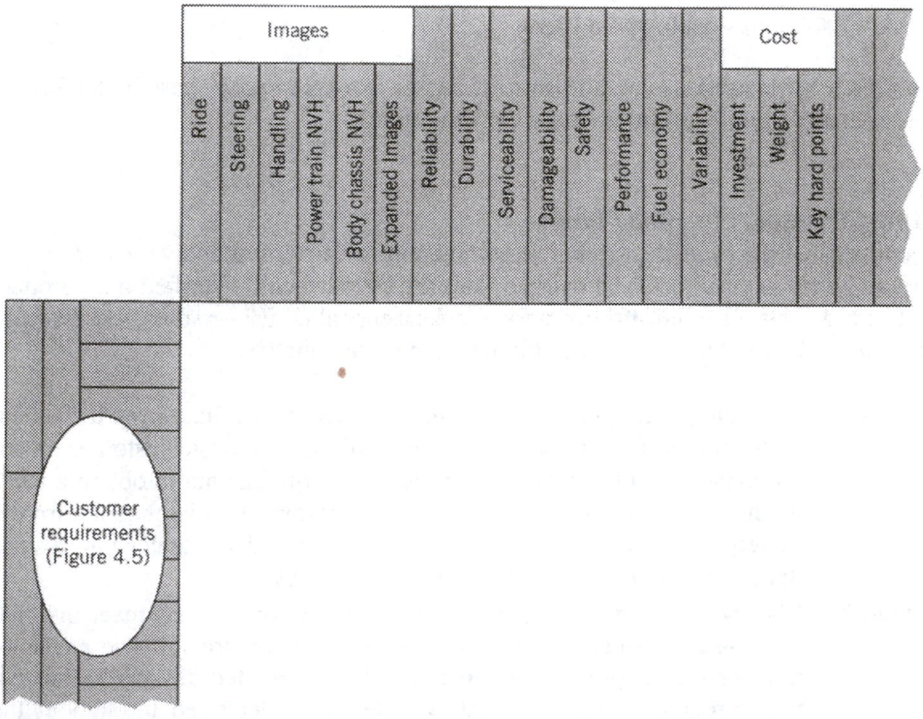
Images
Cost
Ride
Steering
Handling
Power train NVH
Body chassis NVH
Expanded Images
Reliability
Durability
Serviceability
Damageability
Safety
Performance
Fuel economy
Variability
Investment
Weight
Key hard points
Customer requirements (Figure 4.5)

FIGURE 4.6 Step 2: list existing final product control characteristics (NVH = noise, vibration, and harshness). (From Sullivan, 1986; Reproduced with permission from Quality Progress: Sullivan, 1986)

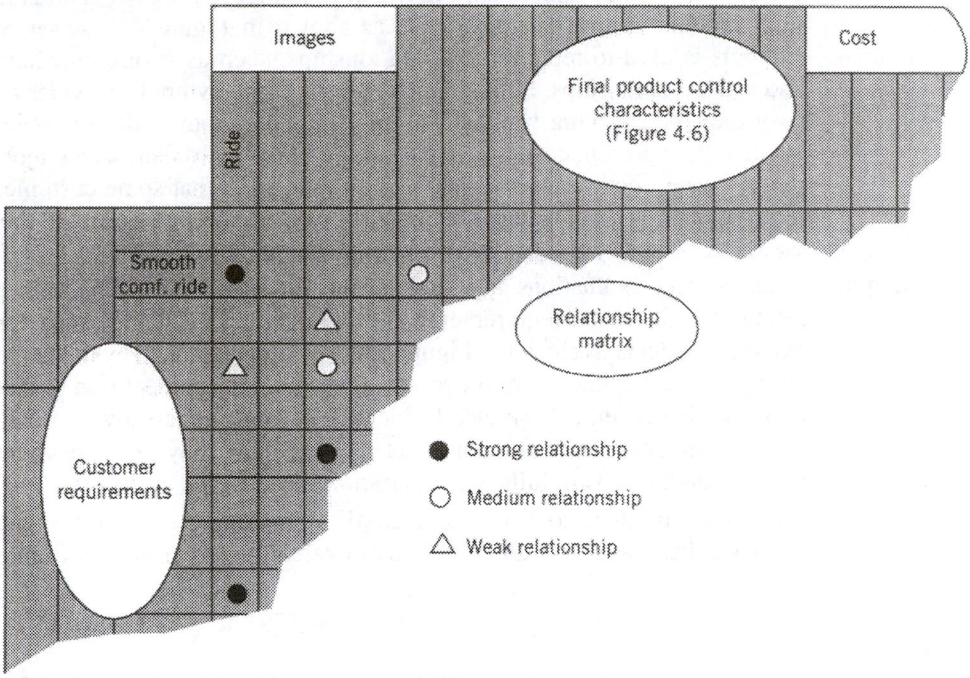

FIGURE 4.7 Step 3: develop a relationship matrix between customer requirements and final product control characteristics. (From Sullivan, 1986; Reproduced with permission from Quality Progress: Sullivan, 1986)

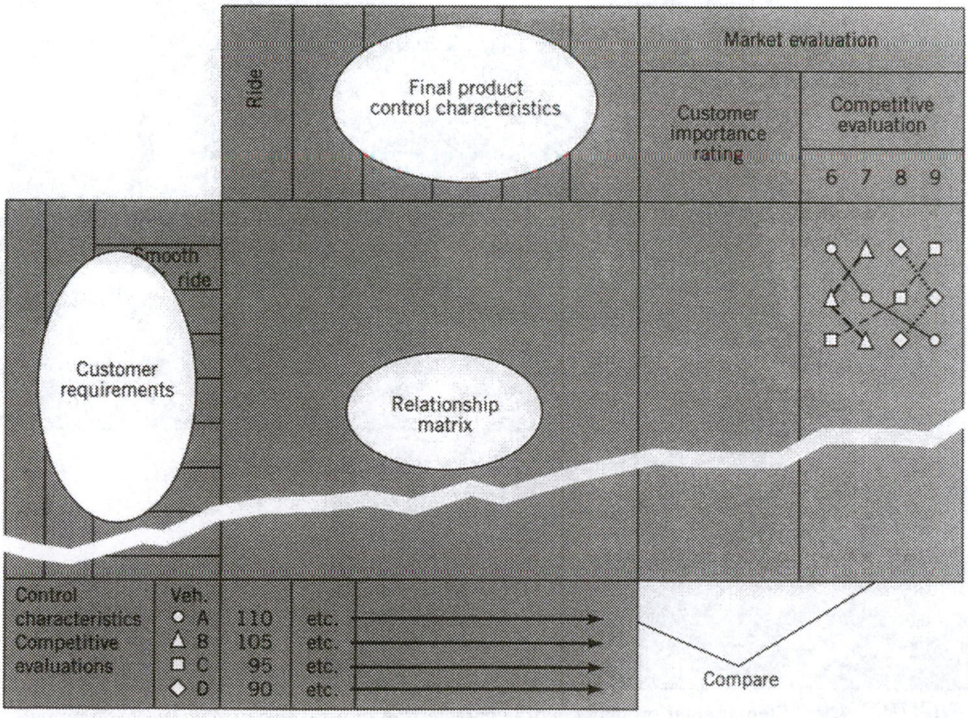

FIGURE 4.8 Step 4: enter market evaluations. (From Sullivan, 1986; Reproduced with permission from Quality Progress: Sullivan, 1986)

Step 3: Develop the relationship matrix between customer requirements and the final product control characteristics as shown in Figure 4.7. A set of symbols is used to represent the relationships, such as strong, medium, and weak relationships. Filling out this matrix using symbols provides an easy tool for checking whether the final product control characteristics adequately represent customer expectations. If the matrix shows a majority of "weak relationship" signs, it is an indication that some customer requirements are not addressed properly. An important aspect of this matrix is its ability to identify conflicting design requirements.

Step 4: Enter market evaluations that include customer-expressed importance ratings for the listed requirements and competitive evaluation data for existing products as shown in Figure 4.8. The objective is to evaluate the strengths and weaknesses of the products vis-à-vis the competition so that areas for improvement are clearly identified. These data show the customers' perceptions about the product. Furthermore, they indicate where your product stands in fulfilling a particular need of the customer.

Step 5: Enter final product control characteristic competitive evaluations and compare these with market competitive evaluations as shown in Figure

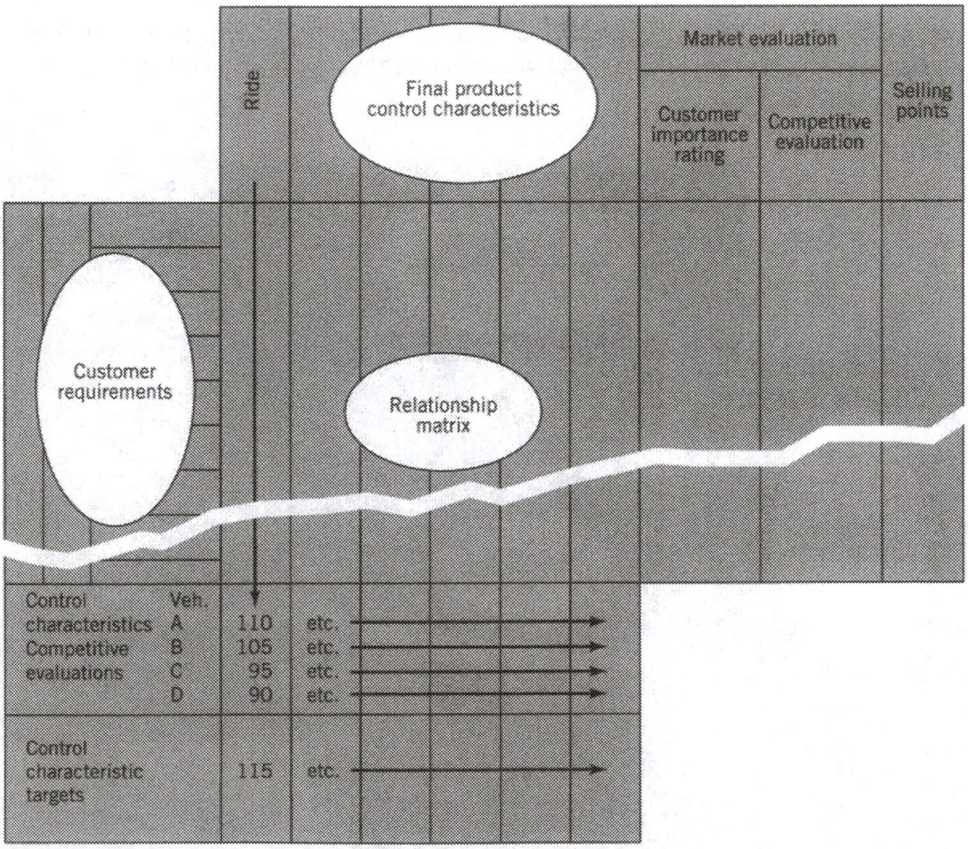

FIGURE 4.9 Step 5: enter product control characteristic competitive evaluations and compare control characteristic competitive evaluations with market competitive evaluations. (From Sullivan, 1986; Reproduced with permission from Quality Progress: Sullivan, 1986)

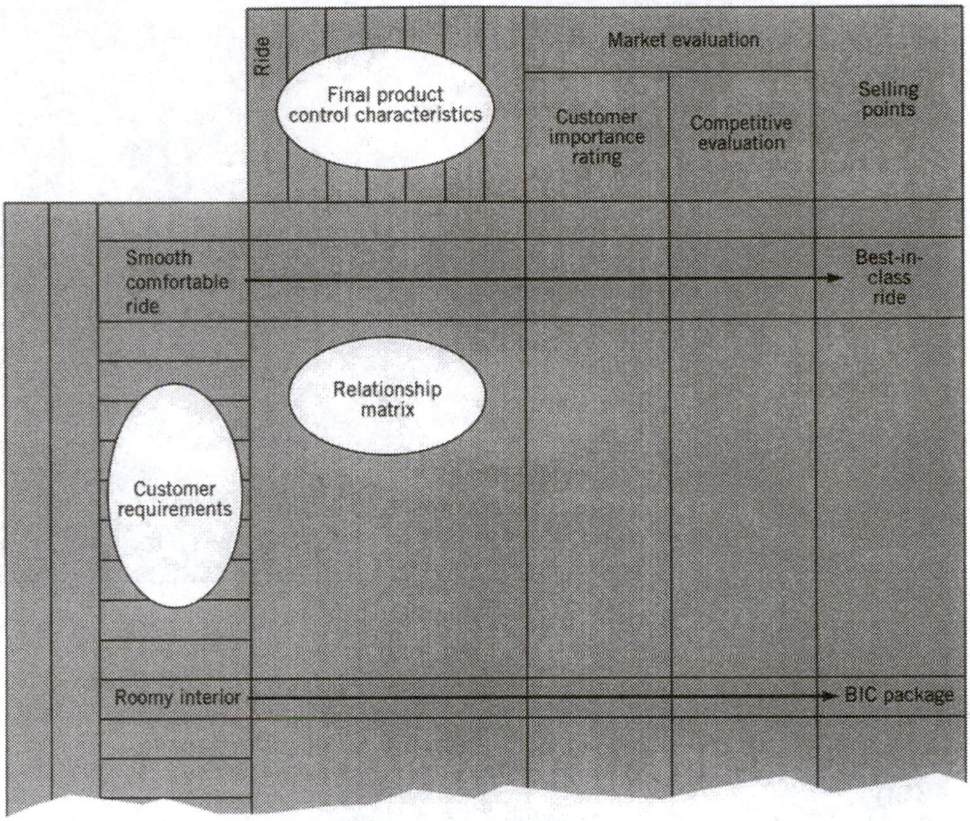

FIGURE 4.10 Step 6: determine selling points for new product (advertisable characteristics pertinent to the market segment). (From Sullivan, 1986; Reproduced with permission from Quality Progress: Sullivan, 1986)

4.9. These evaluation data should be expressed in objective and measurable terms. This helps indicate inconsistencies between customer requirements and your own evaluations. For example, market data may show that a customer requirement is better satisfied by a competitive product than by your product. However, your own evaluation indicates that your product is better in the characteristics related to the requirement of the customer. Then it is logical to conclude that there is something wrong with the internal evaluation or that the wrong characteristic was chosen to meet the customer's need.

Step 6: Determine selling points for the new product, that is, advertisable characteristics pertinent to the market segment as shown in Figure 4.10. Based on these points, product marketing, distribution, and promotion strategies are decided.

Step 7: Develop measurable targets as shown in Figure 4.11 for final product control characteristics based on agreed-upon selling points, the customer importance index, and the current product strengths and weaknesses. The attainment of these targets should be measured at each stage of the product development and testing process.

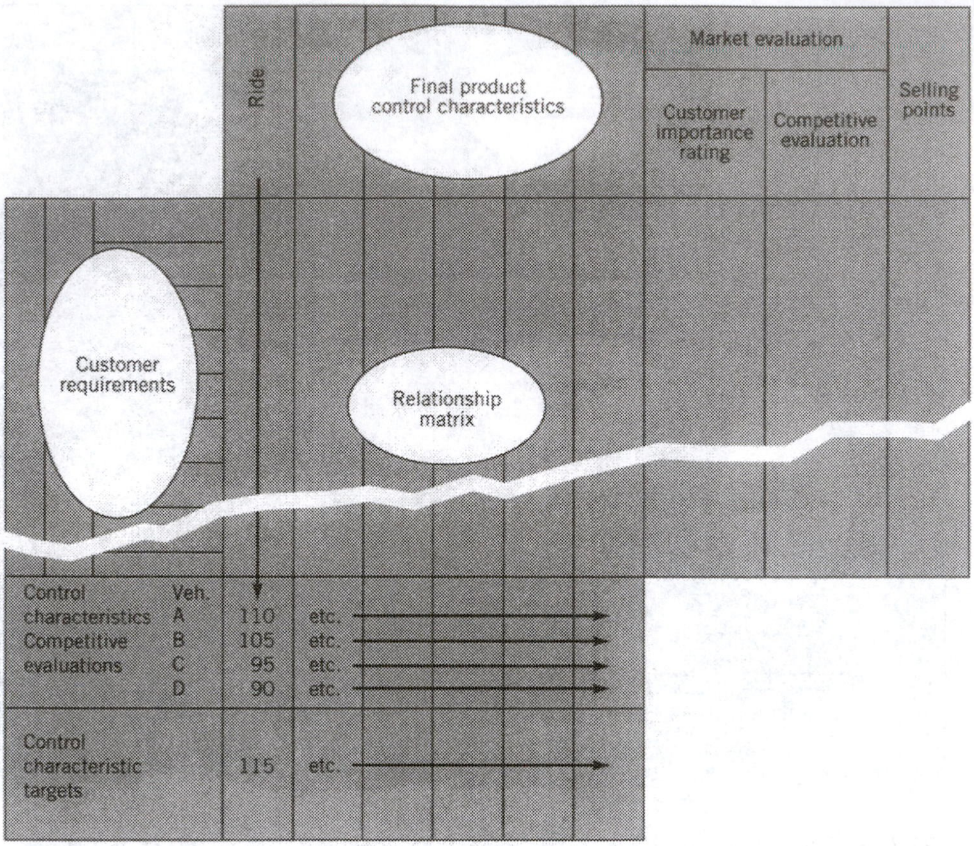

FIGURE 4.11 Develop targets for final product control characteristics. (From Sullivan, 1986; Reproduced with permission from Quality Progress: Sullivan, 1986)

Step 8: Select control characteristics (to be deployed throughout the remainder of the QFD process from planning to production) based on customer importance, selling points, and competitive evaluations as shown in Figure 4.12. The selection is based on customer importance, selling points, competitive evaluations, and the difficulty of achieving the characteristic target. These selected characteristics must be translated into the language of each discipline in terms of actions and controls required to ensure that the customer's voice is heard through every stage of the product life cycle. This also implies that characteristics that are not critical in meeting customer requirements, are not strong selling points, or have easily achievable targets need not go through a rigorous deployment process. Now our planning matrix is complete. We therefore move on to the deployment matrix.

4.10.1.2 Part Deployment Phase

In this phase, the output of the product planning (i.e., final product control characteristics) is translated into critical component characteristics. Therefore, this phase is the first step in materializing the customer needs and a one step forward into the design and assembly process development. For this purpose, a document called the final

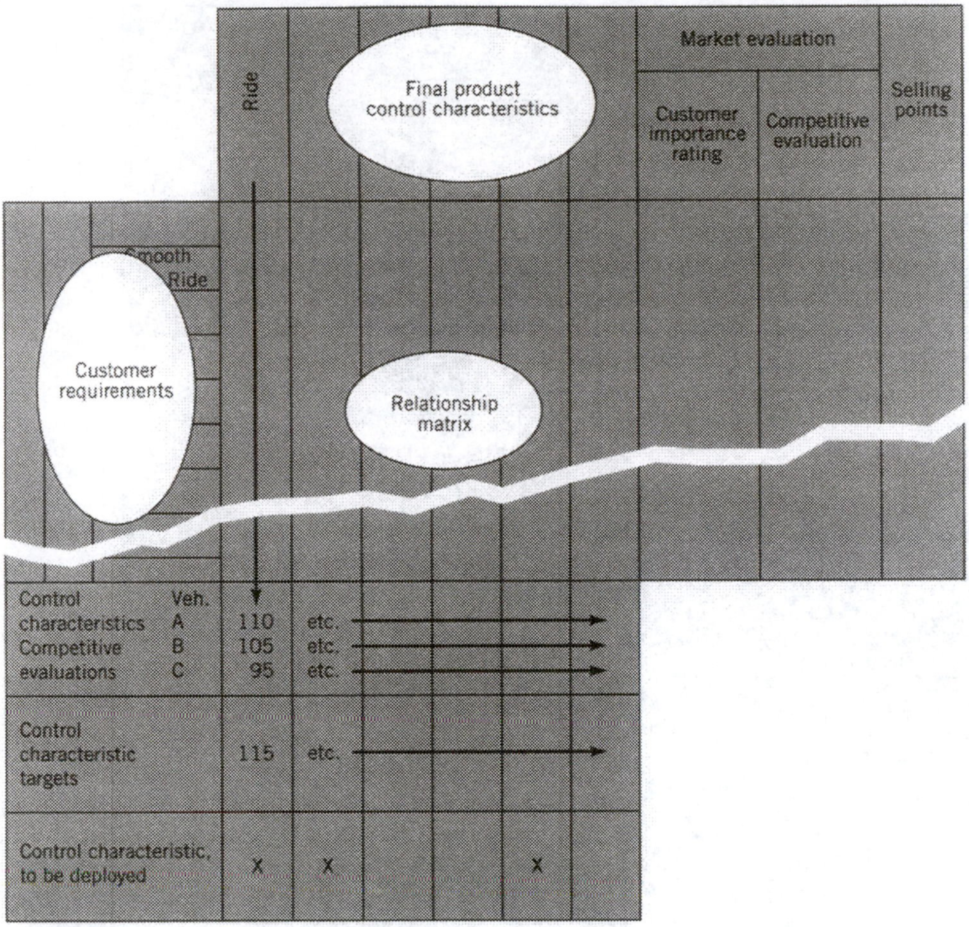

FIGURE 4.12 Select control characteristics to be deployed based on customer importance, selling points, and competitive evaluations. (From Sullivan, 1986; Reproduced with permission from Quality Progress: Sullivan, 1986)

product characteristic deployment matrix, as shown in Figure 4.13, is used. In this matrix, the final product control characteristics are carried from the final assembly (product) level to the subsystem/component level. From the customer requirements and final product control characteristics, the finished component characteristics affecting the final product are identified. The matrix helps identify the critical relationships between component and product characteristics. The critical finished component characteristics are deployed further and monitored in the production planning and control system as shown in Figure 4.14.

4.10.1.3 Process Deployment Phase

In this phase all the critical product and process parameters are identified and quality control checkpoints for each parameter are established. Process plan charts as shown in Figure 4.15 and quality control charts as shown in Figure 4.16 are used for this purpose. A powerful distinction is made in this phase of deployment. If a critical product component parameter is created or directly affected in a given step of a process, that parameter is identified as a control point. These points establish the data

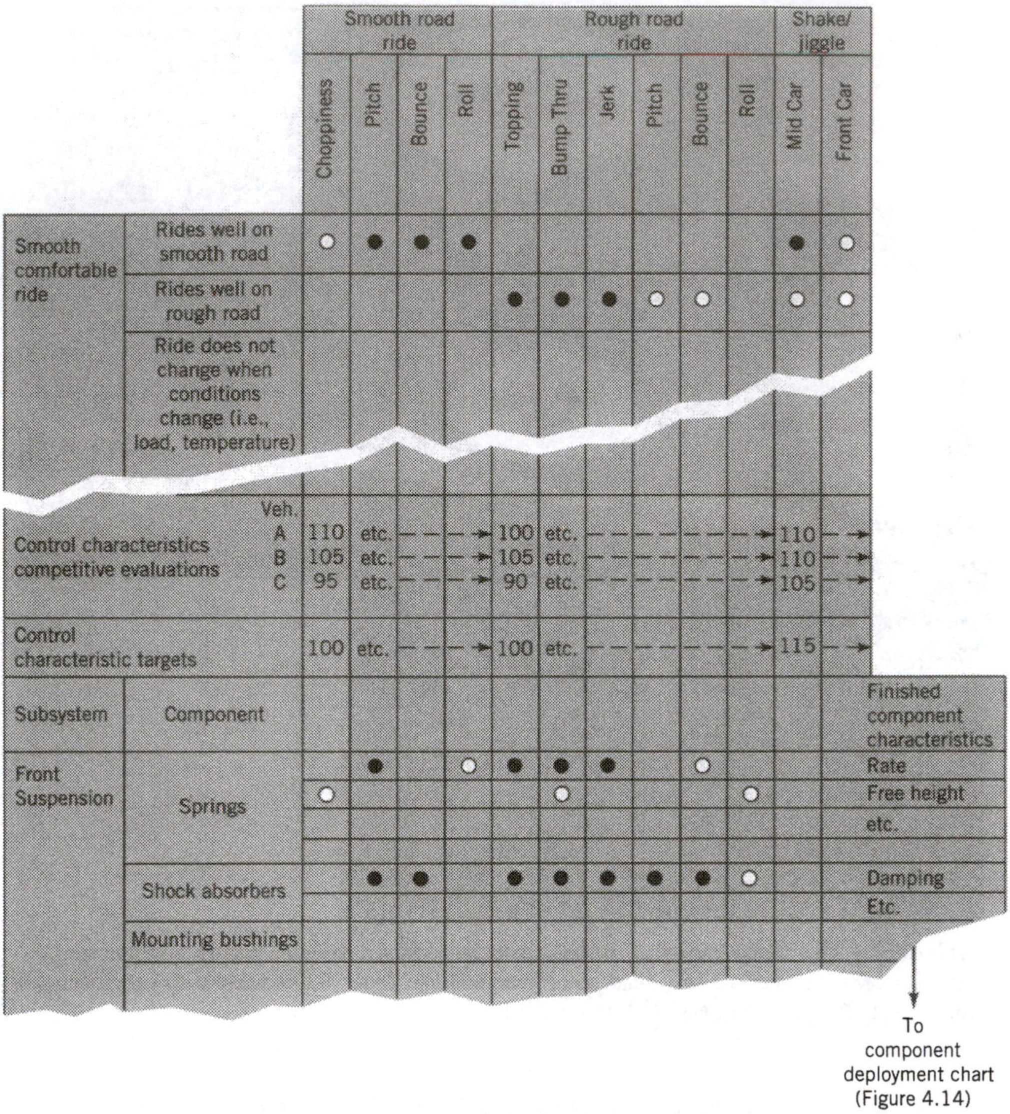

FIGURE 4.13 Finished component characteristic deployment matrix from planning matrix (overall ride target, 115% of competitive vehicle). (From Sullivan, 1986; Reproduced with permission from Quality Progress: Sullivan, 1986)

and strategy for the product quality control plan and are essential for achieving product characteristics that meet the high-priority customer requirements. If critical parameters, such as time, temperature, and pressure, must be monitored to ensure that the component parameters are achieved, these parameters are designated as checkpoints and become the basis for operating instructions and the process control strategy.

4.10.1.4 Production Deployment Phase

The output from the process development and quality control planning phase provides the critical product and process parameters. The objective of the production operating

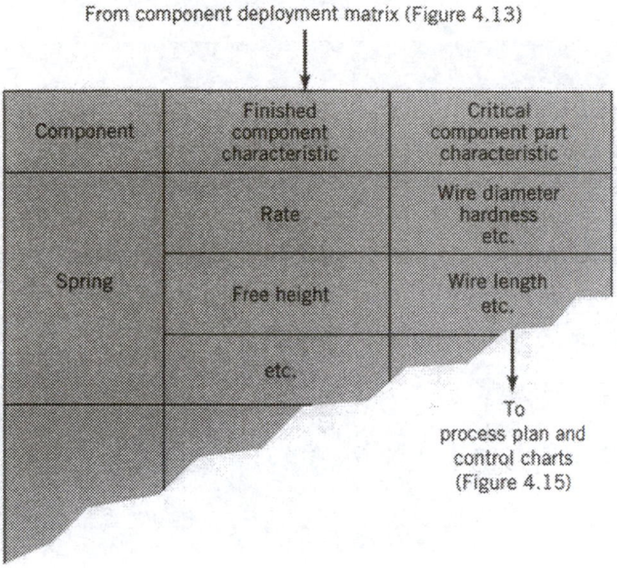

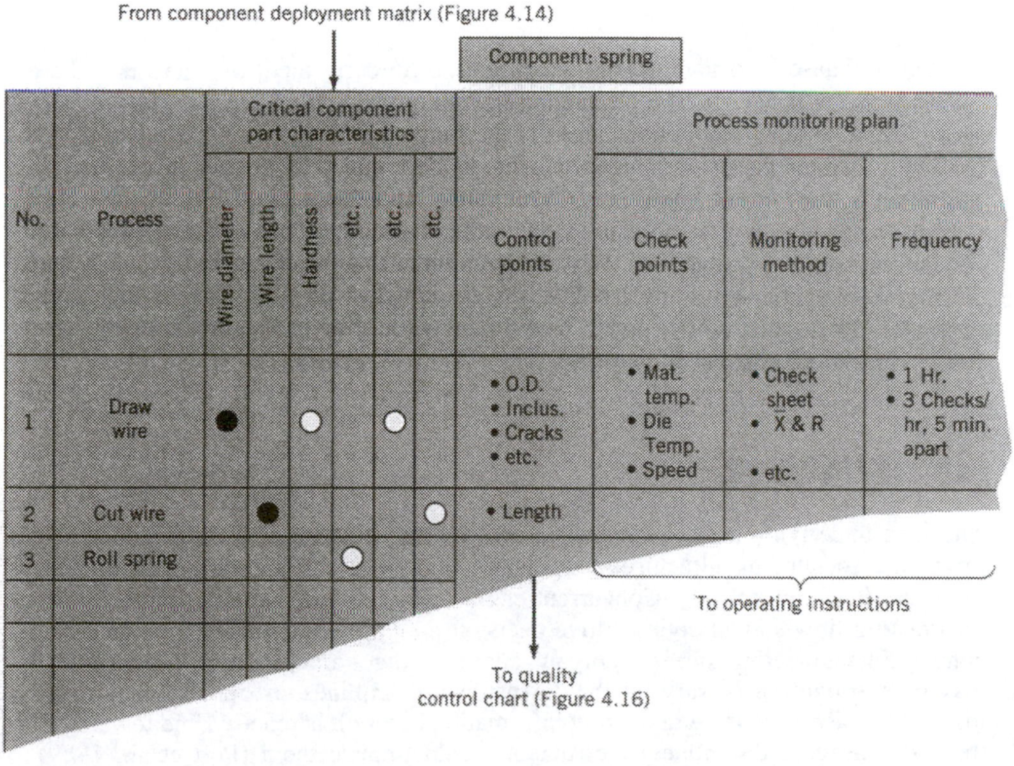

FIGURE 4.15 Process plan chart. (From Sullivan, 1986; Reproduced with permission from Quality Progress: Sullivan, 1986)

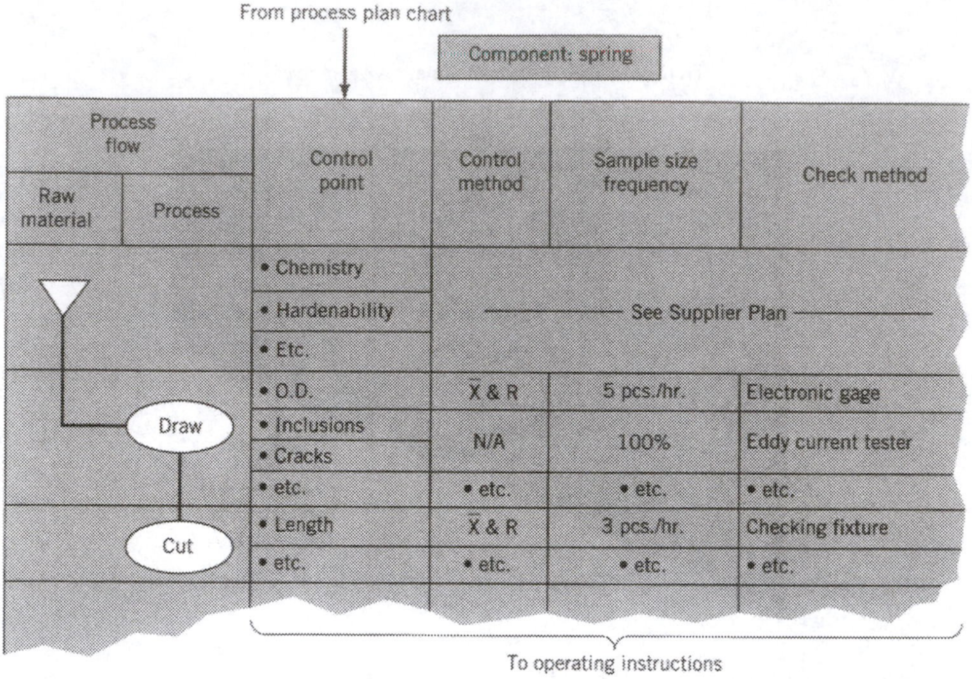
From process plan chart
Component: spring
Process flow
Raw material
Process
Control point
Control method
Sample size frequency
Check method
• Chemistry
• Hardenability
• Etc.
See Supplier Plan
• O.D.
X̄ & R
5 pcs./hr.
Electronic gage
Draw
• Inclusions
• Cracks
N/A
100%
Eddy current tester
• etc.
• etc.
• etc.
• etc.
• Length
X̄ & R
3 pcs./hr.
Checking fixture
Cut
• etc.
• etc.
• etc.
• etc.
To operating instructions

FIGURE 4.16 Control chart. (From Sullivan, 1986; Reproduced with permission from Quality Progress: Sullivan, 1986)

instruction phase is to identify the operations to be performed to ensure that these parameters are achieved. The production operating instructions are used for this purpose. The operating instructions sheet is the fourth and final key QFD document. It basically defines the operator requirements as determined by the actual process requirements, the process plan chart checkpoints, and the quality control plan chart control points. Many variations in the operating instructions can be anticipated based on individual process situations. What is important is that this document, which relates to the checkpoints and control points, clearly conveys the following points to the operator: What parts are involved? How many should he or she check, using what tool? How should the check be made?

4.11 SUMMARY

The idea underlying concurrent engineering is that the design and development of product, associated manufacturing equipment and processes, and other support functions are done concurrently. Concurrent engineering provides a basic framework for information flow so that collaborative decision making is facilitated. For successful concurrent engineering, sweeping organizational changes are required. For example, it may be absolutely necessary for the downstream disciplines, especially manufacturing, to have access to the engineering information before it is released and to veto it if they (downstream disciplines) feel that it would impede them (Port et al., 1989). Although applications of concurrent engineering have produced a number of success stories, its potential has not yet been fully exploited. There is a need to explore implementation issues and develop test beds.

In this chapter a simple modeling framework was proposed for understanding the basic concepts of serial and concurrent engineering. For this purpose a mathematical model was presented for understanding the interactions between design and manufacturing. The interaction between design and manufacturing and differences between serial and concurrent engineering were illustrated by numerical examples. A broader view of designing concurrent engineering programs was presented. The difficulties encountered in carrying out concurrent engineering were highlighted. An architecture for integration in concurrent engineering has been presented.

PROBLEMS

4.1 Discuss the following:
 (a) Serial engineering
 (b) Concurrent engineering

4.2 Discuss the interaction between design and manufacturing.

4.3 NSL, a small company, wants to manufacture a part requiring a drilling operation. The hole is to be drilled to dimensions 2 ± 0.002 in. NSL has decided to use your services as a concurrent engineering consultant. Help NSL develop the design of the part and select the appropriate manufacturing process for minimum total cost if 10,000 parts are delivered. The company has gathered the following data:

Raw material cost per unit = \$2.00

Salvage value per unit = \$0.50

Other data are given in Table P4.1.

TABLE P4.1 **Data on Drilling Operations**

Manufacturing Method	*Process Mean (in.)*	*Standard Deviation (in.)*	*Unit Processing Cost (Dollars)*
Drill press	2.0008	0.007	10.00
Radial drilling machine	2.0008	0.002	12.00
NC drilling machine	2.0008	0.0005	14.00

4.4 A system consisting of a gear-and-pulley assembly on a shaft is used to transmit power as suggested by Enrick (1985). The assembly system arrangement consists of spacer, gear, spacer, pulley, and then spacer. The spacers are produced on an automated punch press with a process standard deviation of 0.0005 in. at a cost of \$0.75 each. There are a number of alternatives for manufacturing the gear and pulley. The following data are available (standard deviation is expressed in inches):

Gear	***Manufacturing Alternative Cost Per Gear***	***Standard Deviation***
GI	\$3.50	0.002
GII	\$7.00	0.001
GIII	\$20.00	0.0005

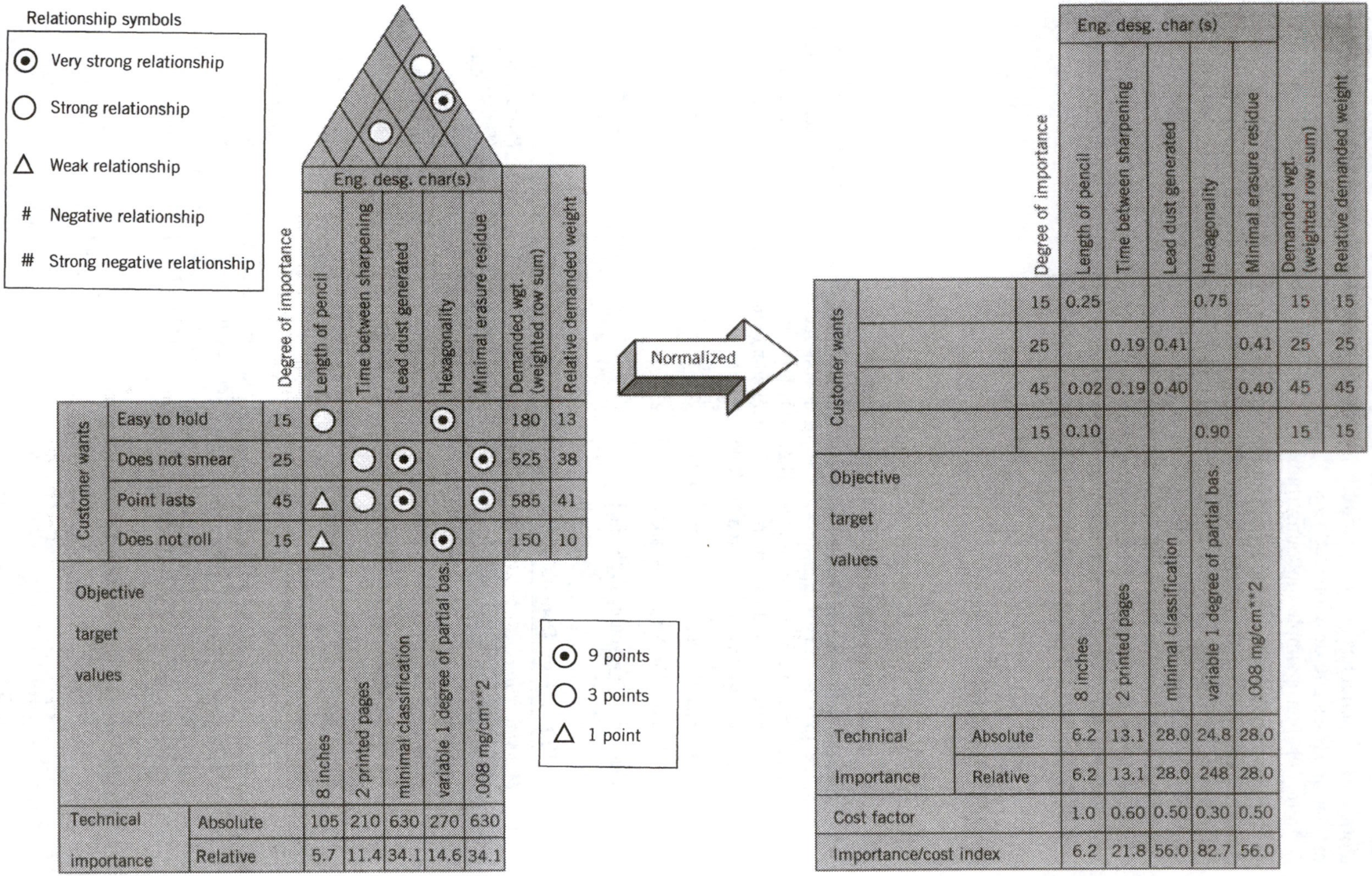

FIGURE P4.1 QFD matrix for a hypothetical writing instrument. (Reproduced with permission from IIE: Wasserman, 1993.)

Pulley	Manufacturing Alternative Cost Per Pulley	Standard Deviation
PI	$2.00	0.005
PII	$3.50	0.003
PIII	$5.00	0.002

There is stacking of tolerances for the system elements. However, the assembly tolerance must not exceed ±0.011.

Using the concurrent engineering approach, suggest the best combination of design and manufacturing for the gear-and-pulley system. Assume other necessary data as required. The component tolerances can be obtained as ±3 times the standard deviation of the process.

4.5 Discuss various difficulties encountered in carrying out concurrent engineering.

4.6 Select a product of your choice or visit a company and carry out a quality function deployment study.

4.7 Discuss various elements to characterize the complexity of the product in Problem 4.6.

4.8 Discuss the following and develop a concurrent engineering environmental profile for the company you are studying in Problem 4.6:

- Organization
- Requirements
- Communications
- Product development methodology

4.9 Select a simple design project with the help of your professor. Set up a multifunctional team in your laboratory class and discuss all the issues from the product conception stage to the final production and distribution phase.

4.10 Suppose a product requires a milling operation. Identify the alternative milling processes that can be used for this purpose. Collect data on the process capabilities of these machine tools and recommend a process based on criteria of cost, quality, and manufacturing lead time.

4.11 Concurrent engineering involves both design process change and organizational change. Discuss.

4.12 Pick a simple product and design a cross-functional multidisciplinary concurrent engineering team.

4.13 Examine the quality function deployment matrix in Figure P4.1 and explain the various steps of phase I of QFD.

REFERENCES AND SUGGESTED READING

Akao, Y. (1990). *Quality Function Deployment.* Productivity Press, Cambridge, Massachusetts.

Bird, S. (1992). Object-oriented expert system architectures for manufacturing quality management. *Journal of Manufacturing Systems* 11(1):50–60.

Chieng, W. H., and Hoeltzel, D. A. (1987). A generic planning model for large scale engineering design optimization with a power transmission case study. *Computers in Engineering,* 1:113–124.

Creese, R. C., and Moore, L. T. (1990). Cost modelling for concurrent engineering. *Cost Engineering,* 32(6):23–27.

Dowlatshahi, S. (1992). Product design in a concurrent engineering environment: An optimization approach. *International Journal of Production Research,* 30(8):1803–1818.

Enrick, N. L. (1985). *Quality, Reliability and Process Improvements.* Industrial Press, New York.

Evans, B. (1988). Simultaneous engineering. *Mechanical Engineering,* 110(2):38–39.

Gu, P., and Kusiak, A. (eds.) (1993). *Concurrent Engineering: Methodology and Applications.* Elsevier, Amsterdam.

Guichelaar, P. J. (1992). *Design for Manufacturability: Integrating Manufacturing and Design to Create a Concurrent Engineering Environment.* DE-Vol. 52. ASME, New York.

Halender, M., and Nagamachi, M. (eds.) (1992). *Design for Manufacturability: A Systems Approach to Concurrent Engineering and Ergonomics.* Taylor & Francis, London.

Harfmann, A. C. (1987). The rationalizing of design. In *Computability of Design* (Y. H. Kaley, ed.). John Wiley & Sons, New York.

Hartley, J. R. (1992). *Concurrent Engineering: Shortening Lead Times, Raising Quality and Lowering Costs.* Productivity Press, Cambridge.

Haug, E. J. (1990). *Concurrent Engineering of Mechanical Systems,* DE-Vol. 22. ASME, New York.

Jakiela, M., Pralambros, P., and Ulsoy, A. G. (1984). Programming optimal suggestions in the design concept phase: Application to the Boothroyd assembly charts. ASME Technical Paper No. 84-DET-77.

Kohli, R.,and Forgionne, G. A. (1992). Knowledge-based system to close gaps in CE decision making for providing intelligent retrieval of corporate knowledge. *Fourth National Seminar on Concurrent Engineering,* National Security Industry Association, Washington, D.C., pp. 100–131.

Kusiak, A. (ed.) (1993). *Concurrent Engineering: Automation, Tools and Techniques,* Wiley-Interscience, New York.

Linton, L., Hall, D., Hutchison, K., Hoffman, D., Evanczuk, S., and Sullivan, P. (1992). First principles of concurrent engineering: A competitive strategy for product development. CALS/CE Electronic Systems Working Group Report, National Security Industry Association, Washington, D.C., 1992.

Meth, A. M. (1991). Concurrent engineering—changing the process of bringing products to market. *Computer,* September, pp. 100–101.

Miller, L. C. G. (1993). *Concurrent Engineering Design: Integrating the Best Practices for Process Improvement.* Society of Manufacturing Department, Dearborn, Michigan.

Parsaei, H. R., and Sullivan, W. G. (eds.) (1993). *Concurrent Engineering: Contemporary Issues and Modern Design Tools.* Chapman & Hall, London.

Pennell, J. P., and Winner, R. I. (1989). *Concurrent Engineering: Practices and Prospects,* Proceedings: IEEE Global Telecommunications Conference & Exhibition (GLOBCOM '89), Part I, Published by IEEE, IEEE Service Center, Piscataway, NJ, USA. (Catlog n 89 CH2682-3), pp. 647–655.

Port, O., Schiller, Z., Miller, G. L., and Schulman, A. (1989). Special report: Smart factories: America's turn? *Business Week,* May 8, pp. 142–148.

Rosenblatt, A. (Managing Editor) (1991). Concurrent engineering: Special report. *IEEE Spectrum,* July, pp. 22–37.

Shigley, J. E., and Mischke, C. R. (1989). *Mechanical Engineering Design.* McGraw-Hill, New York.

Shina, S. G. (1991). *Concurrent Engineering and Design for Manufacture of Electronics Products.* Van Nostrand Reinhold, New York.

Singh, N. (1983). Optimum design of a journal bearing system with multiple objectives: A goal programming approach. *Engineering Optimization,* 6:193–196.

Singh, N., and Falkenburg, D. R. (1994). An analytical framework for understanding concurrent engineering. Working paper, Department of Industrial and Manufacturing Engineering, Wayne State University, Detroit, Michigan.

Singh, N., and Sushil (1990a). A physical system theory framework for modelling manufacturing systems. *International Journal of Production Research,* 28(6):1067–1082.

Singh, N., and Sushil (1990b). Technology selection models for multi-stage production systems: Joint application of physical system theory and mathematical programming. *European Journal of Operational Research,* 47:248–261.

Singh, N., and Wang, M. H. (1994). Concurrent engineering in high variety label printing industry. *International Journal of Production Research,* 32(7):1675–1691.

Smith, L. R. (1991). QFD and its application in concurrent engineering. *Design and Productivity International Conference,* Honolulu, Hawaii, February 6–9, pp. 369–372.

Stoll, H. W. (1988). Design for manufacture. In *Tool and Manufacturing Engineering Handbook,* Vol. 5, *Manufacturing Management* (R. F. Veilleux and L. W. Petro, eds.). Society of Manufacturing Engineers, Dearborn, Michigan, pp. 13.1–13.32.

Sullivan, L. P. (1986). Quality function deployment. *Quality Progress,* June, pp. 39–50.

Turino, J. (1991). Making it work calls for input from everyone, Concurrent engineering: Special report. *IEEE Spectrum,* 28(July):22–37.

Turino, J. (1992). *Managing Concurrent Engineering: Buying Time to Market.* Van Nostrand Reinhold, New York.

Wasserman, G. R. (1993). Technical note on how to prioritize design requirements during QFD planning process. *IIE Transactions,* 25(3):59–65.

Young, R. E., Greef, A., and O'Grady, P. (1992). An artificial intelligence–based constraint network system for concurrent engineering. *International Journal of Production Research,* 30(7):1715–1735.

APPENDIX

FRAMEWORK FOR THE APPLICATION OF CE TO ASSEMBLIES

A Journal Bearing Assembly Example

We now provide an example of an assembly to illustrate the advantages that could be realized through CE. We consider a simple journal bearing system. It is needed to support a flywheel of mass 2000 lb that rotates at a speed of v rev/s. Suppose we require 2000 such units of finished products.

Basically, a journal bearing system consists of a shaft, or journal, that rotates or oscillates within a sleeve or bearing. The journal and the bearing are separated by an oil film, whose thickness depends on the load conditions and the ratio of the diameter and the length of the bearing. To avoid point-to-point contact, it is necessary to maintain a minimum film thickness. For detailed design of a journal bearing system, see Singh (1983) and Shigley and Mischke (1989). The equation for h_0, the minimum oil film thickness, is

$$h_0 = (1 - \varepsilon)c$$

where radial clearance, c, is the difference in radii between the journal and the bearing, eccentricity (e) is the distance between the center of the journal and the bearing radius of the journal (r), and the eccentricity ratio (ε) $= e/c$ as shown in Figure 4.A1.

Furthermore, to maintain a minimum oil film thickness of h_0, an optimal clearance is to be maintained between the journal and the bearing. When designing a journal for thick-film lubri-

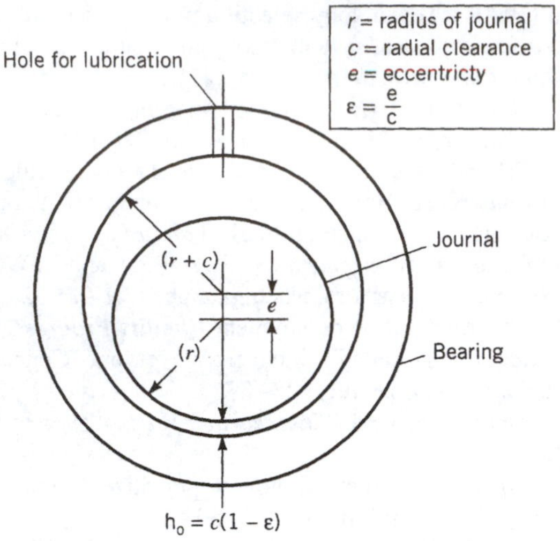

FIGURE 4.A1 A journal bearing system.

cation, the grade of oil to be used and suitable values for pressure, revolutions per minute, radial clearance, the radius of the journal, and the length of the bearing must be selected. Poor selection of these or inadequate control of them during manufacture may result in a film that is too thin, causing the bearing to overheat and eventually fail. A large clearance will permit dirt particles to pass through and will permit a large flow of oil. This lowers the temperature and increases the life of the bearing. However, if the clearance is too large, the bearing becomes noisy and the minimum film thickness begins to decrease. Thus, in between these two limitations, there exists a large range of clearances that would result in a satisfactory bearing performance. This clearance is the result of stacking of tolerances of the journal and the bearing. The implication is that we can have a whole range of tolerances on both the journal and the bearing to meet the range of clearances and thus a number of design options. Corresponding to the design options we can have a number of manufacturing alternatives. From our experience with the shaft example of Sections 4.5 and 4.6, we know that CE helps in deciding the best combination of both design options and manufacturing alternatives to meet the main objectives of quality, cost, and lead time. In CE, we explore the various manufacturing alternatives for all the design options available.

Continuing with our example of the journal bearing, the basic dimensions of design interest are the diameter of the journal and the diameter and length of the bearing. These dimensions can be obtained from bending moment and twist considerations using the methodology suggested in Singh (1983) and Shigley and Mischke (1989). From the functional point of view, a clearance of 0.001 in. is required to permit a minimum oil film thickness of 0.0001 in. To meet this requirement, the design options given in Table 4.A1 are found suitable. The available manufacturing alternatives with associated information are given in Table 4.A2.

Sample Calculations

The following calculations show how tolerances may be combined to satisfy overall tolerance in an assembly. The principle of stacking tolerances is applied with the result that the final tolerance values obtained will permit maximum possible product variation consistent with quality and processing requirements. Thus, statistical methods can help to obtain the cost-saving advantages of maximum allowable tolerances consistent with the requisite quality.

TABLE 4.A1 **Various Design Options**

	Bearing	*Journal*	*Clearance Fit*
Design Option I			
Design size	10,000	9990	10
Tolerance option I	+6	0	
	0	−10	
Average size with product centered between limits	10,003	9985	18
Tolerance from average	±3	±5	
Clearance tolerance $= \sqrt{(3)^2 + (5)^2} = 5.83$			
Expected clearance $= 18 \pm 5.83$			
Design Option II			
Design Size	10,000	9990	10
Tolerance option II	+10	0	
	0	−8	
Average size with product centered between limits	10,005	9986	19
Tolerance	±5	±4	
Clearance tolerance $= \sqrt{(5)^2 + (4)^2} = 6.40$			
Expected clearance $= 19 \pm 6.40$			

Note: All dimensions in ten-thousandths of an inch.

The relationship of tolerances and random assembly will be strictly valid only when the individual parts come from processes under good control, as established by a review of control charts. Such a production process is said to be in statistical control. It is also desirable that frequency distributions derived from control chart data be checked to see that they fall into the approximate pattern of a normal distribution. It is assumed that the tolerance specified by the designer is approximately equal to the natural tolerance of the process. The formula for the assembly tolerance is

$$\text{Assembly tolerance} = \sqrt{\text{sum of squares of component tolerances}}$$

The sample calculations for manufacturing alternatives B1J1 and design option I are shown next. All dimensions are in ten-thousandths of an inch.

TABLE 4.A2 **Information on Manufacturing Alternatives**

Manufacturing Alternative	*Raw Material Cost Per Unit ($)*	*Processing Cost Per Unit ($)*	*Salvage Value Per Unit ($)*	*Standard Deviation*
Bearing				
B1 (machining)	2	15.00	0.50	3
B2 (powder metallurgy)	4	25.00	0	1
Journal				
J1 (machining)	1	4.00	1.00	3
J2 (powder metallurgy)	3	8.50	0	1

TABLE 4.A3 **Tabulation of Results**

			BEARING	
		Tolerance	±3	±5
		Squared tolerance	±9	±25
		Cost	\$24.67 (B1)	\$18.73 (B1)
			\$29.07 (B2)	\$29.00 (B2)
	Tolerance	±5		
	Squared tolerance	±25	±34*	±50
J	Cost	\$5.22 (J1)	\$29.89 (B1J1)**	**\$23.95 (B1J1)**
O		\$12.70 (J2)	\$37.37 (B1J2)	\$31.43 (B1J2)
U			\$34.29 (B2J1)	\$34.22 (B2J1)
R			\$41.77 (B2J2)	\$41.70 (B2J2)
	Tolerance	±4		
N	Squared tolerance	±16	±25	±41
A	Cost	\$5.89 (J1)	\$30.56 (B1J1)	\$24.62 (B1J1)
		\$11.50 (J2)	\$36.17 (B1J2)	\$30.23 (B1J2)
L			\$34.96 (B2J1)	\$34.89 (B2J1)
			\$40.57 (B2J2)	\$40.50 (B2J2)

Note: All dimensions in ten-thousandths of an inch.

* Combined squared tolerances for journal-bearing options.

** Combined costs for journal-bearing options.

For B1:

Process mean (μ) = 10,003

Upper tolerance limit (UTL) = 10,006

Lower tolerance limit (LTL) = 10,000

Tolerance from average = ±3

Therefore, $Z^u = 1$, $Z^l = 1$, SC = 31.74%, $k^s = 0.4649$, and

$$\text{Unit output cost } (X^0) = (1.4649 \times 2) - (0.4649 \times 0.5) + (1.4649 \times 15) = \$24.67$$

For J1:

Process mean (μ) = 9985

Upper tolerance limit (UTL) = 9990

Lower tolerance limit (LTL) = 9980

Tolerance from average = ±5

Therefore, $Z^u = 1.67$, $Z^1 = 1.67$, SC = 4.70%, $K^s = 0.04982$, and

$$\text{Unit output cost } (X^0) = (1.04982 \times 1) - (0.4982 \times 0.5) + (1.04982 \times 4) = \$5.22$$

The results obtained from all the calculations for all the different combinations of manufacturing alternatives and design options are presented in Table 4.A3. It is important to note that the unit costs for the manufacture of journal and bearing reflect the additional cost incurred for scrap. It is clear from Table 4.A3 that the bearing of design option II and journal of design option I, manufactured by alternatives B1 and J1, respectively, would be the most economical means of obtaining a journal bearing assembly.

Expected Number of Assembly Failures

We can also now determine the expected number of failures of assemblies that do not meet the minimum clearance requirement of the assembly. The calculations involved are shown by considering bearing design option II and journal design option I:

1. *Standard deviation of clearance.* Since the clearance tolerance is $\sqrt{(5)^2 + (5)^2} = 7.07$ division by our tolerance factor of 3 yields an estimated standard deviation of 2.356.

2. *Average clearance.* The expected minimum clearance of 12.93 ($20 - 7.07 = 12.93$; from Table 4A.1) is larger by approximately 3 than the allowable minimum clearance of 10. This suggests that if the mean of the bearing were decreased by 1.5, with an increase of 1.5 for the shaft, using up the approximate difference of 3 between nominal and expected clearance, no assembly failures would result. With a shift in dimensional averages by -1.5 and $+1.5$, the old average clearance of 20 has now narrowed to 17.

3. *Difference between clearances.* The difference between the required clearance of 10 and average clearance of 17 is 7. Let us call this difference t.

4. *Look up the normal curve.* The ratio $t/\sigma = Z = 7/2.356 \simeq 3.0$ is now looked up in the table of the normal curve. We find that approximately 0.135% of the assemblies will not be able to meet the minimum clearance requirement and therefore can be considered failed.

The percentage of cases in which minimum clearances will not be achieved is thus negligible for most practical purposes. The conclusion we draw from this example is that CE, used intelligently with knowledge from various areas (statistical tolerancing in the present example), will definitely help to achieve our objectives of least cost and best quality.

CHAPTER 5

COMPUTER-AIDED PROCESS PLANNING

The twenty-first century engineering response to world competition is concurrent engineering (CE). CE requires the integration of all aspects of the product life cycle, that is, design, manufacturing, assembly, distribution, service, and disposal. Two important areas in the life cycle of a product are design and manufacturing. Process planning serves as an integration link between design and manufacturing. Therefore, process planning is one of the most important activities in concurrent engineering to help translate the product design into a final product.

In this chapter we provide answers to some fundamental questions: What is process planning? What are the basic steps in developing a process plan? What is computer-aided process planning (CAPP)? What are the basic features of variant and generative approaches to CAPP? We also provide some discussion of knowledge-based process planning and feature recognition approaches. A number of examples are solved to illustrate process planning concepts.

5.1 OVERVIEW OF MANUFACTURING PROCESSES

In this section we review some basic machining processes, such as turning, drilling, milling, and grinding. Detailed descriptions of these and various other manufacturing processes are given in a number of textbooks on manufacturing (Yankee, 1979; El-Wakil, 1989; Lindberg, 1990; Kalpakjian, 1992).

It is worth mentioning that the manufacturing processes are not necessarily metal-cutting processes. For example, for the production of electronic circuit boards, soldering is a manufacturing process. Generally speaking, manufacturing processes refer to processes that change either the properties or shapes for the purpose of adding value to the products. However, in this section we discuss mainly metal-cutting processes.

5.1.1 Turning Operations

Turning is a common and a versatile machining process for producing cylindrical, conical, or irregularly shaped internal or external surfaces on a rotating workpiece. The

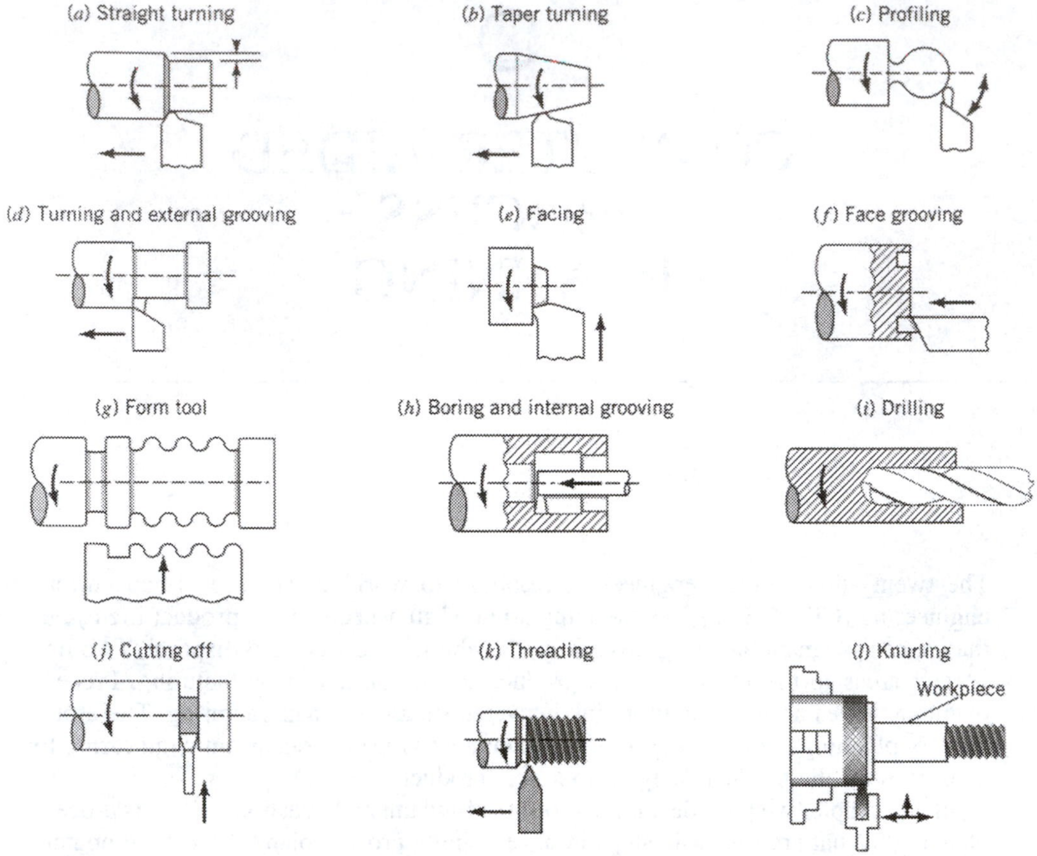

FIGURE 5.1 Various cutting operations that can be performed on lathe machines. (From Kalpakjian, 1992.)

machine tool used is the lathe. Typical parts include pins, shafts, spindles, handles, and various other components having O-ring grooves, holes, threads (both internal and external), and many other shapes. Cutting operations that can be performed on a lathe include straight turning, taper turning, profiling, turning and external grooving, facing, face grooving, drilling, boring and internal grooving, cutting off, threading, and knurling, as shown in Figure 5.1. The various machining parameters, such as cutting speed, feed rate, depth of cut, machining time, and material removal rate, are given for some lathe operations in Figure 5.2.

5.1.2 Drilling Operations

Drilling is another common machining operation for producing through holes or blind holes. For example, assembly processes involving fasteners such as rivets, screws, and bolts require holes. To perform the drilling operations, a cylindrical rotary-end cutting tool called a drill is employed. Different types of drills are used to produce a variety of holes. Various types of drills and drilling operations are shown in Figure 5.3.

Operation		Cutting speed	Machine time	Material removal rate
Turning (external)	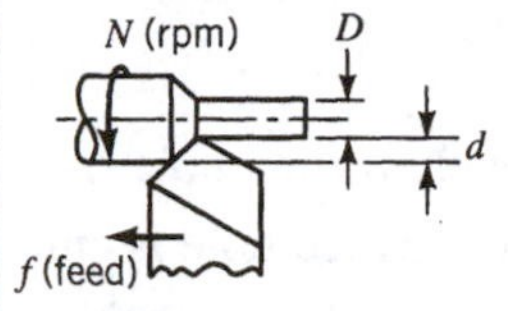	$V = \pi(D + 2d)N$	$T = \frac{L}{fN}$ where $L = L_{workpiece}$ + allowance i.e., length of the workpiece plus allowance	M.R.R. $= \pi(D - d)N{\cdot}f{\cdot}d$
Boring	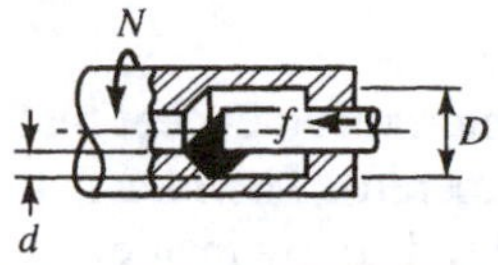	$V = \pi DN$	$T = \frac{L}{fN}$	M.R.R. $= \pi(D - d)N{\cdot}f{\cdot}d$
Facing	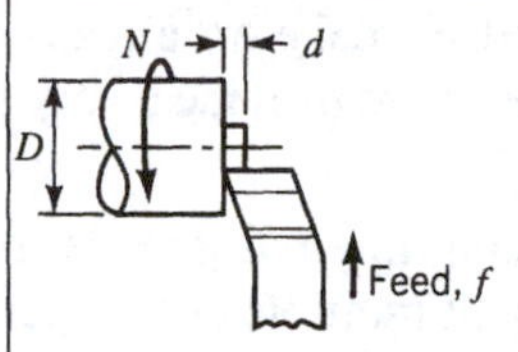	max $V = \pi DN$ min $V = 0$ mean $V = \frac{\pi DN}{2}$	$T = \frac{D + \text{allowance}}{2fN}$	max M.R.R. $= \pi DN{\cdot}f{\cdot}d$ mean M.R.R. $= \frac{\pi DN{\cdot}f{\cdot}d}{2}$
Parting	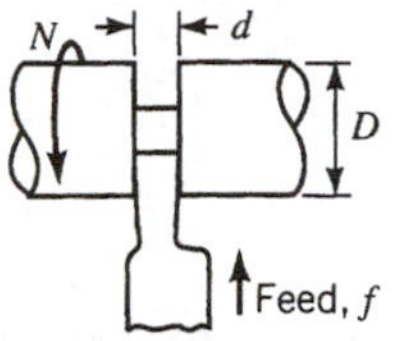	max $V = \pi DN$ min $V = 0$ mean $V = \frac{\pi DN}{2}$	$T = \frac{D + \text{allowance}}{2fN}$	max M.R.R. $= \pi DN{\cdot}f{\cdot}d$ mean M.R.R. $= \frac{\pi DN{\cdot}f{\cdot}d}{2}$

FIGURE 5.2 Various parameter estimation equations for some lathe operations. (From ElWakil, *Processes and Design for Manufacturing,* Prentice Hall (1989). Reproduced with special permission from the author.)

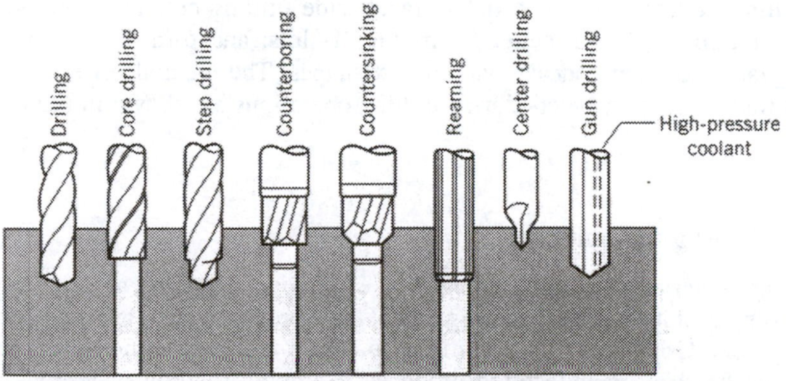

FIGURE 5.3 Various types of drills and drilling operations. (From Kalpakjian, *Manufacturing and Engineering Technology,* Second Edition, © 1992 by Addison-Wesley Publishing Company, Inc. Reprinted by permission of the publisher.)

Other operations that involve hole making include boring, counterboring, spot facing, countersinking, reaming, and tapping. A brief description of each of these processes is given below:

Boring: Boring involves enlarging an already drilled hole.

Counterboring: In counterboring only one end of a drilled hole is enlarged.

Spot facing: Finishing off a small surface area around the opening of a hole involves spot facing.

Countersinking: Countersinking is similar to counterboring except that the hole enlarged at one end is conical (tapered). The idea is to accommodate the conical seat of a flathead screw inside.

Reaming: Reaming is a sizing process used to make an already drilled hole dimensionally more accurate and to provide a very smooth surface.

Tapping: Tapping is the process of producing internal threads in workpieces by using a threaded tool with multiple cutting teeth; the tool is called a tap.

5.1.3 Milling Operations

Milling is used to produce a variety of shapes such as flat, contoured, and helical surfaces. It is also used for thread- and gear-cutting operations, among others. The milling process involves simultaneous rotary motion of the milling cutter and linear motion of the workpiece. Based on the direction of cutter rotation and workpiece feed, the milling process is classified into two basic categories: *up-milling* and *down-milling*. In up-milling the workpiece is fed against the direction of the cutter rotation, whereas in down-milling the cutter rotation coincides with the direction of feed at the contact point between the milling cutter and the workpiece.

A large variety of milling cutters are used to produce different shapes. Examples are plain milling cutters to produce flat surfaces; side milling cutters for cutting slots, grooves, and spines; T-slot cutter for milling T-slots; and form milling cutters for making gears and other concave and convex shapes. The methods of estimating the different machining parameters during milling operations are shown in Figure 5.4.

5.1.4 Grinding Operations

In grinding, material removal is achieved by employing a rotating abrasive wheel. In fact, grinding is quite similar to milling except that abrasive wheels are used in place of milling cutters. Grinding is generally used to obtain the finest dimensional accuracy and surface finish in manufactured products. Common grinding operations include surface grinding, cylindrical grinding, internal grinding, and centerless grinding. The equations to be used for estimating different parameters in surface grinding with both horizontal and vertical grinding are given in Figure 5.5.

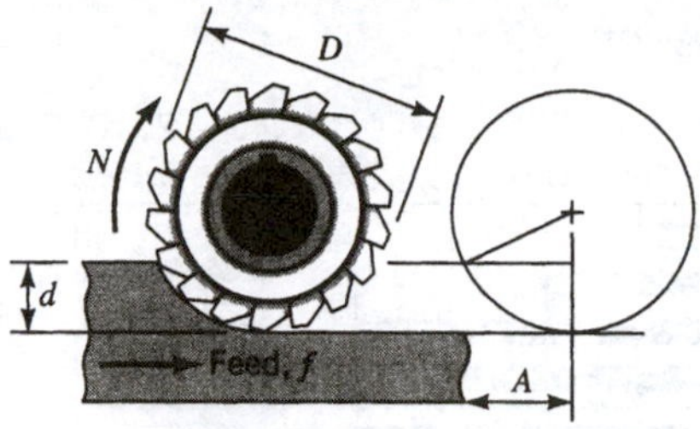

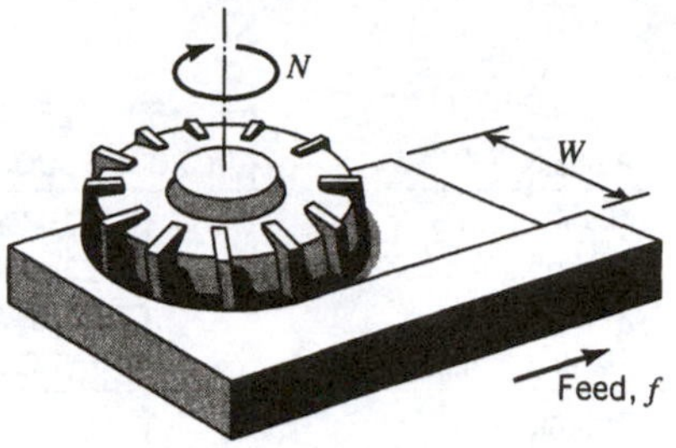

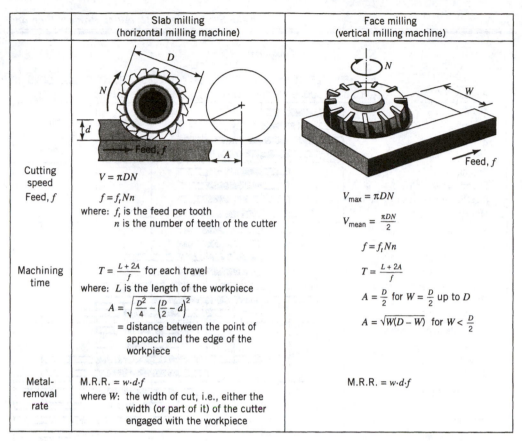

	Slab milling (horizontal milling machine)	Face milling (vertical milling machine)
Cutting speed	$V = \pi DN$	$V_{max} = \pi DN$ $V_{mean} = \frac{\pi DN}{2}$
Feed, f	$f = f_t Nn$ where: f_t is the feed per tooth n is the number of teeth of the cutter	$f = f_t Nn$
Machining time	$T = \frac{L+2A}{f}$ for each travel where: L is the length of the workpiece $A = \sqrt{\frac{D^2}{4} - \left(\frac{D}{2} - d\right)^2}$ = distance between the point of appoach and the edge of the workpiece	$T = \frac{L+2A}{f}$ $A = \frac{D}{2}$ for $W = \frac{D}{2}$ up to D $A = \sqrt{W(D-W)}$ for $W < \frac{D}{2}$
Metal-removal rate	M.R.R. = $w \cdot d \cdot f$ where W: the width of cut, i.e., either the width (or part of it) of the cutter engaged with the workpiece	M.R.R. = $w \cdot d \cdot f$

FIGURE 5.4 Parameter estimation for various milling operations. (From ElWakil, *Processes and Design for Manufacturing,* Prentice Hall (1989). Reproduced with special permission from the author.)

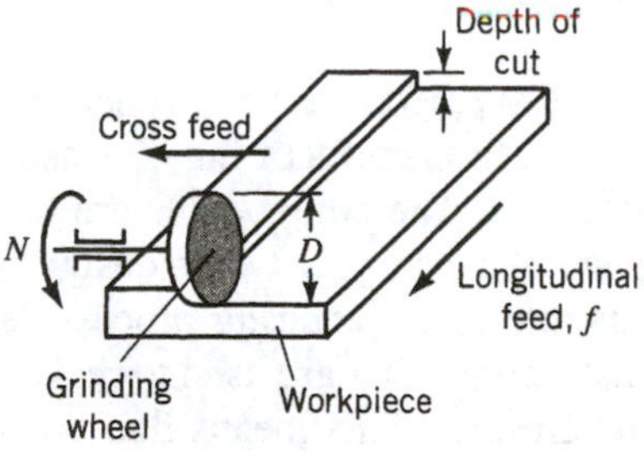

(a)

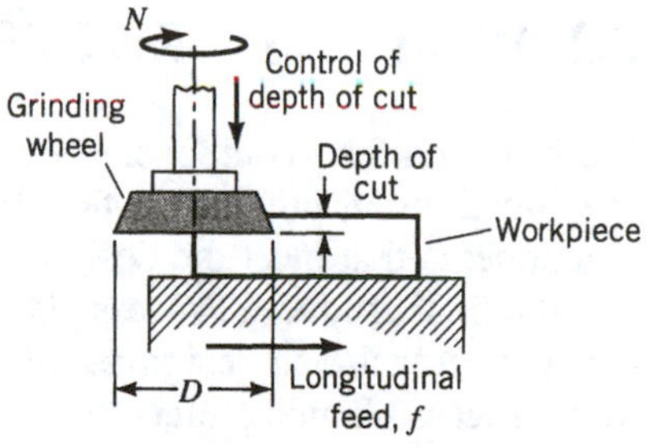

(b)

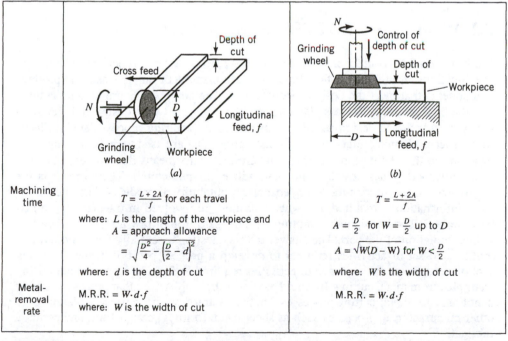

	(a)	(b)
Machining time	$T = \frac{L+2A}{f}$ for each travel where: L is the length of the workpiece and A = approach allowance $= \sqrt{\frac{D^2}{4} - \left(\frac{D}{2} - d\right)^2}$ where: d is the depth of cut	$T = \frac{L+2A}{f}$ $A = \frac{D}{2}$ for $W = \frac{D}{2}$ up to D $A = \sqrt{W(D-W)}$ for $W < \frac{D}{2}$ where: W is the width of cut
Metal-removal rate	M.R.R. = $W \cdot d \cdot f$ where: W is the width of cut	M.R.R. = $W \cdot d \cdot f$

FIGURE 5.5 Parameter estimation for horizontal and vertical surface grinding. (From ElWakil, *Processes and Design for Manufacturing,* Prentice Hall (1989). Reproduced with special permission from the author.)

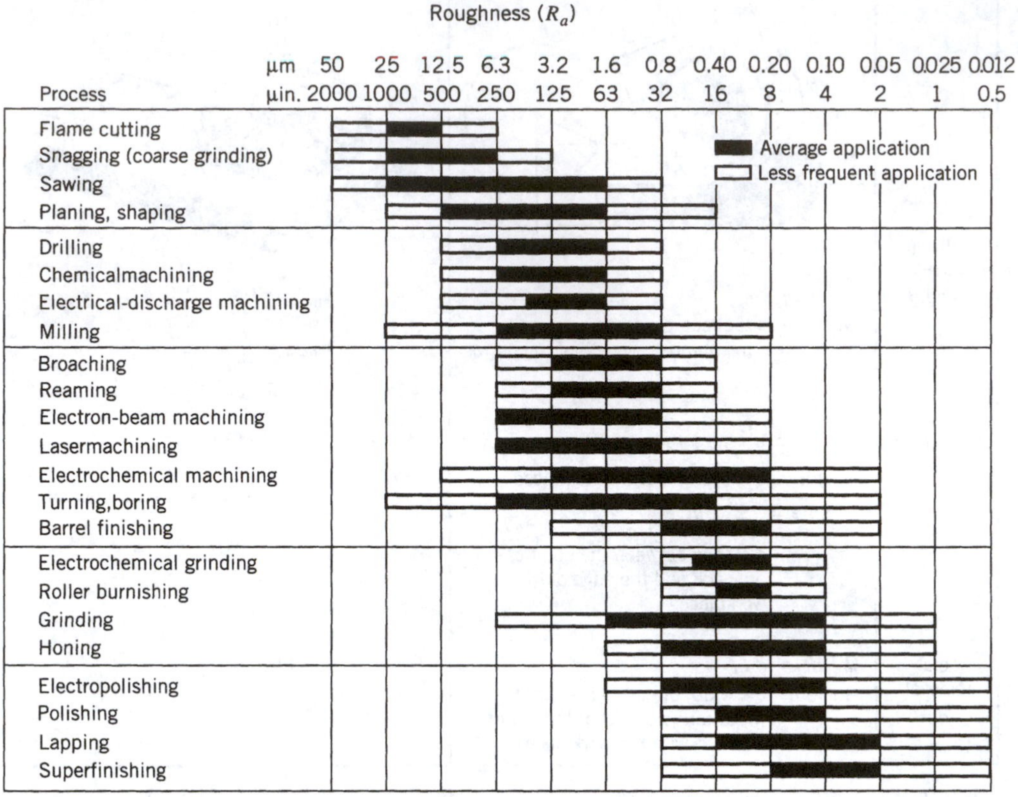

FIGURE 5.6 Surface roughness obtained from different manufacturing processes. (From Kalpakjian, *Manufacturing and Engineering Technology,* Second Edition, © 1992 by Addison-Wesley Publishing Company, Inc. Reprinted by permission of the publisher.)

5.2 WHAT IS PROCESS PLANNING?

Products and their components are designed to perform certain functions. The design specifications ensure the functionality aspects. In manufacturing, the task is to produce components that meet the design specifications. The components are then assembled into the final products. Process planning acts as a bridge between design and manufacturing by translating design specifications into manufacturing process details. Therefore, process planning refers to a set of instructions that are used to make a component or a part so that the design specifications are met. This means that process planning essentially determines how a component will be manufactured. Therefore, it is the major determinant of manufacturing cost and profitability of products. The question is what information is required and what activities are involved in transforming a raw part into a finished component, starting with the selection of raw material and ending with completion of the part. The answer to this question essentially defines the information and set of activities required to develop a process plan(s). In the following section we discuss the sequence of activities required to develop a process plan using examples from metal cutting. It should, however, be emphasized that process planning is not only for metal-cutting processes. On the contrary, we need process planning for other manufacturing processes such as sheet metal forming, composites, and ceramic fabrication.

5.3 BASIC STEPS IN DEVELOPING A PROCESS PLAN

The development of process plans involves a number of activities. In the following sections we describe the activities that are essential in generating a process plan:

- Analysis of part requirements
- Selection of raw workpiece
- Determining manufacturing operations and their sequences
- Selection of machine tools
- Selection of tools, workholding devices, and inspection equipment
- Determining machining conditions (cutting speed, feed and depth of cut) and manufacturing times (setup time, processing time, and lead time)

5.3.1 Analysis of Part Requirements

The primary purpose of process planning is to translate the design requirements for parts into manufacturing process details. The question is, what are the part design requirements? At the engineering design level, the part requirements can be defined as the part features, dimensions, and tolerance specifications. These, in turn, determine the processing requirements. The analysis of finished part requirements is the first step in process planning. First, the features of the parts are analyzed. Examples of geometric features are a plane, cylinder, cone, step, edge, and fillet. These common features can be modified by the addition of slots, pockets, grooves, and holes, among others. For example, consider the part with plane geometric features shown in Figure 5.7*a*. This part is successively modified by adding a step (Figure 5.7*b*), a slot (Figure 5.7*c*), a side step (Figure 5.7*d*), and a blind cylindrical hole (Figure 5.7*e*). After the feature analysis, dimensional and tolerance analyses are performed to provide more information for manufacturing purposes.

5.3.2 Selection of Raw Workpiece

The selection of the raw workpiece is an important element of process planning. It involves such attributes as shape, size (dimensions and weight), and material. For example, a raw part may be in the shape of a rod, a slab, a blank, or just a rough forging. From the point of view of dimensional accuracy as well as economics of manufacturing, it is important to determine the required oversize of the raw part. The weight and the material of the raw part are dictated by the functional requirement of the parts.

5.3.3 Determining Manufacturing Operations and Their Sequences

The next logical step in process planning is to determine the appropriate types of processing operations and their sequence to transform the features, dimensions, and tolerances of a part from the raw to the finished state. There may be several ways to produce a given design. Sometimes constraints such as accessibility and setup may require that some features be machined before or after others. Furthermore, the types

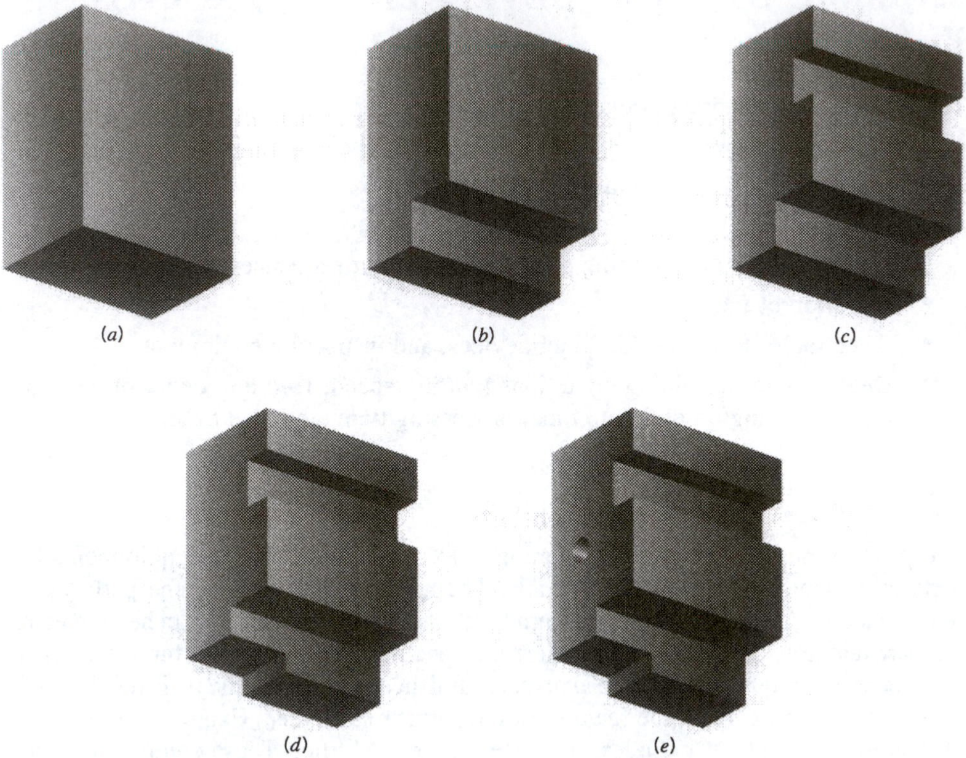

FIGURE 5.7 Successive modification of a part: (*a*) part with plane geometric features; (*b*) step addition; (*c*) slot addition; (*d*) side step addition; (*e*) a blind cylindrical hole addition.

of machines and tools available as well as the batch sizes influence the process sequence. For example, a process plan that is optimal on a three- or four-axis machine may not be optimal on a five-axis machine because of the greater flexibility of higher-axis machines. Similarly, the tools that are available and the tools that can be loaded onto a particular machine might change the sequence. The criteria for evaluating these alternatives include the quality of the product produced and the efficiency of machining.

Surface roughness and tolerance requirements also influence the operation sequence. For example, a part requiring a hole with low tolerance and surface roughness specifications would require a simple drilling operation. The same part with much finer surface finish and closer tolerance requirements would require first a drilling operation and then a boring operation to obtain the desired surface roughness and the tolerance on the hole feature of the part.

Sometimes operations are dependent on one another (Ssemakula and Rangachar, 1989). For example, consider Figure 5.8*a*, in which the operations on the part are dependent. The holes must be drilled before milling the inclined surface because the holes cannot be drilled accurately on an inclined surface. However, if the inclined surface has to be finished before drilling, an end mill should be used to obtain a flat surface perpendicular to the axis of the drill before drilling the hole.

Cutting forces and rigidity of the workpiece-tool machine tool also influence the operation sequence. For example, consider the part shown in Figure 5.8*b*. Hole H2 must be produced before machining the slot. If the hole is machined after finishing the

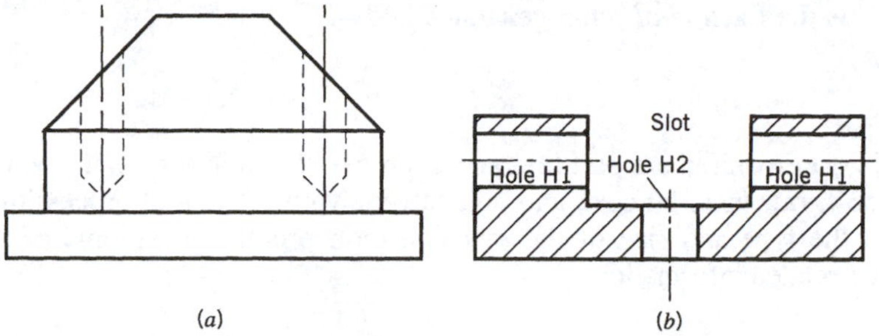

FIGURE 5.8 (*a*) Dependent operations—holes on inclined surfaces; (*b*) a part with interdependent features.

slot, it may bend. These simple examples demonstrate that the part features, dimensions, tolerances, accessibility, and setup constraints are some of the many factors that dictate the processing requirements and their sequences.

5.3.4 Selection of Machine Tools

The next step in process planning after the selection of manufacturing operations and their sequence is to select the machine tools on which these operations can be performed. A large number of factors influence the selection of machine tools:

1. Workpiece-related attributes such as the kinds of features desired, the dimensions of the workpiece, its dimensional tolerance, and the raw material form.
2. Machine tool–related attributes such as process capability, size, mode of operation (e.g., manual, semiautomatic, automatic, numerically controlled), tooling capabilities (e.g., size and type of the tool magazine), and automatic tool-changing capabilities.
3. Production volume–related information such as the production quantity and order frequency.

The three basic criteria for evaluating the suitability of a machine tool to accomplish an operation are unit cost of production, manufacturing lead time, and quality. We provide a simple analytical framework for the selection of machine tools as follows (for details, refer to Chapter 4, Section 4.4):

$$Y^{i} = k^{i}Y^{o} \tag{5.1}$$

$$Y^{s} = k^{s}Y^{o} \tag{5.2}$$

$$X^{o} = k^{i}X^{i} - k^{s}X^{s} + k^{i}f(Y^{i}) \tag{5.3}$$

where X^{i}, X^{o}, and X^{s} represent the unit cost of input, output, and scrap, respectively; Y^{i}, Y^{o}, and Y^{s} represent input, output, and scrap units, respectively; k^{i} and k^{s} represent the technological coefficients of input and scrap, respectively; and $f(Y^{i})$ is the unit processing cost as a function of input.

$$k^{s} = \frac{\text{SC}}{1 - \text{SC}}$$

where SC is the fraction of scrap generated and

$$k^i = 1 + k^s$$

The basic data required are part tolerances, process capability of machine tools, processing cost, raw material cost, and unit salvage value. The unit processing cost depends on the type and size of the machine tool, production volume of parts, and workpiece-related information.

EXAMPLE 5.1

Suppose 500 units of a shaft are to be manufactured within 1 ± 0.003 in. Suppose there are three alternative machine tools with the information given in Table 5.1. Use the models developed in Chapter 4 to select a machine tool to perform the turning operation.

The other data are:

Unit raw material cost = \$10.00

Unit salvage value = \$2.00

Process average = 1.0015 in.

Solution

We provide a detailed calculation for the turret lathe. Assuming that all parts above and below the tolerance limits are scrapped, we get $Z^l = 0.21$ and $Z^u = 0.64$. From normal tables, the percentage of items above the upper tolerance limit is 41.683 and the percentage of items below the lower tolerance limit is 26.109. The total percentage of rejects is 41.683 + 26.109 = 67.792. Therefore, the fraction of scrap SC = 0.67792.

The technological coefficient of scrap,

$$k^s = \frac{\text{SC}}{1 - \text{SC}} = \frac{0.67792}{1 - 0.67792} = 2.1048$$

Accordingly,

Technological coefficient of input $= 1 + k^s = 3.1048$

Number of units scrapped, $Y^s = k^s Y^o = 2.1048 \times 500 = 1052.4$

Number of raw units (input) required, $Y^i = k^i Y^o = 3.1048 \times 500 = 1552.4$

Manufacturing lead time $= S + t \times Y^i = 15 + 1.00 \times 1552.4 = 1567.4$ min

$$\begin{aligned}\text{Unit output cost, } X^o &= k^i X^i - k^s X^s + k^i f(Y^i)\\ &= 3.1048 \times 10.00 - 2.1048 \times 2.00 + 3.1048 \times 7.00\\ &= 48.572\end{aligned}$$

TABLE 5.1 **Basic Data on Types of Machine Tools**

Types of Machine Tools	*Standard Deviation, σ (in.)*	*Processing Cost per Unit, f ($/unit)*	*Processing Time per Unit, t (min/unit)*	*Setup Time, S (minutes)*
Turret lathe	0.007	7.00	1.00	15
Engine lathe	0.001	10.00	0.90	30
Automatic screw machine	0.0005	15.00	0.70	60

TABLE 5.2 **Unit Cost, Quality, and Manufacturing Lead Time for Various Technologies**

Types of Machine Tools	*Unit Cost ($/unit)*	*Scrap (units)*	*Manufacturing Lead Time (mins)*
Turret lathe	48.57	1052	1567.40
Engine lathe	21.28	33	510.06
Automatic screw machine	25.03	1	410.70

Similarly, calculations are done for the engine lathe and the automatic screw machine and are tabulated in Table 5.2. The number of units of scrap generated is indicative of quality.

Analysis of Results

For the data assumed, the results are interesting. The turret lathe is not preferred, because the unit cost, the number of defective units, and the manufacturing lead time are higher than those obtained with other technologies. However, there is trade-off between the unit cost and number of units of scrap as well as the manufacturing lead time for the engine lathe and automatic screw machine. If market forces dictate quick and quality delivery, use the automatic screw machine. From the minimum-unit-cost point of view, the engine lathe is the best option. Similar analyses can be done for other operations in the company and the results can be tabulated. In this section, only a basic framework was provided for the selection of machine tools considering the criteria of unit cost, quality, and manufacturing lead time.

Machine tool selection is quite complex because of the large number of factors involved. The analytical framework proposed in this section does not necessarily capture all the information. For example, qualitative information such as low, medium, or high production rate is not adequately captured. An expert system that embodies some of the qualitative and quantitative knowledge of machine tools, cutting tools, and operations can be useful in process planning. It can suggest alternative machine tools and cutting tools for the various operations on the part. The user can then build alternative process plans using this information.

5.3.5 Selection of Tools, Workholding Devices, and Inspection Equipment

A combination of machine tool and cutting tool is required to generate a feature(s) on the workpiece. Workholding devices are used to locate and hold the workpieces to help generate the features. Inspection equipment is necessary to ensure the dimensional accuracy, tolerances, and surface finish on the features. The major categories include on-line and off-line inspection equipment. The selection of machine tools, cutting tools, fixtures, and inspection equipment is based primarily on part features. For example, if tolerances are to be specified in the range of ± 0.0002 to ± 0.0005 in./in. and surface finishes in the range of 16 to 32 μin., then the Swiss Automatics as a machine tool and a high-speed steel (HSS) single-point cutting tool may be recommended. Furthermore, cutting tool specifications may include various angles such as rakes, clearances, cutting edge, and nose radius.

The primary purpose of a workholding device is to hold the workpiece securely. These devices include clamps, jigs, and fixtures, which are often used interchangeably in manufacturing operations. Jigs, however, are designed to have various reference surfaces and points for accurate alignment of parts and tools. Some of the common examples of workholding devices include:

1. Manually operated devices such as collets, chucks, mandrels, faceplates, and various kinds of fixtures.
2. Designed devices such as power chucks.
3. Flexible fixtures used in flexible manufacturing systems. The objective is to accommodate a range of part shapes and dimensions with the least need for changes and adjustments requiring operator interventions.

The shapes, dimensions, accuracy, production rate, and variety of parts essentially determine the types of workholding devices required. For example, a four-jaw chuck can accommodate prismatic parts, faceplates are used for clamping irregularly shaped workpieces, and collets are used to hold round bars only (and only those within a certain range of diameters). The fixtures are, however, designed for specific shapes and dimensions of parts.

5.3.6 Determining Machining Conditions and Manufacturing Times

Having specified the workpiece material, machine tool, and cutting tool, the question is what can be controlled to reduce cost and increase production rate. The controllable variables are cutting speed (v), feed (f), and depth of cut (d). Jointly, v, f, and d are referred to as machining conditions. There are a number of models for determining the optimal machining conditions. In this section we present two simple models.

5.3.6.1 Minimum Cost per Piece

The average cost per piece to produce a workpiece consists of the following costs:

$$\begin{aligned}\text{Cost per component, } C_u &= \text{nonproductive cost per piece} \\ &\quad + \text{machining time cost per piece} \\ &\quad + \text{tool changing cost per piece} \\ &\quad + \text{tooling cost per piece}\end{aligned} \tag{5.4}$$

Mathematically, this can be expressed as

$$C_u = c_o t_l + c_o t_c + c_o t_d \left(\frac{t_{ac}}{T}\right) + c_t \left(\frac{t_{ac}}{T}\right) \tag{5.5}$$

The tool life equation as a function of cutting speed (v) is expressed as

$$vT^n = C \tag{5.6}$$

where

c_o = cost rate including labor and overhead cost rates ($/min)
c_t = tool cost per cutting edge, which depends on the type of tool used
C = constant in the tool life equation, $vT^n = C$
v = cutting speed in meters/minute
f = feed rate (mm/rev)
d = depth of cut (mm)
n = exponent in the tool life equation
t_l = nonproductive time consisting of loading and unloading the part and other idle time (min)
t_c = machining time per piece (min/piece)
t_d = time to change a cutting edge (min)
t_{ac} = actual cutting time per piece, which is approximately equal to t_c (min/piece)
T = tool life (min)

Consider a single-pass turning operation. If L, D, and f are the length of cut (mm), diameter of the workpiece (mm), and feed rate (mm/rev), respectively, then the cutting time per piece for a single-pass operation is

$$t_c \approx t_{ac} = \frac{\pi LD}{1000vf} \tag{5.7}$$

Upon substituting these values as well as the tool life equation in the cost per piece equation (5.5), we obtain

$$\begin{aligned} C_u = c_o t_l + c_o \left(\frac{\pi LD}{1000vf}\right) + c_o \left(\frac{\pi LD}{1000vf}\right)\left(\frac{v}{C}\right)^{1/n} t_d \\ + c_t \left(\frac{\pi LD}{1000vf}\right)\left(\frac{v}{C}\right)^{1/n} \end{aligned} \tag{5.8}$$

The feed rate and depth of cut are normally fixed to their allowable values. Therefore, the cutting speed v is the decision variable. Upon partially differentiating C_u with respect to v, equating to zero, and solving, we obtain the minimum unit cost cutting speed (v_{min}) as follows:

$$v_{min} = \frac{C}{\left[\left(\frac{1}{n} - 1\right)\left(\frac{c_o t_d + c_t}{c_o}\right)\right]^n} \tag{5.9}$$

Upon substituting the value of cutting speed in the tool life equation (5.6), we obtain the optimal tool life (T_{min}) for minimum unit cost as follows:

$$T_{min} = \left(\frac{1}{n} - 1\right)\left(\frac{c_o t_d + c_t}{c_o}\right) \tag{5.10}$$

5.3.6.2 Maximum Production Rate Model

Another criterion used to determine the optimal machining conditions is maximum production rate. The production rate is inversely proportional to the production time per piece, which is given by

$$\begin{aligned}\text{Time per piece, } T_u = {} & \text{nonproductive time per piece} \\ & + \text{cost of machining time per piece} \\ & + \text{tool changing time per piece}\end{aligned} \tag{5.11}$$

Mathematically, this can be expressed as

$$T_u = t_l + t_c + t_d\left(\frac{t_{ac}}{T}\right) \tag{5.12}$$

Upon substituting the values of T, t_c, and t_{ac} in Equation (5.12) we obtain

$$T_u = t_l + \frac{\pi LD}{1000vf} + \left(\frac{\pi LD}{1000vf}\right)\left(\frac{v}{C}\right)^{1/n} t_d \tag{5.13}$$

Upon partially differentiating T_u with respect to v, equating to zero, and solving for v, we obtain

$$v_{max} = \frac{C}{\left[\left(\frac{1}{n} - 1\right)(t_d)\right]^n} \tag{5.14}$$

and therefore

$$T_{max} = \left[\left(\frac{1}{n} - 1\right)(t_d)\right] \tag{5.15}$$

where v_{max} is the optimal cutting speed that ensures maximum production rate and T_{max} is the tool life corresponding to v_{max} obtained from the tool life equation (5.6).

5.3.6.3 Manufacturing Lead Time

Assuming that the lot size is Q units, then the average lead time to process these units will be

$$\text{Lead time} = \text{major setup time} + T_u Q$$

EXAMPLE 5.2

A lot of 500 units of steel rods 30 cm long and 6 cm in diameter is turned on a numerically controlled (NC) lathe at a feed rate of 0.2 mm per revolution and a depth of cut of 1 mm. The tool life is given by

$$vT^{0.20} = 200$$

The other data are:

Machine labor rate	= \$10/h
Machine overhead rate	= 50% of labor
Grinding labor rate	= \$10/hr
Grinding overhead rate	= 50% of grinding labor
Workpiece loading and unloading time	= 0.50 min/piece

The data related to the tools are:

Brazed inserts

Original cost of the tool	= \$27.96
Grinding time	= 2 min
Tool changing time	= 0.50 min

The tool can be ground only five times before it is discarded.

Determine the following:

(a) Optimum tool life and optimum cutting speed to minimize the cost per piece
(b) Optimum tool life and optimum cutting speed to maximize the production rate
(c) Minimum cost per component, time per component, and corresponding lead time
(d) Maximum production rate, corresponding cost per component, and lead time

Solution

(a) Optimum tool life and optimum cutting speed to minimize the cost per piece:

$$c_o = \text{Machine labor} + \text{overhead rate} = \frac{10 + 0.50 \times 10}{60} = \$0.25 \text{ per minute}$$

$$\begin{aligned} c_t &= \text{Original cost of the tool per cutting edge} \\ &\quad + \text{grinding time} \times (\text{grinding labor rate} + \text{grinding overhead rate}) \\ &= \frac{27.96}{6} + \frac{2\,(10 + 0.50 \times 10)}{60} = \$5.16 \end{aligned}$$

Therefore,

$$\begin{aligned} T_{\min} &= \left[\left(\frac{1}{n} - 1\right)\left(\frac{c_o t_d + c_t}{c_o}\right)\right] \\ &= \left(\frac{1}{0.20} - 1\right)\frac{0.25 \times 0.50 + 5.16}{0.25} = 84.56 \text{ min} \end{aligned}$$

$$V_{\min} = \frac{C}{T_{\min}^n} = \frac{200}{(84.56)^{0.20}} = 82.337 \text{ m/min}$$

(b) Optimum tool life and cutting speed to maximize production rate:

$$T_{\max} = \left(\frac{1}{n} - 1\right) t_d = \left(\frac{1}{0.20} - 1\right)(0.50) = 2 \text{ min}$$

$$V_{\max} = \frac{C}{T_{\max}^n} = \frac{200}{(2)^{0.20}} = 174.11 \text{ m/min}$$

(c) Minimum cost per component, time per component, and corresponding lead time:

$$\frac{\pi LD}{1000V_{\min}f} = \frac{3.14 \times 300 \times 60}{1000 \times 82.337 \times 0.20} = 3.4325$$

$$C_u = 0.25 \times 0.50 + 0.25 \times 3.4325 + 0.25 \times 3.4325 \times \left(\frac{1}{84.56}\right) \times 0.50$$

$$+ 5.16 \times 3.4325 \times \left(\frac{1}{84.56}\right)$$

$$= \$1.197 \text{ per piece}$$

The production time per piece at $V_{\min}$ is

$$T_u = t_1 + \left(\frac{\pi LD}{1000V_{\min}f}\right) + \left(\frac{\pi LD}{1000V_{\min}f}\right)\left(\frac{V_{\min}}{C}\right)^{1/n} t_d$$

$$= 0.50 + 3.4325 + 3.4325 \times (1/84.56) \times 0.50$$

$$= 3.9528 \text{ min}$$

Therefore, the lead time (ignoring major setup time) to produce 500 units is 500 × 3.9528 = 1976.40 min.

(d) Maximum production rate, corresponding cost per component and lead time:

$$\left(\frac{\pi LD}{1000V_{\max}f}\right) = \frac{3.14 \times 300 \times 60}{1000 \times 174.11 \times 0.20} = 1.623$$

The production time per piece at $V_{\max}$ is

$$T_u = t_1 + \left(\frac{\pi LD}{1000V_{\max}f}\right) + \left(\frac{\pi LD}{1000V_{\max}f}\right)\left(\frac{V_{\max}}{C}\right)^{1/n} t_d$$

$$= 0.50 + 1.623 + 1.623 \times (1/2) \times 0.50 = 2.52875$$

Therefore, the lead time to produce 500 units is 500 × 2.52875 = 1264.375 min.

$$C_u = 0.25 \times 0.50 + 0.25 \times 1.623 + 0.25 \times 1.623 \times \left(\frac{1}{2}\right) \times 0.50$$

$$+ 5.16 \times 1.623 \times \left(\frac{1}{2}\right)$$

$$= \$4.8195 \text{ per piece}$$

5.4 THE PRINCIPAL PROCESS PLANNING APPROACHES

The principal approaches to process planning are the *manual experience-based method* and the *computer-aided process planning method.* In the following sections we provide a brief description of each of these approaches.

5.4.1 The Manual Experience–Based Planning Method

The manual experience–based process planning method is most widely used. The basic steps involved are essentially the same as given in Section 5.3. The biggest problem with this approach is that it is time consuming and the plans developed over a period of time may not be consistent. The feasibility of process planning is dependent on many upstream factors such as the design and the availability of machine tools. Also, a process plan has a great influence on many downstream manufacturing activities such as scheduling and machine tool allocation. Therefore, to develop a proper process plan (not to mention an optimal one), process planners must have sufficient knowledge and experience. It may take a relatively long time and is usually costly to develop the skill of a successful planner. Computer-aided process planning has been developed to overcome these problems to a certain extent.

5.4.2 The Computer-Aided Process Planning Method

We discuss various aspects of computer-aided process planning, starting with a basic question that is often asked: Why computer-aided process planning?

5.4.2.1 Why Computer-Aided Process Planning?

As mentioned earlier, the primary purpose of process planning is to translate the design requirements into manufacturing process details. This suggests a feedforward system in which design information is processed by the process planning system to generate manufacturing process details. That is not what we want in a concurrent engineering environment. We want to optimize the system performance in a global context. Therefore, we have to integrate the CAPP system into the interorganizational flow. For example, if we change a design, we must be able to fall back on a module of CAPP to generate cost estimates for these design changes. Similarly, if there is a breakdown of a machine(s) on the shop floor, the CAPP system must be able to generate alternative process plans so that the most economical solution for the situation can be adopted. Such a framework is shown in Figure 5.9. In such a setting of a multitude of interactions among various functions of an organization and dynamic changes that take place in these subfunctional areas, the use of computers in process planning is essential.

By comparison with manual experience–based process planning, the use of computers in process planning also helps to achieve the following:

1. It can systematically produce accurate and consistent process plans.
2. It can reduce the cost and lead time of process planning.
3. The skill requirements of process planners are reduced.
4. It results in increased productivity of process planners.
5. The application programs such as cost and manufacturing lead time estimation and work standards can easily be interfaced.

Two major methods are used in computer-aided process planning: the *variant CAPP method* and the *generative CAPP method.*

5.4.2.2 The Variant CAPP Method

In the variant process planning approach, a process plan for a new part is created by recalling, identifying, and retrieving an existing plan for a similar part and making necessary modifications for the new part. Quite often, process plans are developed for

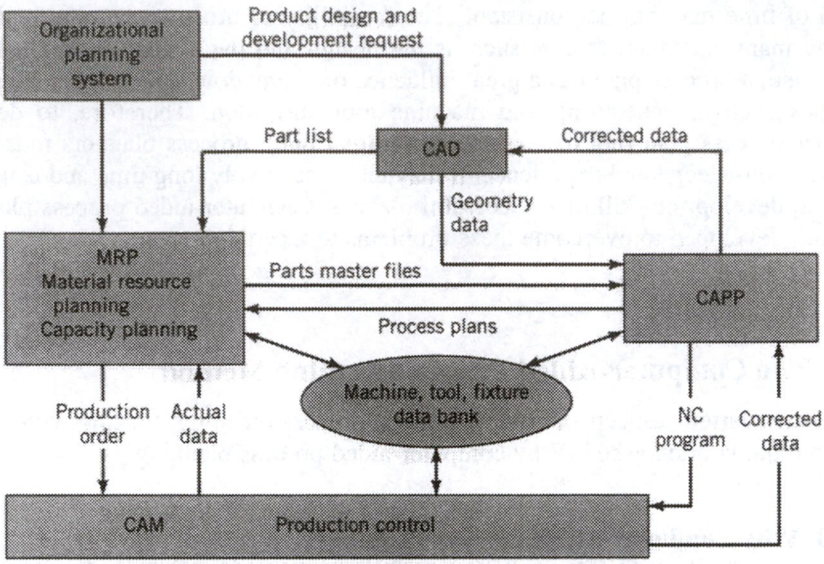

FIGURE 5.9 A computer-aided process planning framework.

parts representing a family of parts. Such parts are called *master parts.* The similarities in design attributes and manufacturing methods are exploited for the purpose of formation of part families. A number of methods have been developed for part family formation using coding and classification systems of group technology (GT), similarity coefficient–based algorithms, and mathematical programming models, among others. A detailed treatment of these approaches to part family and cell formation is given in Chapter 12. Once a new part is identified with a family, the task of developing a process plan is simple. It involves retrieving and modifying the process plan of the master part of that family. Thus, the variant process planning approach can be realized as a four-step process:

1. *Define the coding scheme.* Adopt existing coding or classification schemes to label parts for the purpose of classification. In some extreme cases, a new coding scheme may be developed.
2. *Group the parts into part families.* Group the parts into part families using the coding scheme defined in step 1 based on some common part features. A standard process plan is attached to each part family (see step 3). Often, a number of part types are associated with a family, thereby reducing the total number of standard process plans.
3. *Develop a standard process plan.* Develop a standard process plan for each part family based on the common features of the part types. This process plan can be used for every part type within the family with suitable modifications.
4. *Retrieve and modify the standard plan.* When a new part enters the system, it is assigned to a part family based on the coding and classification scheme. Then the corresponding standard process plan is retrieved and modified to accommodate the unique features of the new part.

These four steps are closely connected. The success of a process planning system largely depends on selection of the coding scheme, the standard process plans, and the underlying modification process. Because the system is usually application oriented, one coding scheme may be more suitable for a company than others.

Variant process planning is quite similar to manual experience–based planning. However, its information management capabilities are much superior because of the use of computers. Advantages of the variant process planning approach include:

- Efficient processing and evaluation of complicated activities and decisions, thus reducing the time and labor requirements.
- Standardized procedures by structuring manufacturing knowledge of the process planners to company's needs.
- Lower development and hardware costs and shorter development times. This is especially important for small and medium-sized companies whose product variety is not high, who have process planners and are interested in establishing their own process planning research activities.

Therefore, variant systems can organize and store completed plans and manufacturing knowledge from which process plans can be quickly evaluated (Alting and Zhang, 1989).

The obvious disadvantages of the variant process planning approach include:

- Maintaining consistency in editing is difficult.
- Adequately accommodating various combinations of material, geometry, size, precision, quality, alternative processing sequences, and machine loading, among many other factors, is difficult.
- The quality of the final process plan generated depends to a large extent on the knowledge and experience of the process planners. This dependence on the process planners is one of the major shortcomings of the variant process planning approach.

A number of variant process planning systems have been developed. One of the most widely used systems is computer-aided process planning, developed by McDonnell-Douglas Automation Company under the direction and sponsorship of Computer-Aided Manufacturing-International (CAM-I). CAPP can be used to generate process plans for rotational, prismatic, and sheet metal parts.

The other popular variant process planning system is MIPLAN, developed in conjunction with the Organization for Industrial Research (OIR) and General Electric Company (Hourzeel, 1976). The MIPLAN system accommodates both rotational and prismatic parts and is based on the MICLASS coding and classification system for part description. A very comprehensive group technology system developed by OIR is called MULTI-II. It consists of a number of task-oriented modules including:

- MultiClass II for group technology classification and retrieval
- Multigroup II for group technology analysis
- Multitrieve II for design retrieval
- MultiCats II for automated time standards
- MultiTrack II for tool tracking and inventory control

5.4.2.3 The Generative CAPP Method

In the generative approach, process plans are generated by means of decision logic, formulas, technology algorithms, and geometry-based data to perform uniquely the many processing decisions for converting a part from raw material to a finished state (Alting and Zhang, 1989). There are essentially two major components of a generative process planning system (Steudel, 1990): a *geometry-based coding scheme* and *process knowledge* in the form of decision logic and data.

Geometry-Based Coding Scheme The objective of a geometry-based coding scheme is to define all geometric features for all process-related surfaces together with feature dimensions, locations, and tolerances and the surface finish desired on the features. The level of detail is much greater in a generative system than a variant system. For example, such details as rough and finished states of the parts and process capability of machine tools to transform these parts to the desired states are provided.

Process Knowledge in the Form of Decision Logic and Data Basically, the matching of part geometry requirements with the manufacturing capabilities is accomplished in this phase using process knowledge in the form of decision logic and data. All the activities of process planning given in Section 5.3 are performed automatically. Examples include the selection of processes, machine tools, tools, jigs or fixtures, inspection equipment, and sequencing of operations. Setup and machining times are calculated. Operations instruction sheets are generated to help the operators run the machines in the case of manual operations. If the machines are numerically controlled, the NC codes are automatically generated.

Manufacturing knowledge is the backbone of process planning. The process of acquisition and documentation of manufacturing knowledge is not a one-time activity but a recurring dynamic phenomenon. Furthermore, the sources of manufacturing knowledge are many and diverse, such as the experience of manufacturing personnel; handbooks; suppliers of major machine tools, tools, jigs or fixtures, materials, and inspection equipment; and customers. To use this wide spectrum of knowledge ranging from qualitative and narrative to quantitative, it is necessary to develop a good knowledge structure to help provide a common denominator for understanding manufacturing information, ensuring its clarity, and providing a framework for future modifications. Tools available for the purpose include flowcharts, decision trees, decision tables, iterative algorithms, concepts of unit-machined surfaces, pattern recognition techniques, and artificial intelligence tools such as expert

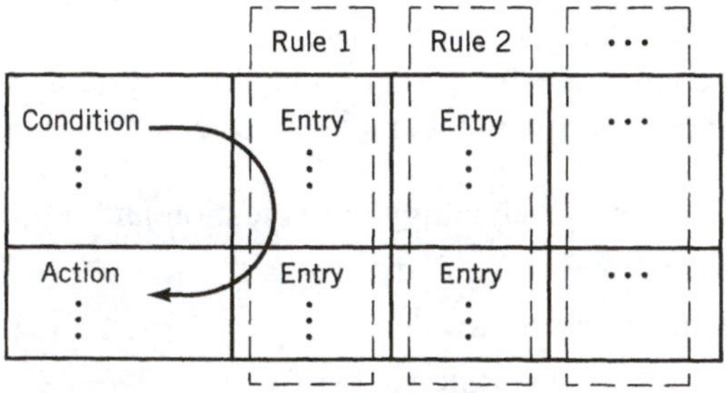

FIGURE 5.10 Format of a decision table.

TABLE 5.3 **Boolean Value-type Entries**

Length of bar ≥ 8 in.	T*	F	
Diameter of bar < 1 in.	T		
Diameter of bar ≥ 1 in.			T
Extra support	T		

* T, true; F, false; blank, do not care.

system shells. We provide a brief description of decision tables in the following section.

Decision Tables Decision tables provide a convenient way to document manufacturing knowledge. They are the principal elements of all decision table–based process planning systems. The elements of a decision table are conditions, actions, and rules. They are organized in the form of an allocation matrix as shown in Figure 5.10, where the conditions state the goal we want to achieve and the actions state the operations we have to perform. The rules, formed by entry values according to the experience of experts, establish the relationship between conditions and actions.

Entries can be either Boolean-type values (true, false, and do not care) or continuous values. See Tables 5.3 and 5.4. The decision-making mechanism works as follows: for a particular set of condition entries, look for its corresponding rule, and from that rule determine the actions. For example, if the condition is to drill a hole, then from the rules we look for the rule that can be applied, and from that rule we get the solution (or action). For more details refer to Metzner and Barnes (1977) and Chang and Wysk (1985).

TABLE 5.4 **Continuous Value-type Entries**

Length of bar (in.)		≤4	≥4	≤16	≥16
Diameter of bar (in.)	≤0.2	>0.2	1 > diameter > 0.2	≥1	
Extra support	T		T		T

* T, true; blank, do not care.

EXAMPLE 5.3

Consider the problem of the selection of lathes or grinding machines for jobs involving turning or grinding operations. Data on conditions such as lot size, diameter, surface finish, and tolerance desired are available. They are compiled in the form of a decision table as shown in Table 5.5. Make a machine selection recommendation if

(a) The lot size of the job is 70 units; diameter is relatively small; the surface roughness desired is 30 μm; and the tolerance range required is ± 0.003 in.

(b) The lot size of the job is less than 10 units; diameter is relatively small; the surface roughness desired is 45 μm; and the tolerance range required is ± 0.004 in.

(c) The lot size is greater than 50 units; diameter is relatively small; surface roughness is 20 μm; and tolerance is less than 0.0008 in.

Solution

(a) From the set of conditions given in the problem, it is easy to see from Table 5.5 that rule 3 is suitable for this situation. The action, therefore, is obviously turret lathe; that is, the operation is performed on a turret lathe.

(b) Similarly, the solution is engine lathe.

(c) From the conditions given in the problem, we find that rule 2 is most suitable. Therefore, the recommended actions are to finish parts on an engine lathe and subsequently on a centerless grinding machine to achieve the desired specifications.

5.4.2.4 Knowledge-Based Process Planning

We provide a brief discussion of knowledge-based process planning. A knowledge-based system refers to a computer program that can store knowledge of a particular domain and use that knowledge to solve problems from that domain in an intelligent way (Hayes-Ruth, 1983). In a knowledge-based process planning system, we use a computer to simulate the decision process of a human expert. Usually, human process planners develop process planning based on their experience, knowledge, and inference. A computer, to some extent, can also be used to perform these functions. By capturing this process through the use of a knowledge-based system, the proper process plan may be developed. In a knowledge-based system, two major problems need to be solved: the knowledge representation and the inference mechanism. The knowledge representation is a scheme by which a real-world problem can be represented in such a way that the computer can manipulate the information. For example, to define a part, we need to define whether there is a hole in it. Given that there is a hole, we next have to define the attributes of the hole, such as the type of hole, the length, and the

TABLE 5.5 **Decision Table for the Selection of a Machine(s) for Turning Operation**

*Conditions**	*Rule 1*	*Rule 2*	*Rule 3*	*Rule 4*
LS $\leq$ 10	X			
LS $\geq$ 50		X	X	
LS $\geq$ 4000				X
Relatively large diameters				
Relatively small diameters	X	X	X	X
SF in the range 40–60 min.	X			
SF in the range 16–32 min.		X	X	X
$\pm 0.003 \leq$ Tol $\leq \pm 0.005$	X			
$\pm 0.001 \leq$ Tol $\leq \pm 0.003$			X	
$\pm 0.0005 \leq$ Tol $\leq \pm 0.001$		X		X
Engine lathe	X	1		
Turret lathe			X	
Automatic screw machine				X
Centerless grinding machine		2		

* LS, lot size; SF, surface finish; Tol, tolerance.

diameter. The reason for this is that the computer is not capable of reading the design from blueprints or databases as humans are. The inference mechanism is the way in which the computer finds the solution. One approach is based on IF–THEN structured knowledge. For example, IF there is a hole, THEN a drill may be used. Through this type of knowledge, the computer can infer what operations are needed. Once the operations are known, it is easy to calculate other details and the process plan can be developed. Other aspects of a knowledge-based system include the interface, which contains the user interface, the interface with the computer-aided design (CAD) database, and the inquiry facility, which explains why a decision is made.

A Knowledge-Based System: EXPLAN Next, the knowledge-based system EXPLAN, is briefly described (for details, refer to Warnecke and Muthsam (1992)). This system is a subproject of the research project on the factory of the future, as part of the European research initiative called EUREKA. To build a comprehensive system, it is important that a proper model is established. This system models the process planning world by three approaches: workpiece geometry, machining, and planning.

In the workpiece geometry model, a part is described in terms of basic processing elements (BEs). Usually, a processing element can be produced through a simple operation. In this way we have established the connection between operations and geometry. It is interesting to note that the concept of BEs is somehow similar to the concept of features, which is discussed in the next section. Figure 5.11*a* illustrates how the BEs are defined.

The machining model encompasses various types of planning knowledge, such as the operations and the sequence of operations needed to remove part of the material. It represents the process plan schematically and includes knowledge of how each sequence of operations, such as setup and clamping, is performed. Rough and finish cutting is also associated with particular machining operations. Figure 5.11*b* shows how a process plan is represented and its structure.

The planning model is the portion in which the clamping positions and other factors are taken into account for the purpose of reducing cost. For example, allocating different sets of BEs to a certain setup may affect the manufacturing cost. Usually, we try to maximize the work content of each individual setup, which helps to achieve the ultimate goal of reducing the total cost of a product.

The overall structure of the EXPLAN system is shown in Figure 5.11*c*. Three basic components of the system are knowledge base, dialogue, and inference engine. The dialogue component connects the users and the system and defines how the users can use the inference engine. Also, the link with external data files such as material requirements planning (MRP) and CAD database is included in this component.

The inference engine is used to apply rules for certain applications and obtain the result. For example, we apply the rules for interpreting geometry data when we try to interpret the geometry data from the CAD database. When generating a detailed process plan, the rules for detailed planning of processing are used by inference engine to obtain a plan to achieve a certain goal.

The knowledge base contains the experience of experts, usually written in a certain format for easy inference. Here the knowledge is in the form of rules. For example, a rule for interpreting the geometry may be: If the angle between two external surfaces of the workpiece is smaller (greater) than 180°, there is an internal (external) edge. From a set of rules, the inference engine may produce some useful new knowledge such as whether the edges form a partcular processing element.

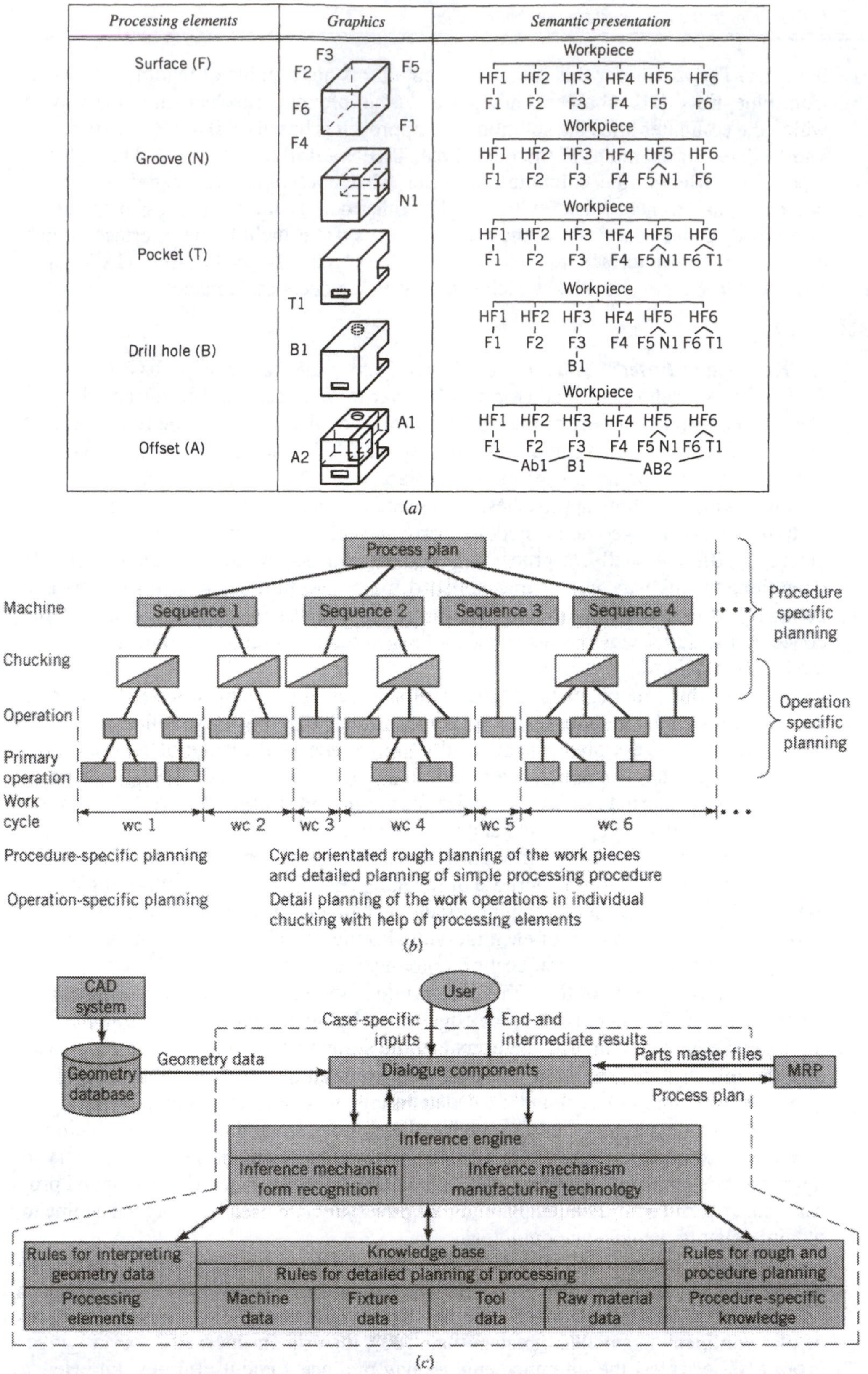

FIGURE 5.11 (*a*) Processing element representation scheme; (*b*) schematic representation of a process plan; (*c*) overall structure of the EXPLAN system. (Reproduced with permission of John Wiley & Sons, Inc from Warnecke and Muthsam (1992).)

TABLE 5.6 **Some of the Variant and Generative CAPP Systems**

CAPP System	*Part Shapes*	*Process Planning Approaches*	*Characteristics and Commercial Situation*	*Programming Languages Used*	*References*	*Developers*
CMPP	Rotational	Generative	Uses English-like language (COPPL)	FORTRAN 77	Roger et al. (1992)	UTRC (USA)
GENPLAN	All	Variant and generative	Interfaced with CAD/CAM		Tulkoff (1987)	Lockheed-Georgia (USA)
GT-CAPP	All	Variant	Part family code used		Strohmeier (1987)	Rockwell Inc. (USA)
KAPPS	Rotational and prismatic	Generative	Part family numbers used	LISP	Iwata and Fukuda (1987)	Kobe University (Japan)
MIPLAN	Rotational and prismatic	Variant	Expert system based on MICLASS		Houtzeel (1976) Lesko (1983)	OIR and GE Co. (USA)
RTCAPP	Prismatic	Generative	Generic shell		Park and Khoshnevis (1993)	University of Southern California (USA)
TURBO-CAPP	Rotational	Generative	Knowledge base interfaced with CAD	PROLOG	Wang and Wisk (1987)	Pennsylvania State University (USA)
XPLAN	All	Generative	Expert system based on DCLASS	FORTRAN 77	Lenau and Alting (1986)	Technical University of DK (Denmark)
XPLAN-R	Rotational	Generative	Expert system based on DCLASS	FORTRAN 77	Zhang (1987)	Technical University of DK (Denmark)
XPLANE	Rotational	Variant	Knowledge based	FORTRAN 77	Erve and Kals (1986)	Twente University Technology (Netherlands)
XPS-1	All	Variant and generative	COPPL used	FORTRAN 77	Groppetti and Semeraro (1986)	UTRC and CAM-I (USA)

Source: Alting and Zhang (1989).

5.5 VARIANT AND GENERATIVE PROCESS PLANNING SYSTEMS

A large number of variant and generative process planning systems have been developed. Alting and Zhang (1989) reviewed 156 CAPP systems and discussed 14 systems in detail. A list of 11 CAPP systems is given in Table 5.6. Some of the well-known generative process planning systems are TIPPS (Chang, 1982), Computer-Managed Process Planner (CMPP), developed by United Technologies Research Center in conjunction with the U.S. Army Missile Command (Rogers et al., 1994), and GENPLAN (Tulkoff, 1987). We provide an overview of CMPP because it is a very comprehensive system for process planning of rotational parts and is available by contacting: The Commander, U.S. Army Missile Command, Attn: AMSMI-RD-SE-MT/Roy Lindberg, Redstone Arsenal, AL 35898-5270 [Phone (205) 876-2147]. The major elements associated with CMPP are:

- Computer-aided design
- CAD-to-CAPP translation
- Process plan generator
- CAPP-to-CAM translator
- Computer-assisted manufacturing

Four types of cylindrical surfaces are allowed in CMPP: diameters, faces, tapers, and circular arcs with noncylindrical features. A blank template is used in the CAD system to prepare a part drawing, which is saved in an automatically created initial graphics exchange specification (IGES) file. The information in the IGES file is then used to convert CAD information into CAPP automatically by CMPP.

5.6 FEATURE RECOGNITION IN COMPUTER-AIDED PROCESS PLANNING

As mentioned in the introduction, CAPP systems usually serve as a link between CAD and CAM. However, it is only a partial link, because most of the existing CAD/drafting systems do not provide part feature information, which is essential data for CAPP. In other words, the CAPP systems do not understand the three-dimensional geometry of the designed parts from CAD systems in terms of their engineering meaning related to manufacturing and assembly. Although this appears to be an interface problem, it is usually harder than it appears. This is a common problem faced by all CAPP process planning methods and systems and is generally referred to as the feature recognition problem. For example, the object shown in Figure 5.12 is defined by a constructive solid geometry (CSG) tree that represents a block primitive and a cylinder primitive combined by the Boolean operator "-" (Li and Singh, 1994). The shape and dimension of the object are uniquely defined by this scheme. However, some useful higher-level information such as whether a hole is a blind hole or a through hole is not provided. This kind of information, defined in terms of feature, is essential to process planning. For example, for the mentioned part, if there is a through-hole, the process plan may be different from that in the blind-hole case. Providing this type of information usually requires human intervention. To solve the CAD/CAPP interface problem, feature recognition is one of the most efficient approaches.

From an engineering point of view, features are regarded as generic shapes of

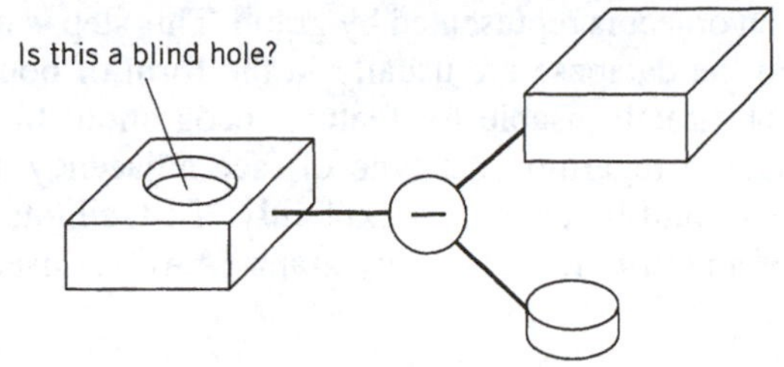

FIGURE 5.12 Useful higher-level information.

objects with which engineers associate certain attributes and knowledge useful in reasoning about or describing the products. Feature recognition converts a general CAD model into an application-specific feature model. A generic part feature recognition system should be able to:

- Extract design information of a part drawn from a CAD database
- Identify all surfaces of the part
- Recognize, reason about, and/or interpret these surfaces in terms of part features

All the functions should be performed automatically, without human interpretation or intervention. Once the features are recognized, CAPP systems can automatically develop the process plans for the part by using the part feature information.

It is worth mentioning that feature recognition is useful not only for computer-aided process planning but also in many other engineering applications that require information about the features of parts. For example, in group technology, the features of a part are helpful for classification or automatic coding. Other applications include assembly, measurement planning, and tolerancing.

5.6.1 A Brief Review of Part Feature Recognition Approaches

A number of approaches to part feature recognition for rotational as well as prismatic parts have been developed. They include syntactic pattern recognition (Jakubowski, 1982; Jakubowski and Flasinski, 1992), geometry decomposition (Woo, 1977, 1984), expert system rule logic (Li and Bedworth, 1988), graph-based (Joshi and Chang, 1988), and set theoretic (Perng et al., 1990).

The feature extraction techniques employed in rotational part feature recognition systems are mainly based on the syntactic pattern recognition and/or expert logic approach (Jakubowski, 1982; Jakubowski and Flasinski, 1992; Kyprianou, 1980; Srinivasan et al., 1985; Rosario, 1990; Sahay, 1990; Singh and Qi, 1992).

For prismatic (or polyhedral) parts, because the rotational property does not exist, the difficulty of both representation of a generic object and recognition of its features increases extensively. In this chapter we limit our exposition to the graph-based approach to feature recognition due to Joshi and Chang (1988).

5.6.2 Graph-Based Approach

Graph-based feature recognition usually consists of three basic steps:

STEP 1: Generating graph-based representation of the object to be recognized
STEP 2: Defining part features
STEP 3: Matching features in the graph representation

In the first step, an object is represented by graph. This step is necessary because the data extracted from the database are usually in the form of boundary representation (BREP) and are not directly usable for feature recognition. In order to recognize a feature, the information regarding the type of face adjacency and relationships between sets of faces should be expressed explicitly. To facilitate the recognition process, the concept of an attributed adjacency graph (AAG) is used.

5.6.2.1 Definition of Attributed Adjacency Graph

An AAG can be defined as a graph $G = (N,A,T)$, where N is the set of nodes, A is the set of arcs, and T is the set of attributes to arcs in A such that:

- For every face f in F, there exists a unique node n in N.
- For every edge e in E, there exists a unique arc a in A, connecting nodes n_i and n_j, corresponding to face f_i and face f_j, which share the common edge e.
- Every arc a in A is assigned an attribute t, where:

$t = 0$ if the faces sharing the edge form a concave angle (or "inside" edge)

$t = 1$ if the faces sharing the edge form a convex angle (or "outside" edge)

The AAG is represented in the computer in the form of a matrix, which is defined as follows:

$$
\begin{array}{c} \\ F_1 \\ F_2 \\ \cdot \\ \cdot \\ \cdot \\ F_n \end{array}
\begin{array}{c} \begin{array}{ccccc} F_1 & F_2 & \cdots & & F_n \end{array} \\
\begin{bmatrix} E_{1,1} & E_{1,2} & \cdots & E_{1,n} \\ & & & \\ \cdot & & & \\ \cdot & & & \\ \cdot & & & \\ E_{n,1} & E_{n,2} & \cdots & E_{n,n} \end{bmatrix} \end{array}
$$

where

$$
E_{i,j} = \begin{cases} 0 & \text{if } F_i \text{ forms a concave angle with } F_j \\ 1 & \text{if } F_i \text{ forms a convex angle with } F_j \\ \Phi & \text{if } F_i \text{ is not adjacent to } F_j \end{cases}
$$

From the preceding definition, we have the following observation: AAG defines the shape of a part uniquely up to its topology, if and only if the faces are cut orthogonally.

5.6.2.2 Definition of Part Features

To achieve feature recognition, we first need to define the feature precisely—that is, what shape we think is a feature. Generally speaking, we can define any shape as a feature; however, only those that have manufacturing meanings should be defined. Six commonly used features in manufacturing are the step, slot, three-side pocket, four-side pocket, pocket (or blind hole), and through hole. The definitions of some of the features are given below. The surfaces are labeled as shown in Figure 5.13.

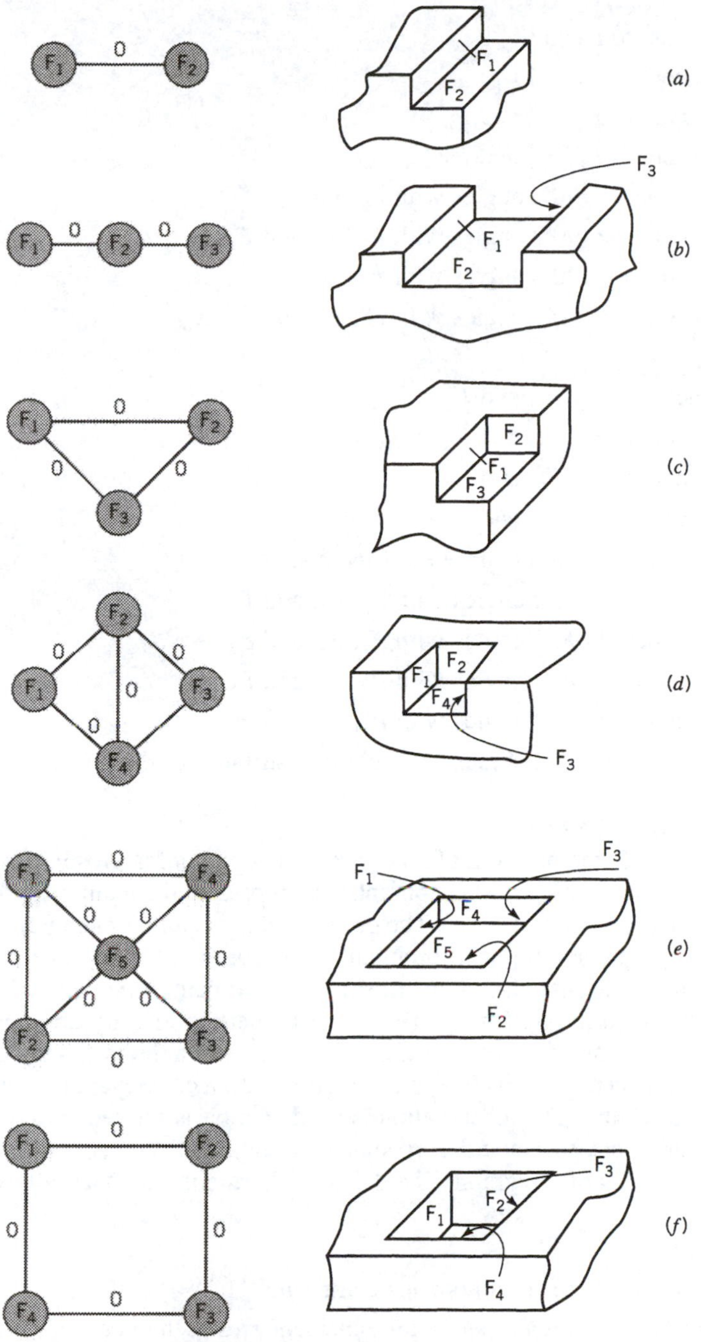

FIGURE 5.13 Defining features.

Four-Side Pocket
F_1 is adjacent to F_2 and F_4
F_3 is adjacent to F_2 and F_4
F_2 is adjacent to F_1, F_3, and F_4
F_4 is adjacent to F_1, F_3, and F_2
F_1 forms concave (90°) angles with F_2 and F_4
F_2 forms concave (90°) angles with F_3, F_1, and F_4
F_3 forms concave (90°) angles with F_2 and F_4
F_4 forms concave (90°) angles with F_1, F_2, and F_4

Blind Hole (Pocket)
F_1 is adjacent to F_2, F_4, and F_5
F_2 is adjacent to F_1, F_3, and F_5
F_3 is adjacent to F_2, F_4, and F_5
F_4 is adjacent to F_1, F_3, and F_5
F_5 is adjacent to all other surfaces of the pocket
F_1 forms concave (90°) angles with F_2, F_4, and F_5
F_2 forms concave (90°) angles with F_1, F_3, and F_5
F_3 forms concave (90°) angles with F_2, F_4, and F_5
F_4 forms concave (90°) angles with F_1, F_3, and F_5
F_5 forms concave (90°) angles with all other surfaces of the pocket

5.6.2.3 Matching the Features

After steps 1 and 2, the problem of recognizing machining features in part changes to the problem of recognizing AAG subgraphs that represent the features in the complete AAG graph that represents the part. The problem of searching for subgraphs in a larger graph is a subgraph isomorphism problem and is computationally exhaustive. There are no known polynomial algorithms to solve the problem in the general case.

An algorithm (Joshi and Chang, 1988) is used here to identify components of the graph that could form a feature. The algorithm is based on the following observation: A face that is adjacent to all its neighboring faces with a convex angle (270°) does not form part of a feature. This observation is used as a basis for separating the original graph into subgraphs that could correspond to features. The separation is done by deleting some nodes of the graph. The delete-node rule is stated as follows:

For all nodes:
If (all incident arcs of a node have attribute ''1'')
Then (delete this node (and all the incident arcs at the node) from AAG)

Because an AAG is represented in the form of a matrix in the program, the delete node rule actually deletes rows and columns that represent the nodes in the matrix.

The subgraphs produced by applying the delete-node rule may correspond directly to features. By applying feature recognition rules, we can determine whether or not a subgraph represents a feature. These rules are written according to the feature definition. Some of the rules used to identify these features are as follows:

Given an AAG graph:

It is a four-side pocket feature *if*

(The AAG subgraph has four nodes) *and*

(The number of arcs with attribute "0" is the number of nodes plus one).

It is a pocket feature *if*

(The AAG subgraph has five nodes) *and*

(The number of arcs with attribute "0" is the number of nodes plus three).

However, the delete-node rule may not succeed in separating a complete graph into subgraphs such that each subgraph corresponds to a feature. This is because of the intersection of features. When features intersect, they usually cannot be separated from a complete AAG by applying the delete-node rule. In fact, the only case in which a graph can be separated into a number of subgraphs with each subgraph representing a feature by the delete-node rule is that in which all the features are disjoint.

For intersecting features, the following procedure is used to separate the subgraphs:

- Delete all 1 arcs.
- Form the subgraphs that may or may not represent features.
- If not all the subgraphs represent features, restore the 1 arcs deleted within a subgraph.

The purpose of this procedure is to attempt to separate the graph into subgraphs. If it is unsuccessful, the graph remains unchanged. However, if the procedure is successful, it greatly reduces the computational effort.

We illustrate the graph-based approach to feature recognition by a small example from Li (1992).

EXAMPLE 5.4

It is easy for a human to see that the part shown in Figure 5.14*a* has a slot and a pocket feature. In this example, however, we simulate the computer to apply the feature recognition algorithm discussed earlier. We therefore want to solve the following:

(a) Develop the AAG of the object.

(b) Give the matrix representation of the AAG.

(c) Recognize the features in this object.

Solution

(a) First, we have to label each surface of the part. Given that the part is labeled as shown in Figure 5.14*a*, we develop the AAG as shown in Figure 5.14*b* from the definition of AAG. By the definition of AAG we mean that each surface of this part is represented by a node and each edge by an arc with attribute 1 or 0.

(b) For the purpose of inputting the AAG graph into the computer, we have to convert the graph to matrix form. The matrix representation of AAG is given as follows:

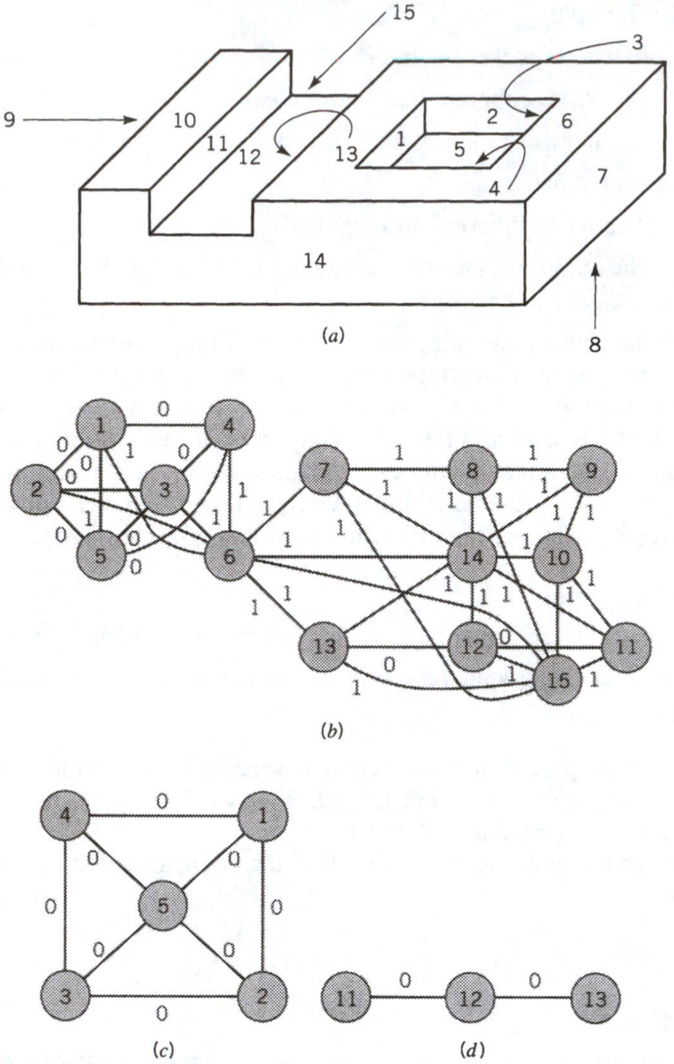

FIGURE 5.14 (*a*) Example part. (*b*) AAG for the example part. (Reproduced with permission from Li, 1992.) (*c*) AAG for slot feature. (*d*) AAG for pocket feature.

	F_1	F_2	F_3	F_4	F_5	F_6	F_7	F_8	F_9	F_{10}	F_{11}	F_{12}	F_{13}	F_{14}	F_{15}
F_1	9	0	9	0	0	1	9	9	9	9	9	9	9	9	9
F_2	·	9	0	9	0	1	9	9	9	9	9	9	9	9	9
F_3	·	·	9	0	0	1	9	9	9	9	9	9	9	9	9
F_4	·	·	·	9	9	1	9	9	9	9	9	9	9	9	9
F_5	·	·	·	·	9	9	9	9	9	9	9	9	9	9	9
F_6	·	·	·	·	·	9	1	9	9	9	9	9	1	1	1
F_7	·	·	·	·	·	·	9	1	9	9	9	9	9	1	1
F_8	·	·	·	·	·	·	·	9	1	9	9	9	9	1	1
F_9	·	·	·	·	·	·	·	·	9	1	9	9	9	1	1
F_{10}	·	·	·	·	·	·	·	·	·	9	1	9	9	1	1
F_{11}	*S*	*y*	*m*	*m*	*e*	*t*	*r*	*y*	·	·	9	0	9	1	1
F_{12}	·	·	·	·	·	·	·	·	·	·	·	9	0	1	1
F_{13}	·	·	·	·	·	·	·	·	·	·	·	·	9	1	1
F_{14}	·	·	·	·	·	·	·	·	·	·	·	·	·	9	9
F_{15}	·	·	·	·	·	·	·	·	·	·	·	·	·	·	9

where 9 represents the null set; that is, two faces are not adjacent or they are the same face.

(c) Apply the delete node rule of the algorithm; that is, delete the nodes connected with all "1" attribute arcs. Also, delete these "1" arcs. Doing this on the adjacent matrix, we remove the rows and columns without 0 elements. For example, row 15 and column 15 represent this type of arc and can be deleted. After all such arcs are deleted, the present matrix will result into two unrelated sub-matrices. Each sub-matrix represents a sub-graph. Observe that we do have "0" in column 12, which is F_{12}. We can see that two disjoint subgraphs are generated (see Figure 5.14*c* and *d*. Figure 5.14*c* has the same structure as the one shown in Figure 5.13*b*, which corresponds to the slot feature. Thus the first feature that is recognized is the slot feature. In the computer this matching is achieved by applying the identifying rules. That is, if AAG sub-graph has three nodes and the number of arcs with attribute "0" is 2, then it is a slot (see, section 5.6.2.3). Also, because Figure 5.14*d* has the same structure as the one shown in Figure 5.13*e*, it is a pocket. As there are no more features to be recognized, we conclude that there are two features in this part, a slot and a pocket.

5.7 FUTURE TRENDS IN COMPUTER-AIDED PROCESS PLANNING

One of the major strategies for reducing cost and lead time is to integrate various functional areas such as design, process planning, manufacturing, and inspection. Most of the systems developed provide a kind of interface among various functional areas. There are a number of difficulties in achieving the goal of complete integration. For example, each functional area has its own stand-alone relational database and associated database management system. The software and hardware incompatibilities among these systems pose difficulties in full integration. There is a need to develop a single-database technology to address these difficulties. Other challenges include automated translation of the design dimensions and tolerances into manufacturing dimensions and tolerances considering process capabilities and dimensional chains, automatic recognition of features, and making the CAPP systems affordable to the small and medium-scale manufacturing companies.

5.8 SUMMARY

Process planning is a link between design and manufacturing. It is therefore an important activity in helping to translate the design of products into salable manufactured products. In this chapter we provided an understanding of what process planning is all about. We discussed and illustrated with examples the elements of process planning, such as analysis of part requirements; selection of the raw workpiece; determining manufacturing operations and their sequences; selection of machine tools; selection of tools, jigs or fixtures, and inspection equipment; and determining machining conditions (cutting speed, feed, and depth of cut) and manufacturing times (setup time, processing time, and lead time). Various computer-aided process planning systems were reviewed. The graph-based approach to feature recognition was discussed and illustrated by an example.

PROBLEMS

5.1 What do you understand by process planning?

5.2 Discuss a variant process planning system.

5.3 Discuss a generative process planning system.

5.4 Discuss the differences between the systems in Problems 5.2 and 5.3.

5.5 A competitive manufacturing company has to deliver 300 units of a cylindrical part to a customer. The critical dimension is the diameter of the part, which is to be machined within 1 ± 0.003 in. Suppose there are three alternative machine tools with the information given in Table P5.1. Three manufacturing alternatives are available: engine lathe, automatic screw machine, and NC lathe. The company wants to know the unit cost of production and the manufacturing lead time as well as the expected number of defects produced on these machines. This information will be helpful to the company in considering a trade-off among the unit cost, manufacturing lead time, and quality represented by the number of defects and selecting a machine tool depending on the customer's requirement. Based on this information, advise the selection of machine tools.

The other data are:

Unit raw material cost = \$15.00

Unit salvage value = \$1.00

Process average = 1.0005 in.

5.6 Goldenburg and Associates (GA) have received an order for 500 gears. The primary dimensional control that GA has to worry about is the pitch circle diameter of the gear,

TABLE P5.1 **Basic Data on Types of Machine Tools**

Types of Machine Tools	*Standard Deviation, σ (in.)*	*Processing Cost per Unit,* f *(\$/unit)*	*Processing Time per Unit,* t *(min/unit)*
Engine lathe	0.001	10.00	1.00
Automatic screw machine	0.0004	15.00	0.90
NC lathe	0.0001	16.00	0.60

which should be within 3 ± 0.002 in. Because this item is being used in a number of products, GA wants to explore the possibility of using alternative technologies for its manufacture. A preliminary analysis indicates that a universal milling machine, a broaching machine with a form type of broaching cutter, and a hobbing machine are available within the company. Estimate the unit cost of production, manufacturing lead time, and expected number of defective gears produced on all these machine tools. The available data are shown in Table P5.2.

The other data are:

Unit raw material cost = \$10.00

Unit salvage value = \$2.00

Process average = 3.0002 in.

5.7 A lot of 1000 units of steel rods 40 cm long and 7 cm in diameter is turned on an NC lathe at a feed rate of 0.2 mm per revolution and depth of cut of 2 mm. The tool life is given by

$$vT^{0.25} = 190$$

The other data are:

Machine labor rate = \$10/h

Machine overhead rate = 200% of labor

Grinding labor rate = \$10/h

Grinding overhead rate = 300% of grinding labor

Loading and unloading time = 2 min/piece

Two types of carbide tools can be used for the turning operation: brazed inserts and throwaway inserts. The data related to the tools are:

Brazed Inserts

Original cost of the tool = \$25.00

Grinding time = 3 min

Tool changing time = 1 min

The tool can be ground only five times before it is discarded.

Throwaway Inserts

Tool cost = \$15.00

Tool changing time = 0.5 min

TABLE P5.2 **Basic Data on Types of Machine Tools**

Types of Machine Tools	*Standard Deviation, σ (in.)*	*Processing Cost per Unit,* f *(\$/unit)*	*Processing Time per Unit,* t *(min/unit)*
Universal milling machine	0.001	20.00	1.00
Broaching machine	0.0007	30.00	0.80
Hobbing machine	0.0001	32.00	0.70

Determine the following (assuming a single pass):

(a) Optimum tool life and optimum cutting speed to minimize the cost per piece
(b) Production rate for the minimum-cost criterion
(c) Optimum tool life and optimum cutting speed to maximize the production rate
(d) Production rate for the maximum production rate criterion
(e) Lead time to process the lot for the criteria of minimum cost per piece and maximum production rate
(f) Which tool should be recommended for minimum cost per piece criterion?
(g) Which tool should be recommended for maximum production rate criterion?

5.8 A 300-mm-diameter part having a 100-mm hole in the center is to be faced starting at the outside. Determine the machining time if the following data are available:

Spindle rotational speed = 10 revolutions per second
Depth of cut = 4 mm
Feed = 0.10 mm per revolution

5.9 A thousand bars 85 mm in diameter and 350 mm in length are to be machined to 84.75 mm in diameter. Only two cuts are permitted: a rough cut and a finishing cut. The following machining conditions are used for these cuts:

Rough cut
Cutting speed = 90 m/min
Feed rate = 0.10 mm/rev
Depth of cut = 0.1 mm

Finishing cut
Cutting speed = 120 m/min
Feed rate = 0.03 mm/rev
Depth of cut = 0.025 mm

Determine the machining time to turn the lot. Also determine the overall production time if the time taken to return to the beginning of the cut is 10 s and the loading–unloading time is 1.5 min.

5.10 A part involves the following turning operations:
(a) Facing
(b) External turning
(c) Drilling
(d) Boring

Determine the machining time for the part if it is processed in a lot of 200 units. The following information is available: The initial solid bar stock has a diameter of 100 mm and length of 150 mm. The external turning operation is performed at a cutting speed of 90 m/min, a feed rate of 0.10 mm/rev, and a depth of cut of 1.00 mm. A through-hole of diameter 15 mm is to be drilled on a lathe followed by a boring operation so that the diameter is 15.5 mm. Cutting speed and feed rate for drilling are 70 m/min and 0.10 mm/rev, respectively, and for boring 60 m/min and 0.05 mm/rev, respectively. The loading and unloading time is 2 min/piece. Assume any missing data.

5.11 Determine the machining time for face milling a workpiece if the cutter width is larger than the workpiece. The following data are given:

Milling cutter has 15 teeth and 60 mm diameter
Rotational speed = 300 rpm
Depth of cut = 4 mm
Feed = 0.020 mm per tooth
Length of workpiece = 400 mm

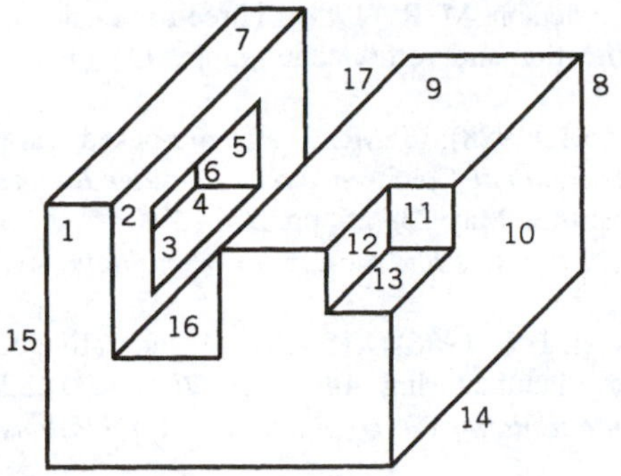

FIGURE P5.1 A part with intersecting features: a slot, a hole, and a three-side pocket.

5.12 Consider the manufacturing of a spur gear from a bar stock. The following operations are required:

(a) Face one end
(b) Turn outer diameter
(c) Part off
(d) Face other end
(e) Machine the internal bore
(f) Perform the boring operation if necessary
(g) Machine the keyway
(h) Gear teeth cutting

Explore possible alternative process plans.

5.13 Is it always justifiable to have a totally automated process planning system? Comment.

5.14 Develop a decision table for the selection of drilling machines using information from handbooks.

5.15 For the object shown in Figure P5.1, use the graph-based feature recognition approach to achieve the following:

(a) Develop the AAG of the object.
(b) Give the matrix representation of the AAG.
(c) Recognize the features in this object.

REFERENCES AND SUGGESTED READING

Alting, L., and Zhang, H. (1989). Computer aided process planning: The state of the art survey. *International Journal of Production Research,* 27(4):553–585.

Bedworth, D. D., Henderson M. R., and Wolfe, P. M. (1991). *Computer-Integrated Design and Manufacturing.* McGraw-Hill, New York.

Chang, T. C. (1982). TIPPS—A Totally Integrated Process Planning System, Ph.D. thesis, Virginia Polytechnic Institute and State University, Blacksburg, Virginia.

Chang, T. C., and Wysk, R. A. (1985). *An Introduction to Automated Process Planning System.* Prentice Hall, Englewood Cliffs, New Jersey.

Chang, T. C., Wysk, R. A., and Wang, H. P. (1991). *Computer-Aided Manufacturing.* Prentice Hall, Englewood Cliffs, New Jersey.

Choi, B. K., and Barash, M. M. (1988). STOPP: An approach to CADCAM integration. *Computer-Aided Design,* 17(4):162–168.

Chuang, S. H., and Henderson, M. R. (1990). Three-dimensional shape pattern recognition using vertex classification and vertex-edge graphs. *Computer Aided Design,* 22(61):377–387.

Dong, X., and Wozny, M. (1988). FRARES, a frame-based feature extraction system. *Proceedings of the International Conference on Computer Integrated Manufacturing,* Rensselaer Polytechnic Institute, May 23–25, pp. 296–305.

ElWakil, S. D. (1989). *Processes and Design for Manufacturing.* Prentice Hall, Englewood Cliffs, New Jersey.

Erve, A. H., and Kals, H. J. J. (1986). XPLANE: A generative computer aided process planning system for part manufacturing. *Annals of CIRP,* 35(1):325–329.

Fu, K. S. (1982). *Syntactic Pattern Recognition and Applications.* Prentice-Hall, Englewood Cliffs, New Jersey.

Gavankar, P., and Henderson, M. R. (1990). Graph-based extraction of protrusions and depressions from boundary representations. *Computer Aided Design,* 22(7):442–450.

Groppetti, R., and Semeraro, Q. (1986). CAPP—computer aided process planning using relational databases. *ISATA,* Flims, Switzerland, October 6–10.

Henderson, M. R., and Chang, G. J. (1988). FRAPP: Automated feature recognition and process planning from solid model data. *ASME Computers in Engineering Proceedings,* Vol. 1, August, pp. 529–536.

Henderson, M. R., and Musti, S. (1988). Automated group technology part coding from a three dimensional CAD database. *Transactions of ASME, Journal of Engineering for Industry,* 110(3):278–287.

Hormoz, Z., and Goulding, J. R. (1992). Neural networks in design of products: A case study. In *Intelligent Design and Manufacturing* (A. Kusiak, ed.), John Wiley & Sons, New York, pp. 179–201.

Houtzeel, A. (1976). *The MICLASS System, Proceedings of the CAM-I's Executive Seminar—Coding, Classification and Group Technology for Automated Process Planning.* CAM-I, Arlington, Texas.

Iwata, K., and Fukuda, Y. (1987). KAPPS: Know-how and knowledge assisted production system in the machine shop. *19th CIRP International Seminar on Manufacturing Systems,* Pennsylvania State University, University Park, June 1–2.

Jakubowski, R. (1982). Syntactic characterization of machined part shapes. *Cybernetics and Systems,* 13:1–24.

Jakubowski, R., and Flasinski, M. (1992). Towards a generalized sweeping model for designing with extraction and recognition of 3D solids. *Journal of Design and Manufacturing,* 2:1–20.

Joshi, S., and Chang T. C. (1987). CAD interface for automated process planning. *Proceedings of the 19th CIRP International Seminar on Manufacturing Systems,* June 1–2, pp. 39–45.

Joshi, S., and Chang, T. C. (1988). Graph-based heuristics for recognition of machined features from a 3D solid model. *Computer Aided Design,* 20(2):58–66.

Kalpakjian, S. (1992). *Manufacturing Engineering and Technology.* Addison-Wesley Publishing Company, New York.

Khoshnevis, B., and Chen, Q. (1990). Integration of process planning and scheduling functions. *Integrated Manufacturing Systems,* 1:165–176.

Kusiak, A. (ed.) (1992). Intelligent Design and Manufacturing. John Wiley & Sons, New York.

Kyprianov, L. K. (1980). Shape Classification in Computer-Aided Design, Ph.D. Thesis, University of Cambridge, England.

Lenau, T., and Alting, L. (1986). XPLAN—an expert process planning system. *Second International Expert Systems Conference,* London, September 30–October 2.

Lesko, J. F. (1983). MIPLAN implementation at Union Switch and Signal. Association for Integrated Manufacturing Technology, 20th Annual Meeting and Technical Conference, April.

Li, L., and Bedworth, D. D. (1988). A semi-generative approach to computer-aided process planning using group technology. *Computers and Engineering,* 14(2):127–137.

Li, R.-K., and Huang, C.-L. (1992). Assembly code generation from a feature-based geometric model. *International Journal of Production Research,* 30(3):627–647.

Li, R. K., Bor-wern Taur, and Hayn-jyu Shyur. (1991). A two-stage feature-based design system. *International Journal of Production Research,* 29(1):133–154.

Li, Y. (1992). A feature recognition algorithm for polyhedral parts. Unpublished Master's Thesis, Department of Industrial Engineering, University of Windsor (Canada).

Li, Y., and Singh, N. (1994). "A Neural Network Based Feature Recognition Algorithm for Polyhedral Parts", Working paper, Department of Industrial and Manufacturing Engineering, Wayne State University, Detroit.

Lindberg, R. A. (1990). *Processes and Materials of Manufacture,* Allyn & Bacon, Boston, chapter 19.

Liu, R. C., and Srinivasan, R. (1984). Generative process planning using syntactic pattern recognition. *Computers in Mechanical Engineering,* March, pp. 63–66.

Metzner, J. R., and Barnes, B. H. (1977). *Decision Table Languages and Systems.* Academic Press, New York.

Mortensen, K. S., and Belnap, B. K. (1989). A rule-based approach employing feature recognition for engineering graphics characterization. *Computer-Aided Engineering Journal,* December, pp. 221–228.

Park, J. Y., and Khoshnevis, B. (1993). A real time computer-aided process planning system as a support tool for economic product design. *Journal of Manufacturing Systems,* 12(2):181–193.

Perng, D. B., Chen, Z., and Li, R. K. (1990). Automatic 3D machining extraction from 3D CSG solid input. *Computer-Aided Design,* 22(5):285–296.

Reinschmidt, K. F., and Finn, G. A. (1992). Integration of expert systems, databases, and computer-aided design. In *Intelligent Design and Manufacturing* (A. Kusiak, ed.). John Wiley & Sons, New York, pp. 133–156.

Rogers, J. S., Farrington, P. A., Schroer, B. J., and Hubbard, R. G. (1994). Automated process planning system for turned parts. *Integrated Manufacturing Systems,* 5(4/5):41–47.

Rosario, L. M., and Knight, W. A. (1989). Design for assembly analysis-extraction of geometric features from a CAD system database. *Annals of CIRP,* Vol. 38, no. 1 pp. 13–16.

Sahay, A., Graves, G. R., Parks, C. M., and Mann, L. Jr. (1990). A methodology for recognizing features in two-dimensional cylindrical part designs. *International Journal of Production Research,* 28(8):1401–1416.

Singh, N., and Qi, Dengzhou (1992). A structural framework for part feature recognition: A link between computer-aided design and process planning. *Integrated Manufacturing Systems,* 3(1):4–12.

Srinivasan, R., Liu, C. R., and Fu, K. S. (1985). Extraction of manufacturing details from geometric models. *Computers and Industrial Engineering,* 9(2):125–133.

Ssemakula, M. E., and Rangachar, R. (1989). The prospects of process sequence optimization in CAPP systems. *Computers and Industrial Engineering,* 16(1):161–170.

Staley, S. M., Henderson, M. R., and Anderson, D. C. (1983). Using syntactic pattern recognition to extract feature information from a solid geometric data base. *ASME Computer Mechanical Engineering,* 2(2):61–66.

Steudel, H. (1990). Process planning. In *Process and Materials of Manufacture* by R. A. Lindberg, Allyn & Bacon, Boston, pp. 823–845.

Strohmeier, A. H. (1987). Implementing computer aided process planning: Rockwell International case study. *CIM Review,* 4(1):34–41.

Tulkoff, J. (1987). Process planning in the computer-integrated factory. *CIM Review,* 4(1):24–27.

Wang, H.-P., and Li, Jian-Kang (1991). *Computer-Aided Process Planning,* Vol. 13. Elsevier Science Publisher, Amsterdam.

Wang, H. P., and Wysk, R. A. (1987). A knowledge-based computer aided process planning system. *19th CIRP International Seminar on Manufacturing Systems,* Pennsylvania State University, University Park, June 1–2.

Wang, H. P., and Wysk, R. A. (1989). A knowledge-based approach for automated process planning. *International Journal of Production Research,* 27(6):999–1014.

Warnecke, H. J., and Muthsam, H. (1992). Knowledge-based systems for process planning. In *Intelligent Design and Manufacturing* (A. Kusiak, ed.). John Wiley & Sons, New York, pp. 377–396.

Woo, T. C. (1977). Computer aided recognition of volumetric designs. In *Advances in Computer-Aided Manufacturing.* North-Holland, Amsterdam, pp. 121–136.

Woo, T. C. (1982). Feature extraction by volume decomposition. *Proceedings of the Conference on CAD/CAM Technology in Mechanical Engineering,* MIT, Cambridge, Massachusetts, pp. 76–94.

Woo, T. C. (1984). Interfacing solid modelling to CAD and CAM data structures and algorithms for decomposing a solid. *Computer,* 17(12):44–49.

Yankee, H. W. (1979). *Manufacturing Processes.* Prentice Hall, Englewood Cliffs, New Jersey.

Zhang, H. C. (1987). Overview of CAPP and Development of XPLAN. Institute of Manufacturing Engineering. Technical University of Denmark, Publication 87-26.

Zhang, K. F., Wright, A. J., and Davies B. J. (1989). A feature recognition knowledge base for process planning of rotational mechanical components. *International Journal of Advanced Manufacturing Technology,* 4(1):13–25.

COMPUTER CONTROL OF MANUFACTURING SYSTEMS*

The utilization of computers in various manufacturing applications has proved to be one of the most significant developments over the last couple of decades in helping to improve the productivity and efficiency of manufacturing systems. In this chapter we look closely at some of the technologies used in the automated control of manufacturing systems. In the first part of the chapter, we look at one of the earliest applications of computers to control of individual manufacturing functions at the shop floor level using numerical control. Later in the chapter, we consider the more recent developments involving the use of programmable logic controllers and computers that can be used to control a variety of functions at the system level.

Numerical control (NC) is a term used to describe the control of the various functions of a machine by the use of numeric data.The term was coined at the Massachusetts Institute of Technology (MIT), where the first successful NC machine was demonstrated under a subcontract from the Parsons Corporation of Traverse City, Michigan, funded by the U.S. Air Force. Numerical control is now applied to a wide range of machines including welding, riveting, bending, hole-making, and drafting machines. However, the vast majority of NC machines in use today are metal-cutting machine tools. In the following discussion of numerical control, we shall concentrate on machine tool applications but keep in mind that the basic principles are applicable to all numerically controlled machines.

6.1 METAL-CUTTING MACHINES

The metal-cutting operation (also called *machining*) is one of the most important manufacturing processes in industry today. In addition to being a primary manufacturing process, it is used as a finishing operation after other processes such as casting or forging because of its ability to achieve very high dimensional accuracy and close surface finish. The nature of the metal-cutting process involves removal of excess

* The author of this chapter is Dr. Mukasa E. Ssemakula, Associate Professor, Division of Engineering Technology, Wayne State University, Detroit, Michigan.

material from a raw workpiece using a cutting tool, thus changing the shape of the workpiece. By controlling how the excess material is removed, we can control what the final shape of the workpiece will be. Material removal is achieved by forcing a sharp cutting edge (the cutting tool or simply tool for short) into the workpiece and causing relative motion between the tool and the workpiece. Thus, the material to be removed is in effect peeled off the raw workpiece. In the metal-cutting context, the material removed is called a chip.

Of course, metals are hard and therefore high forces are required, first to feed the tool into the workpiece and then to force relative motion between the tool and the workpiece so as to remove chips. Power-driven machines (also called machine tools, not to be confused with cutting tools) are used which are capable of generating the high forces required and causing the relative motion between the cutting tool and the workpiece at a sufficiently high rate (called the cutting speed) to achieve a reasonable material removal rate. Relative motion between the cutting tool and the workpiece can be achieved by keeping the workpiece stationary and moving the tool or by keeping the tool stationary and moving the workpiece.

The main function of a machine tool is to control the workpiece–cutting tool positional relationship in such a way as to achieve a desired geometric shape of the workpiece with sufficient dimensional accuracy. Actual machine tool movements are made up of one or more degrees of freedom. By combining these degrees of freedom and controlling their relationships to one another, it is possible to produce various geometric shapes such as cylinders or flat surfaces. In using a machine tool to carry out a machining operation, we need to be able to accomplish the following basic machining functions:

1. Determining the location on the workpiece where machining is to be done
2. Controlling the path followed during the motion of the tool or workpiece
3. Controlling the rate at which the path is traversed
4. Controlling the rate at which the tool is fed into the workpiece

The first two functions in particular are crucial in ensuring that a component of the correct shape is produced. With conventional machine tools, a human operator loads the workpiece onto the machine tool. The operator is also responsible for setting the position of the cutting tool to ensure that the correct amount of material is removed at the right position and maintaining the correct workpiece–cutting tool positional relationship during the machining process. As a rule, it takes longer to position the tool as the accuracy required of the finished component increases. In particular, if shapes other than simple straight lines or straight cylinders are to be produced, simultaneous control of more than one axis of the machine has to be maintained. This can be quite difficult on conventional machines. The final quality of the components made is highly dependent on the knowledge and skill of the machine operator. But even with a skilled operator, it is impossible to guarantee consistent levels of quality over a long production run or from one day to another.

6.1.1 Numerically Controlled Machines

An NC machine tool is functionally the same as a conventional machine. The technological capabilities in terms of machining are no different from those of conventional machines. The difference between NC machines and conventional machines is in the way in which the various machine functions and slide movements are controlled. With

NC machines, functions such as positioning the tool, turning the spindle on and off, setting cutting speeds or feed rates, and turning coolant on and off are removed from the realm of the machine operator and turned over to a machine control unit (MCU) associated with the NC machine. The MCU issues commands in the form of numeric data to motors controlling the individual machine functions. The MCU can be used to control the direction and rate of slide motion, spindle rotation, tool changes, coolant, and so forth. In fact, the first NC machine demonstrated by MIT was a conventional machine retrofitted with appropriate motors and control systems, and many early NC machines were retrofitted conventional machines. Figure 6.1*a* shows a photograph of a

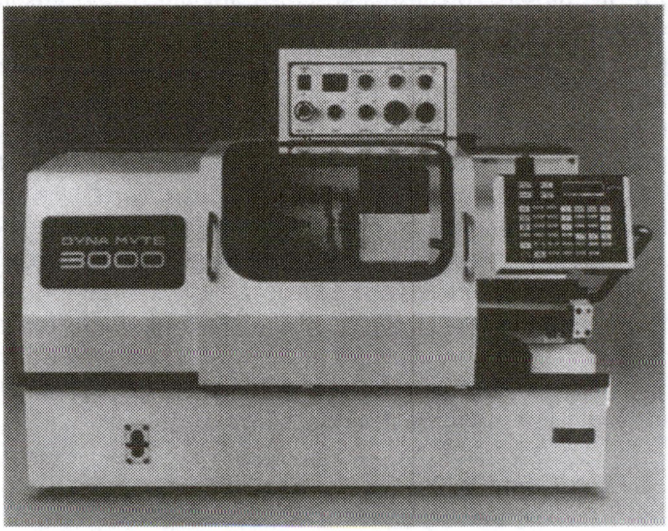

(a)

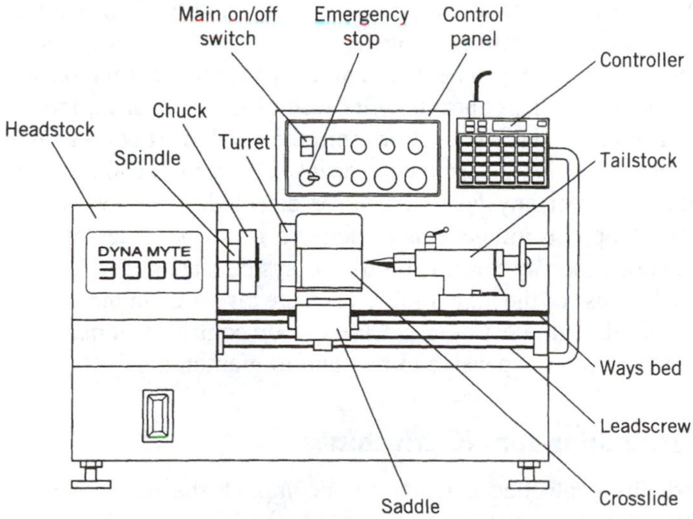

(*b*)

FIGURE 6.1 A typical NC lathe used for teaching purposes. (Used with permission of Dyna Mechatronics.)

tabletop NC lathe, used in teaching environments, and Figure 6.1*b* shows a line drawing of the same machine with its associated nomenclature.

6.1.1.1 Types of NC Control Systems

Two basic types of control systems are used with NC machines. The earliest form of control was open-loop control, and this was followed by closed-loop control.

6.1.1.2 Open-Loop Control

This type of control system is used with a special motor called a stepper motor. With this type of control, signals in the form of current pulses are sent from the MCU to the individual motor being controlled. Each pulse results in a finite predetermined amount of revolution of the motor. To cause a specified amount of movement, the control system determines how many current pulses are required and sends precisely that number to the motor. Thus, the control does not need to monitor specifically where the motor is located; it is assumed that the required motion is achieved if the correct number of pulses is sent. The control system needs only to keep track of how many revolutions (or parts thereof) the motor has gone through, to know the motor's position. With NC machines, it is possible to design the motor to produce a movement of as little as one-thousandth of an inch for each pulse, resulting in precise control of position. Open-loop control systems are less costly, less complex, and easier to maintain and they are popular with smaller NC machines. However, with this type of control system, there is no way to correct any errors that might occur during operation because there is no feedback to the controller. Also, in general, stepper motors cannot generate the same amount of torque as other types of motors and therefore these systems are not suitable for use with large machines that require greater power.

6.1.1.3 Closed-Loop Control

Conventional variable-speed direct current (DC) motors (also called servos) are used with this type of control system. DC motors have the important advantage of being able to generate very high levels of torque, and they can, in essence, be reversed instantly. However, they cannot be caused to move in very precise amounts as stepper motors can. In order to keep track of the position of the motor, a separate position sensor, called a resolver, has to be fitted and the position information so determined is fed back as a signal to the controller. Because of this feedback, the system forms a closed loop. The positional information from the resolver is compared with the target position and any errors are determined. Because DC motors can be reversed instantly, it is possible to correct any positional error detected. This ability to correct errors enables closed-loop control systems to achieve up to an order of magnitude better accuracy than open-loop systems. Closed-loop systems are generally used in the larger NC machines because of the higher load. They are also used in machines where greater accuracy is desired, regardless of size. Closed-loop control systems are more complex, however, and thus more expensive to buy and to maintain.

6.1.2 Programming for NC Machines

For a numerically controlled machine to accomplish the required machining operations, the necessary data have to be entered into the MCU. The MCU can then convert the data into commands that can be issued to the appropriate motors for the necessary functions to be executed. The series of data that is fed into the MCU to generate the required machine tool commands is referred to as an NC part program. (*Note:* A part program refers to the program required to machine a specific part or component; it is not meant to suggest that the program is incomplete!) The process of writing an NC part program is called NC part programming, and the person responsible for writing the part program is called the NC part programmer. The part programming function is clearly a critical function if NC machines are to be used effectively in a production environment. Whereas the use of NC machines leads to a reduction in the need for skilled machine operators to operate the machines directly, it creates a need for people with the appropriate skills to be able to write good part programs that are used in actual machining.

The NC programmer needs to have intimate knowledge of a wide range of manufacturing processes and possess skill as a machine operator. In particular, he or she needs to have a thorough knowledge of the capabilities of the machine for which the program is being written. This ensures that the program written makes maximum use of the machine's capabilities without violating its technological constraints. The current resource availability respecting cutting tools, jigs and fixtures, labor available, or any other material-handling equipment such as robots or automated guided vehicles (AGVs) must also be taken into account. In writing the part program, the programmer generally starts with an engineering drawing of the part to be made. This must be interpreted to determine the individual operations that should be performed on the workpiece to produce the final component according to the design specifications. It is the basis used to determine the order in which the operations should be carried out, establish the cutting conditions to be used during each machining operation, determine associated non-machining operations (e.g., tool changing, machine setup, coolant use), and select the appropriate jigs and fixtures to be used to hold the workpiece while machining is being done. These functions are what we generally associate with process planning, so in fact the NC programmer is frequently responsible for carrying out these process planning tasks for parts made on NC machines. Once all this information has been determined, it must be coded in a form that can be programmed into the MCU that controls the actual machine operation; that is, the part program itself must be written.

6.1.3 Motion and Coordinate System Nomenclature for NC Machines

Remember that a part program is a series of coded instructions for effecting the various machine functions necessary to make a specific part on a particular machine tool. Among the most important of these functions is maintaining the correct tool–workpiece positional relationship during machining. This is achieved by establishing a coordinate system and then defining tool–workpiece motion in terms of the coordinate system. The standard coordinate system used is the right-handed Cartesian coordinate system, with axes designated as x, y, and z. Figure 6.2 shows the relationship between the axes of such a coordinate system and how it can be applied to some common machines.

In relating the various coordinate axes and motions to a particular machine, the following general principles are followed:

1. *z-axis.* This is the most important axis for machining and it is always aligned with the spindle that imparts cutting power. This spindle might rotate the workpiece as in a lathe, or it might rotate a tool as in a milling machine. If no such spindle exists on a specific machine, the z-axis is perpendicular to the

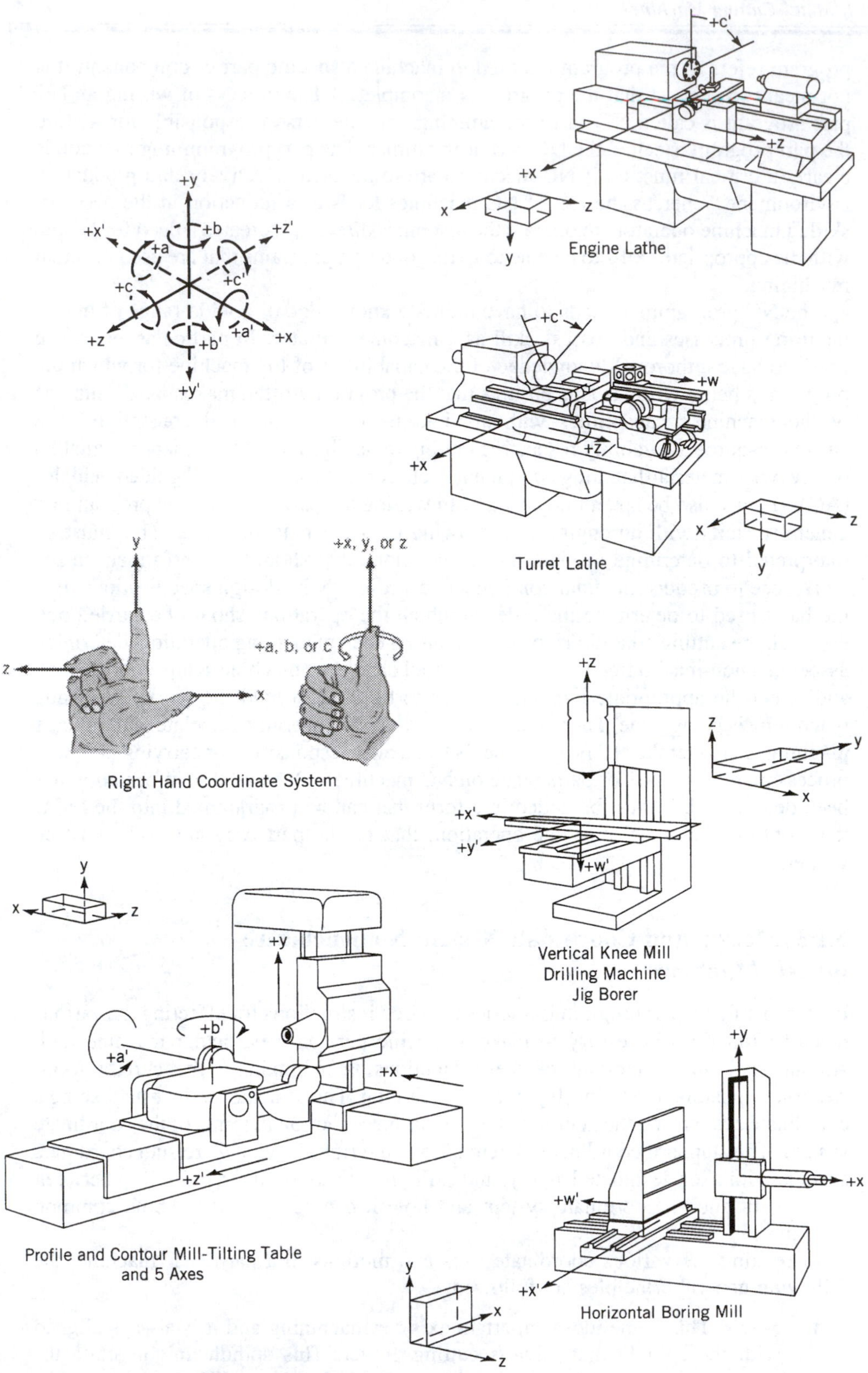

FIGURE 6.2 The right-handed Cartesian coordinate system and its application to some common machines. (*Source:* EIA Standard RS-267 B. Used with permission of the Electronic Industries Association.)

workholding surface. For reasons that will become evident later, positive motion in z tends to increase the separation between the workpiece and the tool.

2. *x-axis.* The x-axis is the principal axis of motion in which the moving element (tool or workpiece) is positioned. It is parallel to the workholding surface and is arranged to be horizontal if possible. On machines with rotating workpieces, it is radial and parallel to the cross-slide. On machines with rotating tools,
   - If the z-axis is horizontal, the positive x motion is to the right when looking from the spindle to the workpiece.
   - If the z-axis is vertical, the positive x motion is to the right when looking from the spindle to the column.

   On machines with nonrotating workpieces and nonrotating tools, the x-axis is parallel to and directed toward the principal cutting direction.
3. *y-axis.* Once the z- and x-axes are established, the y-axis must be in such a direction as to complete a right-handed Cartesian coordinate system.
4. *Supplementary linear motions.* On some machines, there are secondary linear motions parallel to the primary x, y, and z motions. Such supplementary motions are designated U, V, and W respectively.
5. *Rotary motions.* Motions A, B, and C are rotary motions about axes respectively parallel to the x-, y-, and z-axes. A positive rotary motion is in a direction that would cause a right-handed screw to advance in the positive direction of the axis of rotation.
6. *Spindle rotation.* Counterclockwise spindle rotation is considered positive. It is the rotation that would cause a right-handed screw to recede from the workpiece.

6.2 BASICS OF NC PART PROGRAMMING

What moves? We saw in our earlier discussion that machining is achieved by digging the tool into the workpiece and causing relative motion between the two. For some machines, the tool undergoes the primary motion, whereas for some others the workpiece undergoes the primary motion. When writing an NC part program, it is always assumed that it is the tool that undergoes the primary motion. Thus, the part programmer does not have to remember which element moves for which machine. It is easier for the programmer to visualize motion of the tool relative to the workpiece during the programming stage. If it is indeed the tool that moves relative to the workpiece, such as in turning operations, the motions programmed are the motions that actually take place. If it is the workpiece that moves relative to the tool, such as in milling, the programmed motions have to be translated internally by the MCU to cause the workpiece to move in such a way as to achieve the equivalent relative motion that was programmed for the tool.

Where is the tool? The NC part program includes, among other things, commands that move the tool to various locations relative to the workpiece. To be able to specify the required tool positions, some reference point is required. This reference point, used within the program as the basis of defining tool location and other geometric entities, is referred to as the *origin.* The MCU keeps track of current tool location relative to the origin. The tool itself is defined as a point. For single-tooth cutting tools such as those used in turning, the point defining the tool corresponds to the location of the cutting tip of the tool. For multiple-teeth tools such as drills or milling cutters, the point defining the tool is the center of the cutter. In a given program, the origin is usually a point determined by the programmer. Generally, the programmer assumes that at the beginning of the program, the tool is located at some specific point relative to the workpiece, which is designated as the origin. In practice, during setup and before any programmed motion, the machine operator has to move the tool to the position designated by the programmer as the origin and then depress a special button on the control panel that zeros the axis counters in the MCU. Thus, a zero location is set that serves as the origin for the program. Because the designated point could be anywhere within the machine's range of travel, this is called a *floating zero.* (*Note:* For some older NC machines, the origin is a preset fixed location.) In defining the motion of the tool from one point to another, either absolute positioning mode or incremental positioning mode can be used.

1. *Absolute positioning.* In this mode, the desired target position of the tool for a particular move is given relative to the origin point of the program. Because the MCU always keeps track of the current location of the tool, it is a simple matter for it to calculate the actual distance and direction of motion required to go from the current location to the target. This approach, however, is more demanding of the programmer, who has to determine the absolute coordinates of all target points, which may involve many calculations.
2. *Incremental positioning.* In this mode, the next target position for the tool is given relative to the current tool position. In many cases, this is easier for the programmer. The task of calculating absolute tool position is left to the controller, which continues to keep track of the actual tool location at any instant. With this approach, however, it is critical for the programmer to ensure that the final tool position at the end of the program is identical to the initial tool position. If this is not the case, errors can build up during the machining of successive parts using the same program.

Modal and nonmodal commands. Commands issued in the NC program may stay in effect indefinitely (until they are explicitly canceled or changed by some other command), or they may be effective for only the one time that they are issued. The former are referred to as *modal* commands. Examples of modal commands include feed rate selection and coolant selection. Commands that are effective only when issued and whose effects are lost for subsequent commands are referred to as *nonmodal* commands. A dwell command, which instructs the tool to remain in a given configuration for a given amount of time, is an example of a nonmodal command.

6.2.1 Structure of an NC Part Program

An NC program is made up of a series of commands that are input into the MCU in a serial manner. The MCU interprets these commands and generates the necessary signals to each of the drive units of the machine to accomplish the required action. The NC program is required to have a particular structure that the controller can understand and it must follow a specific syntax. Commands are input into the controller in units called *blocks* or *statements*. Each block is made up of one or more machine commands. In general, several commands are grouped together to accomplish a specific machine operation, hence the use of a block of information for each operation. Each command gives a specific element of control data, such as a dimension or a feed rate. Each command within a block is also called a *word.* The way in which individual commands (or words) are arranged within the block is referred to as the *block format.* The three different block formats being used in the industry are:

1. Fixed sequential format
2. Tab sequential format
3. Word address format

The first two were used in earlier machines and are now essentially obsolete. However, some of the machines on which they are implemented are still in service and it is important for the reader to be familiar with all three formats.

6.2.1.1 Fixed Sequential Format

This was the earliest block format used for NC machines and it spawned the name *numerical control* because in this format only numbers are used. With this format, each block in the program consists of exactly the same number of words, entered in a specified sequence, and each word consists of a fixed number of data characters. The data characters are either numbers or signs to indicate whether the associated number is positive or negative. The data are interpreted according to where they are located within the block and thus the data positions are significant. Characters cannot be omitted and no extra characters can be included because doing either would change the meaning of the data. Every word must be represented even if this requires using a series of zero characters or repeating previously entered values. Clearly, this frequently results in giving unnecessary information and leads to very long programs. The programs themselves, being given simply as a series of numbers, are difficult for a human to interpret, let along debug. Exhibit 6.1 shows a sample set of statements in this format. In this exhibit, spaces have been inserted between words to highlight the relationship between words. These spaces would not be used in the actual program. The reader is cautioned here to focus on the structure of the statements. The meaning will be explained later in Section 6.3.1.3.

Exhibit 6.1 Fixed Sequential Format

```
0050 00 +0025400 +0012500 +0000000 0000 00
0060 01 +0025400 +0012500 −0010000 0500 08
0070 01 +0025400 +0012500 +0000000 0500 09
```

6.2.1.2 Tab Sequential Format

This format is essentially the same as the fixed sequential format. The difference is that each word within a block (except for the first word) is preceded by a TAB character. The main improvement over fixed sequential format is that the TAB character for a specific word need not be followed by numeric data if data are not required in that particular block or if they are modal data that have not changed from the previously given value. The TAB character indicates the beginning of a new word but does not specify which type of word; therefore the sequence of the words remains significant. Exhibit 6.2 is a repetition of the commands in Exhibit 6.1, but written in the tab sequential format. Once again, spaces are inserted between words for ease of interpretation. These spaces would not be used in the actual program. The reader is again cautioned to focus on the structure of the statements. The meaning will be explained in Section 6.3.1.3.

Exhibit 6.2 Tab Sequential Format

```
0050 TAB 00 TAB +0025400 TAB +0012500 TAB TAB TAB
0060 TAB 01 TAB TAB TAB −0010000 TAB 0500 TAB 08
0070 TAB 00 TAB TAB TAB +0000000 TAB 0000 TAB 09
```

6.2.1.3 Word Address Format

This is the format that is used on virtually all modern controllers and will be explained in greater detail. With this type of format, each type of word is assigned an address that is identified by a letter code within the part program. Thus, the letter code specifies the type of word that follows and then its associated numeric data is given. For example, the code T represents a tool number. Thus, a word of the form T01 would be interpreted as representing tool number 1. In theory, with this approach, the words in a given block can be entered in any sequence and the controller should be able to interpret them correctly. In practice, however, most controllers have restrictions on the order in which words are entered and this is specified in each controller's manual.

With the word address format, only the needed words for a given operation have to be included within the block. The command to which particular numeric data applies is identified by the preceding address code. Thus, it is easy to omit unneeded commands. Word address format has the additional advantage of making it possible to have more than one command of the same type in a single block, something that would be impossible with the other two formats. Table 6.1 shows a listing of the most widely used word addresses and their meanings. A complete list of address words is given in the Appendix.

The American National Standards Institute (ANSI) has established a standard method of specifying word address data for any controller, which has been adopted by most manufacturers. A typical specification might look as follows:

$$N4G2X\pm 43Y\pm 43Z\pm 43R\pm 43F\pm 40S\pm 40T2M2I43J43K43$$

TABLE 6.1 **Commonly Used Word Addresses**

Address	*Meaning*
F	Feed rate command
G	Preparatory function
I	Circular interpolation: x-axis offset
J	Circular interpolation: y-axis offset
K	Circular interpolation: z-axis offset
M	Miscellaneous commands
N	Sequence number
R	Arc radius
S	Spindle speed
T	Tool number
X	x-axis data
Y	y-axis data
Z	z-axis data

Within the specification, a letter identifies a specific type of word as in Table 6.1. A ± symbol after the letter indicates that sign is significant for the associated numeric data. Generally, a positive sign is assumed if numeric data have no sign specified. If one numeral follows the letter, the data for that word are of integer form with up to the number of digits specified by the numeral. If the letter (and associated sign where applicable) is followed by two numerals, the data for that word are real numbers. The decimal point is not to be programmed explicitly; its position is inferred by counting the number of digits in the actual data associated with the word, counting from the right. The second numeral in the specification gives the number of digits to count in the data before the decimal point. The first numeral in the specification gives the number of allowable digits in the data to the left of the decimal point. In general, it is assumed that leading zeros may be suppressed. So for the sample specification just given we have:

N word can have up to four integer digits with no associated sign.

G word can have up to two integer digits with no associated sign.

X word can have up to seven real digits, which may be positive or negative. The decimal point, which is not explicitly entered, is assumed to be three digits from the right, and there can be up to four digits to the left of the decimal point in metric format.

F word can have up to four real digits, which may be positive or negative. The decimal point, which is not explicitly entered, is in the rightmost position and there can be up to four digits to the left of the decimal point.

I word can have up to seven real digits with no associated sign. The decimal point, which is not explicitly entered, is assumed to be three digits from the right, and there can be up to four digits to the left of the decimal point in metric format.

The reader should now be able to interpret the format for the rest of the words in the sample specification. It is imperative that the programmer know the format specification for the machine for which a particular program is being written in order to be able to write suitable programs. There are variations between machines, and it cannot be assumed that a program written for one machine will run successfully on another machine. For example, some machines do not allow suppression of leading zeros. Other machines have the capability to suppress trailing zeros. Still other machines require that decimal points are entered explicitly as part of the word data. The total number of digits in the word data also varies from machine to machine, as does the number of digits before or after a decimal point (whether implicit or explicit). The commands used in Exhibits 6.1 and 6.2 are repeated in Exhibit 6.3, written in word address format, for a machine that has the preceding format specification. Again, spaces have been inserted between words for ease of interpretation. The reader is still urged to focus on the structure rather than the meaning.

Exhibit 6.3 Word Address Format

```
N50 G00 X25400 Y12500 Z0 F0
N60 G01 Z-10000 F500 M08
N70 Z0 M09
```

It is clear from our example that the word address format is considerably easier to use than the other two formats and that it also results in shorter programs. Note that spaces can be used in the word address format and, when used, are simply ignored by the controller.

6.3 FUNDAMENTALS OF NC PART PROGRAMMING

The first step in writing an NC part program is to determine and organize the data that will be used within the program. As we have seen, the NC programmer has to carry out process planning functions such as selecting specific machining processes to use in making the part, the associated cutting speeds and feeds, the cutting tools to use, and so on. For simple components, these decisions can be made mentally and the program coded directly. For more complicated parts, however, it is preferable to organize the data systematically in a formal process plan. The process plan will list in proper sequence all the individual operations that have to be carried out to make the part, the workholding devices needed, and tools to be used. The programmer will also need to decide whether to use coolant during the machining process and such other details related to each operation. Refer to the previous chapter for more details of process planning. Once all the required data have been determined, the programmer is ready to go ahead and code the program.

A fully coded NC part program generally consists of five broad categories or classes of command. These are listed below in no particular order, followed by a description of each class of command and how the commands can be used in an NC program. Use of the word address format is assumed throughout the following discussion. Because there are wide differences between controllers, it is important to consult the manual for the particular MCU used to determine what commands are actually available for that controller and the specific meaning, usage requirements, and effects of each command as implemented on the controller.

1. *Preparatory functions.* These are used to inform the MCU of the requirements for the machining that is to be carried out and thus to establish the necessary operating conditions.
2. *Axis motion commands.* These are used to control the amount of relative motion between the cutting tool and the workpiece along each machine axis.
3. *Feed and speed commands.* These are used to set and control the cutting conditions for individual machining operations.
4. *Identification commands.* These are used to identify specific entities in the program, such as cutting tools used.
5. *Miscellaneous commands.* These are used to control various other aspects of the machine's operation not addressed elsewhere, such as turning the spindle on and off and changing tools.

6.3.1 Preparatory Functions

Preparatory functions form the largest class of commands used in NC programs. They are identified by the word address letter G followed by two digits. The digits specify the particular type of function. The combination is referred to as a G code. In general, preparatory functions have the effect of making the MCU assume specific operating conditions or command the controller to perform the next task in a particular manner. Preparatory functions generally take effect before execution of the other commands within the block in which the function is programmed. It is usually permissible to program more than one preparatory word in a block provided the words do not have conflicting effects. Most preparatory functions are modal. Efforts have been made to standardize NC commands, and Table 6.2 shows some of the more widely used standard G codes. A complete list of G codes is given in the Appendix. Bear in mind, however, that not all codes are available on all machines and also that a manufacturer may give a particular code a meaning other than the standard meaning. Furthermore, some of the available codes have not been assigned specific meanings in the standard and each MCU maker is free to use such codes for any functions deemed important in a particular application. *Always check the manual to verify the meaning of a particular code on a specific controller.*

6.3.1.1 Explanation of Some Commonly Used G Codes

G00 is a preparatory function to specify that the tool should be moved to a specified location. This function is used only to control the final position of the tool and is not concerned with the path that is followed in arriving at the final destination. For this reason, motion with this function is also referred to as *positioning mode*. The way this code is implemented in most controllers is that all axes that need to be moved in order to get to the target point are moved simultaneously at the beginning of the motion, with each axis being moved at maximum speed. As an example, for motion that occurs in the $x-y$ plane with the same maximum speed for the x- and y-axes, initial motion is at an angle of 45° to the axes until motion in one of the axes is completed and then the balance of the motion occurs in the other axis. This is called point-to-point motion. This function is typically used for positioning the tool without carrying out any machining during the motion of the tool. See path *ABC* illustrated in Figure 6.3.

G01 is another preparatory function to specify that the tool should be moved to a specified location. It differs from the G00 function in that the path followed by the tool in moving to the target point is required to be the straight line connecting the current tool position and the target position. Thus, the path followed by the tool is in effect specified by the programmer. Because this function always causes the tool to follow a linear path between two points, it is also referred to as *linear interpolation*. If motion in more than one axis is involved, the MCU coordinates the simultaneous motions in the axes to generate a straight-line path. The rate of travel during the motion is specified by the programmer giving a feed rate value. This function is typically used to specify machining of straight features such as turning a chamfer on a lathe or cutting a slot on a milling machine. Path *AC* in Figure 6.3 is as an example of linear interpolation.

TABLE 6.2 **Some Common G Codes**

Code	*Function*
G00	Point-to-point positioning, high rate
G01	Linear interpolation, controlled feed rate
G02	Circular interpolation, clockwise
G03	Circular interpolation, counterclockwise
G04	Dwell for programmed duration
G17	Select $x-y$ plane
G18	Select $x-z$ plane
G19	Select $y-z$ plane
G70	Inch units
G71	Metric units
G90	Absolute dimensions
G91	Incremental dimensions

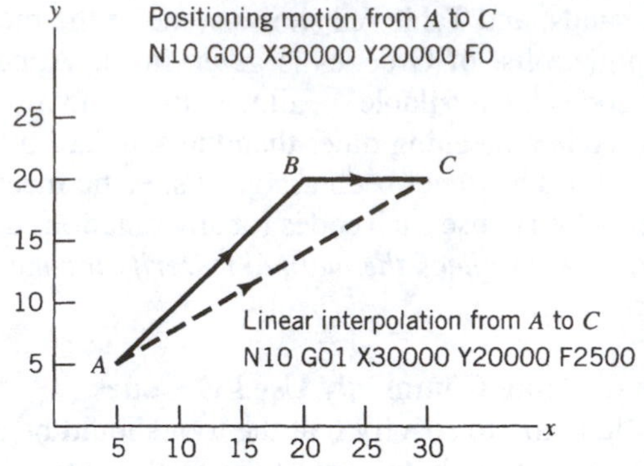

FIGURE 6.3 Positioning and linear interpolation for NC.

G02 is also a preparatory function to specify that the tool should be moved to a specified location. It differs from the G00 and G01 functions in that in this case the path followed by the tool in moving to the target point is required to be a circular arc, starting from the current tool position, moving in a clockwise direction, and ending at the target position. Within the block in which the G02 code is programmed, the center of the arc is given by specifying its location relative to the start of the arc. An appropriate combination of I, J, and K words (depending on the plane in which motion occurs) is used to specify the location of the center of the arc relative to the start of the arc. Thus, the path followed by the tool is again specified by the programmer. This type of motion is referred to as *circular interpolation.* In this case, motion in more than one axis is always involved and the MCU coordinates the simultaneous motions to generate the circular path. An example of circular interpolation is given in Figure 6.4.

On most machines, circular interpolation can be carried out within only one of three possible planes at a time. The available planes are $x-y$, $z-x$, and $y-z$. Usually the $x-y$ plane is assumed if a plane is not explicitly specified. Codes G17–G19 are used to select the plane of operation. A further restriction on many machines is that a circular interpolation command can be effective within only one of the quadrants formed by the intersection of the axes of the coordinate system within the plane of operation, and the maximum angle of the arc is 90°. For such systems, if a circular path is required to

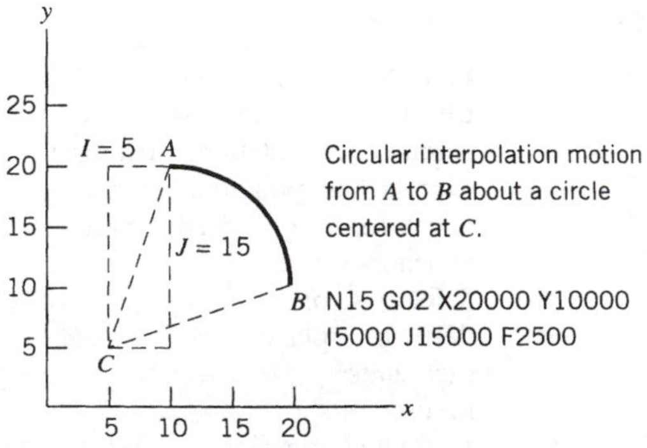

FIGURE 6.4 Circular interpolation for NC.

cross the axes, motion up to the axis has to be programmed in one block, and then further circular motion starting from the axis has to be programmed in the next block. Some sophisticated machines are capable of multiquadrant circular interpolation, which is enabled by a G75 code and disabled by a G74.

G03 is circular interpolation similar to G02 except that all motion occurs in a counterclockwise direction.

6.3.1.2 Canned Cycles

Some sequences of machining operations are used so frequently with different machines and different components that they have been standardized and assigned special preparatory functions. For example, a simple hole-drilling operation involves the following sequence of operations:

1. Position the tool just above the point where the hole is to be drilled.
2. Set the correct spindle speed.
3. Feed the tool into the workpiece at a controlled feed rate to a predetermined depth.
4. Retract the tool at a rapid rate to just above the point where the hole started.

The same sequence of operations is repeated for any simple drilling operation regardless of the machine used. This sequence of operations would require several blocks of code if each motion were programmed individually. However, a special drilling cycle code (G81) has been developed. By using the G81 preparatory function, the programmer achieves the same effect in only one block. The location and depth of the hole to be drilled, speed and feed to be used, and height above the part surface for positioning before and after drilling are all specified in the block. This kind of specialized cycle is referred to as a canned cycle or fixed cycle. Several such cycles have been standardized for use on all controllers, and some others are defined by individual manufacturers to provide more specialized capabilities. Table 6.3 shows the most commonly used standardized canned cycles. The effect of any one of these canned cycles is canceled by programming a G80 function.

Consider the use of the simple drilling cycle, for example. Using the G81 canned cycle, the same set of motions achieved in Exhibits 6.1–6.3 can be attained in a single block as shown in Exhibit 6.4.

Exhibit 6.4 Canned Cycle for Drilling

```
N50G81X25400Y12500Z-10000F500M08
```

TABLE 6.3 **Commonly Used Canned Cycles**

Code	*Function*	*Down Feed*	*At Bottom*	*Retraction*
G81	Drilling	Continuous feed	No action	Rapid
G82	Spot face, counterbore	Continuous feed	Dwell	Rapid
G83	Deep hole drilling	Peck	No action	Rapid
G84	Tapping	Continuous feed	Reverse spindle	Feed rate
G85	Through boring (in and out)	Continuous feed	No action	Feed rate
G86	Through boring (in only)	Continuous feed	Stop spindle	Rapid
G87	Chip breaker drilling	Intermittent	No action	Rapid
G88	Chip breaker drilling	Intermittent	Dwell	Rapid
G89	Through boring with dwell	Continuous feed	Dwell	Feed rate

6.3.1.3 Explanation of Programs in Exhibits 6.1–6.4

The commands given in Exhibits 6.1–6.4 all lead to the same types of motion, as detailed in the following explanation. Using a rapid feed rate, the tool is positioned at the coordinate location (25.4, 12.5, 0). The tool is then advanced −10 units in the z-direction at a feed rate of 500 mm/min, with the flood coolant on. The tool is then retracted back 10 units at the rapid feed rate, and the coolant is turned off. The corresponding motions are shown in Figure 6.5. With the zero datum assumed to be 0.5 unit above the surface of the part, these commands have the effect of drilling a through hole in a workpiece material 9 units thick. The reader can now appreciate the progressive simplification in the programming task for the four examples. Explanations of other G codes and canned cycles similar to the ones given here can always be found in the manual for the controller being used.

6.3.2 Axis Motion Commands

Axis motion commands are used to specify the axes that are required to move during the execution of a given command. They are made up of a letter specifying an axis such as x, followed by dimensional information associated with the motion of the axis in question. The X, Y, and Z commands, respectively, specify motion of the Cartesian coordinate axes themselves; I, J, and K specify offset values relative to the x-, y-, and z-axes, respectively; while A, B, and C specify rotation about the x-, y-, and z-axes. Some controllers support the use of polar coordinates, in which case R and A axes are used to specify the radial and angular directions, respectively. The dimensional data associated with an axis command can represent absolute dimensions (if G90 was specified) or they may be incremental values (if G91 was specified). Most control systems require that I, J, and K data used in specifying circular interpolation be given as incremental values regardless of whether G90 or G91 is in effect elsewhere in the program. The dimensional data associated with axis commands consist of real numbers that may or may not have a sign associated with them. The actual format for the data is given as part of the specification of the controller. Typically, axis motion commands define the target location of the tool after some required motion. As previously discussed, the motion itself may be point to point, linear interpolation, or circular interpolation.

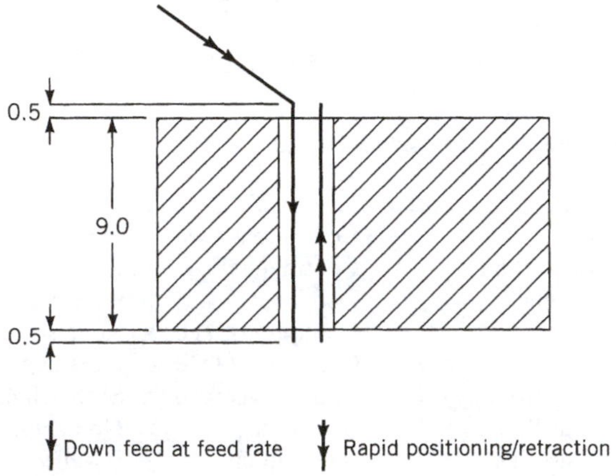

FIGURE 6.5 Drilling motion for Exhibits 6.1–6.4.

An important point to remember is that axis commands guide the motion of the point defining the tool position. For some operations, such as profile milling, the periphery of the cutter moves along the surface to be machined, rather than the tool point (i.e., the center of the cutter). Thus, actual motion of the tool point has to be along a path different from the geometry of the machined surface. This difference is called a tool offset, and the programmer has to account for it when writing the program. Most modern controllers can be programmed using an offset tool by applying a compensating factor called the cutter compensation. With this approach, once the offset between the tool point and the machined surface is specified, the tool motion can be programmed as if the tool point followed the actual machined surface. The controller adjusts internally for the difference in the actual path followed by the tool point. Cutter compensation (where available) is programmed using the G41 and G42 preparatory codes and canceled using the G40 code. The data defining the required tool offsets are entered separately at the MCU.

6.3.3 Feed and Speed Commands

Feed and speed commands are used to specify the feed rate and speed to use during the machining operation. The feed command is specified by the address word F followed by the numerical value of the feed rate required; the speed command is specified by the address word S followed by the required speed. The feed rate and speed used during machining are of crucial importance in determining how long it will take to make a part. Therefore, they play a key role in the overall economics and productivity of the process. Choosing very low values will result in large processing times, low productivity, poor quality, and an uneconomical product. Choosing excessively large values can result in broken tools, damaged workpieces, a high scrap rate, and again, uneconomical products. One of the skills required of the NC programmer is the ability to select optimum cutting conditions given the constraints inherent in the production process. Selection of optimum cutting conditions is discussed in Chapter 5.

The units for cutting conditions can be specified in a variety of ways in the NC program. For example, the feed rate may be specified directly in units per minute or units per revolution, where the units may be inches or millimeters. The cutting speed may be specified in spindle revolutions per minute or directly as a surface cutting speed (ft/min or m/min). The preparatory functions G92–G98 are used to designate how the cutting conditions are to be specified. With many machines, maximum available feed rate can be specified by giving the value as F0.

6.3.4 Identification Commands

Identification commands are used within an NC part program for the simple task of being able to identify certain entities within the program. The N word is the most widely used identification command and it is used to identify individual blocks within the program. The identification data in this case consist of integer numbers written in a format given as part of the machine specification. Usually three or four digits are used and leading or trailing zeros are not suppressed. The N word is purely for the convenience of the humans writing or using the program, so that they can distinguish between the various blocks in the program. The MCU itself does not use the data contained in the N word. Because the controller does not use the block identification data, it is not strictly necessary to number the blocks in any particular order. However, for the convenience of the human users, blocks are generally numbered in ascending order, with increments of 5 or 10 between consecutive blocks. The reason for having increments of 5 or 10 is that, when necessary, additional blocks may be inserted in the program while maintaining the generally ascending order in which blocks are numbered. For example, block N047 may be inserted between blocks N045 and N050. The resulting block numbers are not strictly consecutive, but they are in ascending order.

The other widely used identification command is the T word. This is used to identify individual cutting tools used within the program. For most components, more than one tool is required to complete the machining operations needed to make the part. For many NC machines, multistation tool turrets or tool magazines housing several cutting tools are used. The programmer uses the T word to specify to the controller which of the various tools available should be used for a particular machining operation. The format of the T word usually consists of two unsigned digits after the T. The programmer must also develop a separate tool listing detailing which tool has been assigned what code so that the tools may be set up properly on the machine.

Other identification commands are used to identify special sections of the part program, such as loops and macros, that can be executed more than once during the running of the program. The method of identifying these facilities is not standardized and the reader is advised to consult the manual of a specific controller for details that apply to a particular machine. The use of loops and macros in NC programs is discussed later under advanced features (Section 6.3.7).

6.3.5 Miscellaneous Commands

Miscellaneous commands are used to control a variety of machine functions that are not covered by the other commands. The address word M followed by two unsigned digits is used to specify miscellaneous commands. Examples of functions controlled by miscellaneous commands are turning the spindle on and off, turning coolant on and off, initiating a tool change, clamping and unclamping the workpiece, interrupting and restarting program execution, stopping the program, and rewinding the program. Generally, miscellaneous commands take effect after execution of the other commands in the block in which they are programmed. It is usually permissible to program more than one miscellaneous command in a given block provided they do not have conflicting effects. Many of the M codes have been assigned standardized functions. However, some available codes have not been assigned specific meanings, to afford MCU makers flexibility in providing specific capabilities they consider important. Some of the more commonly used M codes are given in Table 6.4. A complete list of M codes is

TABLE 6.4 **Some Common M Codes**

Code	*Function*
M00	Program stop
M01	Optional stop
M02	End of program
M03	Spindle on CW
M04	Spindle on CCW
M05	Spindle off
M06	Tool change
M07	Mist coolant on
M08	Flood coolant on
M09	Coolant off
M30	End of program—rewind

given in the Appendix. Bear in mind as always that it is necessary to double check with the manual of a particular controller to verify that the codes have been assigned standard meanings by the manufacturer and also to determine what nonstandard codes have been implemented by the manufacturer. The effect of most M codes is self-explanatory.

6.3.6 Special Characters

In addition to the commands outlined in the preceding pages, certain special characters are used in NC part programs to achieve special effects. Some of these special characters are used with all controllers, but others are particular to specific controllers. These characters include the % sign, common to all controllers, which is used as the first line of the NC program. The character signals the controller when the beginning of the program has been reached during a rewind of the program, so that it will stop rewinding. To separate successive blocks within the program, an end-of-block character is used at the end of each block of the program. This special character is produced by hitting a carriage return on a keyboard (or end of line followed by carriage return on older systems). The character itself does not print when the program is printed. During coding, the end-of-block is frequently represented by the * symbol or the letters EOB. Another special character is the / character, which indicates commands that may optionally be skipped during program execution. This is used for making parts that differ slightly in detail or for which the raw material, such as a casting, may vary appreciably from one part to another. The omitted portion of the program would account for the differences. To effect the omission of the optional commands, a special switch on the control unit must be set. The detailed format required for this facility varies between controllers, so again it is imperative to check the manual. Other special characters that are sometimes used include =, #, and $, which are usually related to characterizing special controller capabilities such as defining loops and macros. When available, these special capabilities and how they are utilized would be fully described in the manual.

EXAMPLE 6.1

Write an NC program to machine a $\frac{1}{2}$-in.-wide L-shaped slot in a mild steel workpiece with dimensions 3 × 2.75 × 0.75 in. as shown in Figure 6.6.

Assumptions:

1. The top lower left corner will be used for program zero.
2. Machining motion will start in the indicated position.
3. The tool is $\frac{1}{4}$ in. above the top surface of the part prior to start of machining.
4. The tool diameter used is $\frac{1}{2}$-in., so only one pass is required.
5. A cutting speed of 500 rpm and feed rate of 10 in./min are used for machining.
6. Machine specification: N3G2X±43Y±43Z±43R±43F4S4T2M2.

Solution

The following program can be used to carry out the required machining. A brief explanation of the effect of each command is included.

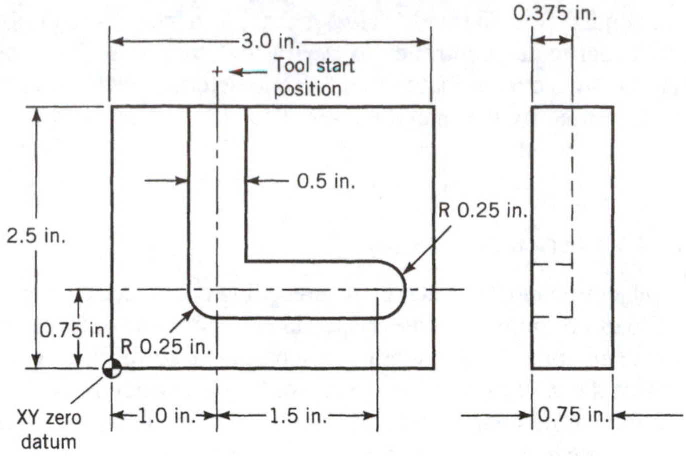

FIGURE 6.6 A slot milling example.

%	Indicates start of program
N005 G90 G70	Specifies absolute dimensions, inch units
N010 G97 G94 T01	Specifies units for speed and feed rate; loads first tool
N015 G00 X1000 Y3000 Z250 F0	Rapid positioning of tool to start point
N020 G01 Z-375 M03 S500 F10	Turns on spindle, feeds tool to required depth
N025 Y750	Machines the vertical portion of the L
N030 X2500	Machines the horizontal portion of the L
N035 Z250	Retracts tool to 0.25 in above part surface
N040 X-1000 Y-1000 F0	Moves to safe location at rapid rate
N045 M30	Turns off all machine functions

EXAMPLE 6.2

Write an NC program to machine the simple aluminum pin shown in Figure 6.7. A 2-in.-diameter blank, $2\frac{1}{2}$-in. long, is to be used.

Assumptions

1. The center of the left face of the pin will be used for program zero.
2. The tool start position is 0.2 in. off the diameter and 0.1 in. off the right face.
3. Two roughing cuts (0.1 in. deep) and one finish cut (0.05 in. deep) will be taken.
4. A spindle speed of 1200 rpm and feed rate of 12 in. /min are used for machining.
5. Machine specification: N3G2X$\pm$43Y$\pm$43Z$\pm$43R$\pm$43F40S4T2M2.
6. X values are to be programmed as diameters.

Solution

The following program can be used to carry out the required machining. A brief explanation of the effect of each command is included.

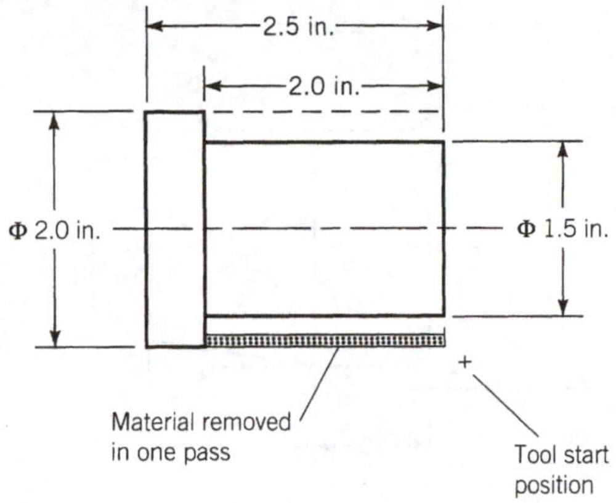

FIGURE 6.7 A simple turning example.

%	Indicates start of program
N005 G90 G70	Specifies absolute programming, inch units
N010 G98 G92 T01	Specifies units for speed and feed rate, loads 1st tool
N015 G00 X2200 Z2600 F0	Rapid positioning of tool to tool start position
N020 X1800 M03 S1200 F0	Position tool to remove 0.1 in. off part diameter, start spindle
N025 G01 Z500 F12	Feed tool into workpiece
N030 X1900	Retract tool (overlap previous cut)
N035 G00 Z2600 F0	Move tool clear of workpiece
N040 X1600 F0	Position tool to remove 0.1 in. off part diameter
N045 G01 Z500 F12	Feed tool into workpiece
N050 X1700	Retract tool (overlap previous cut)
N050 G00 Z2600 F0	Move tool clear of workpiece
N060 X1500 F0	Position tool to take finish cut
N065 G01 Z500 F12	Feed tool into workpiece
N070 X2200	Retract tool clear of the workpiece
N075 G00 X5000 Z5000 F0	Move to safe position
N080 M30	Turn off all machine functions

EXAMPLE 6.3

Write an NC program to machine the aluminum part shown in Figure 6.8. A 50-mm-diameter blank, 65-mm long, is to be used.

Assumptions

This is the process sequence used: face off to final length, rough cut 40-mm diameter in two passes, rough turn taper in two passes, finish machine to final dimensions. Absolute programming has been used; spindle speed is specified in rev/min and feed rate in mm/min. Note the use of F0 to specify rapid feed rate. X values are to be programmed as radii. The specification of the machine to be used is N3G2X± 43Y± 43Z± 43R± 43F4S4T2M2.

Solution

The following program can be used to carry out the required machining. The reader should now be able to interpret most of this program, in light of the preceding examples. Some explanatory comments are given only for the more difficult elements.

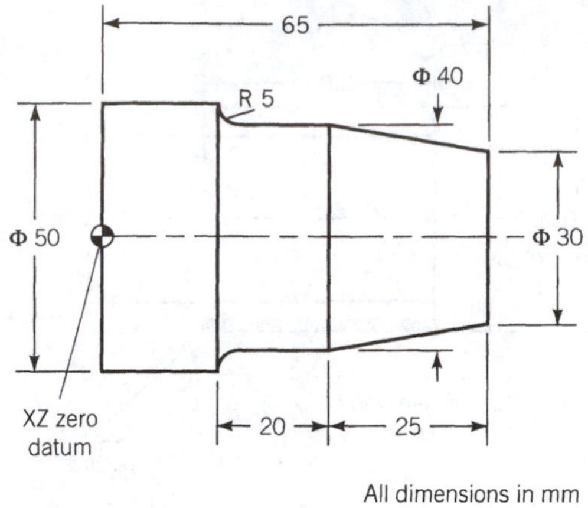

FIGURE 6.8 A more elaborate turning example (Φ = diameter).

```
%
N001 G90 G71
N005 G98 G95 T01
N010 G00 X26000 Z66000 F0                Rapid move to tool start position
N015 M03 S750 M08                        Turn on spindle and coolant
N020 G01 X23000 F225                     Position tool for first cut
N025 Z23000                              First rough cut
N030 X23500
N035 G00 Z66000 F0
N040 G01 X21000 F225                     Position tool for second cut
N045 Z25000                              Second rough cut
N050 X21500
N055 G00 Z66000 F0
N060 G01 X18000 F225                     Position for start of rough taper
N065 X21000 Z50000                       First rough taper
N070 X21500
N075 G00 Z66000 F0
N080 G01 X16000 F225                     Position for second rough taper
N085 X21000 Z40000                       Second rough taper
N090 X21500
N095 G00 Z66000 F0
N100 G01 X15000 F225                     Position for start of finishing cut
N105 X20000 Z40000                       Finish taper
N110 Z25000                              Finish 40 mm diameter
N115 G03 X25000 Z20000 I5000 K5000       Finish 5 mm radius
N120 G01 X26000 M09                      Clear the part, turn off coolant
N125 G00 Z66000 F0 M30                   Move to safe place, turn off all machine
                                         functions
```

EXAMPLE 6.4

Repeat Example 6.3 for the part shown in Figure 6.9, which is made out of steel. The blank is 150 × 135 × 15 mm. Program zero is the lower right corner.

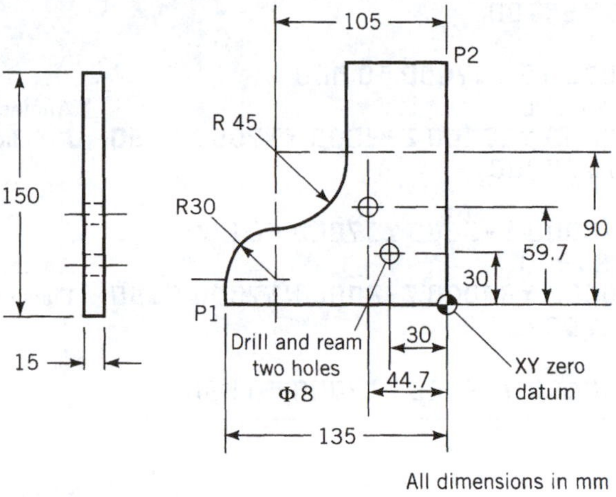

FIGURE 6.9 A more elaborate milling example.

Solution

The following sequence of processes is assumed. Rough machine the profile, finish machine the profile, then center drill, drill, and final ream the two holes. Absolute programming has been used; spindle speed is specified in rev/min and feed rate in mm/rev. Again, explanations are given for the more difficult elements.

%	
N005 G90 G71	
N010 G98 G95 T01	
N012 G00 X50000 Y0 Z17000 F0	Initial tool position
N015 G00 X2000 Y15200 Z17000 M03 S500 F0	Position for first cut, turn on spindle
N020 G01 Z-2000 F375	Feed tool down
N025 X-62000	Start of rough profile
N030 Y90000	
N035 G02 X-105000 Y47000 I43000 J43000	Clockwise rotation for 45-mm radius
N040 G03 X-137000 Y15000 I32000 J32000	Counterclockwise rotation, 30-mm radius
N045 G01 Y-2000	
N050 G00 Z-17000 F0	End of rough profile, retract tool
N055 G00 X2000 Y150000 F0	Position for second cut
N060 G01 Z-2000 F375	
N065 X-60000	Start of finish profile
N070 Y90000	
N075 G02 X-105000 Y45000 I45000 J45000	
N080 G03 X-135000 Y15000 I30000 J30000	
N085 G01 Y-2000	Last part of finish profile
N090 G00 X50000 Y0 Z17000 F0 M00	Move clear of part, stop spindle
N095 T02 M03 S2000	Change tool, restart spindle
N100 G81 X-30000 Y30000 Z12000 R17000 F100	Center drill holes, using drill cycle

```
N105 X-44700 Y59700
N110 G80
N115 G00 X50000 Y0 Z17000 F0 M00
N120 T03 M03 S1000                              Another tool change
N125 G81 X-30000 Y30000 Z-2000 R17000 F150      Drill holes
N130 X-44700 Y59700
N135 G80
N140 G00 X-140000 Y-5000 Z17000 F0 M00
N145 T04 M03 S1200                              Another tool change
N150 G81 X-30000 Y30000 Z-2000 R17000 F150      Finish ream the holes
N155 X-44700 Y59700
N160 G80
N165 G00 X-140000 Y-5000 Z17000 F0 M30
```

6.3.7 Advanced Features

With the progress in controller capabilities, several advanced features are becoming available on NC machines that were not possible with earlier machines. Among these are the ability to take a portion of the program and execute it in a rotated or mirrored position, the ability to scale the program and produce larger or smaller features than those programmed, and capabilities such as three-dimensional circular interpolation, which produces a helical shape (also called helical interpolation), as well as parabolic and cubic interpolation for producing free-form designs. Another useful feature is the ability to execute part of the program more than once. This can be accomplished by the use of either loops or macros. Loops and macros can both be considered to be types of subroutines. The difference is that loops are executed immediately on being encountered in the program. The statement that activates the loop specifies how many times the loop is to be executed. Macros, on the other hand, are not executed immediately. Once defined, a macro can be activated from anywhere within the program, with the calling statement actually activating the macro. Thus, a loop has to be programmed *after* the block that calls it up whereas a macro has to be programmed *before* the block that calls it up. A macro can contain a loop, and a loop may contain a macro provided the macro has been programmed before the loop. Readers familiar with programming in high-level languages such as FORTRAN will see the similarity with DO loops and subroutines.

6.4 LOADING THE PROGRAM

For the NC program to be executed, it has to be loaded into the MCU. A variety of methods can be used to prepare the program for loading into the MCU. One of the most widely used forms of program storage and input to NC machines is the 1-in.-wide punched paper tape. Punched tape uses a binary-based representation code that is efficient for the machine to read and provides a compact storage medium. Numbers in the program are represented in a modified binary form called binary-coded decimal (BCD). Non-numeric characters are also assigned specific codes in this representation scheme. The digit 1 in the BCD representation of a number is represented by a punched hole on the tape, whereas the digit 0 is represented by the absence of a hole. BCD is slightly less efficient for data storage than pure binary but is easier for humans to interpret if the need arises. Two standard coding schemes have emerged and are widely used in industry. One is the Electronic Industries Association (EIA) Standard RS-244A and the other is the American Standard Code for Information Interchange (ASCII) standard. The EIA standard was the earlier one and probably has a larger installed base of machines. The ASCII standard, which developed later, is intended to serve other needs in addition to NC tapes and therefore is more robust. Newer machines now mostly use the ASCII standard, although they also usually have the capability to accept EIA tape.

With each standard, a character is represented by a series of holes punched across the width of the tape. Each character is represented by a specific pattern of holes. A total of eight tracks are available across the width of the tape for punching holes. In each coding scheme, one of the eight channels is reserved for checking the accuracy of the punched information. This is done by using a scheme called parity check. The EIA scheme uses odd parity. This requires that every row of tape have an odd number of punched holes. If the character represented in that row in fact has an odd number of ones (i.e., punched holes), nothing needs to be done. If, however, the actual number of ones for a particular character is even, an extra hole is punched in the parity channel so that this, together with the holes for the character, results in an odd number of holes. Thus, the system can make a rough check on the accuracy of punched data by counting the number of holes. For example, if an even number of holes is found in a given row of the tape in this case, it is recognized as an error. The ASCII scheme follows the same logic but uses even parity. (Parity check is only a rough check and lack of parity error does not guarantee accuracy of data. This has to be verified by other means.) Figure 6.10 shows a comparison of the two standards.

6.4.1 Conventional Numerical Control

With conventional numerical control, once the program is on tape, it is read into the MCU by a tape reader on the controller. The program is read and executed one block at a time. At the end of the program, the tape is physically rewound to get ready for machining the next component. (This is the reason for using the % character described earlier to indicate the beginning of the program and hence the stop of the rewinding.) The tape then has to be stored if it is to be used for making more parts in the future. Perforated paper tape is fragile and can be difficult to handle and store conveniently, especially at a facility with a large number of programs of different lengths. Another problem is that if a program has to be altered, for example, because of program errors or engineering changes, the complete tape must be replaced. Once a program has been verified and there are no errors in it, a more durable material such as Mylar is sometimes used for the production tape.

Another important aspect of conventional numerical control is that, in general, the MCU has only a limited range of capabilities. Most of the functionality of the controller is fixed in the way the controller is built; in other words, the various capabilities are hardwired and cannot be changed. For example, some early NC controllers were capable of incremental programming but not absolute programming; others were capable of linear interpolation but not circular interpolation. The greater the range of capabilities desired in a given controller, the more expensive it was to buy. Consequently the buyer had to make a trade-off between the cost and usefulness of various

	ISO code										EIA code									Meaning
	8	7	6	5	4		3	2	1		8	7	6	5	4		3	2	1	Track Number
Character										Character										
0			O	O		o				0			O			o				Numeral 0
1	O		O	O		o			O	1						o			O	Numeral 1
2	O		O	O		o		O		2						o		O		Numeral 2
3			O	O		o		O	O	3				O		o		O	O	Numeral 3
4	O		O	O		o	O			4						o	O			Numeral 4
5			O	O		o	O		O	5				O		o	O		O	Numeral 5
6			O	O		o	O	O		6				O		o	O	O		Numeral 6
7	O		O	O		o	O	O	O	7						o	O	O	O	Numeral 7
8	O		O	O	O	o				8					O	o				Numeral 8
9			O	O	O	o			O	9				O	O	o			O	Numeral 9
A		O				o			O	a		O	O			o			O	Address A
B		O				o		O		b		O	O			o		O		Address B
C	O	O				o		O	O	c		O	O	O		o		O	O	Address C
D		O				o	O			d		O	O			o	O			Address D
E	O	O				o	O		O	e		O	O	O		o	O		O	Address E
F	O	O				o	O	O		f		O	O	O		o	O	O		Address F
G		O				o	O	O	O	g		O	O			o	O	O	O	Address G
H		O			O	o				h		O	O		O	o				Address H
I	O	O			O	o			O	i		O	O	O	O	o			O	Address I
J	O	O			O	o		O		j		O		O		o			O	Address J
K		O			O	o		O	O	k		O		O		o		O		Address K
L	O	O			O	o	O			l		O				o		O	O	Address L
M		O				o	O		O	m		O		O		o	O			Address M
N		O			O	o	O	O		n		O				o	O		O	Address N
O	O	O			O	o	O	O	O	o		O				o	O	O		Address O
P		O		O		o				p		O		O		o	O	O	O	Address P
Q	O	O		O		o			O	q		O		O	O	o				Address Q
R	O	O		O		o		O		r		O			O	o			O	Address R
S		O		O		o		O	O	s			O	O		o		O		Address S
T	O	O		O		o	O			t			O			o		O	O	Address T
U		O		O		o	O		O	u			O	O		o	O			Address U
V		O		O		o	O	O		v			O			o	O		O	Address V
W	O	O		O		o	O	O	O	w			O			o	O	O		Address W
X	O	O		O	O	o				x			O	O		o	O	O	O	Address X
Y		O		O	O	o			O	y			O	O	O	o				Address Y
Z		O		O	O	o		O		z			O		O	o			O	Address Z

FIGURE 6.10 Comparison of ISO and EIA codes for NC data.

ISO code										EIA code										Meaning
	8	7	6	5	4		3	2	1		8	7	6	5	4		3	2	1	Track Number
Character										Character										
DEL	O	O	O	O	O	o	O	O	O	Del		O	O	O	O	o	O	O	O	Delete (cancel or error punch)
NUL						o				Blank						o				Not punched
BS	O				O	o				BS			O		O	o		O		Backspace
HT					O	o			O	Tab			O	O	O	o	O	O		Tabulator
LF or NL					O	o		O		Cr or EOB	O					o				End of block
SP	O		O			o				SP				O		o				Space
%	O		O			o	O		O	ER					O	o		O	O	Absolute rewind stop
(			O		O	o				(2-4-5)				O	O	o		O		Control out (a comment is started)
)	O		O		O	o			O	(2-4-7)		O			O	o		O		Control in (the end of a comment)
+			O		O	o		O	O	+		O	O	O		o				Positive sign
–			O		O	o	O		O	–		O				o				Negative sign
/	O		O		O	o	O	O	O	/			O	O		o			O	Optional block skip
.			O		O	o	O	O		.		O	O		O	o		O	O	Period (a decimal point)
&	O		O			o	O	O		&					O	o	O	O		Ampersand
,	O		O		O	o	O			,			O	O	O	o		O	O	Comma
CR	O				O	o	O		O		Not assigned									Carriage return
:			O	O	O	o		O			Not assigned									Colon
#	O		O			o		O	O		Not assigned									Sharpe
$			O			o	O				Not assigned									Dollar sign
'			O			o	O	O	O		Not assigned									Apostrophe
*	O		O		O	o		O			Not assigned									Asterisk
;	O		O	O	O	o		O	O		Not assigned									Semicolon
<			O	O	O	o	O				Not assigned									Left angle bracket
=	O		O	O	O	o	O		O		Not assigned									Equal
>	O		O	O	O	o	O	O			Not assigned									Right angle bracket
?			O	O	O	o	O	O	O		Not assigned									Question mark
@	O	O				o					Not assigned									Commercial at mark
"			O			o		O			Not assigned									Quotation
[	O	O		O	O	o		O	O		Not assigned									Left brace
]	O	O		O	O	o	O		O		Not assigned									Right brace

FIGURE 6.10 (continued)

options. This problem was largely overcome with the advent of computer numerical control (CNC), which is discussed in Section 6.4.3.

6.4.2 Direct Numerical Control

In the 1960s a solution to the problems associated with punched tape was found with the use of a central time-sharing computer to store NC programs. The central computer was hardwired to the controller of one or more NC machines on the shop floor. The part program would then be downloaded from the central computer directly to the NC machine, during the actual machining of a component, one block at a time. Several machines could be controlled simultaneously in this way because of the high-speed capabilities of the computer. This eliminated the need to use punched tape. Among other advantages, a large number of programs could be stored more conveniently on the computer, and if a change in the program was required, it could be accomplished easily using a text editor.

There were several disadvantages with this type of direct numerical control (DNC), however. For example, if a problem developed with the central computer, all the machines would have to be shut down. Also, the wiring between the central computer and the machines was vulnerable to significant voltage variations in the manufacturing environment, and the central computer itself was very costly. With the fall in the cost of computing power in the 1970s and 1980s, this method of using computers in numerical control applications was superseded by the use of local computers at each machine as in computer numerical control and distributed numerical control.

6.4.3 Computer Numerical Control

With computer numerical control (CNC), a local dedicated microcomputer with its own memory is used to control the operation of each machine. This is in contrast to the centrally controlled computer used in direct numerical control. Perhaps even more significant, the fall in the cost of computing power that led to the advent of CNC also made it possible to write many of the MCU functions into the software that controlled the MCU rather than having them physically hardwired into the design. This software, called the executive program, is loaded into the CNC's memory and controls how a particular controller operates. The executive program of a CNC unit is analogous to the operating system of a computer. It thus became possible to provide far greater flexibility in the MCU by writing more sophisticated executive programs. For example, the controller could be switched between absolute and incremental programming, or linear and circular interpolation, rather than having these as hardware functions that could not be changed.

With the CNC approach, the NC program is read from a storage medium such as punched tape and stored in the memory of the local computer. The program can then be executed by the MCU reading one instruction at a time from memory, rather than from the original storage medium. With the use of computer diskettes, it became possible to store multiple programs more conveniently. Thus, the advantages of direct numerical control could be provided at the local level without the associated disadvantages. Computer diskettes can also be used to store large programs that cannot fit in the memory of the local computer.

Modern CNCs have display screens on which they can show the program block being executed as well as the next several blocks, the coordinate positions of the slides, and other operational parameters. The MCU may also have an input keypad or even a full keyboard for data entry. This makes it possible to edit the program at the machine and save the changes in the computer memory or to disk. Some controls are designed to have complete programs entered at the control unit itself rather than from some other medium such as tape or disk. Such controls are referred to as manual data input (MDI) controls. Virtually all NC machines currently on the market have CNC capability.

6.4.4 Distributed Numerical Control

Distributed numerical control is known by the same acronym as direct numerical control (i.e., DNC). As mentioned earlier, the original concept of DNC was superseded with the development of CNC. In its current incarnation as *distributed,* DNC is an attempt to combine the best features of CNC and those of the original (*i.e., direct*) DNC. Modern DNC still uses a central time-sharing computer capable of communicating with several machines on the shop floor and storing part programs that are downloaded to individual machines as needed. The important difference is that because modern NC machines have CNC capability, they have memory, and therefore a complete program (or substantial portions thereof in the case of large programs) can be downloaded into the memory of the local computer of the CNC machine, rather than one block at a time as in the original DNC. Thus, the local machine can run autonomously and does not depend on the central computer for execution of each step of the program. The central computer need only play a supervisory role, monitoring the operation of the various machines, archiving programs, and downloading appropriate programs to scheduled machines as needed. Thus, the individual machines can continue to operate even if the central computer fails. This type of DNC is sometimes referred to as *hierarchical numerical control.*

6.5 COMPUTER-AIDED PART PROGRAMMING

From the foregoing examples, it is apparent that writing NC programs can be a tedious and error-prone process. For a program of any sizable length, it is difficult to check the program manuscript and determine all the possible errors there may be in the program. Even after checking the manuscript, the program has to go through a troublesome proving process before it is used for manufacturing real parts. This consumes valuable machine time that would otherwise be used for actual production. Moreover, because of the different capabilities of various machine tools and controllers, the programmer is required to master all the individual functions for all the machines in a shop that he or she will be called upon to program.

It became evident soon after the introduction of NC machines that programmers would benefit substantially from computer assistance during program preparation. Many computer-aided part programming systems (or part programming languages, as they are sometimes called) have since been developed. In the majority of these systems English-like commands, rather than the standard M&G codes, are used to instruct the computer on how the part is to be machined. Advantages of applying computer-aided part programming include the following:

1. It reduces the manual calculations involved in determining the geometric characteristics of the part. By having the bulk of calculations handled by a computer, a significant source of errors is eliminated. For some parts, this may indeed be the only viable way in which to generate the part program.

2. In many cases, the program preparation system includes a proving capability such as path simulation on a computer screen. Therefore, most errors in the program that go beyond the syntactical can be identified before the program is loaded on a machine. This off-line proving offers considerable savings in machine time that would otherwise be required for tape proving.
3. A set of events can be programmed with fewer commands, leading to shorter programs that take less time to prepare and are more convenient to store.
4. The English-like structure of the programming system makes it easier for programmers to learn, which reduces the overhead associated with NC programming. This is especially important in environments where a variety of machines are to be programmed, because most of the standardized programming techniques do not change as one moves between machines.
5. Program preparation is simplified by use of English-like commands that are easy to understand and program. This reduces the likelihood of errors in the program, and when errors do occur they are easier to trace and correct.

The Aerospace Industries Association sponsored the work that led to the first part programming language, developed at MIT in 1955. This was called Automatically Programmed Tools (APT). The system has been under continual development since then. Because of its historical importance, APT is described in some detail here. APT has evolved into the most widely used NC programming language in industry. In addition to the standard, several derivative languages have been developed which are aimed at providing enhanced capabilities not available in standard APT. The derivatives of APT include NELAPT, EXAPT, UNIAPT, ADAPT, and IFAPT. In our discussion here, we will concentrate on the standard APT language, and the reader is referred to the bibliography for more details about the various derivative systems.

An APT programming system consists of two parts: the main language processor and a postprocessor. The main language processor takes the source APT program written by the user and, during a series of runs through the program, checks it for syntactical errors, errors in defined geometry, and errors in required tool motions. During each run, any errors that are found are printed out to a separate file with codes indicating the nature of the error detected. The user then has to correct the errors and resubmit the program for processing, and the whole process is repeated until the program is determined to be error free and runs successfully. When the source program is run successfully, it generates as output all the cutter location data (or CL data) required to create an NC program. This is called the cutter location file (or CLFILE). This output, however, does not include machine-specific data such as tool lengths, cutting speeds, and coolant. Also, the CL data are in machine language, which cannot be utilized directly by an NC controller. Therefore, the second part of the programming system is used to convert the data into NC codes that a particular controller can recognize and use with a specific machine. This second part of the system is called a postprocessor. Because there are many types of NC controllers, which can be used on many different types of machines, each machine–controller combination requires its own postprocessor to be able to take full advantage of all the capabilities available with a given combination. In addition to generating the NC codes from the CL data, the postprocessor generates a list file showing the source file statement that generated each final NC command. Figure 6.11 shows an overview of the structure of the APT system.

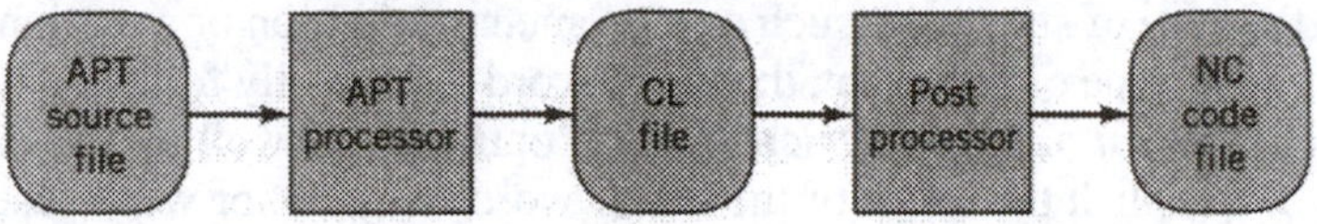

FIGURE 6.11 Structure of the APT system.

6.5.1 APT Language Basics

An APT part program is composed of statements that instruct the machine on what has to be done for the required operation, how it is to be done, and the required tooling. Each statement is analogous to a sentence in English and it must be structured according to a specific syntax. Each statement is made up of words, which can be formed using any of the 26 alphabetical characters as well as any of the digits 0–9. A word can consist of up to six alphanumeric characters, with the first character always being a letter. Certain words are reserved for use by the system and have a defined meaning. Such words are referred to as *key words* and they cannot be used for any other purpose in the program. Since all key words consist of letters only, a simple way to be sure that a reserved key word has not been used for some unacceptable function is always to include at least one digit in user-defined words. Words that are used to define geometric entities are referred to as symbols. Symbols can also be used to store numeric values. Such symbolic values can then be referenced later in the program. Special words called labels can be used to reference statements. A label is the only type of word that can consist entirely of numerals.

To carry out computations, APT provides the following arithmetic operations: addition (+), subtraction (−), multiplication (*), division (/), and exponentiation (**). The language also provides a variety of mathematical functions including the common trigonometric functions, logarithms, and square roots. (Angles are given in degrees and decimal parts of degrees.) Finally, the following punctuation characters may be used:

- / A slash is used to separate a statement into major words and minor words. Major words are to the left and minor words are to the right. Major and minor words are defined later.
- , A comma is used to separate elements in a statement.
- . A decimal point is used to indicate the fractional part of a real number.
- = An equals sign is used to assign values to a symbolic name.
-) A right parenthesis is used to terminate a label.
- ( ) A pair of parentheses is used to enclose nested definitions.
- ; A semicolon is used to separate multiple statements on a single line.
- $ A single dollar sign indicates continuation of a statement on the next line.
- $$ Double dollar signs are used to indicate the start of a program comment that should be ignored by the APT processor.

Blank spaces may be used between elements of a statement to make it easier for a human to interpret, but the computer system itself does not use them and they are optional. Note that blank spaces cannot be used to replace commas.

Each statement within an APT program consists of one *major word.* The major word determines the type of statement, such as a geometry definition or a motion command. Depending on the type of statement, the major word is generally followed by a slash (/) and then some *minor word(s),* which may be optional, as well as the data that are required to accomplish the effect of the major word. Any minor words used typically modify the effect of the major word to meet specific requirements. The APT system allows up to 4092 elements to be specified within a single statement. In this context, an element can be any major or minor word, symbolic name, mathematical operator, punctuation mark, or numeric data. However, a statement label is not considered to be part of the statement. A typical APT part program consists of the following four general types of statements:

1. Initialization and termination statements
2. Geometry definition statements
3. Tool definition and motion statements
4. Postprocessor statements

6.5.2 Initialization and Termination

The first statement in the APT part program initialization sequence is always the major word PARTNO, followed by any text that serves to complete the first statement. The text following the word PARTNO is punched into the NC tape as human-readable characters and is solely for identification purposes. For this reason, the part number is often used as the text, which explains the name of the major word used. In fact, the text after the word PARTNO could be completely omitted although the word PARTNO must always be included. Another statement required as part of the program initialization sequence is the MACHIN statement. This specifies the name of a particular postprocessor that will be used for generating the final NC output from the program.

NOPOST is an optional statement used to indicate that no postprocessing is required for subsequent statements. Another statement that may be used in the initialization sequence is CLPRNT. This causes the system to print out a list of all cutter locations determined by the system (before postprocessing) as well as corresponding postprocessor commands. This can be useful during program proving. For program termination, the END statement is used to indicate to the postprocessor that the end of the machining operations has been reached. This is always followed by the FINI statement, which is the last statement of an APT program. This indicates to the APT processor the end of the actual APT program.

6.5.3 Geometry Definition

Geometry definition statements are used in APT to describe the shape of the part to be machined and the path to be followed by the cutter in generating the required shape. APT can define up to 16 different types of geometric entities including the following commonly used ones: POINT, LINE, CIRCLE, PLANE, CYLNDR, SPHERE, CONE, PATERN. Each entity can be defined in several different ways, and some entities have up to 14 different methods of definition. In general, a geometry definition statement starts with a symbolic name for the element being defined. An entity type and definition are then assigned to this symbolic name. The name of the type of entity being defined is used as the major word. Numeric data and minor words complete the definition. The general syntax of a geometry definition statement would be as follows:

symbol = entity_type/entity_definition

Previously defined symbolic names can be used within a current definition. It is also permissible to nest a definition within another definition. A nested definition is enclosed in parentheses within the statement. An entity in a nested definition does not have to be assigned a symbolic name if it is not to be used again later in the program. If a z-coordinate value is not given for an entity requiring one, the value is assumed to be zero. Exhibit 6.5 gives some examples of geometry definitions that will help in understanding the approach used.

Exhibit 6.5 APT Geometry Definitions

1. P10=POINT/12,5,10
   This defines a point, with symbolic name P10, as having coordinates (12, 5, 10).
2. L10=LINE/P10,(POINT/(0,32,10))
   This defines a line L10, which passes through point P10 and some unnamed point with coordinates (0, 32, 10).
3. CIRCL1=CIRCLE/TANTO,L10,YLARGE,P10,15
   This defines a circle CIRCL1, which is tangent to line L10 and passes through point P10. The y-coordinate of its center is larger than that of point P10 and it has a radius of 15. Modifiers such as YLARGE here are used to choose between multiple valid possibilities.
4. P20=POINT/CENTER, (CIRCL2=CIRCLE/P2,P3,P6)
   This defines a point P20 as being at the center of a circle named CIRCL2. Within this definition is a nested definition of CIRCL2, which is a circle passing through the points P2, P3, and P6.
5. PLN1=PLANE/P6,PERTO,V1
   This defines a plane PLN1, which passes through point P6 and is perpendicular to vector V1.

Note: As used in these definitions, it is assumed that entities P2, P3, P6, and V1 have already been defined elsewhere in the program.

6.5.4 APT Tool Definition and Motion

Actual machining of a workpiece is accomplished by feeding a cutting tool into the workpiece and causing relative motion between the two at an appropriate cutting speed. The tool definition and motion commands have the general effect of describing to the system the specific cutting tools to be used for each machining operation and how those tools are to be moved around the previously defined geometry to generate the required part shape.

6.5.4.1 Tool Definition Commands

Before the machining statements are generated, the tool to be used in the machining operation must be defined completely. The tool definition commands are used to give the system necessary information about the cutter. Supplemental commands define how the cutter is used and give the machine's operating conditions. For the examples given in the following discussion, items enclosed in square brackets such as *[item]* are optional.

The tool is defined using a CUTTER statement. The minimum information required for tool definition is the tool diameter. If only the diameter is given, the tool is assumed to have a flat end. Optionally, an end radius for the tool may also be given. Additional information may be required in case of three-dimensional machining. The format is

CUTTER/d[,r [,e,f,a,b,f]]

To load a tool, a LOADTL command specifying the tool number for the required tool is used. If the tool to be loaded is not the first tool in the program, this causes the processor to issue an automatic tool change statement. As an option, the tool length may be given as part of this statement if tool lengths have to be preset. The format is

LOADTL/n[,LENGTH,l]

The spindle is turned on using a SPINDL command. This command also sets the spindle speed and direction of rotation to be used during machining. Used with different parameters, this command can also turn off the spindle and turn it back on again. The possible formats are

SPINDL/speed,units,direction or
SPINDL/option

When coolant is to be used during machining, it is controlled using the COOLNT command. The minor word (option in the format below) in this statement specifies the use of either MIST or FLOOD coolant. If COOLNT has been previously selected, this command can be used to turn the coolant off or back on again using the option value OFF or ON. The format is

COOLNT/option

The feed rate to be used is specified using a FEDRAT command. The parameters used with the command give the value of the feed rate as well as the feed rate units. Sometimes a RAPID command is used for the feed rate, and this causes the machine to move at its maximum available feed rate. The respective formats are

FEDRAT/value,units
RAPID

With the foregoing commands specified as needed, the tool motion commands can then be programmed.

6.5.4.2 Point-to-Point Tool Motion

In general, the end point of tool motion for a given statement is treated as the start point of motion for the next statement. At the start of all tool motion, however, a start point needs to be specified. This is done using a FROM statement, which helps to establish an initial direction of motion. Its format is

FROM/point_definition

The FROM command itself does not lead to any machine movements, but it causes subsequent motion to be as if the tool started from the specified point. The actual initial tool position does not have to coincide with the specified FROM location. In many cases, the tool-changing position is specified as the FROM location.

Actual tool motion commands are classified into two broad types: *point-to-point* motion and *continuous-path* motion. Point-to-point commands are used to position a tool at a target location without regard to the path taken in getting there. This is analogous to the G00 code in manual programming. This type of motion is most frequently used for hole-making operations or for rapid positioning of the tool. Continuous-path motion commands are used when precise control over the path followed by the tool is required. The two commands GOTO and GODLTA are used to control motion in the point-to-point positioning mode. Their respective formats are

GOTO/point_definition
GODLTA/distance_definition

The GOTO command has the effect of causing the tool to go to the specified point. This may be a predefined point, or the necessary coordinate values may be specified instead. In fact, more than one point may be specified or a pattern name may be given for the GOTO statement if several locations are to be visited in sequence. Usually, the GOTO statement is preceded by a RAPID command to ensure that the ensuing positioning motion occurs at maximum feed rate. The GOTO statement causes motion to the absolute coordinate values specified. The GODLTA statement, on the other hand, causes incremental motion to occur. The parameters given with the command specify the amount of incremental motion to occur from the current tool location along each coordinate axis. If only one parameter value is given, motion is assumed to be along the z-axis. A RAPID command may also be used with a GODLTA statement to cause motion at the maximum feed rate.

The GOTO and GODLTA commands are frequently used together to carry out hole-making types of operations such as drilling, boring, and tapping. Either command can be used to position the tool where the operation is to be carried out (with proper provision for some clearance), then to carry out the machining operation to the appropriate depth, and finally to retract the tool. The process of positioning the tool, machining to the required depth, and subsequent retraction can be accomplished on some machines by use of a CYCLE command. This command is analogous to the use of canned cycles in manual programming. Its format is

CYCLE/type,parameters

where *type* specifies the type of cycle operation to be carried out and *parameters* are the parameters appropriate to the type of cycle, such as depth, feed rate, and direction of spindle rotation. The possible types of cycle include DRILL, BORE, and TAP. The availability of the CYCLE command depends on the particular postprocessor in use and there is some variation in the details of how this command is implemented on different systems; therefore, the manual for each system has to be consulted for the relevant details.

6.5.4.3 Continuous-Path Tool Motion

As mentioned earlier, continuous-path motion (also referred to as contouring) involves precise control of the path followed by the tool as it goes through the required motion.

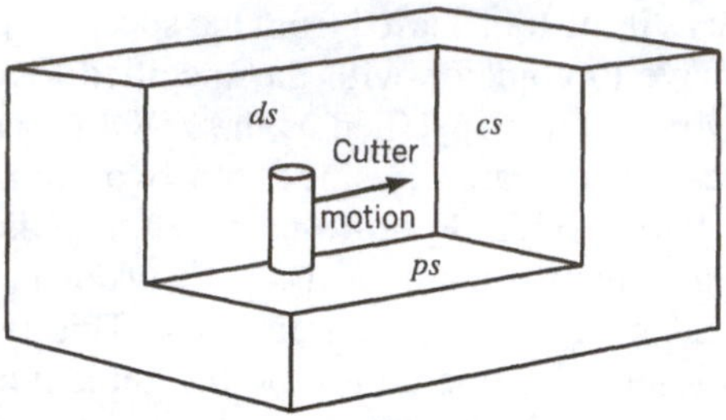

FIGURE 6.12 Control surfaces for continuous-path motion.

In order to achieve this control over the tool motion, APT uses three control surfaces referred to as the *drive surface (ds), part surface (ps),* and *check surface (cs).* During contouring, all three surfaces must be defined either explicitly or implicitly. The cutting tool is required to maintain continuous contact with the drive surface as well as the part surface. The drive surface is used to guide the tool around the part being machined, in a plane perpendicular to the tool axis. The periphery of the tool follows the drive surface. The part surface controls motion along the tool axis and the tip of the tool maintains contact with the part surface. Therefore, the part surface determines how deep the tool cuts into the workpiece. The check surface is used to indicate where the current tool motion stops (which is also where the next tool motion will start). The drive surface must always be given explicitly during a contouring motion, whereas the other surfaces may be given implicitly. Figure 6.12 shows the relationship among the three control surfaces.

A start-up command is required to establish the proper initial tool position relative to all three control surfaces. The GO command is used for this purpose, and it should not be confused with the GOTO command discussed earlier in point-to-point motion. The general format of the GO command is

GO/rel,ds,rel,ps,rel,cs

where *ds*, *ps*, and *cs* specify the control surfaces and *rel* is a modifier that specifies a relationship between the tool and the corresponding control surface. The possible values for *rel* with all three surfaces are TO, ON, and PAST, except that *rel* can also have a value of TANTO with respect to the check surface only. Therefore the GO command causes the tool to move to a position where it can achieve the specified relationships with the control surfaces. The position of the tool relative to a given control surface as a result of the TO, ON, and PAST modifiers is shown in Figure 6.13.

Once the initial relationship between the tool and the control surfaces has been established by means of a start-up statement, tool motion is achieved by driving the tool along the drive surface. The direction that the tool is to take in moving along the drive surface is indicated by one of six possible commands: GOFWD, GOBACK, GOLFT, GORGT, GOUP, GODOWN. The meanings of the various commands can be inferred from their names. The direction specified in each command is given relative to the direction of the immediately preceding motion. Thus, the commands give the directional relationship between a current drive surface and the one for the succeeding motion. These commands are used to specify all subsequent motion. The general format for the commands is

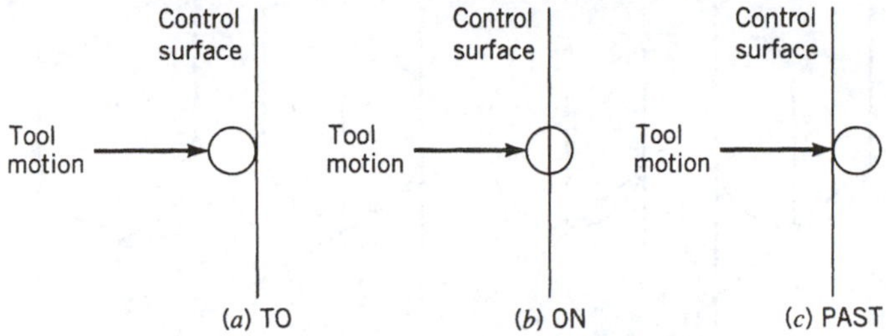

FIGURE 6.13 Effect of modifiers in a GO command.

option,cmnd/ds,rel,cs

where *option* establishes a positional relationship between the tool and the drive surface for the following motion, *cmnd* is one of the six motion commands, *ds* is the drive surface, *cs* is the check surface, and *rel* is the relationship between the tool and the check surface.

The possible relationships between the tool and the drive surface for contouring motion are TLLFT, TLON, and TLRGT. These indicate which side of the drive surface the tool will be on during the motion. Note that these are different from the *ds* positional relationships during start-up. However, the possible relationships between the tool and the check surface during the contouring motion are similar to those during start-up. In many cases, the check surface for a given command becomes the drive surface for the next command. In such cases, it is not necessary to give the check surface explicitly, because the computer can deduce this by looking ahead at commands that have not yet been executed. The relationship between the tool and the part surface is generally specified separately from the motion command itself and the possible values are TLONPS and TLOFPS. These various possible relationships are summarized in Table 6.5 and illustrated in Figure 6.14.

6.5.5 Postprocessor Commands

The postprocessor plays an important role in the application of APT part programming for NC machining. The output of the general language processor is in the form of CLDATA, which defines the location of the cutter for the required machining operations. Thus, the language processor serves primarily as a geometry processor. The geometric data produced have to be converted into a form suitable for a specific machine, taking into account the capabilities of the machine. The various functions of the postprocessor are:

TABLE 6.5 **Possible Tool–Surface Relationships for Contouring**

ps	*ds*	*cs*
TLONPS	TLON	TO
TLOFPS	TLLFT	ON
	TLRGT	PAST
		TANTO

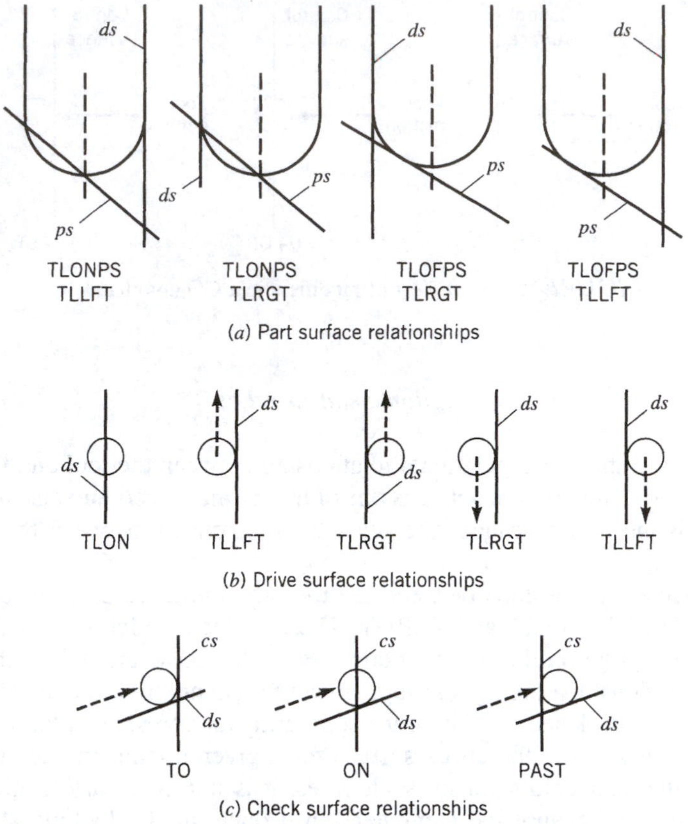

FIGURE 6.14 Illustration of tool–surface relationships.

(a) Convert CLDATA to machine tool coordinate system.
(b) Check for violation of machine tool slide travel limitations.
(c) Check for violation of available spindle speeds and feed rates.
(d) Select available spindle speeds and feed rates.
(e) Develop motion commands using available M & G codes.
(f) Determine slide acceleration and deceleration avoiding overshoots.
(g) Determine other MCU requirements such as servo setting time.
(h) Process machine-specific functions.
(i) Provide output including diagnostics, NC tape, and operator instructions.

Because a different postprocessor is required for each type of machine–controller combination, the way in which these functions are implemented can vary widely. We will not describe this in any great detail here. Various commands intended for postprocessor execution can be written into the source APT program. Such commands have no effect on the language processor, which simply passes them on to the postprocessor for processing. Examples of these include some of the preliminary commands already discussed, such as SPINDL, COOLNT, FEDRAT, and RAPID. The CYCLE command is also passed directly to the postprocessor to select appropriate canned cycles corresponding to the command being processed. Some postprocessor commands when used in the source program change the way in which the CLDATA is handled. For example, the command ARCSLP causes some postprocessors to turn on or off the circular interpolation capabilities. Again, because of the wide variation in postprocessor capabilities, the interested reader is advised to check the documentation for a specific postprocessor to determine its capabilities.

Sometimes the programmer may wish to use specific commands in the final NC program while bypassing the postprocessor. This can be accomplished by using an INSERT command. The data contained in the INSERT command are inserted directly into the NC program by the postprocessor.

EXAMPLE 6.5

The following is an example of an APT program for making the part in Figure 6.9. From Example 6.4, you are already familiar with the machining sequence used for the part and therefore should be able to interpret the program given below with ease. Explanatory comments (starting with the $$ sign) are added to the more significant parts of the program.

```
PARTNO EXAMPLE2
MACHIN/MILL
NOPOST
UNITS/MM
P0=POINT/-150,-20,0            $$ Geometry definition
P1=POINT/-135,0,0              $$ Point coordinates
P2=POINT/0,150,0
P3=POINT/-105,15,0
P4=POINT/-105,90,0
P5=POINT/-30,30,15
P6=POINT/-44.7,59.7,15
L1=LINE/XAXIS                  $$ L1 is the x-axis
L2=LINE/YAXIS                  $$ L2 is the y-axis
L3=LINE/P1,ATANGL,90           $$ vertical line
L4=LINE/P2,ATANGL,0            $$ horizontal line
L5=LINE/YAXIS,-60              $$ -60 from y-axis
C1=CIRCLE/CENTER,P3,RADIUS,30        $$ circle
C2=CIRCLE/CENTER,P4,RADIUS,45
LOADTL/1                       $$ Load first tool
CUTTER/20                      $$ Tool definition
RAPID;GOTO/-150,-20,17               $$ Tool start
RAPID;GOTO/P0
FROM/P0
THICK/2                        $$ 2-mm allowance
FEDRAT/375;GO/TO,L1,TO,L3      $$ Start profiling
TLLFT,GOLFT/L3,TANTO,C1        $$ Tool to the left
GOFWD/C1,TO,C2                 $$ Along C1 to C2
GOFWD/C2,TANTO,L5
GOFWD/L5,PAST,L4
GOLFT/L4,PAST,L2               $$ Complete the profile
RAPID;GODLTA/20                $$ Tool retract
RAPID;GOTO/-150,-20,17
RAPID;GOTO/P0
FROM/P0
THICK/0                        $$ Finish cut
FEDRAT/375;GO/TO,L1,TO,L3
TLLFT,GOLFT/L3,TANTO,C1 $$ Second profile
GOFWD/C1,TO,C2
GOFWD/C2,TANTO,L5
GOFWD/L5,PAST,L4
GOLFT/L4,PAST,L2 $$ End of profile
RAPID;GODLTA/20     $$ Retract tool
RAPID;GOTO/-150,-20,17
LOADTL/2                              $$ Load second tool
CUTTER/2.5                            $$ Define tool
CYCLE/DRILL,3,IPM,100,2             $$ Center drill
GOTO/P5
GOTO/P6
CYCLE/OFF
RAPID;GOTO/-150,-20,17
LOADTL/3                            $$ Load third tool
CUTTER/7.5
CYCLE/DRILL,17,IPM,150,2    $$ Drill holes
GOTO/P5
GOTO/P6
CYCLE/OFF
RAPID;GOTO/-150,-20,17
LOADTL/4                            $$ Load fourth tool
CUTTER/8
CYCLE/DRILL,17,IPM,150,2     $$ Ream holes
GOTO/P5
GOTO/P6
CYCLE/OFF
RAPID;GOTO/-150,-20,17
SPINDL/OFF                          $$ Stop spindle
COOLNT/OFF                          $$ Stop coolant
END
FINI
```

6.5.6 Advanced APT Programming Features

As the APT programming system has evolved, a variety of advanced programming features have been added that help to simplify the programming task. Among these is the use of logical operators for conditional testing and branching, looping capabilities, and macros. These features give APT some of the versatility of high-level programming languages such as C. The use of statement labels is essential to testing, branching, and looping. A label, like any other word, can consist of up to six alphanumeric characters, although for labels, unlike other words, all characters may be numeric. The label is terminated by a right parenthesis, which is not considered part of the label. When used, the label must be the first part of a statement and it identifies that statement uniquely. Branching causes program operation to cease sequential execution of statements and go to another part of the program identified by a statement label. This branching may be unconditional, or it maybe the result of some specific logical condition.

Another feature that increases the versatility of the APT system is the use of macros. A macro is essentially a subroutine that is defined once and can then be recalled an unlimited number of times for execution. Variables can be passed to the macro at the time of execution, and the values passed can change every time the macro is executed. A macro is assigned a symbolic name as part of the definition. When the macro is to be executed, a CALL statement is used, which calls up the macro and passes any required variable values. A macro definition is ended by the command TERMAC. Note that a macro cannot be defined inside another macro, although a similar effect can be achieved by calling a macro from inside another macro.

6.5.7 Other Part Programming Systems

Other programming systems have been developed that tend to provide capabilities similar to those of APT although they are not strictly APT derivatives. Examples of such systems include GNC, developed in Britain; ELAN, developed in France; GTL, developed in Italy; and COMPACT II, developed in the United States. The concepts used with these systems are generally similar to those of the APT system. Some of these started as proprietary systems or as systems for use with specific types of computers. The interested reader is referred to the suggested readings at the end of the chapter for sources of information about these systems.

6.6 CAD/CAM-BASED PART PROGRAMMING

The reader will have seen from the foregoing discussion of the APT computer-aided part programming system that one of its major functions is to give a description of the geometry of the part and of the tool path to be followed in machining the part. This is the main function of the preprocessor in APT (and in other similar systems). The geometric description provides the key data on which the rest of the programming functions are based. Advances in computer capabilities, together with the fall in the cost of computing, have led to the development of more sophisticated and affordable computer-aided design (CAD) systems, with far better part definition capabilities than APT. CAD systems have been discussed extensively in Chapter 2, and with that knowledge, the reader can make a comparison with the capabilities just described for APT. It was a logical progression to combine the well-developed part definition capabilities of CAD systems with the machining capabilities of part programming systems, to develop computer-aided design and manufacturing (CAD/CAM) systems. These are now far more widely used in industry than just CAD alone or part programming alone.

For our present purposes, we note that the CAD database contains a complete geometric description of the part. It is logical to use this design database as the basis for generating the geometry description of the part needed to meet the NC programming requirements. A great deal of work in both industry and academia has gone into efforts to provide NC program generation capabilities from the CAD system database. Most CAD/CAM systems on the market today can generate tool path information from the geometric model of the part contained in the CAD database. In general, with these systems a part design is developed using the CAD modules of the system and stored as a drawing file. (See Chapter 2 for details.) The cutting tool(s) to be used for machining and the required machining parameters are then defined interactively. The system then uses the part geometry information together with the defined tool data to decide how the required part can be made. The computer determines the tool paths needed to produce the required shape and generates the corresponding NC program.

Most systems can directly generate a CLFILE, which can be postprocessed for use on specific machines. Some systems generate output in the form of an APT (or similar

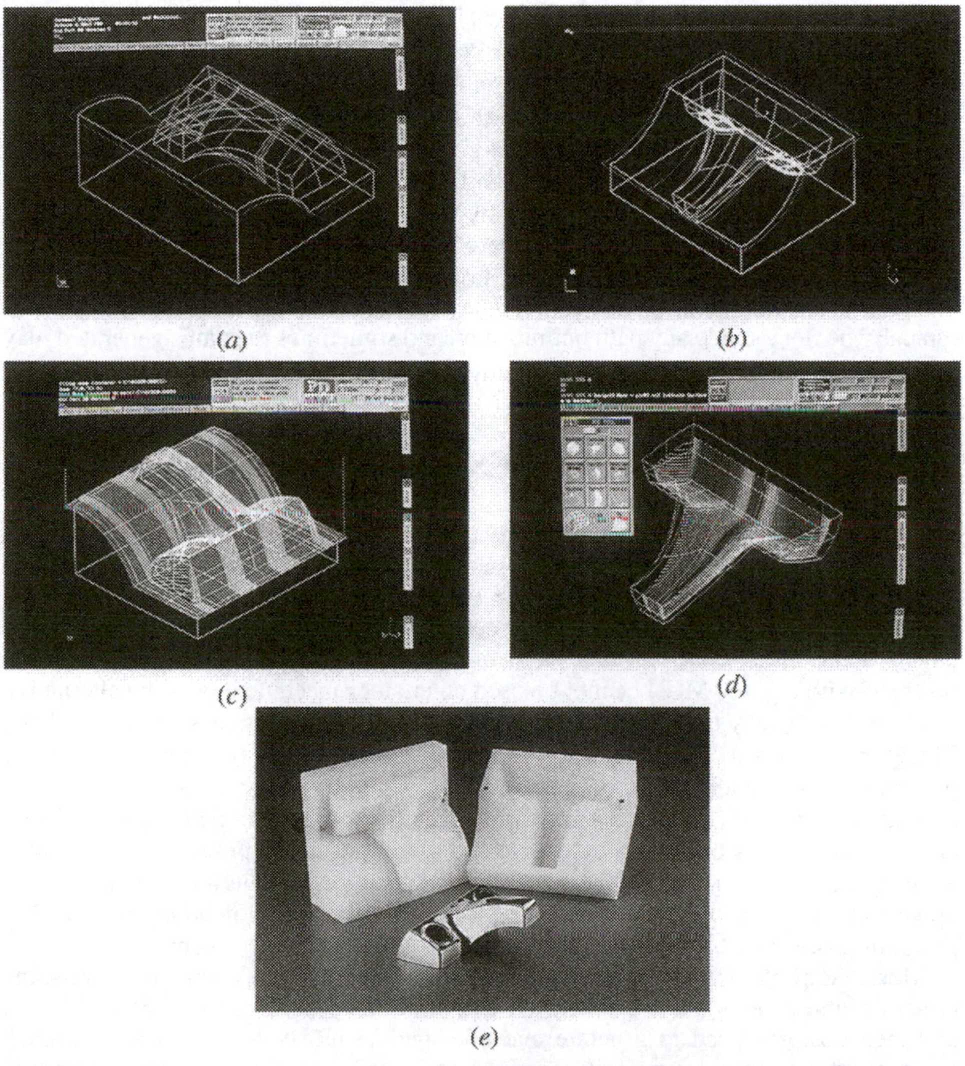

FIGURE 6.15 CAD/CAM-based NC program generation using Personal Machinist. (Used with permission of Computervision Corp.)

language) program for processing and postprocessing in the traditional way. In either case, postprocessing is still required before the program is submitted to the machine for execution. The postprocessing functions given in Section 6.5.5 must still be carried out before the NC program is usable. Examples of commercial CAD/CAM systems with NC program generation capabilities are Computervision, CATIA, CADAM, and ProEngineer. CAD/CAM systems do not operate in a standardized way and therefore, to retain generality, specific details of how these systems operate are not given here. Most universities and colleges have access to one or more CAD/CAM systems that can be used to demonstrate the concepts discussed and to develop skills in using such systems.

One of the major benefits of CAD/CAM-based program generation is the capability to plot the tool path on a graphics screen and check for errors before running the program on a machine. This tool path verification function can also be used to check for possible collision of the tool with jigs and fixtures that may be used in holding the part, if the design of these fixtures is available on the CAD database. Although tool path plots can be made with the traditional programming languages, the collision-checking capability in CAD/CAM-based systems adds a powerful feature not available before. In addition, using the design data as the basis for generating the NC program avoids the problem of duplicating geometry data in the NC system, assures data consistency, and makes it easier to accommodate any design changes that might occur. Figure 6.15 shows a set of molds that were designed on Personal Machinist (a product of Computervision Corp.) at Adams Mold and Engineering of Peoria, Arizona. The NC program was generated and proved on the same system, and the resulting molds and a sample product made with those molds are shown at the bottom of the illustration. A limitation of many CAD/CAM-based systems, however, is that they typically do not include any path optimization and sometimes the paths generated may have to be modified interactively to improve on machining efficiency.

6.7 BEYOND POSTPROCESSORS

As we saw earlier, because there are many types of NC controllers that can be used on many different types of machines, each machine–controller combination requires its own postprocessor. This means that in a typical shop with multiple machines from multiple suppliers, a large library of postprocessors has to be developed and maintained. It also leads to the practical problem that an NC program developed for a given machine with a given MCU cannot be used on another machine unless the alternative machine has exactly the same configuration and capabilities and has the same MCU. Therefore, if the part has to be made on a machine other than the one for which the program was originally developed, the program has to be postprocessed again for the second machine, proved out, and possibly modified through several iterations before it can be used. This is clearly an expensive and time-consuming process. This problem arises quite frequently in practice for a variety of reasons, including machine breakdown, scheduling conflicts, and the need for extra capacity. A new approach to NC program processing has been developed to try to address this problem.

Most NC programs today are generated from CAD/CAM systems or from some type of high-level language such as APT that has to be processed to generate CL data and then postprocessed to generate machine-specific NC codes. The new approach removes the postprocessing task from the realm of the programming system and transfers it to specially equipped MCUs that then, in effect, carry out the postprocessing task. EIA standard 494, "32-Bit Binary CL Exchange Input Format for Numeri-

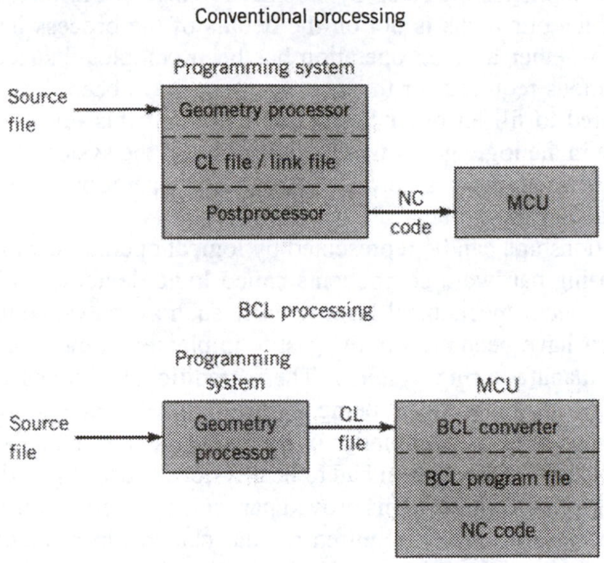

FIGURE 6.16 Conventional versus BCL NC processing.

cally Controlled Machines'' (BCL for short), gives the formal specification. The basic concept is quite simple. The CL data obtained from the processing stage of the programming system are downloaded directly to the BCL-equipped MCU. Because the data are downloaded before postprocessing, they are in ''part-oriented'' form rather than ''machine-oriented'' form and are thus machine independent. The BCL converter incorporated within the MCU then converts the CL data into the neutral BCL file format, consisting of a series of 32-bit binary integer words. All postprocessor commands in the original file are represented as integer codes. The MCU then converts the BCL program into machine-specific NC codes for machining the part. Therefore, in effect, the postprocessing function is carried out at the machine itself. However, the BCL file is independent of the machine as well as the original programming system. Figure 6.16 shows a comparison of conventional NC processing and BCL-type processing.

Because the final conversion into NC code is done at the machine itself, use of BCL makes it possible for NC files to be moved between BCL-equipped machines without difficulty, provided the machines are capable of making the part. The inherent machine capabilities might be quite different (e.g., three-axis versus five-axis), but this would not matter as long as the machine's MCU is BCL capable. It is even possible to fit a BCL front end to a conventional MCU and make it BCL capable. The use of BCL eliminates the need to have postprocessors written for each machine–controller combination and frees the programmer to concentrate on machine capabilities and machining requirements rather than postprocessor capabilities. BCL is still a relatively new concept; its use is not yet widespread but its potential is considerable.

6.8 PROGRAMMABLE LOGIC CONTROLLERS

In the preceding sections, we have been discussing control of manufacturing at the process level. We were interested in the technical details of how the manufacturing operation is accomplished on a step-by-step basis. There is a different level of control, however, at which our focus is not on the details of the process itself but rather on issues such as whether a given operation has been completed successfully, whether pertinent conditions required for the next operation have been satisfied, and whether the parts required to fill an order have been made. At this level of control, we are interested more in the logic governing the operation of the system than in the technology. The logical relationships between the various operation parameters determine what the next action should be.

Logical relationships can be represented by logical operators, which in turn can be implemented using hardware components called logic devices. Various mechanical, pneumatic, and electromechanical logic devices such as relays, counters, timers, and drum sequencers have been used in the past to implement logical functions including the control of manufacturing systems. These traditional systems had a number of shortcomings, the most significant being that the control logic had to be implemented by physical means such as pneumatics or hardwired relays. Thus, any change in the control logic meant that the system had to be physically reconfigured, which was both expensive and time consuming. This proved particularly onerous for industries such as the automotive industry, which required regular changes in products or models and hence, changes in manufacturing control logic. Another factor was the need for increasing accuracy and speed of response from these logic devices. This, together with advances in semiconductors, led to the development of microprocessor-based replacements for the traditional logic devices. These new electronic logic devices offer the same functional capabilities as the mechanical, pneumatic, and electromechanical devices, coupled with the greater reliability of electronics-based systems, while offering the versatility and flexibility of the computer because the control logic is implemented in software rather than system hardware.

Programmable logic controllers (PLCs), as these systems have come to be known, are among the most widely used electronic devices for implementing automatic control of manufacturing systems today. Originally, these devices were called programmable controllers (PCs), but with the popularization of small desktop computers starting with the IBM personal computer in the early 1980s, the acronym PC became generally associated with these small general-purpose computers. Consequently, the makers of the programmable controllers started referring to their products as programmable logic controllers to differentiate them from personal computers. What distinguishes PLCs from other computer applications in manufacturing is that whereas computers can be used to run a wide range of programs during routine operation, PLCs are typically programmed to control particular functions or processes according to a specified control logic. The controller monitors the function or process being controlled by taking input signals from a variety of sensors that characterize the function or operation, evaluating the logical relationships between the inputs, and setting the output signals to accomplish various actions according to the programmed control logic. Hence it would be appropriate to think of the PLC as a special-purpose computer.

Nevertheless, a programmable logical controller has many characteristics similar to those of a general-purpose computer. It is made up of a power supply, main processor, memory, inputs and outputs, and possibly some peripheral equipment. The PLC's power supply operates on mains AC voltage (110 or 220 V), which it converts to the DC voltage required for the controller's internal operation. The main processor or central processing unit (CPU) is responsible for carrying out the logical and other computational operations required and generating any required outputs. The memory is used to store the control program as well as the status of inputs and outputs used in computing. The PLC has multiple inputs and outputs (I/Os), generally of modular form and sometimes combined in one unit, allowing it to accept inputs from (and generate outputs to) a variety of devices. The status of each input or output is assigned a specific location in memory that can be referenced by the control program as needed. Peripheral equipment is used for purposes such as preparing, storing, and loading control programs; system monitoring; and, for more sophisticated systems, communicating with other computers with which the PLC may be networked. Figure 6.17 shows a block diagram of a typical PLC.

A PLC is intended to carry out logical operations as opposed to the extensive computation that is associated with more general-purpose computers. An example of an operation that is in the scope of a PLC is controlling the operation of a robotic work cell, which is interfaced with an automated material transportation system using AGVs. When an AGV docks into position, the robot is required to unload a processed part from the machine onto the AGV and then pick up a new workpiece from the AGV and load it onto the machine tool. This process can be controlled using fairly simple logic that would be implemented in the control program of a PLC. A simple program for this task would involve monitoring the status of the machine and the robot, whether the AGV has docked at the load–unload station, whether there is space on the AGV into which to place a finished part, and whether the AGV is carrying a new part that should be loaded onto the machine tool. Thus, a series of logical decisions have to be made and a variety of actions taken on the basis of input that is obtained from appropriate sensors.

There are no extensive computing requirements for the preceding task. What is needed is a means of rapidly processing logical information and quickly responding with appropriate actions. This is the strength of the PLC, which checks sensor inputs rapidly and repeatedly. In a typical PLC, the control program is in general executed thousands and even millions of times before the control strategy (or program) needs to be changed, and sometimes only one program may be used for the life of the PLC. However, the control logic can be changed easily because it is stored in software. In many manufacturing applications, the control logic is fairly simple and is expected to be stable over a large number of cycles. The control program is executed once every cycle, but the execution time for the program is very short, sometimes on the order of

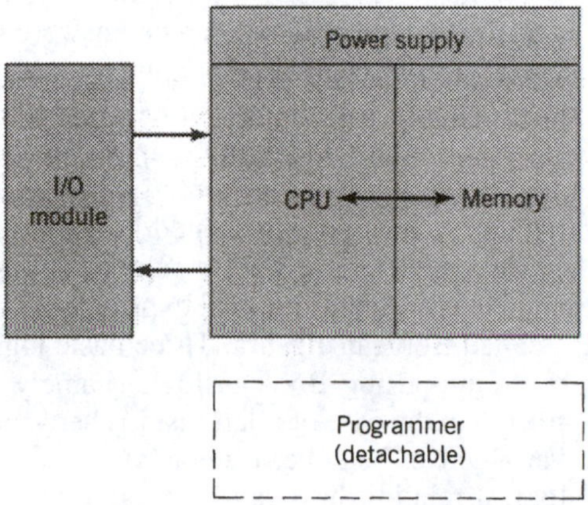

FIGURE 6.17 Modular structure of a typical PLC.

nanoseconds, and for all practical purposes the individual steps in the program are considered to be executed simultaneously. Because the program is executed repeatedly at a very high frequency, virtual real-time control becomes feasible. This characterizes the two major differences between PLCs and general-purpose computers: dedicated application to a specific function using a relatively small control program and rapid, simultaneous execution of the individual steps in the program.

6.8.1 Logical Control

As just explained, PLCs are widely used in manufacturing as a means of implementing logical control of the manufacturing system. Control actions are taken by making decisions depending on the values associated with various inputs or variables and the control logic in the program. If a particular decision can be made by answering yes or no to a given question, it is referred to as a decision by attributes. Examples of this include:

1. Is the machine turned on?
2. Is the gate to the work cell open?
3. Has the AGV arrived at the docking station?

Decisions by attributes are particularly amenable to implementation using logical control. These decisions are also referred to as go–nogo decisions. They can also be envisioned as on–off conditions. Because there are only two possible answers or states, binary representation in a computer (or PLC) is simple, with one state corresponding to 1 and the other to 0. If a particular decision cannot be made by answering yes or no to a question, it is referred to as a decision by variables. Generally, these types of decisions are based on values that can vary widely. Examples of these include:

1. How deep is the hole?
2. What is the cutting speed?
3. What is the required surface finish?
4. How many parts are to be made?

Attribute-type questions can generally be considered candidates for automation using logical control, whereas variable-type questions would be less amenable to logical control. A variable-type question can be made suitable for logical automation, however, if it can be broken down into a series of elementary attribute-type questions.

As we have seen, an attribute-type question can be answered by yes or no, so there are only two possible answers or states. Correspondingly, a logical variable can have only two possible values, namely true–false, which are comparable to an on–off setting in a mechanical system, high–low voltage in an electronic device, or 1/0 in binary data representation. Accordingly, an attribute-type question can be expressed as a logical variable, which can in turn be represented by appropriate settings in a mechanical system or electronic device or as binary data. Relationships between logical variables constitute a logical expression. Logical expressions can be represented by a special algebra of logic called Boolean algebra. Three basic logical operators are used to construct logical expressions using Boolean logic, namely AND, OR, and NOT. These are shown in Table 6.6 in the case of relationships between two logical variables X and Y, where each variable can be either true or false.

More complicated logical relationships can be obtained by using combinations of the three operators given above or by extending to relationships between any number

TABLE 6.6 **Boolean Logic Operators**

Relationship	*Meaning*
X AND Y	Both variables are true
X OR Y	Either one of the variables is true
NOT X	The specified variable is not true

of variables. Extending the electrical analogy, simple semiconductor devices called *gates* can be constructed that allow current to flow depending on the status of the input contacts. Considering a simple example with two inputs, an AND gate will allow current to flow if both inputs are high but not otherwise, whereas an OR gate will allow current to flow if either one of the inputs is high (or both are high). Thus, with a high corresponding to a logical value of true and a low corresponding to a logical value of false, an AND gate would correspond to the logical AND operator. Other types of logical relationships can easily be imagined and can be extended to multiple inputs or variables. The logical relationships can be represented in a diagram called a logic network diagram. The symbols used in a logic network diagram corresponding to the basic Boolean operators are shown in Figure 6.18*a*.

The devices implementing the various logical relationships are what we refer to as logic devices. These logic devices are used in constructing PLCs. Although logic network diagrams could be used to represent the logic in a PLC control program, another logic diagramming technique referred to as the *ladder logic diagram* is used more widely in industry. The reason for this is that ladder logic diagramming was already well established in industry in relation to the traditional electromechanical logic devices. Thus, when PLCs were introduced, this standard logic diagramming technique was retained to ease the transition, especially for technicians who were involved in wiring the various systems that were being controlled.

The ladder logic diagram makes use of representations similar to electrical circuits in which a series connection represents a logical AND and a parallel connection represents a logical OR. A ladder logic diagram is made up of inputs and outputs connected according to the appropriate logic. Each rung in the ladder represents a set of logical relationships between the inputs that leads to a particular output. The output from one rung of the ladder could be used as an input in another rung of the same ladder. Except when special provisions are made, it is considered that all rungs in a

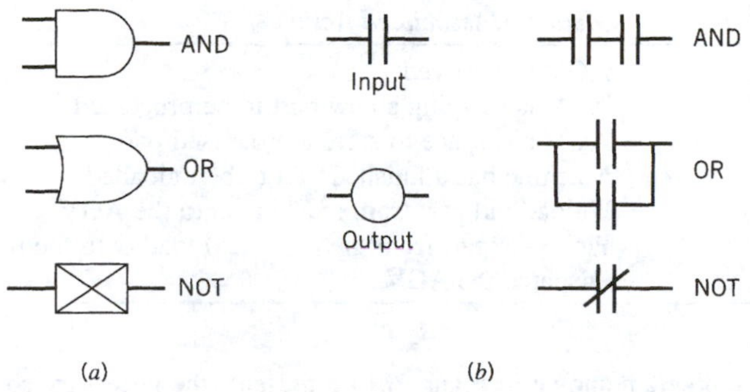

FIGURE 6.18 (*a*) Symbols used in logic network diagrams. (*b*) Symbols used in ladder logic diagrams.

given ladder logic diagram are executed simultaneously, so the order of the rungs on the ladder in general does not matter. Figure 6.18*b* shows the symbols used in a ladder logic diagram and their use in representing logical operators. The reader is cautioned not to confuse the symbol for an input in a ladder logic diagram with the symbol for a capacitor used in electrical circuits.

6.8.2 Programming the PLC

Typically, PLCs are programmed by entering the program on an external unit called a programmer, although personal computers are being used increasingly for this task. The program can then be downloaded to the memory of the PLC, from which it is executed as needed. Although the PLC can be programmed using a variety of languages such as BASIC and FORTRAN, or using Boolean functions directly, the predominant method of programming is by use of ladder logic and this is the method that will be used in this book. A simple example will illustrate the concepts.

EXAMPLE 6.6

A robot is to be used to unload finished parts from a machine onto an AGV and to load raw parts from the AGV to the machine as outlined in Section 6.8. Assume that there are sensors at the AGV's docking station to indicate the arrival of a vehicle and onboard sensors indicating whether the vehicle has brought a raw part to be processed as well as whether the AGV has space to carry away a finished part. Also assume there are sensors on the machine to indicate whether the machine is loaded with a part and also to signal completion of part processing. The robot is required to unload a processed part from the machine onto the AGV, pick up a new part for processing from the AGV, and load it onto the machine. The AGV is to be dispatched after completion of the cycle. Construct a ladder logic diagram for this task.

Solution

In the following solution, it is assumed that we are interested not in the details of the robot motion, but rather in the overall logic of the system. For example, we could give a signal to unload the machine tool that would trigger the robot to execute a "machine unload program." In this case, we are not concerned about the path of the robot, its velocity, and such details which would be taken care of within the robot program itself. We will use the following I/O assignments:

(I/O)	*Meaning/Associated Action*
01	AGV has arrived
02	AGV is carrying a new part to be processed
03	AGV has space to store a processed part
04	Machine has a finished part to be unloaded
20	Unload old part from machine onto the AGV
21	Pick new part from the AGV and load onto the machine
22	Dispatch the AGV

The ladder logic diagram shown in Figure 6.19 represents the necessary control logic for this situation. To understand the ladder logic diagram, note that the logic flows from left to right and from top to bottom. The ladder logic diagram of Figure 6.19 is interpreted as follows:

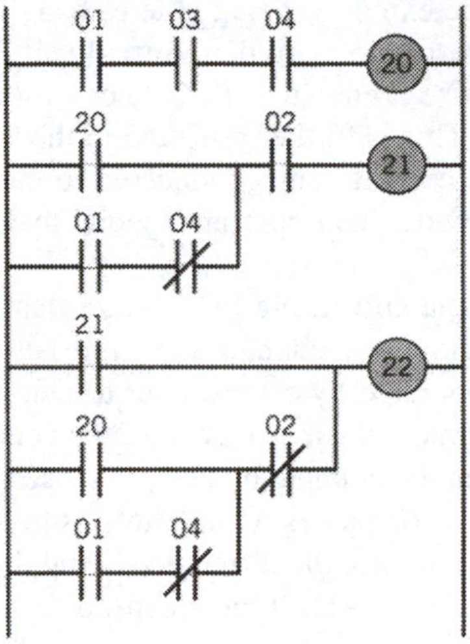

FIGURE 6.19 Ladder logic diagram for Example 6.6.

1. The first rung states that if inputs 01, 03, and 04 are all true, then output 20 is true. This is interpreted as meaning that if the AGV has arrived, and the AGV has space to store a processed part, and the machine has a finished part to be unloaded, then the robot should unload the old part from the machine onto the AGV.
2. The second rung states that if (input 20 is true AND input 02 is true), OR (input 01 is true, and input 04 is not true, and input 02 is true), then output 21 is true. This rung thus illustrates the use of OR in a ladder logic diagram. The rung is interpreted as meaning that if the machine has been unloaded, and the AGV is carrying a new part to be processed; or if the AGV has arrived, and the machine has no part to be unloaded, and the AGV is carrying a new part to be processed; then the robot should load the new part from the AGV onto the machine. In this case there are two scenarios in which the same output may be obtained. Note in particular that output 20 from the previous rung is being used as an input on the current rung. This should not be misinterpreted as meaning that the machine can be unloaded before the AGV arrives, which could be a possible interpretation if the flow of the logic is forgotten, but remember that the input 20 can be true only if inputs 01, 03, and 04 are all true according to the logic of the first rung!
3. The third rung contains the logic for dispatching the AGV after it arrives at the docking station. The reader is invited to figure out the logic in light of the preceding discussion.

The attentive reader will have noticed from this example that a given input may be used repeatedly on different rungs of the ladder. For example, input 01 has been used on all three rungs, and input 20 has been used on the second and third rungs. This is perfectly legitimate and should not cause difficulty if the reader bears in mind that the inputs represent logical variables and each rung of the ladder logic diagram represents a set of logical relationships. The ladder logic diagram should not be confused with an electrical circuit through which current is flowing. It should also be noted that although a rung in the ladder may have several inputs, it has only one output.

6.8.3 Counters and Timers

As demonstrated, PLCs are highly suited to making decisions on the basis of attribute-type questions. With the use of timers and counters, the versatility of a PLC can be greatly expanded, even to the extent of being able to handle variable-type questions. This increase in versatility is so important that virtually all PLCs on the market today include this capability, because it enables a PLC to control a much greater variety of functions in manufacturing. This is further reflected in the fact that although counters and timers could be used as external units connected to the inputs of the PLC, most manufacturers choose to provide this important special feature by building them into the PLC.

Counters can be used in manufacturing to measure quantities such as production stock, inventory, and packaging. The counter accomplishes its task by counting voltage pulses, which can be generated by a sensor set to detect the event whose occurrence is to be noted. Every time a pulse is received, the count is changed by one. For example, production stock can be counted by using a sensor that emits a voltage pulse every time a part on a conveyor passes a specific position in the conveyor's path. Counters and timers are similar, with the difference being that timers are used specifically to count clock pulses. As a result, timers can be seen as clock driven whereas regular counters are event driven.

A counter can be constructed to count up or count down, and the more versatile ones are capable of counting both up and down. In the case of an up–down counter, different input lines are used for counting up and counting down. Counters have another input line that is used to reset the counter to its initial value (usually zero). Some also have an extra input line that forces certain preset values into the counter regardless of the states of the other inputs. Depending on the intended application, the counter may have more than one output. For example, some counters have CARRY and BORROW outputs in addition to the regular output. The CARRY output occurs when the counter exceeds its maximum count value when counting up, and BORROW occurs when the counter goes beyond the minimum value when counting down. Such counters can be connected in cascade fashion with a CARRY/BORROW from one counter connected to the input of the next counter, increasing the overall range of counting.

When used in a ladder logic diagram, a counter or timer (or any other special device for that matter) is represented by a rectangular box. An identifier for the type of device is written inside the box. In the case of a counter or timer, the maximum count value is also written in the box. Example 6.7 illustrates the use of the timing function.

EXAMPLE 6.7

During the powder metallurgy process, a punch is used to press blended metal powder into a compact inside a die. A pushbutton is used to start the process. When the start button is pressed, the die is filled with powder. The punch is then advanced and it applies pressure to the powder for a duration of 10 s, after which it is retracted. The pressed compact is then ejected from the die and the cycle repeats. The cycle can be interrupted by pressing a stop button. If the stop button is pressed, the punch is required to retract (if it had been advanced) before the process is stopped. We are required to construct a ladder logic diagram for this task.

Solution

The following I/O assignments are used:

(I/O)	*Meaning*
01	Start button
02	Stop button
T1	Timer (with a limit of 10 s)
30	Fill die
31	Advance punch
32	Retract punch
34	Eject part (i.e., compact)
35	Stop cycle

The ladder logic diagram shown in Figure 6.20 represents a possible solution.

The logic in Figure 6.20 is explained as follows: When the start button is pushed to initiate the process, or if a part has been ejected successfully from the die (accounts for the process already being in progress), and if the stop button has not been pushed, the die is filled with a predetermined amount of powder. After the die is filled, the punch is advanced to start applying

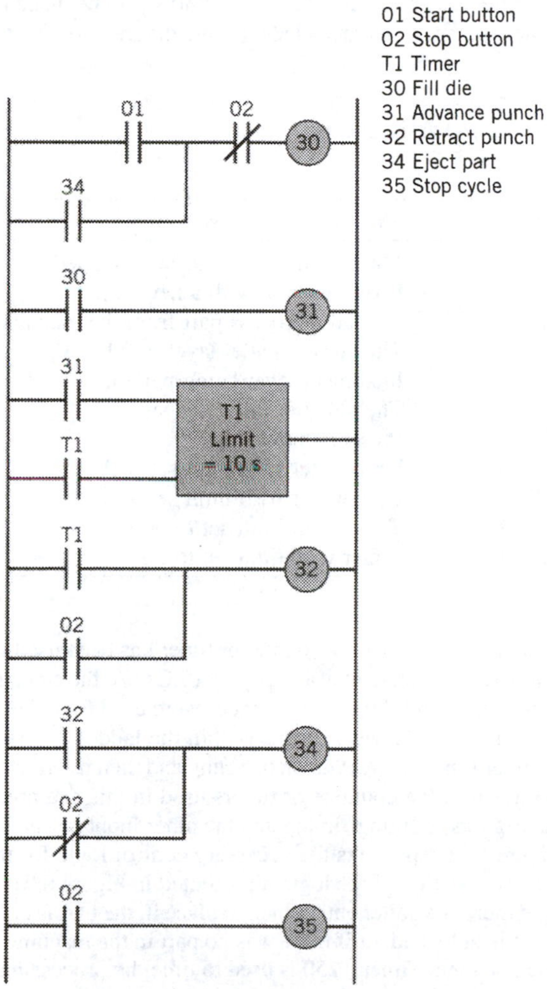

FIGURE 6.20 Ladder logic diagram for Example 6.7.

pressure on the powder. The pressing is timed to last for 10 s, after which the timer resets itself. After the 10 s, or any time the stop button is pressed, the punch retracts. After the punch retracts and provided the stop button has not been pressed, the part is ejected. After the part is ejected, the cycle repeats from the beginning. Whenever the stop button is pressed, the punch is retracted (if it was already advanced) and the cycle stops.

EXAMPLE 6.8

This example illustrates the use of both the timing and counting functions. Consider a production line in which parts requiring processing are brought to a machine by a conveyor. A robot is used to load parts from the conveyor onto the machine and, after the part has been processed, unload the part from the machine and place it on a pallet. The cycle time for processing each part is 10 min. The robot is to palletize the parts by placing 125 parts on each pallet. The parts are to be arranged on the pallet in five layers of 25 parts each. Once a pallet is complete, it is dispatched and a new pallet is started. An allowance of 30 s is to be made for pallet dispatching and presentation of a new pallet. Construct a ladder logic diagram to effect the required control.

Solution

We will use the following I/O assignments:

(I/O)	*Meaning/Associated Action*
10	Machine has a part to be unloaded
30	Load machine with a new part
40	Unload a process part from the machine
45	The current pallet layer is full
48	Increment layer being palletized by 1
50	The pallet is full—dispatch
60	Present a new pallet
C100	Up counter with limit set to 25
C200	Up counter with limit set to 5
T250	Timer with limit set to 600 s
T300	Timer with limit set to 30 s

Notice that no identifying number for a counter or timer has been used more than once. This is a good practice that is recommended because many PLCs use the same memory location for storing counter and timer data, and if the same number were used for different devices, the PLC would not be able to distinguish between them. Within the ladder diagram, the reader should note that a counter or timer function is set up on one rung and then referenced on another rung(s) to trigger its function. Each of the counters or timers used in this example has two inputs and one output. One input triggers counting/timing and the other input resets the device. The ladder diagram shown in Figure 6.21 represents the necessary control logic for this situation.

The following is an explanation of the logic represented in Figure 6.21: If the machine has a part to be unloaded and there is a pallet onto which to place it, the part is unloaded and placed on the pallet. After the part is unloaded, or if there was no part in the machine to begin with, a new part is loaded onto the machine. Timer T250 is used to time the processing operation, and after the 10 min it takes to process the part, the robot is signaled that there is a part to be unloaded from the machine, T250 resets itself, and the cycle is repeated. Counter C100 is used to count parts as they are unloaded from the machine. When C100 counts 25 parts, a signal is generated

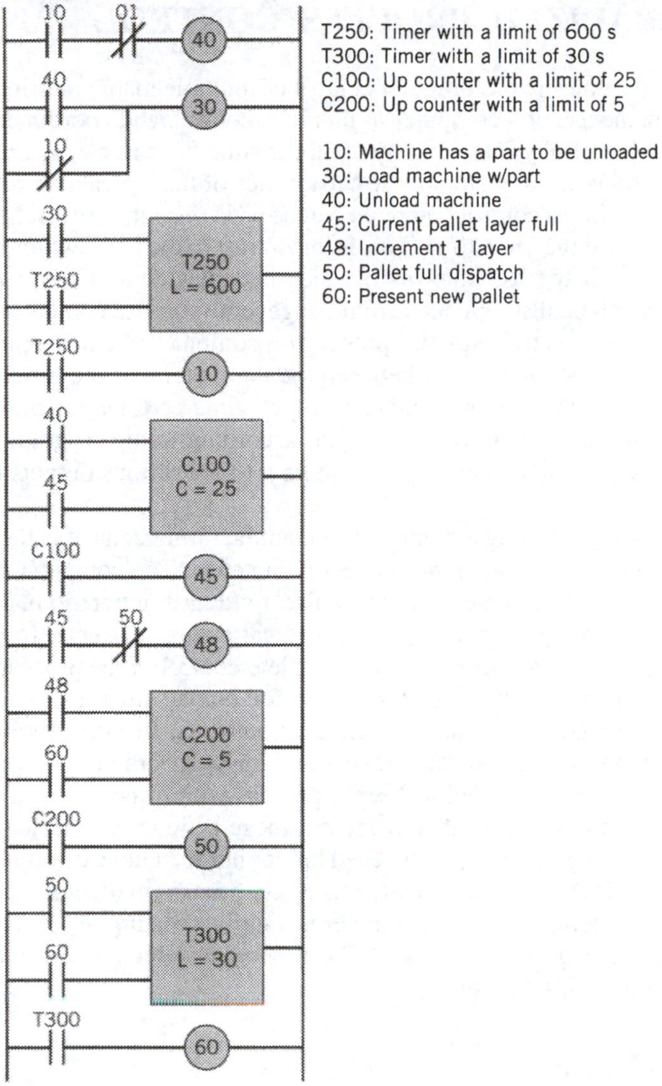

FIGURE 6.21 Ladder logic diagram for Example 6.8.

indicating that the current layer on the pallet is full and C100 is reset. Counter C200 is used to count the number of full layers on the pallet. If the layer just completed is not the fifth layer, pallet loading is continued. When the number of layers on a pallet reaches five, a signal that the pallet is full is generated, the pallet is dispatched, and a signal is generated to present a new pallet. Timer T300 is used to time the dispatch and presentation of pallets, for which a time of 30 s is allowed. After the 30 s, T300 resets itself and C200 is also reset. The whole cycle can now be repeated with the newly presented pallet.

As in Example 6.6, the PLC in this case plays a supervisory role, controlling the overall process rather than the details of individual actions such as robot motions or moving the pallets. For simplicity, a number of issues have been ignored in this example—what happens when tools have to be changed on the machine, how pallets are presented, how the robot recognizes the presence of the part on the conveyor, and so forth. The simplified problem should make it easier for the reader to understand the concepts involved.

6.9 GENERALIZED PROCESS CONTROL

We now turn to the concept of computer control of multiple manufacturing processes. By this we mean the use of a computer to monitor, control, and coordinate the operation of various types of physical equipment on the shop floor in a concurrent manner. This type of control is an extension of the capabilities of the logical control associated with PLCs. Specifically, a control computer can be used to control several processes or pieces of equipment at the same time. This is in contrast to the PLC, which is dedicated to a single process, or the NC controller, which is dedicated to a single machine. A control computer can be distinguished from the general-purpose computer by its ability to communicate directly with the process or equipment being controlled. This capability for direct communication between the computer and the process is called *on-line control.* Thus, the computer takes as input some pertinent information about the process parameters. It then uses this input, according to the programmed control logic, as the basis for making decisions about how to set various outputs that control the process.

The main rationale for using a computer in manufacturing control is the speed with which it can respond to the changing process parameters. The computer can respond almost instantaneously to an input, it is not subject to fatigue or boredom, and it has far greater reliability than equivalent electromechanical control systems. In its most sophisticated form, the on-line computer has complete control of the process, forming a closed control loop in which there is no need for human intervention except in a supervisory role to take care of unforeseen developments. In other applications, the computer can be used to monitor the process and make specific recommendations to the operator about actions needed to keep a process within the required operational parameters. The operator would then carry out those actions or override the recommendations of the computer if experience led him or her to believe this more appropriate. The difference is that in this case there is direct human involvement in executing the required control action, and the computer is simply assisting the human operator. In light of the foregoing discussion, a PLC can be considered a rudimentary control computer dedicated to a single process.

6.9.1 Process Interface

The control computer has the usual interfaces such as a keyboard, a printer, and a display screen for communication with humans. But, unlike the general-purpose computer, a control computer also needs some means of communication with the process being controlled. Therefore, there is a direct physical connection with the process being controlled. This includes contacts to inputs such as sensors, meters, and valves for monitoring the process parameters, as well as output contacts to equipment such as motors, relays, and actuators in the case of direct process control.

For its internal operation, the computer must operate on binary data. Thus the inputs and outputs to the computer are required to be in binary form. To make matters awkward, however, only integers have direct binary equivalents. Other data are represented in binary by using special binary codes according to a data-coding scheme. The most widely used coding scheme is ASCII (which we discussed earlier in connection with NC tapes). At the process level however, the process parameters could be in either digital or analog form. Digital parameters are generally logical variables based on attributes such as those we have seen for PLCs. It follows that they are easy to represent in binary form to be operated on by the computer. Analog parameters, however, are of the variable type and have to be converted to binary digital form before the computer can operate on them. Thus, for input to the computer, analog data must be converted to digital form. Similarly, if an output to the process from the computer has to be in analog form, the computer's digital output must be converted to analog form before it is fed to the process.

The need for analog-to-digital (A/D) conversion is encountered far more frequently in manufacturing control applications than that for digital-to-analog (D/A) conversion. This is because although there are many process parameters that are of analog form, most types of control action dictated by a control computer are of digital form. For example, while tracking the position of an AGV on the shop floor requires analog input to the computer, a corresponding control action from the computer may be to stop the AGV when it reaches a given workstation or to dispatch it once it has been loaded or unloaded. Furthermore, the control computer is typically more involved in process monitoring than actual control, which adds to the importance of A/D conversion in manufacturing control applications. The process of A/D conversion is called encoding, and D/A conversion is called decoding. The reason is that the conversions involve approximation and the converted value will in general not be exactly equal to the original value but will be some close equivalent. The accuracy of conversion depends on the number of binary digits used to store the digital representation of the value being converted and the range of possible values to be represented.

6.9.2 Data Communication

Let us now consider how data are handled internally in a computer and communicated with external devices or processes. We know that data are represented in binary form within the computer. Each digit is called a *bit* (short for binary digit). A group of eight bits is called a *byte*. The computer normally manipulates data in bytes. A *register* is hardware used to store bytes of data, so the register sizes are 8-bit, 16-bit, 32-bit, and so on, depending on the number of bytes the register can handle. A *data bus* is used to move data between registers, and thus the data bus also has a size such as 8-bit or 16-bit. The size of the data bus is used to characterize the central processing unit (CPU) of the computer. To communicate with external devices, I/O ports are used. The data can be transmitted (or received) through the communication ports in either serial or parallel mode.

6.9.2.1 Serial Communication

For serial communication, a byte of data is serialized and sent out 1 bit at a time on a single line. The number of bits transmitted or received per second is referred to as the baud rate. Typical values of baud rate include 1200, 2400, 9600, and 14,400. For transmission, one of the bits is used for parity, which may be odd or even. In addition, start and stop bits are added to the signal from the transmitting end so that the receiver can tell when a byte starts and when it ends. At the receiving end, the data are sent to a shift register, converted back to the byte format, and are then ready to be sent onto the data bus. The transmitting and receiving ends must be set at the same baud rate and with the same type of parity. This process is repeated until data byte transmission is completed. A serial port typically has three contacts, one for sending, one for receiving, and one for the ground wire.

6.9.2.2 Parallel Communication

For parallel communication, a complete byte is sent out together, with each bit transmitted on a separate line. Because all the data bits are transmitted simultaneously, the data are said to be handled in parallel. A parallel port therefore has to have at least eight lines. It is also possible to group together two or more 8-bit ports with each group programmed as either an input or output port. In addition, it is possible to program individual bits within an 8-bit port as either inputs or outputs.

Generally, serial communication is used between computers transferring data and parallel communication is used between a computer and other external devices. A control computer is required to control multiple processes or pieces of equipment on a real-time basis. The actual data transfer between the computer and the external devices must be accomplished according to a specific discipline to ensure that each device is serviced at the appropriate time. Two techniques used for this purpose are polling and interrupts.

6.9.2.3 Polling

With the polling technique, the computer periodically checks the status of all process variables being monitored. The control logic then determines what action needs to be taken (if any) depending on the status of the variable at the time it is polled. A real-time clock within the computer is used to trigger the polling action at regular intervals. If the computer is involved in some other task at the time the polling is triggered, the other task is interrupted in order to service the polling request. The main disadvantage of polling is that it takes place regardless of whether the status of the process itself warrants such action. This imposes a significant computational overhead on the system. Also, if the timing of the interrupt is not properly selected, some process data may be lost between polling actions.

6.9.2.4 Interrupts

The alternative approach uses the status of the process itself to trigger an interrupt. This would be appropriate when some condition within the process being controlled is of such urgency that it must be attended to immediately without waiting for a periodic computer check. In that case, the status of the process condition itself causes an interrupt of the computer. In fact, periodic polling can be dispensed with completely. Under normal conditions, the process does not need to be attended to by the computer. When unsafe or other anomalous conditions arise, the control system simply relies on the status of the process variables to cause the necessary interrupt. This reduces the computational overhead and allows the computer to attend to other tasks during normal operation.

6.9.2.5 Priorities

For a computer controlling several processes, it is possible to imagine a situation in which multiple processes attempt to cause an interrupt at the same time. In that case, there has to be a means of prioritizing the interrupt requests and attending to the most urgent condition first. What is more, if during the servicing of a given interrupt condition another even more critical condition should arise, it should be possible to have another interrupt. Thus one of the tasks involved in designing the control system is to analyze the various potential interrupts from the several devices being controlled and assign them priority levels. During normal operating conditions, the computer may be idle or it may be assigned some routine background task. When an anomalous condition occurs and an interruption is requested, the computer checks on the priority of the interrupt request and compares it with that of the task currently under way (if any). If the interrupt has higher priority, the current task is suspended and the interrupt is serviced. If the interrupt is of lower priority than the current task, the task is completed before the interrupt is serviced. Properly selecting the priority levels prevents situations in which the computer is constantly interrupted and unable to complete a single task.

6.9.3 Local Area Networks

In the manufacturing environment, a control computer needs to communicate with the several processes or devices being controlled and possibly with other computers. Data have to be communicated between all these systems. It would be a daunting task to have one-to-one connection between all of the computers and devices that need to communicate with one another. This combinatorial problem would result in $n!/2(n-2)!$ interconnections for n systems. As an alternative, networks can be used to meet the need for intercommunication between several computers and/or other devices. A network enables communication between many devices without having direct connections between the individual devices. An example of a familiar network is the telephone network. Calls between subscribers are routed through an exchange, and all subscribers on the exchange can reach each other without having direct connection. Moreover, by interconnecting the exchanges, subscribers on different exchanges can reach each other. The networking technology used for the telephone system was the basis for today's computer networking technology.

The computer networks used to connect computers up to 10 km apart are referred to as local area networks (LANs). Clearly, LANs can be used to connect devices in a manufacturing facility. A network consists of a medium for carrying the data signals, software to control data handling and error recovery, and the transmitting and receiving devices connected to the network. Each device on the network has equal access to the network. To avoid "hogging" the network during transmission of large messages, the message to be transmitted is split into manageable portions called *packets*. A packet includes source and destination information on the data being transmitted. At the receiving end, the packets are reassembled into the complete message. Coaxial cable similar to that used for cable television is frequently used as the transmission medium in LANs. A detailed description of network technology, topology, and architecture is given in Chapter 14.

6.10 SUMMARY

The foregoing discussion has provided a basis for understanding the capabilities and applications of computer control in manufacturing. The computer plays a key role in modern manufacturing industry, in controlling both the individual pieces of equipment used in manufacturing and the overall logical operation of the manufacturing system. The computer may be used in different roles, including direct control of the equipment in question, or may act in a supervisory capacity, monitoring equipment and advising the equipment operator on a real-time basis. The computer can also serve in a support role, helping in managerial decision making. It is important for the person involved in the study, design, or analysis of manufacturing systems to have a clear understanding of the capabilities and limitations of computers in this important arena.

PROBLEMS

6.1 What are the functions of an NC controller?

6.2 What is the difference between fixed sequential format and word address format?

6.3 What is a modal command?

6.4 What is a preparatory function?

6.5 Explain the difference between incremental and absolute programming.

6.6 What is the difference between linear and circular position interpolation?

6.7 What is a canned cycle?

6.8 What are the advantages of computer-aided part programming?

6.9 What are the functions of a postprocessor?

6.10 What is the general format of a geometry definition statement in APT?

6.11 What is continuous-path motion?

6.12 Explain the difference between the GOTO and GO commands in APT.

6.13 What are the advantages of using BCL?

6.14 What is the difference between a PLC and a computer?

6.15 List the three basic logical operators.

6.16 What capabilities do counters and timers introduce in a PLC?

6.17 How does a control computer differ from a general-purpose computer?

6.18 What is the purpose of A/D and D/A conversion in relation to computer control?

6.19 Why are LANs used in interconnecting computers?

6.20 Describe how data transmission is controlled in an Ethernet network.

6.21 Rewrite the solution to Example 6.1 using incremental programming.

6.22 Rewrite the solution to Example 6.2 using incremental programming.

6.23 Write an NC program to machine the first letter of your last name.

6.24 Write an APT program to machine the letter B.

6.25 A PLC is to be used to control the operation of an automatic door. A camera is used to detect a person's approach. When the person is within 2 ft of the door, the door is to be opened automatically. An infrared beam in the doorway is used to detect the actual entrance of the person. Ten seconds after the person enters, the door is closed unless there is someone else within 2 ft of the door. If the person does not enter 30 s after the door has opened, it is closed again. Construct a ladder logic diagram for this task. What suggestions could you make to improve on this logic?

6.26 A PLC is used to control the operation of a spot welding machine. Sheets of 6 × 3 ft are to be welded along their 6-ft-long sides allowing for 1.5 in. overlap. The first spot weld is to be 2 in. from the edge and successive welds are to be 4 in. apart. During welding, a preset pressure and current are to be applied. Pressure is applied for 10 s during each weld, and 1 s after the start of pressure application current flow is to start and is to last for 8 s. After all the welds in a pair of sheets are complete, there is an allowance of 1 min to unload and load the next pair of sheets. The cycle is then repeated. Construct a ladder logic diagram for this task.

Laboratory Exercises

In the following exercises, the student is required actually to make the relevant parts on the equipment available at his or her institution. The instructor will give guidance to the students about any site-specific requirements and procedures. Where appropriate, the student should develop a process plan and make the decisions regarding tooling, cutting conditions, and part fixturing.

6.27 Prove out the program you developed for Problem 6.23 and use it actually to make the relevant part.

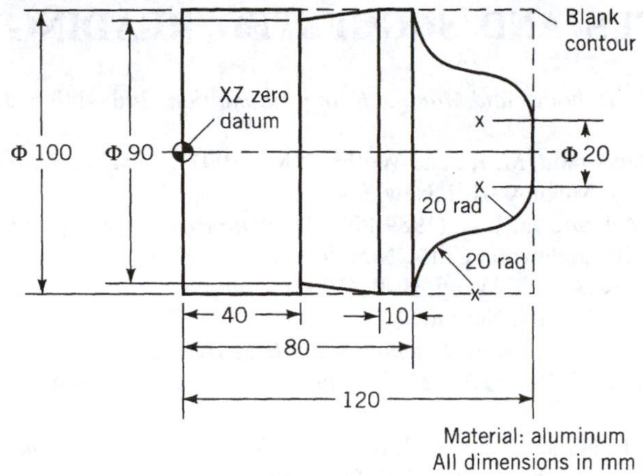

FIGURE P6.1

6.28 Prove out the program you developed for Problem 6.24 and use it actually to make the relevant part.

6.29 *(For those with access to an APT system)* Develop an APT program to make the part shown in Figure P6.1. Postprocess your APT program to generate an NC program and use this to make the part.

6.30 *(For CAD/CAM-based systems)* Generate a design of the part shown in Figure P6.2 on your CAD/CAM system. Use the system's machining functions to generate an NC program for making the part, and use that program to make the part.

6.31 *(For CAD/CAM-based systems)* Generate a design of the part shown in Figure P6.1 on your CAD/CAM system. Use the system's machining functions to generate an NC program for making the part, and use that program actually to make the part.

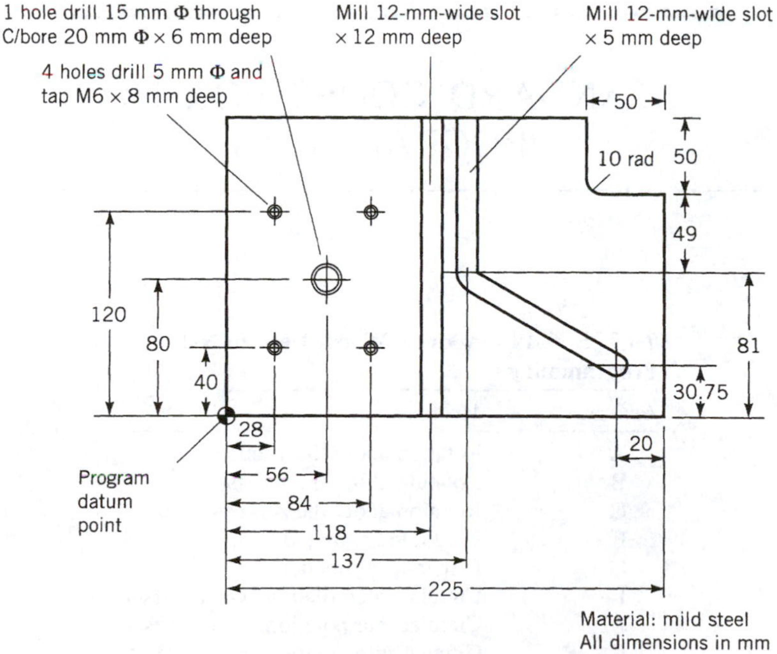

FIGURE P6.2

REFERENCES AND SUGGESTED READING

Asfahl, C. R. (1992). *Robotics and Manufacturing Automation,* 2nd edition. John Wiley & Sons, New York.

Bedworth, D. D., Henderson, M. R., and Wolfe, P. M. (1991). *Computer Integrated Design and Manufacturing.* McGraw-Hill, New York.

Chang, C.-H., and Melkanoff, M. A. (1989). *NC Machine Programming and Software Design.* Prentice-Hall, Englewood Cliffs, New Jersey.

Chang, T.-C., Wysk, R. A., and Wang, H.-P. (1991). *Computer Aided Manufacturing.* Prentice-Hall, Englewood Cliffs, New Jersey.

CNC fundamentals. (1992). *Modern Machine Shop,* 64(10A): 129–214.

Kenlay, G., and Harris, K. W. (1979). *Manufacturing Technology.* Edward Arnold Publishers, London.

Kundra, T. K., Rao, P. N., and Tewari, N. K. (1988). *Numerical Control and Computer Aided Manufacturing.* Tata McGraw-Hill Publishing Co., New Delhi.

Luggen, W. W. (1988). *Fundamentals of Numerical Control.* Delmar Publishers, Albany, New York.

Needler, M. A., and Baker, D. E. (1985). *Digital and Analog Controls.* Reston Publishing Co., Reston, Virginia.

Seames, W. S. (1990). *Computer Numerical Control: Concepts and Programming.* Delmar Publishers, Albany, New York.

Stanton, G. C. (1988). *Numerical Control Programming.* John Wiley & Sons, New York.

Thyer, G. E. (1991). *Computer Numerical Control of Machine Tools.* Newnes, Boston, Massachusetts.

Zahner, S. P. (1991). The value of BCL to the CAD/CAM user. *Modern Machine Shop,* July, pp. 72–80.

APPENDIX

STANDARD CODES FOR NC PROGRAMMING

TABLE 6.A1 **Address Words Used in NC Programming**

Address	*Meaning*
A	Rotation about the x-axis
B	Rotation about the y-axis
C	Rotation about the z-axis
F	Feed rate command
G	Preparatory function
I	Circular interpolation: x-axis offset
J	Circular interpolation: y-axis offset
K	Circular interpolation: z-axis offset

TABLE 6.A1 **(continued)**

Address	*Meaning*
M	Miscellaneous commands
N	Sequence number
R	Radius of arc or circle
S	Spindle speed
T	Tool number
U	Supplemental coordinate parallel to x-axis
V	Supplemental coordinate parallel to y-axis
W	Supplemental coordinate parallel to z-axis
X	x-axis data
Y	y-axis data
Z	z-axis data

Note: Additional nonstandard address words may be used by an individual manufacturer to meet specific needs.

TABLE 6.A2 **Preparatory Word Functions**

Code	*Usage*
G00	Point-to-point positioning
G01	Linear interpolation
G02	Circular interpolation (clockwise)
G03	Circular interpolation (counterclockwise)
G04	Dwell for programmed duration
G05	Delay or hold (until resumed by operator)
G06	Parabolic interpolation
G08	Controlled acceleration of feed rate to programmed value
G09	Controlled deceleration of feed rate to programmed value
G10	Linear interpolation (long dimensions)
G11	Linear interpolation (short dimensions)
G12	Three-dimensional interpolation
G13–G16	Axis selection for machines with multiple heads
G17	$x-y$ Plane Selection
G18	$z-x$ Plane Selection
G19	$y-z$ Plane Selection
G20	Circular interpolation (clockwise, long dimensions)
G21	Circular interpolation (clockwise, short dimensions)
G30	Circular interpolation (counterclockwise, long dimensions)
G31	Circular interpolation (counterclockwise, short dimensions)
G33	Thread cutting, constant lead
G34	Thread cutting, increasing lead
G35	Thread cutting, decreasing lead
G40	Cancel cutter compensation (see G41 and G42)
G41	Cutter compensation, left (cutter to the left of the workpiece)
G42	Cutter compensation, right (cutter to the right of the workpiece)
G43	Cutter compensation, positive (re: radius of single-point lathe tool)
G44	Cutter compensation, negative (re: radius of single-point lathe tool)
G53	Cancel linear shift values (see G54–G59)
G54	Linear shift, x
G55	Linear shift, y
G56	Linear shift, z
G57	Linear shift, xy

TABLE 6.A2 **(continued)**

Code	Usage
G58	Linear shift, *xz*
G59	Linear shift, *yz*
G62	Fast positioning (rarely used since advent of CNC)
G63	Tapping (rarely used since advent of CNC)
G64	Change feed rate (not required with CNC)
G70	Input dimensions in inches
G71	Input dimensions in metric units
G80	Cancel canned cycle (see G81–G89)
G81	Canned cycle for drilling
G82	Canned cycle for spot face/counterbore
G83	Canned cycle for deep hole drilling
G84	Canned cycle for tapping
G85	Canned cycle for through boring (in and out)
G86	Canned cycle for through boring (in only)
G87	Canned cycle for chip breaker drilling
G88	Canned cycle for chip breaker drilling (with dwell)
G89	Canned cycle for through boring (with dwell)
G90	Input in absolute dimensions
G91	Input in incremental dimensions
G92	Preset absolute registers
G94	Feed rate specified in millimeters (or inches) per minute
G95	Feed rate specified in millimeters (or inches) per revolution
G96	Constant cutting speed specified in millimeters (or inches) per minute
G97	Spindle speed in revolutions per minute

Note: Omitted sequences represent nonstandard codes that may be used by individual manufacturers to implement other functions deemed important.

TABLE 6.A3 **Miscellaneous Functions**

Code	Usage
M00	Program stop
M01	Optional program stop
M02	End of program
M03	Spindle on—clockwise rotation
M04	Spindle on—counterclockwise rotation
M05	Spindle off
M06	Tool change
M07	Mist coolant on
M08	Flood coolant on
M09	Coolant off
M10	Clamp on
M11	Clamp off
M13	Spindle on CW* and coolant on
M14	Spindle on CCW* and coolant on
M15	Rapid slide motion in positive direction
M16	Rapid slide motion in negative direction
M19	Stop spindle in oriented position
M30	End of tape—rewind
M31	Interlock bypass
M32–M35	Constant cutting speed codes

TABLE 6.A3 **(continued)**

Code	*Usage*
M36	Feed range 1
M37	Feed range 2
M38	Spindle speed range 1
M39	Spindle speed range 2
M50	Coolant no. 3 on
M51	Coolant no. 4 on
M55	Linear tool shift position 1
M56	Linear tool shift position 2
M60	Change workpiece
M61	Linear workpiece shift position 1
M62	Linear workpiece shift position 2
M68	Clamp workpiece
M69	Unclamp workpiece
M71	Angular workpiece shift position 1
M72	Angular workpiece shift position 2
M78	Clamp slide
M79	Unclamp slide

Note: Omitted sequences represent nonstandard codes that may be used by individual manufacturers to implement other functions deemed important.

* CW = clockwise; CCW = counterclockwise.

CHAPTER 7

AUTOMATED MATERIAL-HANDLING AND STORAGE SYSTEMS

Automated guided vehicle systems (AGVSs), popularly known as driverless vehicles, are becoming an integral part of automated manufacturing systems. With the growth of mid-volume mid-variety production systems such as flexible manufacturing systems (FMSs), which require not only machine flexibility but also material-handling, storage, and retrieval flexibility, it is common to see AGVSs and automated storage and retrieval systems (AS/RSs) interfaced with FMSs. It is therefore important to understand these systems.

In this chapter we study types of AGVSs, their applications, and types of guide paths. System design issues of automated guided vehicle systems such as AGV and guide path selection, guide path design, and determining number of vehicles are analyzed. Similarly, types of AS/RSs, their applications, and AS/RS design and selection aspects are studied. We provide quantitative analysis of single- and dual-command cycle time for the storage systems as well as utilization of S/R machines. A brief discussion of various types of conveyors is also given.

7.1 WHAT IS A MATERIAL-HANDLING SYSTEM?

A material-handling system can be simply defined as an integrated system involving such activities as handling, storing, and controlling of materials. The word material has a very broad meaning, covering all kinds of raw materials, work in progress, subassemblies, and finished assemblies. The primary objective of using a material-handling system is to ensure that the material in the right amount is safely delivered to the desired destination at the right time and at minimum cost.

Material handling is an integral part of any manufacturing activity. The material-handling cost component may vary from 10 to 80% of the total cost. Furthermore, material-handling equipment is prone to accidents because of its moving nature. It is therefore important that the material-handling system is properly designed not only to ensure the minimum cost and compatibility with other manufacturing equipment but also to meet safety concerns. In the next section we discuss some of the principles that have proved to be useful in designing efficient material-handling systems.

7.2 PRINCIPLES OF MATERIAL HANDLING

The Material Handling Institute has compiled 20 basic guidelines for designing and operating material-handling systems. These guidelines are referred to as principles of material handling. In the following section we provide a brief discussion of these principles:

1. *Orientation principle.* Study the system relationships thoroughly prior to preliminary planning in order to identify existing methods and problems, physical and economic constraints, and to establish future requirements and goals.
2. *Planning principle.* Establish a plan to include basic requirements, desirable options, and consideration of contingencies for all material-handling and storage activities.
3. *Systems principle.* Integrate the handling and storage activities that are economically viable into a coordinated system of operation including receiving, inspection, storage, production, assembly, packaging, warehousing, shipping, and transportation.
4. *Unit load principle.* Handle product in as large a unit load as practical.
5. *Space utilization principle.* Make effective utilization of all cubic space.
6. *Standardization principle.* Standardize handling methods and equipment whenever possible.
7. *Ergonomic principle.* Recognize human capabilities and limitations by designing material-handling equipment and procedures for effective interaction with the people using the system.
8. *Energy principle.* Include energy consumption of the material-handling systems and material-handling procedures when making comparisons or preparing economic justifications.
9. *Ecology principle.* Minimize adverse effects on the environment when selecting material-handling equipment and procedures.
10. *Mechanization principle.* Mechanize the handling process where feasible to increase efficiency and economy in handling of materials.
11. *Flexibility principle.* Use methods and equipment that can perform a variety of tasks under a variety of operating conditions.
12. *Simplification principle.* Simplify handling by eliminating, reducing, or combining unnecessary movements and/or equipment.
13. *Gravity principle.* Utilize gravity to move material whenever possible, while respecting limitations concerning safety, product damage, and loss.
14. *Safety principle.* Provide safe material-handling equipment and methods that follow existing safety codes and regulations in addition to accrued experience.
15. *Computerization principle.* Consider computerization in material-handling and storage systems, when circumstances warrant, for improved material and information control.
16. *System flow principle.* Integrate data flow with the physical material flow in handling and storage.
17. *Layout principle.* Prepare an operational sequence and equipment layout for all viable system solutions, then select the alternative system that best integrates efficiency and effectiveness.
18. *Cost principle.* Compare the economic justification of alternative solutions in

equipment and methods on the basis of economic effectiveness as measured by expense per unit handled.

19. *Maintenance principle.* Prepare a plan for preventive maintenance and scheduled repairs on all material-handling equipment.
20. *Obsolescence principle.* Prepare a long-range and economically sound policy for replacement of obsolete equipment and methods with special consideration of after-tax cycle costs.

7.3 MATERIAL-HANDLING EQUIPMENT

Material-handling equipment can be classified into the following basic categories:

- Industrial trucks include hand trucks such as two-wheeled, four-wheeled, hand lift, and forklift and powered trucks such as forklift, tractor–trailer trains, industrial crane trucks, and side loaders. They have platforms with wheels for manual movement of items in the case of hand trucks and mechanized movement of items in the case of industrial trucks.
- Conveyors such as belt, chute, roller, wheel, slat, chain, bucket, trolley, tow, screw, vibrating, and pneumatic.
- Monorails, hoists, and cranes such as bridge, gantry, tower, and stacker.
- Automated guided vehicle systems such as unit load carriers, towing, pallet trucks, fork trucks, and assembly line.
- Automated storage and retrieval systems such as unit load, miniload, person-on-board, deep lane, and storage carousel systems.

A detailed discussion of industrial trucks, conveyors, monorails, hoists, and cranes is given in a number of material-handling textbooks (Tompkins and White, 1984; Sule, 1994). In this chapter we provide a detailed treatment of AGVSs and AS/RSs followed by a brief discussion of conveyors.

7.4 AUTOMATED GUIDED VEHICLE SYSTEMS

An automated guided vehicle system is a battery-powered driverless vehicle with programming capabilities for destination, path selection, and positioning. The AGVS belongs to a class of highly flexible, intelligent, and versatile material-handling systems used to transport materials from various loading locations to various unloading locations throughout the facility. The collision avoidance capability is an interesting feature of the AGVS. That is, the vehicle comes to a dead stop before any damage is done to personnel, materials, or structures. AGVSs are becoming an integral part of flexible manufacturing system installations. Koff (1987) provides a detailed discussion of vehicle types, their applications, basic functions, traffic, and system management.

The modern AGVS owes its reputation as a versatile and flexible material-handling system to modern microprocessor technology. An on-board microprocessor on each vehicle is used to guide a vehicle along the prescribed path and makes corrections if the vehicle strays from the path. A system controller receives instructions directly from the host computer, communicates with other vehicles, and issues appropriate move commands to each vehicle. Communication with the vehicles occurs either through a wire in the floor or by radio.

7.4.1 The Components of an AGVS

There are four main components of an automated guided vehicle system:

1. *The vehicle.* It is used to move the material within the system without a human operator.
2. *The guide path.* It guides the vehicle to move along the path.
3. *The control unit.* It monitors and directs system operations including feedback on moves, inventory, and vehicle status.
4. *The computer interface.* It interfaces with other computers and systems such as the mainframe host computer, the automated storage and retrieval system (AS/RS), and the flexible manufacturing system (FMS).

7.4.2 The Types of AGVSs

Several different types of automated guided vehicles are available to meet different service requirements (Koff, 1987). The vehicle types include:

- AGVS towing vehicles
- AGVS unit load transporters
- AGVS pallet trucks
- AGVS forklift trucks
- AGVS light-load transporters
- AGVS assembly-line vehicles

The different types of AGVS vehicles are illustrated in Figure 7.1. A typical unidirectional unit load carrier is shown in Figure 7.2. These vehicles are built with a variety of cargo decks. These decks include lift-and-lower type, powered or nonpowered roller,

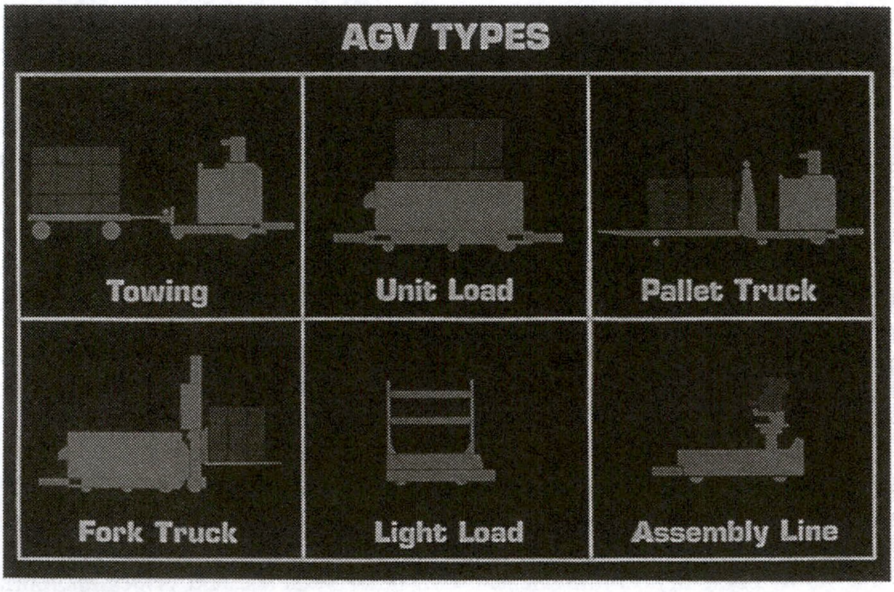

FIGURE 7.1 Different types of automated guided vehicle systems. (Courtesy of Rapistan Demag Corporation.)

FIGURE 7.2 A heavy-duty unidirectional unit load carrier. (Courtesy of Rapistan Demag Corporation.)

chain, or belt decks, and custom decks with multiple compartments. Other features include interface with conveyor systems and on-board robots to load and unload cargo and/or perform operations. They are also often equipped with special tooling and perform assembly operations such as lifting engines into car bodies that are riding on overhead conveyors.

The level of sophistication of the AGVSs has increased to allow automatic positioning and pickup and drop-off (P/D) of cargo, or they may perform P/D services between machining work centers, storage racks, and the AS/RS. They are also capable of two-way travel on the same path (with passing zones) and real-time dispatching under computer control. Other AGVSs may travel between the buildings of a plant, opening and closing doors en route, or travel between floors in a loft building or hospital via automatic call and dispatch of elevators. AGVSs can also be modified, adapted, and redesigned to operate in hostile atmospheres and environments.

7.4.2.1 AGVS Towing Vehicles

AGVS towing vehicles were the first type introduced and are still one of the popular types (Koff, 1987). A towing vehicle is an automated guided tractor. A wide variety of trailers can be used, such as flatbed trailers, pallet trucks, custom trailers, and bin trailers. The types of loading equipment used for loading and unloading the trailer include an AGV-pulled train, hand pallet truck, cranes, forklift truck, automatic transfer equipment, manual labor, shuttle transfer, and programmed automatic loading and unloading device.

Usually, towing applications involve the bulk movement of product into and out of warehouse areas (Figure 7.3*a*). Towing vehicles are better used for large volumes with long moving distances of 1000 ft or more. Moreover, the trailers have capacities ranging from 8000 to 50,000 lb. The train speed is 264 ft/min, and the minimum turning radius is 7 ft.

7.4.2.2 AGVS Unit Load Transporters

AGVS unit load transporters are equipped with decks that permit transportation of an individual unit load on board the vehicle. The deck can be a powered or nonpowered roller, chain or belt deck, lift-and-lower type, or custom deck with multiple compartments. Thus the deck can be interfaced with powered or nonpowered conveyors. Push–pull stations can also be incorporated. Furthermore, the loads can be inserted and removed by forklift truck, pallet truck, automatic loading and unloading device, and other equipment. Unit load transporters are often equipped with automatic load transfer. They are usually independent of one another and can pass each other to get to specific destinations. This is the reason why unit load transporters can be used effectively in a variety of situations. Moreover, they are capable of bidirectional movement.

Unit load transporters are normally used in warehousing and distribution systems where the guide path lengths are relatively short but the volumes are high (Figure 7.3b). They are efficient in horizontal transportation between hardware-intensive material-handling subsystems. The unit load transporter can handle a high volume of material over a moderate distance, linking other automated subsystems in a totally integrated facility. It normally travels at 176 ft/min. Moreover, the vehicles have capacities ranging from 500 to 1000 lb and the turning radius is 2 ft.

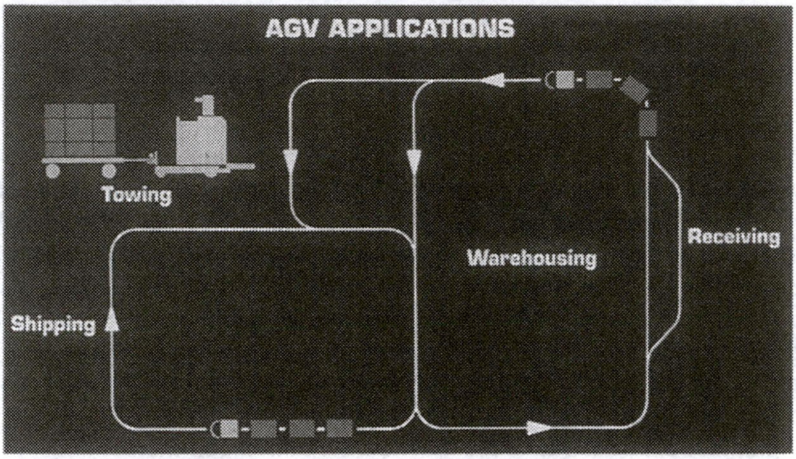

(*a*)

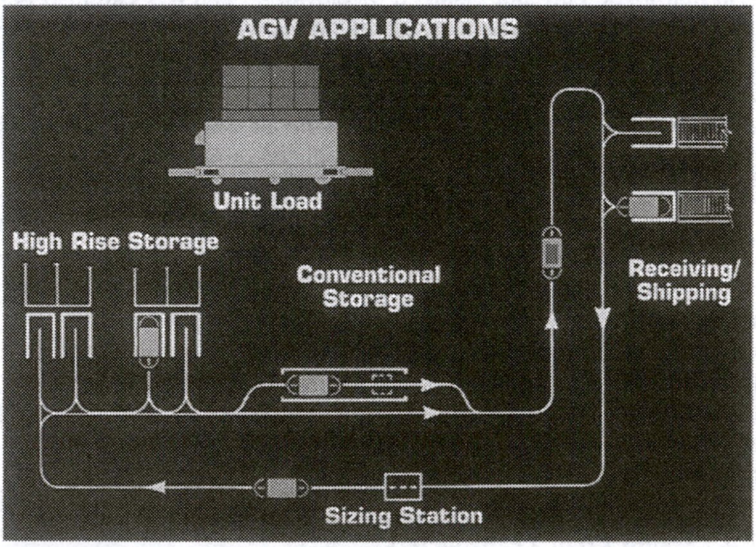

(*b*)

FIGURE 7.3 AGVS applications: (*a*) towing vehicles; (*b*) unit load transporters; (*c*) pallet truck; (*d*) forklift; (*e*) light load; (*f*) assembly line. (Courtesy of Rapistan Demag Corporation.)

7.4.2.3 AGVS Pallet Trucks

AGVS pallet trucks are designed to lift, maneuver, and transport palletized loads. They are still widely used in distribution functions. The vehicle is used for picking up and dropping off loads from and to floor level, thus eliminating the need for fixed load stands (Figure 7.3*c*). No special device is necessary for loading and unloading the AGVS pallet truck except that the loads should be on a pallet. The AGVS pallet truck is limited to floor-level loading and unloading with a palletized load. The vehicle has capacities ranging from 1000 to 2000 lb. The speed of the vehicle is 264 ft/min and it has a minimum turning radius of 7 ft.

The AGVS pallet truck can be loaded and unloaded in two ways: automatically or manually. For load transportation, the vehicle normally proceeds along the path to a specific storage area destination, pulls off onto a spur, lowers the pallet forks to the

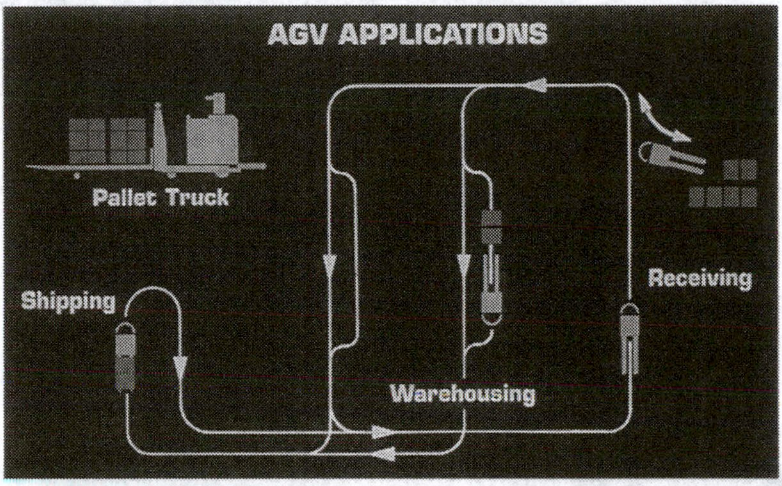

(*c*)

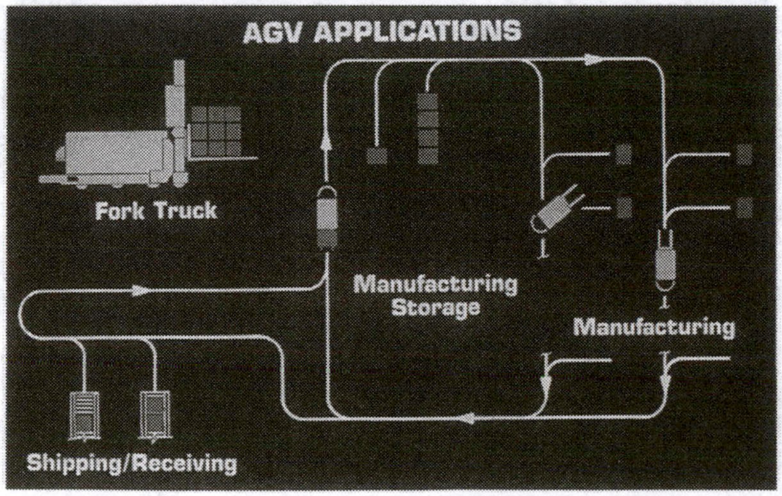

(*d*)

FIGURE 7.3 (continued)

floor, pulls out from the pallet, and then automatically returns empty to the loading area.

An AGVS pallet truck with automatic loading and unloading requires accurate positioning of loads on the floor for picking up and a sensor for locating the pallet to be picked up. This is a considerable expense to the system. Manually loading the vehicle gives operators flexibility to position loads anywhere off the path and still be able to

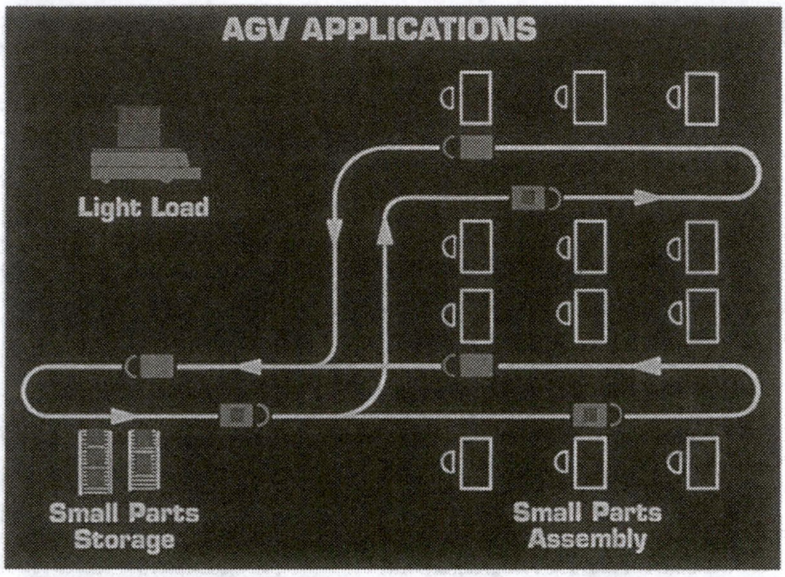

(*e*)

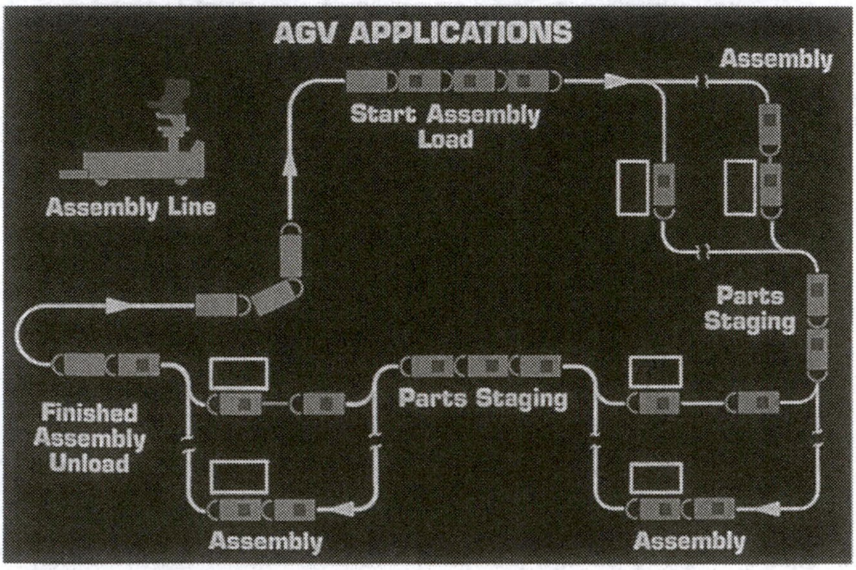

(*f*)

FIGURE 7.3 (continued)

retrieve them with the vehicles, which then automatically proceed without operators into the warehouse drop-off location.

7.4.2.4 AGVS Forklift Trucks

AGVS forklift trucks are relatively new. An AGVS forklift truck has the ability to pick up and drop off palletized loads both at floor level and on stands, and the pickup height can be different from the drop-off height. In some cases, these vehicles can also stack loads in a rack. The guided forklift truck is capable of picking up and dropping off a palletized load automatically without a human operator. The vehicles can position its forks at any height so that conveyors or load stands with different heights in the material-handling system can all be serviced (Figure 7.3*d*).

AGVS forklift trucks are one of the most expensive AGVS types (except for vehicles with special tooling such as robot or air-bearing devices), so they are applied only in systems where full automation is required. The truck is equipped with sensors at the fork end, so it can handle high-level stacking on its own. A system with these vehicles requires a more intricate path layout and a method for accurately positioning the loads on the floor or on a stand. It also requires greater discipline than other systems. However, these systems have the advantage of greater flexibility in integrating with other subsystems with various loading and unloading heights through the material-handling system.

The AGVS forklift truck is limited to a palletized load with the ability to service different height facilities. The vehicles have capacities ranging from 1000 to 2000 lb, a speed of 264 ft/min, and a minimum turning radius of 7 feet.

7.4.2.5 AGVS Light-Load Transporters

AGVS light-load transporters are vehicles with capacities less than 500 lb. They are used to handle small, light parts over a moderate distance and to distribute the parts between storage and a number of workstations (Figure 7.3*e*). Light-load transporters normally travel at 100 ft/min and have a turning radius of 2 ft. They are designed to operate in areas with limited space. Electronic fabrication, small-assembly manufacturing, parts-kitting applications, and mail are proper uses for the AGVS light-load transporters.

7.4.2.6 AGVS Assembly-Line Vehicles

AGVS assembly line vehicles are an adaptation of the light-load transporter for applications involving serial assembly processes (Figure 7.3*f*). The AGVS assembly line system has been introduced in the United States recently. The guided vehicle carries major subassemblies such as motors, transmissions, or even automobiles. As the vehicle moves from one station to the next, succeeding assembly operations are performed.

After the part is loaded on the vehicle, the vehicle proceeds to an assembly area and stops for assembly. When the assembly is complete, the operator releases the vehicle, which proceeds to the next parts staging area for new parts. After that, the vehicle moves forward to the next assembly station. The process is repeated until the final unloading station is reached.

This system provides manufacturing flexibility by permitting parallel operations in the manufacturing process. The vehicle can be tracked individually and work rate can be measured. The major advantage of the AGVS assembly line is lower expense and ease of installation compared with "hard" assembly lines. The line can easily be changed by adjusting the guide path if necessary and by reprogramming. Moreover, variable speeds and dwell intervals can be programmed into the system. However, complex computer control is required to integrate the system into the overall production system and extensive planning is necessary.

An AGVS assembly line can be as small as the light-load transporter or large enough to transport an automobile. The speed of the vehicle is in the range of 100 to 200 ft/min. Moreover, the vehicles have capacities of 500 to 2000 lb, and the turning radius can be 2 to 7 ft.

The following are some of the important issues that must be considered for the proper management of automated guided vehicle systems:

- Guidance systems
- Routing
- AGVS control systems
- Load transfer
- Interfacing with other subsystems

Koff (1987) provides a detailed treatment of some of these issues. A brief summary of various guidance systems is also given in Luggen (1991).

7.4.3 AGVS Guidance Systems

The primary objective of a guidance system is to keep the vehicle in the predesignated path. The main advantage of AGVS guidance is that the guide path can be changed easily at low cost compared with the high cost of modifying fixed-path equipment such as conveyors, chains, and tow lines. Moreover, the guide path is flexible; that is, crossover of path is possible and the path does not obstruct other traffic. A number of guidance systems are available. The selection will depend on need, application, and environmental constraints.

7.4.3.1 Wire-Guided Guidance System

In this system, an energized wire is embedded in the floor along the AGV guidepath. The antenna of the AGV senses and follows the embedded wire.

7.4.3.2 Optical Guidance System

Colorless fluorescent particles are painted or taped on to the carpeted, tiled, or concrete floor. Photosensors on the vehicle read and track these colorless particles. This system permits a clean operating environment.

7.4.3.3 Inertial Guidance System

The system has an onboard microprocessor that is used to steer the vehicle on a preprogrammed path. A sonar system is used for obstacle detection and a gyroscope for directional change.

7.4.3.4 Infrared Guidance System

This system consists of infrared light transmitters, reflectors mounted in the roof of the facility to reflect the light, and radar-like detectors to relay reflected light signals to the computer. The computer then determines the position and direction of travel of the vehicle.

7.4.3.5 Laser Guidance System

In this system a laser beam is used to scan wall-mounted bar-coded reflectors. Accurate location and maneuvering of an AGV are achieved through known distances.

7.4.3.6 Teaching-Type Guidance System

In this system, neural network concepts are used. A programmed vehicle learns the guidepath by "walking through" the desired route. It then informs the host computer what it has learned about the new path. The host computer, in turn, passes information about the new path to other automated guided vehicles.

7.4.4 AGVS Steering Control

The steering control of an AGVS can control the vehicle to negotiate a turn and to maneuver physically in different ways. Two basic types of AGVS steering control systems are used for this purpose: *differential-speed* steer control and *steered-wheel* steer control.

7.4.4.1 Differential-Speed Steer Control

The differential-speed steer control system uses an amplitude-detection type of guidance sensor. The control is based on balancing of signals from the left and right sensors in front of the vehicle. Whenever a difference exists between the amplitudes of the right and left signals, the steering system compensates by correcting the steering. Vehicles with differential-speed steer control have less tracking tolerance than vehicles with steered-wheel steer control.

7.4.4.2 Steered-Wheel Steer Control

This system uses a phase-detection type of guidance sensor to determine whether the vehicle is to the left or right of the path by detecting the positive or negative phase of the sensor signal received from the guided path wire. The vehicle uses this information to steer so that there is no phase difference. Vehicles with steered-wheel steer control have excellent tolerance along the guide path.

7.4.5 AGVS Routing

AGVS routing means determining how the vehicle negotiates the path to take the shortest route from one point to another. The commonly used methods are the *frequency select method* and the *path-switch select method.*

7.4.5.1 Frequency Select Method

Consider the simple layout given in Figure 7.4*a*. The frequency select method is demonstrated in Figure 7.4*b*. The location where a path splits into two or more than two separate directions is called a decision point. At the decision point the vehicle reads a marker (a passive code device in the form of a buried magnet, metal plate, or other code device) in the floor, where multiple frequencies are present to allow the vehicle to go into multiple directions. The vehicle selects a frequency for the direction it wants to follow. The frequencies loop through the system in a continuous wire and are always active.

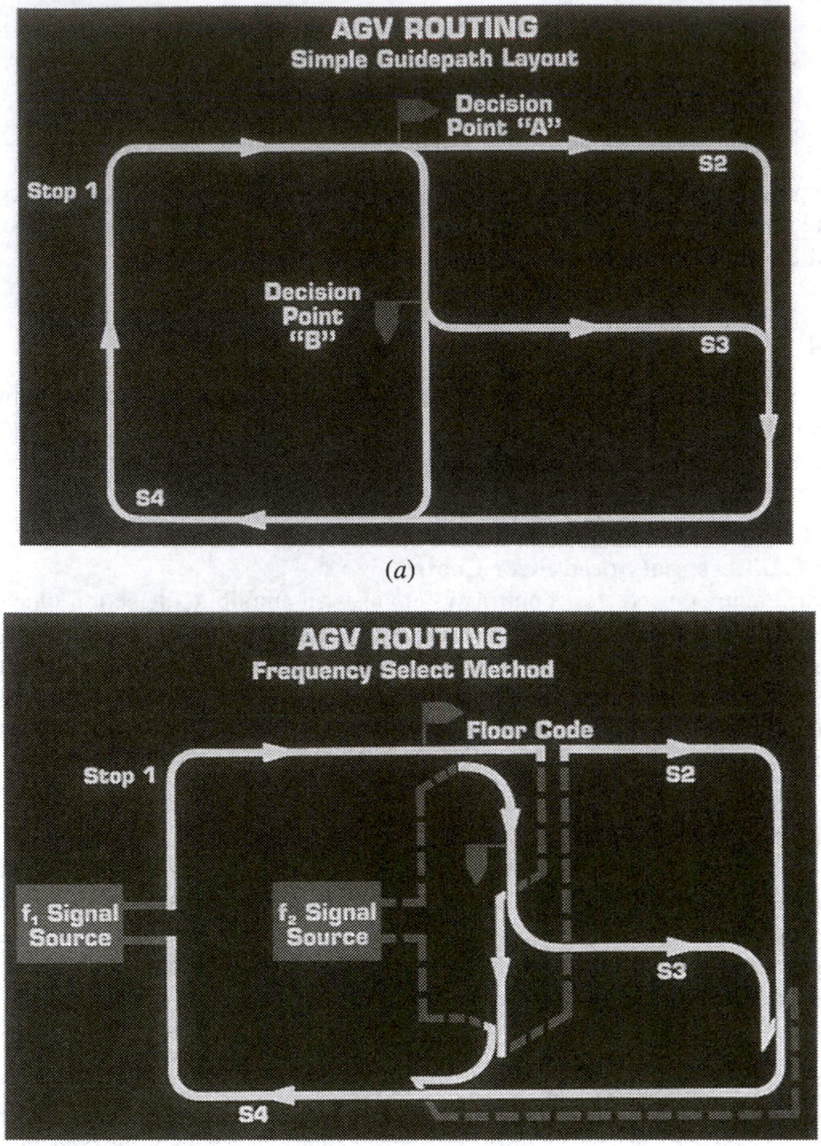

(b)

FIGURE 7.4 AGV routing. (*a*) Simple guidepath layout; (*b*) frequency-select method; (*c*) path-switch method. (Courtesy of Rapistan Demag Corporation.)

7.4.5.2 Path-Switch Select Method

In this system the guide path is divided into segments that are switched on and off by separate floor controls, as shown in Figure 7.4*c*. Only one frequency is used. At the decision points the controls are switched on and off depending on the path to be followed. Remember, the vehicle chooses the proper path in the frequency select method. For this reason the path-switch select method is less preferred than the frequency select method.

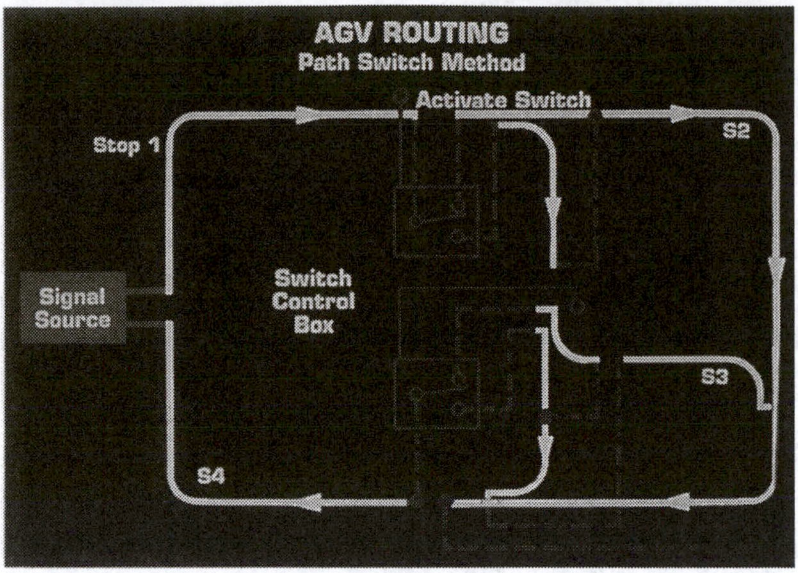

(c)

FIGURE 7.4 (continued)

7.4.6 AGVS Control Systems

Three types of AGVS control systems are available:

- Computer-controlled system
- Remote dispatch control system
- Manual control system

7.4.6.1 Computer-Controlled System

In this system, all the transactions and AGVS vehicle movements are controlled and monitored by the system controller. A diagram of the computer-controlled system is shown in Figure 7.5. The guidepath controller controls the guidepath of the AGVS and

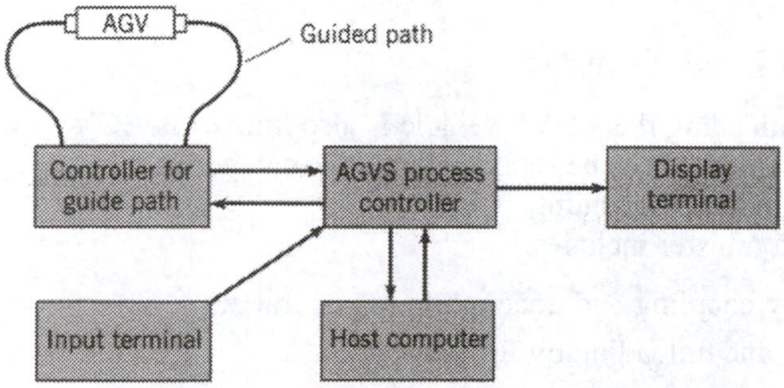

FIGURE 7.5 Computer control architecture for AGVS control.

transfers the information to the AGVS process controller. The AGVS process controller directs the movement of the AGVS vehicles. For monitoring purposes this information is displayed at the display monitor. Moreover, the AGVS process controller interchanges information with the host computer. The host computer is used for process accounting, financial, and other data for management uses. An AGVS computer-controlled system is most efficient, but it is also the most expensive and complex type of control system.

7.4.6.2 Remote Dispatch Control System

In this system a human operator is required to issue instructions to the vehicle through a remote control station. The control system sends destination instructions directly to the vehicle. Therefore, the human operator does not have any direct control over the AGVS vehicle. Most remote dispatch control systems have automatic loading and unloading capability.

7.4.6.3 Manual Control System

In the manually controlled system, the operator loads the vehicle and enters a destination into the onboard control panel on the vehicle. The vehicle is routed by itself to the designated destination through the guide path. After reaching the final destination, the vehicle stops and waits for an operator to perform or direct unloading. A manually controlled system is simple and the least expensive of all control systems. The efficiency of the system depends on the skill and performance of the operator.

7.4.7 Interface with Other Subsystems

The computer-controlled system may interface the AGVS materials-handling system with other subsystems in the organization. These subsystems include:

1. Automated storage and retrieval systems
2. Flexible manufacturing systems
3. Computer numerical control (CNC) machines
4. Process control equipment
5. Shop floor control system

This interface may be through either a distributed data processing network or the host computer. In the distributed data processing network, the system control computers communicate with each other directly without the intermediate or host computer.

7.4.8 AGVS Load Transfer

Loading and unloading the AGVS vehicle is also known as AGVS load transfer. The load transfer operations can be separated into two categories: manual load transfer and automatic loading and unloading.

Manual load transfer includes:

- Manually coupling and uncoupling towed trailers
- Loading and unloading by forklift truck
- Loading and unloading by roller
- Manually loading and unloading the AGVS vehicle

Automatic loading and unloading of the AGVS vehicle is essential for top efficiency in a system. If automatic loading and unloading is not available, manual loading and unloading will be required. In this case, there will be little advantage to automating the rest of the AGVS.

Automatic loading and unloading can be accomplished in many different ways:

- Automatic couple and uncouple
- Powered roller, belt, and chain
- Powered lift and lower device
- Powered push or pull device

7.4.9 AGVS Design Features

Several design features of an AGVS are common to all other material-handling systems. However, there are several special features unique to the AGVS, such as stopping accuracy, facilities, safety, and maintenance.

Stopping accuracy is an important attribute of an AGVS and varies considerably with the nature and requirements of the system. A system with automatic load transfer requires high stopping accuracy. However, lower stopping accuracy is possible in case of manual load transfer. Moreover, unit load transporters are used for systems that require higher accuracy. A system of mechanisms or computer control with feedback could be used to provide the stopping accuracy in an AGVS. Stopping accuracies depend on the applications, for example, ± 0.001 in. for machine tool interfaces, ± 1 in. or more for towing and light-load vehicles, and ± 3 in. for a manual system.

Automatic door-opening devices, elevators, environmental compatibility (as in cold and hot working places), and grades are several facilities and features that must be considered in the design of AGVSs. Safety features such as emergency contact bumpers and stop buttons, object detectors, automatic warning signals, and stopping devices must be built into an AGVS. These features are necessary to avoid human injuries and damage to other equipment, materials, and the vehicle itself.

Every AGVS vehicle must have a service manual detailing routine and repair maintenance activities. Preventive maintenance intervals for important parts should be specified and usage-based checking for lubrication, batteries, electrical system, and so forth should be provided.

7.4.10 System Design of Automated Guided Vehicle Systems

The system design of automated guided vehicle systems is a complex decision process. A number of issues must be resolved, including:

- Selection of guidepath type and vehicle type
- Flow path design
- Guidepath layout
- Type of flow path within the layout (unidirectional, bidirectional, or combinations)
- Number and location of load transfer points and load transfer station storage space
- Number of vehicles required

There are also operational issues such as the routes used by vehicles during operation and the dispatching rules used during operation (both vehicle initiated and work center initiated). The interaction between the design and operational issues must be considered for any system design to be successful.

7.4.10.1 Attributes for Selection of Guidance and AGVS

Shelton and Jones (1987) proposed a multiattribute value approach for the selection of an AGVS. A number of ranking approaches can also be used if information about their attributes, user requirements, and user preferences for AGV attributes is available. Lists of a number of attributes of AGVSs related to the vehicle as well as vendor support and services are given here and should be considered in the selection of an AGVS.

The vehicle-related attributes include:

- Cost of the guidance and vehicle systems
- Guidepaths such as magnetic, optical, chemical, laser, teaching type, and so forth
- Off-path travel capability
- Vehicle width
- Load capacity attributes such as weight, height, and depth
- Maximum loaded and unloaded speeds
- Charging related attributes such as run time between charges, charging time required, and on-line recharging capability
- Bidirectional movement along a path
- Maintenance facilities such as light-emitting diode (LED) lights for self-diagnosis, low-level power indicators, vehicle jack stands, and modular components for maintenance
- Safety features such as pressure-sensitive bumpers, emergency stop buttons, warning lights, warning beeps and messages, and vehicle restart (manual, automatic, or both)
- Turning radius
- Position sensors
- Plane of movement such as horizontal and vertical
- Light height (meters)
- System capabilities such as transport only unit loads, mobile assembly or pickup, transport, unload to floor, conveyor, shelves, and common carrier
- Loading system such as unit load, pallet, roll, special attachments required

Vendor support and services–related attributes include:

- Customization of vehicle
- Warranty coverage (length of time)
- Reputation of vendor
- Commitment to AGV

All of the listed attributes fall in one of four categories:

1. Those in which higher values are preferred (capacity, speed, run time between charges)

2. Those in which lower values are preferred (cost, charging time required)
3. Those that are available or not (discrete attributes)
4. Those that have several options

The selection procedures would normally involve the following steps:

1. A feasible set of AGV models is chosen, based on user specifications for attribute values.
2. The feasible set is ranked according to preferences expressed by the user.

7.4.10.2 Flow Path Design

The flow path design is one of the most important processes in the AGV system design. Some of the important decisions involved in flow path design are:

- The type of guidepath layout
- The type of flow path within the layout (unidirectional, bidirectional, or combinations)
- The number and location of load transfer (pickup and delivery or deposit, also known as P/D station) points
- Load transfer station storage space

The type of application, such as FMS, assembly, or warehousing, essentially determines guide path layout, P/D location points, and load transfer station storage space. On the other hand, the complexity of controls and economic considerations influence the direction of flows. For example, unidirectional flow restricts the vehicle travel to one direction along a given segment of the flow path, resulting in more vehicle travel than with bidirectional flow. However, unidirectional flows require fewer controls and are more economical.

The flow path design for any real-life situation would require consideration of such issues as vehicle blocking, vehicle congestion, and unloaded vehicle travel, which would depend on the number of vehicles and the requests for vehicles from various pickup and delivery stations. To develop realistic designs under these circumstances, it is advisable to use simulation. A number of user-friendly simulation packages are now available (for details, see ''Simulation software buyers' guide,'' 1994). The type of information required for developing a simulation model would include layout of departments, aisles, location of load transfer stations, and from–to charts containing the material flow intensities between departments.

7.4.10.3 Number of Automated Guided Vehicles Required

Another important element of system design is estimation of the number of automated guided vehicles required. In this section we provide a simple analysis to determine the number of vehicles. The following notation is used:

D_d = total average loaded travel distance
D_e = total average empty travel distance
N_{dr} = number of deliveries required per hour
T_h = loading and unloading time
T_f = traffic factor that accounts for blocking of vehicles and waiting of vehicles in line and at intersections. If there is no congestion (that means there is only one vehicle in the system), the traffic factor is 1. However, when more vehicles are involved, the traffic factor value will certainly be less than 1. Normally, T_f lies between 0.85 and 1.
v = vehicle speed

Then the total time per delivery per vehicle (T_{dv}) is given by the sum of loaded travel time, loading and unloading time, and empty travel time as follows:

$$T_{dv} = \frac{D_d}{v} + T_h + \frac{D_e}{v}$$

Number of deliveries per vehicle per hour

$$N_d = \frac{60T_f}{T_{dv}}$$

Number of automated guided vehicles = N_{dr}/N_d.

The approach presented in this section provides an approximate estimate of number of vehicles. A number of analytical and simulation approaches have appeared in the literature [Maxwell (1981); Maxwell and Muckstadt (1982); Newton (1985); Egbelu (1987); Tanchoco et al. (1987); Leung et al. (1987); and many others] considering more detailed analysis.

EXAMPLE 7.1

Johnson and Johnson (JJ) is planning to integrate the AGVS and AS/RS with their flexible manufacturing system. JJ is interested in estimating the number of AGVSs required to satisfy the needs of the manufacturing system; that means the system must be capable of making 51 deliveries per hour. JJ has already decided to install a laser guide path system and the unit load AGVS adequately serves the company needs. The following data have been collected:

Vehicle speed	= 180 ft/min
Average loaded travel distance per delivery	= 540 ft
Average empty travel distance per delivery	= 360 ft
Pickup time	= 0.50 min
Drop-off time	= 0.50 min
Traffic factor	= 0.85

Solution

The total time per delivery per vehicle (T_{dv}) is given by

$$T_{dv} = \frac{D_d}{v} + T_h + \frac{D_e}{v}$$

$$= \frac{540}{180} + 0.50 + 0.50 + \frac{360}{180}$$

$$= 3.00 + 0.50 + 0.50 + 2.00 = 6.00$$

Number of deliveries per vehicle per hour,

$$N_d = \frac{60T_f}{T_{dv}} = \frac{60(0.85)}{6.0} = 8.5$$

Therefore, the number of vehicles required = 51/8.5 = 6 vehicles.

EXAMPLE 7.2

Determining the Number of AGVSs in an Automated Manufacturing System

Consider an automated manufacturing system for machining engine blocks in an automobile manufacturing corporation. There are five computer numerical control (CNC) workstations (A, B, C, D, and E) and a load–unload station (F). The estimated time of moving an engine block on an AGVS between stations is as follows:

From–To Chart

	A	*B*	*C*	*D*	*E*	*F*
A	—	1.5				0.5
B	1.5	—	2.5			
C		2.5	—	1.0		
D			1.0	—	0.5	
E				0.5	—	1.0
F	0.5				1.0	

One hundred engine blocks are machined every 8-h shift and the operations on the engine blocks are performed in sequence from station A through E. Assuming that every pickup and drop-off takes approximately 0.50 min, determine the number of AGVSs to meet the demand of moving 100 engine blocks. The load factor is assumed to be 0.65 and the traffic factor 0.95.

Solution

In this problem we do not know the empty travel time of the AGVS. However, we know the load factor. The load factor refers to the percentage of time the AGVS carries loads.

Total travel time of an engine block from pickup to drop-off = 0.5 + 1.5 + 2.5 + 1.0 + 0.5 + 1.0 = 7.00.

Total pickup and drop-off time = 3.00 min, because there are only six stations including the pickup and drop-off station and each takes 0.50 min.

Total transit time = 7.00 + 3.00 = 10.00 min.

Considering that there are delays due to congestion and that there is empty travel of AGVs:

Total AGVS travel time for one engine block = 10.00/(traffic factor × load factor) = 10.00/(0.95 × 0.65) = 16.19 min.

Total available time per shift = 8 hr/shift × 60 min/h = 480 min per shift.

Therefore, the number of AGVs = (number of engine blocks × total time per engine block)/available time = 100 × 16.19/480 = 3.37 vehicles.

This means that approximately four vehicles are required.

7.4.11 Advantages of AGVSs Over Other Material-Handling Systems

AGVSs have many advantages over other material-handling systems. These include:

- Flexibility
- Higher reliability
- Higher operating savings and lower investment
- Unobstructed movements
- Easy interfacing with other systems

7.4.11.1 Flexibility

Automated guided vehicle systems are very flexible compared with other automated material-handling systems. The AGVS provides flexibility in several ways, such as the ease with which changes in the number of vehicles being used, and the path, can be made. The AGVS also permits better use of existing space. The changes in the number of vehicles being used, movement of vehicles as well as location of pickup or drop-off stations can be easily accomplished by reprogramming.

It is relatively easy to make changes in the guide path systems. For example, for the magnetic guide path system, the wire guidepath in the floor can be relocated by cutting a groove into the floor, inserting the wire, and filling the groove with an epoxy. For an optical guidance system, the path can be changed by simply removing the old reflective stripe and painting a new one. This can be done over a weekend or other period when the system is not operating. The control program can be revised without interfering with operations.

Compared with a fixed conveyor, it is very easy to fit an AGVS into an existing space. Furthermore, an AGVS provides operational flexibility because the turning radius of the vehicle is small.

7.4.11.2 Higher Reliability

The AGVS is very reliable compared with other automated material-handling systems. For example, in case of a breakdown, a spare vehicle can replace an AGV with negligible interruption in service and the replaced AGV can be sent for repair. This may not be true in other automated material-handling systems. For example, replacing a conveyor system is not easy and failure may render the whole manufacturing system inoperable. Also, the degree of environmental problems is less for an AGVS. For example, a magnetic guidepath system with an in-floor wire is impervious to environmental contamination such as dirt, oil spills, and noise. The AGVS provides operational reliability. For example, small objects on the guidepath seldom deflect the vehicle enough to interrupt operations. Of course, large objects on the path activate the emergency contact bumper and stop the vehicle.

7.4.11.3 Higher Operating Savings and Lower Investment

The operating costs of an AGVS are less than those of other material-handling systems. For example, with an AGVS labor requirements are minimal; maintenance of the system is easier and less expensive. Moreover, downtime of the system seldom occurs. Furthermore, power is usually a negligible expense factor. The power expenses are for battery recharging and replacement.

In the case of a magnetic guidepath, the track of the AGVS is only a wire in the floor or a reflective stripe on the floor for an optical guidance system. Therefore, the investment cost is less than that of many other automatic material-handling systems. The cost of vehicle, hardware, and software systems is, however, comparable to that of many other material-handling systems.

7.4.11.4 Unobstructed Movements

There is free movement of personnel and other vehicles over the guide path because the guide path is either embedded in the floor (magnetic guide path system) or painted on the floor (optical guidance system). This also ensures smoothness and flexibility by allowing narrower aisles and multiple use by forklift trucks and other variable-path vehicles.

7.4.11.5 Easy Interfacing with Other Systems

An AGVS is a natural material-handling choice for interfacing with FMS, AS/RS, and other material-handling systems such as conveyors or other vehicles. Robots can be mounted on the AGVS to perform loading and unloading operations. Even machines such as drilling machines can be mounted on the AGVS to perform operations on parts located at different stations. Moreover, the AGVS can deliver unit loads of product from a distant warehouse to an AS/RS or miniload system for order picking and distribution.

7.4.12 Applications of AGVSs

AGVSs have numerous applications and have already been applied by many manufacturing plants and companies. Various types of AGVSs discussed in Section 7.4.2 have different applications. New applications are being developed as technology improves and as experience is gained. Some of the most common applications of the AGVS are:

- Raw material storage
- Finished goods storage
- Assembly operations
- Flexible manufacturing systems
- Manufacturing operations

7.5 AUTOMATED STORAGE AND RETRIEVAL SYSTEMS

Automated manufacturing systems such as flexible manufacturing systems can provide quick changeovers to different part types and their cost-effective production only if we can get the right parts, pallets, fixtures, and tools to the right place at the right time. For this purpose an efficient system for their storage and retrieval together with a material transportation system is required. An integrated FMS, AGVS, and AS/RS system provides an efficient production system for manufacturing low- to medium-volume and middle- to high-variety products. In this section we address a number of issues related to the design and analysis of automated storage and retrieval systems.

7.5.1 Functions of Storage Systems and Definition of AS/RS

Receiving, identification and sorting, dispatching to storage, placing in storage, storage, retrieving from storage, order accumulation, packing, shipping, and record keeping for raw materials, purchased parts, work in process, finished product, pallets, fixtures, tools, spare parts, rework and scrap, office supplies, and so forth have traditionally been considered the functions of storage systems. An AS/RS attempts to achieve these functions by automating most of these procedures in a cost-effective and efficient manner.

An automated storage and retrieval system is defined by the Materials Handling Institute as

> *A combination of equipment and controls which handles, stores and retrieves materials with precision, accuracy and speed under a defined degree of automation.*

In general, an AS/RS performs a basic set of operations without human intervention, regardless of the specific type of system that is employed. These operations are:

- Automatic removal of an item from a storage location
- Transportation of this item to a specific processing or interface point
- Automatic storage of an item in a predetermined location, having received an item from a processing or interface point.

Furthermore, operational control of all actions performed is automated by use of a microprocessor or computer with appropriate software. However, in practice, the term AS/RS has come to mean a specific type of system using multitiered racks and a vehicle that stores and retrieves loads from a rack position in an aisle. A computerized system is used to regulate its performance.

7.5.2 AS/RS Components and Terminology Used

An automated storage and retrieval system comprises the following:

- A series of storage aisles having storage racks
- Storage and retrieval (S/R) machines, normally one machine per aisle, to store and retrieve materials
- One or more pickup and delivery stations where materials are delivered for entry to the system and materials are picked up from the system.

Some of the components are indicated in Figure 7.6. Brief explanations are given below:

Storage space Storage space is the three-dimensional space in the storage racks that is normally required to store a single load unit of material.

Bay Vertical stack of storage locations from floor to the ceiling.

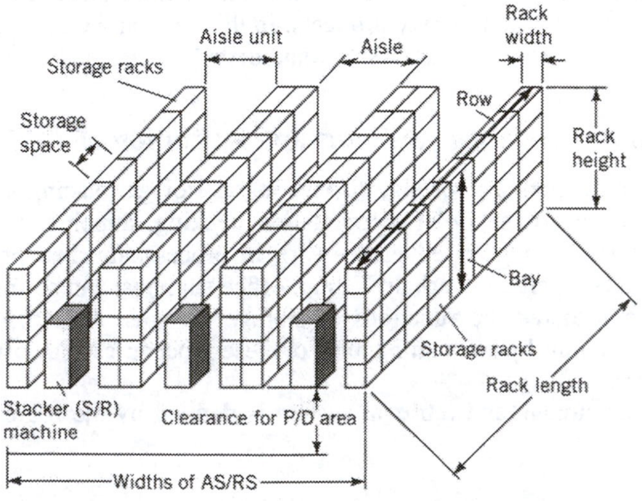

FIGURE 7.6 Generic structure of an AS/RS.

Row	A series of bays placed side by side.
Aisle	The space between two rows for the AS/RS machine operations
Aisle unit	Aisle space and racks adjacent to an aisle constitute an aisle unit.
Storage racks	A structural entity comprising storage locations, bays, and rows.
Storage structure	A storage structure comprises storage racks and is used to store inventory items. Usually, it is a steel frame structure that is designed to handle the expected size and weight of the stored items.
Storage/retrieval machine	An S/R machine moves items in and out of inventory. The S/R machine must be capable of both vertical and horizontal movements and must be able to place and remove items from storage, as well as interfacing to entry and exit points of the AS/RS. The entry and exit stations are sometimes referred to as input–output stations and also as pickup and deposit stations. A rail system along the floor guides the machine and an overhead rail maintains its alignment.
Storage modules	Storage modules are used to hold the inventory items. The modules may be pallets, bins, wire baskets, pans, or other containers. The storage modules must be designed so that they are of a standard size capable of being stored in the structure and moved by the S/R machines.
Pickup and deposit stations	To allow inventory into the system, it is necessary to have pickup-and-deposit (P/D) stations. These are generally located at the end of aisles so that they can be accessed by the S/R machines from the external material-handling system. The location and number of P/D stations depend on the quantity and type of inventory that flows through the AS/RS system. These are also known as I/O stations.

7.5.3 Why an AS/RS?

The several reasons why a company would choose to use an AS/RS include:

- An AS/RS is highly space efficient. Space now occupied by raw stock, work in process, or finished parts and assemblies can be released for valuable manufacturing space.
- Increased storage capacity to meet long-range plans.
- Improved inventory management and control.
- Quick response time to locate, store, and retrieve items.
- Reduced shortages of inventory items due to real-time information and control.
- Reduced labor costs due to automation.

- Improved stock rotation.
- Improved security and reduced pilferage because of closed storage area.
- Flexibility in design to accommodate a wide variety of loads.
- Flexibility in interfacing with other systems such as AGVS, FMS, and inspection systems such as coordinate measuring machines.
- Reduced scrap and rework due to automatic handling of parts.
- Reduced operating expenses for light, power, and heat.
- Helps implement just-in-time (JIT) concepts by getting the right parts, tools, pallets, and fixtures to the right place at the right time because of automatic control of storage and retrieval functions and accurate inventory management.

7.5.4 Types of AS/RS

Several types of AS/RSs are distinguished based on certain features and applications. Some of the important categories include:

1. Unit load AS/RS
2. Miniload AS/RS
3. Person-on-board AS/RS
4. Deep-lane AS/RS
5. Automated item retrieval system

7.5.4.1 Unit Load AS/RS

The unit load AS/RS is used to store and retrieve loads that are palletized or stored in standard-size containers. The loads are generally over 500 lb per unit. In general, a unit load system is computer controlled, having automated S/R machines designed to handle unit load containers. Each S/R machine is guided by rails in the floor. On the frame of the S/R machine itself is a shuttle, which is the load-supporting mechanism that moves loads to and from storage locations and the pickup-and-deposit stations. Usually, a mechanical clamp mechanism on the S/R machine handles the load. However, other mechanisms can be used, such as a vacuum or a magnet-based mechanism for handling sheet metal. A typical S/R machine is shown in Figure 7.7*a* and a typical unit load AS/RS in Figure 7.7*b*.

7.5.4.2 Miniload AS/RS

A miniload system is designed to handle small loads such as individual parts, tools, and supplies. The system is suitable for use where there is a limit on the amount of space that can be utilized and where the volume is too low for a full-scale unit load system and too high for a manual system. A smaller investment and flexibility of handling small items make it a popular choice in industry.

7.5.4.3 Person-on-Board System

The person-on-board system allows storage of items in less than unit load quantities. A person rides on a platform with the S/R machine to pick up individual items from a bin or drawer. This provides in-aisle order-picking ability, which can reduce the time it takes to fill an order. The operator can select the items and place them in a tote or module, which is then carried by the S/R machine to the end of the aisle or to a conveyor to reach its destination. The platform the operator is on may contain additional devices, some automatic, to facilitate lifting heavy items.

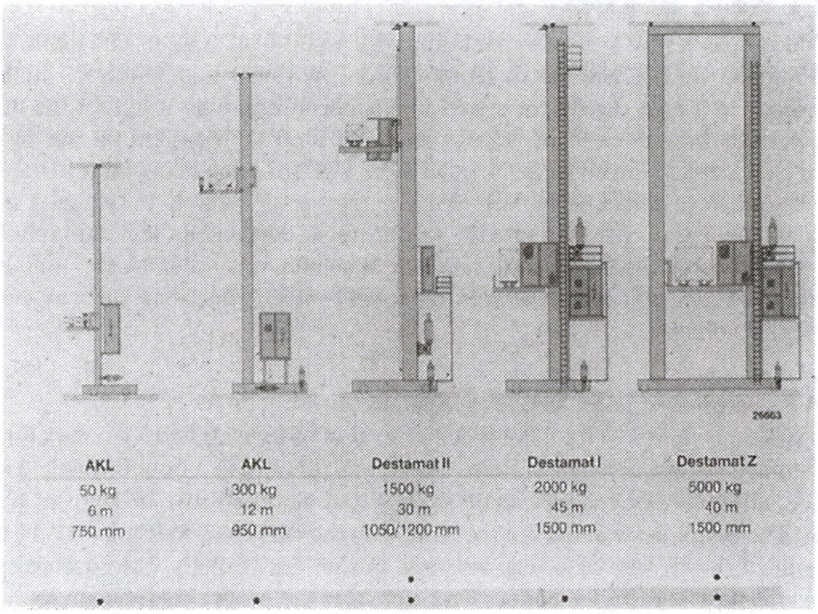

(*a*)

(*b*)

FIGURE 7.7 (*a*) S/R machine; (*b*) unit load AS/RS. (Courtesy of Rapistan Demag Corporation.)

7.5.4.4 Deep-Lane AS/RS

The deep-lane AS/RS is another variation on the unit load system. The items are stored in multideep storage with up to 10 items per row rather than single or double deep. This leads to a high density of stored items, permitting high usage of the unit. Each rack permits flow-through of items; that is, an item is deposited on one side of the storage rack and removed from the other side. The S/R vehicle operates in the aisle and delivers loads to a rack-entry vehicle. The rack-entry vehicle is typically a moving platform that carries the load into the storage rack, deposits it there, and returns to the S/R machine for the next load. The S/R machine is similar to the unit load S/R machine, except that S/R machines have specialized functions such as controlling rack-entry vehicles.

7.5.4.5 Automated Item Retrieval System

This system is designed for automatic retrieval of individual items or cases for storage. The storage system consists of items stored individually in a flow-through system that can be automatically released from storage and automatically brought to a required point. The items are stored from the rear, as in the deep-lane system, and are retrieved from the front by use of a rear-mounted pusher bar, usually onto a conveyor. The picking head moves to the correct lane, activates the pusher mechanism to the correct position, and pushes to release only the required number of units from storage.

7.5.5 Design of an AS/RS

A large number of user- and supplier-related decisions must be made in the design of an automated storage and retrieval system. Bozer and White (1980) and the Material Handling Institute provide a list of user- and supplier-related issues that must be considered. In this section we discuss the following important issues related to the layout and design of AS/RS:

1. Determining load sizes
2. Determining the dimensions of an individual storage space
3. Determining the number of storage spaces considering
   - Dedicated storage
   - Randomized storage
4. Determining the system throughput and number of S/R machines
5. Determining the size parameters of the storage and retrieval system
   - Determining the number of rows and number of bays in each row
   - Determining bay width, rack length, system length, bay depth, aisle unit, and system width
6. Determining single- and dual-command cycle times
7. Determining utilization of S/R machines

7.5.5.1 Determining Load Sizes

The variety and volume of part types and the type of production system used essentially determine the overall work flow, that is, the movement frequency of parts, tools, fixtures, pallets, and other supplies. The work flow information is required to determine load size, which is the most important element in the design of an AS/RS. The load size refers to depth, width, and height. Normally, items are palletized into unit loads. The dimensions of the unit loads with appropriate clearances provide the individual storage space dimensions. The idea is to have uniform storage spaces that are large enough to accommodate most of the materials. AS/RS is not necessarily designed to store all kinds of items; some unique items of unusual shape and size may be excluded from the AS/RS design. The weight of the unit load is another important element that affects the structural design.

7.5.5.2 Determining the Dimensions of an Individual Storage Space

Height of a storage space $= h + c_1$.

Length of a storage space $= l + c_2$.

Width of individual storage space $= u(w + c_3)$.

Normally, the storage space depth (width) is up to a maximum of three unit loads ($u = 3$).

where h = height of a unit load
l = length of a unit load
w = width of a unit load
c_1 = height clearance required for a unit load
c_2 = length clearance required for a unit load
c_3 = width clearance required for a unit load
u = storage depth in number of unit loads

EXAMPLE 7.3

Determine the size of a single storage space. The dimensions of a unit load are 48 (width) × 52 (length) × 52 (height). The clearances are $c_1 = 10$ in., $c_2 = 8$ in., $c_3 = 6$ in., and $u = 3$.

Solution

Height of an individual storage space $= h + c_1 = 52 + 10 = 62$ in.

Length of an individual storage space $= l + c_2 = 52 + 8 = 60$ in.

Width of individual storage space $= u(w + c_3) = 3(48 + 6) = 162$ in.

7.5.5.3 Determining the Number of Storage Spaces

We consider dedicated and randomized storage policies (Tompkins and White, 1984) to determine the number of storage spaces. The number thus determined should be revised considering future needs.

7.5.5.3.1 Determining the Number of Storage Spaces Considering Dedicated Storage Policy Let us first understand what dedicated storage policy (also known as fixed-slot storage) means. In this policy, a particular set of storage slots or locations is assigned to a specific product. Therefore, the number of slots required to store the products equals the sum of the maximum inventory levels for all the products.

7.5.5.3.2 Determining the Number of Storage Spaces Considering Randomized Storage Policy In randomized storage (also known as floating-slot storage) each empty storage slot is equally likely to be selected for storage when a storage operation is performed. Likewise, each unit of a particular product is equally likely to be retrieved when a retrieval operation is performed. Therefore, in the long run, the number of storage spaces required equals the maximum of the aggregate inventory level of all the products.

We illustrate two policies by a small example.

EXAMPLE 7.4

Four products are received by a warehouse according to the schedule given in Table 7.1. Determine the number of storage spaces that a storage and retrieval system should be designed for considering dedicated and randomized storage policies.

TABLE 7.1 **Pallet Loads of Products**

	Product Type				*Aggregate Inventory Level*
Period	*1*	*2*	*3*	*4*	
1	1000*	1500	500	2000	5000
2	2500	700	800	500	4500
3	1500	3000	200	1300	6000
4	500	1000	3500	4000	9000
5	1100	900	200	300	2500

* Inventory level expressed in pallet loads.

Solution

Number of storage spaces required according to the dedicated storage policy is the sum of individual maximum inventory levels = 2500 + 3000 + 3500 + 4000 = 13,000 pallet loads.

Number of storage spaces required according to the randomized storage policy is the maximum of aggregate inventory level = 9000 pallet loads.

The randomized storage policy results in less storage than the dedicated storage policy. Two basic reasons for this (Tompkins and White, 1984) are:

1. If an out-of-stock condition exists for a given stock-keeping unit (SKU), the empty slot continues to remain active with dedicated storage whereas it would not with randomized storage.
2. If there are multiple slots for a given SKU, empty slots will develop as the inventory level decreases.

There will, however, be no differences in the storage requirements for the dedicated and randomized storage policies when occurrences of inventory shortages are seldom and single slots are assigned to SKUs. Many carousel and miniload systems meet these conditions.

7.5.5.4 Determining the System Throughput and the Number of S/R Machines

The system throughput refers to the number of loads to be stored and number of loads to be retrieved per hour. These numbers are, of course, a function of production activity. Factors that influence the throughput include:

1. Speed of S/R machine
2. Mix of single- and dual-cycle transactions
3. Percent utilization of the storage racks
4. Arrangement of stored items
5. AS/RS control system speed
6. Speed and efficiency of the material-handling equipment such as AGVs, conveyors, and forklifts used to move loads to the input and remove loads from the output

To carry out the production activity efficiently, the calculation of the number of S/R machines should be based on the maximum number of loads in and loads out per hour. The number of S/R machines can be determined as follows:

$$\text{Number of S/R machines} = \frac{\text{system throughput}}{\text{S/R machine capacity in cycles per hour}}$$

EXAMPLE 7.5

Suppose the single command cycle system for the S/R machine is recommended. The average cycle time per operation is 1 min. The desired system throughput is 360 operations per hour. An operation refers to either storage or retrieval and both take approximately the same time. Determine the number of S/R machines.

Solution

Number of cycles per hour per machine = 60 because the cycle time is 1 min

Therefore, the number of S/R machines = system throughput/(S/R machine capacity in cycles per hour) = (360 operations/h)/(60 cycles/h per machine) = 6

7.5.5.5 Determining the Size Parameters of the Storage and Retrieval System

The sizing of an AS/RS system involves determining the system length, width, and height. For this purpose it is required to determine the number of rows in a system, number of bays in each row, number of loads per height, number of bays required per row, bay width, aisle width, bay depth, and aisle unit. We provide a simple analysis of the AS/RS sizing problem and illustrate the concept by an example in the following section.

7.5.5.5.1 Determining the Number of Rows and the Number of Bays in Each Row in a System The S/R machines are used to store and retrieve materials and their number is determined primarily by the system throughput and the cycle time. Normally, the S/R machines are dedicated to one aisle; however, the machines may be used to serve more than one aisle. Each aisle has two rows. Therefore, in the case of one S/R machine per aisle, the number of rows would be

$$\text{Number of rows in the system} = 2 \times \text{Number of S/R machines in the system}$$

The number of bays can be determined as follows:

$$\text{Number of bays} = \frac{\text{number of storage spaces required}}{\text{number of rows per S/R machine} \times \text{number of S/R machines} \times \text{number of storage spaces per system height}}$$

$$\text{Number of storage spaces per system height} = \frac{\text{Desired system height}}{\text{Storage space height}}$$

The desired system height normally varies between 30 to 90 ft.

EXAMPLE 7.6

Using the data from Examples 7.4 and 7.5, determine the number of rows and the number of bays in each row in the system.

Solution

The number of S/R machines from Example 7.5 is 6. Therefore,

$$\text{Number of rows in the system} = 2 \times 6 = 12$$

$$\text{Number of storage spaces per system height} = \frac{\text{Desired system height}}{\text{storage space height}} = \frac{(77.5 \text{ ft})(12 \text{ in./ft})}{62 \text{ in.}} = 15$$

The total number of storage spaces using a randomized policy from Example 7.4 is 9000.

$$\text{Number of bays in each row} = \frac{9000 \text{ storage spaces}}{2 \text{ rows per S/R machine} \times 6 \text{ machines} \times 15 \text{ storage spaces in the system height}} = 50 \text{ bays}$$

7.5.5.5.2 Determining Bay Width, Rack Length, System Length, Bay Depth, Aisle Unit, and System Width The bay width equals the length of a single storage space plus the center-to-center rack support width. That is,

$$\text{Bay width} = \text{length of a storage space} + \text{center-to-center rack support width} = l + c_2 + c_4$$

where c_4 is center-to-center rack support width.

$$\text{Rack length} = \text{bay width} \times \text{number of bays}$$

$$\text{System length} = \text{rack length} + \text{clearance for S/R machine run-out} + \text{clearance for the P/D area}$$

$$\text{Bay depth} = \text{width of individual storage space} + \text{bay side support allowance}$$
$$= u(w + c_3) + c_5$$

where c_5 is bay side support allowance.

$$\text{Aisle unit} = \text{aisle width} + (2 \times \text{bay depth})$$

$$\text{System width} = \text{aisle unit} \times \text{desired number of aisles}$$

EXAMPLE 7.7

Determine the following AS/RS sizing parameters using data from Examples 7.3, 7.4, and 7.5. Assume that a randomized storage policy is used.

- Bay width
- Rack length
- System length
- Bay depth
- Aisle unit
- System width

Additional data are: $c_4 = 6$ in., $c_5 = 6$ in., desired system height = 77.5 ft, clearance for S/R machine run-out = 10 ft, clearance for P/D area = 15 ft, aisle width = 72 in.

Solution

$$\text{Bay width} = 1 + c_2 + c_4 = 52 + 8 + 6 = 66 \text{ in.}$$

$$\text{Rack length} = \text{bay width} \times \text{number of bays}$$
$$= 66 \text{ in.} \times 50 = 3300 \text{ in.} = 275 \text{ ft}$$

$$\text{System length} = \text{rack length} + \text{clearance for S/R machine run-out and for P/D area}$$
$$= 275 + 10 + 15 = 300 \text{ ft}$$

$$\text{Bay depth} = u(w + c_3) + c_5$$

If $u = 1$, bay depth $= 1(48 + 6) + 6 = 60$ in.
If $u = 2$, bay depth $= 2(48 + 6) + 6 = 114$ in.
If $u = 3$, bay depth $= 3(48 + 6) + 6 = 168$ in.

$$\text{Aisle unit} = \text{aisle width} + 2 \times \text{bay depth}$$
$$= 72 + 2 \times 60 = 192 \text{ in.} \qquad \text{for } u = 1$$
$$= 72 + 2 \times 114 = 300 \text{ in.} \qquad \text{for } u = 2$$
$$= 72 + 2 \times 168 = 408 \text{ in.} \qquad \text{for } u = 3$$

$$\text{System width} = \text{aisle unit} \times \text{desired number of aisles}$$
$$= 192 \times 6 = 1152 \text{ in.} \qquad \text{for } u = 1$$

7.5.5.6 Determining Single- and Dual-Command Cycle Times for Unit Load AS/RS

A detailed analysis for determining the cycle time for both single- and double-command cycles for unit load AS/RS is given in Bozer and White (1984) and is also described in Tompkins and White (1984).

Single-Command Cycle In a single-command cycle either a storage or a retrieval operation is performed, but not both. To determine cycle time, a storage cycle is assumed to begin with the S/R machine at the P/D station. The machine picks up a load, travels to the storage location, deposits the load, and returns empty to the P/D station. Similarly, a retrieval cycle consists of the following steps: the S/R machine begins at the P/D station, travels empty to the retrieval location, picks up the load, travels to the P/D station, and deposits the load.

Dual-Command Cycle To determine cycle time, a dual-command cycle is assumed to begin with the S/R machine at the P/D station. The machine picks up a load, travels to the storage location and deposits the load there, travels empty to the retrieval location and retrieves a load from there, travels back to the P/D station, and deposits the load.

The cycle time expressions derived in Bozer and White (1984) are based on the following assumptions:

- Randomized storage policy
- Constant horizontal and vertical velocities
- Single-sized rack openings
- P/D station located at the base and at the end of the aisle
- S/R machine travels simultaneously in the aisle both horizontally and vertically

The time required to travel from a P/D station to a storage or a retrieval station would be the maximum of the horizontal and vertical travel times because of simultaneous travel of the S/R machine.

The length (L) and height (H) of an AS/RS aisle are easily obtained from the storage space dimensions as follows:

$$L = n(l + c_2)$$

$$H = m(h + c_1)$$

where n = number of bays

m = number of storage spaces per system height

If the length and height of an aisle are known and the average horizontal and vertical speeds of S/R machines are V_h and V_v, respectively, then the time required to travel the full horizontal length and vertical height of an aisle is given by

$$t_h = \frac{L}{V_h} \qquad \text{and} \qquad t_v = \frac{H}{V_v}$$

Single-command cycle time:

$$T_{sc} = T\left(\frac{Q^2}{3} + 1\right) + 2T_{pd}$$

Dual-command cycle time:

$$T_{dc} = \frac{T}{30}(40 + 15\,Q^2 - Q^3) + 4T_{pd}$$

where $T = \max(t_h, t_v)$,
$Q = \min(t_h/T, t_v/T)$
T_{pd} = time to perform either a pick up or deposit
t_h = time required to travel full horizontal aisle distance
t_v = time required to travel full vertical aisle distance

EXAMPLE 7.8

Johnson and Johnson has a unit load AS/RS with six aisles. Six S/R machines are used, one for each aisle. From Example 7.7, the aisle length (rack length) is 275 ft and aisle height is 77.5 ft. The horizontal and vertical speeds are 300 ft/min and 70 ft/min, respectively. A P/D operation of the S/R machine takes approximately 0.35 min. Determine the single- and dual-command cycle times for a unit load AS/RS of JJ company.

Solution

Length of an aisle = 275 ft, height of an aisle = 77.5 ft, horizontal speed V_h = 300 ft/min, and V_v = 70 ft/min. Therefore,

$$t_h = \frac{L}{V_h} = \frac{275 \text{ ft}}{300 \text{ ft/min}} = 0.9167 \text{ min}$$

$$t_v = \frac{H}{V_v} = \frac{77.5 \text{ ft}}{70 \text{ ft/min}} = 1.107 \text{ min}$$

$$T = \max(t_h, t_v) = \max(0.9167, 1.107) = 1.107$$

$$Q = \min\left(\frac{t_h}{T}, \frac{t_v}{T}\right) = \min\left(\frac{0.9167}{1.107}, \frac{1.107}{1.107}\right) = 0.828$$

The single-command transaction cycle time is

$$T_{sc} = 1.107\left(\frac{0.828^2}{3} + 1\right) + 2(0.35) = 2.059 \text{ min}$$

The dual-command transaction cycle time is

$$T_{dc} = \left(\frac{1.107}{30}\right)[40 + 15(0.828)^2 - (0.828)^3] + 4(0.35) = 3.2345$$

7.5.5.7 Determining the Utilization of S/R Machines

The S/R machine is the most critical component of a storage and retrieval system. Therefore, the percent utilization of S/R machines is an interesting statistic for the performance evaluation of an automated storage and retrieval system.

Suppose the system throughput (ST) for an AS/RS is known. Remember, the system throughput is defined as the number of loads to be stored and number of loads to be retrieved per hour. Suppose each aisle is served by one S/R machine and there are N S/R machines. Then the number of transactions per S/R machine per hour is

$$n_t = \frac{\text{ST}}{N}$$

Now suppose that the system permits a mixture of single- and dual-command transaction cycles and α and β are the percentages of operations (storage and retrievals) done by single- and dual-command cycles, respectively ($\alpha + \beta = 1$).

Assuming the numbers of storages and retrievals are equal in the long run, the workload per S/R machine can be defined as

$$\text{Workload per machine} = \alpha n_t T_{sc} + \beta(n_t/2)T_{dc} \text{ min/h}$$

The $(n_t/2)$ appears in the second term in this expression because in a dual-command cycle both a storage and a retrieval are done in one cycle.

EXAMPLE 7.9

Suppose the system throughput is 300 storage and retrievals per hour. The AS/RS has 10 aisles and each is served by one S/R machine. Furthermore, 30% of the operations are performed as single-command and the rest as dual-command operations. Determine the percent utilization of the machine. Other data from Example 7.8 apply to this problem. Determine the number of transactions at which the S/R machine is 100% utilized.

Solution

The number of operations per machine per hour is

$$n_t = \frac{\text{ST}}{N} = \frac{300}{10} = 30$$

Therefore, the number of storage operations per hour is 15 and the number of retrievals per hour is 15. We have $\alpha = 0.30$, $\beta = 0.70$, and from Example 7.8, $T_{sc} = 2.059$ min, $T_{dc} = 3.2345$ min. Therefore,

$$\begin{aligned}\text{Workload per machine per hour} &= \alpha n_t T_{sc} + \beta(n_t/2)T_{dc} \\ &= 0.30(30)(2.059) + 0.70(30/2)(3.2345) \text{ min} \\ &= 52.49325 \text{ min}\end{aligned}$$

$$\begin{aligned}\text{Percent utilization of the S/R machine} &= (52.49325/60) \times 100 \\ &= 87.488\%\end{aligned}$$

For 100% utilization of the S/R machine

$$\alpha n_t T_{sc} + \beta(n_t/2)T_{dc} = 60$$

Therefore,

$$\begin{aligned}n_t &= \frac{120}{2\alpha T_{sc} + \beta T_{dc}} \\ &= \frac{120}{(2)(0.30)(2.059) + (0.70)(3.2345)} = 34.29\end{aligned}$$

This means that if the number of operations per machine per hour exceeds 34, the machine utilization is 100% and there is a need to look into AS/RS capacity expansion. Remember, if the utilization is less than 50%, one S/R machine can serve two aisles.

7.6 A DISTRIBUTED COMPUTER CONTROL ARCHITECTURE FOR AGVSs AND AS/RSs

There are two prominent computer control architectures, central control and distributed control, that can be used to control the flow of materials and information. The bottom line in the design of a control system is to ensure that the automated systems keep running even if a control component fails. In a manufacturing environment that requires integration of its various components such as AGVS, AS/RS, and FMS, distributed control is the logical choice. Distributed control makes it possible to debug the system level by level, does not require a large central computer, and permits easy addition of components and expansion to integrate other systems. A generic distributed control system architecture is shown in Figure 7.8. Starting from the lowest level, the programmable logic controllers (PLCs) control and execute movements of AGVs, S/R machines, other carriers, and equipment such as conveyors, monorails, and robots. The PLCs receive instructions from a group of microcomputers at the middle level (sometimes called system directors) that oversee the operations of systems such as AGVS, AS/RS, conveyors, and monorail systems. In turn, the microcomputers receive instructions from a minicomputer at the top level, called the system manager, which schedules material movements through the system. Backup units are maintained at each level to ensure reliable system operation. This control system is only one of the modules of a complete manufacturing control system. The other modules are machine tool control, management control, part control, tool control, and service control.

A computerized control system can be used to monitor the AS/RS system constantly. The system normally operates in a real-time mode, but manual data input is also permitted. The locations of machines and movement of loads are continuously monitored through a system of manual key entry, bar-code scanners, and photoelectric sensors. Such a system increases the speed of storage and retrievals by reducing to a minimum the number of moves and distances moved required to locate a load. Full/

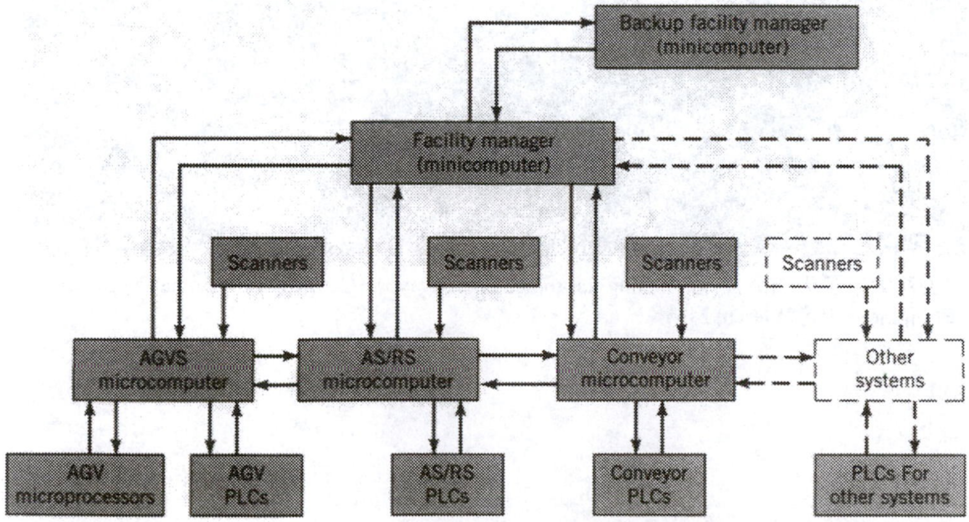

FIGURE 7.8 A distributed control architecture for AS/RSs and AGVSs.

empty bin detectors are used by S/R machines to determine the presence or absence of a load in the storage area. This increases the S/R machine productivity by preventing it from making any unnecessary or damaging actions, such as inserting a load into a location that is already occupied.

7.7 CONVEYORS

A conveyor is a convenient and cost-effective means of moving materials over a fixed path. Whenever there is a need to move materials frequently between specific points, conveyors are the logical choice for material handling. Depending on the circumstances, the conveyors can be designed to suit specific applications. Often, the

FIGURE 7.9 (*a*) A side-flexing flat-top chain conveyor. (Courtesy of Automation Service Equipment, Inc, Warren, MI.)

conveyors are classified into two broad categories according to

- The type of product being handled, that is, bulk or unit
- The location of the conveyor, that is, overhead or floor

This classification is not unique. For example, a belt conveyor can be used for bulk and unit materials, and it can be located overhead as well as on the floor. Within these categories, a number of types of conveyors can be designed to meet the requirements of the customers. Examples include belt, roller, wheel, bucket, slat, vibrating, screw, pneumatic, and tow, among many others.

It is important to emphasize that conveyor systems are normally designed to meet specific application requirements. Accordingly, the type and configuration change from one application to another. We provide some photographs of conveyor systems used in different industrial applications. For example, a side-flexing flat-top chain conveyor is shown in Figure 7.9*a*. It is a versatile conveyor system used for transportation in bottling plants, automotive plants, and so forth. Figure 7.9*b* and *c* show roller conveyors used in production operations in an automotive seating facility. Conveyors used in an electronic assembly line are shown in Figure 7.9*d* and *e*. Conveyors used for fabricated metals, drum filling, and engine assembly are shown in Figures 7.9*f*, *g*, and *h*, respectively. Conveyors are used for in-line storage as well as transportation. Figure 7.9*i* shows a gravity helical storage unit used in automotive parts assembly.

FIGURE 7.9 (*b*) Roller conveyors used in production operations in an automotive seating facility. (Courtesy of Rapistan Demag Corp., Grand Rapids, MI.).

FIGURE 7.9 (*c*) Roller conveyors used in production operations in an automotive seating facility (Courtesy of Rapistan Demag Corp., Grand Rapids, MI.).

FIGURE 7.9 (*d*) Conveyors in an electronic assembly line (Courtesy of Rapistan Demag Corp., Grand Rapids, MI.).

FIGURE 7.9 (*e*) Conveyors in an electronic assembly line (Courtesy of Rapistan Demag. Corp., Grand Rapids, MI.).

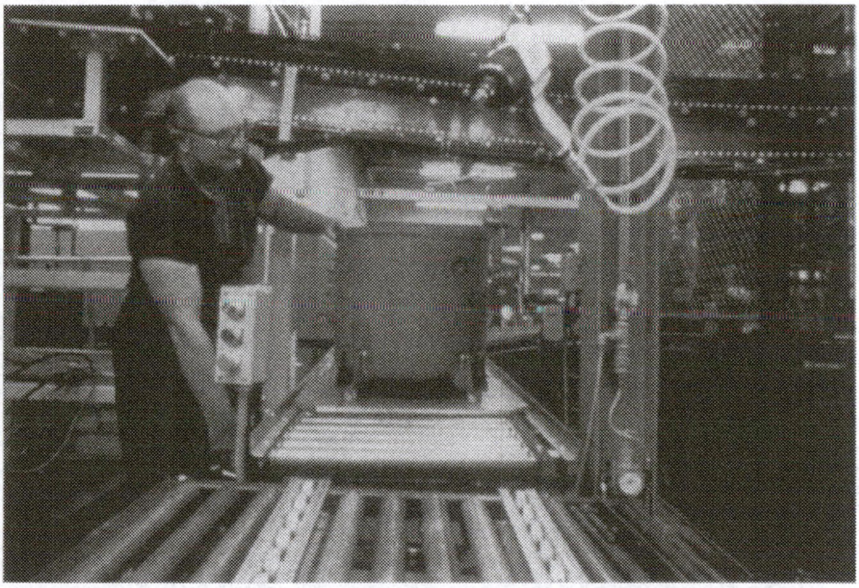

FIGURE 7.9 (*f*) Conveyors used for fabricated metals (Courtesy of Rapistan Demag Corp., Grand Rapids, MI.).

FIGURE 7.9 (*g*) Drum filling (Courtesy of Rapistan Demag Corp., Grand Rapids, MI.).

FIGURE 7.9 (*h*) Engine assembly (Courtesy of Rapistan Demag Corp., Grand Rapids, MI.).

FIGURE 7.9 (*i*) Gravity storage unit used in automotive assembly. (Courtesy of Automation Service Equipment, Inc., Warren, MI.).

7.8 SUMMARY

Automated guided vehicle systems are material-handling systems that are flexible, reliable, inexpensive to operate, and easy to interface with systems such as FMSs, AS/RSs, and other material-handling systems. The automated storage and retrieval systems offer many advantages over conventional storage systems. AS/RSs provide efficient inventory management with reduced space requirements, faster throughput, and flexibility in operations. Conveyor systems are relatively inexpensive automated material-handling systems used in a variety of industrial environments. Conveyor systems can be designed to suit many applications. In this chapter we attempted to provide coverage of the design and analysis of AGVSs and AS/RSs. The concepts have been illustrated by a number of figures and solved examples. Brief coverage of various types of conveyors was also given.

PROBLEMS

7.1 Discuss various types of material-handling systems.

7.2 What are the principles of material handling?

7.3 Discuss the following types of AGVSs and their applications:
- (a) AGVS towing vehicles
- (b) AGVS unit load transporters
- (c) AGVS pallet trucks
- (d) AGVS forklift trucks
- (e) AGVS light-load transporters
- (f) AGVS assembly-line vehicles

7.4 Discuss various types of guidance systems.

7.5 Describe the following types of AGVS steering control:
(a) Differential-speed steer control
(b) Steered-wheel steer control

7.6 Describe the following types of AGVS routing methods:
(a) Frequency select method
(b) Path-switch select method

7.7 Describe the following types of AGVS control systems:
(a) Computer-controlled system
(b) Remote dispatch control system
(c) Manual control system

7.8 Discuss the following issues involved in the system design of an AGVS:
(a) Selection of guidepath type and vehicle type
(b) Flow path design
(c) Guidepath layout
(d) Type of flow path within the layout (unidirectional, bidirectional, or combinations)
(e) Number and location of load transfer points and load transfer station storage space
(f) Number of vehicles required

7.9 Discuss various attributes of guidance and AGVSs.

7.10 Johnson and Johnson is planning to modernize their spark plug assembly operations. There are four assembly workstations (A, B, C, and D) and a load/unload station (E). The parts are moved in unit loads. The estimated time to move a unit load on an AGVS between assembly and load/unload stations is given in the following chart:

From–To Chart

	A	*B*	*C*	*D*	*E*
A	—	1.0			0.8
B	1.0	—	1.2		
C		1.2	—	1.6	
D			1.6	—	0.4
E	0.8			0.4	—

Two hundred unit loads of spark plugs are finished and packed every 8-h shift and the spark plug assembly operations are performed in sequence from station A through D. Assuming that every pickup and drop-off takes approximately 0.50 min, determine the number of AGVs to meet the demand of moving 200 unit loads. The load factor is assumed to be 0.60 and the traffic factor 0.90.

7.11 What are advantages of AGVSs over other material-handling systems?

7.12 What is meant by an automated storage and retrieval system?

7.13 Describe the following types of storage and retrieval systems:

- Unit load AS/RS
- Miniload AS/RS
- Deep-lane system
- Person-on-board system

7.14 Five products are received by a warehouse according to the schedule given in Table P7.1. Determine the number of storage spaces that a storage and retrieval system should be designed for considering dedicated and randomized storage policies.

7.15 Suppose the dual-command cycle system for the S/R machine is recommended. The average cycle time is 2 min. The desired system throughput is 240 operations per hour.

TABLE P7.1 **Pallet Loads of Products**

Period	Product Type 1	2	3	4	5	Aggregate Inventory Level
1	2000*	2500	1500	1000	4100	11100
2	1500	3700	700	1500	900	8300
3	1500	3000	1200	1300	500	7500
4	1000	3500	3000	1100	700	9300
5	1900	1200	3300	1200	3000	10600
6	2000	500	600	700	900	4700

* Inventory level expressed in pallet loads.

An operation refers to either storage or retrieval and both take approximately the same time. Determine the number of S/R machines.

7.16 Using the data from Problem 7.15, determine the number of rows in the system.

7.17 Determine the following AS/RS sizing parameters using data from Problems 7.14, 7.15, and 7.16. Assume that a randomized storage policy is used.
(a) Bay width
(b) Number of storage spaces per system height
(c) Number of bays
(d) Rack length
(e) System length
(f) Bay depth
(g) Aisle unit
(h) System width

Additional data are: $c_4 = 6$ in., $c_5 = 6$ in., desired system height = 80 ft, clearance for S/R machine runout = 10 ft, clearance for P/D area = 15 ft, aisle width = 6 ft.

7.18 Thompson and Thompson (TT) has a unit load AS/RS with 10 aisles. Ten S/R machines are used, one for each aisle. The aisle length (rack length) is 300 ft and aisle height is 80 ft. The horizontal and vertical speeds are 350 ft/min and 90 ft/min, respectively. A P/D operation of an S/R machine takes approximately 0.30 min. Determine the single- and dual-command cycle times for a unit load AS/RS of TT company.

7.19 The AS/RS at Thompson and Thompson has 10 aisles and each is served by one S/R machine. Suppose the system throughput is 200 storage and retrievals per hour. Furthermore, 40% of the operations are performed as single-command and the rest as dual-command operations. Other data from Problem 7.18 for aisle length and height as well as horizontal and vertical speeds of S/R machines apply to this problem. Determine the percent utilization of the machine. Also determine the number of transactions at which the S/R machine is 100% utilized.

REFERENCES AND SUGGESTED READING

Allegri, T. H. (1989). *Advanced Manufacturing Technology.* TAB Professional and Reference Books, Blue Ridge Summit, Pennsylvania, pp. 168–170.

Blair, E. L., Charnsethikul, P., and Vasques, A. (1985). Optimal routing of driverless vehicles in a flexible material handling system. Texas Tech University and Rensselaer Polytechnic Institute, November.

Blair, E. L., Charnsethikul, P., and Vasques, A. (1987). Optimal routing of driverless vehicles in a flexible material handling system. *Material Flow,* 4(1):73–83.

Bozer, Y. A., and White, J. A. (1980). Optimum designs of automated storage/retrieval systems. Presented to the TIMS/ORSA Joint National Meeting, Washington, DC.

Bozer, Y. A., and White, J. A. (1984). Travel time models for automated storage/retrieval systems. *IIE Transactions,* 24:329–338.

Bredenbeck, J. E., Shirk, W. T., and Majure, J. C. (1989). Small parts handling needs are met by installing a vertical storage system. *Industrial Engineering,* 21(7):34–38.

Brian, T., and Pulat, M. (1989). Software tool automates AS/RS error recovery and preventive maintenance scheduling. *Industrial Engineering,* February, p. 43.

Eastman, R. M. (1987). *Materials Handling.* Marcel Dekker, New York, pp. 301–318.

Erickson, B. E. (1987). Electronic diagnostics for enhanced automatic guided vehicle safety and maintainability. *Material Flow,* 4(1):109–115.

Egbelu, P. J. (1987). The use of non-simulation approaches in estimating vehicle requirements in an automatic guided vehicle based transport system. *Material Flow,* 4(1):17–32.

Egbelu, P. J., and Roy, N. (1988). Material flow control in AGV/unit load based production lines. *International Journal of Production Research,* 26(1):81–94.

Egbelu, P. J., and Tanchoco, J. M. A. (1984). Characterization of automatic guided vehicle dispatching rules. *International Journal of Production Research,* 22(3):359–374.

Egbelu, P. J., and Tanchoco, J. M. A. (1986). Potentials for bi-directional guidepath for automated guided vehicle based systems. *International Journal of Production Research,* 24(5):1075–1097.

Gaskins, R. J., and Tanchoco, J. M. A. (1987). Flow path design for automated guided vehicle systems. *International Journal of Production Research,* 25, (5):667–676, 1987.

Groover, M. P. (1987). *Automation, Production Systems and Computer-Integrated Manufacturing.* Prentice-Hall, Englewood Cliffs, New Jersey.

Hackman, S., and Rosenblatt, M. (1990). Allocating items to an automated storage and retrieval system. *IIE Transactions,* 22(1):7–14.

Hodgson, T. J., King, R. E., Monteith, S. K., and Schultz, S. R. (1987). Developing control rules for an AGVS using Markov decision processes. *Material Flow,* 4(1):85–96.

Hwang, M., and Lee, M. K. (1988). Order batching algorithms for a man-on-board automated storage and retrieval system. *Engineering Costs and Production Economics,* 13:285–294.

Hwang, M., Beak, B., and Lee, M. K. (1988). Clustering algorithms for order picking in an automated storage and retrieval system. *International Journal of Production Research,* 26(2):189–201.

Koff, G. A. (1987). Automatic guided vehicle systems: Applications, controls and planning. *Material Flow,* 4(1):3–16.

Kulwiec, R. A. (1985). *Material Handling Handbook.* Wiley Interscience, New York.

Landers, T. L., Whitt, W. A., and Ogle, M. K. (1988). Computer integration of automatic guided vehicle systems. International Industrial Engineering Conference Proceedings, pp. 165–169.

Lee, J., Choi, R. H. G., and Khaksar, M. (1990). Evaluation of automated guided vehicle systems by simulation. *Computers Industrial Engineering,* 19(1–4):318–321.

Lee, M. K., and Hwang, M. (1988). An approach in the design of a unit-load automated carousel storage system. *Engineering Optimization,* 13:197–210.

Leung, L. C., Khator, S. K., and Kimbler, D. L. (1987). Assignment of AGVS with different vehicle types. *Material Flow,* 4(1):65–72.

Lindkvist, R. G. T. (1985). *Handbook of Material Handling.* Ellis Horwood, Chichester, England, pp. 186–191.

Luggen, W. M. (1991). *Flexible Manufacturing Cells and Systems.* Prentice Hall, Englewood Cliffs, New Jersey.

Maleki, R. A. (1991). *Flexible manufacturing systems: the technology and management.* Prentice Hall, Englewood Cliffs, New Jersey.

Malmborg, C. J. (1989). A compendium of archival literature in AGVS modeling. International Industrial Engineering Conference Proceedings. pp. 185–190.

Malmborg, C. J. (1990). Simulation evaluation of model based AGVS fleet sizing. International Industrial Engineering Conference Proceedings, pp. 205–210.

Maxwell, W. L. (1981). Solving material handling design problem with OR. *Industrial Engineering,* 13(4):58–69.

Maxwell, W. L., and Muckstadt, J. A. (1982). Design of automatic guided vehicle systems. *IIE Transactions,* 14(2):114–124.

McAllister, R. L., and Lucchesi, D. A. (1987). An AGV supported pull system on the manufacturing floor. International Industrial Engineering Conference Proceedings, pp. 267–271.

Newton, D. (1985). Simulation model helps determine how many automatic guided vehicles are needed. *Industrial Engineering,* 17(2):68–79.

O'Neal, K. R. (1986). AS/RS at Delta Air Lines reaps high dividends. *Industrial Engineering,* 18(11):60–66.

Ozden, M. (1988). A simulation study of multiple load carrying automatic guided vehicles in a flexible manufacturing system. *International Journal of Production Research,* 26(8):1353–1366.

Pan, L. L., Alasya, D., and Richards, L. D. (1992). Using material handling in the development of integrated manufacturing. *Industrial Engineering,* 24(3):43–48.

Rabeneck, C. W., Usher, J. S., and Evans, G. W. (1989). An analytical model for AGVS design. International Industrial Engineering Conference Proceedings, pp. 191–195.

Schuler, J. (1987). Mobile robots. *Material Flow,* 4(1):117–126.

Shelton, D., and Jones, M. S. (1987). A selection method for automatic guided vehicles. *Material Flow,* 4(1):97–107.

Sims, R. Jr. (1990). AGVs are flexible and trainable. *Industrial Engineering,* 22(12):16–17.

Simulation software buyers' guide. (1994). *IE Magazine,* 26(5):58–71.

Taghaboni, F., and Tanchoco, J. M. A. (1988). A LISP base controller for free ranging automatic guided vehicle systems. *International Journal of Production Research,* 26(2):173–188.

Tanchoco, J. M. A., Egeblu, P. J., Taghaboni, F. (1987). Determination of the total number of vehicles in an AGV based material transport system. *Material Flow,* 4(1):33–52.

Tompkins, J. A., and White, J. A. (1984). *Facilities Planning.* John Wiley & Sons, Toronto, pp. 187–189.

Usher, J. S., Evan, G. W., and Wilhelm, M. R. (1988). AGV Flow Path Design and Load Transfer Point Location, International I.I.E. Conference Proceedings, pp 174–178.

Wilhelm, M. R., and Evans, G. W. (1987). The state-of-the-art in AGV systems analysis and planning. Proceedings of the AGVS '87, Pittsburgh, October.

Wysk, R. A., Egbelu, P. J., Zhou, C., and Ghosh, B. K. (1987). Use of spreadsheet analysis for evaluating AGV systems. *Material Flow,* 4(1):53–64.

CHAPTER 8

ROBOTIC SYSTEMS

Since the development of the first articulated arm in the 1950s and subsequent developments in the area of microprocessor technology, robots have become available in a variety of types, styles, and sizes. They are capable of performing a wide variety of tasks. In fact, the driving force for the purchase of robots is their applicability in hostile, strenuous, and repetitive environments as well as in highly competitive situations with strong economic pressure to perform. Such applications include welding, painting, and pick-and-place material handling, among others. Robotics is now becoming an integral part of automated discrete-parts manufacturing systems such as flexible manufacturing systems.

In this chapter we provide a basic understanding of the fundamentals of robotics and robot technology. Issues such as spatial resolution, accuracy, and repeatability are discussed. Robotic joints are classified and joint notation is described. Understanding the principles of robot motion analysis is necessary for the design of robots for specific applications. Forward and backward kinematic analyses are provided. Programming languages are discussed, followed by robotic applications. Economic justification of robot applications is considered. A number of solved examples are included in the chapter to illustrate these concepts.

8.1 WHAT IS AN INDUSTRIAL ROBOT?

The word "robot" is derived from a satirical fantasy play, "Rossum's Universal Robots," written by Karel Capek in 1921. In his play, Capek used the word to mean "forced labor." The Robotics Industries Association (RIA), formerly known as the Robotics Institute of America, defines robot in the following way:

> *An industrial robot is a programmable, multi-functional manipulator designed to move materials, parts, tools, or special devices through variable programmed motions for the performance of a variety of tasks.*

The first articulated arm was developed in the 1950s. There have been many advances

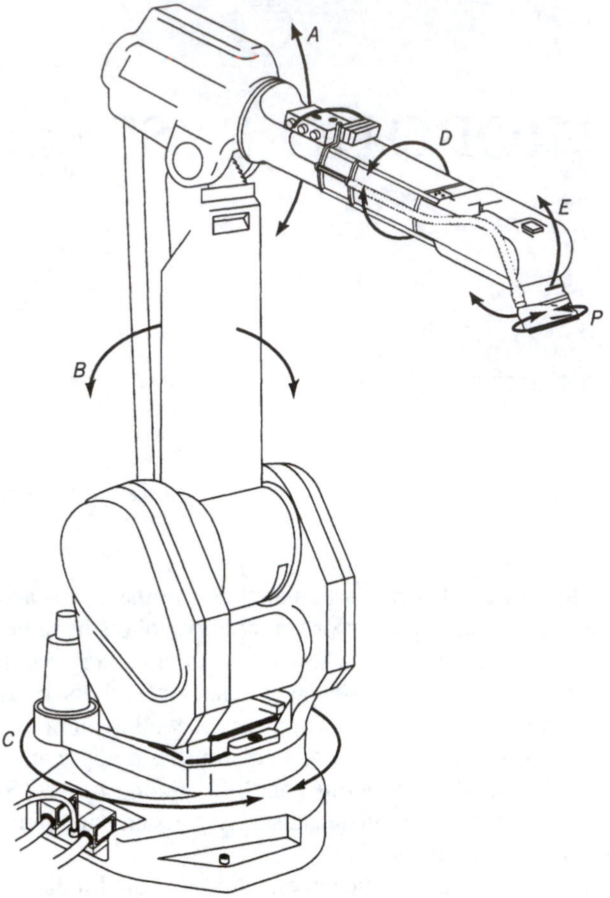

FIGURE 8.1 A typical industrial robot with six-degrees of freedom. The robot's movement pattern is briefly described as follows: Axis 1 (*C*), turning of the complete mechanical robot; Axis 2 (*B*), forward and reverse movement of the lower arm; Axis 3 (*A*), up and down movement of the upper arm; Axis 4 (*D*), turning of the complete wrist center; Axis 5 (*E*), bending of wrist around the wrist center; Axis 6 (*P*), turning of mounting flange (turn disk). (Courtesy of ABB Robotics, Inc.).

in the area of robotics since then, motivated primarily by the developments in the area of industrial automation in particular and computer-integrated manufacturing systems in general.

An industrial robot consists of a number of rigid links connected by joints of different types, controlled and monitored by a computer. To a large extent, the physical construction of a robot resembles a human arm. The link assembly mentioned above is connected to the body, which is usually mounted on a base. This link assembly is generally referred to as a robot arm. A wrist is attached to the arm. To facilitate gripping or handling, a hand is attached at the end of the wrist. In robotics terminology, this hand is called an end-effector. The complete motion of the end-effector is accomplished through a series of motions and positions of the links, joints, and wrist. A typical industrial robot with six-degrees of freedom is shown in Figure 8.1.

8.2 FUNDAMENTALS OF ROBOTICS AND ROBOTICS TECHNOLOGY

In this section we provide a basic understanding of the fundamentals and technology of robotics. The basic components of a robot include the manipulator, the controller, and the power supply sources. The types and attributes of these components are discussed next.

8.2.1 Power Sources for Robots

An important element of a robot is the drive system. The drive system supplies the power, which enables the robot to move. The dynamic performance of the robot is determined by the drive system adopted, which depends mainly on the type of application and the power requirements. The three types of drive systems are generally used for industrial robots:

1. Hydraulic drive
2. Electric drive
3. Pneumatic drive

8.2.1.1 Hydraulic Drive

A hydraulic drive system gives a robot great speed and strength. These systems can be designed to actuate linear or rotational joints. The main disadvantage of a hydraulic system is that it occupies floor space in addition to that required by the robot. Also, there are problems of leaks, making the floor messy. Because they provide high speed and strength, hydraulic systems are adopted for large industrial robots. Hydraulic robots are preferred in environments in which the use of electric-drive robots may cause fire hazards, for example, in spray painting.

8.2.1.2 Electric Drive

Compared with a hydraulic system, an electric system provides a robot with less speed and strength. Accordingly, electric drive systems are adopted for smaller robots. However, robots supported by electric drive systems are more accurate, exhibit better repeatability, and are cleaner to use. Electrically driven robots are the most commonly available and used industrial robots. Like numerically controlled (NC) machines, electrically driven robots can be classified into two broad categories: stepper motor-driven and direct current (DC) servo-motor driven. Most stepper motor–driven robots are of the open-loop type, but feedback loops can be incorporated in stepper-driven robots. Servo-driven robots invariably have feedback loops from the driven components back to the driver.

8.2.1.3 Pneumatic Drive

Pneumatic drive systems are generally used for smaller robots. These robots, with fewer degrees of freedom, carry out simple pick-and-place material-handling operations, such as picking up an object at one location and placing it at another location. These operations are generally simple and have short cycle times. The pneumatic power can be used for sliding or rotational joints. Pneumatic robots are less expensive than electric or hydraulic robots. Normally, shop air compressed at approximately 90 pounds per square inch (psi), which is used on machine tools and presses, is available for use in robots without extra cost. But mostly pneumatic robots operate at mechanically fixed end points for each axis. That means these are limited sequence robots. A big advantage of such robots is their simple modular construction, using standard commercially available components. This makes it possible for a firm to build its own robots at substantial cost savings for simple tasks such as pick and place, machine loading and unloading, and so forth.

8.2.2 Robotic Sensors

The motion of a robot is obtained by precise movements at its joints and wrist. While the movements are obtained, it is important to ensure that the motion is precise and smooth. The drive systems should be controlled by proper means to regulate the motion of the robot. Along with controls, robots are required to sense some characteristics of their environment. These characteristics provide the feedback to enable the control systems to regulate the manipulator movements efficiently. Sensors provide feedback to the control systems and give the robots more flexibility. Sensors such as visual sensors are useful in the building of more accurate and intelligent robots. The sensors can be classified in many different ways based on their utility. In this section we discuss a few typical sensors that are normally used in robots:

- Position sensors
- Range sensors
- Velocity sensors
- Proximity sensors

8.2.2.1 Position Sensors

Position sensors are used to monitor the position of joints. Information about the position is fed back to the control systems that are used to determine the accuracy of joint movements. Accurate joint movements are reflected in correct positioning of the end-effector, which eventually carries out the prescribed task.

8.2.2.2 Range Sensors

Range sensors measure distances from a reference point to other points of importance. Range sensing is accomplished by means of television cameras or sonar transmitters and receivers. The major drawback of range sensing is that it may miss certain points that cannot be seen from the positions of the transmitters. This problem may be reduced by using a greater number of sensors.

8.2.2.3 Velocity Sensors

Velocity sensors are used to estimate the speed with which a manipulator is moved. The velocity is an important part of the dynamic performance of the manipulator. Variations in acceleration during the movements between points give rise to the dynamic nature of the manipulator. Inertial forces due to changes in acceleration, damping forces due to changes in velocity, and spring forces due to elongations in the links caused by gravity and the weights carried should be monitored and controlled to fine-tune the dynamic performance of the manipulator. The DC techometer is one of the most commonly used devices for feedback of velocity information. The techometer, which is essentially a DC generator, provides an output voltage proportional to the angular velocity of the armature. This information is fed back to the controls for proper regulation of the motion.

8.2.2.4 Proximity Sensors

Proximity sensors are used to sense and indicate the presence of an object within a specified distance or space without any physical contact. This helps prevent accidents and damage to the robot. These sensors act on reflected signals that they receive from the object. The signals are generated using a light-emitting diode transmitter and are received by a photodiode receiver. Range sensors can, in fact, replace proximity sensors.

There are many other types of sensors with different sensing abilities. Acoustic sensors sense and interpret acoustic waves in a gas, liquid, or solid. Touch sensors sense and indicate physical contact between the sensor-carrying object and another object. Force sensors measure all the components of force and torque between two objects. Tactile sensors are being developed to provide more accurate data on the position of parts that are in contact than is provided by vision.

The sophistication of a sensor is reflected in the flexibility, accuracy, and repeatability of robots. Machine vision, an important sensor technology, has been developed significantly during the past decade and is being applied in various robot applications. This technology is also applied in inspection systems and thus discussed in the chapter on quality design, control, and automated inspection systems. Sensors are important for both the safety of robotic systems and the safety of workers.

8.2.3 The Hand of a Robot: End-Effector

The end-effector (commonly known as robot hand) mounted on the wrist enables the robot to perform specified tasks. Various types of end-effectors are designed for the same robot to make it more flexible and versatile. End-effectors are categorized into two major types: *grippers* and *tools.*

Grippers are generally used to grasp and hold an object and place it at a desired location. Grippers can be further classified as mechanical grippers, vacuum or suction cups, magnetic grippers, adhesive grippers, hooks, scoops, and so forth. Mechanical grippers are further classified as single grippers and double grippers. A double gripper can handle two objects at the same time, and the two gripping devices can be actuated separately. More than two grippers can also be used when needed; however, such occasions are not common. Grippers may also be classified as external or internal, depending on whether the part is grasped on its external or internal surface. A detailed discussion of grippers is beyond the scope of this book but is given in a number of books on robotics (Groover, et al., 1984; Asfahl, 1992).

At times, a robot is required to manipulate a tool to perform an operation on a workpart. In such applications the end-effector is used as a gripper that can grasp and handle a variety of tools and the robot has multitool handling function. However, in most robot applications in which only one tool is to be manipulated, the tool is directly mounted on the wrist. Here the tool itself acts as end-effector. Spot-welding tools, arc-welding tools, spray-painting nozzles, and rotating spindles for drilling and grinding are typical examples of tools used as end-effectors.

8.2.4 Robot Movement and Precision

Speed of response and stability are two important characteristics of robot movement. Speed defines how quickly the robot arm moves from one point to another. Stability refers to robot motion with the least amount of oscillation. A good robot is one that is fast enough but at the same time has good stability. Speed and stability are often conflicting goals. However, a good controlling system can be designed for the robot to facilitate a good trade-off between the two parameters.

The precision of robot movement is defined by three basic features:

1. Spatial resolution
2. Accuracy
3. Repeatability

These attributes of precision are discussed below.

8.2.4.1 Spatial Resolution

The spatial resolution of a robot is the smallest increment of movement into which the robot can divide its work volume. It depends on the system's control resolution and the robot's mechanical inaccuracies. The control resolution is determined by the robot's position control system and its feedback measurement system. The controller divides the total range of movements for any particular joint into individual increments that can be addressed in the controller. The bit storage capacity of the control memory defines this ability to divide the total range into increments. For a particular axis, the number of separate increments is given by

$$\text{Number of increments} = 2^n \tag{8.1}$$

where n is the number of bits in the control memory.

EXAMPLE 8.1

A robot's control memory has 8-bit storage capacity. It has two rotational joints and one linear joint. Determine the control resolution for each joint, if the linear link can vary its length from as short as 0.2 m to as long as 1.2 m.

Solution

Control memory = 8 bit

From equation (8.1), number of increments = $2^8 = 256$

(a) Total range for rotational joints = 360°
Control resolution for each rotational joint = 360/256 = 1.40625°

(b) Total range for linear joint = 1.2 − 0.2 = 1.0 m
Control resolution for linear joint = 1/256 = 0.003906 m = 3.906 mm

This example shows how control resolutions are computed for different joints. To obtain the control resolution for the entire robot, component resolutions would have to be summed up vectorially. However, the robot's control resolution is a complex quantity to determine because joints of different types (rotatory and linear) are present.

Elastic deformations in the links due to gravity and other forces result in mechanical inaccuracies. These inaccuracies are greater for larger robots simply because they are magnified by the larger components. Other factors creating inaccuracies include the speed with which the arm is moving, condition of the robot, stretching of pulley cords, and leakage of hydraulic fluids. The spatial resolution can be improved by enhancing the control bit capacity.

8.2.4.2 Accuracy

Accuracy can be defined as the ability of a robot to position its wrist end at a desired target point within its reach. In terms of control resolution, the accuracy can be defined as one-half of the control resolution. This definition of accuracy applies in the worst case when the target point is between two control points. The reason is that displacements smaller than one basic control resolution unit (BCRU) can be neither programmed nor measured and, on average, they account for one-half BCRU. The accuracy of a robot is affected by many factors. For example, when the arm is fully stretched out, the mechanical inaccuracies tend to be larger because the loads tend to

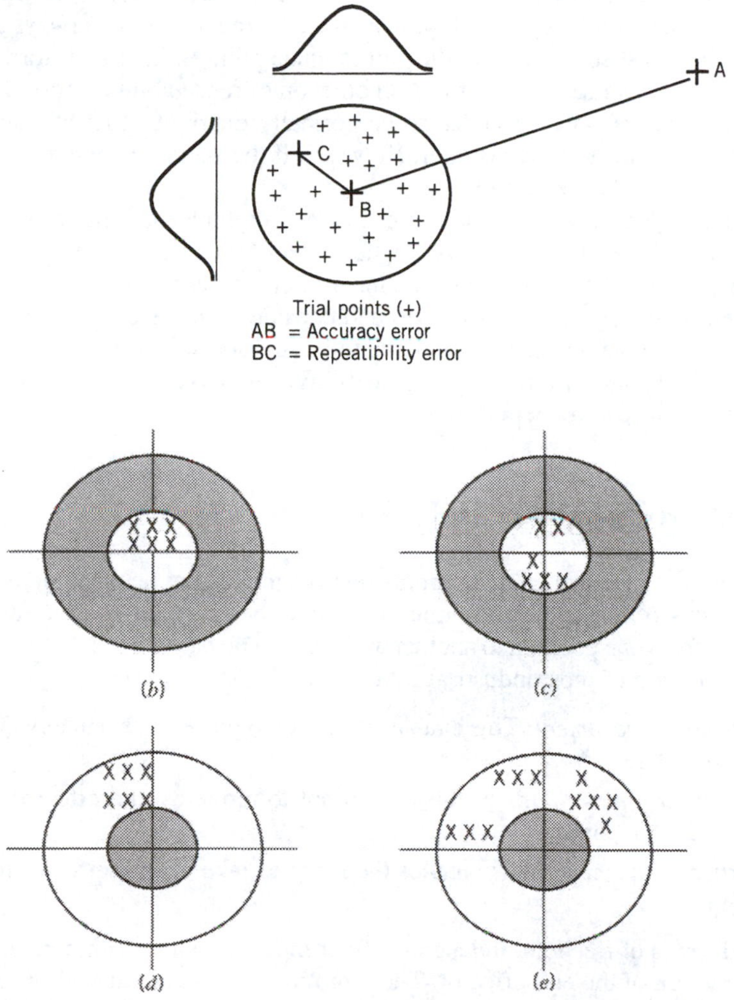

FIGURE 8.2 (*a*) Accuracy and repeatability; (*b*), high accuracy and high repeatability; (*c*) high accuracy and low repeatability; (*d*) low accuracy and high repeatability; (*e*) low accuracy and low repeatability.

cause larger torques at the joints, resulting in greater deformations. When the arm is closer to its base, the inaccuracies tend to be minimal and better accuracy is observed. In robots with only linearly varying links, ideally the accuracy may be considered uniform. However, for robots with other configurations that employ rotational and/or linear joints, it is difficult to combine the effect of all joints and define accuracy.

8.2.4.3 Repeatability

Repeatability refers to the robot's ability to position its end-effector at a point that had previously been taught to the robot. The repeatability error differs from accuracy as described below (Figure 8.2).

Let point A be the target point as shown in Figure 8.2*a*. Because of the limitations of spatial resolution and therefore accuracy, the programmed point becomes point B. The distance between points A and B is a result of the robot's limited accuracy due to the spatial resolution. When the robot is instructed to return to the programmed point B, it returns to point C instead. The distance between points B and C is the result of limitations on the robot's repeatability. However, the robot does not always go to point C every time it is asked to return to the programmed point B. Instead, it forms a cluster of points. This gives rise to a random phenomenon of repeatability errors. The repeatability errors are generally assumed to be normally distributed. If the mean error is large, we say that the accuracy is poor. However, if the standard deviation of the error is low, we say that the repeatability is high.

We pictorially represent the concept of low and high repeatability as well as accuracy in Figure 8.2*b*, *c*, *d*, and *e*. Consider the center of the two concentric circles as the desired target point. The diameter of the inner circle represents the limits up to which the robot end-effector can be positioned and considered to be of high accuracy. Any point outside the inner circle is considered to be of poor or low accuracy. A group of closely clustered points implies high repeatability, whereas a sparsely distributed cluster of points indicates low repeatability.

8.3 THE ROBOTIC JOINTS

A robot joint is a mechanism that permits relative movement between parts of a robot arm. The joints of a robot are designed to enable the robot to move its end-effector along a path from one position to another as desired. The basic movements required for the desired motion of most industrial robots are:

- *Rotational movement:* This enables the robot to place its arm in any direction on a horizontal plane.
- *Radial movement:* This enables the robot to move its end-effector radially to reach distant points.
- *Vertical movement:* This enables the robot to take its end-effector to different heights.

These degrees of freedom, independently or in combination with others, define the complete motion of the end-effector. These motions are accomplished by movements of individual joints of the robot arm. The joint movements are basically the same as relative motion of adjoining links. Depending on the nature of this relative motion, the joints are classified as *prismatic* or *revolute.*

Prismatic joints are also known as sliding as well as linear joints. They are called prismatic because the cross section of the joint is considered as a generalized prism. They permit links to move in a linear relationship.

Revolute joints permit only angular motion between links. Their variations include:

- Rotational joint (R)
- Twisting joint (T)
- Revolving joint (V)

Revolute joints are also referred to as rotational joints. Schematic representations of the joints are shown in Figure 8.3.

In a prismatic joint, also known as a sliding or linear joint (L), the links are generally parallel to one another. In some cases, adjoining links are perpendicular but one link slides at the end of the other link. The joint motion is defined by sliding or translational movements of the links. The orientation of the links remains the same after the joint movement, but the lengths of the links are altered.

A rotational joint (R) is identified by its motion, rotation about an axis perpendicular to the adjoining links. Here, the lengths of adjoining links do not change but the relative position of the links with respect to one another changes as the rotation takes place.

A twisting joint (T) is also a rotational joint, where the rotation takes place about an axis that is parallel to both adjoining links. Here the rotation involves the twisting of one link with respect to another, hence the name twisting joint.

A revolving joint (V) is another rotational joint, where the rotation takes place about an axis that is parallel to one of the adjoining links. Usually, the links are aligned perpendicular to one another at this kind of joint. The rotation involves revolution of one link about another, hence the name.

In addition to the movements of the robot's arm and body, the movements of its wrist are also important. The orientation of the end-effector is obtained by proper movement of the joint between wrist and end-effector. The wrist movement is designed to enable the robot to orient its end-effector so that the task is carried out properly. Usually, the wrist is designed with rotations about three different axes. See Figure 8.1 for the robot's movement pattern.

8.3.1 The Joint Notation

A robot's physical configuration can be described by the notation discussed in this section. This notation basically identifies the types of joints used in the configuration

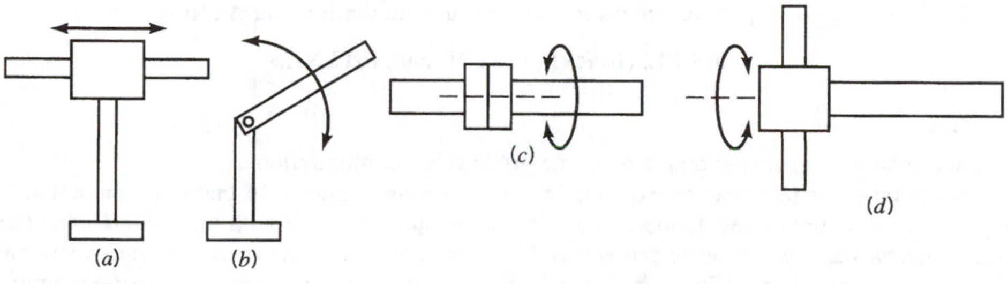

FIGURE 8.3 Types of joints: (*a*) linear joint; (*b*) rotational joint; (*c*) twisting joint; (*d*) revolving joint.

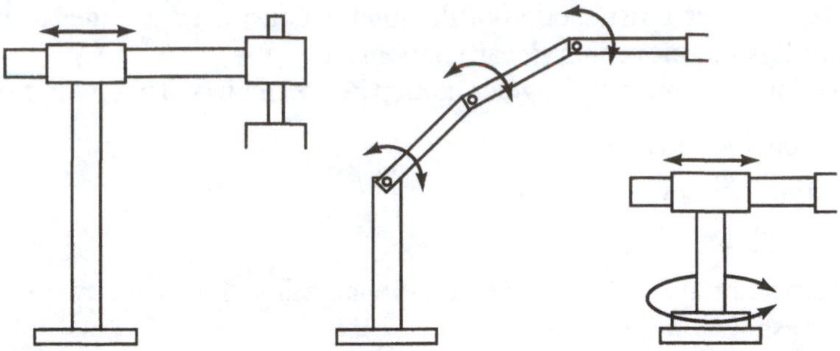

FIGURE 8.4 Robot configurations for Example 8.2: (*a*) LL robot; (*b*) RRR robot; (*c*) TL robot.

of the robot. As just discussed, the joints can be denoted by the letters L, R, T, and V for linear, rotational, twisting, and revolving, respectively. We consider the arm and body first and use these letters to designate the particular robot configuration. The letter corresponding to the joint closest to the base is written first and letters for succeeding joints follow. For example, the designation TRR means that the base joint is a twisting joint and the succeeding joints of the arm are rotational joints. Various robot configurations are described in the following sections and corresponding designations are listed for reference.

EXAMPLE 8.2

Designate the robot configurations shown in Figure 8.4, using the joint notation scheme.

Solution

(a) This configuration has two linear joints. Hence, it is designated LL.

(b) This configuration has three rotational joints. Hence, it is designated RRR.

(c) This configuration has one twisting joint and one linear joint. This is indicated by TL.

EXAMPLE 8.3

For the following joint notation, give sketches to illustrate the robot arm configuration.

(a) LRL, (b) RRL, (c) TRL and, (d) LVL.

Solution

Figure 8.5 shows schematic diagrams of the given robot configurations.

This notation scheme can be expanded to include wrist motions. In that case, the notation begins with the joint closest to the arm and proceeds up to the joint with the end-effector. For example, a two-axis wrist can be denoted as RT, which means that the wrist joints are rotational and twisting, respectively. The complete designation for a robot with arm and wrist configurations similar to those discussed here is TRR:RT.

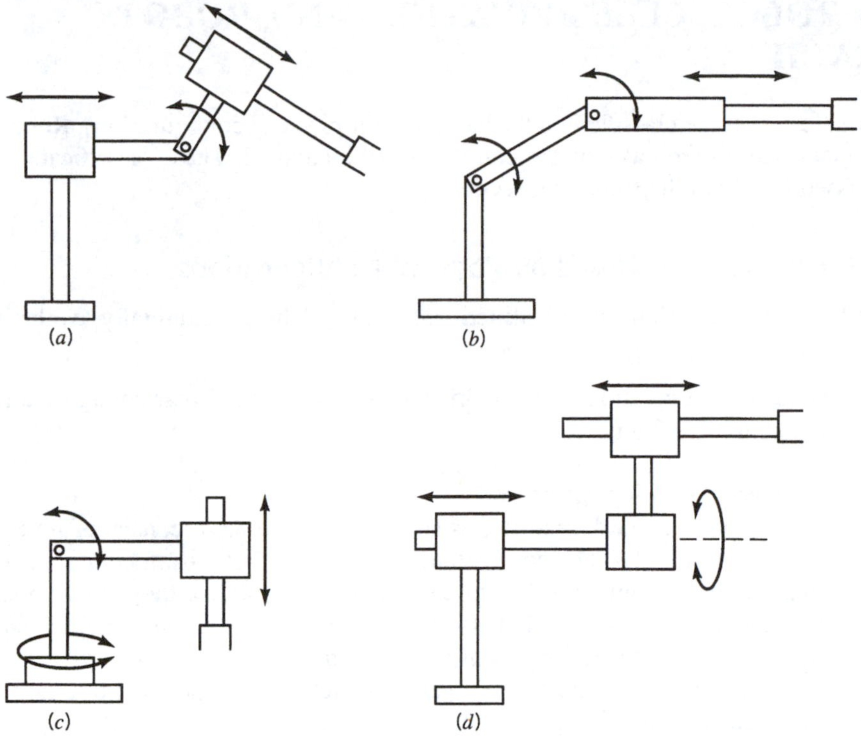

FIGURE 8.5 Robot configurations for Example 8.3: (*a*) LRL robot; (*b*) RRL robot; (*c*) TRL robot; (*d*) LVL robot.

EXAMPLE 8.4

The robots described in Examples 8.2 and 8.3 are equipped with a wrist that has twisting, rotatory, and twisting joints in sequence from the arm to the end-effector. Give the designation for the complete configuration of each robot.

Solution

The wrist has three joints denoted by T, R, and T (T for twisting and R for rotation). Using the joint notation scheme for the wrist, the wrist can be designated as TRT.

For the robots in Example 8.2, the complete designation is as follows:

(a) LL:TRT
(b) RRR:TRT
(c) TL:TRT

For the robots in Example 8.3, the complete designation is as follows:

(a) LRL:TRT
(b) RRL:TRT
(c) TRL:TRT
(d) LVL:TRT

8.4 ROBOT CLASSIFICATION AND ROBOT REACH

Normally robots are classified on the basis of their physical configurations. Robots are also classified on the basis of the control systems adopted. These classifications are discussed briefly in the following sections.

8.4.1 Classification Based on Physical Configurations

Four basic configurations are identified with most of the commercially available industrial robots. They are:

1. Cartesian configuration; 2. Cylindrical configuration; 3. Polar configuration; 4. Jointed-arm configuration.

8.4.1.1 Cartesian Configuration

Robots with Cartesian configurations, as shown in Figure 8.6*a*, consist of links connected by linear joints (L). The configuration of the robot's arm can be designated as LLL. Because the configuration has three perpendicular slides, they are also called rectilinear robots. Another robot that is similar to this configuration is a *gantry robot.* The structure of a gantry robot resembles a gantry-type crane. Gantry robots are Cartesian robots that are mounted on a gantry structure and operate from the top to perform the specified task.

8.4.1.2 Cylindrical Configuration

In the cylindrical configuration, as shown in Figure 8.6*b*, robots have one rotatory (R) joint at the base and linear (L) joints succeed to connect the links. The robot arm in this configuration can be designated as TLL. The space in which this robot operates is cylindrical in shape, hence the name cylindrical configuration.

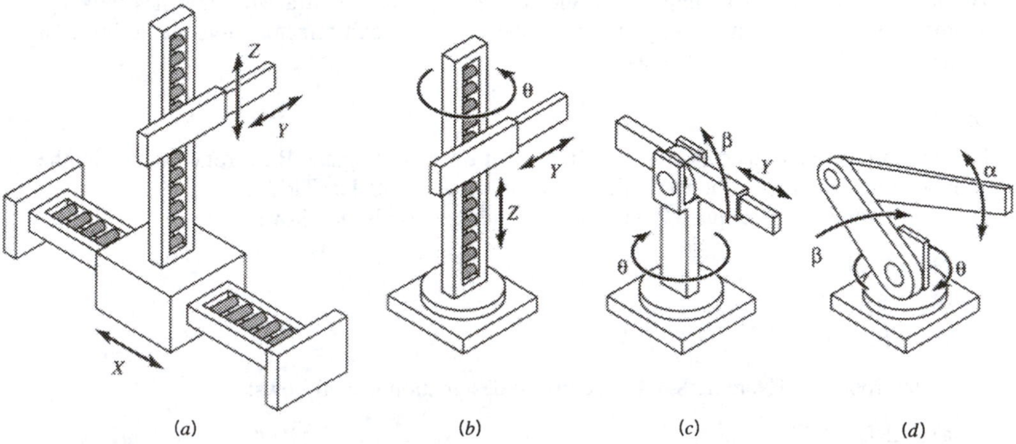

FIGURE 8.6 Robot classification: (*a*) Cartesian robot; (*b*) cylindrical robot; (*c*) polar robot; (*d*) jointed-arm (revolute) robot. (Reprinted with the permission of the publisher from *Robotics in Practice* by J. F. Engelberger, page 31 © 1980 by J. L. Engelberger, published in the U.S.A. by AMACOM, a division of American Management Association, New York, all rights reserved.)

8.4.1.3 Polar Configuration

Polar robots, as shown in Figure 8.6*c*, have a work space of spherical shape. Generally, the arm is connected to the base with a twisting (T) joint and rotatory (R) and/or linear (L) joints follow. The designation of the arm for this configuration can be TRL or TRR. Robots with the designation TRL are also called spherical robots. Those with the designation TRR are also called articulated robots. An articulated robot more closely resembles the human arm.

8.4.1.4 Jointed-Arm Configuration

The jointed-arm configuration, as shown in Figure 8.6*d*, is a combination of cylindrical and articulated configurations. The arm of the robot is connected to the base with a twisting joint. The links in the arm are connected by rotatory joints. The rotations generally take place in the vertical plane. Several commercially available robots have this configuration. The most popular robot, which is very close to this configuration, is SCARA (selective compliance assembly robot arm). However, in the SCARA robot rotations take place in horizontal planes, thus reducing the possibility of large deformations in the links. This configuration gives the robot substantial vertical rigidity, which makes it ideal for many assembly tasks.

EXAMPLE 8.5

Describe and identify the robot configurations given in Example 8.2.

Solution

(a) This configuration consists of two linear joints. Hence it is a Cartesian configuration.

(b) This configuration consists of three rotational joints. It can be called a jointed-arm configuration.

(c) This configuration has one twisting joint and one linear joint. It is a cylindrical configuration.

The classification of robots broadly described here provides a framework for complex configurations. It is possible to have robots with configurations formed by combining two or more of the basic ones described in this section. For example, the robot configurations in Example 8.3 are combinations of two or more basic configurations. The configuration is designed to meet the requirements of the task the robot is assigned to perform.

8.4.2 Classification Based on Control Systems

Based on the control systems adopted, robots are classified into the following categories:

1. Point-to-point (PTP) control robot
2. Continuous-path (CP) control robot
3. Controlled-path robot

8.4.2.1 Point-to-Point (PTP) Control Robot

The PTP robot is capable of moving from one point to another point. The locations are recorded in the control memory. PTP robots do not control the path to get from one point to the next point. The programmer exercises some control over the desired path to be followed by programming a series of points along the path. Common applications include component insertion, spot welding, hole drilling, machine loading and unloading, and crude assembly operations.

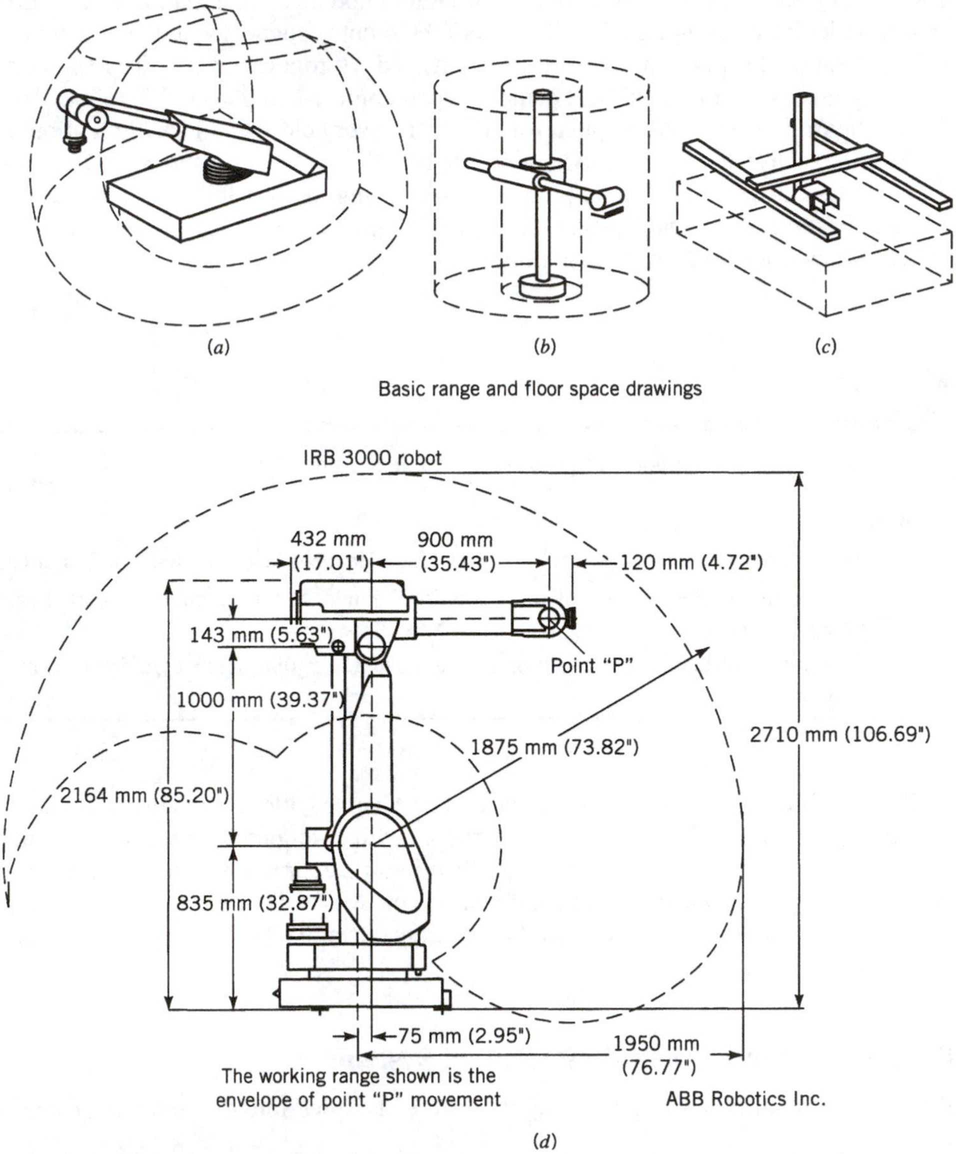

FIGURE 8.7 Robot reach (work envelope): (*a*) polar; (*b*) cylindrical robot; (*c*) Cartesian. (Source: Toepperwein and Blackman, 1980.) (*d*) Joint arm (revolute) robot. (Courtesy of ABB Robotics, Inc.)

8.4.2.2 Continuous-Path (CP) Control Robot

The CP robot is capable of performing movements along the controlled path. With CP control, the robot can stop at any specified point along the controlled path. All the points along the path must be stored explicitly in the robot's control memory. Straight-line motion is the simplest example for this type of robot. Some continuous-path controlled robots also have the capability to follow a smooth curve path that has been defined by the programmer. In such cases the programmer manually moves the robot arm through the desired path and the controller unit stores a large number of individual point locations along the path in memory. Typical applications include spray painting, finishing, gluing, and arc welding operations.

8.4.2.3 Controlled-Path Robot

In controlled-path robots, the control equipment can generate paths of different geometry such as straight lines, circles, and interpolated curves with a high degree of accuracy. Good accuracy can be obtained at any point along the specified path. Only the start and finish points and the path definition function must be stored in the robot's control memory. It is important to mention that all controlled-path robots have a servo capability to correct their path.

8.4.3 Robot Reach

Robot reach, also known as the work envelope or work volume, is the space of all points in the surrounding space that can be reached by the robot arm or the mounting point for the end-effector or tool. The area reachable by the end-effector itself is not considered part of the work envelope. Reach is one of the most important characteristics to be considered in selecting a suitable robot because the application space should not fall out of the selected robot's reach.

Robot reach for various robot configurations is shown in Figure 8.7. For a Cartesian configuration the reach is a rectangular-type space. For a cylindrical configuration the reach is a hollow cylindrical space and for a polar configuration it is part of a hollow spherical shape. Robot reach for a jointed-arm configuration does not have a specific geometric shape as shown in Figure 8.7.

8.5 ROBOT MOTION ANALYSIS: FORWARD AND BACKWARD KINEMATIC TRANSFORMATION

In robot motion analysis we study the geometry of the robot arm with respect to a reference coordinate system, while the end-effector moves along the prescribed path. This kinematic analysis involves two different kinds of problems: (1) determining the coordinates of the end-effector or end of arm for a given set of joints coordinates and (2) determining the joints coordinates for a given location of the end-effector or end of arm. Before describing these problems in detail, we need to understand the position representations.

The position, V, of the end-effector can be defined, in the Cartesian coordinate system, as

$$V = (x, y) \tag{8.2}$$

Generally, for robots the location of the end-effector can be defined in two systems: *joint space* and *world space* (also known as *global space*).

In joint space, the joint parameters such as rotating or twisting joint angles and variable link lengths are used to represent the position of the end-effector.

$$\begin{aligned} V_j &= (\theta, \alpha) && \text{for RR robot} \\ &= (L_1, L_2) && \text{for LL robot} \\ &= (\alpha, L_2) && \text{for TL robot} \end{aligned} \tag{8.3}$$

where V_j refers to the position of the end-effector in joint space.

In world space, rectilinear coordinates with reference to the basic Cartesian system are used to define the position of the end-effector. Usually the origin of the Cartesian axes is located in the robot's base.

$$V_w = (x, y) \tag{8.4}$$

where V_w refers to the position of the end-effector in world space.

The transformation of coordinates of the end-effector point from the joint space to the world space is known as forward kinematic transformation. Similarly, the transformation of coordinates from world space to joint space is known as backward or reverse kinematic transformation. We discuss these transformations for robot arms with two degrees of freedom. For this purpose three cases, LL robot, RR robot, and TL robot, as shown in Figure 8.8, are analyzed in the following sections.

In this section we provide a framework for analysis of the forward and backward kinematic transformations. Various simple cases are analyzed that form the building blocks for advanced analyses.

8.5.1 Forward Kinematic Transformation

We illustrate the concepts of kinematic transformations using specific configurations.

8.5.1.1 LL Robot

Let us consider a Cartesian LL robot as shown in Figure 8.8*a*. Joints J_1 and J_2 are linear joints with links of variable lengths L_1 and L_2. Let joint J_1 be denoted by (x_1, y_1) and joint J_2 by (x_2, y_2).

From geometry, we can easily get the following:

$$x_2 = x_1 + L_2 \tag{8.5}$$

$$y_2 = y_1 \tag{8.6}$$

These relations can be represented in homogeneous matrix from (for details of homogeneous transformations, refer to Chapter 2) as

$$\begin{bmatrix} x_2 \\ y_2 \\ 1 \end{bmatrix} = \begin{bmatrix} 1 & 0 & L_2 \\ 0 & 1 & 0 \\ 0 & 0 & 1 \end{bmatrix} \cdot \begin{bmatrix} x_1 \\ y_1 \\ 1 \end{bmatrix} \tag{8.7}$$

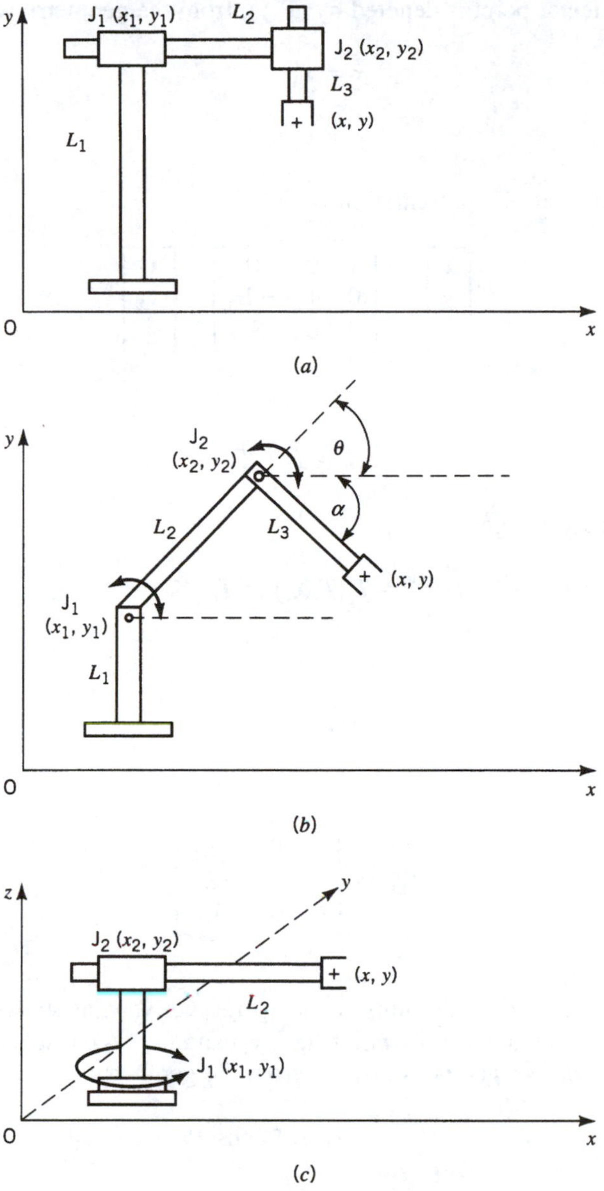

FIGURE 8.8 Robot arms of two degrees of freedom: (*a*) LL robot; (*b*) RR robot; (*c*) TL robot.

or

$$X_2 = T_1 \cdot X_1$$

where

$$X_2 = \begin{bmatrix} x_2 \\ y_2 \\ 1 \end{bmatrix}, \qquad T_1 = \begin{bmatrix} 1 & 0 & L_2 \\ 0 & 1 & 0 \\ 0 & 0 & 1 \end{bmatrix}, \qquad X_1 = \begin{bmatrix} x_1 \\ y_1 \\ 1 \end{bmatrix}$$

If the end-effector point is denoted by (x, y), from the geometry we can get

$$x = x_2 \tag{8.8}$$

$$y = y_2 - L_3 \tag{8.9}$$

Its homogeneous matrix representation is

$$\begin{bmatrix} x \\ y \\ 1 \end{bmatrix} = \begin{bmatrix} 1 & 0 & 0 \\ 0 & 1 & -L_3 \\ 0 & 0 & 1 \end{bmatrix} \cdot \begin{bmatrix} x_2 \\ y_2 \\ 1 \end{bmatrix} \tag{8.10}$$

or

$$X = T_2 \cdot X_2$$

Substituting for X_2, we get

$$X = T_2(T_1 X_1) = T_{LL} X_1 \tag{8.11}$$

where

$$T_{LL} = T_2 T_1 \tag{8.12}$$

and

$$T_{LL} = \begin{bmatrix} 1 & 0 & L_2 \\ 0 & 1 & -L_3 \\ 0 & 0 & 1 \end{bmatrix} \tag{8.13}$$

8.5.1.2 RR Robot

Let θ and α be the rotations at joints J_1 and J_2, respectively, as shown in Figure 8.8*b*. Let joints J_1 and J_2 be denoted by points (x_1, y_1) and (x_2, y_2), respectively.

Accordingly, we can get the following from the geometry:

$$x_2 = x_1 + L_2 \cos(\theta) \tag{8.14}$$

$$y_2 = y_1 + L_2 \sin(\theta) \tag{8.15}$$

In matrix form this can be represented as

$$\begin{bmatrix} x_2 \\ y_2 \\ 1 \end{bmatrix} = \begin{bmatrix} 1 & 0 & L_2 \cos(\theta) \\ 0 & 1 & L_2 \sin(\theta) \\ 0 & 0 & 1 \end{bmatrix} \cdot \begin{bmatrix} x_1 \\ y_1 \\ 1 \end{bmatrix} \tag{8.16}$$

or

$$X_2 = T_1 \cdot X_1$$

Suppose the end-effector point is represented by (x, y). Then from the geometry it is easy to obtain

$$x = x_2 + L_3 \cos(\alpha - \theta) \tag{8.17}$$

$$y = y_2 - L_3 \sin(\alpha - \theta) \tag{8.18}$$

In matrix form, this can be represented as

$$\begin{bmatrix} x \\ y \\ 1 \end{bmatrix} = \begin{bmatrix} 1 & 0 & L_3 \cos(\alpha - \theta) \\ 0 & 1 & -L_3 \sin(\alpha - \theta) \\ 0 & 0 & 1 \end{bmatrix} \cdot \begin{bmatrix} x_2 \\ y_2 \\ 1 \end{bmatrix} \tag{8.19}$$

or

$$X = T_2 \cdot X_2$$

Substituting for X_2, we get

$$X = T_2(T_1 X_1) = T_{RR} X_1 \tag{8.20}$$

where

$$T_{RR} = T_2 T_1 \tag{8.21}$$

$$T_{RR} = \begin{bmatrix} 1 & 0 & L_2 \cos(\theta) + L_3 \cos(\alpha - \theta) \\ 0 & 1 & L_2 \sin(\theta) - L_3 \sin(\alpha - \theta) \\ 0 & 0 & 1 \end{bmatrix} \tag{8.22}$$

8.5.1.3 TL Robot

Suppose α is the rotation at twisting joint J_1 and L_2 is the variable link length at linear joint J_2, whose position is given by (x_2, y_2) as shown in Figure 8.8*c*. If the end-effector point is (x, y), then from the geometry we can easily get

$$x = x_2 + L_2 \cos \alpha \tag{8.23}$$

$$y = y_2 + L_2 \sin \alpha \tag{8.24}$$

In matrix form we can represent this as follows:

$$\begin{bmatrix} x \\ y \\ 1 \end{bmatrix} = \begin{bmatrix} 1 & 0 & L_2 \cos \alpha \\ 0 & 1 & L_2 \sin \alpha \\ 0 & 0 & 1 \end{bmatrix} \cdot \begin{bmatrix} x_2 \\ y_2 \\ 1 \end{bmatrix} \tag{8.25}$$

or

$$X = T_{TL} \cdot X_2$$

8.5.2 Backward Kinematic Transformation

In this section we illustrate the concepts of backward kinematic transformations using specific robot configurations.

8.5.2.1 LL Robot

In backward kinematic transformation, the objective is to derive the variable link lengths from the known position of the end-effector in world space. The position of the end-effector is given by

$$X = T_{\text{LL}} \cdot X_1$$

Rewriting this equation in expanded form, we get

$$x = x_1 + L_2$$

$$y = y_1 - L_3 \qquad \text{and} \qquad y_1 = y_2$$

A simple manipulation of equations yields the variable lengths as

$$L_2 = x - x_1 \tag{8.26}$$

$$L_3 = -y + y_2 \tag{8.27}$$

8.5.2.2 RR Robot

In the case of the RR robot, the objective in backward transformation is to derive the joint angles from the known position of the end-effector in world space. We know from equation (8.20) that

$$X = T_{\text{RR}} \cdot X_1$$

Expanding this equation, we get

$$x = x_1 + L_2 \cos(\theta) + L_3 \cos(\alpha - \theta)$$

$$y = y_1 + L_2 \sin(\theta) - L_3 \sin(\alpha - \theta)$$

On simplification we can easily get the following:

$$\cos \alpha = \frac{[(x - x_1)^2 + (y - y_1)^2 - L_2^2 - L_3^2]}{2L_2L_3} \tag{8.28}$$

and

$$\tan \theta = \frac{(y - y_1)(L_2 + L_3 \cos \alpha) + (x - x_1)\, L_3 \sin \alpha}{(x - x_1)(L_2 + L_3 \cos \alpha) - (y - y_1)\, L_3 \sin \alpha} \tag{8.29}$$

It is pertinent to emphasize here that the reverse transformation becomes more and more cumbersome with increasing degrees of freedom.

8.5.2.3 TL Robot

For the TL robot the objective is to derive the variable link length and the twist angle from the known position of the end-effector in world space. The expanded version of the equation $X = T_{\text{TL}} \cdot X_2$ gives

$$x = x_2 + L \cos \alpha$$

$$y = y_2 + L \sin \alpha$$

Simplification of these equations yields

$$L = \sqrt{(x - x_2)^2 + (y - y_2)^2} \tag{8.30}$$

and

$$\sin \alpha = \frac{y - y_2}{L} \tag{8.31}$$

We illustrate these concepts in the following examples.

EXAMPLE 8.6

An LL robot has two links of variable length. Assuming that the global coordinate system is defined at joint J_1, determine the following:

(a) The coordinates of the end-effector point if the variable link lengths are 3 m and 5 m as shown in Figure 8.8*a*.

(b) Variable link lengths if the end-effector is located at (3, 5).

Solution

(a) We are given $(x_1, y_1) = (0, 0)$. Using equation (8.13):

$$T_{\text{LL}} = \begin{bmatrix} 1 & 0 & 3 \\ 0 & 1 & -5 \\ 0 & 0 & 1 \end{bmatrix}$$

$$\begin{bmatrix} x \\ y \\ 1 \end{bmatrix} = T_{\text{LL}} \cdot \begin{bmatrix} x_1 \\ y_1 \\ 1 \end{bmatrix}$$

$$= \begin{bmatrix} 1 & 0 & 3 \\ 0 & 1 & -5 \\ 0 & 0 & 1 \end{bmatrix} \cdot \begin{bmatrix} 0 \\ 0 \\ 1 \end{bmatrix}$$

$$= \begin{bmatrix} 3 \\ -5 \\ 1 \end{bmatrix}$$

Therefore, the end-effector point is given by (3, −5).

(b) The end-effector point $(x, y) = (3, 5)$. Accordingly,

$$L_2 = x - x_1 = 3 - 0 = 3 \text{ m}$$

$$L_3 = -y + y_1 = -5 + 0 = -5 \text{ m}$$

The variable link lengths are 3 m and 5 m, because the minus sign is due to the coordinate system used.

EXAMPLE 8.7

An RR robot has two links of length 1.0 m. Assuming that the global coordinate system is defined at joint J_1, determine the following:

(a) The coordinates of the end-effector point if the joint rotations are 30° at both joints as shown in Figure 8.8*b*.

(b) Joint rotations if the end-effector is located at (1.8667, 0.5)

Solution

(a) We are given $(x_1, y_1) = (0, 0)$. Using equation (8.22):

$$T_{RR} = \begin{bmatrix} 1 & 0 & \frac{\sqrt{3}}{2} + 1 \\ 0 & 1 & \frac{1}{2} + 0 \\ 0 & 0 & 1 \end{bmatrix} = \begin{bmatrix} 1 & 0 & 1.8667 \\ 0 & 1 & 0.50 \\ 0 & 0 & 1 \end{bmatrix}$$

$$\begin{bmatrix} x \\ y \\ 1 \end{bmatrix} = T_{RR} \cdot \begin{bmatrix} x_1 \\ y_1 \\ 1 \end{bmatrix} = \begin{bmatrix} 1 & 0 & 1.8667 \\ 0 & 1 & 0.50 \\ 0 & 0 & 1 \end{bmatrix} \cdot \begin{bmatrix} 0 \\ 0 \\ 1 \end{bmatrix} = \begin{bmatrix} 1.8667 \\ 0.50 \\ 1 \end{bmatrix}$$

Therefore, the end-effector point is given by (1.8667, 0.5).

(b) The end-effector is located at (1.8667, 0.5), so using equation (8.28):

$$\cos\alpha = \frac{x^2 + y^2 - L_2^2 - L_3^2}{2L_3L_2} = \frac{1.8667^2 + 0.5^2 - 1^2 - 1^2}{2} = 0.866$$

Therefore,

$$\alpha = \arccos(0.866) = 30°$$

Also, using equation (8.29), we have:

$$\tan\theta = \frac{0.5(1 + 0.866) + (1.8667 \cdot 0.5)}{1.8667 \cdot (1 + 0.866) - 0.5 \cdot 0.5} = 0.5773$$

Therefore,

$$\theta = 30°$$

EXAMPLE 8.8

A TL robot has a variable link as shown in Figure 8.8*c*. Assuming that the coordinate system is defined at joint J_2, determine the following:

(a) The coordinates of the end-effector point if joint J_1 twists by an angle of 30° and the variable link has a length of 1 m.

(b) Variable link length and angle of twist at J_1 if the end-effector is located at (0.867, 0.5).

Solution

(a) We know that $(x_2, y_2) = (0, 0)$; $L = 1$ m, $\alpha = 30°$. Accordingly, from equation (8.25)

$$T_{\mathrm{TL}} = \begin{bmatrix} 1 & 0 & \frac{\sqrt{3}}{2} \\ 0 & 1 & \frac{1}{2} \\ 0 & 0 & 1 \end{bmatrix}$$

Therefore,

$$\begin{bmatrix} x \\ y \\ 1 \end{bmatrix} = \begin{bmatrix} 1 & 0 & \frac{\sqrt{3}}{2} \\ 0 & 1 & \frac{1}{2} \\ 0 & 0 & 1 \end{bmatrix} \cdot \begin{bmatrix} 0 \\ 0 \\ 1 \end{bmatrix}$$

$$= \begin{bmatrix} \frac{\sqrt{3}}{2} \\ \frac{1}{2} \\ 1 \end{bmatrix}$$

(b) We are given that $(x, y) = (0.867, 0.5)$

$$\begin{aligned} L &= \sqrt{(x - x_2)^2 + (y - y_2)^2} \\ &= \sqrt{(0.867 - 0)^2 + (0.5 - 0)^2} \\ &= 1.0 \text{ m} \end{aligned}$$

From equation (8.31),

$$\sin \alpha = \frac{y - y_2}{L} = \frac{0.5 - 0}{1.0} = 0.5$$

Therefore,

$$\alpha = \text{arc} \sin(0.5) = 30°$$

8.5.3 Basic Homogeneous Transformations

In Chapter 2 on computer-aided design, a detailed discussion of the basic homogeneous transformations is provided. In this section we apply the homogeneous transformations to solve the kinematic equations of a robot with many joints. In fact, Denavit and Hartenburg (1955) proposed the use of homogeneous matrices to describe the relationships between the robot links. Denavit–Hartenburg (DH) use a 4 × 4 matrix to transform a vector from one coordinate system to another. As mentioned earlier, to compute the position of the end-effector of a robot arm, each joint is taken as the center of a new coordinate system. The DH system starts by expressing the base reference point of the robot in a homogeneous coordinate matrix. Then a second homogeneous matrix is written describing the relationship between the center of coordinates of the first and second joints. We continue to write such matrices for subsequent pairs. Finally, the matrices are multiplied in the sequence in which they were developed to obtain the position of the end-effector from the point in the base reference coordinates. We elaborate on these concepts in the following sections with illustrations.

8.5.3.1 Translation

Suppose we want to translate the end-effector position of a robot in two-dimensional space by a distance x_1 in the x-direction and a distance y_1 in the y-direction. This transformation is accomplished by the transformation matrix T, given by

$$T = \begin{bmatrix} 1 & 0 & x_1 \\ 0 & 1 & y_1 \\ 0 & 0 & 1 \end{bmatrix} \tag{8.32}$$

Extending the same concept to three-dimensional space, where a point vector is to be translated by a distance of x_1 in the x-direction, y_1 in the y-direction, and z_1 in the z-direction, the transformation matrix T is given by

$$T = \begin{bmatrix} 1 & 0 & 0 & x_1 \\ 0 & 1 & 0 & y_1 \\ 0 & 0 & 1 & z_1 \\ 0 & 0 & 0 & 1 \end{bmatrix} \tag{8.33}$$

If a point vector $\mathbf{V} = r\mathbf{i} + s\mathbf{j} + t\mathbf{k}$ is translated as described above, the new translated point vector $\mathbf{V}'$ is given by the following equation:

$$\mathbf{V}' = T\mathbf{V} \tag{8.34}$$

where scalar a of point vector $\mathbf{V}$ is given by

$$a = \begin{bmatrix} r \\ s \\ t \\ 1 \end{bmatrix} \tag{8.35}$$

EXAMPLE 8.9

The end-effector position of a robot is translated in the x-, y-, and z-directions by distances of 5, 10, and 15, respectively. Write the transformation matrix. If the initial point position of the end-effector is (2, 1, 2), what is the final position of the end-effector?

Solution

Using equation (8.33), the transformation matrix is written as

$$T = \begin{bmatrix} 1 & 0 & 0 & 5 \\ 0 & 1 & 0 & 10 \\ 0 & 0 & 1 & 15 \\ 0 & 0 & 0 & 1 \end{bmatrix}$$

$$\mathbf{V} = \begin{bmatrix} 2 \\ 1 \\ 2 \\ 1 \end{bmatrix}$$

$$\mathbf{V}' = T \cdot \mathbf{V}$$

$$= \begin{bmatrix} 1 & 0 & 0 & 5 \\ 0 & 1 & 0 & 10 \\ 0 & 0 & 1 & 15 \\ 0 & 0 & 0 & 1 \end{bmatrix} \cdot \begin{bmatrix} 2 \\ 1 \\ 2 \\ 1 \end{bmatrix} = \begin{bmatrix} 7 \\ 11 \\ 17 \\ 1 \end{bmatrix}$$

where **V** is the initial position of the end-effector, and **V**′ is the final position of the end-effector. Hence, the final position of the point is (7, 11, 17).

8.5.3.2 Rotation

The transformation matrices for rotation were discussed in Chapter 2. We reproduce the relevant formulas for ready use in robot applications. Accordingly, the transformations for rotation of a point vector about each coordinate axes are as follows.
About the x-axis:

$$R_{x,\alpha} = \begin{bmatrix} 1 & 0 & 0 & 0 \\ 0 & \cos\alpha & -\sin\alpha & 0 \\ 0 & \sin\alpha & \cos\alpha & 0 \\ 0 & 0 & 0 & 1 \end{bmatrix} \tag{8.36}$$

where α = rotation about the x-axis.
About the y-axis:

$$R_{y,\beta} = \begin{bmatrix} \cos\beta & 0 & \sin\beta & 0 \\ 0 & 1 & 0 & 0 \\ -\sin\beta & 0 & \cos\beta & 0 \\ 0 & 0 & 0 & 1 \end{bmatrix} \tag{8.37}$$

where β = rotation about the y-axis.
About the z-axis:

$$R_{z,\gamma} = \begin{bmatrix} \cos\gamma & -\sin\gamma & 0 & 0 \\ \sin\gamma & \cos\gamma & 0 & 0 \\ 0 & 0 & 1 & 0 \\ 0 & 0 & 0 & 1 \end{bmatrix} \tag{8.38}$$

where γ = rotation about the z-axis.

If a point vector $\mathbf{V} = r\mathbf{i} + s\mathbf{j} + t\mathbf{k}$ is rotated about the x-axis as described above, the final location of the point vector $\mathbf{V}'$ is given by

$$\mathbf{V}' = R_{x,\alpha}\mathbf{V} \tag{8.39}$$

where

$$a = \begin{bmatrix} r \\ s \\ t \\ 1 \end{bmatrix}$$

For the robot arm with two degrees of freedom shown in Figure 8.8*b*, the final point of the end-effector due to rotations $\Delta\theta$ and $\Delta\alpha$ at joints J_1 and J_2, respectively, about the z-axis is given by

$$\mathbf{X}_{\text{final}} = T(x_1, y_1, 0)T(L_2, 0, 0)R(z, \Delta\theta)T(L_3, 0, 0)R(z, \Delta\alpha)X_{\text{initial}} \tag{8.40}$$

where

$$\mathbf{X}_{\text{final}} = \begin{bmatrix} x_{\text{final}} \\ y_{\text{final}} \\ 0 \\ 1 \end{bmatrix}$$

$$\mathbf{X}_{\text{initial}} = \begin{bmatrix} x_{\text{initial}} \\ y_{\text{initial}} \\ 0 \\ 1 \end{bmatrix}$$

EXAMPLE 8.10

A point vector (end-effector position) is rotated about the x-axis by an angle of 90°. Write the transformation matrix. The initial position of the end-effector before rotation is (5, 2, 4). Determine the new position of this point.

Solution

The transformation matrix using equation (8.36) can be written as

$$R_{(x,90°)} = \begin{bmatrix} 1 & 0 & 0 & 0 \\ 0 & 0 & -1 & 0 \\ 0 & 1 & 0 & 0 \\ 0 & 0 & 0 & 1 \end{bmatrix}$$

$$V = \begin{bmatrix} 5 \\ 2 \\ 4 \\ 1 \end{bmatrix}$$

$$V' = R_{(x,90°)} \cdot V$$

$$= \begin{bmatrix} 1 & 0 & 0 & 0 \\ 0 & 0 & -1 & 0 \\ 0 & 1 & 0 & 0 \\ 0 & 0 & 0 & 1 \end{bmatrix} \cdot \begin{bmatrix} 5 \\ 2 \\ 4 \\ 1 \end{bmatrix} = \begin{bmatrix} 5 \\ -4 \\ 2 \\ 1 \end{bmatrix}$$

Hence, the new position of the end-effector is (5, −4, 2).

8.6 ROBOT PROGRAMMING AND LANGUAGES

The primary objective of robot programming is to make the robot understand its work cycle. The program teaches the robot the following:

- The path it should take
- The points it should reach precisely
- How to interpret the sensor data
- How and when to actuate the end-effector
- How to move parts from one location to another, and so forth

A computer-like program that is user friendly is most suitable for these purposes. Programming of conventional robots normally takes one of two forms:

(1) Teach-by-showing, which can be divided into

- Powered leadthrough or discrete point programming
- Manual leadthrough or walk-through or continuous path programming

(2) Textual language programming

Teach-by-showing methods were introduced in the 1960s. In teach-by-showing programming the programmer is required to move the robot arm through the desired motion path and the path is defined in the robot memory by the controller. Control systems for this method operate in either teach mode or run mode. Teach mode is used to program the robot, and run mode is used to run or execute the program. In this section we briefly discuss the methods of powered and manual leadthrough programming.

Powered leadthrough programming uses a teach pendant to instruct a robot to move in the working space. By its nature, it is also called pendant teaching. A teach pendant is a small handled control box equipped with toggle switches, dials, and buttons used to control the robot's movements to and from the desired points in the space. These points are recorded in memory for subsequent playback. For playback robots, this is the most common programming method used. However, it has its limitations. It is largely limited to point-to-point motions rather than continuous movement, because of the difficulty in using a teach pendant to regulate complex geometric paths in space. In cases such as machine loading and unloading, transfer tasks, and spot welding, the movements of the manipulator are basically of a point-to-point nature and hence this programming method is suitable.

Manual leadthrough programming is for continuous-path playback robots. In pendant programming, if we decided to program a straight-line path between two points, we could employ the teach pendant to teach the robot the locations of the points. The robot controller computes the trajectory to be followed between the two points. In walk-through programming, on the other hand, the programmer simply moves the robot physically through the required motion cycle. The robot controller records the position and speed as the programmer leads the robot through the operation. If the robot is too big to handle physically, a replica of the robot that has basically the same geometry is substituted for the actual robot. It is easier to manipulate the replica during programming. A teach button connected to the wrist of the robot or replica acts as a special programming apparatus. When the button is pressed, the movements of the manipulator become part of the program. This permits the programmer to make moves of the arm that will not be part of the program. The programmer is able to define movements that are not included in the final program with the help of a special programming apparatus.

Teach-by-showing methods have their limitations, which in fact led to the development of textual languages in the 1970s. Teach-by-showing methods take time for programming. Hence the lot sizes in production lines, where the robot is adopted should be sufficiently large, or the contribution of the programming time cost becomes uneconomical. Another limitation is that these methods are not suitable for certain complex functions, whereas with textual methods it is easy to accomplish the complex functions. Also, teach-by-showing methods are not suitable for ongoing developments such as computer-integrated manufacturing (CIM) systems. Thus, textual robot languages have found their way into robot technology.

Textual language programming methods use an English-like language to establish the logical sequence of a work cycle. A cathode ray tube (CRT) computer terminal is used to input the program instructions, and to augment this procedure a teach pendant might be used to define on line the location of various points in the workplace. Off-line programming is used when a textual language program is entered without a teach pendant defining locations in the program. In the following section we briefly discuss the development of textual programming languages.

8.6.1 Programming Languages

In this section we discuss robot programming languages for computer-controlled manipulators. A manipulator of this kind moves through a path in space under the direction of a program. Other actions included in the path are controlling the end-effector and receiving signals from sensors. Different languages can be used for robot programming, and their purpose is to instruct the robot in how to perform these actions. Most robot languages implemented today are a combination of textual and teach-pendant programming. Programming in these languages is much like computer programming. These languages can also provide robots with limited intelligence by way of error recovery procedures and subroutines, defining a necessary action or set of actions in case of an error or emergency. These programs can be extended by the user, which enables the user to handle more sophisticated items at a future time, such as the requirements of future applications, future sensing devices, and future robots. Some of the languages that have been developed are WAVE, VAL, AML, RAIL, MCL, TL-10, IRL, PLAW, SINGLA, and VAL II.

VAL II is one of the most commonly used and easily learned languages. VAL II is a computer-based control system and language designed for the industrial robots at Unimation, Inc. The VAL II robot language is permanently stored as a part of the VAL II system. This includes the programming language used to direct the system for user-defined applications. The VAL II instructions are clear, concise, and generally self-explanatory and the language is easily learned. Control programs are written on the same computer that controls the robot.

As a real-time system, VAL II computes a continuous trajectory that permits complex motions to be executed quickly, with efficient use of system memory and reduction in overall system complexity. The VAL II system continuously generates robot commands and can simultaneously interact with a human operator, permitting on-line program generation and modification.

A convenient feature of VAL II is the ability to use libraries of manipulation routines. Thus, complex operations can be easily and quickly programmed by combining predefined subtasks.

8.6.1.1 Programming with VAL II

In this section we provide the basic framework for programming in VAL II. The first step in any robot programming exercise is the physical identification of location points using the teach pendant. We do not have to teach all the points that the robot is programmed to visit; only a few key points have to be shown (e.g., the corner of a pallet). Other points to which it can be directed can be referenced from these key points. The procedure is simple. First use the keys or button of the teach pendant to drive the robot physically to the desired location and then type the command HERE with the symbolic name for that location. For example,

HERE P1

This command will identify the present location as P1. Rules for the location name are as follows:

1. It is any string of letters, numbers, and periods.
2. The first character must be alphabetic.
3. There must be no intervening blank.
4. Every location name must be unique.
5. There may be a limit on the maximum number of characters that can be used.

Just as locations are named, every VAL program must have a name so that program can be referred to when required. The same rules apply for the program name as for the location name.

A VAL program has one instruction per line and the principal field is the instruction word, which is separated from other fields by a space. Variables or arguments used to specify the instructions further are separated by commas. Instructions may be labeled if it is desired to refer to that instruction from elsewhere in the program. The following example illustrates the general command format for VAL II.

100 APPRO P1 15

In this example, 100 is the label that refers to this instruction, APPRO is the instruction to the robot to approach the location named P1 by a distance of 15 mm. A VAL program is made of several such commands, which are logically connected to perform the desired tasks upon execution of the program by the robot manipulator.

In the following section we describe the most commonly used VAL II commands.

MOVE P1	This causes the robot to move in joint interpolation motion from its present location to location P1.
MOVES P1	Here, the suffix S stands for straight-line interpolation motion.
MOVE P1 VIA P2	This command instructs the robot to move from its present location to P1, passing through location P2.
APPRO P1 10	This command instructs the robot to move near to the location P1 but offset from the location along the tool z-axis in the negative direction (above the part) by a distance of 10 mm.

DEPART 15	Similar to APPRO, this instructs the robot to depart by a specified distance (15 mm) from its present position. The APPRO and DEPART commands can be modified to use straight-line interpolation by adding the suffix S.
DEFINE PATH 1 = PATH (P1, P2, P3, P5)	
MOVE PATH 1	The first command (DEFINE) defines a path that consists of series of locations P1, P2, P3, and P5 (all previously defined). The second command (MOVE) instructs the robot to move through these points in joint interpolation. A MOVES command can be used to get straight-line interpolation.
ABOVE & BELOW	These commands instruct the elbow of the robot to point up and down, respectively.
SPEED 50 IPS	This indicates that the speed of the end-effector during program execution should be 50 inch per second (in./s).
SPEED 75	This instructs the robot to operate at 75% of normal speed.
OPEN	Instructs end effector to open during the execution of the next motion.
CLOSE	Instructs the end-effector to close during the execution of the next motion.
OPENI	Causes the action to occur immediately.
CLOSEI	Causes the action to occur immediately.

If a gripper is controlled using a servo-mechanism, the following commands may also be available.

CLOSE 40 MM	The width of finger opening should be 40 mm.
CLOSE 3.0 LB	This causes 3 lb of gripping force to be applied against the part.
GRASP 10, 100	This statement causes the gripper to close immediately and checks whether the final opening is less than the specified amount of 10 mm. If it is, the program branches to statement 100 in the program.
SIGNAL 4 ON .. .. **SIGNAL 4 OFF**	This allows the signal from output port 4 to be turned on at one point in the program and turned off at another point in the program.
WAIT 10 ON	This command makes the robot wait to get the signal on line 10 so that the device is on there. Similarly, there can be an off option.

The standard set of mathematical operators consists of +, −, *, /, **, and = with their usual meaning. VAL II also has the capability to calculate common trigonometric, logarithmic, exponential, and similar functions. The following relational and logical operators are also available.

EQ	Equal to
NE	Not equal to
GT	Greater than
GE	Greater than or equal to
LT	Less than
LE	Less than or equal to
AND	Logical AND operator
OR	Logical OR
NOT	Logical complement

TYPE "text" This statement displays the message given in the quotation marks. The statement is also used to display output information on the terminal.

PROMPT "text", INDEX This statement displays the message given in the quotation marks on the terminal. Then the system waits for the input value, which is to be assigned to the variable INDEX.

In most real-life problems, program sequence control is required. The following statements are used to control logic flow in the program.

GOTO 10 This command causes an unconditional branch to statement 10.

IF (Logical expression) THEN
.. .. ..
(Group of instructions)
.. .. ..
ELSE
.. .. ..
(Group of instructions)
.. .. ..
END

If the logical expression is true, the group of statements between THEN and ELSE is executed. If the logical expression is false, the group of statements between ELSE and END is executed. The program continues after the END statement.

DO
.. .. ..
(Group of instructions)
.. .. ..
UNTIL (Logical expression)

The group of instructions after the DO statement makes a logical set whose variable value would affect the logical expression with the UNTIL statement. After every execution of the group of instructions, the logical expression is evaluated. If the result is false, the DO loop is executed again; if the result is true, the program continues.

SUBROUTINES can also be written and called in VAL II programs.

Monitor mode commands are used for functions such as entering locations and systems supervision, data processing, and communications. Some of the commonly used monitor mode commands are as follows:

EDIT (Program name) This makes it possible to edit the existing program or to create a new program by the specified program name.

EXIT	This command stores the program in controller memory and quits the edit mode.
STORE (Program name)	This allows the program to be stored on a specified device.
READ (Program name)	Reads a file from storage memory to robot controller.
LIST (Program name)	Displays program on monitor.
PRINT (Program name)	Provides hard copy.
DIRECTORY	Provides a listing of the program names that are stored either in the controller memory or on the disk.
ERASE (Program name)	Deletes the specified program from memory or storage.
EXECUTE (Program name)	Makes the robot execute the specified program. It may be abbreviated as EX or EXEC.
ABORT	Stops the robot motion during execution.
STOP	The same as abort.

We provide a simple robot program in VAL II to acquaint the reader with some of the basic concepts and statements of the VAL II language.

EXAMPLE 8.11

Develop a program in VAL II to command a PUMA robot to unload a cylindrical part of 10 mm diameter from machine 1 positioned at point P1 and load the part on machine 2 positioned at P2. The speed of robot motion is 40 in./s. However, because of safety precautions, the speed is reduced to 10 in./s while moving to a machine for an unloading or loading operation.

Solution

A robot program in VAL II:

```
      SIGNAL 5
      SPEED 40 IPS
      OPEN 100
      APPRO P1, 50
      SPEED 10 IPS
      MOVE P1
      GRASP 10, 100
50    TYPE "THE OPENING IS NOT 10mm."
      PROMPT "ENTER : 1 TO PROCEED OR 0 TO STOP.", INDEX
      CASE INDEX OF
      VALUE 1
      TYPE "I AM PROCEEDING."
      GO TO 100
```

```
       VALUE 0
       TYPE "I STOPPED ON YOUR INSTRUCTIONS."
       STOP
       ANY
       TYPE "ERROR IN INPUT."
       GO TO 50
       END
100    DEPART P1, 50
       SPEED 40 IPS
       APPRO P2, 50
       SPEED 10 IPS
       MOVE P2
       BELOW
       OPENI 100
       ABOVE
       DEPART P2, 50
       STOP
```

The program is self-explanatory.

8.7 ROBOT SELECTION

With the growth in robot applications, there has been exponential growth in the variety of robots being manufactured. For example, in an industrial robot survey (Penington et al., 1986), 676 robot models were identified that were available in the market. This phenomenal growth in the variety of robots has made the robot selection process difficult for applications engineers. Once the application is selected, which is the primary objective, a suitable robot should be chosen from the many commercial robots available in the market. The technical features are the prime considerations in the selection of a robot. These include features such as (1) degrees of freedom, (2) control system to be adopted, (3) work volume, (4) load-carrying capacity, and (5) accuracy and repeatability. The characteristics of robots generally considered in a selection process include (Penington, et al., 1986):

1. Size of class
2. Degrees of freedom
3. Velocity
4. Actuator type
5. Control mode
6. Repeatability
7. Lift capacity
8. Right-Left-Traverse
9. Up-down-traverse
10. In-Out-Traverse

11. Yaw
12. Pitch
13. Roll
14. Weight of the robot

We elaborate on some of these characteristics.

1. *Size of class.* The size of the robot is given by the maximum dimension (x) of the robot work envelope. Four different classes are identified:

- Micro ($x \leq 1$ m)
- Small ($1 < x \leq 2$ m)
- Medium ($2 < x \leq 5$ m)
- Large ($x > 5$ m)

2. *Degrees of freedom.* The degrees of freedom can be one, two, three, and so on. The cost of the robot increases with increasing number of degrees of freedom.

3. *Velocity.* Velocity considerations are affected by the robot's arm structure. There are various types of arm structures. For example, the arm structure can be classified into the following categories:

- Rectangular
- Cylindrical
- Spherical
- Articulated horizontal
- Articulated vertical

4. *Actuator types.* Actuator types have been discussed in the earlier sections. They are:

- Hydraulic
- Electric
- Pneumatic

Sometimes, a combined electrical and hydraulic control system may be preferred.

5. *Control modes.* Possible control modes include:

- Nonservo
- Servo point-to-point (PTP)
- Servo continuous path (CP)
- Combined PTP and CP

Characteristics such as lift capacity, weight, velocity, and repeatability are divided into ranges. Based on the ranges, the characteristics are categorized in subclasses. For example, lift capacity can be categorized as 0–5 kg, 5–20 kg, 20–40 kg, and so forth.

A simple approach to selecting a robot is to identify all the required features and the features that may be desirable. The desirable features may play an important role in the selection of robots. These desirable features in an individual robot may be ranked on a scale of, say, 1 to 10 and the desirability of these features itself may be assigned weights. Finally, rank the available robots that have these features based on cost and quality considerations.

In the following example we illustrate a procedure for the selection of robots based on required and desirable features.

EXAMPLE 8.12

A manufacturing company is planning to buy a robot. For the type of application, the robot should have at least six required features. It will be helpful to have more features that would add some flexibility in its usage capabilities. The company is looking at six more desirable features. Five robots are selected from the initial elimination process based on required features. The rating score matrix R is given as

$$R = \begin{bmatrix} 9 & 4 & 3 & 5 & 2 & 6 \\ 5 & 9 & 6 & 4 & 6 & 4 \\ 7 & 6 & 8 & 6 & 3 & 5 \\ 6 & 5 & 4 & 9 & 2 & 7 \\ 8 & 7 & 4 & 7 & 4 & 6 \end{bmatrix}_{5\times 6}$$

The entry in position (i, j) represents the score given to the ith robot model based on how well it satisfies the jth desirable feature. The score is given on a scale of 0 to 10. These scores are assigned by the applications engineers based on their experience and practical requirements. Furthermore, if the importance of desirable features is given by the following weight vector, determine the priority ranking of robots for the given application.

$$\mathbf{W} = (\,0.9\ 0.3\ 0.6\ 0.5\ 0.8\ 0.4\,)_{1\times 6}$$

Solution

The total scores (T) can be computed using the formula

$$T = R \cdot W'$$

Substituting for R and W, we get

$$T = \begin{bmatrix} 9 & 4 & 3 & 5 & 2 & 6 \\ 5 & 9 & 6 & 4 & 6 & 4 \\ 7 & 6 & 8 & 6 & 3 & 5 \\ 6 & 5 & 4 & 9 & 2 & 7 \\ 8 & 7 & 4 & 7 & 4 & 6 \end{bmatrix} \cdot \begin{bmatrix} 0.9 \\ 0.3 \\ 0.6 \\ 0.5 \\ 0.8 \\ 0.4 \end{bmatrix}$$

$$= \begin{bmatrix} 17.6 \\ 19.2 \\ 20.3 \\ 18.2 \\ 20.8 \end{bmatrix}$$

The ranking based on desirable attributes is 5, 3, 2, 1 and 4. This means that the fifth robot is the most preferable and so on. However, the final selection should be based on a number of other considerations, such as initial purchasing cost and system support available.

8.8 ROBOT APPLICATIONS

Robotics is becoming an integral part of automated manufacturing systems. Originally, robots were thought of as equipment to be used to perform operations such as painting, welding, and material movement in foundries and in environments subject to personnel safety hazards where it is difficult for human beings to work. The scenario is now changing, and the scope of robot applications is increasing. Robots are seen as the archetypes of flexible automation. In this section our focus is on robots performing loading and unloading operations as an integral part of flexible automation.

The common industrial applications of robots in manufacturing involve loading and unloading of parts. They include:

- The robot unloading parts from die-casting machines
- The robot loading a raw hot billet into a die, holding it during forging, and unloading it from the forging die
- The robot loading sheet blanks into automatic presses, with the parts falling out of the back of the machine automatically after the press operation is performed
- The robot unloading molded parts formed in injection molding machines
- The robot loading raw blanks into NC machine tools and unloading the finished parts from the machines

Safety and relief from handling heavy loads are the key advantages of using robots for loading and unloading operations.

8.8.1 A Single-Machine Robotic Cell Application

Consider a machining center with input–output conveyors and a robot to load the parts onto the machine and unload the parts from the machine as shown in Figure 8.9. A typical operation sequence consists of the following steps:

- The incoming conveyor delivers the parts to a fixed position.
- The robot picks up a part from the conveyor and moves to the machine.
- The robot loads the part onto the machine.
- The part is processed on the machine.

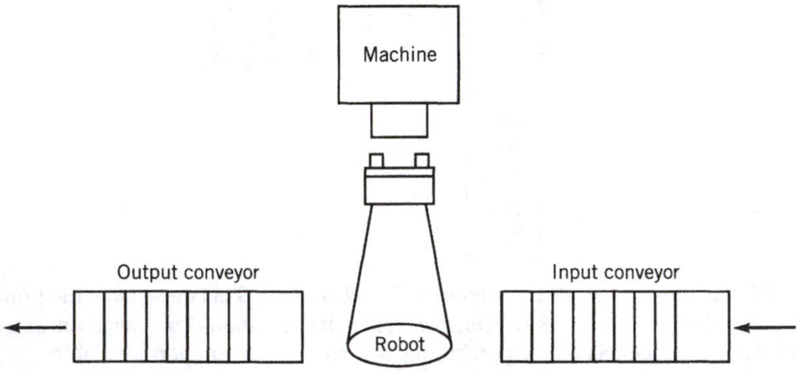

FIGURE 8.9 A single-machine robotic cell.

- The robot unloads the part from the machine.
- The robot puts the part on the outgoing conveyor.
- The robot moves from the output conveyor to the input conveyor.

This operation sequence of the robotic cell is accomplished by a cell controller. Production rate is one of the important performance measures of such cells. We provide an example of determining the cycle time and production rate of a robotic cell.

EXAMPLE 8.13

Compute the cycle time and production rate for a single-machine robotic cell for an 8-h shift if the system availability is 90%. Also determine the percent utilization of machine and robot. On average, the machine takes 30 s to process a part. The other robot operation times are as follows:

Robot picks up a part from the conveyor	3.0 s
Robot moves the part to the machine	1.3 s
Robot loads the part onto the machine	1.0 s
Robot unloads the part from the machine	0.7 s
Robot moves to the conveyor	1.5 s
Robot puts the part on the outgoing conveyor	0.5 s
Robot moves from the output conveyor to the input conveyor	4.0 s

Solution

The total cycle time of 42 s is obtained by summing all the robot operation times (12 s) and the machining time (30 s). The production rate is the reciprocal of cycle time. The production rate considering system availability is therefore

$$\text{Production rate} = \left(\frac{1\text{ unit}}{42\text{ s}}\right)\left(\frac{60\text{ s}}{\text{min}}\right)\left(\frac{60\text{ min}}{\text{h}}\right)\left(\frac{8\text{ h}}{\text{shift}}\right)(0.90\%\text{ uptime})$$

$$= 617\text{ units per shift}$$

$$\text{Machine utilization} = \frac{\text{machine cycle time}}{\text{total cycle time}} = \frac{30}{42} = 71.4\%$$

$$\text{Robot utilization} = \frac{\text{robot cycle time}}{\text{total cycle time}} = \frac{12}{42} = 28.6\%$$

8.8.2 A Single-Machine Cell with a Double-Gripper Robot

A double-gripper robot has two gripping devices attached to the wrist. The two gripping devices can be actuated independently. The double gripper can be used to handle a finished and an unfinished workpiece at the same time. This helps increase productivity, particularly in loading and unloading operations on machines. For example, with the use of a double-handed gripper, the following robot operations could be performed during the machine operation cycle time:

1. Move to conveyor
2. Deposit a part and pick up a new part
3. Move to the machine

However, it must be mentioned that this is possible only if the machine operation cycle time is more than the combined time for activities 1, 2, and 3. Furthermore, there is no need to move the robot arm from the output conveyor to the input conveyor.

EXAMPLE 8.14

In this example we illustrate the improvement in productivity with the use of double-handed grippers using the data in Example 8.13.

Solution

The operation sequence with double-handed gripper is:

Machine cycle time	30.0 s
Robot unloads the part from the machine	0.7 s
Robot loads the part onto the machine	1.0 s

The total cycle time is 31.7 s.

The production rate considering system availability is therefore

$$\text{Production rate} = \left(\frac{1\text{ unit}}{31.7\text{ s}}\right)\left(\frac{60\text{ s}}{\text{min}}\right)\left(\frac{60\text{ min}}{\text{h}}\right)\left(\frac{8\text{ h}}{\text{shift}}\right)(0.90\text{ uptime})$$
$$= 817\text{ units per shift}$$

The productivity increase obtained by using a double-handed gripper is (817 − 617)/617 = 32.4%.

8.8.3 Multimachine Robotic Cell Applications

The most interesting application of robots in flexible automation is in cellular and flexible manufacturing. Two or three NC machines are served by a robot. The cell layout is normally circular. The robot is used to perform loading and unloading operations. Machines in a cell are used to perform machining operations such as turning, milling, and drilling. A detailed scheduling analysis of robot operations for two- and three-machine cells with a serving robot is given in Chapter 13, on flexible manufacturing systems.

8.8.4 Welding

Welding is one of the most visible applications of robots in industry. The reason for using robots in welding is that the work environment is tedious, repetitive, hot, and cramped and therefore unhealthy for human beings. Furthermore, the productivity increase with the use of robots in welding is high. Almost all automobile assembly plants in North America, Japan, and Europe use robots for spot welding in the automobile body assembly lines. Arc welding is another important application of industrial robots. Ship building, aerospace, and construction industries are among the many areas

FIGURE 8.10 A group of robots used in car body welding. (Courtesy of Guiddings & Lewis.)

of applications of industrial robots for spot and arc welding. Figure 8.10 shows a group of robots used in car body welding.

8.8.5 Spray Painting

Besides welding, spray painting is an important application of robots in automobile and other manufacturing industries. The robots with spray guns painting bodies and thousands of body parts are now commonly seen in automobile factories. The primary reason for the increased use of robots in painting is their high level of consistency, which is difficult to achieve with human operators. Furthermore, spray painting poses health risks and is environmentally undesirable for human operators.

8.8.6 Assembly

Assembly of components is yet another but difficult area of application for robots. The difficulty arises because of the complexity of the assembly process, which involves orientation, alignment, and joining operations such as welding, riveting, and press fitting. Because the assembly process is mostly manual, assembly tasks sometimes take more time than is spent on producing parts. Therefore, there is a need to make concerted efforts to automate the assembly process. However, not every final product may qualify for automated assembly. Boothroyd et al. (1982) provided a number of guidelines for evaluating the assemblability of objects. Redford (1986) considered the following requirements necessary for improved, more efficient robotic assembly:

- Faster robots
- Limited-capability, cheap robots

- Versatile, inexpensive grippers
- Identification of assembly families
- Improved assembly efficiency
- Low-cost feeders

The design for robotic assembly should evolve from the design of the product. For example, establishing assembly sequences requires identification of potential jigging and gripping surfaces, grip and assembly forces, clearances and tolerances, and other issues that must be accounted for in the component design. For machine assembly, the tolerances on grip and jig surfaces must be adequate with respect to mating surfaces. This aspect may not be critical in the case of manual assembly. Figure 8.11 shows a robot with special engineered tooling, inserting four valves into an engine cylinder head.

8.8.7 Other Applications

There are many other application areas for robots in industry and business. Typical ones include material handling, inspection (such as checking container labels, inspecting parts, gauging); fire fighting (where the heat and the smoke would prevent the fire fighters from being deployed with conventional equipment); filling, sealing, packaging, gluing, and gasketing; nuclear reactor operation; warehousing, polishing; and surface preparation, among many others. Figure 8.12*a–c* show various applications of robots palletizing boxes, deburring transmission housing, and applying sealant to an automobile headlamp.

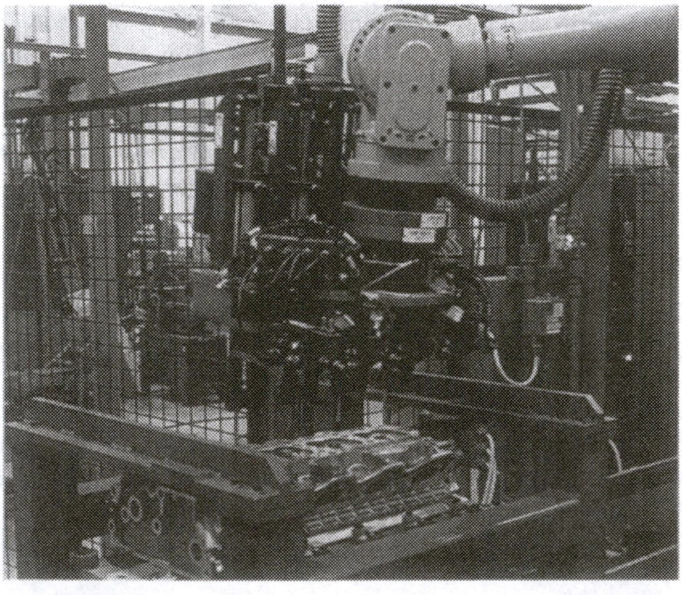

FIGURE 8.11 A robot with special engineered tooling inserts four valves into an engine cylinder head. (Courtesy of Guiddings & Lewis.)

(*a*)

(*b*)

FIGURE 8.12 (*a*) Mounted on a riser, IRB 6000 palletizes different sizes of boxes. (*b*) IRB 3000 deburs transmission housing. (*c*) IRB 2000 applies sealant to headlamp. (Courtesy of ABB Robotics, Inc.)

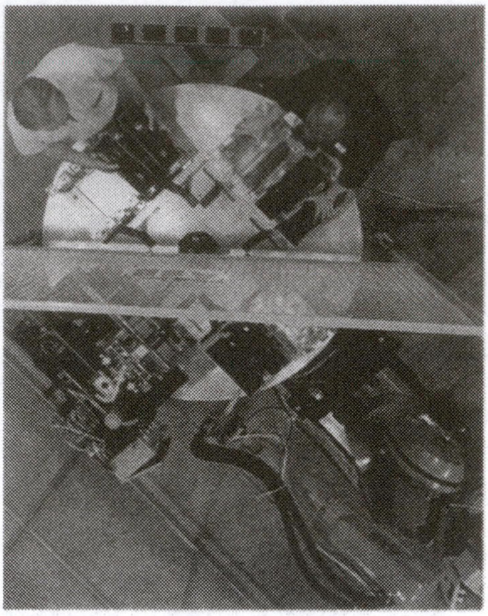

(c)

FIGURE 8.12 (continued)

8.9 ECONOMIC JUSTIFICATION OF ROBOTS

We have seen in the previous section on robot applications that robots are being used in a variety of industrial and domestic environments. Some of these applications are justified on the basis that the type of work, such as welding or painting, is dangerous and unhealthy for humans. It is, however, equally important to study whether the robotization is also economically justified. A large number of models for economic evaluation exist (for details, refer to White et al., 1989). In this section we provide a simple treatment by considering the payback period as a measure of economic justification of robots.

8.9.1 Payback Period Method

The primary idea behind the payback period method is to determine how long it takes to get back the money invested in a project. The payback period n can be determined from the following relation:

$$n = \frac{\text{net investment cost (NIC) of the robot system including accessories}}{\text{net annual cash flows}}$$

Net investment cost = total investment cost of robot and accessories − investment tax credits available from the government, if any

Net annual cash flows = annual anticipated revenues from robot installation including direct labor and material cost savings − annual operating costs including labor, material, and maintenance cost of the robot system

We now illustrate the payback period method using a simple example.

EXAMPLE 8.15

Detroit Plastics is planning to replace a manual painting system by a robotic system. The system is priced at $160,000.00, which includes sensors, grippers, and other required accessories. The annual maintenance and operation cost of the robot system on a single-shift basis is $10,000.00. The company is eligible for a $20,000.00 tax credit from the federal government under its technology investment program. The robot will replace two operators. The hourly rate of an operator is $20.00 including fringe benefits. There is no increase in production rate. Determine the payback period for one- and two-shift operations.

Solution

Net investment cost = capital cost − tax credits = $160,000 − $20,000.00 = $140,000.00

Annual labor cost = operator rate ($20/hr) × number of operators (2) × days per year (250 d/yr) × single shift (8 h/d).
= $80,000 (for a single shift)

For double-shift operation, the annual labor cost is $160,000.00.
For a single-shift operation:

Annual savings = annual labor cost − annual robot maintenance and operating cost
= $80,000.00 − $10,000.00 = $70,000.00

The payback period for single-shift operation is $140,000.00/$70,000.00 = 2 years
For double-shift operation,

Annual savings = $160,000.00 − $20,000.00
= $140,000.00

Therefore, the payback period for double-shift operation is 140,000.00/140,000.00 = 1.00 years.

A payback period of 2 years or less is a very attractive investment. In this example we have not considered any production rate increase with the robot system installation. Typically, such a system results in 30 to 75% increase in productivity. Based on these figures, this is an attractive proposal.

8.10 SUMMARY

Industrial automation owes its present status to developments in robotic technology along with other technologies such as programmable controllers, microprocessors, process control computers, industrial logic control systems, computer numerical control (CNC) machines, automated guided vehicles, and automated storage and retrieval systems. Industrial robots now perform a wide variety of tasks and are used in all kinds of applications. For effective management of robot technology, it is important to understand the basics of robotics. In this chapter we attempted to cover such basic aspects as robot joints, kinematic analysis, robot programming, robot selection, economic justification of robots, and their applications.

PROBLEMS

8.1 Describe the physical components of a typical industrial robot.

8.2 What do you understand by the following?
(a) Spatial resolution

(b) Accuracy
(c) Repeatability

8.3 Discuss the following robotic joints.
(a) Linear joint
(b) Rotational joint
(c) Twisting joint
(d) Revolving joint

8.4 Discuss the following robot configurations
(a) Cartesian robot configuration
(b) Cylindrical robot configuration
(c) Polar robot configuration
(d) Jointed-arm configuration

8.5 What do you mean by work envelope of a robot? Discuss the work envelope for various types of robots.

8.6 Give machine size and determine the reach of a cylindrical robot.

8.7 A robot's control memory has 12-bit storage capacity. It has two rotational joints, one twisting joint, and one linear joint. Determine the control resolution for each joint, if the linear link can vary its length from as short as 0.1 m to as long as 1.0 m.

8.8 For the following joint notation, make sketches to illustrate the robot arm configuration:
(a) TRR
(b) TLR
(c) TLV
(d) RLR

8.9 An LL robot has two links of variable length. Assuming that the global coordinate system is defined at joint J_1, determine
(a) The coordinates of the end-effector point if the variable link lengths are 1 m and 2 m as shown in Figure 8.8*a*.
(b) Variable link lengths if the end-effector is located at (1, 2).

8.10 An RR robot has two links of length 0.50 m and 1.0 m, respectively. Assuming that the global coordinate system is defined at joint J_1, determine
(a) The coordinates of the end-effector point if the joint rotations are 45° at both joints as shown in Figure 8.8*b*.
(b) Joint rotations if the end-effector is located at (1,414 0.5)

8.11 A point vector is translated in *x*-, *y*-, and *z*-directions by a distance of 1, 2, and 1, respectively. Write the transformation matrix for the translation. If the point is (3, 2, 1), determine the position of this point after translation. Afterwards the point vector is rotated about the *x*-, *y*-, and *z*-axes by angles of 30°, 45°, and 60°, respectively. Write the transformation matrices for the rotations and also the total transformation matrix from the initial position of (3, 2, 1). Also find the new position of this point.

8.12 A manufacturing application requires a robot with 15 technical features. Out of 15 features, 9 are required features and the remaining 6 are desirable features. Ten robots are selected from the initial elimination process based on required features. The rating score matrix is given as

$$S = \begin{bmatrix} 7 & 3 & 2 & 5 & 1 & 6 \\ 4 & 8 & 5 & 3 & 5 & 3 \\ 8 & 7 & 9 & 7 & 4 & 6 \\ 5 & 4 & 4 & 8 & 3 & 8 \\ 5 & 7 & 8 & 4 & 2 & 5 \\ 1 & 3 & 8 & 6 & 6 & 9 \\ 9 & 8 & 4 & 2 & 7 & 8 \\ 3 & 7 & 9 & 9 & 4 & 6 \\ 7 & 2 & 1 & 4 & 9 & 8 \\ 6 & 8 & 3 & 8 & 3 & 8 \end{bmatrix}_{10\times 6}$$

In the matrix, each row corresponds to a robot model and each column corresponds to a desirable feature. The entry in position (i, j) represents the score given to the ith robot model based on how well it satisfies the jth desirable feature. The score is given on a scale of 0 to 10. If the importance of desirable features is given by the weight vector as follows, determine which robot best suits the application.

$$W = (0.7 \quad 0.6 \quad 0.9 \quad 0.4 \quad 0.3 \quad 0.6)_{1\times 6}$$

8.13 Compute the cycle time, the production rate, and the percent utilization of machine and robot for a single-machine robotic cell for an 8-h shift if the system availability is 95%. The machine takes 25 s to process a part, on average. The other robot operation times are:

Robot picks up a part from the conveyor	4.0 s
Robot moves the part to the machine	1.4 s
Robot loads the part onto the machine	1.0 s
Robot unloads the part from the machine	0.6 s
Robot moves to the conveyor	1.6 s
Robot puts the part on the outgoing conveyor	0.4 s
Robot moves from the output conveyor to the input conveyor	3.0 s

8.14 Illustrate the improvement in productivity with the use of double-handed grippers using the data in Problem 8.13.

8.15 One of the big three automobile manufacturing companies in Detroit is planning to make a capital investment of $2.00 million in a robotic welding system with 20 robots for their car assembly plant. One of the primary reasons for this investment is to improve productivity and quality of the welding process. At present, the company employs 25 workers on this assembly process. The workers are paid $30.00 per hour including benefits and work an average of 6 h during a shift of 8 h. The production rate is approximately 50 units per hour. The approximate annual maintenance cost of the manual system is $10,000.00

On the contrary, the robotic system is estimated to produce at the rate of 110 units per hour in an 8-h shift with an annual cost of $1.2 million. The operating cost of the robotic system is $100.00 per hour including a maintenance cost of $10.00 per hour for one-shift operation and $11.00 for two-shift operation.

(a) Determine the payback period for the robot system.
(b) Determine the unit production costs for both systems based on one- and two-shift operation.

8.16 The Cool-Age Corporation Inc. (CACI) manufactures a line of refrigerators. CACI wants to mechanize its painting shop, which currently employs 2 persons. The management of CACI is planning to buy a robotic system, which is expected to cost the company $200,000.00 with an operating and maintenance cost of $2.50 per hour. At present the manual labor cost is $25 per hour per person including all benefits. Determine the payback period for this proposed investment in the robotic system. Is the investment justified?

8.17 Visit some industries and develop a list of existing and potential robot applications. Suggest an integrated material-handling system involving robots.

Laboratory Assignments

8.18 Develop a program for a robot to pick up four blocks of size 10 × 15 × 5 cm that are stacked at a fixed position and to stack them over each other at another fixed position.

8.19 Develop a program for a robot to pick up five blocks of size 10 × 10 × 10 cm that are stacked at a fixed position and place them at the corners and the center of a square table of size 50 × 50 cm.

8.20 Program a robot to write the word ROBOT using a pen mounted in the robot gripper. The letters should be rectangular in shape and approximately 5 in. high.

8.21 Program a robot to palletize parts of size 10 × 15 × 5 by picking them from a fixed position on a conveyor belt and placing them on a pallet that has four rows and six columns. The center-to-center distance between two rows is 16 cm and between two columns 20 cm.

REFERENCES AND SUGGESTED READING

Asfahl, C. R. (1992). *Robots and Manufacturing Automation.* John Wiley & Sons, New York.

Booth D. E., Khouza, M., and Hu, M. (1992). A robust multivariate statistical procedure for evaluation and selection of industrial robots. *International Journal of Operations and Production Management,* 12(2):15–24.

Boothroyd, G. C., Poli, C., and Murck, L. (1982). *Automatic Assembly.* Marcel Dekker, New York.

Brady, M., Hollerbach, J. M., Johnson, T. C., Perez, T. L., and Mason , M. T. (1982). *Robot Motion: Planning and Control.* MIT Press, Cambridge, Massachusetts.

Critchlow, A. J. (1985). *Introduction to Robotics.* Macmillan Publishing Company, New York.

Denavit, J., and Hartenburg, R. S. (1955). A kinematic notation for lower pair mechanisms based on matrices. *ASME Journal of Applied Mechanics,* 22:215–221.

Dickenson, S. (1984). Report on Robot Joint Notation Scheme. Lehigh University, Bethlehem, Pennsylvania.

Engelberger, J. F. (1980). *Robotics in Practice.* AMACOM, New York.

Fu, K. S., Gonzalez, R. C., and Lee, C. S. G. (1987). *Robotics: Control, Sensing, Vision, and Intelligence.* McGraw-Hill, New York.

Groover, M. P., Mitchell, W., Nagel, R. N., and Odrey, N.G. (1984). *Industrial Robotics.* McGraw-Hill Publications, Toronto.

Horn, B. K. P. (1979). Kinematics, statics and dynamics of 2D-manipulators. In *Artificial Intelligence: An MIT Perspective,* Vol. 2. MIT Press, Cambridge, Massachusetts.

Koren, Y. (1985). Robotics for Engineers, McGraw-Hill Publishing Company, New York.

Lee, C. S. G., and Ziegler, M. (1983). A geometric approach in solving the inverse kinematics of PUMA robots. Conference Proceedings, 13th International Symposium on Industrial Robots and Robots 7. Society of Manufacturing Engineers, Chicago.

Nnaji, B. O., and Yannacopoulou, M. (1988). A utility theory–based robot selection and evaluation for electronic assembly. *Computers and Industrial Engineering,* 14:477–493.

Paul, R. P. (1981). *Robot Manipulators: Mathematics, Programming, and Control.* MIT Press, Cambridge, Massachusetts.

Penington, R. A., Fisher, E. L., and Nof, S. Y. (1986). Survey of industrial robot characteristics: General distributions, trends, and correlations. *Material Flow,* 3:35–54.

Redford, A. H. (1986). Design for assembly. In *Computer-Aided Design and Manufacturing* U. Rembold and R. Dillmann, eds.), Springer-Verlag, New York.

Sumanth, D. J. (1984). *Productivity Engineering and Management.* McGraw-Hill Book Company, New York.

Savariano, J. W. (1980). Industrial robots today and tomorrow. *Robotics Age,* X, Y, 4–17.

Toepperwein, L. L., Blackman, M. T., et al. (1980). ICAM robotics application guide. Technical Report AFWAL-TR-80-4042, Vol. II. Materials Laboratory, Air Force Wright Aeronautical Laboratories, Ohio.

Unimation, Inc., a Westinghouse Company. (1984). *Programming Manual—User's Guide to VAL II.* Unimation, Inc., Danbury, Connecticut.

White, J. A., Agee, M. H., and Case, K. E. (1989). *Principles of Engineering Economic Analysis* (3rd ed.). John Wiley & Sons, New York.

CHAPTER 9

QUALITY ENGINEERING, STATISTICAL PROCESS CONTROL, AND AUTOMATED INSPECTION SYSTEMS

Market share and profitability are two of the major determinants of the success of any organization. The cornerstone of increased market share and profitability is the competitive edge an organization has over its competitors. The factors that influence and improve the competitive edge of a company are unit cost of products, product quality, and lead time. Quality is one of the major salable attributes of products. The best approach to improving product quality is to build quality into the product and process right at the product and process design stages. Quality may also be improved during the production stage. For this purpose techniques such as statistical process control (SPC) are helpful in reducing the number of out-of-specification products, thereby contributing to product quality. Quality is a vast topic that has numerous dimensions and cuts across various functional boundaries of any organization. Our exposure to quality in this chapter is limited mainly to some of the analytical tools used for improving quality of products. We present answers to some of the basic questions: What is quality? What are the dimensions of quality? What are the approaches to improving quality? What is Taguchi's approach to designing quality into the products and processes? What are various SPC tools for quality control?

9.1 UNDERSTANDING THE MEANING OF QUALITY

The basic question that is often asked is, what is quality? Quality is a relative term. For example, a product considered to be of good quality by one person could be considered of poor quality by another person and vice versa. Quality, like beauty, is in the eye of the beholder. From the functional point of view, a product is considered to be of good quality if it meets the desired functional requirements adequately over the intended period of its use under the intended conditions.

Can we provide a precise definition of quality? Yes, quality has a precise meaning. It is defined in American National Standards Institute/American Society of Quality Control (Glossary and Tables for Statistical Quality Control) Standard A3-1987 as:

The totality of features and characteristics of a product or service that bear on its ability to satisfy a given need.

The features and characteristics of the products or services describe their performance relative to customer requirements and expectations. The quality characteristic is the window through which you can observe the performance of products and processes. In fact, the quality of a product is measured in terms of these characteristics. Characteristics such as durability of batteries, picture quality of a television, fuel economy of a car, quietness of operation of a refrigerator, cooling abilities of an air conditioner, softness of tissue paper, and failure time of a product are typical examples of product characteristics that are of concern to the customer.

Because the products are designed to satisfy the needs of the customers and the processes are designed to produce quality products, it is crucial first to understand the customer requirements or expectations and then translate these customer requirements into measurable quality characteristics. Quality function deployment (QFD) is a technique that is often used to translate the customer requirements into quality characteristics. A detailed discussion of QFD is given in Chapter 4. The quality dimensions provide a link between the customer requirements and the measurable quality characteristics. Moen et al. (1991) expanded the eight dimensions of quality proposed by Garvin (1987) as discussed next.

9.2 THE DIMENSIONS OF QUALITY

Quality is characterized by multiple dimensions. Garvin (1987) provided a list of eight dimensions, which were subsequently expanded by Moen et al. (1991), as follows:

Performance	Primary operating characteristics
Features	Secondary operating characteristics such as added touches
Time	Time waiting in line, time from concept to production of a new product, time to complete a service
Reliability	Extent of failure-free operation
Durability	Amount of use until replacement is preferable to repair
Uniformity	Low variation among repeated outcomes of a process
Consistency	Match with documentation, advertising, deadlines, or industry standards
Serviceability	Resolution of problems and complaints
Aesthetics	Characteristics related to the senses
Personal interface	Characteristics such as punctuality, courtesy, and professionalism
Harmlessness	Characteristics related to safety, health, or environment
Perceived quality	Indirect measures or inferences about one or more of the dimensions, reputation

9.3 QUALITY COSTS

Before undertaking any quality improvement project in a company, it is important to understand the relationship between quality and costs. As we know, one of the important aspects of the product development process is to translate the customer requirements into product specifications. Manufactured products that do not meet the specifications should be identified and repaired if possible, otherwise discarded. In any case, such defective products should not reach the customer. The prime quality costs for supplying satisfactory products to customers include producing, identifying, avoiding, or repairing products that do not meet customer requirements. Quality costs have been classified in a number of categories, and different companies follow different classification schemes. Many manufacturing and service organizations have classified the quality costs in the following categories:

- Prevention costs
- Appraisal costs
- Internal failure costs
- External failure costs

We provide a brief explanation of these costs; a detailed account is given in Montgomery (1991).

9.3.1 Prevention Costs

There is an old adage that an ounce of prevention is worth a pound of cure. The prevention philosophy is essentially concerned with making the product right the first time so that the product performs well during its intended period of use. Accordingly, prevention costs include all the efforts that go into designing and manufacturing a product that meets customer requirements by preventing nonconformance. The elements of such prevention costs include activities involving quality planning and engineering, new product reviews, product and process design, process control, training, and quality data acquisition and analysis.

9.3.2 Appraisal Costs

As the name suggests, appraisal costs include all those costs involved in measuring, evaluating, or auditing products, components, and purchased materials to ensure conformance with the standards and specifications. Specifically, appraisal costs include costs of activities such as inspection and test of incoming material, product inspection and test, materials and services consumed, and maintaining accuracy of test equipment.

9.3.3 Internal Failure Costs

Internal failure occurs when products fail to meet the customer quality requirements before being shipped to the customers. Internal failure costs include all the cost elements involved in rectifying this situation. Examples of internal failure cost elements are failure analysis, scrap, repair, retest, downtime, yield losses, and downgrading of usual specifications.

9.3.4 External Failure Costs

External failures occur when products do not function satisfactorily after being supplied to the customer. All kinds of costs are incurred for activities such as complaint adjustment and dealing with returned products. Other costs include warranty charges and liability costs. In addition to these costs, there are indirect costs due to the external failure of products, such as loss of market share and, consequently, loss of revenue and profits because of bad reputation.

Another question that is frequently asked is, how large are quality costs? There is no specific answer to this question. These costs may vary from as low as 4 percent to as high as 40 percent of sales. Quality costs differ from industry to industry and from one company to another even in the same industry. What is needed in all cases is to control the quality costs. Obviously, the most pertinent question is how to control these costs. The best approach to controlling quality costs is to focus on designing quality into the products and processes followed by process control. In the following section we provide a framework for quality improvement including designing quality into products and processes as well as controlling and improving quality during production.

9.4 A FRAMEWORK FOR QUALITY IMPROVEMENT

To be successful in a competitive business environment, it is important to deliver products that meet the customer requirements with respect to quality, cost, and delivery schedule. But to continue to be successful in a global competitive environment, it is important to improve product quality continuously. The question is, where are the opportunities for product quality improvement? Let us look at a typical product life cycle. The product life cycle starts with product planning and continues through such phases as:

- Product design
- Production process design
- Production
- Maintenance and product service

As we said earlier, "an ounce of prevention is worth a pound of cure." That means that by building in quality right at the design stage the cost of quality control at the production stage can be considerably reduced. Therefore, the preferable approach to improving product quality is to build quality into the products at the product design stage, followed by improvements at the process design stage and then at the production engineering, maintenance, and product service stages. These efforts to improve quality can be classified into the following categories:

- Off-line quality control activities conducted at the product and process design stages in the product development cycle.
- On-line quality control activities conducted at the manufacturing stage to keep the process in statistical control and to reduce manufacturing imperfections in the product.
- Activities conducted during the product usage stage to provide maintenance and after-sales product service.

In this chapter we concentrate on both off-line and on-line quality control and improvement activities.

9.4.1 Designing Quality into Products and Processes

Product design is the prime activity in the process of realizing a product. Therefore, it has the greatest impact on the product quality. Loss of quality occurs when there is deviation of functional characteristics of the product from the target values. Therefore, to improve product quality at the design stage it is necessary to consider:

- All aspects of design that influence the deviations of functional characteristics from the target
- Methods for reducing undesirable and uncontrollable factors that cause functional deviations

Taguchi has proposed a philosophy and methodology for designing quality into products and processes. He postulates that the process of designing a product or process should be viewed as a three-phase program:

1. System design
2. Parameter design
3. Tolerance design

By designing product and processes, we mean assigning nominal values and tolerances to products and process design characteristics.

9.4.1.1 System Design

System design is the process of applying scientific and engineering knowledge to produce a basic functional prototype design. In the system design phase, new concepts, ideas, and methods are synthesized to provide new or improved products to customers. That means that the basic design concept is established during this stage, including the selection of materials, parts, and subassemblies. For example, consider designing a car: Should the internal combustion engine block be of cast iron or aluminum alloy? Should the brakes be antilock brakes? The relationship between the inputs and outputs is established. Also, the functions of the subsystems and parts are determined during this phase. Techniques such as quality function deployment are helpful in translating the customer needs into design requirements and finally into the product quality characteristics. A detailed discussion of QFD was provided in Chapter 4.

9.4.1.2 Parameter Design

In the parameter design phase, levels for the product/process design parameters (inputs) are set to make the system performance less sensitive to causes of variation, thus minimizing quality loss. In parameter design, wide tolerances on the noise factors are assumed to allow low manufacturing cost, as it is costly to control noise factors. During the parameter design stage, the quality is improved without controlling or removing the cause of variation by making the design robust, that is, making the product insensitive to noise. Design of experiments (DOE), simulation, and optimization are the techniques used during the parameter stage.

9.4.1.3 Tolerance Design

The tolerance design phase usually follows the parameter design phase. Quality improvement is achieved by tightening tolerances around the chosen target values of the control factors so as to reduce performance variation. However, with quality improvement—that is, reduction in quality loss—there may be an increase in manufacturing cost. Thus, there is a trade-off between these two conflicting requirements.

What is required is to reduce tolerances selectively and specify high-grade material or high-precision manufacturing processes.

9.4.1.4 What Is Quality Loss?

The traditional understanding of quality loss is explained in Figure 9.1*a*. The objective in the traditional quality approach is to ensure that the manufactured products fall within specification limits. All items meeting specification limits are considered of good quality. Those not meeting the specifications are considered of bad quality and are either rejected or reworked. Loss is incurred only when the quality characteristic falls outside the specification limits. However, the modern approach to quality considers that loss is always incurred whenever the functional quality characteristic of a product deviates from its target value, denoted by T, regardless of how small the deviation is. A simplified relationship between quality loss and deviation from the target is shown in Figure 9.1*b*. The increase in the value of the functional characteristic from the target in either direction results in increasing quality loss. However, at the limiting values of the quality characteristic (lower and upper specification limits), the loss equals the cost of manufacturing or disposal of the product. Taguchi provides a simple quality loss function that quantifies the variability present in the process.

9.4.1.5 Taguchi Loss Function

Taguchi's quadratic loss function is a simple and meaningful function for approximating the quality loss in most situations (Phadke, 1989). It quantifies the variability

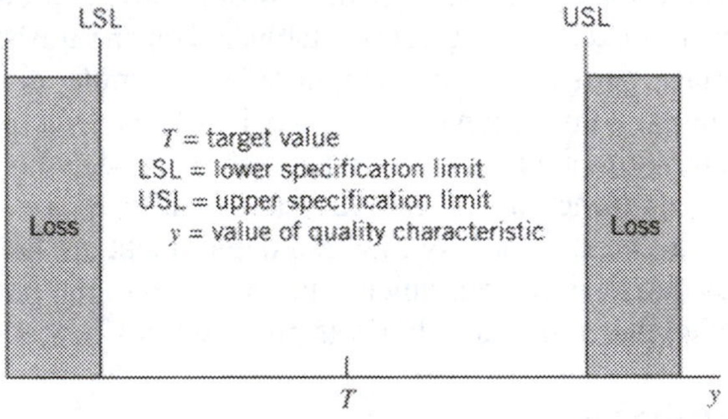

(*a*)

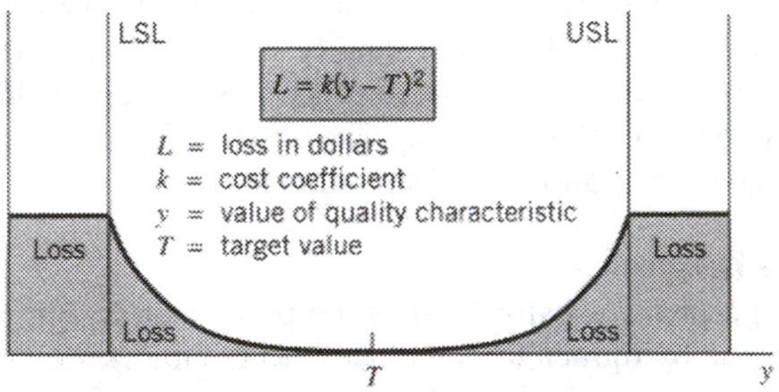

(*b*)

FIGURE 9.1 (*a*) Traditional approach to quality loss. (*b*) The quadratic loss function.

present in a process. Therefore, it is an effective measure for evaluating the effect of quality improvements, determining the economic consequences of tightening tolerances as a way to improve quality, and justifying the quality improvements. The loss function is defined as

$$L(y) = k(y - T)^2 \tag{9.1}$$

where k = quality loss coefficient, a constant
y = quality characteristic of a product
T = target value for y

9.4.1.6 The Average Quality Loss

There will always be variation in the quality characteristic due to noise factors from unit to unit and from time to time during usage of the product. If y_i $(i = 1, 2, \ldots, n)$ is the ith representative measurement of the quality characteristic y, then the average quality loss can be computed as follows:

$$\begin{aligned}\text{Average quality loss} &= \frac{1}{n}[L(y_1) + L(y_2) + \ldots + L(y_n)] \\ &= \frac{k}{n}[(y_1 - T)^2 + (y_2 - T)^2 + \ldots + (y_n - T)^2] \\ &= k\left[(\mu - T)^2 + \frac{n-1}{n}\sigma^2\right]\end{aligned}$$

If n is large, the average quality loss (AQS) is equivalent to

$$\text{AQS} = k[(\mu - T)^2 + \sigma^2] \tag{9.2}$$

where

$$\mu = \frac{1}{n}\sum_{i=1}^{n} y_i \quad \text{and} \quad \sigma^2 = \frac{1}{n-1}\sum_{i=1}^{n}(y_i - \mu)^2$$

Therefore, the average quality loss is made up of two components:

1. The loss, $k(\mu - T)^2$, due to the deviation of the average value of y from the target
2. The loss, $k\sigma^2$, due to the mean squared deviation of y around its own mean

9.4.1.7 Common Variations of Loss Functions

Product characteristics are the barometers of quality of products in the sense that they describe and measure the performance of products relative to customer requirements and expectations. From the customer point of view, the loss is minimum if the quality characteristic is at the target value. However, the expectations of the customers would differ from product to product, and this can be characterized by their target values. For example,

1. Nominal is best when y is at the target. Examples include dimension, viscosity, and clearance.

2. Smaller is better; that is, y tends to zero, where target is zero. Examples of quality characteristics include wear, shrinkage, deterioration, friction loss, and microfinish of a machined surface, among others.
3. Larger (bigger) is better; y tends to infinity when target is at infinity. Examples include fuel efficiency, ultimate strength, and life.

The quadratic loss functions according to these classifications of the product characteristics are defined as

$$\text{Nominal-the-best type:} \qquad L(y) = k(y - T)^2 \tag{9.3}$$

$$\text{Smaller-the-better type:} \qquad L(y) = k(y)^2 \tag{9.4}$$

$$\text{Larger-the-better type:} \qquad L(y) = k\left(\frac{1}{y^2}\right) \tag{9.5}$$

The value of k for the nominal-the-best case given by Equation (9.3) is determined from the functional limits $T \pm d$ for the value of y; that is, the product is considered to have failed or is scrapped beyond these limits and should be repaired or replaced at a cost of A dollars. Accordingly, we obtain from Equation (9.3)

$$A = k(d)^2 \qquad \text{or} \qquad k = \frac{A}{d^2} \tag{9.6}$$

The quality loss coefficient k, in the case of either smaller-the-better or larger-the-better, is determined from the functional limit d and associated quality loss A using Equation (9.4) and Equation (9.5), respectively. Accordingly,

$$k = \frac{A}{d^2} \qquad \text{(for smaller-the-better type)} \tag{9.7}$$

$$k = Ad^2 \qquad \text{(for larger-the-better type)} \tag{9.8}$$

The average quality loss for these functions can be shown to be

$$\text{Nominal-the-best type:} \qquad L(y) = k[\sigma^2 + (\mu - T)^2] \tag{9.9}$$

$$\text{Smaller-the-better type:} \qquad L(y) = k[\sigma^2 + (\mu)^2] \tag{9.10}$$

$$\text{Larger-the-better type:} \qquad L(y) = k\left(\frac{1}{\mu^2}\right)\left(1 + 3\frac{\sigma^2}{\mu^2}\right) \tag{9.11}$$

In the case of larger-the-better problems, the following questions often may be asked: Why do we have to take the reciprocal of a larger-the-better characteristic and treat it as a smaller-the-better type of quality characteristic? Why do we not maximize the mean quality characteristic? The answer to these questions follows directly from the expression for the mean square reciprocal quality characteristic value given by Equation (9.11). Minimizing the mean square reciprocal quality characteristic implies maximizing μ and minimizing σ^2, which is the right thing to do.

9.4.1.8 Applications of Quality Loss Function

The quality loss function has been used as a decision support tool in a number of situations involving variability (Ross, 1988; Taguchi et al., 1990). In this section we present a few examples to illustrate various applications of the Taguchi loss function.

Determining Best Factory Tolerances The loss function can be used to determine economical factory tolerances, as illustrated in the following example:

EXAMPLE 9.1

Consider the production of automatic transmissions for trucks. The transmission shift point is one of the critical quality characteristics. Truck drivers would feel very uneasy if the transmission shift point was farther than the transmission output speed on the first-to-second gear shift by 35 rpm. Suppose it costs the manufacturer \$200.00 to adjust a valve body to fix the shift point problem. However, it may cost only \$16.40 for labor charges to make adjustments during the manufacturing and testing phase. Determine the factory tolerances (manufacturer's specifications).

Solution

The loss caused by product variations from the target value, $L(y)$, is

$$L(y) = k(y - T)^2, \quad \text{where } y = T \pm d$$

Accordingly, from Equation (9.6) $k = A/d^2 = 200.00/(35)^2 = 0.164$ \$/rpm^2

The factory tolerances should be determined based on the \$16.40 loss incurred because of adjustments at the factory. Therefore, from Equation (9.6)

$$16.4 = 0.164(d)^2$$

$$d = \pm 10 \text{ rpm}$$

Therefore, the factory tolerances should be $\pm$ 10 rpm. This means that if the transmission shift point is farther than 10 rpm from nominal, it is cheaper to adjust at the factory than to wait for a complaint and make adjustments under warranty at a much higher cost and considerable inconvenience to the customer.

Product Selection The loss function can be used to select products as illustrated by the following example.

EXAMPLE 9.2

High-Tech Rotor Dynamics Inc. is planning to buy a couple of thousand bolts to be used in their systems. The system requires highly reliable bolts. In case of bolt failure the system repair cost is estimated to be \$15.00. Two companies that use different kinds of alloys in their products bid to supply the bolts. High-Tech decides to go for destructive testing using 20 specimens. The criterion used for testing is the ultimate tensile strength measured in kgf/mm^2. The test data for both products are given in Table 9.1.

The lower specification limit is 11 kgf/mm^2, and purchase quantity is 20,000. The unit costs of products A and B are \$0.14 and \$0.13, respectively. Advise High-Tech Rotor Dynamics about its purchasing decision.

TABLE 9.1 Data on UTS of Bolts

Product (bolt)	*Ultimate Tensile Strength Data (kgf/mm²)*									
A	15.5	13.8	15.1	15.3	13.7	15.5	13.8	15.1	15.2	13.6
	14.2	14.1	14.9	14.8	15.5	14.2	14.5	14.6	14.4	15.4
B	15.5	10.8	15.1	16.3	13.7	10.5	13.8	15.1	12.2	17.6
	11.2	14.1	11.9	14.8	17.5	14.2	17.5	14.6	18.4	13.4

Solution

In this case it is better to have higher ultimate tensile strength. Therefore, the formula used to calculate the quality loss will be of higher-the-better type, as given below:

$$\text{Larger-the-better type:} \qquad L(y) = k\left(\frac{1}{\mu^2}\right)\left(1 + 3\frac{\sigma^2}{\mu^2}\right)$$

$$\mu = \frac{1}{n}\sum_{i=1}^{n} y_i \qquad \text{and} \qquad \sigma^2 = \frac{1}{n-1}\sum_{i=1}^{n}(y_i - \mu)^2$$

Accordingly,

$$\mu_A = 14.66, \qquad \sigma_A = 0.656$$

$$\mu_B = 14.41, \qquad \sigma_B = 2.327$$

For the larger-the-better type of quality characteristic, the estimation of k values is based on the lower specification limit. Therefore, from Equation (9.8)

$$k_A = 15.00(11.00)^2 = 1815$$

$$k_B = 15.00(11.00)^2 = 1815$$

Therefore, using Equation (9.11)

$$L_A = 1815\left[\frac{1}{(14.66)^2}\right]\left[1 + 3\left(\frac{0.656}{14.66}\right)^2\right]$$

$$= \$8.48$$

$$L_B = 1815\left[\frac{1}{(14.41)^2}\right]\left[1 + 3\left(\frac{2.327}{14.41}\right)^2\right]$$

$$= \$9.40$$

Quality loss for the lot of 20,000 units of product A is less than that of B. Therefore, based purely on the quality loss criterion, product A is preferable. However, if we consider only purchasing cost, product B is cheaper by $200.00. A more realistic approach is to consider both cost due to quality loss and purchasing. In that case, product A is cheaper.

9.4.2 Robust Design of Products and Processes

Robust design is an approach to designing a product or process that emphasizes reduction of performance variation through the use of design techniques that reduce sensitivity to sources of variation. Simply stated, we want to achieve the target of the quality characteristic but at the same time we want to minimize the variation in a product's functional characteristics to ensure minimum quality loss. We will illustrate this idea using a classical example of design of an electrical power circuit. But first let us understand the different types of variables. The target and the variance of a product's quality characteristic are affected by certain variables which can be classified as *controllable factors* and *uncontrollable factors,* also known as *noise factors.*

Figure 9.2 illustrates the relationship between various factors of an engineered system that affect the response.

9.4.2.1 Controllable Factors

Controllable factors are those that can easily be controlled, such as choice of material, mold temperature, and cutting speed on a machine tool. They can be separated into two major groups: factors controlled by the user/operator and factors controlled by designers.

Factors Controlled by the User/Operator These are also known as signal factors. A signal factor carries the intent to the system from a customer's point of view to attain the target performance or to express the intended output. Consider the steering system of a car. A driver's intent is to change direction. For this purpose, the driver changes the steering wheel position, thus giving a signal to the automobile to change directions. In this case the signal factor is the angular displacement of the steering wheel. Other examples of signal factors include setting a remote control button of a television set to control volume and brightness and setting the temperature control knob of a refrigerator to get the desired cooling effect.

Factors Controlled by Designers There are three types of factors in this category:

1. *Variability control factors.* Those that affect the variability in a response are called variability control factors or simply control factors. For example, transistor gain in an electrical power circuit is a variability control factor.

2. *Target control factors.* These factors can easily be adjusted to achieve the desired functional relationship between the user input (signal) and the response. For example, the gear ratio in the steering mechanism of an automobile can be selected during the product design stage to get the required sensitivity of the turning radius to a change in the steering angle.

3. *Neutral factors.* These are factors that do not affect either the mean response or the variability in the response. They are also known as neutral factors. It is important to know these neutral factors, since cost savings can be obtained by setting them at their most economic levels.

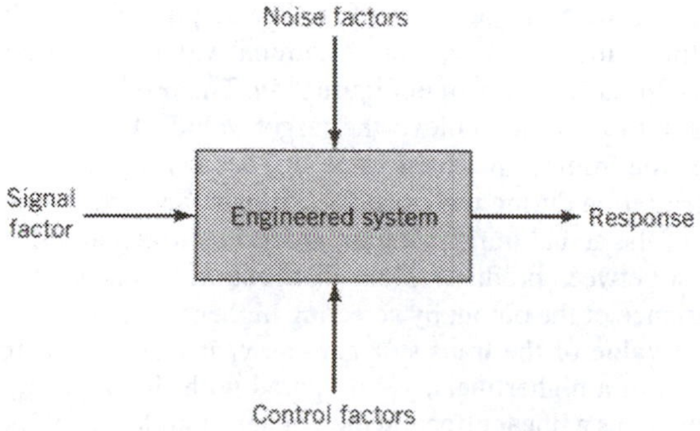

FIGURE 9.2 Relationship between various factors of an engineered system.

9.4.2.2 Noise Factors

Noise factors are, in general, responsible for the functional characteristic(s) of a product deviating from the target value. Remember, deviation from the target value results in quality loss. Noise factors can be classified as:

- Outer (external factors) noise
- Inner noise
- Between-product noise

Outer Noise The variables external to a product that affect the product performance are known as external noise factors. Examples include variations in temperature, humidity, and dust.

Inner Noise Inner noise is a result of variations due to the deterioration of parts and materials. Examples include loss of resilience of springs, wearing out of parts due to friction, and increase in resistance of resistors with age.

Between-Product Noise Between-product noise is due to the variation in the product variables from unit to unit, which is inevitable in a manufacturing process. Examples include material variations.

Noise factors, as the name suggests, are uncontrollable factors. Trying to control noise factors may be a very expensive proposition, if not impossible.

Taguchi's approach to robust design of products and processes attempts to reduce variability by changing the variability control factors while maintaining the required average performance through appropriate adjustments in the target control factors. Therefore, the objective of robust design engineering is to select values of controllable factors such that the product or process is least sensitive to changes in the noise variables. The intent is to remove or reduce the impact of the noise factors rather than find and eliminate them.

EXAMPLE 9.3

Electrical Power Circuit Design

An electrical power circuit design example given by Taguchi (1986) is used here to illustrate the separation of variability control and target control variables. The quality characteristic of interest is the output voltage, y, with a target value of y_0. The output voltage is largely determined by the gain of a transistor in the circuit, x, whose nominal value can be controlled. The input–output relationship is nonlinear as shown in Figure 9.3*a*. The product design engineer can select the nominal value of x to be x_0 to achieve the target value of y_0. However, in real life the transistor gain can deviate from the nominal value (x_0) because of manufacturing imperfections in the transistor, deterioration during the circuit's life span, and environmental variations. This deviation (variation) of the actual transistor gain around its nominal value is essentially due to internal noise (inner or between product). If the distribution of x is as shown in the figure, then we can reduce the variance of the output by selecting higher values of the input. For example, if we select the nominal value of the transistor gain as x_1 instead of x_0, the output variance is reduced but this results in a higher mean y_1 compared with the target y_0. Suppose we have a resistor in the circuit that has a linear effect on the voltage at all levels of the transistor gain; then we can easily change the mean y_1 to the desired target value y_0 by changing the resistance of the resistor as shown in Figure 9.3*b*.

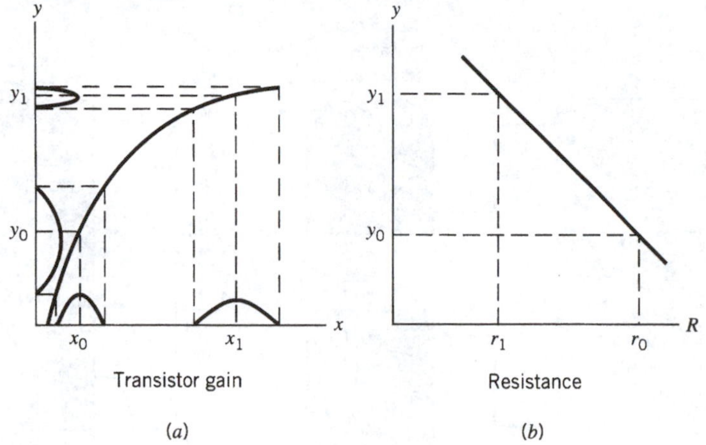

FIGURE 9.3 (*a*) Nonlinear input–output relationship. (*b*) Linear relationship between the output voltage and resistance.

We have achieved what we wanted: the output (response) is on target and the variability in the output is minimized. We can therefore categorize transistor gain as a variability control factor and resistance as a target control factor. You will notice that we essentially exploited the nonlinear effects of the product or process controllable variables to reduce the performance variation of the product (or process). This is an important feature of Taguchi's parameter design.

Taguchi has developed a systematic approach for robust design of products and processes. The details of the approach are given in a six-step procedure in Section 9.4.3. Taguchi uses a performance measure known as signal-to-noise (*S/N*) ratio to decide on the best combination of controllable factors that remove or reduce the impact of the noise factors. In the following section we discuss the concept of *S/N* ratio.

9.4.2.3 Signal-to-Noise Ratio

Traditionally, a product or process design is chosen that maximizes or minimizes the average performance. However, one can generalize this concept and choose a design to optimize some measure of performance. The measure of performance may not necessarily be average.

Taguchi chooses a measure called the signal-to-noise ratio. To estimate the *S/N* ratio, experiments are conducted in a systematic manner. Taguchi's idea is to recognize controllable and noise factors and to treat them separately as a design parameter matrix and a noise factor matrix, respectively. Experiments are organized according to orthogonal arrays (OAs). Some discussion of OAs is given in Taguchi and Konishi (1987), Phadke (1989), and Taguchi and Clausing (1990)*. Noise factors are changed in a balanced fashion during experimentation. Consider a simple scenario in which

---

* An orthogonal array can be thought of as a distillation mechanism through which the engineer's experimentation passes. Its great power lies in its ability to separate the effect each factor has on the average and the dispersion of the experiment as a whole. By exploiting this ability to sort out individual factors, engineers may track a large number of factors simultaneously in each experimental run without confusion, thereby obviating the need to try all possible combinations or to wait for the results of one experiment before proceeding with the next.

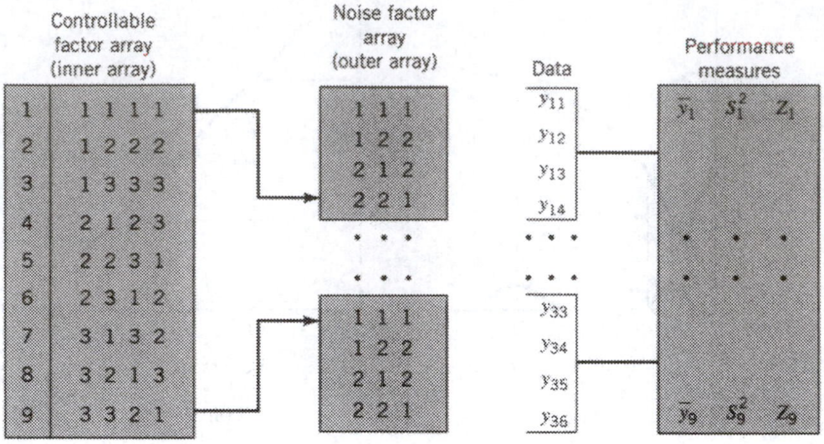

FIGURE 9.4 A sample experimental design.

there are four controllable factors at three levels and three noise factors that can be studied at two levels as shown in Figure 9.4.

The next step is to identify the type of quality characteristic, that is, smaller-the-better, nominal-the-best, or larger-the-better. The *S/N* ratios for various classifications of quality characteristics discussed in Section 9.4.1.7 are given below.

Smaller-the-better:

$$Z_i = -10 \log_{10}\left(\frac{1}{n}\sum_{j=1}^{n} y_{ij}^2\right)$$

($n = 3$ in the outer array in the present illustration.)

Nominal-the-best:

$$Z_i = 10 \log_{10}\left(\frac{\bar{y}_i^2}{S_i^2}\right)$$

Larger-the-better:

$$Z_i = -10 \log_{10}\left(\frac{1}{n}\sum_{j=1}^{n} \frac{1}{y_{ij}^2}\right)$$

where Z_i is the *S/N* ratio for the ith run and

$$\bar{y}_i = \frac{1}{n}\sum_{j=1}^{n} y_{ij} \qquad \text{and} \qquad S_i^2 = \frac{1}{n-1}\sum_{j=1}^{n} (y_{ij} - \bar{y}_i)^2$$

It is important to understand that we always maximize the *S/N* ratio regardless of whether the quality characteristic is smaller-the-better, nominal-the-best, or larger-the-better.

The question is how to use information on the *S/N* ratio to determine the optimal setting of control factors. The following procedure, based on Taguchi philosophy, is suggested:

Using analysis of variance (ANOVA) of the *S/N* ratio, determine factors that have a significant effect on the *S/N* ratio. Then select levels of these factors to maximize the overall *S/N* ratio. This is normally done using main effect graphs if no interaction among factors is significant. The main effect graph is a plot for the average value of Z at each level for each factor. In case interactions are significant, information obtained from the plots of interactions is used to decide the optimal setting for the corresponding factors. The factors that are not significantly affecting the *S/N* ratio are analyzed further to see if any of these factors has a significant effect on the mean value of the quality characteristic. The factors that significantly affect the mean quality characteristic but not the *S/N* ratio are used to adjust its mean value on the target. These steps are explained in detail in the analysis step of the case study in the following section.

9.4.3 A Case Study to Illustrate the Taguchi Approach to Parameter Design

A typical parameter design study using the Taguchi approach can be conducted using the following steps (Phadke, 1989; Wille, 1990; Unal and Bush, 1992):

1. Identify the quality characteristic to be observed and the objective function to be optimized.
2. Identify the design parameters and alterative levels.
3. Define possible interactions between these parameters.
4. Design the matrix experiment and the define-data analysis procedure.
5. Conduct the matrix experiment.
6. Analyze the data to determine the optimum levels of design parameters and verify through confirmation experiments.

The first four steps are used for planning the experiment. In the fifth step, the experiment is conducted. The controllable process can be an actual hardware experiment. However, in most cases, costly hardware experiments are not necessary. Computer models of the response of many products and processes can be used adequately to conduct the controlled matrix experiments.

In the sixth step, the experimental results are analyzed (using analysis of variance) to determine the factors and their interactions that significantly affect the signal-to-noise ratio (Z). Also, the factors that do not significantly affect Z are further analyzed to see their effect on the quality characteristic to achieve the target. Confirmation experiments are conducted to verify the results. The details of these steps are described below using a case study of heat treatment of leaf springs for a truck.

EXAMPLE 9.4

Heat Treatment Case Study

The heat treatment of leaf springs for a truck considered here is based on Pignatiello and Ramberg (1985) and a personal communication from Professor Abrahim Bovas (1993). The leaf spring assembly is transported by a conveyor system through a high-temperature furnace. Upon exiting the furnace, the part is transferred to a forming machine, where the camber (curvature) of the spring is induced by holding the spring in a high-pressure press for a short length of time. Next, the spring is submersed into an oil quench and then removed from the processing area.

Step 1: Identify the quality characteristic.
The quality characteristic is free height of the spring in the unloaded condition. This free height is obtained during the heat treatment process while the camber is being formed. The target value for the free height is 8 in. Deviations above or below this nominal value are considered undesirable.

Step 2: Identify the design (controllable) and noise parameters and their levels.
Four controllable design factors affect the free height:

- Furnace temperature
- Heating time
- Transfer time (length of time to transfer a part from the heat furnace to the camber former)
- Hold-down time (length of time that a camber former is closed on a hot part)

These are represented by *B*, *C*, *D*, and *E*, respectively. The engineers felt that the quench oil temperature would be difficult to control during production and treated it as a noise factor (*O*).

The next step involves the selection of feasible ranges over which each parameter would be varied in the analysis process. In parameter design, generally two or three levels or settings are selected for each parameter (Phadke, 1989). The level of a parameter refers to how many test values of the parameter are to be analyzed over the feasible range. In this study, two levels of each parameter were studied. The levels and ranges of the four variables selected for study are given in Table 9.2.

Step 3: Define possible interactions between these parameters.
Simultaneously varying several design parameters may have interactive effects on the quality characteristic that can affect the optimum solution. An interaction is said to exist whenever the effect of one parameter depends on the level of another. The engineers were interested in the interactions *BC*, *BD*, and *CD*. They felt that the quench oil temperature would be difficult to control during production and treated it as a noise factor (*O*). Thus, the objective is to find combinations of *B*, *C*,

TABLE 9.2 **Controllable and Noise Factors and Their Levels**

	Levels	
Controllable and Noise Factors	*Low*	*High*
B. furnace temperature (°F)	1840	1880
C. heating time (s)	25*	23
D. transfer time (s)	12*	10
E. hold-down time (s)	2	3
O. quench oil temperature (°F)	130–150†	150–170 (was not held constant)

Source: Pignatiello and Ramberg, 1985. Reproduced with permission from the American Society for Quality Control.

* Notice that heating time refers to the time taken by the conveyor to transport the leaf spring through the furnace. Accordingly, we consider a heating time of 25 s at the low level and 23 s at the high level because a higher transportation time implies a lower rate. Similarly, the levels for the transfer time are established.

† Note that oil quench temperature was not held constant within its limits.

D, and *E* that would yield a free height of 8 in. while being insensitive to *O*. They also wanted to know which factors to adjust when the free height deviated from the target and in which direction to adjust them.

Step 4: Design the matrix experiment and the define-data analysis procedure.
With the objective of studying a large number of decision variables with a small number of experiments, the Taguchi method uses orthogonal arrays based on the design-of-experiments theory. There is a significant reduction in the number of experimental configurations. A set of 18 standard OAs and corresponding linear graphs are given in Taguchi and Konishi (1987) and Phadke (1989). These arrays can be used directly in many cases or modified to suit a specific problem. However, to select an appropriate OA to fit a specific case, a count of the total degrees of freedom is required in order to determine the minimum number of experiments that must be performed to reach a near-optimum parameter set (American Supplier Institute, 1989; Phadke, 1989; Wille, 1990). For details of degrees of freedom and orthogonal arrays, refer to Appendix B.

An L_8 array is used in the present case study. In the matrix design given in Table 9.3, there are four main factors, *B*, *C*, *D*, and *E*, each at two levels. The full factorial is $2^4 = 16$ runs. It is more economical to run $2^{4-1} = 8$ experiments without loss of vital information. This design allows us to estimate *B*, *C*, *BC*, *D*, *DC*, and *E* assuming that the other effects are negligible. Note that of the seven degrees of freedom available for effect estimation, four degrees of freedom are used for estimating the main effects and the three remaining degrees of freedom are used for estimating the interaction effect.

Step 5: Conduct the matrix experiment.
The Taguchi approach to parameter design can be used in any situation involving a controllable process (Phadke, 1989; Meisl, 1990; Wille, 1990; Unal and Bush, 1992). The controllable process can be an actual hardware experiment or a computer experiment. In this case study, actual experiments were conducted based on the design matrix in step 4. The outer array of this experiment consists of three replicates of the two levels of oil quench temperature factor *O*. That is, for each factor–level combination in the inner array, the free height was observed six times: three times at the low level of *O* and three times at the high level of *O*. Thus, a total of 48 observations were made. The experimental observations are shown in Table 9.3.

Step 6: Analyze the data to determine the optimum levels of design parameters and verify.
Remember, the quality characteristic is the free height of the spring in the un-

TABLE 9.3 **Experimental Observations**

Inner Array							Outer Array					
1	2	3	4	5	6	7						
B	*C*	*BC*	*D*	*BD*	*CD*	*E*	O^-			O^+		
−	−	+	−	+	+	−	7.78	7.78	7.81	7.50	7.25	7.12
+	−	−	−	−	+	+	8.15	8.18	7.88	7.88	7.88	7.44
−	+	−	−	+	−	+	7.50	7.56	7.50	7.50	7.56	7.50
+	+	+	−	−	−	−	7.59	7.56	7.75	7.63	7.75	7.56
−	−	+	+	−	−	+	7.96	8.00	7.88	7.32	7.44	7.44
+	−	−	+	+	−	−	7.69	8.09	8.06	7.56	7.69	7.62
−	+	−	+	−	+	−	7.56	7.62	7.44	7.18	7.18	7.25
+	+	+	+	+	+	+	7.56	7.81	7.69	7.81	7.50	7.59

Source: Pignatiello and Ramberg, 1985. Reproduced with permission from the American Society of Quality Control.

loaded condition. Furthermore, it is required to achieve the target free height of 8 in.; deviations above and below this are considered undesirable. Therefore, this situation can be characterized as nominal is best. Accordingly, we calculate $Z_i = 10\log[(\bar{y}_i)^2/(S_i)^2]$ for each test condition. For the first experiment, sample calculations are given below:

$$\bar{y} = \frac{7.78 + 7.78 + 7.81 + 7.50 + 7.25 + 7.12}{6} = 7.54$$

$$S^2 = \frac{(7.78 - 7.54)^2 + (7.78 - 7.54)^2 + (7.81 - 7.54)^2 + (7.50 - 7.54)^2 + (7.25 - 7.54)^2 + (7.12 - 7.54)^2}{6 - 1}$$

$$= 0.090$$

$$Z_1 = 10 \log_{10}\left(\frac{7.54^2}{0.09}\right) = 28.00$$

The results are shown in Table 9.4. From the analysis of variance (ANOVA) table, Table 9.5, we find that the factor C and the interaction CD are significant at α equal to 0.05 and 0.01, respectively. Although D is not significant by itself, it is important to control D because its interaction with C is significant. Therefore, to decide optimal level setting for C and D, we have to review the CD interaction plot as shown in Figure 9.5. It is clear from Figure 9.5 that the combination of C^+ and D^- maximizes the *S/N* ratio.

Since factors B and E are not significant, the combination (C^+, D^-) maximizes Z. Taguchi does not stress understanding the underlying phenomena. Instead, he suggests confirmation experiments. Taguchi's objective is to find a combination of the controllable factors that maximize Z. He then uses the factors that do not have an effect on Z to adjust the mean free height to the desired value.

The next step in the analysis is to determine whether there are any factors among those that did not significantly affect Z that can be used to adjust the mean leaf spring height. For this, the analysis of the original $(\bar{y}_i)$ quantities is necessary. B and E were found to be significant at α equal to 0.01 when the original responses were analyzed, but they were not significant in the analysis of the signal-to-noise ratio (Z). Therefore, we conclude that B and E can be used to control the free height of the leaf spring without having a detrimental effect on the process variability. Thus, if we find that the process mean is out of control, B and/or E are the factors to adjust to bring the process back to control without affecting the process variability. It may be

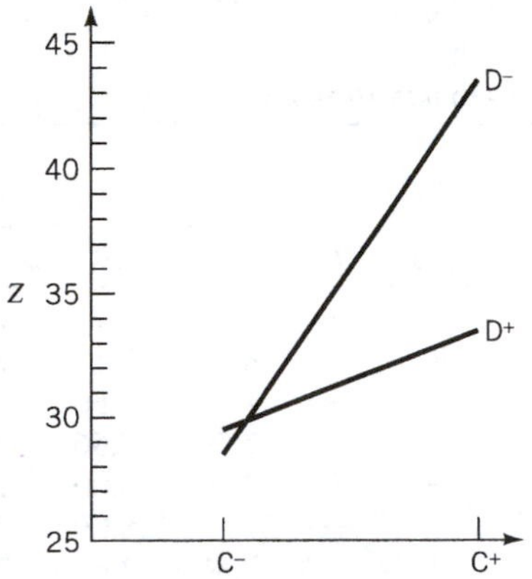

FIGURE 9.5 Plot of the *CD* interaction effect on Z. (© 1985. Reproduced with permission from the American Society of Quality Control.)

TABLE 9.4 **Experimental Results of the Case Study**

B	*C*	*BC*	*D*	*BD*	*CD*	*E*	$\bar{y}$	S^2	*Z*
−	−	+	−	+	+	−	7.54	0.09	28.00
+	−	−	−	−	+	+	7.90	0.07	29.46
−	+	−	−	+	−	+	7.52	0.001	47.70
+	+	+	−	−	−	−	7.64	0.01	38.68
−	−	+	+	−	−	+	7.67	0.09	28.11
+	−	−	+	+	−	−	7.79	0.05	30.59
−	+	−	+	−	+	−	7.37	0.04	31.55
+	+	+	+	+	+	+	7.66	0.02	35.31

Source: Pignatiello and Ramberg, 1985. Reproduced with permission from the American Society of Quality Control.

emphasized that confirmation experiments are required before implementing the outcome of the study.

Oil Quench Temperature as a Controllable Variable

In the previous analysis, oil quench temperature (*O*) was not a controllable variable. If we treat it as a controllable variable, we get the design matrix as given in Table 9.6. Here we have a 2^{5-1} design studying the effect of five factors. The replications are treated as the noise array. If we follow the same procedure as before (analyze *Z*), we will find that the results are somewhat different. *B*, *DO*, and *BCO* are significant at α equal to 0.01, 0.05, and 0.05, respectively. This implies that *B*, *C*, and *D* have a significant effect on signal-to-noise ratio. Therefore, factor *E* alone is left to adjust the free height of the leaf spring without having a detrimental effect on the process variability.

Two Strategies for the Analysis of Results

We present two strategies for the analysis of results as follows:

1. The oil quench temperature (*O*) cannot be controlled during normal production. Factors *C* and *D* should be held in the (C^+, D^-) combinations to control the leaf spring height variability. Factors *B* and *E* should then be used to move the leaf spring height mean to the target.

TABLE 9.5 **ANOVA Table**

Source	*SS*	*df*	*F*	*P Value*	*Mean Effect*
B + *CDE*	0.224	1	—	—	−0.335
C + *BDE*	171.810	1	31.80	0.03	9.269
BC + *DE*	10.585	1	—	—	−2.301
D + *BCE*	41.742	1	7.72	0.11	−4.569
BD + *CE*	23.826	1	4.40	0.17	3.452
CD + *BE*	53.862	1	9.96	0.09	−5.190
E + *BCD*	17.294	1	3.20	0.21	2.941
Error	10.809*	2			
Total	319.342				

Source: Pignatiello and Ramberg, 1985. Reproduced with permission from the American Society of Quality Control.

* Error is the result of pooling all terms that contribute less than 5% of the total sum of squares, namely *B* and *BC*.

TABLE 9.6 **Oil Quench Temperature as a Controllable Factor**

B	*C*	*D*	*O*	(*BCD*) *E*	y^2	*S*	*Z*
−	−	−	−	−	7.76	0.0003	53.06
+	−	−	−	+	8.07	0.0273	33.78
−	+	−	−	+	7.52	0.0012	46.73
+	+	−	−	−	7.63	0.0104	37.47
−	−	+	−	+	7.94	0.0036	42.43
+	−	+	−	−	7.95	0.0496	31.05
−	+	+	−	−	7.54	0.0084	38.31
+	+	+	−	+	7.69	0.0156	35.77
−	−	−	+	−	7.29	0.0373	31.54
+	−	−	+	+	7.73	0.0645	29.67
−	+	−	+	+	7.52	0.0012	46.73
+	+	−	+	−	7.65	0.0092	38.02
−	−	+	+	+	7.40	0.0048	40.57
+	−	+	+	−	7.62	0.0042	41.38
−	+	+	+	−	7.20	0.0016	45.02
+	+	+	+	+	7.63	0.0254	33.60

Source: Pignatiello and Ramberg, 1985. Reproduced with permission from the American Society of Quality Control.

2. The oil quench temperature (*O*) can be controlled during production. Then *B*, *C*, *D*, and *O* should be held at the low levels to reduce variability of the process. This factor–level combination produces the maximum response. Factor *E* can then be adjusted to control the mean free height to the target value. For a detailed analysis of this case, refer to Pignatiello and Ramberg (1985).

Confirmation experiments are needed for both of the strategies.

Alternative Policies for Robust Design

Instead of $Z_i = 10 \log[(\bar{y}_i)^2/(S_i)^2]$, consider $Z_1 = 10 \log S^2$. This means that our objective is to minimize the logarithmic function of variance. An analysis of Z_1 will reveal that *B*, *DO*, *BC*, *CDO*, and *CD* are significant. This is basically the same as the previous analysis with *O* as a controllable factor.

Since $Z_i = 10 \log[(\bar{y}_i)^2/(S_i)^2] = 10[\log(\bar{y}_i)^2 - \log(S_i^2)]$, a large negative or positive effect on $\bar{y}_i$ will cause $\log(\bar{y}_i)^2$ to be large. Small variability will cause $-\log S_i^2$ to be large. Taguchi's *S/N* ratio simultaneously measures the effect of a factor on the mean responses and on variability. In many cases (as in this example), the best operating strategy is strengthened by studying the variability by itself.

9.5 FAILURE MODE AND EFFECT ANALYSIS

Failure mode and effect analysis (FMEA) is another important technique that is widely used in industry, including the big three auto manufacturers, for continuous product quality improvement to satisfy the needs of the customer. FMEA (Automotive Industry Action Group [AIGG], 1993) can be described as a systemized group of activities intended to:

- Recognize and evaluate the potential failure of a product/process and its effects
- Identify actions that could eliminate or reduce the chance of potential failure occurring
- Document the process

It is complementary to the design process of defining positively what a design and process must do to satisfy the customer. FMEA is a generic approach that can be used to identify failure modes and analyze their effects on the system performance with the objective of developing a preventive strategy. FMEA can be used successfully at any stage of product life cycle. Software packages (for example, Formuser, 1992) have been developed that include features such as process FMEA, design FMEA, quality control plan, dimensional control plan, process flow diagrams, and design verification plans. In this section we provide some basic understanding of FMEA methodology as applied to process improvement.

Process FMEA is a methodology for evaluating the process for possible ways in which failures can occur. The primary objective in process FMEA is to eliminate potential production failure effects (if possible, otherwise reduce possible limits to a minimum) by identifying important characteristics that have to be measured, controlled, and monitored. Therefore, process FMEA is conducted during quality planning and before beginning production. The FMEA philosophy is based on the characterization of potential failures. Failures are characterized by the following tuple (occurrence, severity, and detection):

- Occurrence: how often the failure occurs
- Severity: how serious the failure is
- Detection: how easy or difficult it is to detect the failure

Examples of typical failure modes include cracked, dirty, deformed, bent, and burred components; worn tools; and improper setup.

To implement process FMEA, the following steps may be taken:

1. Identify problems for each operation using brainstorming and committee discussions. Cause-and-effect diagrams can be used. For example, the potential causes of machine failures could involve mechanical or electrical subsystem failure, tools, inspection equipment, operators, and so forth.
2. Use flow process charts as a basis for understanding the problem. This provides a common basis for communication among the committee members.
3. Collect data. Data collection may be necessary if data are not already available.
4. Prioritize the problems to be studied. The ranking of priorities is based on the following:

   $$\text{RPN (risk priority number)} = \text{occurrence} \times \text{severity} \times \text{detection}$$

   This is based on the notion that not all the problems are important and that the resources are too limited to handle all the problems.

5. Use appropriate tools to analyze the problems by making use of the data.
6. Implement the suggestions.
7. Confirm and evaluate the results by doing some experiments and ask whether you are better or worse off or the same as before.
8. The FMEA is a continuous improvement tool. Repeat the FMEA process as often as necessary.

EXAMPLE 9.5

Real-Life Illustration of the Use of Process FMEA

This simple example is adapted from the process FMEA application in Ford (AIGG, 1993). The process involves manual application of wax inside a car door, with the objective of retarding corrosion. A detailed analysis is given in Figure 9.6, which provides a sample format. This may be modified depending on the process requirements. We provide a brief explanation for this example. In items 1 through 8 (Figure 9.6) information such as part identification, names of team members, and date is provided. Items 9 through 22 systematically describe the process FMEA approach. In this example, the problem of corrosion in the car door is considered. To retard corrosion, manual application of wax is considered. The manner in which this process could potentially fail to meet the process requirements and/or design intent is defined by the potential failure mode.

In our example, the failure mode is insufficient wax coverage over the specified surface. We have to determine the effect of failure in terms of what the customer might experience. Here it would be unsatisfactory appearance due to rust and impaired function of the interior door hardware. The next step is to assess the seriousness of the effect based on a severity scale of 1 to 10 (the more severe, the higher the number). A severity index of 7 is assigned by the team, as shown in column 12. We have to define the potential cause of failure in terms of something that can be corrected or controlled. For example, this failure may be due to the fact that a manually inserted spray head has not been inserted far enough. For every potential cause, frequency of occurrence should be estimated on a scale of 1 to 10. Here the ranking 10 means that failure is almost inevitable. The estimated occurrence ranking for all the causes is given in column 15. We have to analyze and collect information regarding current practices for preventing the potential cause of failure as given in column 16. Now we have to assess the probability of detection of the cause of failure by current practice. This is also on a scale of 1 to 10, where 1 denotes a very low probability of detection; this implies that control will not or cannot detect the existence of a defect. In our example, the value is 5, implying a moderate chance of detection.

The next step is to calculate the risk priority number, which is used to rank order the concerns in the process. RPN may vary from 1 to 1000. If it is high, corrective action must be taken. In practice, regardless of the resultant RPN, special attention should be given when severity is high. The idea is to recommend corrective actions to reduce severity, occurrence, and detection ranking. At the same time, the organization and individuals responsible for the recommended action and target completion date should be scheduled as shown in column 20. These actions have to be implemented. A new RPN may be calculated upon implementation. All resulting RPNs should be reviewed. If future actions are required, steps 19 to 22 may be repeated.

POTENTIAL
FAILURE MODE AND EFFECTS ANALYSIS
(PROCESS FMEA)

Item Front Door L.H./H8HX-0000-A (2)
Model Year(s)/Vehicle(s) 199X/Lion 4-dr/Wagon (5)
Process Responsibility Body Engrg./Assembly Operations (3)
Key Date 9X 03 01 ER 9X 08 26 Job #1 (6)
Suppliers and plants effected (8)
FMEA Number 1450 (1)
Page 1 of 1
Prepared By xxxx - X6521 - Assy Ops (4)
FMEA Date 10/23/9X 06 17 Original and revised (7)

Process Function (9) Requirements	Potential Failure Mode (10)	Potential Effect(s) of Failure (11)	(12) Sev	Class	(13) Potential Cause(s)/ Mechanism(s) of Failure (14)	Occur	(15) Current Process Controls (16)	(17) Detec	R.P.N.	(18) Recommended Action(s) (19)	Responsibility & Target Completion Date (20)	Action Results (22) Actions Taken (21)	Sev	Occ	Det	R.P.N.
Manual application of wax inside door To cover inner door, lower surfaces at minimum wax thickness to retard corrosion	Insufficient wax coverage over specified surface	Deteriorated life of door leading to: ■ Unsatisfactory appearance due to rust through paint over time ■ Impaired function of interior door hardware	7		Manually inserted spray head not inserted far enough	8	Visual check each hour-1/shift for film thickness (depth meter) and coverage	5	280	Add positive depth stop to sprayer	MFG Engrg 9X 10 15	Stop added, sprayer checked on line	7	2	5	70
										Automatic spraying	MFG Engrg 9X 12 15	Rejected due to complexity of different doors on same line				
					Spray heads clogged -Viscosity too high - Temperature too low - Pressure too low	5	Test spray pattern at start-up and after idle periods, and preventative maintenance program to clean heads	3	105	Use Design of Experiments (DOE) on viscosity vs. temperature vs. pressure	MFG Engrg 9X 10 01	Temp and press limits were determined and limit controls have been installed - control charts show process is in control Cpk = 1.85	7	1	3	21
					Spray head deformed due to impact	2	Preventative maintenance programs to maintain head	2	28	None						
					Spray time insufficient	8	Operator instructions and lot sampling (10 doors / shift) to check for coverage of critical areas	7	392	Install spray timer	Maintenance 9X 09 15	Automatic spray timer installed - operator starts spray, timer controls shut-off -control charts show process is in control Cpk = 2.05	7	1	7	49

SAMPLE

FIGURE 9.6 Process failure mode effect analysis. (Courtesy of the Automotive Industry Action Group.)

9.6 IMPROVING PRODUCT QUALITY DURING THE PRODUCTION PHASE

The bottom line is that the very survival of companies depends on continuous improvement of quality. Quality can be designed into a product(s), as we have seen in the previous section, but then the product must be manufactured. During the manufacturing process, assignable causes may occur, seemingly at random. These assignable causes result in a shift in the process to an out-of-control state, resulting in output that may not conform to requirements. To produce quality output it is necessary to have a process that is stable or repeatable, a process capable of operating with little variability around the target or nominal dimension of the product's quality characteristic(s). The idea behind improving quality is to reduce variability and eliminate waste. The quality improvement process is illustrated by Figure 9.7.

Statistical process control is very useful in monitoring process stability and improving process capability by reducing variability. It should be emphasized here that SPC alone cannot reduce variability. However, with the aid of process improvement tools such as design of experiments, process variability can be reduced. The following SPC tools, popularly known as the magnificent seven (Montgomery, 1991), are effective process improvement tools:

1. Histogram
2. Check sheet
3. Pareto chart
4. Cause-and-effect diagram
5. Defect concentration diagram
6. Scatter diagram
7. Control chart

These SPC tools are useful for the motivative-participative approach to quality improvement, such as quality circles. A group of workers and their supervisors organize themselves into teams for the purpose of reviewing problems related to quality, cost, productivity, and safety and jointly seek an effective solution to the problem. The

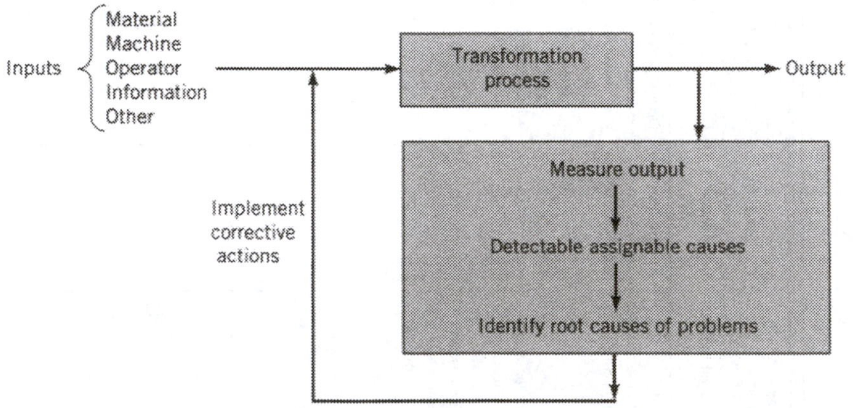

FIGURE 9.7 Quality improvement process during the production stage.

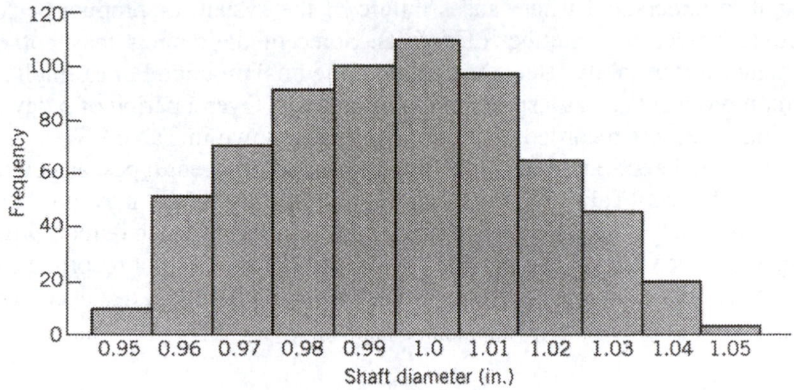

FIGURE 9.8 Histogram of shaft diameter as a quality characteristic.

SPC tools provide vital information about the process and causes of quality problems. However, management involvement and commitment to the quality improvement process is the most vital component of its potential success.

9.6.1 Histogram

Suppose it is required to produce a shaft within 1 ± 0.05 in. on a numerically controlled turning machine. The shaft diameters are plotted against frequency as shown in Figure 9.8. This plot is known as a histogram, and it provides information on the central tendency, spread, and shape. We see that the distribution of the shaft diameter is symmetric with the mean at around 1 in. and variability between 0.95 and 1.05 in. This information is valuable in showing how the process is behaving and whether the process is capable of producing the desired output meeting the tolerances.

9.6.2 Check Sheet

A check sheet serves as a useful tool for collecting historical or current operating data for the process under investigation. In the early stages of implementation of SPC, it is

TABLE 9.7 **Check Sheet for the Spark Plug Defects**

	Days				
Type of Defect	*1*	*2*	*3*	*4*	*5*
Dirty cores	500	800	2150	1440	1100
Raised studs	1100			270	680
Off-center wire	140		560	450	
Mixed plugs	450	1200		900	800
Bad platting	800				620
Chipped cores			1300		
Dirty Insulators			70		900
Poor gapping	125		400		
Cement on core				450	
	3115	2000	4480	3510	4100

important to understand what causes failure of the system or product performance. This could be due to a number of defects. Some of the defects may not affect the performance but certainly affect the quality of the final product. For example, consider a common product such as a spark plug used in a car. Over a period of 5 days, a list of spark plug defects is recorded on a check sheet as shown in Table 9.7.

Some of the defects are due to tool changeovers to different types, as you notice for raised stud defects (Table 9.7). This means that the machines may not be properly tooled. This check sheet helps in identifying the sources of these defects with respect to time. We notice that, except for dirty cores, the defects are not recorded every day. Cores are supplied from outside vendors. Therefore, the problem lies in controlling the quality of incoming parts.

9.6.3 Pareto Chart

The origin of the Pareto chart or diagram is the famous concept known as Pareto's law developed by the noted economist Alfred Pareto. The Pareto law states that on average 80 percent of the problems stem from 20 percent of the causes. For example, in the case of spark plugs, most of the quality problems (dirty cores, mixed plugs, and raised studs) come from only three out of nine or more problem areas (Figure 9.9). A Pareto diagram is helpful in identifying the fact that taking care of these few problems takes care of 80 percent of all causes of the problem situation.

9.6.4 Cause-and-Effect Diagram

A cause-and-effect (CAE) diagram is a technique for systematically listing the various causes of a problem. The CAE diagram, also known as a fishbone diagram and credited to Dr. Kaoru Ishikawa, serves as a tool to indicate how various causes can operate independently as well as simultaneously to produce an eventual effect on the manufactured product. For example, consider the quality of a turned part such as a shaft. Poor quality may be caused by several factors, such as workmanship, worn tool, or nonoptimal machining conditions (in terms of cutting speed, feed, and depth of cut), as

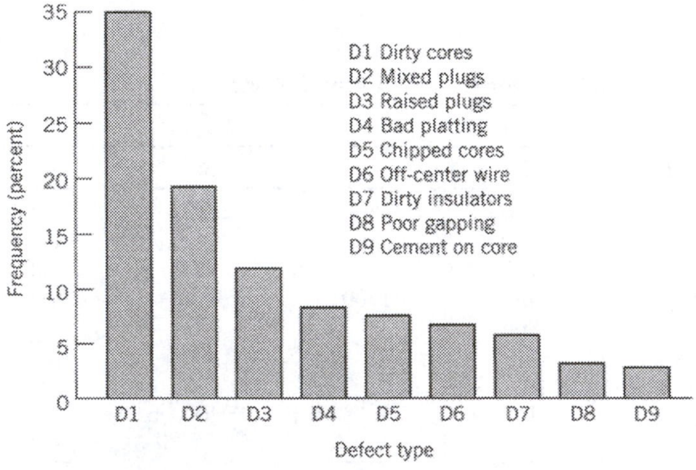

FIGURE 9.9 Pareto chart for defect types.

shown in Figure 9.10. This CAE diagram immediately identifies all the relevant factors that may be responsible for poor quality.

9.6.5 Defect Concentration Diagram

A defect concentration diagram is a visual representation of the unit under study showing all possible views with all possible defects identified on it. This type of representation is useful in understanding the types of defects and their possible causes.

9.6.6 Scatter Diagram

A scatter diagram is useful in establishing a relationship between two variables. The shape of the scatter diagram is obtained by plotting the two variables. It may indicate a positive or negative correlation between the variables or no correlation at all. Such information helps in developing control strategy for these variables.

9.6.7 Control Chart

We mentioned earlier that the key to improving quality lies in reducing the variability of the quality characteristic of interest. Variation in the outcome of a process is principally due to two types of causes: chance (also known as common) causes and assignable (special) causes. This fundamental concept was introduced by Shewhart (1931). The inherent variability in the process is due to the cumulative effect of many small but essentially unavoidable random (chance) causes. A process is said to be in statistical control if only chance causes are present. However, there are other causes of variability that may create a shift in the process to an out-of-control state resulting in a significant proportion of output not conforming to specifications. Such causes are known as assignable causes and could include improperly adjusted machines, operator errors, or defective raw materials. Control charts are effective means of detecting the occurrence of assignable causes so that corrective measures are undertaken before defective units are produced.

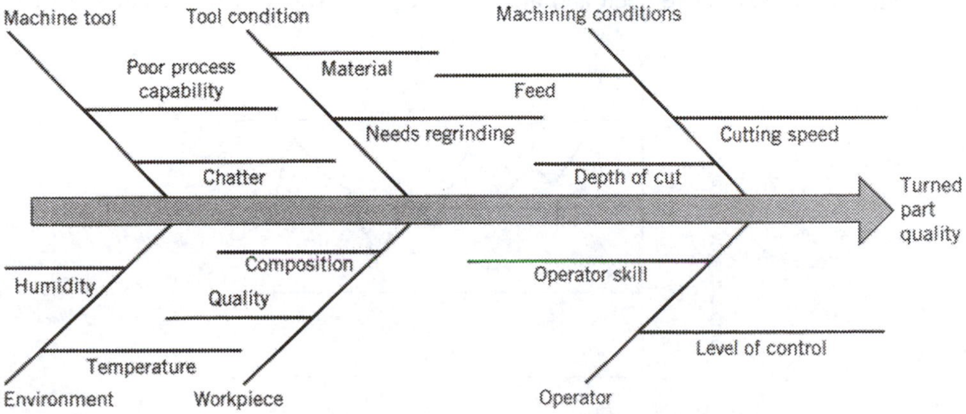

FIGURE 9.10 The cause-and-effect diagram.

A typical control chart is a graphical display of a quality characteristic measured on a sample versus the sample number or time as shown in Figure 9.11. There are three essential elements of a control chart:

1. Center line (CL) representing the average value of the quality characteristic corresponding to the in-control state
2. Upper control limit (UCL) represented by the upper horizontal line of the chart
3. Lower control limit (LCL) represented by the line below the center line

The selection of upper and lower control limits is based on the notion that all the sample points should fall between them if the process is in control. Points lying outside these limits signal the presence of assignable causes. The process should then be investigated to eliminate the assignable causes.

9.6.7.1 A General Model of a Control Chart

Suppose y is a sample statistic that measures some quality characteristic of interest, and let μ_y and σ_y be the mean and the standard deviation. Then the CL, UCL, and LCL are given by

$$\mathrm{UCL} = \mu_y + k\sigma_y$$

$$\mathrm{CL} = \mu_y$$

$$\mathrm{LCL} = \mu_y - k\sigma_y$$

where k is the distance (in standard deviation units) of the control limits from the center line. If $k = 3$, the control limits are typically called ''three-sigma'' control limits.

Control charts are classified into two general categories: *variable control chart* and *attribute control chart.*

9.6.7.2 Variable Control Chart

If the quality characteristic can be measured and expressed as a continuous variable, then it can be conveniently characterized by measures of central tendency and variability. Variable control charts can explain process data in terms of both location (process average) and spread (piece-to-piece variability). For this reason, control charts for variables are always developed and analyzed in pairs. The $\bar{x}$ (x-bar) chart is widely

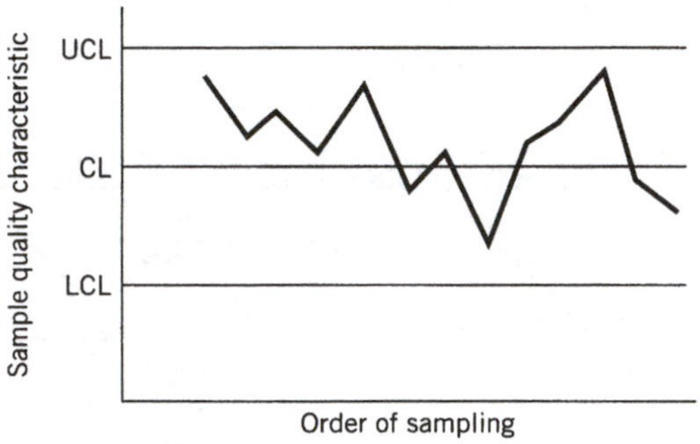

FIGURE 9.11 A sample control chart.

used for controlling central tendency. Charts based on either the sample range (R chart) or the sample standard deviation (S chart) are used to control process variability. The range chart is relatively efficient for small subgroup sample sizes, especially below 8. The S chart is used with larger sample sizes.

9.6.7.3 Attribute Control Chart

Many quality characteristics cannot be measured on a continuous scale. This happens when the quality of an item is judged as either conforming or not conforming to specifications. For example, items which have cracks, missing components, appearance defects, or other visual imperfections may be rendered as rejects, defective or nonconforming items. Control charts to control such quality characteristics are called attribute control charts. There are a variety of attribute control charts depending on the situation such as:

- The p chart for proportion of units nonconforming (from samples not necessarily of constant size),
- The np chart for number of units nonconforming (from samples of constant size)
- The c chart for number of nonconformities or defects (from samples of constant size)
- The u chart for number of nonconformities per unit (from samples not necessarily of constant size).

The control limits for various types of charts are given in the appendix.

9.6.7.4 Benefits of Control Charts

Control charts provide a large number of benefits. The compound effect of all these benefits is improvement in product quality. Some of the distinct benefits are as follows:

- Control charts are effective means of monitoring statistical control.
- Control charts help predict the performance of a process when the process is in a state of statistical control.
- They provide a common language for communication about the process, such as between two or three shifts, between production or maintenance supervisors, or between suppliers and producers.
- Control charts help direct corrective measures in a logical manner by identifying the occurrence of assignable causes. Some of the assignable causes may require special resources and involvement of the management. This helps in avoiding confusion, frustration, and the high cost of possible misdirected efforts to solve the problem.

We provide an illustrative example for constructing an $\bar{x}$ and R chart.

EXAMPLE 9.6

Control charts are to be maintained to monitor the diameter of a pin shaft manufactured using centerless grinding. The diameter of the shaft is the quality characteristic of interest. Ten samples of five observations each are taken every hour. The sample data, their averages, and the ranges are given in Table 9.8.

TABLE 9.8 Sample Averages and Ranges for Pin Shaft Diameters

Sample Number	Sample Values				Mean, $\bar{x}$	Range, R
1	5.010	5.011	5.010	5.011	5.0105	0.001
2	5.011	5.012	5.011	5.010	5.011	0.002
3	5.013	5.012	5.011	5.012	5.0115	0.002
4	5.011	5.012	5.014	5.013	5.0125	0.003
5	5.011	5.011	5.012	5.012	5.0115	0.001
6	5.013	5.012	5.013	5.010	5.012	0.003
7	5.011	5.012	5.011	5.012	5.0115	0.001
8	5.011	5.011	5.011	5.014	5.012	0.003
9	5.011	5.012	5.012	5.011	5.0115	0.001
10	5.013	5.012	5.013	5.012	5.0125	0.001

An R chart is constructed first. The mean value of range is $\bar{R} = 0.0018$. Using the control limits for the R chart from Appendix A, we have

$$\text{UCL}_R = 2.115(0.0018) = 0.003807$$
$$\text{LCL}_R = 0(0.0025) = 0$$

where $D_4 = 2.115$, $D_3 = 0.0$, and $A_2 = 0.577$ for a sample size of $n = 5$ from the American Society for Testing and Materials (1951) manual.

Using these limits, the R chart is constructed as shown in Figure 9.12*a*. Because all the values are within control limits, the R chart is accepted as a means of assessing subsequent process variation. If a point had fallen outside the calculated limits, that point would have been discarded and the limits recalculated.

We now develop an $\bar{x}$ chart as shown in Figure 9.12*b*. The mean of the sample means is 5.01165. The preliminary control limits are calculated using the control limit relations given in Appendix A as follows:

$$\text{UCL}_{\bar{x}} = 5.01165 + 0.577(0.0018) = 5.0126886$$
$$\text{LCL}_{\bar{x}} = 5.01165 - 0.577(0.0018) = 5.0106114$$

We observe that the first sample mean is below the lower control limit. This means that the universe from which this sample was selected was not exhibiting a stable pattern of variation. Further information revealed that the grinding wheels were dressed after the first sample, leading to improvement in the process output. The data for the first sample should be discarded and the control limits recalculated for the remaining pattern of the variation. You can now easily verify that no sample means exceed the recalculated limits and therefore no further changes are necessary.

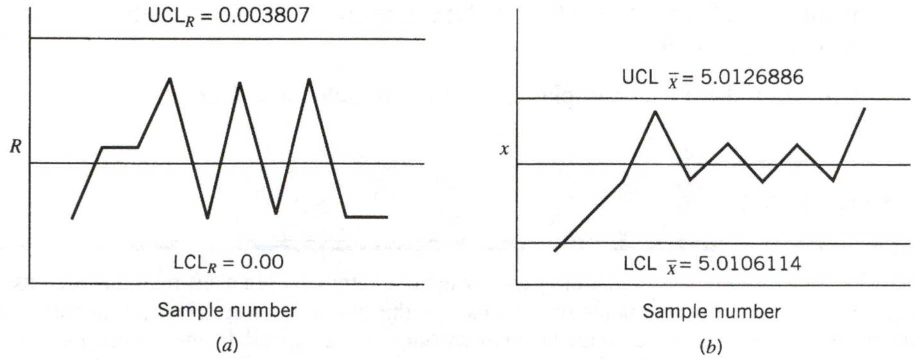

FIGURE 9.12 (*a*) Range chart. (*b*) $\bar{x}$ chart.

9.7 AUTOMATED INSPECTION

The prime requirement for the success of any quality improvement effort is the appropriateness and accuracy of the data collection process. Inspection systems are the basic tools used for collecting data on the features and characteristics of products and processes. The primary objectives of an inspection system or program are to assure product conformance to given specifications and to detect machine malfunctions that result in parts deviating from specifications. This helps in taking appropriate steps to correct the process. There are many kinds of inspection equipment, which can be classified into two basic categories: *on-line* and *off-line.* On-line inspection can be further subclassified into the following categories: *on-line/in-process* and *on-line/postprocess* inspection.

9.7.1 On-Line/In-Process and On-Line/Postprocess Inspection Methods

As the name suggests, the task of inspection in on-line methods is performed as the parts are being made. There are two variations of on-line inspection. If the inspection is performed during the manufacturing operation, it is called on-line/in-process inspection. If the inspection is performed immediately following the production process, it is called on-line/postprocess inspection.

Inspection probes are the classical examples of on-line inspection. These probes can be used in a large variety of ways. For example, they can be mounted in holders, inserted into machine-tool spindles, or stored in a tool magazine to be exchanged by an automatic tool exchanger just as tools are. Machine-tool spindle–mounted probes are commonly used in flexible manufacturing systems. Sensors in the probe are the primary inspection elements. When contact is made with the part surface, signals are transmitted to the controller. Various technologies are available for transmitting the signals, such as direct electrical connection, induction coil, or infrared data transmission. The task of data processing and interpretation is performed by the controller. Figure 9.13 shows a probe being used to measure the dimensions of a part.

9.7.2 Off-Line Inspection Methods

In off-line inspection, the inspection equipment is usually dedicated and does not make any physical contact with machine tools. A coordinate measuring machine (CMM) is an example of off-line inspection. CMMs are measuring devices capable of moving a probe and/or part within a three-dimensional rectilinear and/or polar coordinate system. They are capable of accurately establishing and recording the spatial coordinate location of selected contact points between the probe and the part or its features. CMMs are available in a number of configurations. We provide a brief discussion of some selected CMM configurations:

The primary configurations of CMMs available are cantilever, bridge, column, gantry, and horizontal arm. A brief description of each, along with their potential uses, is provided next.

9.7.2.1 Cantilever-Type CMM

This type of construction uses three movable components as shown in Figure 9.14*a* and *b*. These components move along mutually perpendicular guideways. The workpiece is supported on the worktable with a CMM holding fixture. Three-dimensional

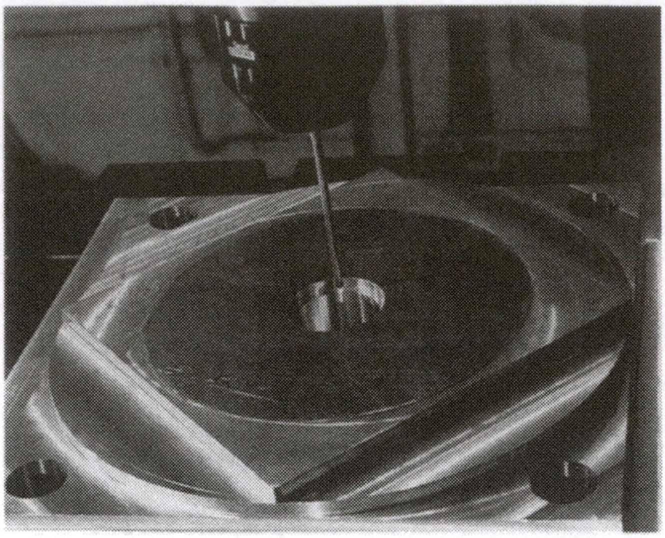

FIGURE 9.13 Probe being used to measure the dimensions of a part. (Courtesy of Giddings & Lewis.)

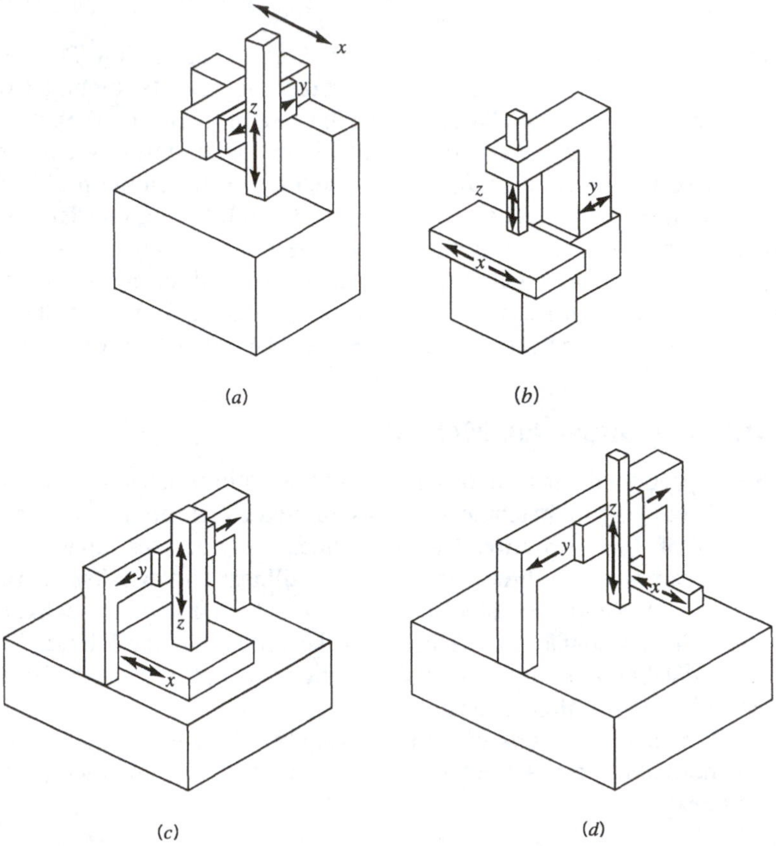

FIGURE 9.14 Various types of coordinate measuring machines: (*a* and *b*) cantilever type; (*c–f*) bridge type; (*g*) column type; (*h*) gantry type; (*i–k*) horizontal arm type. (Courtesy of the American Society of Mechanical Engineers.)

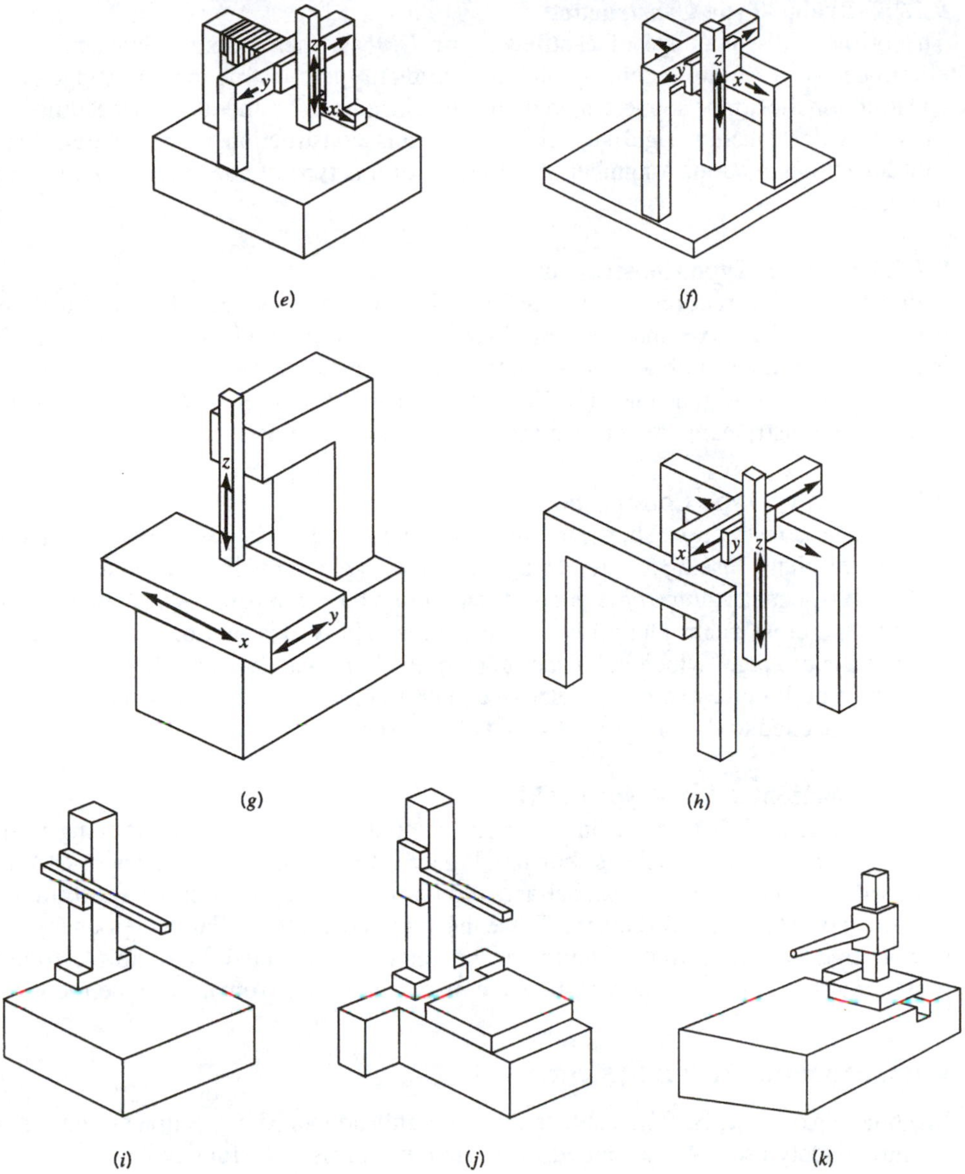

FIGURE 9.14 (continued)

measurements are accomplished by having the probe attached to the vertical quill, which moves vertically in the *z*-direction relative to the horizontal arm. The quill can also move horizontally in the *y*-direction along the length of the arm to achieve *y*-axis motion. The arm is supported at one end only in a cantilever fashion and moves horizontally in the *x*-direction relative to the machine base.

Features of cantilever-type CMMs include small size, low cost, and minimum floor space requirement. Another interesting feature is that it permits a completely unobstructed work area, allowing full access to load, inspect, and unload parts that may be larger than the table (Wick and Veilleux, 1986). The disadvantage of this type of construction is limited accuracy due to the cantilever nature of the system.

9.7.2.2 Bridge-Type Construction

The primary disadvantage of cantilever-type CMMs, their possible inaccuracy, is eliminated to a certain extent by having a bridge-type construction. In bridge-type construction the arm is supported on both ends like a bridge rather than as a cantilever. This provides inherent rigid support, making this construction more accurate than cantilever construction. A number of variations of this type of construction are shown in Figure 9.14*c*–*f*.

9.7.2.3 Column-Type Construction

Column-type construction is quite similar to that of a machine tool. The worktable is used to obtain the x-axis and y-axis motions as shown in Figure 9.14*g*. The probe quill is moved vertically to obtain z-axis motion. These machines are often referred to as universal measuring machines (UMMs) rather than CMMs. They are often used as gauge-room instruments rather than production-floor machines.

9.7.2.4 Gantry-Type Construction

This type of construction, shown in Figure 9.14*h*, is used for inspection of large parts such as airplane fuselages, diesel engine blocks, ship propellers, and automobile bodies. It is a gantry crane type of construction in which x-axis motion is obtained by moving the cross beam along two elevated rails. The y-axis motion is obtained by moving the carriage (which holds the probe quill) horizontally along the cross beam. The probe quill moves vertically relative to a cross beam to obtain z-axis motion. The probe is attached to the probe quill to obtain measurement signals.

9.7.2.5 Horizontal-Arm-Type CMM

Horizontal arm CMMs come in a variety of configurations such as moving ram, moving table, and fixed table as shown in Figure 9.14*i*–*k*, respectively. These CMMs are used to inspect the dimensional and geometric accuracy of a broad spectrum of machined or fabricated workpieces. These machines are quite similar in their operation to horizontal machine tools. Therefore, the parts are inspected using an electronic probe in a way similar to the way they are machined on horizontal machine tools.

9.7.3 Machine Vision Systems

Machine vision systems form another class of highly advanced inspection systems that are now widely used. A machine vision system performs three functions:

- Image acquisition and digitization
- Image processing and analysis
- Interpretation of the data for inspection purposes

The essential elements of a machine vision system include a lighting source, a camera, a digitizer and frame buffers, a computer, and a plotter. The basic diagram connecting these elements is shown in Figure 9.15.

The images may be formed by light scattering or diffraction from the surface of parts or specimens to be inspected. In light-scattering methods, the image is formed by using a white light source. In diffraction methods, a diffraction pattern (Fourier pattern) is formed at infinity when the surface is illuminated by a monochromatic light source such as a helium–neon (He–Ne) laser. Using a system of lenses, this pattern can be focused on the image plane of a camera. Charge-coupled device (CCD) cameras

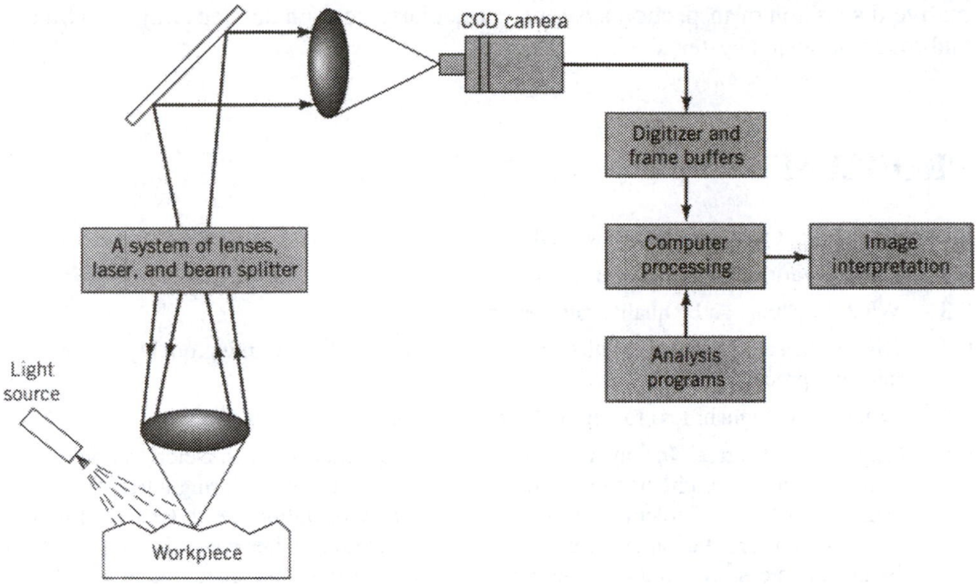

FIGURE 9.15 Elements of a machine vision system.

operate by focusing the image onto a two-dimensional array of very small, finely spaced photosensitive elements. An image is obtained by dividing the viewing area into a matrix of discrete picture elements, or pixels. A CCD camera is used to capture the reflected light in light-scattering methods. The next step is to transfer the analog signal from the camera to a frame grabber. The frame grabber digitizes the image into $512 \times 512 \times 8$-bit pixels. A frame is a set of pixel values. A computer memory device called a frame buffer, available on the frame grabber board, stores each frame. The frame grabber board can use the computer bus and is capable of image capturing and digitization in 1/30 s. The digitized image can be displayed on a high-resolution monitor.

Applications of vision systems (Schaffer, 1984) include inspection such as measurement and gauging, verification of the location of features such as holes and the existence of components, surface roughness measurement, and flaw detection (Cuthbert et al., 1990).

9.8 SUMMARY

In this chapter we provided a framework for quality improvement during product and process design as well as during the production phases of the product life cycle. We have discussed the Taguchi method, which is a systematic and efficient approach to robust design of products and processes. Using the Taguchi method, information on variable trends and interactions can be identified efficiently, leading to good solutions and considerable time and resource savings. Use of the Taguchi method should be encouraged early in the design phase, where the cost and risk of design changes are low.

A brief discussion of failure mode and effect analysis was included. FMEA is now being used in all major manufacturing companies as a preventive approach to quality problems. Statistical process control tools were discussed. We also provided an informative discussion of inspection systems, particularly coordinate measuring machines and machine vision systems.

PROBLEMS

9.1 Define what you understand by quality.

9.2 Discuss various dimensions of quality.

9.3 What do you mean by quality engineering?

9.4 Discuss three phases of a quality engineering program for designing quality into products and processes.

9.5 What is the Taguchi loss function? Discuss various types of loss functions.

9.6 High-Tech Electrical, Inc. manufactures high-voltage transformers. Deterioration of resistors in the power circuit causes changes in the output voltage during a transformer's operational life. The tolerance limits for satisfactory operation are $\pm$ 10 V. A loss of \$500.00 is incurred upon exceeding these limits. However, adjustments in the plant can be done at a cost of \$5.00 by simply changing a resistor. If the target voltage is 110 V, determine the factory tolerances so that it is cheaper to adjust in the factory while the product is being manufactured.

9.7 Johnson and Johnson (JJ) is planning to buy 1000 steel plates used in their steel cylinder manufacturing. Two companies bid to supply these plates. There is a slight variation in the material used in the plates from different suppliers. JJ decided to go for destructive testing using 20 specimens. The criterion used for testing is the ultimate tensile strength measured in kgf/mm^2. The test data for two products are given in Table P9.1.

The lower specification limit is 511 kgf/mm^2. The purchase quantity is 1000. The unit costs of products SCP1 and SCP2 are \$15.00 and \$13.00, respectively. Advise JJ about its purchasing decision.

9.8 Discuss various SPC tools that are used.

9.9 Discuss salient features of failure mode and effect analysis.

9.10 Discuss various types of factors in robust design of products and processes.

9.11 The objective of this example is to design a robust grinding process. Surface-ground parts are used in the aerospace industry. Therefore, the quality of the parts has to be very high. The measure of quality is the surface roughness (in micrometers). Grinding wheel speed, table speed, and depth of cut are the three dominant controllable factors that influence the surface roughness of the ground parts. The wheel must be dressed frequently because dressing frequency affects the surface roughness. However, it is difficult

TABLE P9.1 **Data for Problem 9.7**

Product (Steel Cylinder Plates)	*Ultimate Tensile Strength Data (kgf/mm^2)*							
SCP1	515.5	513.8	515.1	515.3	513.7	515.5	513.8	515.1
	515.2	513.6	514.2	514.1	514.9	514.8	515.5	514.2
	514.5	514.6	514.4	515.4				
SCP2	515.5	510.8	515.1	516.3	513.7	510.5	513.8	515.1
	512.2	517.6	511.2	514.1	511.9	514.8	517.5	514.2
	517.5	514.6	518.4	513.4				

TABLE P9.2 **Data on Levels of Various Factors for Problem 9.11**

Factor	*Levels*	
A Work speed	0.082 m/s	0.119 m/s
B Wheel speed	25.82 m/s	32.6 m/s
C Depth of cut	5×10^{-6} m	20×10^{-6} m

to determine a precise dressing interval. Therefore, dressing interval is considered as a noise variable. Levels of various factors are given in Table P9.2.

A full factorial experiment was conducted on a surface grinding machine in a laboratory environment at four dressing intervals. The mean and standard deviation of surface roughness are given in Table P9.3.

Using Taguchi's approach to robust design, determine the best setting of the controllable variables that maximize the *S/N* ratio.

9.12 A spot-welding process is used to weld a bracket that is used in the rear axle assembly of a car. The quality of the weld is determined by the pull force to tear the bracket off during the assembly. It is desired to have a minimum pull force of 2000 in.-lb. On investigation it was found that a number of factors, such as heat, pressure, weld time, hold time, and squeeze time, were affecting the quality of weld. Cleanliness and dimensional accuracy were noise factors that also affected the pull force of the weld. These act as noise variables and were varied at two levels each. The ranges of the controllable variables are shown in Table P9.4.

Using an L16 array, the mean and variance of the pull force for the 16 test conditions are given in Table P9.5.

Determine the optimal process settings by using the Taguchi parameter approach.

TABLE P9.3 **Various Experimental Observations**

	Surface Finish ($m \times 10^{-6}$)	
Control Factor Levels	*Mean*	*Standard Deviation*
A1 B1 C1	0.12675	0.09280
A2 B1 C1	0.16000	0.05340
A1 B2 C1	0.11675	0.02076
A2 B2 C1	0.11200	0.01853
A1 B1 C2	0.31050	0.07122
A2 B1 C2	0.32375	0.06080
A1 B2 C2	0.18575	0.03260
A2 B2 C2	0.20425	0.02266

TABLE P9.4 **Data for Problem 9.12**

Controllable Variables	*Levels*	
A Heat (°C)	100.00	120.00
B Pressure (psi)	8.00	10.00
C Weld time (s)	3.00	4.00
D Hold time (s)	1.50	2.50
E Squeeze time (s)	6.00	8.00

TABLE P9.5 **Experimental Data for Problem 9.12**

Trial Number	Column Number															Mean Pull	Variance of Pull
	A	*B*	*(AB)*	*C*	*(AC)*	*(BC)*	*(DE)*	*D*	*(AD)*	*(BD)*	*(CE)*	*(CD)*	*(BE)*	*AE*	*E*		
1	1	1	1	1	1	1	1	1	1	1	1	1	1	1	1	1000	10
2	1	1	1	1	1	1	1	2	2	2	2	2	2	2	2	1500	15
3	1	1	1	2	2	2	2	1	1	1	1	2	2	2	2	1600	16
4	1	1	1	2	2	2	2	2	2	2	2	1	1	1	1	950	9
5	1	2	2	1	1	2	2	1	1	2	2	1	1	2	2	1200	12
6	1	2	2	1	1	2	2	2	2	1	1	2	2	1	1	900	13
7	1	2	2	2	2	1	1	1	1	2	2	2	2	1	1	850	10
8	1	2	2	2	2	1	1	2	2	1	1	1	1	2	2	1050	11
9	2	1	2	1	2	1	2	1	2	1	2	1	2	1	2	2200	20
10	2	1	2	1	2	1	2	2	1	2	1	2	1	2	1	1850	22
11	2	1	2	2	1	2	1	1	2	1	2	2	1	2	1	2100	18
12	2	1	2	1	2	1	2	1	2	1	2	1	2	1	2	2300	20
13	2	2	1	1	2	2	1	1	2	2	1	1	2	2	1	2400	23
14	2	2	1	1	2	2	1	2	1	1	2	2	1	1	2	2700	24
15	2	2	1	2	1	1	2	1	2	2	1	2	1	1	2	2600	27
16	2	2	1	2	1	1	2	2	1	1	2	1	2	2	1	2500	26

TABLE P9.6 **Factors and Interactions**

		Low	*High*
A	Mold temperature	A1	A2
B	Chemical temperature	B1	B2
A × B	Mold temperature × chemical temperature interaction		
D	Throughput	D1	D2
E	Index	E1	E2
B × D	Chemical temperature × throughput interaction		
G	Cure time	G1	G2

9.13 ABC Company is a supplier of reaction injection molded polyurethane bumpers for light truck applications. It was observed that the front fender flares were not meeting quality standards. Therefore, a study on front fender flares was planned. Through Pareto analysis, porosity was proven to be the major flaw. A designed experiment was conducted in an effort to:

1. Identify process variables that significantly contributed to porosity.
2. Determine optimum operating levels for the conditions studied.

During a brainstorming session, the following cause and effect diagram for porosity was constructed.

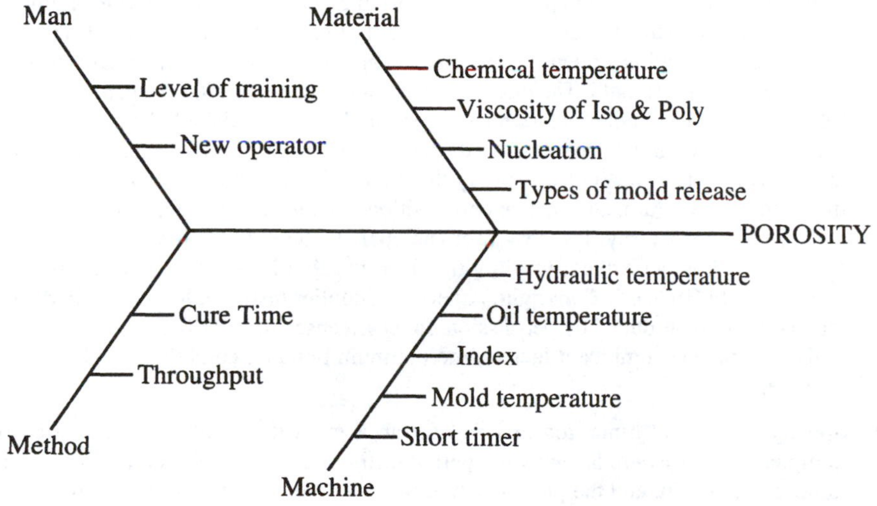

As a result, five factors and two interactions were selected as shown in Table P9.6.

It was decided that an L8 orthogonal array with 2 replicates was best for the experiment. Porosity is the quality characteristic being evaluated. In this case, porosity is a smaller-the-better characteristic. Because porosity is virtually undetectable to the human eye until the flares are primed, 32 flares were sent through the prime process before evaluation. After the flares were primed, the porosity on each was measured. Since counting each hole of porosity would have been an enormous task, a grid was developed by copying a sheet of graph paper (each square had $\frac{1}{5}$ inch sides) onto an overhead

TABLE P9.7 **Experimental Data for the Front Fender Flare Study**

	Experiment Runs									
	A	*A × B*	*B*	*G*	*B × D*	*D*	*E*	*Porosity*		
No.	*1*	*2*	*3*	*4*	*5*	*6*	*7*	*Count*		*S/N*
1	1	1	1	1	1	1	1	26	38	−30.25
2	1	1	1	2	2	2	2	16	6	−21.64
3	1	2	2	1	1	2	2	3	17	−21.73
4	1	2	2	2	2	1	1	18	16	−24.62
5	2	1	2	1	2	1	2	0	5	−10.97
6	2	1	2	2	1	2	1	0	0	− 3.01
7	2	2	1	1	2	2	1	4	5	−13.12
8	2	2	1	2	1	1	2	5	3	−12.30

transparency. By placing the transparency over the affected area, it was possible to count the total number of squares containing porosity. The experimental observations are summarized in Table P9.7.

Using Taguchi's approach to robust design, identify the significant factors and suggest the optimal operating conditions to minimize the porosity. [This problem is adapted from Angsten and Law (1987). © Copyright, American Supplier Institute, Inc., Allen Park, Michigan (USA). Reproduced by permission under License No. 950304.]

9.14 This study is concerned with process design for the manufacture of a plastic product. The quality characteristic of interest is the bonding strength of the plastic product. The factors that affect the bonding strength are given in Table P9.8. It is desirable to have the highest possible bonding strength. The quality loss is estimated to be \$76.00 when the consumer tolerance of 10 kgf/cm^2 for the bonding strength is not satisfied. The objective is to determine the optimum bonding conditions. Accordingly, seven factors are studied at three levels. It is also decided to study the effect of two factor interactions among etch time, etch temperature, and etchant composition. Factors and interactions are assigned to an L27 orthogonal array. Two test pieces are manufactured for each set of conditions and a pull-off test is performed, yielding the data in Table P9.9. [This problem is adapted from Taguchi (1990). © Copyright, American Supplier Institute, Inc., Allen Park, Michigan (USA). Reproduced by permission under License No. 950304.]

Determine the significant factors, the optimum bonding conditions, and the process average.

9.15 Specify the control limits for an $\bar{x}$ and for an R chart if the following data are given: Samples ($n = 10$) were taken over a period of time. The process average was estimated to be $\bar{x} = 0.050$ in. and the process range was estimated to be $\bar{R} = 0.0040$ in.

TABLE P9.8 **Factors and Levels**

A. Etch time (min)	5	10	15
B. Etch temperature (°C)	60	65	80
C. Etchant composition	C1	C2	C3
D. Preprocessing	None	Solvent	Warm water
E. Accelerator	E1	E2	E3
F. Catalyst	Present	Proposed$_1$	Proposed$_2$
G. Neutralizing method	G1	G2	G3

TABLE P9.9 **Layout and Data**

No.	A 1	B 2	A × B 3	 4	C 5	A × C 6	 7	B × C 8	D 9	E 10	B × C 11	F 12	G 13	Data		Decibel Value (η − 20)
1	1	1	1	1	1	1	1	1	1	1	1	1	1	6	5	− 5.3
2	1	1	1	1	2	2	2	2	2	2	2	2	2	10	8	− 1.1
3	1	1	1	1	3	3	3	3	3	3	3	3	3	10	12	0.7
4	1	2	2	2	1	1	1	3	2	2	3	3	3	3	10	− 7.8
5	1	2	2	2	2	2	2	1	3	3	1	1	1	18	18	5.1
6	1	2	2	2	3	3	3	2	1	1	2	2	2	23	18	6.0
7	1	3	3	3	1	1	1	2	3	3	2	2	2	9	13	0.4
8	1	3	3	3	2	2	2	3	1	1	3	3	3	33	30	9.9
9	1	3	3	3	3	3	3	1	2	2	1	1	1	29	29	9.2
10	2	1	2	3	1	2	3	1	2	3	1	2	3	6	8	− 3.4
11	2	1	2	3	2	3	1	2	3	1	2	3	1	7	11	− 1.6
12	2	1	2	3	3	1	2	3	1	2	3	1	2	23	24	7.4
13	2	2	3	1	1	2	3	3	3	1	3	1	2	1	1	− 20.0
14	2	2	3	1	2	3	1	1	1	2	1	2	3	31	31	9.8
15	2	2	3	1	3	1	2	2	2	3	2	3	1	32	35	10.5
16	2	3	1	2	1	2	3	2	1	2	2	3	1	16	20	4.9
17	2	3	1	2	2	3	1	3	2	3	3	1	2	32	35	10.5
18	2	3	1	2	3	1	2	1	3	1	1	2	3	29	32	9.7
19	3	1	3	2	1	3	2	1	3	2	1	3	2	1	1	− 20.0
20	3	1	3	2	2	1	3	2	1	3	2	1	3	37	34	11.0
21	3	1	3	2	3	2	1	3	2	1	3	2	1	33	28	9.6
22	3	2	1	3	1	3	2	2	1	3	3	2	1	13	16	3.1
23	3	2	1	3	2	1	3	3	2	1	1	3	2	37	35	11.1
24	3	2	1	3	3	2	1	1	3	2	2	1	3	31	33	10.1
25	3	3	2	1	1	3	2	3	2	1	2	1	3	28	28	8.9
26	3	3	2	1	2	1	3	1	3	2	3	2	1	35	38	11.2
27	3	3	2	1	3	2	1	2	1	3	1	3	2	36	35	11.0

TABLE P9.10 **Data on Steel Cylinders for Defects**

Date	Number of Defects	Date	Number of Defects
1	3	11	3
2	4	12	2
3	3	13	8
4	5	14	7
5	4	15	4
6	5	16	2
7	2	17	5
8	4	18	4
9	3	19	2
10	2	20	3

9.16 Windsor Steel Manufacturing Company inspects steel cylinders before shipping them to a defense contractor. Over a 4-week period, a number of defects were found as listed in Table P9.10 for 200 cylinders. Construct a c chart for these data. Do you notice any assignable cause of variation during the inspection period?

9.17 Control charts for $\bar{x}$ and R are to be established on a certain dimension part measured in millimeters. Data were collected in subgroup sizes of 5 and are given in Table P9.11. Determine the trial center line and control limits. If you notice assignable causes, revise the center line and limits.

9.18 Prepare a detailed report how you will implement an SPC program in the following cases:
(a) High-variety, low-volume company.
(b) Low-variety, high-volume company.

9.19 Distinguish between off-line and on-line inspection methods.

9.20 Describe various types of coordinate measuring machines.

TABLE P9.11 **Data for $\bar{x}$ and R Control Charts**

Subgroup Number	$\bar{x}$	R	Subgroup Number	$\bar{x}$	R
1	120.53	0.35	11	120.14	0.63
2	121.45	0.45	12	120.65	0.91
3	122.21	0.53	13	121.01	0.97
4	121.12	0.76	14	122.21	0.56
5	120.99	0.44	15	121.59	0.41
6	121.53	0.52	16	121.14	0.63
7	120.45	0.97	17	120.56	0.49
8	121.25	0.29	18	121.41	0.87
9	121.62	0.46	19	121.71	0.76
10	121.99	0.86	20	122.24	0.85

REFERENCES AND SUGGESTED READING

American Society for Testing and Materials. (1951). *Manual on Quality Control of Materials.* STP 15C. ASTM, Philadelphia.

American Supplier Institute, Inc. (1989). *Taguchi Methods: Implementation Manual.* ASI, Dearborn, Michigan.

Automotive Industry Action Group. (1993). *Potential Failure Mode and Effects Analysis (FMEA) Reference Manual.* AIGG, Dearborn, Michigan.

Barker, T. B. (1990). *Engineering Quality by Design: Interpreting the Taguchi Approach.* Marcel Dekker, New York.

Bedworth, D. D., Henderson, M. R., and Wolfe, P. M. (1991). *Computer-Integrated Design and Manufacturing.* McGraw-Hill Book Company, New York.

Bendell, A. (1988). Introduction to Taguchi methodology. In *Taguchi Methods: Proceedings of the 1988 European Conference,* London, pp. 1–14. Elsevier Applied Science, New York.

Bonner, E., Clever, W., and Dunn, K. (1989). Aerodynamic Preliminary Analysis System II, Part I—Theory. NASA CR165627. National Aeronautics and Space Administration, Washington, DC.

Bovas, A. (1993). Personal communication. Department of Statistics and Actuarial Sciences, University of Waterloo, Canada.

Cuthbert, L., Kurada, S., and Huynh, V. (1990). Application of machine vision to surface texture measurements. *Proceedings: Vision, '90,* MS90-588, SME (Society of Manufacturing Engineers) November 12–15.

Dehnad, K. (1989). *Quality Control, Robust Design and the Taguchi Method.* Wadsworth & Brooks Cole Advanced Books & Software, Pacific Grove, California.

Enrick, N. L. (1985). *Quality, Reliability and Process Improvement.* Industrial Press, New York.

Formuser, developed by Engineered Work Systems, Inc. Rochester, Michigan.

Garvin, D. A. (1987). Competing on the eight dimensions of quality. *Harvard Business Review* 87(6):101–109.

Groover, M. P. (1987). *Automation, Production, Systems, and Computer-Integrated Manufacturing.* Prentice Hall, Englewood Cliffs, New Jersey.

Kackar, R. (1985). Off-line quality control, parameter design and Taguchi method. *Journal of Quality Technology* 17:176–188.

Logothetis, N. and Wynn, H. P. (1989). *Quality Through Design.* Oxford Science Publications, New York.

Meisl, C. J. (1990). Parametric cost analysis in the TQM environment. 12th Conference of International Society of Parametric Analysts, San Diego.

Moen, R. D., Nolan, T. W., and Provost, L. P. (1991). *Improving Quality Through Planned Experimentation.* McGraw-Hill Book Company, New York.

Montgomery, D. C. (1991). *Introduction to Statistical Quality Control.* John Wiley & Sons, New York.

Ott, E. R., and Schilling, E. G. (1990). *Process Quality Control.* McGraw-Hill Book Company, New York.

Phadke, M. S. (1989). *Quality Engineering Using Robust Design.* Prentice Hall, Englewood Cliffs, New Jersey.

Pignatiello, J. J., Jr., and Ramberg, J. S. (1985). Discussion of off-line quality control, parameter design and the Taguchi method. *Journal of Quality Technology* 17:198–206.

Ross, P. J. (1988). *Taguchi Techniques for Quality Engineering.* McGraw-Hill Book Company, New York.

Roy, R. (1990). *A Primer on the Taguchi Method.* Van Nostrand Reinhold, New York.

Schaffer, G. H. (1984). Machine vision: A sense for CIM. *American Machinist,* Special Report 767, pp. 101–120.

Shewhart, W. A. (1931; reprinted 1980). *The Economic Control of Quality of Manufactured Product.* American Society for Quality Control, Milwaukee.
Taguchi, G. (1986). *Introduction to Quality Engineering.* Asian Productivity Organization; distributed by American Supplier Institute, Dearborn, Michigan.
Taguchi, G. (1987). *System of Experimental Design* (D. Clausing, ed.), Vols. 1 and 2. UNIPUB/Kraus International Publications, New York.
Taguchi, G., and Clausing, D. (1990). Robust quality. *Harvard Business Review* 68(1):65–75.
Taguchi, G., and Konishi, S. (1987). *Orthogonal Arrays and Linear Graphs.* ASI Press, Dearborn, Michigan.
Taguchi, G., Elsayed, A. E., and Hsiang, T. (1990). *Quality Engineering in Production Systems.* McGraw-Hill Book Company, New York.
Taylor, W. A. (1991). *Optimization and Variation Reduction in Quality.* McGraw-Hill Book Company, New York.
Unal, R., and Bush, L. B. (1992). Engineering design for quality using the Taguchi approach. *Engineering Management* 4(1):37–47.
Wetherill, G. B., and Brown, D. W. (1991). *Statistical Process Control: Theory and Practice.* Chapman & Hall, London.
Wick, C., and Veilleux, R.S. (eds.) (1987). *Tool and Manufacturing Engineers Handbook, Vol. 4: Quality Control and Assembly,* 4th Edition, SME, Dearborn, Michigan.
Wille, R. (1990). Landing gear weight optimization using Taguchi analysis. 49th Annual International Conference of Allied Weight Engineers, Chandler, Arkansas.

APPENDIX A

CONTROL LIMITS FOR VARIABLE AND ATTRIBUTE CHARTS

Control Charts for Variables

$\bar{x}$ and R Charts

$\bar{x}$ chart:

$$\mathrm{UCL}\bar{x}, \mathrm{LCL}_{\bar{x}} = \bar{\bar{x}} \pm A_2\bar{R}$$

R chart:

$$\mathrm{UCL}_R = D_4\bar{R}$$

$$\mathrm{LCL}_R = D_3\bar{R}$$

$\bar{x}$ and S Charts

$\bar{x}$ chart:

$$\mathrm{UCL}_{\bar{x}}, \mathrm{LCL}_{\bar{x}} = .\bar{\bar{x}} \pm A_3\bar{S}$$

S chart:

$$\mathrm{UCL}_s = B_4\bar{S}$$

$$\mathrm{LCL}_s = B_3\bar{S}$$

TABLE 9.A1 **Factors for Constructing Variables Control Charts**

Observations in	*Chart for Averages*			*Chart for Standard Deviations*						*Chart for Ranges*						
	Factors for Control Limits			*Factors for Center Line*		*Factors for Control Limits*				*Factors for Center Line*		*Factors for Control Limits*				
Sample, n	A	A_2	A_3	c_4	$1/c_4$	B_3	B_4	B_5	B_6	d_2	$1/d_2$	d_3	D_1	D_2	D_3	D_4
2	2.121	1.880	2.659	0.7979	1.2533	0	3.267	0	2.606	1.128	0.8865	0.853	0	3.686	0	3.267
3	1.732	1.023	1.954	0.8862	1.1284	0	2.568	0	2.276	1.693	0.5907	0.888	0	4.358	0	2.575
4	1.500	0.729	1.628	0.9213	1.0854	0	2.266	0	2.088	2.059	0.4857	0.880	0	4.698	0	2.282
5	1.342	0.577	1.427	0.9400	1.0638	0	2.089	0	1.964	2.326	0.4299	0.864	0	4.918	0	2.115
6	1.225	0.483	1.287	0.9515	1.0510	0.030	1.970	0.029	1.874	2.534	0.3946	0.848	0	5.078	0	2.004
7	1.134	0.419	1.182	0.9594	1.0423	0.118	1.882	0.113	1.806	2.704	0.3698	0.833	0.204	5.204	0.076	1.924
8	1.061	0.373	1.099	0.9650	1.0363	0.185	1.815	0.179	1.751	2.847	0.3512	0.820	0.388	5.306	0.136	1.864
9	1.000	0.337	1.032	0.9693	1.0317	0.239	1.761	0.232	1.707	2.970	0.3367	0.808	0.547	5.393	0.184	1.816
10	0.949	0.308	0.975	0.9727	1.0281	0.284	1.716	0.276	1.669	3.078	0.3249	0.797	0.687	5.469	0.223	1.777
11	0.905	0.285	0.927	0.9754	1.0252	0.321	1.679	0.313	1.637	3.173	0.3152	0.787	0.811	5.535	0.256	1.744
12	0.866	0.266	0.886	0.9776	1.0229	0.354	1.646	0.346	1.610	3.258	0.3069	0.778	0.922	5.594	0.283	1.717
13	0.832	0.249	0.850	0.9794	1.0210	0.382	1.618	0.374	1.585	3.336	0.2998	0.770	1.025	5.647	0.307	1.693
14	0.802	0.235	0.817	0.9810	1.0194	0.406	1.594	0.399	1.563	3.407	0.2935	0.763	1.118	5.696	0.328	1.672
15	0.775	0.223	0.789	0.9823	1.0180	0.428	1.572	0.421	1.544	3.472	0.2880	0.756	1.203	5.741	0.347	1.653
16	0.750	0.212	0.763	0.9835	1.0168	0.448	1.552	0.440	1.526	3.532	0.2831	0.750	1.282	5.782	0.363	1.637
17	0.728	0.203	0.739	0.9845	1.0157	0.466	1.534	0.458	1.511	3.588	0.2787	0.744	1.356	5.820	0.378	1.622
18	0.707	0.194	0.718	0.9854	1.0148	0.482	1.518	0.475	1.496	3.640	0.2747	0.739	1.424	5.856	0.391	1.608
19	0.688	0.187	0.698	0.9862	1.0140	0.497	1.503	0.490	1.483	3.689	0.2711	0.734	1.487	5.891	0.403	1.597
20	0.671	0.180	0.680	0.9869	1.0133	0.510	1.490	0.504	1.470	3.735	0.2677	0.729	1.549	5.921	0.415	1.585
21	0.655	0.173	0.663	0.9876	1.0126	0.523	1.477	0.516	1.459	3.778	0.2647	0.724	1.605	5.951	0.425	1.575
22	0.640	0.167	0.647	0.9882	1.0119	0.534	1.466	0.528	1.448	3.819	0.2618	0.720	1.659	5.979	0.434	1.566
23	0.626	0.162	0.633	0.9887	1.0114	0.545	1.455	0.539	1.438	3.858	0.2592	0.716	1.710	6.006	0.443	1.557
24	0.612	0.157	0.619	0.9892	1.0109	0.555	1.445	0.549	1.429	3.895	0.2567	0.712	1.759	6.031	0.451	1.548
25	0.600	0.153	0.606	0.9896	1.0105	0.565	1.435	0.559	1.420	3.931	0.2544	0.708	1.806	6.056	0.459	1.541

For $n > 25$,

$$A = \frac{3}{\sqrt{n}},\ A_3 = \frac{3}{c_4\sqrt{n}},\ c_4 \simeq \frac{4(n-1)}{4n-3},\ B_3 = 1 - \frac{3}{c_4\sqrt{2(n-1)}},\ B_4 = 1 + \frac{3}{c_4\sqrt{2(n-1)}},\ B_5 = c_4 - \frac{3}{\sqrt{2(n-1)}},\ B_6 = c_4 + \frac{3}{\sqrt{2(n-1)}}.$$

Source: Montgomery (1991).

The *p* Control Chart

$$\text{UCL}_p, \text{LCL}_p = \bar{p} \pm \frac{3\sqrt{\bar{p}(1-\bar{p})}}{\sqrt{n}}$$

The constants A_2, A_3, B_3, B_4, D_3, and D_4, are given in Table 9.A1 for various sample sizes.

Control Charts for Attributes

The *p* Control Chart

$$\text{UCL}_p, \text{LCL}_p = \bar{p} \pm \frac{3\sqrt{\bar{p}(1-\bar{p})}}{\sqrt{n}}$$

The *np* Control Chart

$$\text{UCL}_{np}, \text{LCL}_{np} = n\bar{p} \pm \frac{3\sqrt{n\bar{p}(1-n\bar{p})}}{\sqrt{n}}$$

The *c* Control Chart

$$\text{UCL}_c, \text{LCL}_c = \bar{c} \pm \frac{3\sqrt{\bar{c}}}{\sqrt{n}}$$

The *u* Control Chart

$$\text{UCL}_u, \text{LCL}_u = \bar{u} \pm \frac{3\sqrt{\bar{u}}}{\sqrt{n}}$$

APPENDIX B

BASIC CONCEPTS ON DESIGNING MATRIX EXPERIMENTS USING ORTHOGONAL ARRAYS

In this appendix we provide some basic concepts of designing matrix experiments based on orthogonal arrays. A matrix has a number of columns equal to the number of factors (parameters) to be considered, each column representing a specific factor. Within each column we specify the levels (parameter setting) at which the factors are kept for experiments. The number of rows in a matrix represents the number of experiments that are to be performed. As the name suggests, the columns of orthogonal array are mutually orthogonal. Here, orthogonal is interpreted in the combinatoric sense; that is, for any pair of columns, all combinations of factor levels occur and they occur equal numbers of times. An orthogonal array design gives more reliable estimates of factor effects with fewer experiments than are needed in traditional methods, such as one-factor-at-a-time experiments.

Taguchi (1987) has tabulated 18 basic arrays that we call standard orthogonal arrays. An array's name indicates the number of rows and columns it has and also the number of levels in each of the columns. For example, L_8 (2^7) has 8 rows and 7 columns each at 2 levels. For brevity, we generally refer to an array by the number of rows. The 18 standard orthogonal arrays with the number of columns at different levels for these arrays are listed in Table 9.B1. These arrays can be used directly in many cases or modified to suit a specific problem. However, to select an appropriate OA to fit a specific case, the count of the total degrees of freedom is required in order to determine the minimum number of experiments that must be performed to reach a near-optimum parameter set (American Supplier Institute, 1989; Phadke, 1989; Wille, 1990). To start with, one degree of freedom is associated with the overall mean regardless of the number of control factors considered. In general, the number of degrees of freedom associated with a factor is one less than the number of levels for that factor. The degrees of freedom associated with interaction between two factors, called P and Q, is equal to the product of the degrees of freedom for each of the two factors. For example, let n_P and n_Q be the number of levels for factors P and Q. Then the total combinations of the levels of these two factors will be $n_P n_Q$. The degrees of freedom for interaction P·Q can be obtained by subtracting one degree of freedom for the overall mean, $(n_P - 1)$ for the degree of freedom of P and $(n_Q - 1)$ for the degrees of freedom of Q. Thus,

Degrees of freedom for interaction P·Q

$$= n_P n_Q - 1 - (n_P - 1) - (n_Q - 1) = (n_P - 1)(n_Q - 1)$$

The number of rows of an orthogonal array represents the number of experiments. For an array to be a viable choice, the number of rows must be at least equal to the degrees of freedom required for the case study. The number of columns of an array represents the maximum number

TABLE 9.B1 **List of Standard Orthogonal Arrays**

Orthogonal Arrays	*Number of Rows*	*Maximum Number of Factors*	*Maximum Number of Columns at These Levels*			
			2	*3*	*4*	*5*
L_4	4	3	3	—	—	—
L_8	8	7	7	—	—	—
L_9	9	4	—	4	—	—
L_{12}	12	11	11	—	—	—
L_{16}	16	15	15	—	—	—
L'_{16}	16	5	—	—	5	—
L_{18}	18	8	1	7	—	—
L_{25}	25	6	—	—	—	6
L_{27}	27	13	—	13	—	—
L_{32}	32	31	31	—	—	—
L'_{32}	32	10	1	—	9	—
L_{36}	36	23	11	12	—	—
L'_{36}	36	16	3	13	—	—
L_{50}	50	12	1	—	—	11
L_{54}	54	26	1	25	—	—
L_{64}	64	63	63	—	—	—
L'_{64}	64	21	—	—	21	—
L_{81}	81	40	—	40	—	—

of factors that can be studied using that array. Furthermore, in order to use a standard orthogonal array directly, we must be able to match the number of levels of the factors with the numbers of levels of the columns in the array. Usually, it is expensive to conduct experiments. Therefore, we use the smallest possible orthogonal array that meets the requirements of the case study.

To understand these ideas, let us consider the case study discussed in Example 9.4. In this example, we have four factors, *B*, *C*, *D*, and *E*, each at two levels and three two-factor interaction effects, *BC*, *BD*, and *CD*. The total number of degrees of freedom can be calculated as given in Table 9.B2. Based on the total degrees of freedom (8), number of factors (7), and their levels (2), it can be seen from Table 9.B1 that an L_8 array is the best choice for this case study.

TABLE 9.B2 **Calculation of Degrees of Freedom for Example 9.4**

Factor/Interactions	*Degrees of Freedom*
Overall mean	1
B, *C*, *D*, *E*	$4 \cdot (2 - 1) = 4$
BC, *BD*, *CD*	$3 \cdot (2 - 1)(2 - 1) = 3$
Total	$1 + 4 + 3 = 8$

CHAPTER 10

MANUFACTURING PLANNING AND CONTROL SYSTEMS

The cost of manufacturing products and their quality and lead time are three major determinants of the market share and profitability of any organization. The manufacturing planning and control functions are key to achieving the goals of minimum cost, high quality, and minimum lead time. It is therefore important to understand the basic principles of manufacturing planning and control. In this chapter we provide a basic framework of a manufacturing planning and control system (MPCS). We discuss various elements of an MPCS such as demand management, aggregate production planning, product structure, master production scheduling, material requirements planning (MRP), MRP lot sizing and algorithms, inventory management, capacity planning, order release, and shop-floor scheduling and control. A number of numerical examples are included to illustrate these concepts.

10.1 A BASIC FRAMEWORK FOR A MANUFACTURING PLANNING AND CONTROL SYSTEM

The primary objective of an MPCS in any organization is to ensure that the desired products are manufactured at the right time, in the right quantities, meeting quality specifications, and at minimum cost. The MPCS in a company encompasses in an integrated manner such activities as determining end-item demand, translating end-item demand into feasible manufacturing plans, establishing detailed planning of material flows and capacity to support the overall manufacturing plans, and finally helping to execute these plans by such actions as detailed cell scheduling and purchasing. Among the benefits achieved through use of an integrated manufacturing planning and control system are:

- Reduced inventories
- Reduced capacity
- Reduced labor and overtime costs

- Shorter manufacturing lead times
- Faster responsiveness to internal and external changes such as machine and other equipment failures, product mix and demand changes, and so on.

In this chapter we provide a basic framework for developing a manufacturing planning and control system in any organization. The major elements of an integrated manufacturing planning and control system are:

1. Demand management
2. Aggregate production planning
3. Master production schedule
4. Rough-cut capacity planning
5. Material requirements planning
6. Capacity planning
7. Order release
8. Shop-floor scheduling and control

The flow of information among various elements of an MPCS is shown in Figure 10.1. The elements of an integrated manufacturing planning and control system interact with each other. The driving force behind any manufacturing activity is the demand for the products. Therefore, the demand management module is one of the most important elements of an MPCS. This module has the primary function of demand forecasting. It not only provides an estimate of the demand of each type of product but also provides a link between the manufacturing planning and control system and the mar-

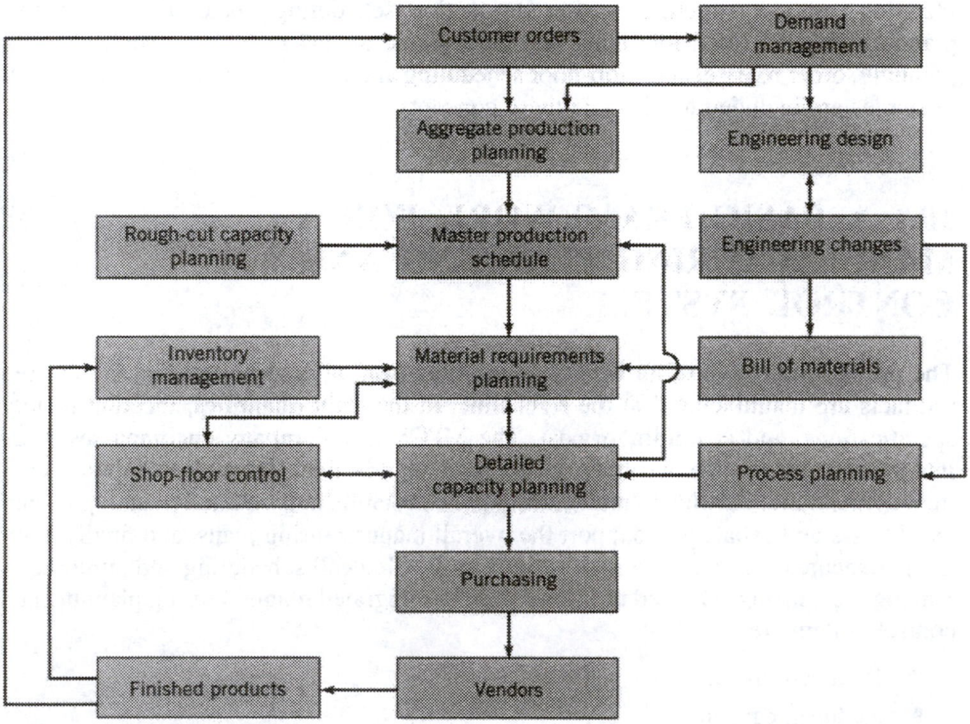

FIGURE 10.1 A basic framework for a manufacturing planning and control system.

ketplace. It helps establish a channel of communication between manufacturing and customers.

The physical resources of firms are normally fixed during the planning horizon. If a firm has a number of product types with time-varying demands, which is normally the case in discrete-product manufacturing environments, then the production should be planned in an aggregate manner to utilize the resources effectively. Demand forecasting is an important input to aggregate production planning. The objective of aggregate production planning is to rationalize the differences between the forecast demand of products and capacity over the planning horizon. In aggregate production planning, the demand and production requirements are represented in common aggregate units such as plant hours or direct labor hours. The aggregate production plan must be disaggregated to determine the quantity of each product to be produced in each period during the planning horizon. Such a disaggregate plan for each product is known as a master production schedule (MPS).

The feasibility of the MPS is assured based on rough-cut capacity planning. However, the final assembly of each end item (product) consists of a number of subassemblies and several components. In a real-life manufacturing environment, inventories exist for some of the components and subassemblies. Under these circumstances, the MPS cannot be used to develop detailed production plans for end items.

The material requirements planning system is used to determine the detailed production plans. The MPS and information on on-hand stock, purchased and manufacturing order status, order quantity, lead time and safety stock, and product structure are inputs to the MRP system. The output from the MRP determines how many of each item in each period from the bill of materials must be manufactured.

It may happen that the production plan suggested by the MRP system exceeds available capacity for some of the components. Such infeasibilities are determined by what is known as detailed capacity analysis. There are a number of ways to resolve capacity limitation problems. For example, we can look into possible alternatives such as multiple shifts, overtime, subcontracting, varying production rate by hiring and layoffs, and building inventories. If these solutions do not work, then there is no alternative but to modify the MPS. Every modification in the MPS results in changes in MRP calculations; consequently, the MPS and MRP are usually derived by an iterative process.

Once the feasibility of the detailed production plans is assured, the next step in the process is order release. Order release refers to the process of issuing directives to work. That means releasing production orders for the parts to be manufactured and purchase orders for the parts to be purchased. Once the orders are released, the most complex next step is production control.

Many random and complex events take place once production is started. For example, tools and machines exhibit random failure phenomena causing variations in production rates; work centers may "starve" because of nonarrival of parts ordered in time due to inherent uncertainties in the purchase process. The objective of the production control function is to accommodate these changes by scheduling of work orders on the work centers, sequencing of jobs in a work order at a work center, and monitoring of purchase orders from vendors. The production control activities of scheduling and sequencing are known as shop-floor control. Once all the items are manufactured, they are assembled into subassemblies and then assemblies. The final assemblies can then be shipped to customers according to the shipping schedule.

The framework outlined in this chapter forms a foundation for an integrated manufacturing planning and control system. The detailed system may, however, differ from one organization to another. In the following sections we provide a basic understanding of each of the elements of an MPCS.

10.2 DEMAND MANAGEMENT

Demand for products is a prime mover of any production activity. Demand management is therefore an important input to production planning. It encompasses such activities as demand forecasting, order transactions entry, customer contact–related activities, and physical distribution management, among others. Demand forecasting is one of the most critical activities in the demand management process. In the following section we discuss some of the simple approaches to demand forecasting.

10.2.1 Demand Forecasting

Forecasting is concerned with estimating future demand (or requirements) for products. For the purposes of making decisions with respect to planning production, inventories and workforce levels and economic lot sizes, it is necessary to know the requirements of products covering planning horizons into the future. The length of the planning horizon depends on a number of factors, such as types of products and their volume–variety relationships. A number of modeling approaches have been proposed for demand forecasting and are discussed in detail in a number of books in the area of production management and forecasting (e.g., Johnson and Montgomery, 1974; Hax and Candea, 1984; Bedworth and Bailey, 1987). The three broad approaches to forecasting are:

1. The qualitative approach
2. The explanatory approach
3. The descriptive approach

Qualitative approaches rely on the opinions of experts to predict certain events of interest. For example, what kinds of technological breakthroughs are possible in the field of personal computers by the year 2020? There are some well-established techniques for obtaining this information. For example, in the Delphi technique a structured questionnaire is mailed to experts and modified in subsequent rounds based on the responses. These techniques are useful for making predictions for technological forecasting and long-range planning. How long is long range? It may be 5, 10, 15, even 20 or more years.

Causal relationships form the basis of explanatory approaches to forecasting. Typical examples of explanatory models are econometric models and system dynamics models. Proper identification of causal relationships is an important aspect of this approach. For example, growth in economic activity increases employment, which in turn increases the buying power of the people. This, in turn, increases the demand for various products. Econometric models have been used successfully for planning and resource allocations for national economies.

Descriptive approaches to forecasting include statistical models. The basic assumption in these approaches is that the underlying demand-generating process is an extension of its past performance into the near-term future. The planning horizon normally varies from months to a year. The demand history in the form of time series can be analyzed for the constant component, trends, seasonalities, and so forth and then extrapolated into the future.

In this section we illustrate two widely used short-term forecasting approaches: *moving average* and *exponential smoothing.* [For further details on forecasting and time series analysis, refer to Montgomery and Johnson (1976).]

10.2.1.1 Moving Average

The moving-average approach is simple to implement. An average of N (a constant number) past observations is computed in order to eliminate the random variations. Every time a new observation is available, the oldest observation is discarded to compute the new average. However, all the data for the most recent N observations must be stored and often the data are assigned equal weights. These disadvantages are eliminated by exponential smoothing. Consider the time series model generated by a constant process as follows.

For a constant process:

$$x_t = a_0 + \varepsilon_t \tag{10.1}$$

The forecast for any future period considering only N recent observations is given by

$$\hat{x}_{T+\tau} = M_T = \frac{1}{N}\left(\sum_{t=T-N+1}^{T} x_t\right) \tag{10.2}$$

where ε_t = a random variable with zero mean and variance σ_ε^2
x_t = demand observations through period t ($t = 1, 2, \ldots, T$)
a_0 = constant
M_T = average of the most recent N observations

EXAMPLE 10.1

In the last 7 days the demand for spark plugs (in boxes) for four-cylinder cars was: $x_1 = 20$, $x_2 = 26$, $x_3 = 19$, $x_4 = 24$, $x_5 = 23$, $x_6 = 21$, $x_7 = 28$. Each box contains 250 spark plugs. Develop a forecast for the eighth day.

Solution

The 7-day moving average is

$$M_7 = \frac{20 + 26 + 19 + 24 + 23 + 21 + 28}{7} = 23$$

The forecast for the next day is

$$\hat{x}_8 = M_7 = 23 \text{ boxes of spark plugs}$$

Now suppose the actual demand for the eighth day is 34; then x_1 is dropped and x_8 is added to obtain the new moving average. Accordingly,

$$M_8 = \frac{26 + 19 + 24 + 23 + 21 + 28 + 34}{7} = 25$$

Therefore, the forecast for the next day is

$$\hat{x}_9 = M_8 = 25 \text{ boxes of spark plugs}$$

10.2.1.2 Exponential Smoothing

As the name suggests, in exponential smoothing more weight is attached to the recent data and the weight decreases with the age of the data. Furthermore, the storage requirements are considerably reduced compared with moving averages. For example, a constant model requires only three data elements. These features of exponential smoothing make it more appropriate when the number of items to be forecast is large. In this section we illustrate exponential smoothing only for a constant process. Details of linear and higher-order polynomial models are given in a number of books (e.g., Johnson and Montgomery, 1974). For a constant process, the procedure for revising the smoothed statistic considering current forecast error is

$$\hat{S}_T = \alpha x_T + (1 - \alpha)\hat{S}_{T-1} \tag{10.3}$$

where x_T is the actual demand for period T. $\hat{S}_T$ is the smoothed statistic for period T and α is the smoothing constant.

The forecast for τ future periods for the constant model is

$$\hat{x}_{T+\tau} = \hat{S}_T \tag{10.4}$$

In most cases, τ is one period.

The starting value of $\hat{S}_{T-1}$ required in Equation (10.3) is normally determined by averaging the demand of the first $(T - 1)$ periods. The variable α is used to change the weight of recent data relative to the older data; α usually lies between 0.10 and 0.30.

EXAMPLE 10.2

Windsor Steel Cylinder Manufacturing (WSCM) Company manufactures a large variety of high-pressure steel cylinders for its domestic and defense markets. WSCM wishes to forecast the number of cylinders per week for one of their recent products (3-in. size). The data given in Table 10.1 are available.

Forecast the demand for the 11th week using exponential smoothing. Use $\alpha = 0.20$.

Solution

The data reveal that a constant model can be assumed. Accordingly, using Equation (10.3) we get

$$\begin{aligned}\hat{S}_{10} &= (0.20)x_{10} + (0.80)\hat{S}_9 \\ &= (0.20)210 + (0.80)220 \\ &= 218 \text{ cylinders}\end{aligned}$$

The forecasted demand for the eleventh week from Equation (10.4) is 218 cylinders. The value of $\hat{S}_9$ is obtained by averaging the first nine observations.

TABLE 10.1 **Demand Data for 3-in. Size Cylinders**

Week	*1*	*2*	*3*	*4*	*5*	*6*	*7*	*8*	*9*	*10*
Number of cylinders	200	230	190	220	240	210	240	220	230	210

10.3 AGGREGATE PRODUCTION PLANNING

In a high-variety discrete-product manufacturing environment, the demand for products fluctuates considerably. However, the resources of a firm, such as capacity of machines and workforce, normally remain fixed during the planning horizon of interest, which varies from 6 to 18 months. For most production planning and control systems, 12 months is a suitable figure. Under such circumstances (a large variety of products, time-varying demand, a long planning horizon, and fixed available resources), the best approach to obtaining feasible solutions is to aggregate the information being processed. For example, similar items can be grouped into product families, machines processing these similar products into machine cells, and workers with different skills into labor centers. For aggregation purposes the product demand should be expressed in a common measurement unit such as production hours or plant hours.

Production planning is concerned primarily with determining optimal production, inventory, and work force levels to meet demand fluctuations. A number of strategies are available to management to absorb the demand fluctuations:

- Maintain uniform production rate and absorb demand fluctuations by accumulating inventories.
- Maintain uniform work force but vary production rate by permitting planned overtime, idle time, and subcontracting.
- Change the production rate by changing the size of the work force through planned hiring and layoffs.
- Explore the possibility of planned backlogs if customers are willing to accept delays in filling their orders.

A suitable combination of these strategies should be explored to develop an optimal aggregate production plan. First, we will illustrate by a simple example the implications of various alternative aggregate production plans and then present a simple linear programming formulation for determining an optimal aggregate production plan.

EXAMPLE 10.3

Data on the expected aggregated sales of three products, A, B, and C, over a planning horizon of six 4-week periods are given in Table 10.2 and the aggregate demand forecast in cell-hours is

TABLE 10.2 **Demand Forecast in Units for Products A, B, and C**

	Product A		*Product B*		*Product C*	
Period	*Units*	*Equivalent Cell-hours*	*Units*	*Equivalent Cell-hours*	*Units*	*Equivalent Cell-hours*
1	60	120	40	80	100	100
2	70	140	50	100	160	160
3	50	100	70	140	210	210
4	55	110	65	130	170	170
5	45	90	55	110	100	100
6	40	80	40	80	80	80

TABLE 10.3 **Expected Aggregate Demand Forecast for Six 4-Week Periods**

Period	*Expected Aggregate Demand (Equivalent Cell-hours)*	*Cumulative Aggregate Demand (Cell-hours)*
1	300	300
2	400	700
3	450	1150
4	410	1560
5	300	1860
6	240	2100

given in Table 10.3. The company has developed machining-cell hours as a common unit for aggregation purposes. In this case products A and B require 2 cell-hours per unit whereas product C requires only 1 cell-hour per unit. The company has a regular production capacity of 300 units per period, which can be varied up to 350 units per period. Overtime is permitted up to a maximum of 60 units per period. Requirements exceeding overtime capacity can be satisfied by subcontracting. Two alternative production policies are developed as follows:

Plan I: Produce at the constant rate of 350 units per period for the entire planning horizon.

Plan II: Produce at the rate of 400 units per period for the first four periods and then at the rate of 250 units per period for the subsequent periods.

Analyze two aggregate production plans suggested by the production department of Windsor Steel Manufacturing Company.

Analysis

Assuming that there is no initial inventory, all shortages are back-ordered, and the regular time capacity can be varied up to 350 units per period, plan I, given in Table 10.4, results in backorders in three periods with very little inventory. Plan II, given in Table 10.5, almost eliminates the backlogs, and inventory buildup is higher and results in more overtime and subcontracting. The change in production capacity is measured from the regular production capacity. For example, with plan I, the production rate is 350 whereas the regular production capacity is 300. Therefore, the change in capacity is + 50 units. Similarly, with plan II (Table 10.5), the change in capacity in period 5 from the regular production capacity of 300 to 250 is only − 50 units and not − 150 units, as it may appear as if the capacity is changing from 400 to 250.

We analyzed only two alternatives. There could, however, be a large number of such alternative aggregate production plans. The question is which one is the best considering all the relevant costs and system constraints. In the following section we present a mathematical programming model for obtaining an optimal aggregate production plan.

TABLE 10.4 **Plan I: Uniform Regular Production Rate Policy**

Period	*Production Rate*	*Inventory*	*Back Orders*	*Change in Capacity*	*Overtime*	*Subcontract*
1	350	50	0	+ 50	50	0
2	350	0	0	0	50	0
3	350	0	100	0	50	0
4	350	0	160	0	50	0
5	350	0	110	0	50	0
6	350	0	0	0	50	0

TABLE 10.5 **Plan II: Varying Regular Production Rate Policy**

Period	Production Rate	Inventory	Back Orders	Change in Capacity	Overtime	Subcontract
1	400	100	0	+ 100	60	40
2	400	100	0	0	60	40
3	400	50	0	0	60	40
4	400	40	0	0	60	40
5	250	0	10	− 50	0	0
6	250	0	0	0	0	0

10.3.1 A Mathematical Programming Model

Several mathematical models have been developed that seek an optimal combination of various strategies outlined earlier (for details of a number of models see Johnson and Montgomery, 1974; Hax and Candea, 1984). In this section we present a simple linear programming model for this purpose.
Minimize

$$Z = \sum_{t=1}^{T} (c_x X_t + c_w W_t + c_o O_t + c_u U_t + c_i I_t + c_s B_t + c_h H_t + c_f F_t) \quad (10.5)$$

subject to:

$$X_t + I_{t-1} - B_{t-1} - I_t + B_t = d_t \quad \text{for } t = 1, 2, 3, \ldots, T \quad (10.6)$$

$$W_t = W_{t-1} + H_t - F_t \quad (10.7)$$

$$O_t - U_t = kX_t - W_t \quad (10.8)$$

$$X_t, W_t, O_t, I_t, B_t, H_t, F_t, U_t \geq 0 \quad (10.9)$$

where Z = total system cost
d_t = aggregate demand in period t
X_t = production units scheduled in period t
c_x = variable cost of production excluding labor per hour
O_t = overtime scheduled in period t
c_o = overtime labor cost per hour
U_t = undertime allowed in period t
c_u = opportunity cost of not using the equipment per hour
W_t = regular time work force level in period t
c_w = cost of regular time labor per hour
H_t = new labor force added in hours in period t
c_h = cost of hiring regular time labor per hour
F_t = layoffs in hours in period t
c_f = cost of layoffs per hour

I_t = inventory in stock at the end of period t (used as variable I in the detailed formulation given in the appendix to this chapter)

c_i = cost of unit inventory holding per hour

B_t = shortages at the end of period t (used as variable B in the detailed formulation given in the appendix to this chapter)

c_s = cost of a shortage per hour

k = labor hours required to produce a unit

T = number of periods in the planning horizon

The objective function is given by Equation (10.5), which includes costs of production, regular time work force, overtime, undertime, inventory, shortages, hiring, and layoffs for all the periods in the planning horizon. Equation (10.6) provides the inventory balance considering demand and production in all periods. Labor balance is given by Equation (10.7), and the relationship between overtime, undertime, work force, and production is given by Equation (10.8). Non-negativity constraints are given by Equation (10.9).

Example 10.4

Develop an optimal aggregate production plan in terms of cell-hours for the forecast demand data given in Example 10.3. Other data are: c_x = \$100/h, c_o = \$20/h, c_w = \$14/h, c_h = \$14/h, c_f = \$30/h, c_i = \$3/unit/h, c_s = \$400/unit/h, c_u = \$50/h, $k = 1$. The initial regular work force level $W^0 = 240$ labor-hours per hour.

Solution

The objective function and the constraints are given in the Appendix at the end of this chapter. Upon solving the linear programming model presented earlier, an aggregate production plan is obtained as given in Table 10.6.

We see from Table 10.6 that the demand fluctuations are absorbed by using overtime permitted. Accordingly, no hiring, firing, inventory, or shortages are incurred. However, if the overtime is restricted, the scenario will change. For example, if the overtime is restricted to 50 units in periods 1 through 4, the output of the aggregate production planning model is as given in Table 10.7.

We see from Table 10.7 that the optimal plan is now different and requires the use of overtime, hiring, lay-offs, inventory, and back orders for absorbing the demand fluctuations.

TABLE 10.6 **Output of Aggregate Production Planning Model**

Period	d_t	X_t	W_t	O_t	H_t	F_t	U_t	I_t^+	I_t^-
1	300	300	240	60	00	00	00	00	00
2	400	400	240	160	00	00	00	00	00
3	450	450	240	210	00	00	00	00	00
4	410	410	240	170	00	00	00	00	00
5	300	300	240	60	00	00	00	00	00
6	240	240	240	00	00	00	00	00	00

TABLE 10.7 **Output of Aggregate Production Planning Model**

Period	d_t	X_t	W_t	O_t	H_t	F_t	U_t	I_t^+	I_t^-
1	300	290	240	50	00	00	00	00	10
2	400	430	380	50	140	00	00	20	00
3	450	430	380	50	00	00	00	00	00
4	410	410	380	30	00	00	00	00	00
5	300	300	300	00	00	80	00	00	00
6	240	240	240	00	00	60	00	00	00

10.4 MASTER PRODUCTION SCHEDULE

When a large number of products are manufactured in a company, the primary use of an aggregate production plan is to level the production schedule so that the production costs are minimized. However, the output of an aggregate production plan does not indicate individual products. This means the aggregated plan must be disaggregated into individual products. A number of disaggregation methodologies have been developed (Bitran and Hax, 1977, 1981). The treatment of these approaches is beyond the scope of this book. The result of such a disaggregation is what is known as master production schedule. Does a master production schedule present an executable manufacturing plan? Not really, because the capacities and the inventories have not been considered at this stage. Therefore, further analysis for the material and capacity requirements is required to develop an executable manufacturing plan. In the following sections we discuss the basic concepts of rough-cut capacity planning, material requirements planning, and capacity planning, which are used to develop executable production plans.

10.5 ROUGH-CUT CAPACITY PLANNING

The primary objective of rough-cut capacity planning is to ensure that the master production schedule is feasible. For each product family the average amount of work needed on key work centers per unit can be calculated from each item's bill of materials and routings. The resource profile, defined as the amount of work in some meaningful unit of measure by resource per unit of output, is developed. For example, consider two families of steel cylinders and the resource profile developed in standard hours of resources per 200 units of end-product family given in Table 10.8.

TABLE 10.8 **Resource Profile for Two Product Families**

Work Center	Product Family I (Standard Hours per 200 Units)	Product Family II (Standard Hours per 200 Units)	Total Resources Required for all Families
1100	14	7	21
2100	7	20	27
3100	6	14	20
4500	25	9	34
6500	9	16	25

The available resources are compared with the resource requirements profile obtained for all the work centers considering all the product families. If the available resources are less than are required, the problem can be resolved by management decisions related to overtime, subcontracting, hiring, and so on.

10.6 MATERIAL REQUIREMENTS PLANNING

The material requirements planning system is essentially an information system consisting of logical procedures for managing inventories of component assemblies, subassemblies, parts, and raw materials in a manufacturing environment. The primary objective of an MRP system is to determine how many of each item in the bill of materials must be manufactured or purchased and when. The key concepts used in determining the material requirements are:

- Product structure and bill of materials
- Independent versus dependent demand
- Parts explosion
- Gross requirements
- Common-use items
- Scheduled receipts
- On-hand inventories
- Net requirements
- Planned order releases
- Lead time

Brief discussions of these concepts are given next.

10.6.1 Product Structure and Bill of Materials

Product is the single most important identity in an organization. The product is what a company sells to its customers. The survival of a company depends on the profit on the sales of the products. A product may be made from one or more assemblies, subassemblies, and components. The components are made from some form of raw materials. However, the types of raw materials, components, subassemblies, and final assemblies vary from product to product. For example, the types and quantities of raw materials, components, and subassemblies for a household refrigerator are different from those for a color television. To manufacture the products, it is therefore important to understand the product structure and have correct information on the components, subassemblies, and assemblies.

A bill of materials is an engineering document that specifies the components and subassemblies required to make each end item (product). It can be represented as a symbolic exploded view of the end item structure. Consider a hypothetical product called end item E1 (at level 0), which is made up of two subassemblies S1 and S2 at level 1 as shown in Figure 10.2. Subassemblies S1 and S2 at level 1 consist of two and three components at level 2, respectively. A complete product structure for product E1 is shown in Figure 10.2. The end item E1 is called a parent item to subassemblies S1 and S2, which are called component items. Similarly, subassembly S1 is a parent item to components C1 and C2 and S2 is a parent item to C3, C4, and C5. At level 3, the raw material becomes input to the components at level 2.

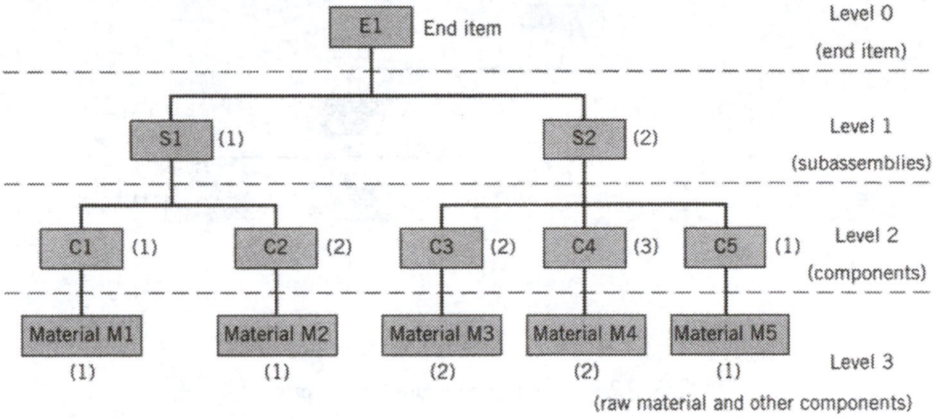

FIGURE 10.2 Product structure for hypothetical product and bill of materials.

10.6.2 Independent versus Dependent Demand

The demand for the end items originates from customer orders and forecasts. Such a demand for end items and spare parts is called independent demand. The demand by a parent item for its components is called dependent demand. For example, if the end-item demand is X number of units and one unit of end item requires Y units of a subassembly, then the demand of that subassembly is XY units.

10.6.3 Parts Explosion

The process of determining gross requirements for component items, that is, requirements for the subassemblies, components, and raw materials for a given number of end-item units, is known as parts explosion. Therefore, parts explosion essentially represents the explosion of parents into their components.

10.6.4 Gross Requirements of Component Items

To compute the gross requirements of component items, it is necessary to know the amounts of each component item required to obtain one parent item. This information is available from the product structure and the bill of materials (as indicated in parentheses beside each component item). For example, if the demand for end product E1 from a market survey in period 7 is 50 units (for product structure and the bill of materials, refer to Figure 10.2), we can determine the dependent demand (gross requirements) for the subassemblies and the components as follows:

$$\text{Demand of S1} = 1 \times \text{demand of E1} = 50 \text{ units}$$
$$\text{Demand of S2} = 2 \times \text{demand of E1} = 100 \text{ units}$$
$$\text{Demand of C1} = 1 \times \text{demand of S1} = 50 \text{ units}$$
$$\text{Demand of C2} = 2 \times \text{demand of S1} = 100 \text{ units}$$
$$\text{Demand of C3} = 2 \times \text{demand of S2} = 200 \text{ units}$$
$$\text{Demand of C4} = 3 \times \text{demand of S2} = 300 \text{ units}$$
$$\text{Demand of C5} = 1 \times \text{demand of S2} = 100 \text{ units}$$

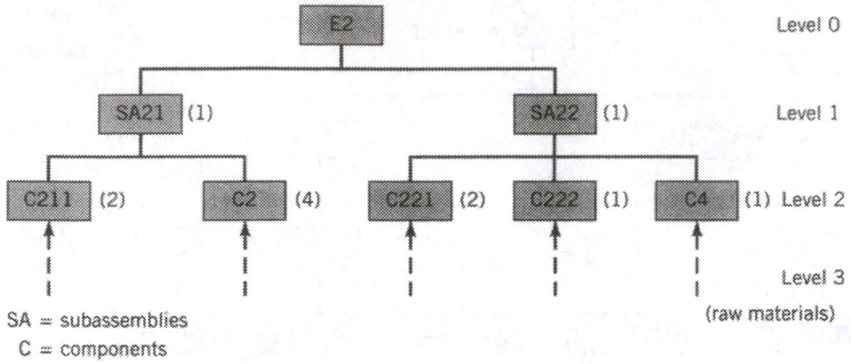

FIGURE 10.3 Product structure for end product E2.

10.6.5 Common-Use Items

Many raw materials and components may be used in several subassemblies of an end item and several end items. For example, consider the product structure for end products E1 and E2 given in Figure 10.2 and Figure 10.3, respectively. Components C2 and C4 are common to both E1 and E2. In the process of determining net requirements, common-use items (C2 and C4 in this case) must be collected from different products to ensure economies in manufacturing and purchasing these items.

10.6.6 On-Hand Inventory, Scheduled Receipts, and Net Requirements

In some cases, when there is ongoing production activity, initial inventory for some of the component items is available from previous production runs. Also, to maintain continuous production from one planning horizon to another, some inventory is planned to be available at the end of the planning horizon. This inventory is referred to as *on-hand inventory* for the current planning period. Furthermore, it takes some time for orders to arrive. Therefore, the orders placed now are delivered into some future periods. These are known as *scheduled receipts.* The *net requirements* in a period are thus obtained by subtracting the on-hand inventory and items already on order to be available in that period for these component items from the gross requirements.

10.6.7 Planned Order Releases

Planned order releases refer to the process of releasing a lot of every component item for production or purchase. The question is how the economic lot sizes of component items are determined. Because shortages are not permitted in an MRP system, the lot sizes are determined by trading off the inventory holding costs and setup costs. Although the manufacturing system is a multistage production system, the demand at each stage (level) is deterministic and time varying. Lot sizes in an MRP system are determined for component items for each stage sequentially starting with level 1, then level 2, and so on. A number of lot-sizing techniques have been developed; only that in Wagner and Whitin (1958) is optimal. A comparative analysis of some heuristic algorithms is given in Naidu and Singh (1987).

10.6.8 Lead Time and Lead Time Offsetting

The lead time is the time it takes to produce or purchase a part. In manufacturing, the lead time depends on the setup time, production time, lot size, sequence of machines on which operations are performed, queuing delays, and so forth. The purchasing lead time is the time that elapses between placing an order with a vendor and receipt of the order.

We know from the parts explosion and gross to net requirements how many of each component item (subassemblies, components, and raw materials) are needed to support a desired finished quantity of an end item. Information on the sequence in which the operations must be done and the amount of time it takes to perform these operations for a given lot size, is required to schedule the component items. The manufacture or purchase of component items must be offset by at least their lead times to ensure availability of these items for assembly into their parent items at the desired time.

EXAMPLE 10.5

Consider the product structure of end item El in Figure 10.2. The end-item demands from the master production schedule for the period of weeks 3 through 10 are 20, 30, 10, 40, 50, 30, 30, and 40 units, respectively.

TABLE 10.9 **MRP Planned Order Releases of Component Items**

	Period (Weeks)									
	1	*2*	*3*	*4*	*5*	*6*	*7*	*8*	*9*	*10*
End Item El; Lead Time 3 Weeks										
Gross requirements			20	30	10	40	50	30	30	40
On-hand inventory (50)										
Scheduled receipts										
Net requirements					10	40	50	30	30	40
Planned order release		10	40	50	30	30	40			
Component Item S2; Lead Time 2 Weeks										
Gross requirements		20	80	100	60	60	80			
On-hand inventory (100)										
Scheduled receipts	100	30								
Net requirements					30	60	80			
Planned order release			30	60	80					
Component Item C4; Lead Time 1 Week										
Gross requirements			90	180	240					
On-hand inventory (50)										
Scheduled receipts	50	20								
Net requirements				150	240					
Planned order release			150	240						
Component Item M4; Lead Time 1 Week										
Gross requirements			300	480						
On-hand inventory (150)										
Scheduled receipts	50			300						
Net requirements			100	180						
Planned order release		100	180							

The manufacturing/assembly lead times for E1, S2, and C4, ordering lead time for M4, information on on-hand inventory, and scheduled receipts are given in Table 10.9 (the solution table). Carry out the material requirements planning procedure for raw material M4 required to manufacture component C4.

Solution

The solution is presented in Table 10.9. There is on-hand inventory of 50 units for end item E1. The net requirements are obtained by first satisfying the demand from the on-hand inventory. The net requirements for E1 are then offset by three periods to obtain the planned order releases of 10, 40, 50, 30, 30, and 40 in periods 2, 3, 4, 5, 6, and 7, respectively. Now two subassemblies of S2 are needed to support E1. Accordingly, the gross requirements for S2 are obtained by doubling the planned order releases of E1. Similarly, calculations for the net requirements of S2 are carried out and the requirements are offset by 2 weeks to obtain the planned order releases. A similar process is continued for component items C4 and M4 as shown in Table 10.9.

10.7 MRP LOT-SIZING PROBLEM

The first phase of MRP is to convert the master production schedule of an end item into net requirements of a component item. The second phase is the planned coverage of such requirements, involving the problem of discrete lot sizing. Because shortages are not permitted, the problem is to determine optimal production policy to minimize the total cost, consisting of costs of setup and holding.

Mathematically, the single-item multiperiod lot-sizing problem can be stated as

Minimize

$$TC = \sum_{j=1}^{T} [(S_j + c_j x_j)a_j + h_j I_j] \tag{10.10}$$

subject to:

$$x_j + I_{j-1} - I_j = d_j \quad \text{for } j = 1, 2, \ldots, T \tag{10.11}$$

$$x_j \geq 0 \tag{10.12}$$

$$I_j \geq 0 \tag{10.13}$$

where $j = 1, 2, \ldots, T$

T = number of periods in the planning horizon

$$a_j = \begin{cases} 1 & \text{for } x_j > 0 \\ 0 & \text{for } x_j = 0 \end{cases}$$

d_j = demand in period j

x_j = production quantity in period j (a decision variable)

I_j = inventory level in period j (a decision variable)

h_j = holding cost per unit in period j

c_j = variable production cost per unit in period j

S_j = setup cost in period j

Equation (10.10) represents the total cost function consisting of setup and holding costs for all periods. The constraints given by Equation (10.11) are material balance equations that relate the inventory variables to the production variables. The constraints (10.12) ensure non-negative production levels whereas the constraints (10.13) ensure that shortages are not allowed.

10.7.1 Solution Algorithms

In this section we present two algorithms for solving the single-item multiperiod unconstrained lot-sizing problem given by Equations (10.10) and (10.11): the *Wagner and Whitin (1958) algorithm,* which assures optimal solution, and the *Naidu and Singh (1986) algorithm,* which is an efficient heuristic.

10.7.1.1 Wagner and Whitin Algorithm

The Wagner and Whitin (W–W) algorithm is based on dynamic programming (for details, see Wagner and Whitin, 1958). The following property allows us to obtain the optimal solution in an efficient manner:

$$I_{(t-1)}\, x_t = 0, \quad \text{for } t = 1, 2, \ldots, T.$$

This means that the demand in a period must be satisfied either by producing in that period or by inventory from the previous period, but not both. Accordingly, it is necessary to consider only the following values for production quantity in period t,

$$x_t\text{: } 0, d_t, d_t + d_{t+1}, \ldots, d_t + d_{t+1} + \ldots + d_T.$$

Consider a period between time instant j and k such that $I_j = 0$ and $I_k = 0$ at the end of j and k, respectively. The end of period j and k with zero level of inventory are known as regeneration points. The dynamic programming recursion that results in an optimal solution for periods 1, 2, . . . k, given $I_k = 0$, is given by the following relation:

$$Z_k = \min_{0 \le j \le k-1} (Z_j^* + C_{jk}) \qquad (k = 1, 2, \ldots, T) \tag{10.14}$$

where

$$C_{jk} = \left(S_{j+1} + c_{j+1}x_{j+1} + \sum_{t=j+1}^{k-1} h_t I_t \right)$$

and,

$$x_{j+1} = d_{j+1} + d_{j+2} + \ldots + d_k$$

$$I_t = x_{j+1} - \sum_{r=j+1}^{t} d_r = \sum_{r=t+1}^{k} d_r \qquad (t = j+1, j+2, \ldots, k-1)$$

and C_{jk} represents the total cost of production in period $j + 1$ to satisfy demand in periods $(j + 1, j + 2, \ldots, k; j = 0, 1, 2, \ldots, T - 1; k = j + 1, j + 2, \ldots, T)$. The total cost C_{jk} includes the cost of setup in period $j + 1$ given by S_{j+1}, production cost given by $c_{j+1}x_{j+1}$, and inventory holding cost over the subperiod j to k of a total planning horizon of T $(k = 1, 2, \ldots, T)$ given by $\Sigma_{t=j+1}^{k-1} h_t I_t$. Z_j^* denotes the cost of the optimal program up to the jth period and $Z_0^* = 0$.

Equation (10.14) attempts to minimize the combination of the cost of producing between two regeneration points j and k and the optimal production cost up to period j. The recursive process is carried out for all k $(k = 1, 2, \ldots, T)$ with Z_0^* equal to zero. The complexity of the W–W algorithm is $O(T^2)$. The W–W algorithm is illustrated by an example.

EXAMPLE 10.6

Consider a four-period problem having no initial inventory. The data are given in Table 10.10.

Solution

$$Z_0^* = 0$$

$$Z_1 = \min C_{01} = S_1 + c_1(d_1) = 15 + 4(20) = 95$$

Therefore, $Z_1^* = 95$.

$$Z_2 = \min \begin{cases} Z_0^* + C_{02} = S_1 + c_1(d_1 + d_2) + h_1(d_2) = 15 + 4(20 + 30) + 2(30) = 275 \\ Z_1^* + C_{12} = Z_1^* + S_2 + c_2(d_2) = 95 + 25 + 4(30) = 240 \end{cases}$$

Therefore, $Z_2^* = 240$.

$$Z_3 = \min \begin{cases} Z_0^* + C_{03} = S_1 + c_1(d_1 + d_2 + d_3) + h_1(d_2 + d_3) + h_2(d_3) \\ \qquad = 15 + 4(20 + 30 + 40) + 2(30 + 40) + 2(40) = 595 \\ Z_1^* + C_{13} = 95 + S_2 + c_2(d_2 + d_3) + h_2(d_3) = 95 + 4(30 + 40) + 2(40) \\ \qquad = 455 \\ Z_2^* + C_{23} = 240 + S_3 + c_3(d_3) = 240 + 25 + 4(40) = 425 \end{cases}$$

Therefore, $Z_3^* = 425$.

$$Z_4 = \min \begin{cases} Z_0^* + C_{04} = S_1 + c_1(d_1 + d_2 + d_3 + d_4) + h_1(d_2 + d_3 + d_4) + h_2(d_3 + d_4) \\ \qquad + h_3(d_4) \\ \qquad = 15 + 4(20 + 30 + 40 + 10) + 2(30 + 40 + 10) + 2(40 + 10) \\ \qquad + 1(10) = 685 \\ Z_1^* + C_{14} = 95 + S_2 + c_2(d_2 + d_3 + d_4) + h_2(d_3 + d_4) + h_3(d_4) \\ \qquad = 95 + 25 + 4(30 + 40 + 10) + 2(40 + 10) + 1(10) = 550 \\ Z_2^* + C_{24} = 240 + S_3 + c_3(d_3 + d_4) + h_3(d_4) = 240 + 25 + 4(40 + 10) \\ \qquad + 1(10) = 475 \\ Z_3^* + C_{34} = 425 + S_4 + c_4(d_4) = 425 + 20 + 4(10) = 485 \end{cases}$$

Therefore, $Z_4^* = 475$.

The optimal production schedule can be obtained from $Z_4^* (= Z_2^* + C_{24} = Z_1^* + C_{12} + C_{24} = C_{01} + C_{12} + C_{24})$ by tracing the solution backward. The optimal production policy can be stated as follows:

Produce 20 units in the first period to satisfy the demand of the first period.

Produce 30 units in the second period to satisfy the demand of the second period.

Produce 50 units in the third period to satisfy the demand of the third and fourth periods.

TABLE 10.10 **Data for the MRP Single-Item Multiperiod Lot-Sizing Problem**

Period j	Demand d_j	Setup Cost S_j	Unit Variable Cost c_j	Unit Holding Cost per Period h_j
1	20	15	4	2
2	30	25	4	2
3	40	25	4	1
4	10	20	4	1

10.7.1.2 Naidu and Singh Algorithm

Naidu and Singh (N–S) algorithm is based on the concept of the incremental cost approach. The basic idea is to shift the jth period demand to the preceding period p ($p < j$). By doing this, we eliminate a setup in period j and save on the cost of one setup in period j. But as a consequence of this policy, we incur a holding cost in period p. The incremental cost (IC) is then defined as the amount of change in the total cost, consisting of setup and holding cost, that would result from this proposed change in the production policy. Mathematically, it is expressed as

$$\begin{aligned} \text{IC}_j &= M && \text{for } j = 1 \text{ and } x_j = 0 \\ &= -S_j + (c_p - c_j)x_j + \sum_{q=p}^{j-1} h_q x_j && \text{for } x_j > 0 \end{aligned} \tag{10.15}$$

If variable cost of production is the same for each period, we get

$$\text{IC}_j = -S_j + \sum_{q=p}^{j-1} h_q x_j \tag{10.16}$$

where M is a large positive value to ensure production in the first period of at least the quantity sufficient to meet its requirement and also to prevent the possibility of production in the periods already having production quantity equal to zero. For other periods, the incremental cost is defined by Equation (10.15). Other parameters are defined as follows:

S_j = setup cost in period j
c_p = unit variable cost in preceding period p
c_j = unit variable cost in period j
h_q = unit holding cost per period
x_j = production quantity to be shifted into preceding period p

If the minimum of the incremental costs obtained using Equation (10.15) is negative, the maximum possible cost reduction is realized reducing the setups from t to $t - 1$ by incorporating the corresponding changes in the production policy. Similarly, minimum-cost production policies having $t - 2, t - 3, \ldots, 1$ setups can be determined by following the same logic. If the minimum of the incremental costs obtained while trying to reduce the present number of setups by one is positive, then the present production policy may be optimal or near optimal. Computational details and comparison with other heuristic algorithms are given in Naidu and Singh (1986, 1987). The computational complexity of the algorithm is $O(T)$.

The steps of the algorithm are:

Step 1: Take the demand schedule as the initial production policy, that is, $x_j = d_j$ $(j = 1, 2, \ldots, T)$.

Step 2: Compute the incremental cost for all periods except the first period using Equation (10.15). Since shortages are not permitted, the first-period demand should be satisfied from on-hand inventory if it is available; otherwise satisfy the demand through production.

Step 3: Identify the period having minimum incremental cost obtained in step 2. If the cost is negative, shift the demand of this period to its immediate preceding period, p. In case of a tie, select arbitrarily.

Step 4: Repeat steps 2 and 3 until the minimum incremental cost identified in step 2 is non-negative, signifying that the present production policy is optimal (or near optimal).

EXAMPLE 10.7

Using the Naidu and Singh heuristic, determine the lot sizing for the data given in Example 10.6.

Solution

Step 1: In the first iteration, the initial production policy is the demand schedule itself. That is, $x_j = d_j$ $(j = 1, 2, \ldots, 4)$ involving four setups.

Step 2: Compute incremental cost for all periods as shown in Table 10.11. For example, for period 2, $IC_2 = -S_2 + (c_1 - c_2)x_2 + h_1x_2 = -25 + 0 + 2(30) = +35$.

Step 3: Identify the minimum incremental cost. $IC_4 = -10$. Update the production quantities by shifting the lot from the minimum incremental cost period to the preceding period. That is, the production quantity is now (40 + 10) in period 3 and zero in period 4.

Step 4: Continue to iterate till the incremental cost is non-negative. All the costs are non-negative in the second iteration as shown in Table 10.11.

The production schedule from iteration 2 from Table 10.11 is $x_1 = 20$, $x_2 = 30$, $x_3 = 50$, and $x_4 = 0$, which is the same as obtained by the W–W algorithm for this particular example.

TABLE 10.11 **Calculations for the N–S Algorithm**

Iteration	Periods	1	2	3	4
1	x_j	20	30	40	10
	IC_j	M	+35	+55	−10
2	x_j	20	30	50	0
	IC_j	M	+35	+75	M

10.8 CAPACITY PLANNING

The planned order releases, obtained independently for each item from the MRP calculations, are tentative because the capacity limitations of the work centers have not been taken into account considering all the items to be produced during a period. To develop an executable manufacturing plan, it is essential to establish the feasibility of the planned order releases obtained from the MRP system. Capacity planning is concerned with ensuring the feasibility of production plans. The question is what to do if the plans are infeasible—how to make them feasible. Capacity planning is concerned primarily with determining resources such as labor and equipment with a view to developing what is known as an executable manufacturing plan. The capacity planning may necessitate changes in the master production schedule. The process is complex and involves a number of decisions. For example,

- Exploring overtime/multiple shifts/subcontracting options
- Developing alternative process plans for effective resource utilization
- Splitting lots
- Increasing or decreasing employment levels to respond to capacity changes
- Inventory options
- Increasing capacity by adding capital equipment such as machine tools

10.9 ORDER RELEASE

An order release essentially means a directive to work. Once it is ascertained that the production plans obtained from the MRP system are executable manufacturing plans, the orders are released to the shop floor. The documents that accompany an order include the following:

- Material inventories allocated to the order
- Routing sheets having information on operation sequences, machines, work centers, tool and fixture allocations, batch sizes, standard machine time allowed for each operation, shrinkage factor, and so forth
- Appropriate shop records such as job cards, move cards, and parts' lists for assembly jobs

These documents provide information required for completing the job order as well as monitoring the status. The order release triggers a number of activities at the shop floor. Some of the important activities are:

- Scheduling of job orders on the work centers
- Sequencing of jobs on a work center
- Allocation of jigs and fixtures
- Loading of work centers considering optimal loading conditions. For example, cutting speed, feed rate, and depth of cut in the case of metal cutting operations
- Coordination of material handling, storage, warehousing, and machine tools

In the following section we discuss some of the shop-floor control activities.

10.10 SHOP-FLOOR CONTROL

When the planned orders are released to the shop floor for manufacturing, the primary objective is to deliver the product at the right time, in the right quantities, meeting quality specifications. Schedule adherence is of primary concern for the work centers and the vendors. It is, however, important to recognize that many random events may occur that will affect schedule adherence and the eventual delivery of the products. These random events include failure of machine tools, tools, and other equipment; shortage of parts and supplies; and absence of workers. These events may force changes in the schedule. To minimize the impact of these events, what is required for production control is an efficient shop-floor data collection and information system that can be linked with the higher-level planning of orders, order releases, and detailed scheduling. Such a system must be able to provide accurate and timely information on the job orders, status of all the resources in the shop, and work status.

A number of methods are used for data collection in industries, such as

- Handwritten reports.
- Manual data entry terminals.
- Bar code readers and sensors such as optical and magnetic reading devices that automatically update an item's progress through the shop floor. (A detailed discussion of bar-coding shop-floor control systems is provided in the next section.)
- Voice data entry system, among others, depending on the type of organization.

The major functions of a shop-floor control system are to schedule job orders on the work centers, to sequence the jobs in order on a work center, and to provide accurate and timely order status information. This information includes order batch sizes, job completions, remaining jobs and operations, and time for all remaining jobs and operations.

The order status information should be updated several times per week. The work order status information thus obtained is used:

1. To monitor the progress of manufacturing activities
2. To determine priorities for scheduling jobs in the shop in response to changes in job order status
3. To maintain and control work in process
4. To provide output data for capacity control purposes

10.10.1 Bar Code Systems for Shop-Floor Control

Bar-coding technology is being used in industry for data storage and data entry for computerized information management systems. The most common types of data stored in bar codes include

- Item identification information used for inventory control
- Work-in-process tracking
- Distribution tracking
- Other manufacturing control functions such as assembly steps or process steps for monitoring the status of items in manufacturing or repair environments, inspection results, equipment settings, and failure mode.

Major elements of a bar code system include symbology, media, printer, operator, scanner, and decoder. The bar code symbology is the process of converting a computer message into bar code symbol. This may be accomplished in four steps:

Step 1: Establish the type of data to be represented and the number of characters in the message.

Step 2: Translate the human-readable information into a binary sequence. The bar code symbology used determines the number and value of the binary bits. For example, Figure 10.4 shows the human-readable character 72 being translated into the binary sequence prescribed by the 2 of 5 bar code family.

Step 3: Create a bar–space pattern that represents the binary word defined in step 2. In Figure 10.4 the narrow bar represents a logic zero and a wide bar represents a logic one for the industrial 2 of 5 code used.

Step 4: Format the individual bar code characters into a symbol that represents the complete message. The elements of a bar code symbol are start and stop margins, start and stop character patterns, data or message characters, and an optional checksum character. The optional character is used to ensure that a message character other than the one originally encoded does not enter the database.

Various bar code systems have been introduced to industry. Table 10.12 summarizes the characteristics of the six most commonly used bar codes.

10.10.1.1 Medium and Printer Selection

The medium is an optical storage device on which bar code symbols are printed. The most commonly used media in industrial applications include adhesive labels, cards, and documents. The selection criteria include optical characteristics and mechanical properties of the media. Optical characteristics of the media, for example, include surface reflectivity at a specific optical wavelength, radiation pattern, and transparency or translucency. Reflectivity means the amount of light reflected when an optical emitter irradiates the surface of the medium. Media reflecting between 70 and 90

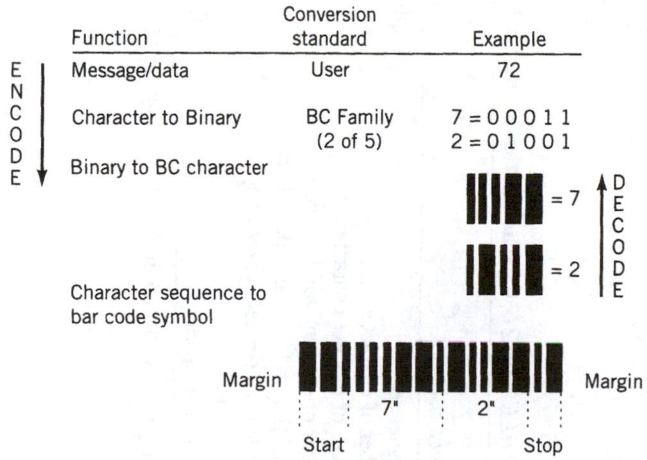

FIGURE 10.4 Symbol encode–decode sequence. (Courtesy of Hewlett-Packard Company, Components Group.)

TABLE 10.12 **Characteristics of the Six Most Commonly Used Bar Codes**

Characteristic	*3 of 9 Code*	*Industrial 2 of 5*	*Matrix 2 of 5*	*Interleaved 2 of 5*	*Codabar Code*	*Code 11*
Character set	Alphanumeric	Numeric	Numeric	Numeric	Numeric	Numeric
Number of characters	43	10	10	10	16	11
Number of bits per character	9	5	5	5	7	5
Number of element widths used	2	2	2	2	10	3
Information in both bars and spaces	Yes	No	Yes	Yes	Yes	Yes
Discrete (independent characters)	Yes	Yes	Yes	No	Yes	Yes
Self-checking	Yes	Yes	Yes	Yes	Yes	No
Checksum character	Optional	Optional	Optional	Optional	None	Recommended

Courtesy of Hewlett-Packard Company, Components Group.

percent of incident light are considered optimal. The optical pattern of light that leaves the medium surface is the reflected radiation pattern. A shiny surface results in a narrow radiation pattern that may cause operational problems for the scanner. Normally, a dull, or matte, surface is recommended to ensure that the radiation pattern will be acceptable to the scanner over a wide range of scan angles. Besides optical characteristics of the medium, durability aspects should also be considered. It is important to ensure the durability of the medium for the application; it should be given a protective coating if necessary.

Bar codes store data in a series of bars and spaces. These bars and spaces are produced when a printing mechanism deposits ink on the medium. A variety of printing techniques can be used to produce bar codes, depending on the applications. Bar code symbols on packages, containers, and cartons have been printed by commercial processes such as letterpress, lithography, offset, gravure, and flexography. Computer-controlled page printers such as ink-jet, laser, and electrostatic printers are widely used for large volumes.

10.10.1.2 Scanners

The binary data encoded in a bar code symbol are extracted by an optical system that consists of an emitter, a detector, and an optical lens. The emitter scans a beam of light over the symbol while the detector simultaneously responds to changes in the reflected light levels. In general, scanners can be classified into three categories: hand-held contact type, hand-held noncontact type, and fixed station system. Figure 10.5*a* shows a laser bar code scanner that can scan at rates up to 1000 scans per second and can read at distances in the range 1 to 50 in. Figure 10.5*b* shows a moving-beam laser scanner designed for use in material handling, warehousing, and manufacturing applications. The scan rate is over 1700 scans per second.

10.10.1.3 Bar Code Readers

A bar code decoder acts as data interpreter or translator of the data provided by the scanner. It converts the serial data into ASCII data or other binary-coded data, which

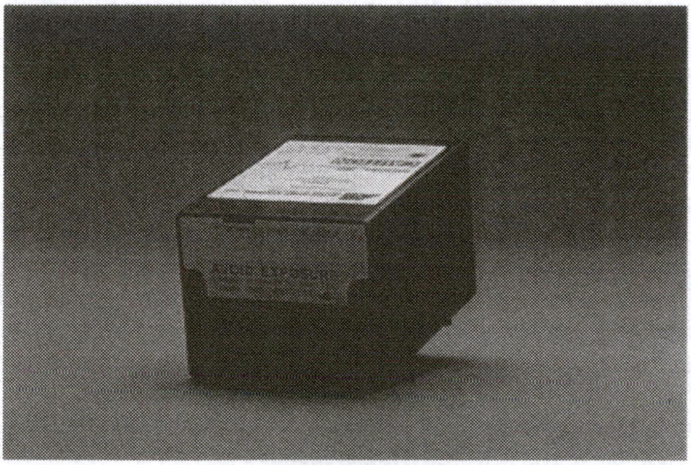

(*a*)

FIGURE 10.5 (*a*) Bar code laser scanner (courtesy of ACCU-SORT Systems, Inc.). (*b*) Moving-beam bar code laser scanner (courtesy of ACCU-SORT Systems, Inc.).

(*b*)

FIGURE 10.5 (continued)

are then formatted into a specific communication protocol for transmission to the host computer. The bar code reader that houses the decoder generally includes a scanner and also performs other functions in addition to decoding and data transmission. These functions may include any or all of the following:

- Audio operator feedback (beeper)
- Visual operator feedback
- Alternative data entry technique (keyboard, magnetic strip)
- User programming of feedback, data formatting, and terminal functions.

10.10.1.4 A Framework for Shop-Floor Control Using Bar Codes

A bar code system may be a very efficient, effective, and economical means of shop-floor control by making information available in real time. Bar codes can be used to encode information such as order and component identification, component location, process routing and assembly steps, equipment configuration settings, and quality and reliability tests.

Let us consider a typical discrete-part manufacturing facility to understand the applications of a bar code system for shop-floor control. This manufacturing facility receives several orders every day with unique requirements. Every order may have a due date and processing, quality, and shipping requirements. Orders may also have different priorities for processing. For example, the company may entertain rush orders. In such a situation shop control can be facilitated by making real-time information available to all the processing workstations. Furthermore, information will be collected from these workstations to update shop-floor information, such as number of components produced, quality test results, and equipment status. As soon as an order arrives, it is assigned a bar code encoding all the relevant information. In certain cases, an order may be split into several lots. In that case, each lot will be assigned a bar code. Resources (e.g., material, tools, jigs, fixtures, pallets) required for this order or lot will be released to the shop with attached bar codes. When an order arrives at a work center, the operator will scan the bar code with the help of a bar code reader attached to a microcomputer. As shown in Figure 10.6, these microcomputers are linked to a main

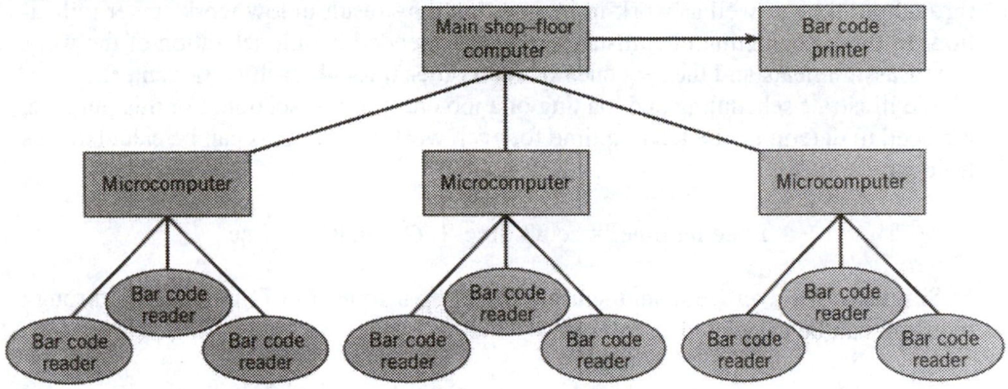

FIGURE 10.6 A framework for shop-floor control using bar codes.

shop-floor computer for immediate database update. The operator retrieves updated process planning and scheduling information from the main computer. Once the order is processed at the workstation, the operator again enters the required data and routes the order to the next station.

At the final processing and assembly station, when the order is complete, the operator enters the actual number of parts produced and the number of carton labels required. The bar code label for the finished product may be printed on a printer located in the receiving–shipping area. Having the labels printed in this area alerts warehouse personnel that the order is ready to be received into inventory and final shipment.

10.10.2 Operations Scheduling

What happens when work orders are released to the shop floor? Two major but very difficult activities are performed:

1. The work orders are assigned to the work centers such that due dates are satisfied. Allocation of jobs to work centers is referred to as machine loading.
2. The sequence of each work order through each work center is determined. This process is referred to as job sequencing.

Machine loading and job sequencing are two of the several important functions of a shop-floor control system. There could be a number of scheduling objectives, depending on the manufacturing situation. However, some of the objectives that typically apply to scheduling problems are:

- Meeting due dates
- Minimizing manufacturing throughput time
- Minimizing work-in-process
- Maximizing work center utilization

These objectives may sometimes be conflicting. For example, consider work center capacity that is not sufficient to meet due dates for the work orders. All the capacity is used, and consequently the work center utilization is very high. Now, if we add more work center capacity, the possibility of meeting due dates is high but work center utilization may be low. Similarly, more capacity can reduce the manufacturing throughput time as well as work-in-process but may result in low work center utilization. In these conflicting circumstances, what is needed is rationalization of the work center assignments and the sequence of each order through each work center.

We illustrate scheduling and loading of a job order in this section. For this purpose, we need to determine the loading time for each work center. This can be calculated as follows:

$$\text{Loading time} = \text{setup time} + Q * \text{unit run time}$$

Similarly, the average manufacturing throughput time (MTT) of an order through the shop can be calculated as follows:

$$\text{MTT} = \text{setup time} + Q * \text{unit run time} + \text{move and queue time}$$

where Q is the order size and unit run time is the time to process one job (or operation). Move and queue time refers to time spent in moving from one work center to another and waiting in a queue before being processed. It accounts for 80 to 90 percent of manufacturing throughput time, and it depends on the scheduling rules as well. For certain operations, such as heat treating, plating, and inspection, the standard time estimates per piece are not usually available. Therefore, for such operations, the time allowances are used for the setup, run, move and queue times.

In the following example we illustrate detailed scheduling and loading of a job order on five work centers and one inspection center having a coordinate measuring machine.

EXAMPLE 10.8

The Detroit-Any-Job Finishing (DAJF) company received an order for 1000 steel parts to be delivered on day 1 of week 12 from now. The job order requires turning, drilling, face milling, gear teeth cutting, and broaching operations in that sequence. Inspection is done on a coordinate measuring machine for which the time standards are available. The setup and unit run times for these workstations are (3, 0.02), (2, 0.01), (5, 0.03), (9, 0.05), (6, 0.04), and (5, 0.005), respectively. The first entry in the parentheses is setup time and the second is the unit run time. The DAJF has two-shift operation. To allow for efficiency and unmeasured activities as well as indirect work, the standard hours available to work each day are 12. Develop a detailed scheduling and loading for the example data. The allowance for move and queue time between operations in the departments is one work day.

Solution

The solution, given in Table 10.13, is obtained by starting at the finish date and working backward up the routing.

Each week consists of 5 working days. The due date is week 12, day 1. The inspection work is worth one day ($5 + 0.005 \times 1000 = 10$ hrs $\simeq$ one work day). Accordingly, the start date is week 11, day 5. Because there is one work day allowance for move and queue time between operations in the departments, the due date for the broaching operation is week 11, day 4. The broaching operation takes a total of 46 hours, approximately four work days. Therefore, the start date is week 10, day 5. The complete schedule and loading for the problem are given in Table 10.13.

TABLE 10.13 **Scheduling and Loading for Example 10.8**

Part Number: DAJFS1000 Order Number: DAJF-WPP10
Quantity = 1000 Due Date: Week 12, Day 1 Start Date: Week 7, Day 5

Work Center	*Setup Time (h)*	*Unit Run Time (h)*	*Loading Time (Setup + Run Time) (h)*	*Start Date*	*Due Date*
Turning	3	0.02	23	Week 7, day 5	Week 8, day 2
Drilling	2	0.01	12	Week 8, day 3	Week 8, day 4
Face milling	5	0.03	35	Week 8, day 5	Week 9, day 3
Gear teeth cutting	9	0.05	59	Week 9, day 4	Week 10, day 4
Broaching	6	0.04	46	Week 10, day 5	Week 11, day 4
Inspection	5	0.005	10	Week 11, day 5	Week 12, day 1

10.10.3 Job Sequencing and Priority Rules

In real-life discrete-part manufacturing situations, the total number of jobs normally exceeds the number of work centers, resulting in a queue of jobs to be processed. To process the jobs in the queue, we need to develop priority rules to determine the sequence in which to process the jobs on a work center. A number of priority rules have been used in industry; Panwalkar and Iskander (1977) have listed 113 such scheduling rules. Some of the simple rules used in industry include:

1. *First-come, first-served* (FCFS) rule assigns jobs on a first-come, first-served basis. This rule is "blind" with respect to all other important information such as due dates and urgent jobs
2. *Shortest processing time* (*SPT*) rule gives the highest priority to the job with the shortest processing time. This rule results in the lowest mean completion time (that is, average manufacturing lead time) and consequently the lowest work-in-process inventory.
3. *Earliest due date* (*EDD*) rule gives the highest priority to jobs with the earliest due date.
4. *Least slack* (*LS*) rule assigns the highest priority to the job with least slack. The slack is defined as follows:

$$\text{Slack} = \text{time remaining until due date} - \text{lead time remaining}$$

5. *Least slack per operation* (*LSPO*) rule assigns priority based on the smallest value obtained by dividing the slack by the number of remaining operations.
6. *Critical ratio* (*CR*) rule assigns priority based on a critical index defined as follows:

$$\text{Critical ratio} = \frac{\text{time remaining until due date}}{\text{lead time remaining}}$$

where

$$\text{Time remaining until due date} = \text{due date} - \text{now}$$

and lead time includes setup, run, move, and queue times.

The least slack, least slack per operation, critical ratio, and earliest due date rules consider the relative urgency of jobs. We illustrate these rules by a simple example.

EXAMPLE 10.9

The Windsor Steel Cylinder Manufacturing company has received orders for type A, B, C, and D cylinders on day 10 on the production schedule calendar at a finishing workstation in that order. The orders are coded as A, B, C, and D for ease of presentation in this example. The following data are available:

Job Types	*Due Date*	*Remaining Process Time*	*Number of Remaining Operations*
A	17	4	8
B	29	18	18
C	27	8	16
D	26	12	2

Determine the order in which the jobs should be processed according to the FCFS, EDD, SPT, LS, SPO, and CR rules. Also determine the mean completion time and average job lateness for each priority rule.

Solution

FCFS Rule

According to the first-come, first-served rule, the sequence is A, B, C, and D.

SPT Rule

According to the SPT rule, the sequence is A, C, D, and B.

EDD Rule

According to the earliest due date rule, the sequence is A, D, C, and B.

Least Slack Rule

To use the slack rule, we first determine the slack using the following formula:

$$\text{Slack} = \text{time remaining until due date} - \text{lead time remaining}$$

For job A, slack $= (17 - 10) - 4 = 3$ days

For job B, slack $= (29 - 10) - 18 = 1$ day

For job C, slack $= (27 - 10) - 8 = 9$ days

For job D, slack $= (26 - 10) - 12 = 4$ days

Therefore, the job sequence according to the least slack rule is B, A, D, and C.

Least Slack per Operation Rule

To use this rule, we determine the slack per operation as follows:

$$\text{Slack} = \frac{\text{time remaining until due date} - \text{lead time remaining}}{\text{number of operations remaining}}$$

For job A, the slack per operation = 3/8 = 0.375

For job B, the slack per operation = 1/18 = 0.055

For job C, the slack per operation = 9/16 = 0.5625

For job D, the slack per operation = 4/2 = 2

Therefore, the job sequence according to least slack per operation is B, A, C, and D.

Critical Ratio Rule

We determine the critical ratios for all jobs by using the formula

$$\text{Critical ratio} = \frac{\text{time remaining until due date}}{\text{lead time remaining}}$$

For job A, slack = (17 − 10)/4 = 1.75 days

For job B, slack = (29 − 10)/18 = 1.05 days

For job C, slack = (27 − 10)/8 = 2.125 days

For job D, slack = (26 − 10)/12 = 1.33 days

The sequence is therefore B, D, A, and C.

The sequences obtained by using different rules defined earlier are summarized below:

Sequencing Priority Rule	***Sequence of Jobs***
FCFS rule	A, B, C, D
SPT rule	A, C, D, B
EDD rule	A, D, C, B
LS rule	B, A, D, C
LSPO rule	B, A, C, D
CR rule	B, D, A, C

For this example, we have different sequences of jobs corresponding to each rule. This is typical of any discrete manufacturing environment. Therefore, the selection of rules to sequence the jobs should be carefully made to reflect the need of the shop floor. This issue is discussed in section 10.10.4.

10.10.4 Comparison of Various Scheduling Rules

The various scheduling rules can be compared if we have some common performance measures. We discuss two important performance measures: *mean completion time,* and *average lateness.*

10.10.4.1 Mean Completion Time

The mean completion time depends on the sequence of jobs and is given by

$$\text{Mean completion time} = \sum_{i=1}^{m} \frac{(m - i + 1)p_{[i]}}{m}$$

where $p_{[i]}$ denotes processing time for a job in the ith position in the sequence in a set of m jobs.

10.10.4.2 Average Lateness

The lateness is defined as $L_i = C_i - d_i$, where C_i is the completion time of the ith job and d_i is the due date for the ith job. Accordingly, the average lateness is defined as

$$\text{Average lateness} = \sum_{i=1}^{m} \frac{C_i - d_i}{m}$$

Remember, lateness is a measure that considers both early and late completions. However, we may be interested in knowing late completions only. A measure known as tardiness considers such a situation and is defined as follows:

$$\text{Tardiness for job } i \qquad T_i = \max(0, L_i).$$

Accordingly, the average tardiness is defined as

$$\text{Average tardiness} = \sum_{i=1}^{m} \frac{T_i}{m}$$

EXAMPLE 10.10

Consider the data of Example 10.9. Determine the mean completion time and the average tardiness for all the scheduling rules considered in that example.

Solution

Mean Completion Time

Consider the SPT rule. The sequence is A, C, D, and B and the respective processing times are 4, 8, 12, and 18 days. The number of jobs $m = 4$ and $p_{[1]} = 4$, $p_{[2]} = 8$, $p_{[3]} = 12$, $p_{[4]} = 18$.

We first have to determine the completion times of the jobs in the sequence.

Completion time of job A, $C_1 = 4$ days

Completion time of job C, $C_2 = 4 + 8 = 12$ days

Completion time of job D, $C_3 = 4 + 8 + 12 = 24$ days

Completion time of job B, $C_4 = 4 + 8 + 12 + 18 = 42$ days

Therefore

$$\text{Mean completion time} = \frac{C_1 + C_2 + C_3 + C_4}{4}$$

$$= \frac{4 + 12 + 24 + 42}{4} = 20.5 \text{ days}$$

Average Tardiness

Since the orders are received on day 10, the due dates have to be adjusted by subtracting 10 from due dates given in Example 10.9. Therefore,

$$\text{Tardiness of job A} = \max(0, C_1 - d_1) = \max(0, 4 - 7) = 0$$

$$\text{Tardiness of job C} = \max(0, C_2 - d_2) = \max(0, 12 - 17) = 0$$

$$\text{Tardiness of job D} = \max(0, C_3 - d_3) = \max(0, 24 - 16) = 8$$

$$\text{Tardiness of job B} = \max(0, C_4 - d_4) = \max(0, 42 - 19) = 23$$

Therefore,

$$\text{Average tardiness} = \frac{0 + 0 + 8 + 23}{4} = 3.875 \text{ days}$$

The mean completion time and average tardiness for all the rules are summarized below:

Scheduling Rules	*Mean Completion Time (Days)*	*Average Tardiness (Days)*
FCFS	24.5	10.50
SPT	20.5	3.875
EDD	25	7.50
LS	29	14.50
LSPO	28	13.50
CR	31	17.00

This example reveals that the SPT rule outperforms all other rules with respect to mean completion time and average tardiness for the given data. However, the conclusions might change if the data were altered or there was a different assessment criterion.

Scheduling n job orders on a single work center was attempted and illustrated by examples. The scheduling of n job orders on m work centers to minimize makespan subject to due date constraints is known to be a very difficult problem; in operations research terminology it is known as an NP-hard problem. Such a treatment is beyond the scope of this book. Normally, Gantt charts are used to help develop feasible schedules for a set of job orders on a set of work centers.

10.11 SUMMARY

Manufacturing planning and control is concerned with manufacturing the right product types, in the right quantities, at the right time, at minimum cost and meeting quality standards. Manufacturing planning and control is the heart of manufacturing firms. Market barriers are coming down, and the market is now open to global competition. Furthermore, the technical complexity of products is increasing; the market demands shorter product life cycles, high quality, and low costs. To compete in such an environment, it is important to have an integrated manufacturing planning and control system. It is all the more important to understand various aspects of a manufacturing planning and control system and their interactions in designing and developing an integrated system.

In this chapter, an attempt was made to provide a framework for understanding the basic elements of an integrated manufacturing planning and control system. A conceptual understanding of demand management, aggregate production planning, master production schedule, rough-cut capacity planning, material requirements planning, detailed capacity planning, order release, and shop-floor scheduling and control was provided. These concepts were illustrated by numerical examples.

PROBLEMS

10.1 Discuss the following elements of a manufacturing planning and control system:
(a) Demand management
(b) Aggregate production planning
(c) Master production schedule
(d) Rough-cut capacity planning
(e) Material requirements planning
(f) Capacity planning
(g) Order release
(h) Shop-floor scheduling and control

10.2 Discuss advantages of an integrated manufacturing planning and control system.

10.3 Demand forecasting is an important input to aggregate production planning. Discuss.

10.4 For the last 8 weeks the demand for a $\frac{1}{2}$-in. high-pressure steel cylinder for the Windsor Steel Cylinder Manufacturing Company was: $x_1 = 200$, $x_2 = 220$, $x_3 = 190$, $x_4 = 240$, $x_5 = 230$, $x_6 = 231$, $x_7 = 228$, $x_8 = 210$. Develop the forecast for the ninth week using a four-period moving-average method.

10.5 For the data given in Problem 10.4, use the simple exponential smoothing method to forecast the demand of steel cylinders for the ninth week. Use $\alpha = 0.30$.

10.6 Data on the expected aggregated sales of four products, A, B, C, and D, over a planning horizon of six 4-week periods are given in Table P10.1. The company has developed machining-cell hours as a common unit for aggregation purposes. In this case products A and C require 2 cell-hours per unit whereas products B and D require only 1 cell-hour per unit. The company has a regular production capacity of 400 cell-hours per period, which can be varied up to 500 cell-hours per period. Overtime is permitted up to a maximum of 180 cell-hours per period. Requirements exceeding overtime capacity can be satisfied by subcontracting. Two alternative production policies are developed as follows:

Plan I: Produce at the constant rate of 600 cell-hours per period for the entire planning horizon.

Plan II: Produce at the rate of 700 cell-hours per period for the first four periods and then at the rate of 400 cell-hours per period for the subsequent periods.

TABLE P10.1 **Demand Forecast (in Units) for Products A, B, C, and D**

Period	*Product A*	*Product B*	*Product C*	*Product D*
1	50	60	70	80
2	80	80	40	100
3	110	40	120	70
4	70	210	190	40
5	160	180	200	50
6	100	60	70	110

Analyze two aggregate production plans suggested by the production department of the company.

10.7 Develop an optimal aggregate production plan in terms of cell-hours for the forecast demand data given in Problem 10.6. Other data are: c_x = \$120/h, c_o = \$40/h, c_w = \$24/h, c_h = \$24/h, c_f = \$40/h, c_i = \$5/unit/h, c_s = \$500/unit/h, c_u = \$60/h. The initial regular work force level W_0 = 240 labor hours per hour.

10.8 Consider the product structure of end item PR-1 given in Figure P10.1. The end-item demand from the master production schedule for the period of weeks 3, 4, 5, 6, 7, 8, 9, and 10 is 40, 30, 20, 10, 50, 30, 70, and 20 units, respectively.

The manufacturing and assembly lead times for PR-1, SA-12, and C-122 and the ordering lead time for M-4 are given below. Carry out the material requirements planning procedure for raw material M-4 required to manufacture component C-122 if one unit of M-4 is required to produce one unit of C-122.

Lead time for assembling PR-1 = 1 week.

Lead time for assembling SA-12 = 1 week.

Lead time for manufacturing C-122 = 2 week; 100 units on-hand inventory are given and 40 units are scheduled to arrive in period 2.

Procurement lead time for raw material M4 = 1 week; 40 units on-hand inventory are available.

10.9 Consider a five-period problem having an initial inventory of 30 units. The data are given in Table P10.2: Using W-W algorithm, determine optimal lot sizes.

10.10 Using the Naidu and Singh heuristic, determine the lot sizing for the data given in Problem 10.9.

10.11 The Johnson and Johnson (JJ) Company has received an order for 10,000 spark plugs from Canadian Tires. The order must be delivered on day 1 of week 18 from now. The job order requires five operations, including assembly, designated as O1, O2, O3, O4, and O5 in that sequence. The setup and unit run times in hours for these work stations are (5, 0.002), (4, 0.001), (5, 0.003), (8, 0.005), and (4, 0.004) respectively. The first

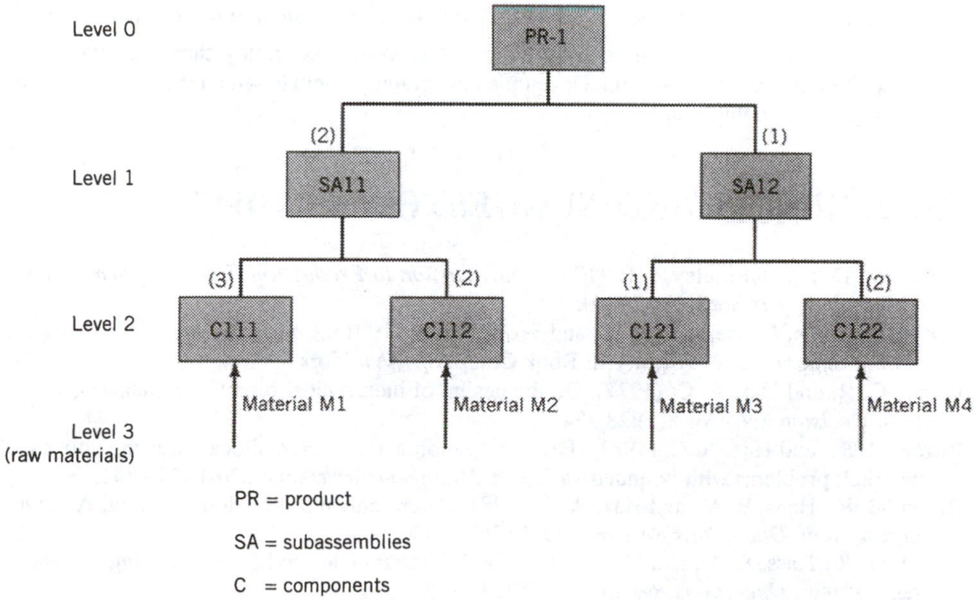

FIGURE P10.1 Product structure for end item PR-1.

TABLE P10.2 **Data for the MRP Single-Item Multiperiod Lot-Sizing Problem**

Period j	Demand d_j	Setup Cost S_j	Unit Variable Cost c_j	Unit Holding Cost per Period h_j
1	20	10	4	3
2	30	20	4	3
3	50	20	4	1
4	10	10	4	2
5	60	30	4	2

entry in parentheses is setup time and the second is the unit run time. JJ has two-shift operation. To allow for efficiency, unmeasured activities, and indirect work, the standard hours available to work each day are 12. Develop detailed scheduling and loading for the example data given.

10.12 The Washington-Any-Job-Finished company has received four job orders A, B, C, and D on day 10 on the production schedule calendar for machining work on their vertical numerical control (NC) milling center in that order. The orders are coded A, B, C, and D for ease of presentation in this example. The following data are available:

Job Type	***Due Date***	***Remaining Process Time***	***Number of Remaining Operations***
A	23	4	8
B	15	8	16
C	13	9	18
D	22	7	14

Determine the order in which the jobs should be processed according to the FCFS, EDD, SPT, LS, SPO, and CR rules. Also, determine the mean completion time and average job lateness for each priority rule.

10.13 Consider the data of Problem 10.12. Determine the average manufacturing lead time and the average tardiness for all the scheduling rules considered in Problem 10.12.

10.14 Visit at least one manufacturing company in your area. Study their manufacturing planning and control system. Develop an integrated system based on the generic system suggested in this chapter.

REFERENCES AND SUGGESTED READING

Bedworth, D. D., and Bailey, J. E. (1987). *Introduction to Production Control Systems,* 2nd ed. John Wiley & Sons, New York.

Bedworth, D. D., Henderson, M. R., and Wolfe, P. M. (1991). *Computer-Integrated Design and Manufacturing.* McGraw-Hill Book Company, New York.

Bitran, G. R. and Hax, A. C. (1977). On the design of hierarchical production planning systems. *Decision Sciences* 8(1):28–54.

Bitran, G. R., and Hax, A. C. (1981). Dis-aggregation and resource allocation using convex knapsack problems with bounded variables. *Management Science* 27(4):431–441.

Bitran, G. R., Haas, E. A., and Hax, A. C. (1981). Hierarchical production planning: A single stage system. *Operations Research* 29(4):717–743.

Bitran, G. R., Hass, E. A., and Hax, A. C. (1982). Hierarchical production planning: A two stage system. *Operations Research* 30(2):232–251.

Collins, D. J., and Whipple, N. N. (1990). *Using Bar Code: Why It's Taking Over.* Data Capture Institute, Dusbury, Massachusetts.

Eric, T., and Orr, J. N. (1987). *Computer-Integrated Manufacturing Handbook.* McGraw-Hill Book Company, New York.

Groover, M. P., and Zimmers, E. W., Jr. (1984). *CAD/CAM Computer-Aided Design and Manufacturing.* Prentice Hall, Englewood Cliffs, New Jersey.

Hax, A. C., and Candea, D. (1984). *Production and Inventory Management.* Prentice Hall, Englewood Cliffs, New Jersey.

Hewlett-Packard. (1983). Elements of a bar code system. Application Note 1013. Hewlett-Packard Corporation, San Jose, California.

Johnson, L. A., and Montgomery, D. C. (1974). *Operations Research in Production Planning, Scheduling, and Inventory Control.* John Wiley & Sons, New York.

Montgomery, D. C. and Johnson, L. A. (1976). *Forecasting and Time Series Analysis.* McGraw Hill Book Company, New York.

Naidu, M. M., and Singh, N. (1986). Lot sizing for material planning systems—an incremental cost approach. *International Journal of Production Research* 24(1):223–240.

Naidu, M. M., and Singh, N. (1987). Further investigations on the performance of incremental cost approach for lot sizing for material requirements planning systems. *International Journal of Production Research* 25(8):1241–1246.

Orlicky, J. A. (1975). *Material Requirements Planning: The New Way of Life in Production and Inventory Management.* McGraw-Hill, New York.

Panwalkar, S. S., and Iskander, W. (1977). A survey of scheduling rules. *Operations Research* 25(1):45–61.

Sobczak, T. V., and King, R. E. (1985). *Applying Industrial Bar Coding.* Society of Manufacturing Engineers, Dearborn, Michigan.

Vollman, T. E., Berry, W. L., and Whyback, D. C. (1984). *Manufacturing Planning and Control Systems.* Richard D. Irwin, Homewood, Illinois.

Wagner, H., and Whitin, T. (1958). Dynamic version of economic lotsize model. *Management Science* 5:89–96.

APPENDIX

DETAILED FORMULATION FOR EXAMPLE 10.4

MIN 100X1 + 14W1 + 20O1 + 50 U1 + 3I1 + 400B1 + 14H1 + 30F1
100X2 + 14W2 + 20O2 + 50 U2 + 3I2 + 400B2 + 14H2 + 30F2
100X3 + 14W3 + 20O3 + 50 U3 + 3I3 + 400B3 + 14H3 + 30F3
100X4 + 14W4 + 20O4 + 50 U4 + 3I4 + 400B4 + 14H4 + 30F4
100X5 + 14W5 + 20O5 + 50 U5 + 3I5 + 400B5 + 14H5 + 30F5
100X6 + 14W6 + 20O6 + 50 U6 + 3I6 + 400B6 + 14H6 + 30F6

SUBJECT TO:

X1 − I1 + B1 = 300
X2 + I1 − B1 − I2 + B2 = 400
X3 + I2 − B2 − I3 + B3 = 450
X4 + I3 − B3 − I4 + B4 = 410
X5 + I4 − B4 − I5 + B5 = 300
X6 + I5 − B5 − I6 + B6 = 240
− W1 + H1 − F1 = 0
− W2 + W1 + H2 − F2 = 0
− W3 + W2 + H3 − F3 = 0
− W4 + W3 + H4 − F4 = 0
− W5 + W4 + H5 − F5 = 0
− W6 + W5 + H6 − F6 = 0
O1 − U1 − X1 + W1 = 0
O2 − U2 − X2 + W2 = 0
O3 − U3 − X3 + W3 = 0
O4 − U4 − X4 + W4 = 0
O5 − U5 − X5 + W5 = 0
O6 − U6 − X6 + W6 = 0
X_t, W_t, O_t, U_t, I_t, B_t, H_t, F_t, 7, 0 for all t
END

Note: The letters B and I refer to backorders and inventory, which are represented by I^- and I^+, respectively, in the model in Section 10.3.1. Add overtime constraints as needed.

CHAPTER 11

JUST-IN-TIME MANUFACTURING SYSTEMS

In this chapter we discuss the Toyota production system, which pervades all aspects of the production and inventory flow process. The Toyota production system covers areas such as process design, job design, job standardization, economic lot sizes, accelerated setup times, just-in-time production, autonomation, kanban, jidoka, andon, and yo-i-don. The most distinctive and dominant among these is the just-in-time production system. In a just-in-time (JIT) production system, only the necessary products, at the necessary time, in the necessary quantity are manufactured and stock on hand is held to a minimum. We discuss various design, planning, and control aspects of a JIT production system. Other issues such as alternative JIT systems, JIT purchasing, total quality control, potential problems in JIT implementation, and potential benefits of JIT are also covered.

11.1 TOYOTA PRODUCTION SYSTEM: AN OVERVIEW

The Toyota production system is a production flow and inventory control system. It is designated as the Toyota production system because it was developed by Mr. Taiichi Ohno, a vice president of Toyota Motor Company, to achieve objectives that include:

- Reducing costs by eliminating all kinds of waste
- Making it easier to achieve and assure product quality
- Attempting to create work sites that respond quickly to change
- Organizing work sites based on human dignity, mutual trust and support, and allowing workers to realize their potential to the fullest.

The system has been in operation for more than 20 years. It is now being used in many Japanese and North American automobile companies and other manufacturing plants.

11.1.1 Components of the Toyota Production System

The Toyota production system (TPS) (Sugimori et al., 1977; Pegels, 1984; Monden,1983) is an integrated approach to production, utilizing existing facilities, materials, and labor as efficiently as possible and making all-out efforts to eliminate muda (waste), mura (unevenness), and muri (overburden). The TPS pervades all aspects of the production and inventory flow process. The TPS covers areas such as

- Process design, job design, and job standardization
- Economic lot sizes and accelerated setup times
- Just-in-time production
- Autonomation
- Kanban
- Jidoka/andon
- Yo-i-don

Autonomation is not misspelled; it is a Toyota-coined word that refers to manual or automatic stopping of production if a defective part is produced.

Kanban is a system of cards used to control work-in-process, production, and inventory flow.

Jidoka refers to a production problem warning system consisting of a battery of yellow and red lights called *andon.* A yellow light indicates a minor problem or a slight delay, whereas a red light is indicative of serious problems such as production or assembly line stoppage.

Yo-i-don refers to a coordinated approach to simultaneous production of parts or subassemblies for assembly into a next-stage subassembly.

The most distinctive and dominant among these is the *just-in-time* production subsystem, which is the cornerstone of the Toyota production system. The key element of JIT production is the kanban system of tags or cards attached to the parts and subassembly containers. The kanban system is an essential tool for managing and controlling the pull type (just-in-time) of production inherent in the Toyota production system. We will discuss these two subsystems in detail.

Let us first understand the problem areas in any production situation that are primarily responsible for higher production costs, low quality, and increased delivery times. We will then discuss the need for rationalized production methods and how implementation of the JIT production philosophy helps achieve the goals of minimum production costs, higher quality, and quick delivery times. In this context we discuss the elements of waste known as the three Ms of muda, mura, and muri in the TPS.

11.1.2 Three Ms: Muda (Waste), Mura (Unevenness), and Muri (Overburden)

Unit cost, quality, and lead time are three major determinants of market share and profitability of any organization. To a large extent, the costs depend on the production methods and the way the production is organized. Therefore, to achieve the objectives of minimum production costs and reduced lead times while maintaining total quality, it is necessary to use rational manufacturing techniques that help eliminate muda, mura, and muri.

Let us understand muda and its various elements. *Muda* is a Japanese word referring to any work or any element of production that does not add value to the product. In contrast, *shigoto* refers to the actual work that adds value to the product. In most manufacturing situations, shigoto is relatively small compared with muda. Therefore, it is important to eliminate muda. We need to design, plan, and control manufacturing systems such that waste is eliminated. The job attitude of looking for muda and finding ways to eliminate it is called *kaizen.* Kaizen is central to the TPS way of thinking.

In TPS, muda has been classified into a number of categories, such as correction, overproduction, processing, conveyance, inventory, motion, and waiting. There is essentially nothing new in these concepts. As engineers and managers we have been taught that only operations add value to the product and other functions such as inspection, transportation, and delays of a permanent or temporary nature should be eliminated, if possible, or reduced to the minimum possible limits. We provide a brief discussion of various types of muda in the following.

1. *Muda for correction.* The rework process necessary for correcting a defective part means extra costs that should have been avoided in the first place.

2. *Muda of overproduction.* Overproduction may result from either producing more than necessary or producing at a higher rate than required or both. Overproduced items have to be stocked, thus unnecessarily using production and material-handling equipment. Moreover, the chances of *kaizen* are reduced, thereby increasing costs. The just-in-time principle in TPS takes care of these problems by producing the right product in the right quantities at the right time.

3. *Muda for processing.* This refers to unnecessary processing work that has no connection to adding value to the product.

4. *Muda in conveyance.* Material handling is an important element of production. However, it does not add value to the product and is therefore a kind of muda. Thus any material handling (conveyance) not required in the just-in-time production system is a waste of resources.

5. *Muda for inventory.* Inventory may be considered a necessary evil. It is necessary because it helps absorb shocks due to uncertainties in supplies and acts as insurance against emergencies. It is an evil because inventories mean loss of investment opportunity. Implementation of the JIT production philosophy helps eliminate uncertainties, so that inventory can be reduced to the minimum necessary.

6. *Muda of motion.* Any unnecessary movement of workers, materials, or production and material-handling equipment that does not add value to the product is a muda of motion. Proper workplace layout design having the necessary materials and tools can help eliminate muda of motion.

7. *Muda for waiting.* Normally, in automated production situations, workers may find themselves idle waiting for the machine to complete its stage of automatic processing. Productive use of workers' time is a key to improving productivity and reducing costs. Constant awareness of muda of this kind helps achieve these objectives.

We now turn our attention to the other concepts, known as mura and muri, that TPS uses to limit production costs and preserve quality.

Mura literally means unevenness. There can be a number of reasons for unevenness; for example, irregular production volumes, changing work flows, and changing production schedules may cause mura. This essentially means that the workloads on the machines are not balanced. In such a situation, in order to avoid shortages, capacity is usually planned considering the peak level of production. This, obviously, increases the cost of production.

Muri essentially means stretching beyond capacity limits, overburdening the capacities of people as well as machines. An excessive workload on the people beyond their normal capacities leads to safety and quality problems. Similarly, too much loading of machines results in breakdowns and defects, resulting in increased costs and lead time as well as poor quality.

We mentioned earlier that the unit cost, quality, and lead time are the three major determinants of market share and profitability. Therefore, it is essential to have rational production methods in which all employees work together to help achieve the goals of low cost, high quality, and reduced delivery times. One of the key elements of rational production methodology is the just-in-time philosophy. In the following sections we present a thorough understanding of JIT methodology, analytical modeling, and application of JIT principles to various industries.

The production control system used in most North American companies is normally based on a material requirements planning (MRP) system. It is also known as a *push system.* The work-in-process inventory is used as a means of absorbing uncertainties in the processes and changes in demand. In practice, however, such a system often creates the following problems:

- It may lead to starvation and excessive stocks simultaneously at different stages because of imbalances of stocks between the stages.
- It may lead to conditions of having excessive equipment and a surplus of workers.

In order to avoid these problems of dead stocks, excessive equipment, and surplus workers, it is necessary to have a rational production control methodology that is adjustable to conform with changes due to internal failures in processes and equipment and external demand fluctuations. Just-in-time production control based on the *pull system* used in the Toyota production system offers such an integrated methodology.

11.2 PULL VERSUS PUSH SYSTEM

Let us first understand the push system. A push system is essentially a material requirements planning–based production planning and inventory control system. In MRP, the master production schedule (MPS) of end products is transformed into parts requirements. Work orders are then launched to build (or purchase) the parts in lot sizes using the lot-sizing logic of MRP. The work orders push materials to the manufacturing floor to produce the parts required. The lot sizes are normally large and consequently production lead times are long. During the planning horizon, MRP works on a fixed master production schedule. The MPS is altered only at the beginning of the planning horizon, which is typically 1 week to 1 month. However, there will be changes in the schedule and delays during this time because of the dynamic nature of the demand and production processes. Therefore, the lot being produced is not correct in relation to the master production schedule of end items. Coordination is lost because of lack of feedback on the status of materials previously released. The parts are pushed to the successive stages as soon as the work is completed at a particular stage as shown in Figure 11.1*a*. A problem is created when some parts are not completed and required at the successive processes (stages), causing shortages. This phenomenon is also re-

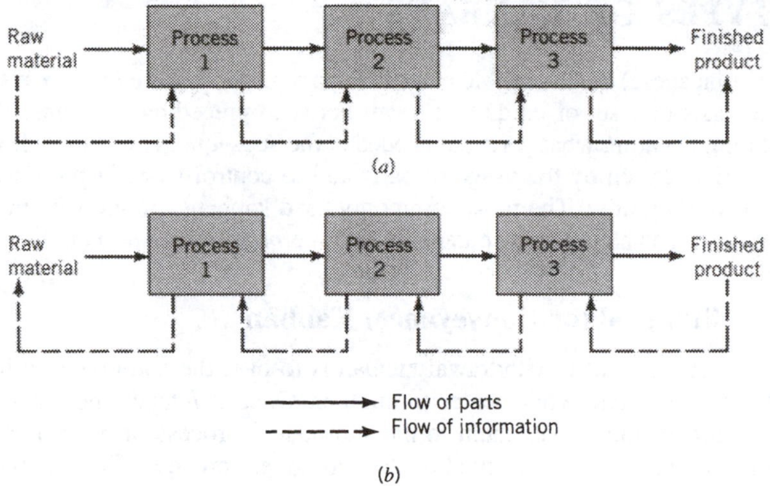

FIGURE 11.1 The material and information flow process in (*a*) a push system and (*b*) a pull system.

ferred to as starving the successive stage. On the other hand, there will be too much inventory of some components, causing what is known as blocking the preceding stage. Remember, inventory is a form of muda (waste) and too much inventory is too much waste.

As seen in Figure 11.1*a*, the push system is a single flow process in which both the build schedules (information) and materials flow in the same direction from one stage to another. The transmittal of information distinguishes a pull system from a push system. In a pull system, there is always feedback from the subsequent to preceding stages as shown in Figure 11.1*b*.

In a pull system, the MPS is used only to give a broad outline of the requirements for resources at different work centers. The major difference in a pull system is that although the MPS is used for the purpose of deciding approximate resource requirements of workstations, it is not used to decide the production rate for each workstation. In a pull system, the materials move in the same direction as in a push system but the information concerning processing of the parts (build schedules) is given by the subsequent process. Therefore, the build schedules travel in the opposite direction. A kanban system is used to communicate the schedule from one station to another. A kanban in a pull system is a card attached to a standard container that issues the production and withdrawal of parts between workstations. It is usually viewed as an information system that controls production of parts. The major strength of a kanban system is its simplicity, which makes it possible for a worker to make a decision at the workstation level concerning the production rate. Any change in demand is communicated to the final assembly level, and this change, in turn, is communicated through kanbans to every other workstation upstream exactly at the required time.

In a nutshell, the differences between push and pull systems can be summarized as follows. In a pull system, kanban is used to trigger production at every stage. A kanban represents the immediate requirements of the next stage. On the contrary, in a push system every workstation produces according to the work orders issued for one planning horizon. The major difference lies in short-term scheduling and production control; long-term and midterm planning is similar for both of them. Types of kanbans and their functions are discussed more in the following sections.

11.3 TYPES OF KANBANS

Kanban (in Japanese) means visible record. Toyota developed the *kanban* system. The system consists of a set of cards that travel between preceding and subsequent processes, communicating what parts are needed at the subsequent processes. It is used to move materials driven by the usage of parts and to control work-in-process, production, and inventory flow. The most commonly used kanbans are the *withdrawal kanban* (also known as a conveyance kanban) and the *production kanban.*

11.3.1 Withdrawal (or Conveyance) Kanban

The primary function of a withdrawal kanban is to pass the authorization for movement of parts from one work center to another. Once it fetches the parts from the preceding process and moves them to the subsequent process, it remains with them until the last part has been consumed by the subsequent process. Then the withdrawal kanban travels back to the preceding process to fetch parts and the cycle continues.

The withdrawal kanban should have information such as the part number and part name, lot size and routing process, name and location of the subsequent process, name

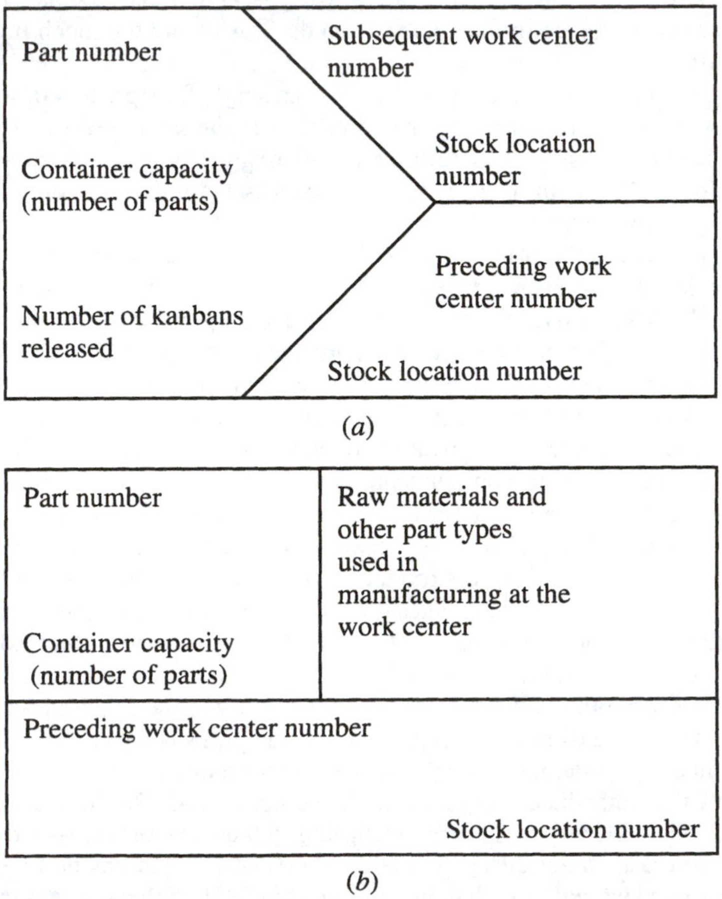

FIGURE 11.2 Sample layouts of (*a*) a withdrawal kanban and (*b*) a production kanban.

and location of the preceding process, container type and container capacity, and number of containers released. The withdrawal card layout can be designed in a number of ways to display this information. One such layout of a withdrawal kanban for a hypothetical shop is shown in Figure 11.2*a*.

11.3.2 Production Kanban

The main function of a production kanban is to release an order to the preceding process to build parts equal to the lot size specified on the card. Therefore, the production kanban card should have information on the materials and parts required as inputs at the preceding process in addition to what is present on a withdrawal kanban. This information is not required on the withdrawal kanban card, since it is used only as a means of communication authorizing movement of parts between work centers. A sample layout for a production kanban is shown in Figure 11.2*b*.

11.3.3 Flow of Withdrawal and Production Kanbans and Their Interactions

Let us understand the flow of withdrawal and production kanbans as well as the flow path of containers. Consider a simplified example (Ebrahimpour and Fathi, 1985) of controlling work flow between preceding and succeeding processing stages, PPS1 and SPS2, separated by a stacking area (SA) as shown in Figure 11.3.

The sequence of movements of kanbans (withdrawal as well as production) and containers between the processing centers and the stacking areas is described as follows:

1. Suppose you start at point P1 in the staging area. Move the full parts container to the subsequent processing stage, SPS2.
2. Detach the attached withdrawal card and send it to kanban collection box at point P2. Meanwhile, the parts in the container are being used by the subsequent stage.

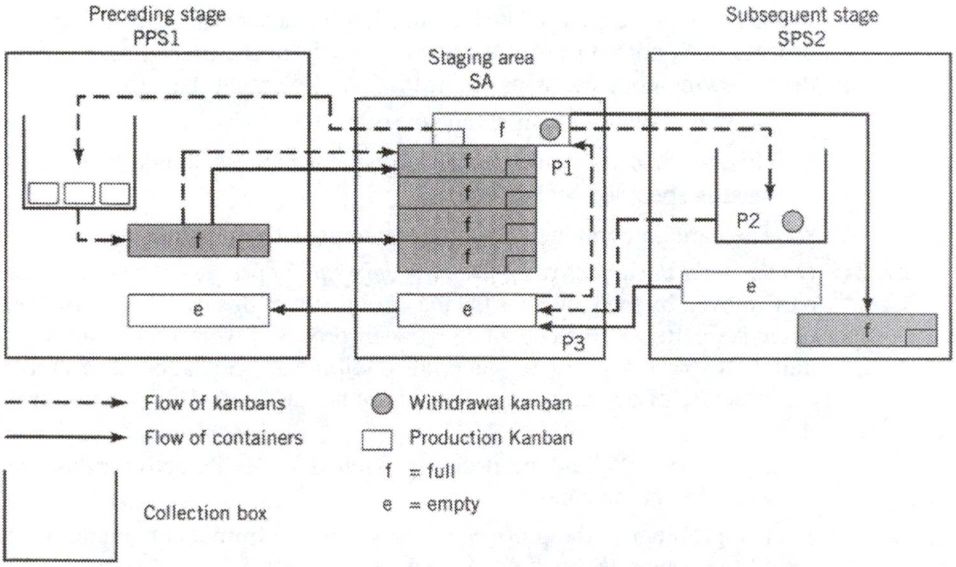

FIGURE 11.3 Flow sequences in a kanban production system.

3. Once all the parts in a container are consumed at SPS2, attach a withdrawal kanban from the kanban collection box to the empty container and move it from SPS2 to location P3 in the stacking area, SA.
4. Now at the P3 location:
   - Detach the withdrawal kanban from the empty container.
   - Attach it to a full parts container.
   - Remove a production kanban from the container to be sent to subsequent stage SPS2.
   - Send it to the preceding stage PPS1 to trigger production of a full container.
   - Empty container is sent from P_3 to the proceeding stage.
5. Put all the parts produced in the empty container and send to stacking area SA with the production kanban attached to it.

This completes one cycle, and the process is similarly repeated cycle after cycle.

11.3.4 Preconditions (Rules) for Operating Kanban

Kanban is essentially a tool created to manage the workplace effectively. In this section we discuss the rules that govern the operational environment of a kanban system. The preconditions (often called the basic rules) for effectively operating the kanban are:

Rule 1: *No withdrawal of parts without a kanban.* We now know that a kanban is a mechanism that controls production on a just-in-time basis, producing necessary parts in the right quantities at the right time. Only a kanban can authorize the flow of parts from a preceding process to the subsequent process.

Rule 2: *The subsequent process comes to withdraw only what is needed.* Muda (waste) of all types, as discussed in Section 11.1, would occur if the preceding process supplied more parts than are actually needed. This can be avoided if the subsequent process comes to the preceding process to withdraw required parts at the time needed. To ensure that the subsequent process does not arbitrarily withdraw parts from the preceding process, the following concrete steps are needed to implement the second rule:

- No withdrawal without a kanban (rule 1).
- Number of parts issued to the subsequent process should be exactly what is specified by the kanban.
- The parts in containers must be accompanied by kanbans.

Rule 3: *Do not send the defective parts to the subsequent process.* The quality of parts moved by the kanban is the major concern of this rule. Furthermore, defective parts would necessitate work-in-process inventories besides requiring extra resources of material, equipment, and labor. Therefore, manufacture of defective parts should not be tolerated. This rule requires that:

- The process should be designed such that the defective parts are identified at the source.
- The problem in the process is brought to the immediate attention of all the concerned workers and supervisory staff.

This rule implies a strong relationship between total quality control (TQC) and JIT manufacturing. For JIT to be successful it is important to implement total quality control concepts. TQC concepts are discussed in Section 11.10.

Rule 4: *The preceding process should produce only the exact quantity of parts withdrawn by the subsequent process.* This rule is a logical extension of the third rule. The basic premise behind this rule is to restrict the inventory at the preceding process to the absolute minimum. To ensure mini mum inventory, it is necessary to have:

- No more production than is required by the number of kanbans, and
- Production in every work center is strictly in the sequence in which the kanbans are received.

Rule 5: *Smoothing of production.* Previous rules imply that the subsequent process comes to the preceding process to withdraw the necessary parts in the necessary quantities at the necessary time. However, if the withdrawals fluctuate in quantity or time, then the peak demand will decide the inventory levels, equipment, and workers. It is, therefore, important to smooth (to minimize the fluctuations of) production.

Rule 6: *Fine tuning of production using kanban.* Small variations in production requirements are adjusted by

- Stopping the process if the production requirements decrease, and
- Using overtime and improvements in the processes if the production requirements increase.

We must remember that overtime is a kind of muda (waste) and should not be encouraged.

11.4 KANBAN PLANNING AND CONTROL MODELS

Kanban is the heart of the JIT system. The number of kanbans plays the most important part in planning, controlling, and reducing the work-in-process inventories. In this section we illustrate a number of deterministic and probabilistic analytical models for determining the optimal number of kanbans.

11.4.1 A Deterministic Model for Determining the Number of Kanbans

Let us first understand how the number of kanbans is determined at a work center in Toyota Motor Company, which has been successful in using the JIT system. Toyota uses the following formula (Sugimori et al., 1977; Monden, 1983):

$$\text{Number of kanbans, } y \geq \frac{D(T_w + T_p)(1 + \alpha)}{a} \tag{11.1}$$

where y = number of kanbans

D = demand per unit time

T_w = waiting time of kanban

T_p = processing time

a = container capacity (not more than 10 percent of daily requirement)

α = a policy variable

α is a policy variable which is used as a means of managing external disturbances such as changes in demand and variability in processing and delivery times. D is determined as a smoothed demand. y is normally fixed even if there are variations in demand. In that case, when D increases the value of the lead time must be reduced accordingly. If it is not possible to reduce the lead time, it may be necessary to have overtime or even line stops.

Improvements in order to reduce the values of a, α, and lead time ($T_p + T_w$) should be continuously pursued. These reductions will lead to reduced work-in-process inventory.

In this section we use two examples to explain the following:

1. How to determine the number of kanbans.
2. Impact of lead time on the number of kanbans and work-in-process inventory.
3. Interactions between the withdrawal and production kanbans.

EXAMPLE 11.1

Consider the production of a certain item manufactured in XYZ company. Its requirements are 10,000 units per month. Suppose the company has just started implementing the JIT system. Accordingly, the policy variable is set at $\alpha = 0.40$. The container capacity is fixed at 50 items and the production lead time is 0.50 days.

1. Determine the number of production kanbans.
2. Suppose the company has stable production environment and the policy variable can be fixed at $\alpha = 0.00$. Determine the number of kanbans and the resulting impact on work-in-process inventory.
3. What happens if the lead time is increased to 1 day because of labor shortages and failure of machines?
4. What happens if the lead time is reduced to 0.25 days because of process improvements? The value of α is 0.30 as a result of these process improvements.

Solution

1. We now know that number of kanbans is given by the following formula:

$$\text{Number of kanbans} = \frac{\text{(daily demand)(lead time)(safety factor)}}{\text{container capacity}}$$

Assuming 20 work days in a month, the daily demand is 10,000/20 = 500 parts. Accordingly,

$$\text{Number of kanbans} = \frac{(500)(0.50)(1.40)}{50} = 7$$

2. If $\alpha = 0.00$, then the safety factor is 1.00. Accordingly,

$$\text{Number of kanbans} = \frac{(500)(0.50)(1.00)}{50} = 5$$

The safety factor of 1 implies that a withdrawal kanban must always be delivered on time, whenever parts are needed. The implication of this change in the operation of processes on work in process can be explained as follows.

Assume that the usage of parts is at a uniform rate. Then the average inventory in case 1 is equal to the average inventory in case 2 plus inventory of two extra containers. Accordingly, the average inventory in case 1 is 100 units [(2)(50) = 100] more than that in case 2. This is because two more containers of 50 units each are also available as a safety stock over and above that of case 1.

3. $$\text{Number of kanbans} = \frac{(500)(1.00)(1.40)}{50} = 14$$

The implication of this change in the system operation is that the average inventory increases by 350 units [(7)(50) = 350] compared with case 1. This is because seven extra containers are available as safety stock.

4. $$\text{Number of kanbans} = \frac{(500)(0.25)(1.30)}{50} = 3.25.$$

If the number of kanbans determined by the formula is not an integer, the next integer may be taken as the number of kanbans required. Therefore, the number of kanbans in this case is 4. The implication of this rounding off to the next integer is an increase in α from 0.30 to 0.60. This essentially works against what we achieved through the process improvements. In a situation like this, management may work on further process improvements to reduce α. For example, if α is 0.20, the required number of kanbans is 3. The other option for the management could be to reduce the container size if further process improvements are not feasible at this time.

In the following example, we analyze a two-stage system involving manufacturing at the preceding stage and assembly at the subsequent stage.

EXAMPLE 11.2

Consider the manufacture of product Z in a company. Product Z is assembled from two parts, X and Y, that are manufactured in the company. A schematic layout depicting preceding stage, staging area, subsequent stage, and the flow of production and withdrawal kanbans is given in Figure 11.4. The data given in Table 11.1 are available.

1. Determine the number of withdrawal and production kanbans.
2. Now suppose the assembly process is shifted to Mexico as part of a reorganization. The lead time to travel between the new location in Mexico and the present plant location is

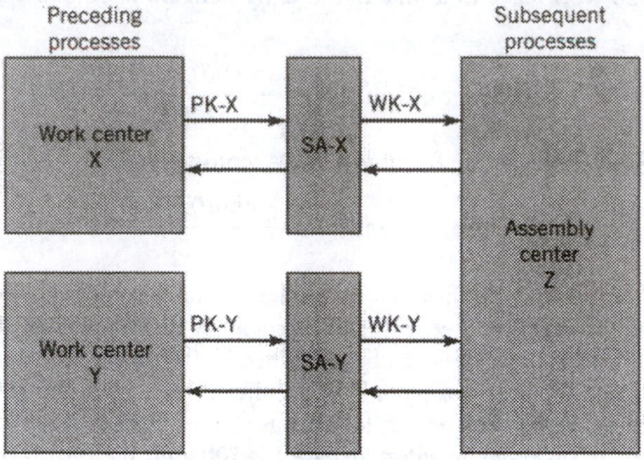

FIGURE 11.4 Layout for Example 11.2.

4 days each for parts X and Y. Determine the number of withdrawal and production kanbans and the impact of this policy on work-in-process inventory.

In Figure 11.4:

PK-X = production kanban for part X

PK-Y = production kanban for part Y

WK-X = withdrawal kanban for part X

WK-Y = withdrawal kanban for part Y

SA-X = staging area for part X

SA-Y = staging area for part Y

Solution

1. (a) *Determining withdrawal kanbans.* The lead time used for determining withdrawal kanbans is the time it takes the parts to travel from the preceding stage work centers (X and Y) to the subsequent assembly stage Z. Using Monden's formula [Equation (11.1)], the numbers of withdrawal kanbans for parts X and Y are 20 and 10, respectively.

   (b) *Determining production kanbans.* Similarly, the lead time for determining the production kanbans for parts X and Y is the time it takes to manufacture these parts. Again using Monden's formula, the numbers of production kanbans for parts X and Y are 12 and 16, respectively.

TABLE 11.1 **Data for Example 11.2**

Part	*Demand (Units/day)*	*Lead Time (Days)*	α	*Container Capacity*
Assembly stage				
X	2000	1.0	0.00	100
Y	800	0.5	0.25	50
Manufacturing stage				
X	2000	0.50	0.20	100
Y	800	1.00	0.00	50

2. Since the lead time is now 4 days, the numbers of withdrawal kanbans for parts X and Y are 80 and 80, respectively. The impact of this decision is that 60 containers for part X and 70 containers for part Y remain in the pipeline. There is no change in the number of production kanbans.

11.4.2 A Probabilistic Cost Model for Determining Optimal Number of Kanbans

Typically, in a JIT operation the master production schedule is frozen for 1 month and the number of kanbans at each work center is set based on the average demand for the period (Monden, 1983).

We now understand that there will be variations in the lead time because of uncertainties and, consequently, variations in the demand during the lead time. In this section we develop a cost model considering the expected cost of holding and shortages. It is assumed that the probability mass function (pmf) of the number of kanbans required is known. The methodology for determining the pmf for the number of kanbans is given in Appendix A.

Let us assume the following notation:

$p(x)$ = probability mass function for the number of kanbans required

c_h = holding cost per container per unit time at a work center

c_s = cost of a shortage per container per unit time at a work center

Suppose there are n kanbans circulating in the system. There are two possibilities:

Case I: The actual requirement for the kanbans, x, is less than n. In that case holding cost will be incurred. Accordingly,

$$\text{Expected holding cost} = c_h \sum_{x=0}^{n} (n - x)p(x) \qquad (11.2)$$

Case II: The actual requirement for the kanbans, x is more than n. In that case shortage costs will be incurred. Accordingly,

$$\text{Expected shortage cost} = c_s \sum_{x=n+1}^{\infty} (x - n)p(x) \qquad (11.3)$$

Therefore, the total expected cost, TC(n) is given by

$$\text{TC}(n) = c_h \sum_{x=0}^{n} (n - x)p(x) + c_s \sum_{x=n+1}^{\infty} (x - n)p(x) \qquad (11.4)$$

The optimal value of n that gives the minimum value of TC(n) is the smallest integer satisfying the following:

$$\Delta\,\text{TC}(n) = \text{TC}(n + 1) - \text{TC}(n) > 0$$

$$\Delta\,\text{TC}(n - 1) = \text{TC}(n) - \text{TC}(n - 1) < 0$$

Accordingly, for minimum TC(n), the condition is

$$\Delta\, \mathrm{TC}(n-1) < 0 < \Delta\, \mathrm{TC}(n)$$

Taking the first forward difference, we obtain

$$\Delta\, \mathrm{TC}(n) = c_{\mathrm{h}} \sum_{x=0}^{n} p(x) - c_{\mathrm{s}} \sum_{x=n+1}^{\infty} p(x) > 0$$

Upon simplification, we obtain

$$(c_{\mathrm{h}} + c_{\mathrm{s}})P(n) - c_{\mathrm{s}} > 0$$

$$P(n) > \frac{c_{\mathrm{s}}}{c_{\mathrm{h}} + c_{\mathrm{s}}}$$

where $P(n) = \sum_{x=0}^{n} p(x)$ is the cumulative distribution function of n.

Similarly, from first backward difference we can obtain

$$P(n-1) < \frac{c_{\mathrm{s}}}{c_{\mathrm{h}} + c_{\mathrm{s}}}$$

Therefore, the optimal number of kanbans can be obtained from

$$P(n-1) < \frac{c_{\mathrm{s}}}{c_{\mathrm{h}} + c_{\mathrm{s}}} < P(n) \tag{11.5}$$

EXAMPLE 11.3

Suppose that the probability mass function of the number of kanbans is known and is given in Table 11.2. Furthermore, suppose the holding and the shortage costs per container per unit time are \$50 and \$200, respectively. Determine the optimum number of kanbans to minimize the total expected cost.

Solution

Using the probabilistic model, the value of $c_{\mathrm{s}}/(c_{\mathrm{s}} + c_{\mathrm{h}})$ is $200/(200 + 50) = 0.80$. From Table 11.2, the value of n that gives $P(n)$ greater than or equal to 0.80 and $P(n - 1)$ less than 0.80 is 3. Therefore, from Equation (11.5) the optimal number of kanbans is equal to 3.

TABLE 11.2 **Data for Example 11.3**

Cumulative Probability	*0.00*	*0.20*	*0.30*	*0.35*	*0.10*	*0.05*
Number of kanbans	0	1	2	3	4	5

11.4.3 Relationship between JIT Manufacturing, Setup Time, and Cost

JIT manufacturing is often understood to mean a manufacturing system with lot size approaching unity. It is important to understand the conditions under which this goal may be achieved. The answer may come directly from the classical economic production quantity inventory model. In a JIT manufacturing environment the intent is not to permit shortages. Accordingly, the total variable cost consisting of setup and holding as a function of economic production quantity Q, is given by

$$\mathrm{TC}(Q) = \frac{AD}{Q} + CD + \frac{iCQ}{2}(1 - D/P) \tag{11.6}$$

where A = setup cost

C = unit cost

i = inventory carrying cost rate

D = demand rate

P = production rate

Q = economic production quantity

The optimal economic production quantity Q^*, which minimizes the total cost function given by Equation (11.6), is given by

$$Q^* = \sqrt{\frac{2AD}{iC(1 - D/P)}} \tag{11.7}$$

A plot of the holding cost as well as the setup cost as a function of Q is shown in Figure 11.5. As we can see from the figure, with reduced setup cost, the total cost function is pulled toward the origin. This is because the annual setup cost function with a low unit setup is pulled toward the origin. Therefore, for a given demand and production rate, the JIT objective of Q equal to 1 can be achieved only if the setup cost (and accordingly setup time) tends to zero, as seen from Figure 11.5. We illustrate this by a simple example.

EXAMPLE 11.4

Consider a product with the following data:

Unit cost, C = \$100.00

Annual inventory carrying cost rate, i = 10%

Demand rate, D = 10,000 units per year

Production rate, P = 15,000 units per year

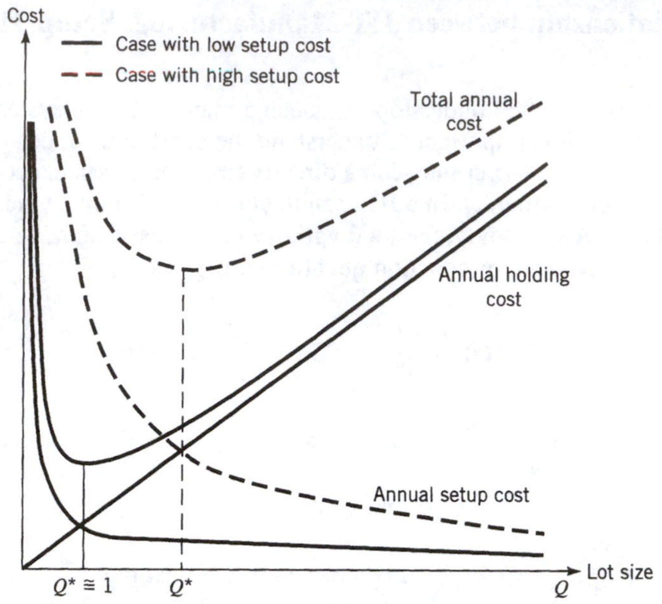

FIGURE 11.5 Relationship between economic production quantity and setup and holding costs.

Determine optimal lot sizes for various values of setup costs varying from \$400.00 to \$0.00016.

Solution

We now solve for the optimal Q^* from Equation (11.7) by varying the setup cost from \$400.00 per setup to \$0.00016. The results are presented in the following four cases.

Case I: Setup cost, $A = \$400.00$
The optimal value of the economic production quantity, $Q^* = 1549$.

Case II: Setup cost, $A = \$100.00$
The optimal value of the economic production quantity, $Q^* = 775$.

Case III: Setup cost, $A = \$1.00$
The optimal value of the economic production quantity, $Q^* = 78$.

Case IV: Setup cost, $A = \$0.00016$
The optimal value of the economic production quantity, $Q^* = 1$.

As we can see from this simple example, the JIT goal of unit production quantity can be achieved only if the setup cost tends to zero. The answer to such a problem lies in developing setup time reduction technologies such as quick tool and die changers. Another approach is to use the cellular manufacturing concepts based on exploiting similarities among components requiring similar tooling, holding devices and machines. The principles of cellular manufacturing are discussed in detail in the following chapter.

If the setup time is not negligible, that does not mean we cannot implement JIT concepts. In such cases we have to use a modified version of the kanban system called signal kanban.

11.5 SIGNAL KANBAN

One of the important conditions for the implementation of JIT with kanbans is to have low setup times relative to processing times. However, there are situations in manufacturing companies, such as forging, die casting, and press operations, in which the setup time is not small relative to processing times. The standard kanban system approach discussed in the previous sections does not work under these circumstances. We use a special type of kanban known as a *signal kanban* at the work centers with large setup time. In effect, a signal kanban triggers the production of a lot that consists of more than one container at these work centers. However, standard kanbans at normal work centers concurrently trigger the production of one container at a time.

Normally there are two types of signal kanbans. The first is rectangular and is known as a *raw material ordering kanban.* It is used to withdraw material from the preceding stage. The other type, known as a *production ordering kanban,* is triangular and is used to trigger the production of a lot at the work center where the signal kanban system is used. The flow of kanbans and material is shown in Figure 11.6. In the standard kanban process, whenever a withdrawal is made, a production kanban is sent back to the preceding stage to trigger the production of a container. In a signal kanban system, a production kanban is not sent back to trigger production after every withdrawal of a container. A triangular production-ordering signal kanban is attached at the reorder point of the lot. This triangular kanban initiates the setup process to produce the whole lot at the signal kanban work center as soon as the container to which it is attached is withdrawn by the succeeding stage. In a way the operation of a signal kanban system is quite similar to the classical reorder point system of inventory control.

In addition to a production-ordering kanban, a rectangular material-ordering kanban may also be attached to the lot to order material from storage. As soon as the container with a material kanban is withdrawn, the material signal kanban is sent to the preced-

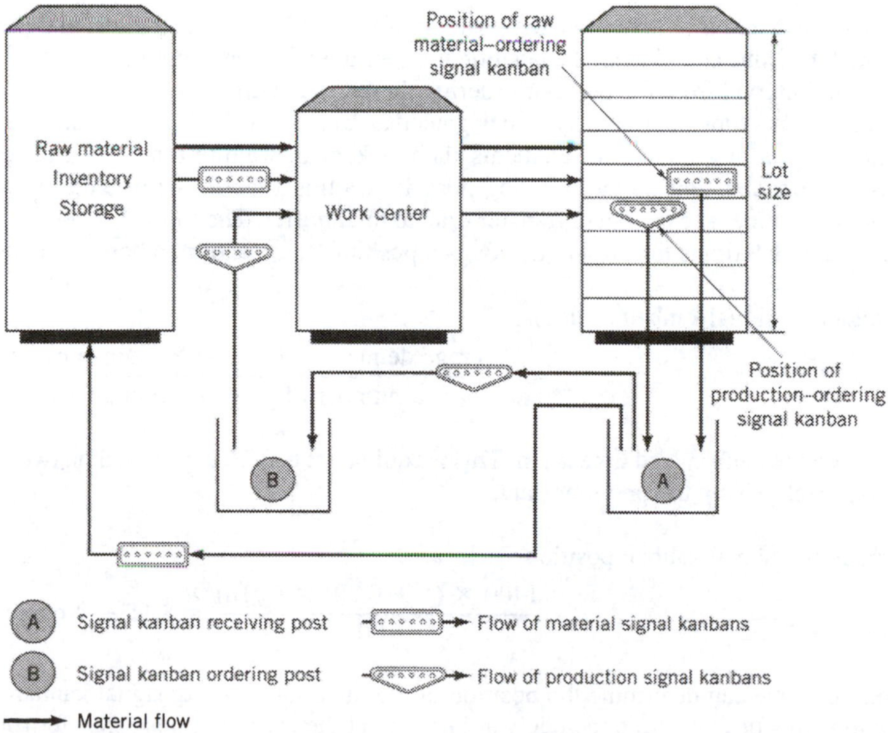

FIGURE 11.6 Flow of signal kanbans.

ing stage to withdraw the required items. These items will be needed at the work center to process the entire lot. When raw material reaches the workcenter, the production-ordering signal kanban may not be there to trigger production. However, raw material will be waiting for the arrival of the triangular signal kanban to initiate the production setup for the lot. Normally, a triangular kanban is attached to the next container in a lot where a rectangular kanban is attached. In other words, rectangular and triangular signal kanbans are attached to subsequent containers. It may be emphasized here that a rectangular kanban goes to the preceding stage whenever a container to which it is attached is withdrawn by the succeeding stage.

There are two important aspects of a signal kanban system: the determination of lot size and the position of both production-ordering as well as material-ordering signal kanbans. We illustrate these aspects by a simple example.

Consider an automobile company that manufactures three types of die-casting products at a diecasting station. Suppose the factory operates on two-shifts. The die-casting machine is utilized at 80 percent of its capacity for processing parts, leaving 20 percent operating time for setups. Over a period of two shifts, the time available for setups is equal to 3.2 hours (2 shifts $\times$ 8 h per shift $\times$ 20 percent). Suppose the average setup time is 32 min. A maximum of two setups per part is possible ($3.2 \times \frac{60}{32} \times \frac{1}{3}$). If the demand for a part is 1400 per day with α equal to 20 percent (α has the same meaning as explained in Munden's formula), the minimal lot size for the part can be calculated as follows:

$$\text{Minimal lot size per setup} = (\tfrac{1}{2}) \times 1400 \times 120 \text{ percent} = 840$$

Suppose the container capacity is 100 parts. We then need nine containers after rounding off ($840/100 = 8.4 \approx 9$). That means the lot size in terms of containers is nine containers.

The next step is to determine the position of the production-ordering signal kanban in the lot of nine containers. The position is determined by consumption of parts during the time interval from the point of ordering the lot to the arrival of the lot to its stock location. This time interval may be designated as *kanban cycle time*. The kanban cycle time consists of a number of elements such as kanban waiting time at the receiving post, its transfer time to the ordering post, its waiting time in the ordering post, lot processing time, and container transfer time to final buffer. The following formula can be used to determine the production kanban position in terms of number of containers:

$$\text{Production signal kanban position} = \frac{\text{Average demand} \times (1 + \alpha) \times \text{kanban cycle time}}{\text{number of parts per container}}$$

Suppose the kanban lead time is 3 h. This is equivalent to 3/16 days based on two shifts of 8 h each. Using the previous data,

$$\text{Production signal kanban position} = \frac{1400 \times (1 + 0.20) \times (3/16)}{100} = 3.15 \approx 4 \text{ containers}$$

Similarly, we can determine the position of the material-ordering signal kanban. The components of cycle time include waiting time at the receiving post, transfer time to raw material storage, waiting as well as withdrawal time at raw material storage, material transfer time to the work center, lot processing time, and container transfer time to final buffer. Notice that lot processing time and container transfer time to final buffer are common to both production and material signal kanbans. The material and production kanban cycle times may be equal or either one may be greater than the other. Often the material-ordering signal kanban cycle time is greater than the production-ordering signal kanban cycle time. Suppose the material-ordering signal kanban cycle time is 4 h. Then, using the previous data, we have:

Material-ordering signal kanban position

$$= \frac{1400 \times (1 + 0.20) \times (4/16)}{100} = 4.2 \approx 5 \text{ containers}$$

The position of these kanbans is shown in Figure 11.6.

Philipoom et al. (1990) have discussed and analyzed signal kanbans for work centers with relatively high setup times and developed mathematical programming models to determine the optimal lot size used in conjunction with the signal kanban. In the following section we discuss their mathematical programming approach for determining optimal lot sizes for signal kanbans.

11.5.1 Integer Programming Model for Determining Signal Kanbans

In developing this model it is assumed that the work centers can be decoupled from each other and considered in isolation if we do not allow any back orders at these work centers. The following sets of constraints ensure that no back orders occur at a signal kanban work center:

$$t_i \geq \sum_{j=1}^{n} (q_{ij}\mathrm{PT}_j + Y_{ij}S_j) \quad \text{for } i = 1, 2, \ldots, m \tag{11.8}$$

$$\sum_{i=1}^{m} Y_{ij} = 1 \quad \text{for } j = 1, 2, \ldots, n \tag{11.9}$$

$$q_{ij} \leq MY_{ij} \quad \text{for } i = 1, 2, \ldots, m, j = 1, 2, \ldots, n \tag{11.10}$$

$$Q_j \leq d_j t_i + (1 - Y_{ij})M \quad \text{for } i = 1, 2, \ldots, m, j = 1, 2, \ldots, n \tag{11.11}$$

$$Q_j \geq d_j t_i - (1 - Y_{ij})M \quad \text{for } i = 1, 2, \ldots, m, j = 1, 2, \ldots, n \tag{11.12}$$

$$Q_j = \sum_{i=1}^{m} q_{ij} \quad \text{for } j = 1, 2, \ldots, n \tag{11.13}$$

$$Y_{ij} = \text{binary} \quad \text{for } i = 1, 2, \ldots, m, j = 1, 2, \ldots, n \tag{11.14}$$

$$q_{ij} \text{ and } Q_{ij} \text{ are integers} \quad \text{for } i = 1, 2, \ldots, m, j = 1, 2, \ldots, n \tag{11.15}$$

where m = number of machines

n = number of items produced at a work center

q_{ij} = lot size in containers for item j processed on machine i

Q_j = sum of lot sizes for all machines at a work center

t_i = production cycle time for the ith machine at the signal kanban work center

PT_j = processing time for containers of item j

S_j = setup time for item j

Y_{ij} = a binary variable that assumes a value 1 if $q_{ij} > 0$ and otherwise takes a value of zero

M = a large positive constant

d_j = demand in containers per unit time for item j

Equation (11.8) ensures that there is no back order at the ith machine by forcing the cycle time for each machine to be greater than or equal to the production time including the setup time. Equation (11.9) ensures that only one machine produces each item at a work center. Equation (11.10) ensures that if the jth item is produced on the ith machine, Y_{ij} is one, so that the setup time for that item is included. Equations (11.11) to (11.13) ensure that demand for the jth item produced on the ith machine during the production cycle is exactly equal to the lot size for that item. These constraints ensure that there are neither back orders nor inventory buildup. Equations (11.14) and (11.15) represent the zero–one and integer variables.

There could be a number of objectives in the context of JIT manufacturing. Minimization of inventory is normally the desired objective. Another objective could be minimization of total cost consisting of the holding and setup costs. Accordingly, the integer programming models are as follows.

Problem P1:

$$\text{Minimize} \quad Z_1 = \sum_{j=1}^{n} Q_j$$

subject to: constraints (11.8) to (11.15)

Problem P2:

$$\text{Minimize} \quad Z_2 = \sum_{j=1}^{n} \left(C_j \frac{R_j}{Q_j} + C_{H_j} \frac{Q_j}{2} (1 - d_j \text{PT}_j) \right)$$

subject to: constraints (11.8) to (11.15)

where problems P1 and P2 represent minimization of inventory and total cost objective functions. The objective function Z_2 is based on the rotation cycle policy (Johnson and Montgomery, 1974). Here, C_j, R_j and C_{H_j} are the cost of a setup, annual demand, and unit annual holding cost for the jth item, respectively.

TABLE 11.3 **Data for Example 11.4**

Item	*Daily Demand (Containers)*	*Container Processing Time (hours)*	*Setup Time (hours)*
A	40	0.10	0.50
B	30	0.10	0.50
C	30	0.20	0.30

EXAMPLE 11.5

Consider three items, A, B, and C, that are produced at a work center having two machines. The available data are given in Table 11.3 Determine the number of kanbans considering a minimum-inventory goal.

Solution

It is assumed in formulating the model that available time during a day is 8 h. Since we want to minimize total inventory, we solve the integer programming model P1. We obtain the following solution:

$$q_{11} = 0 \text{ containers}, \quad q_{21} = 40 \text{ containers}, \quad Q_1 = Q_A = q_{11} + q_{21} = 40 \text{ containers}$$

$$q_{12} = 0 \text{ containers}, \quad q_{22} = 30 \text{ containers}, \quad Q_2 = Q_B = q_{12} + q_{22} = 30 \text{ containers}$$

$$q_{13} = 5 \text{ containers}, \quad q_{23} = 0 \text{ containers}, \quad Q_3 = Q_C = q_{13} + q_{23} = 5 \text{ containers}$$

$$t_1 = 1.3 \text{ h}, \quad t_2 = 8 \text{ h}$$

Therefore, items A and B are produced on machine 2 with a production cycle time of 8 h, whereas item C is produced on machine 1 with a production cycle time of 1.3 h. It is important to point out that on machine 2, we are producing to satisfy the demand for 1 day in one setup. On the contrary, on machine 1, we need approximately six setups to satisfy daily demand. The set of constraints and objective function for this problem are given in Appendix B.

11.6 OTHER TYPES OF KANBANS

So far we have studied the most commonly used production and conveyance (withdrawal) kanbans. However, other types of kanbans are used in specific situations. We provide a brief description of some of them in this section.

11.6.1 Express Kanban

An express kanban is used when shortages of parts occur. It must be withdrawn after its use. The presence of an express kanban in a red post (also known as the express kanban post) triggers the following activities:

1. A button for the machining line making the part is switched on, activating a light on the light board known as the andon for the part.
2. The worker at the location where the light has come on must immediately produce the part and deliver it personally to the subsequent process.

11.6.2 Emergency Kanban

This kanban is used as a temporary measure to make up for the defective units and other uncertainties such as machine failures or fluctuations in daily or weekly production.

11.6.3 Through Kanban

In production situations in which two or more work centers are located close to each other, there is no need to exchange production and conveyance kanbans between these work centers. Only one kanban, known as a through kanban, is used, which is similar to a through ticket between two adjacent railways.

11.7 LEVEL SCHEDULES FOR MIXED-MODEL ASSEMBLY LINES

Mixed-model assembly lines are used to manufacture many products without carrying large inventories. Each product assembled on a mixed-model assembly line requires a variety of parts. Often these parts vary from product to product. For a balanced schedule, the quantity of each part used by the mixed-model assembly lines per unit time should be kept as constant as possible. That is, there should be little variability in the usage of each part from one time period to the next.

The question is what causes variability in usage of parts. For example, if a part is needed only for certain products, its usage is high when those products are being assembled and low otherwise. Also, all products do not have the same operation time at each station on the line. Some may even have operation times at certain stations that exceed the predetermined cycle time. The assembly line may be able to adjust to this without slowing down or stopping. However, if products with longer operation times than the line cycle time are scheduled successively, delays and line stoppage will occur. That is why we need to level our schedule.

In the following section we present a model due to Miltenburg (1989) to develop a level schedule for a mixed-model assembly line assuming that products require approximately the same number and mix of parts. In that case, we can achieve the constant rate of part usage by considering only the demand rates for the products and ignoring the resulting part demand rates. However, if the number and mix of parts change from product to product, the model due to Miltenburg and Sinnamon (1989) can be used to address such variabilities.

11.7.1 A Mathematical Model to Obtain Level Schedules

Our objective is to minimize the variation in the usage of each part by sequencing products in small lots. Normally, in a JIT environment, setup time and cost of setups are low. Therefore we can change the setup after producing each item, making the batch size one. For a batch size of one, the total number of stages (k) for which a schedule is to be developed may be assumed to be equal to the total number of units to be produced (D_T). Accordingly,

$$\sum_{i=1}^{n} d_i = D_T$$

where k represents the stage ($k = 1, 2, \ldots, D_T$), and at every stage only one item is produced, and d_i is the demand for product i ($i = 1, 2, \ldots, n$).

This reduces to the problem of producing all the products in D_T stages. At the same time, ideally a fraction r_i [where $r_i = (d_i/D_T)$] of ith item should be produced at every stage so that the cumulative production of the ith item up to k stages is $k(r_i)$. Essentially, this means proportionate production of d_i units in D_T stages. In reality, we can produce only one item at a stage. That means the actual production of the ith item up to k stages will be x_{ik}. Our objective is to minimize the difference between the ideal and the actual production for all the items. Mathematically, using the model developed by Miltenburg (1989), this can be expressed as follows:

$$\text{Minimize} \sum_{k=1}^{D_T} \sum_{i=1}^{n} (x_{i,k} - kr_i)^2$$

$$\text{subject to} \sum_{i=1}^{n} x_{i,k} = k, \qquad k = 1, 2, \ldots, D_T.$$

$x_{i,k}$ is a non-negative integer.

The objective function of this model minimizes the variation of actual production (x_{ik}) from the desired production (kr_i). The first set of constraints ensures that exactly k products are scheduled during k stages. The last constraint is the non-negativity constraint. That is, it is not possible to schedule less than zero unit of any product.

If we consider only the first constraint, the problem reduces to minimizing a convex function subject to a set of linear constraints. The solution is found by inspection: $x_{ik} = kr_i$. The objective function is equal to zero and the constraints are satisfied:

$$\sum_{i=1}^{n} x_{ik} = \sum_{i=1}^{n} kr_i = k \sum_{i=1}^{n} r_i = k$$

It is relatively simple to adjust the solution to accommodate the non-negative integer constraint. We define the point $X_k = (x_{1,k}, x_{2,k}, \ldots, x_{n,k}) \in R^n$, where $x_{i,k} = kr_i$, $\Sigma_{i=1}^n x_{i,k} = k$, and R is the set of real numbers. Our problem is to find the "nearest" integer point $M_k = (m_{1,k}, m_{2,k}, \ldots, m_{n,k}) \in Z^n$ to the point X_k, where $\Sigma_{i=1}^n m_{i,k} = k$, and Z is the set of non-negative integers. "Nearest" means the point that minimizes $\Sigma_{i=1}^n (m_{i,k} - x_{i,k})^2$.

We now provide a heuristic procedure developed by Miltenburg (1989) to solve the proposed model:

11.7.1.1 Algorithm I

For each stage, the following algorithm finds the nearest integer point $M = (m_1, m_2, \ldots, m_n) \in Z^n$ to a point $X = (x_1, x_2, \ldots, x_n) \in R^n$ where $\Sigma\, m_i = \Sigma\, x_i = k$.

Step 1: Determine x_i where $x_i = kr_i$

Step 2: Find the nearest non-negative integer m_i to each coordinate x_i. That is, find m_i so that $|m_i - x_i| \leq 0.5$, $i = 1, 2, 3, \ldots, n$.

Step 3: Calculate $I_m = \Sigma\, m_i$.

Step 4: (a) if $k - I_m = 0$, stop. The nearest integer point is $M = (m_1, m_2, \ldots, m_n)$.

(b) if $k - I_m > 0$, go to step 5.
(c) if $k - I_m < 0$, go to step 6.

Step 5: Find the coordinate x_i with the smallest $m_i - x_i$. Increment the value of this m_i; $m_i \rightarrow m_i + 1$. Go to step 3.

Step 6: Find the coordinate x_i with the largest $m_i - x_i$. Decrement the value of this m_i; $m_i \rightarrow m_i - 1$. Go to step 3.

The first two steps of the algorithm are used to round off x_i values to the nearest integer. In the third and fourth steps we are checking whether this rounding off satisfies the constraint $\Sigma_{i=1}^{n} x_{i,k} = k$. If I_m is greater than k, it implies that we should reduce some of our m_i by the difference $(I_m - k)$. We choose the m_i that is farthest from its $x_{i,k}$ value (it is the least deserving candidate). We reduce the value of this m_i by one and proceed in a similar manner. If I_m is less than k, we should increase some of our m_i by the difference $(k - I_m)$. We choose the m_i that is nearest its $x_{i,k}$ value (it is the most deserving candidate). We increase the value of this m_i by one and proceed in a similar manner. Elements of M_k represent the cumulative production of ith item up to stage k. The value of these elements can not be decreased at subsequent stages. Therefore, $m_{i,k} - m_{i,k-1} < 0$ implies infeasibility.

If we do not get a feasible schedule by using the preceding algorithm, we use algorithm II.

11.7.1.2 Algorithm II

Step 1: Solve the problem by using algorithm I, and determine whether the schedule is feasible. If the schedule is feasible, stop. This is the optimal schedule. Otherwise, go to step 2.

Step 2: For the infeasible schedule determined in step 1, find the first (or next) stage s where the problem is infeasible, that is, $m_{i,s} - m_{i,s-1} < 0$. Set δ = number of products i for which $m_{i,s} - m_{i,s-1} < 0$, and beginning at stage $s - \delta$ use step 3 to schedule stages $s - \delta$, $s - \delta + 1, \ldots,$ $s + \omega$, where $\omega \geq 0$ and $s + \omega$ is the first stage where the schedule determined by the heuristic matches the schedule determined in step 1.

Step 3: For a stage k, schedule the product i with the lowest $x_{i,k-1} - kr_i$.

Step 4: Repeat step 2 for other stages where $m_{i,k} - m_{i,k-1} < 0$. Then stop.

EXAMPLE 11.6

We have three products with demands of 5, 6, and 2 units, respectively. These products are to be assembled on a mixed-model assembly line. Determine the level schedule.

Solution

For the given data, we have $d_1 = 5$, $d_2 = 6$, and $d_3 = 2$. Accordingly, $D_T = 5 + 6 + 2 = 13$. That means, $k = 1, 2, \ldots, 13$. Now $r_1 = d_1/D_T = 5/13$; similarly, $r_2 = 6/13$ and $r_3 = 2/13$.

At stage 1, we have $k = 1$.

Step 1: $X_1 = (5/13, 6/13, 2/13)$.

Step 2: $M_1 = (0, 0, 0)$ since $m_{1,1} = 0$ because 5/13 is less than 0.5. Therefore, the nearest integer is 0. Similarly, $m_{2,1} = 0$ and $m_{3,1} = 0$.

Step 3: $I_m = \Sigma_{i=1}^{3} m_{i,1} = 0 + 0 + 0 = 0$.

Step 4: $k - I_m > 0$; therefore we go to step 5.

Step 5: $m_{1,1} - x_{1,1} = -5/13$, $m_{2,1} - x_{2,1} = -6/13$, $m_{3,1} - x_{3,1} = -2/13$. The smallest value is for the second product. Therefore, the new $m_{2,1}$ = the old $m_{2,1} + 1 = 1$. Accordingly, $M_1 = (0, 1, 0)$, which means that product 2 is scheduled at this stage.

At stage 2, we have $k = 2$.

Step 1: $X_2 = (10/13, 12/13, 4/13)$.

Step 2: $M_2 = (1, 1, 0)$ since $m_{1,2} = 1$ because 10/13 is greater than 0.5. Therefore, the nearest integer is 1. Similarly, $m_{2,2} = 1$ and $m_{3,2} = 0$.

Step 3: $I_m = \Sigma_{i=1}^{3} m_{i,2} = 1 + 1 + 0 = 2$.

Step 4: $k - I_m = 0$; therefore we stop and the final $M_2 = (1, 1, 0)$. That means product 1 is scheduled at this stage.

At stage 3, we have $k = 3$.

Step 1: $X_3 = (15/13, 18/13, 6/13)$.

Step 2: $M_3 = (1, 1, 0)$ since $m_{1,3} = 1$ because 15/13 is less than 1.5. Therefore, the nearest integer is 1. Similarly, $m_{2,3} = 1$ and $m_{3,3} = 0$.

Step 3: $I_m = \Sigma_{i=1}^{3} m_{i,3} = 1 + 1 + 0 = 2$.

Step 4: $k - I_m > 0$; therefore we go to step 5.

Step 5: $m_{1,3} - x_{1,3} = -2/13$, $m_{2,3} - x_{2,3} = -5/13$, $m_{3,3} - x_{3,3} = -6/13$. The smallest value is for the third product. Therefore, the new $m_{3,3}$ = the old $m_{3,3} + 1 = 1$. Accordingly, $M_3 = (1, 1, 1)$, which means that product 3 is scheduled at this stage.

At stage 4, we have $k = 4$.

Step 1: $X_4 = (20/13, 24/13, 8/13)$.

Step 2: $M_4 = (2, 2, 1)$ since $m_{1,4} = 2$ because 20/13 is greater than 1.5. Therefore, the nearest integer is 2. Similarly, $m_{2,4} = 2$ and $m_{3,4} = 1$.

Step 3: $I_m = \Sigma_{i=1}^{3} m_{i,4} = 2 + 2 + 1 = 5$.

Step 4: $k - I_m < 0$; therefore we go to step 6.

Step 6: $m_{1,4} - x_{1,4} = 6/13$, $m_{2,4} - x_{2,4} = 2/13$, $m_{3,4} - x_{3,4} = 5/13$. The largest value is for the first product. Therefore, the new $m_{1,4}$ = the old $m_{1,4} - 1 = 1$. Accordingly, $M_4 = (1, 2, 1)$, which means that product 2 is scheduled.

Similarly, we can proceed up to stage 13. The final schedule is 2-1-3-2-1-2-1-2-1-2-3-1. Since the schedule developed by the algorithm I is feasible, the second algorithm is not required. However, it is possible that the algorithm I may not yield feasible schedule. In that case, algorithm II should be applied with algorithm I. This is illustrated in the next example.

EXAMPLE 11.7

We have three products with demands of 12, 12, and 2 units, respectively. These products are to be assembled on a mixed-model assembly line. Determine the level schedule.

Solution

Applying algorithm I, we get

$$M_1 = (0, 1, 0), \quad M_2 = (1, 1, 0), \quad M_3 = (1, 2, 0), \quad M_4 = (2, 2, 0),$$
$$M_5 = (2, 2, 1), \quad M_6 = (3, 3, 0)$$

You will notice that the schedule suggested at stage 6 is not feasible. This is because the third product is scheduled in stage 5 for production, but its cumulative production at stage 6 is zero, which is impossible. We use algorithm II to remove this infeasibility.

Algorithm II

Step 1: The problem is solved by using algorithm I. Since it is infeasible at stage 6, we move to step 2.

Step 2: $s = 6$, $\delta = 1$; we reschedule from stage $(s - \delta) = (6 - 1) = 5$.

Step 3: For all the products at stage 5, we determine the value of $(x_{i,k-1} - kr_i)$ and schedule the product with the lowest value. Accordingly, $x_{1,5-1} - 5r_1 = 48/26 - 5(12/26) = -12/26$. Similarly, $x_{2,5-1} - 5r_2 = -12/26$, $x_{3,5-1} - 5r_3 = -2/26$. Since there is a tie, we may select either product 1 or product 2. We choose product 2. Therefore, the new $M_5 = (2, 3, 0)$. Similarly, we find the new $M_6 = (3, 3, 0)$. Since the new and old M_6 are the same, we move to step 4.

Step 4: Repeat step 2 for other stages where $m_{i,k} - m_{i,k-1} < 0$. Then stop.

This illustrates how to remove infeasibility using algorithm II. In a similar manner, we can use steps 1–4 of algorithm II to remove any infeasibility that may occur during subsequent stages.

11.8 ALTERNATIVE JIT SYSTEMS

Some alternative control structures for JIT manufacturing have been presented by various authors. Although JIT is usually understood as a pull system in which the amount of material flow at the immediately preceding station is determined by the stock consumption at the subsequent station, there are a number of alternative methods of control for JIT production. We discuss some of them in this section.

11.8.1 Periodic Pull System

Kim (1985) discusses a periodic pull system in which the manual information processing time of a kanban method was replaced by on-line computerized processing. This results in better system performance, such as reduced lead time and inventory and faster system response.

11.8.2 Constant Work-in-Process System

Spearman et al. (1990) described a pull-based production system called constant work-in-process (CONWIP). In contrast to kanban cards, which are part number specific, CONWIP production cards are assigned to the entire production line. The advantage of this system over the kanban system is that it can be used in environments where the kanban system is impractical because of a large number of part types or significant setup times.

11.8.3 Long Pull System

In the long pull system, the triggering mechanism works in the same way as in a pull system. However, the control of the long pull encompasses more than one workstation (Lambrecht and Segaert, 1990). In this system one unit is allowed to enter the system at the same time that one unit is pulled at the end of the pull. The individual buffers are not limited, but the total number of units in the span of the long pull is limited. In

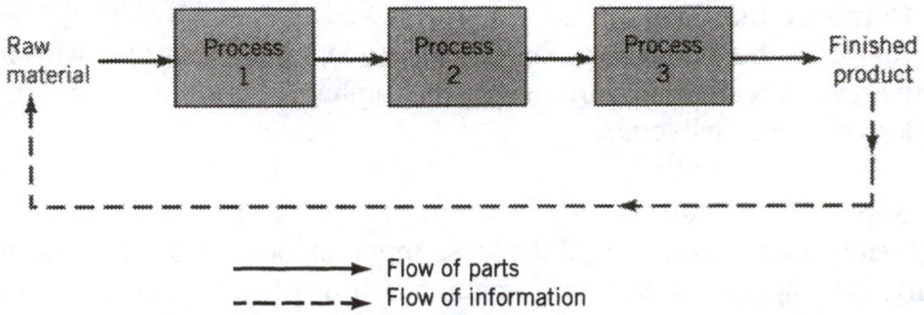

FIGURE 11.7 Flow of parts and information in a long pull JIT system.

Figure 11.7 the span of the pull is located from process 3 and creates a pull on process 1 when the trigger level at process 3 is activated. Once process 1 is started, the unit produced is pushed through the subsequent processes (2 and 3) in a manner similar to a push system. A trigger may be active but process 1 may not produce an additional part if the maximum inventory allowed within the span of the pull is reached.

Lambrecht and Segaert (1990) compared the long pull strategy with other allocation strategies such as push as well as pull and concluded that it out-performs them. Lee and Singh (1994) provide a detailed simulation analysis to find the location of the long pull, span of control of each long pull, and corresponding amount of work-in-process inventory to be allocated.

11.9 JUST-IN-TIME PURCHASING

Every manufacturing company is involved in purchasing raw materials, semifinished parts, and in some cases even subassemblies. It is therefore important to consider the integration of purchasing activities with manufacturing in the context of the just-in-time philosophy. In this section we discuss the activities involved in JIT purchasing and how they differ from traditional North American practices.

11.9.1 Major Purchasing Activities

In any company, the major activities involved in purchasing (Lee and Ansari, 1986) are:

1. Determining the purchase lot size
2. Selecting suppliers
3. Evaluating suppliers
4. Receiving inspection
5. Negotiating and bidding process
6. Determining mode of transportation
7. Determining product specification
8. Paperwork
9. Packaging

We now provide a comparative analysis of the JIT and traditional North American purchasing practices considering these purchasing activities (Lee and Ansari, 1986).

11.9.1.1 Purchase Lot Size

In JIT purchasing, the emphasis is on purchasing in small quantities with more frequent deliveries. In traditional purchasing, the emphasis is on buying in large quantities with less frequent deliveries.

11.9.1.2 Supplier Selection

Supplier (vendor) selection is one of the most important activities in purchasing. In JIT purchasing, the emphasis is on a smaller number of nearby suppliers, ideally one, and establishing good long-term relationships. The benefits of having a smaller number of suppliers are:

- Consistent quality
- Saving resources
- Lower costs
- Special attention
- Savings on tooling
- Long-term relationship

However, in traditional purchasing the emphasis is on multiple sourcing with split orders. The arguments in favor of multiple sourcing are:

- It provides a better technical base for the buyer.
- It protects the buyer in times of uncertain supplies.
- Competitive prices are obtained.

11.9.1.3 Supplier Evaluation

Product quality, delivery performance, and price are the three major criteria used for the evaluation and rating of suppliers (vendors) in both traditional and JIT purchasing. The goal in JIT purchasing is to have zero percent defectives. In traditional purchasing, however, rejects up to 2 percent are normally acceptable.

11.9.1.4 Receiving Inspection

Receiving, counting, and inspecting all incoming parts are the responsibility of the buyer in traditional purchasing. However, in JIT purchasing the inspection function for quality of the incoming parts is extended to the supplier's plant.

11.9.1.5 Negotiating and Bidding Process

In the traditional bidding process, the lowest price bid meeting the exact product specifications customarily gets the contract. Furthermore, the supplier offers very short term contracts and may be terminated for reasons of competitive price.

In JIT purchasing the emphasis is not on the lowest price bid but on product quality and establishing a long-term relationship with a view to establishing a fair price for both buyer and supplier and encouraging the suppliers to be innovative in meeting the specifications.

11.9.1.6 Mode of Transportation

Outgoing freight and internal plant material handling are the two major transportation activities in a manufacturing company. In the JIT system the concern is for both inbound and outbound freight and on-time delivery. The delivery schedule is left to the buyer. However, in traditional purchasing there is more concern for outbound freight and lower outbound costs. The delivery schedule is often left to the supplier.

11.9.1.7 Product Specifications

In traditional purchasing the buyer relies more on design specifications than on product performance. The suppliers have little freedom in developing the design specifications. However, in JIT purchasing the emphasis is more on product performance. For this purpose an interaction between the supplier and the buyer is encouraged to evolve design specifications leading to least manufacturing costs without sacrificing functional requirements.

11.9.1.8 Paperwork

Normally, purchase orders are issued for nearly all requirements, such as purchase requisitions, packing lists, shipping documents, and invoices. This takes a great deal of time and formal paperwork. In JIT purchasing there is less formal paperwork. The delivery schedule and quantities can be changed by telephone calls.

11.9.1.9 Packaging

In JIT purchasing the emphasis is on packaging exact quantities of parts in small standard containers. That makes handling easy and facilitates accurate counts of parts. In traditional purchasing practices there is regular packaging for every part and part type with no clear specifications on product content.

From this discussion it is evident that the benefits of JIT purchasing practices outweigh those of traditional purchasing practices.

11.10 TOTAL QUALITY CONTROL AND JIT

Total quality control is really "total" in the sense that it pervades all departments of a manufacturing company as well as the supplier company. TQC means an integrated approach to sharing responsibility for quality production of products; it requires a commitment from every individual from all functional departments in the company to achieve the goal of quality production. Because defects are not permitted in the JIT production system, it is important to have a TQC program for successful implementation of JIT production in the company. In this section we discuss various aspects of total quality control.

11.10.1 TQC Responsibilities

The vital links in the chain of manufacturing quality products are the supplier(s) of parts and the manufacture of product(s) using parts supplied by the supplier. It is therefore important to have a system defining responsibilities for quality for suppliers as well as all the functional areas in the company. Brief descriptions of the responsibilities of the functional departments for achieving total quality control are given below:

- Design department: designing proper specifications for manufacturability, quality, and reliability of products.
- Materials department: purchasing quality parts from the suppliers.

- Manufacturing department: manufacturing quality products meeting design specifications and educating workers about process control and their responsibilities for quality production.
- Quality control department: setting and implementation of quality standards, inspection procedures, and training programs; implementation of supplier quality audit programs; implementation of quality audit programs in the manufacturing line in the company; and coordination of quality problems between the manufacturer and the supplier.
- Sales and service department: providing quality (after sales) service and feedback on the product performance to the design, manufacturing, and quality control departments.

The emphasis in TQC is prevention and permanent removal of problems. Therefore, the major responsibility for the quality production should lie with the workers.

11.10.2 Principles of Quality

Schonberger (1982) discusses the following seven principles of quality; in each the production worker has the central role to play:

1. Process control: controlling production by checking the quality while the work is being done.
2. Easy-to-see quality: developing measurable standards of quality and making process quality visible.
3. Insistence on compliance: insisting on quality and not on production output.
4. Line stop: production line is stopped for identification and correction of major problems.
5. Correcting one's own errors: the worker(s) performs the rework itself to correct the errors.
6. 100 percent check: inspection of every part is the goal and is adhered to as far as possible.
7. Project-by-project improvement: quality improvements achieved and in progress are displayed on easy-to-see boards.

11.10.3 Quality Culture

What is needed in a JIT manufacturing environment is a quality culture. The concept of responsibility for quality and the establishment of quality principles in a company provide a basic fabric for quality culture. However, having established such a quality culture, it is equally important to maintain it. The following are some of the action plans useful for this purpose:

1. Establish total quality control teams in the factory.
2. Establish standard procedures for detecting and solving problems.
3. Establish good housekeeping practices in the plant.
4. Reinforce JIT manufacturing practices, such as small lots and less than full-capacity scheduling.
5. Establish a feedback mechanism to monitor customer quality needs and change quality standards to meet customer satisfaction.

6. Establish a quality inspection information system with the suppliers to eliminate receiving inspection.
7. Develop and organize quality training programs on a regular basis. Involve suppliers in such programs.

In brief, it is appropriate to say that TQC is an integrated approach to quality involving all functional areas in the company as well as the suppliers. It involves team efforts, attention to small details, attention to customer needs, and above all sharing of responsibility for quality by all concerned.

11.11 BARRIERS TO JIT IMPLEMENTATION

Implementing JIT principles in any company is not an easy task. A number of barriers or obstacles have to be overcome to achieve the goal of zero inventory. Some of the challenging problem areas are:

1. Frequent changes in production planning.
2. Inaccurate forecasting procedures resulting in under- or overforecasting of demand.
3. Equipment failures creating capacity problems.
4. Employee turnover, absenteeism, and so forth.

11.12 POTENTIAL BENEFITS OF JIT IMPLEMENTATION

Proper implementation of JIT principles may lead to a number of benefits for a company:

1. Increased productivity
2. Better quality
3. Reduced lead time
4. Reduced setup times
5. Less scrap and rework and consequently reduced requirements for raw material, personpower, and machine capacity
6. Less work in progress
7. Higher worker motivation and increased teamwork
8. Saved space
9. Increased worker and equipment efficiency

The benefits of JIT cut across functional boundaries within an organization. The functional areas benefited by JIT include:

1. Manufacturing
2. Manufacturing engineering
3. Purchasing
4. Sales and marketing
5. Accounting

6. Quality control
7. Assembly

11.13 SUMMARY

In this chapter we focused on basic understanding of the Toyota production system and JIT manufacturing philosophy. The primary objective has been to present material that would be useful to students, professors, researchers, and particularly professional engineers working in industries who would like to implement these principles. Accordingly, the emphasis was on qualitative as well as quantitative analysis. We discussed kanban operating principles and the interaction between withdrawal and production kanbans. A number of analytical procedures for determining the number of kanbans were presented. Also, we provided algorithms for scheduling parts in multi-model assembly lines.

Other issues included in this chapter were alternative JIT systems, JIT purchasing, total quality control, barriers to JIT implementation, potential benefits of JIT implementation, and a comprehensive literature review on various aspects of JIT manufacturing.

PROBLEMS

11.1 Discuss the following concepts in the context of the Toyota production system:
   (a) Process design, job design, and job standardization
   (b) Economic lot sizes and accelerated setup times
   (c) Just-in-time production
   (d) Autonomation
   (e) Kanban
   (f) Jidoka/andon
   (g) Yo-i-don
   (h) Muda
   (i) Mura
   (j) Muri

11.2 Differentiate between the push and the pull system. Explain why blocking does not occur in case of the pull system.

11.3 Discuss the rationale behind the preconditions (or rules) for operating a kanban system.

11.4 Discuss the following types of kanbans:
   (a) Production kanban
   (b) Conveyance or withdrawal kanban
   (c) Express kanban
   (d) Emergency kanban
   (e) Through kanban

11.5 Discuss in detail the following alternative concepts in JIT production system:
   (a) Periodic pull system
   (b) Constant work-in-process system
   (c) Long pull system
   (d) Integrated push and pull system

11.6 Johnson and Johnson (JJ), a private limited company, supplies parts to a spark plug manufacturing company. JJ is now planning to introduce JIT production concepts for their shell manufacturing section. The following data are available: The requirements-are 25,000,000 units per month. Since the company has just started implementing the

JIT system, the policy variable is set at $\alpha = 0.20$. The container capacity is fixed at 500 shells and the production lead time is 0.10 days.

(a) Since it is the first time that JJ is implementing JIT, advise JJ in developing a kanban operating system. How many kanbans will be needed?

(b) Suppose the company has a stable production environment and the policy variable can be fixed at $\alpha = 0.10$. Determine the number of kanbans and the resulting impact on work-in-process inventory.

(c) What happens if the lead time is reduced to 0.08 days because of process improvements? ($\alpha = 0.10$)

11.7 Johnson and Johnson (JJ) is also planning to introduce a kanban system in their assembly section. However, there is variability in the lead times. Furthermore, the assembly operation is the last operation before the shells are shipped to the spark plug company. Therefore there is considerable value addition. The company industrial engineer, Mr. John Spillane, has conducted a simulation study and developed the probability mass function of demand during lead time as follows:

Probability	*0.00*	*0.15*	*0.20*	*0.30*	*0.20*	*0.15*
Number of kanbans	0	1	2	3	4	5

Suppose the holding and shortage costs per container per unit time are \$50 and \$250, respectively. Determine the optimum number of containers to minimize the total expected cost consisting of holding and shortage.

11.8 JJ company manufactures three types of items at a work center on two machines. Since the setup times are relatively high compared with the processing times, JJ has been advised to implement the signal kanban operating policy. The following data are available:

Holding cost = 25 percent per year of the container cost

Setup cost = \$65 per hour

Item	*Container Cost (\$)*	*Daily Demand (Containers)*	*Container Processing Time (hours)*	*Setup Time (hours)*
1	500	300	0.10	0.20
2	1000	100	0.15	0.40
3	1500	200	0.25	0.50

Determine the optimal number of signal kanbans for the following situations:

(a) Minimum inventory level

(b) Minimum total cost consisting of setup and holding

The JJ company is also planning to make some investments in reducing the setup times. Before making these investments, JJ would like to know what the level of reduction in inventory and the total cost will be if there are 10, 20, and 30 percent decreases in setup times.

11.9 Determine the number of kanbans required for the following:

Item	*X*	*Y*	*Z*
Usage	120 per day	100 per week	20,000 per month
Lead time	3 weeks	1 week	1 week
Container size	100 units	10 units	200 units
Safety factor	0.00	0.10	0.20

11.10 Write short notes on the following:
   (a) Potential benefits of JIT implementation
   (b) Barriers to JIT implementation
   (c) Functional areas likely to be influenced by JIT implementation
   (d) JIT purchasing
   (e) Total quality control and JIT

11.11 Develop a level schedule for three products with demands (6, 6, 1) for a mixed-model JIT assembly line.

11.12 Visit a small-scale company manufacturing automotive parts. Design a JIT manufacturing system for the company.

REFERENCES AND SUGGESTED READING

Baker, K. R., Powell, G. S., and Pyke, F. D. (1990). The performance of push and pull systems: A corrected analysis. *International Journal of Production Research* 28(9):1731–1736.

Bartezzaghi, E., and Turco, F. (1989). The impact of just-in-time on production system performance: An analytical framework. *International Journal of Operations and Production Management* 8:40–62.

Bitran, G. R., and Chang, L. (1987). A mathematical programming approach to a deterministic kanban system. *Management Science* 33(4):427–441.

Box, G. E. P., and Jenkins, G. M. (1976). *Time Series Analysis: Forecasting and Control* (revised edition). Holden-Day, San Francisco.

Brar, J. K., and Singh, N. (1992). System dynamics approach to analysis of scheduling policies in an assembly plant. *System Dynamics: International Journal of Policy Modelling* 5(1):1–21.

Buzacott, J. A. (1989). Queuing models of kanban and MRP controlled production systems. *Engineering Costs and Production Economics* 17:3–20.

Carnall, C. A., and Wild, R. (1976). The location of variable work stations and the performance of production flow lines. *International Journal of Production Research* 14(6):703–710.

Chapman, S. N. (1989). Just-in-time supplier inventory: An empirical implementation model. *International Journal of Production Research* 27(12):1993–2007.

Conway, R., Maxwell, W., McClain, O. M., and Thomas, L. J. (1988). The role of work-in-process inventory in serial production lines. *Operations Research* 136(2):229–241.

Crawford, K. M., Blackstone, J. H., Jr., and Cox, J. F. (1988). A study of JIT implementation and operating problems. *International Journal of Production Research* 26(9):1561–1568.

Davis, W. J., and Stubitz, S. J. (1987). Configuring a kanban system using a discrete optimization of multiple stochastic responses. *International Journal of Production Research* 25(5):721–740.

Deleersynder, J., Hodgson, T. J., Muller, H., and O'Grady, P. J. (1989). Kanban controlled pull systems: An analytic approach. *Management Science* 35(9):1079–1091.

Ebrahimpour, M., and Fathi, B. M. (1985). Dynamic simulation of a kanban production inventory system. *International Journal of Operations and Production Management* 5(1):5–14.

Egbelu, P. J., and Wang, H. P. (1989). Scheduling for just-in-time manufacturing. *Engineering Costs and Production Economics* 16:117–124.

Fallon, D., and Browne, J. (1987). Simulating just-in-time systems. *International Journal of Operations and Production Management* 18(6):30–45.

Gelders, L., and Van Wassenhowe, L. N. (1981). Production planning: A review. *European Journal of Operational Research* 7:101–110.

Goldratt, E. M. (1988). Computerized shop floor scheduling. *International Journal of Production Research* 26(3):443–455.

Gravel, M., and Price, W. L. (1988). Using the kanban in a job shop environment. *International Journal of Production Research* 26(6):1105–1118.

Groeflin, H., Luss, H., Rosenwein, M. B., and Wahls, E. T. (1989). Final assembly sequencing for just-in-time manufacturing. *International Journal of Production Research* 27(2):199–213.

Gupta, Y. P., and Gupta, M. G. (1989a). A system dynamics model of a JIT–kanban system. *Engineering Costs and Production Economics* 18:117–130.

Gupta, Y. P., and Gupta, M. G. (1989b). A system dynamics model for a multi-stage multi-line dual-card JIT–kanban system. *International Journal of Production Research* 27(2):309–352.

Hernandez, A. (1989). *Just-in-Time Manufacturing: A Practical Approach.* Prentice Hall, Englewood Cliffs, New Jersey.

Hillier, S. F., and Boling, R. W. (1966). The effect of some design factors on the efficiency of production lines with variable operation times. *Journal of Industrial Engineering* 17(12):651–658.

Im, J. H., and Lee, S. M. (1988). Implementation of just-in-time systems in US manufacturing firms. *International Journal of Operations and Production Management* 9(1):5–14.

Johnson, L. A., and Montgomery, D. C. (1974). *Operations Research in Production Planning, Scheduling and Inventory Control.* John Wiley & Sons, New York.

Karmarkar, U. S., and Kekre, S. (1987). Batching policy in kanban systems. Working paper QM8706, Graduate School of Business, University of Rochester, Rochester, New York.

Kim, T. (1985). Just-in-time manufacturing system: A periodic pull system. *International Journal of Production Research* 23(3):553–562.

Kimura, O., and Terada, H. (1981). Design and analysis of pull system, a method of multi-stage production control. *International Journal of Production Research* 19(3):241–253.

Lambrecht, M., and Segaert, A. (1990) Buffer stock allocation in serial and assembly type of production lines. *International Journal of Operations and Production Management* 10(2):47–61.

Lee, L. C. (1987). Parametric appraisal of JIT system. *International Journal of Production Research* 25(10):1415–1429.

Lee, L. C. (1989). A comparative study of push and pull production system. *International Journal of Operations and Production Management* 9(4):5–18.

Lee, L. C., and Seah, K. H. W. (1987). JIT and the effects of varying process and set-up times. *International Journal of Operations and Production Management* 8(1):19–35.

Lee, S., and Singh, N. (1994). Understanding dynamic behaviour of long pull JIT system. Working paper, Department of Industrial and Manufacturing Engineering, Wayne State University, Detroit, Michigan.

Lee, S. M., and Ansari, A. (1986). Comparative analysis of Japanese just-in-time purchasing and traditional US purchasing. *International Journal of Operations and Production Management* 5(4):5–14.

Lu, D. J. (1985). *Kanban: Just-In-Time at Toyota.* Productivity Press, Cambridge, U.K.

Martin-Vega, L. A., Pipin, M., Gerdon, E., and Burcham, R. (1989). Applying just-in-time in a wafer fab: A case study. *IEEE Transactions on Semiconductor Manufacturing* 2(1):16–22.

Miltenburg, J. (1989). A theoretical basis for scheduling mixed-model assembly lines for just-in-time production systems. *Management Science* 35:192–207.

Miltenburg, J., and Sinnamon, G. (1989) Scheduling mixed-model multi-level just-in-time production systems. *International Journal of Production Research* 27(9):1487–1509.

Mitra, D., and Mitrani, I. (1990). Analysis of a kanban discipline for cell coordination in production lines. I. *Management Science* 36(12):1548–1566.

Mitwasi, M. G., and Askin, R. G. (1994). Production planning for a multi-item, single stage kanban system. *International Journal of Production Research* 32(5):1173–1196.

Miyazaki, S., Ohta, H., and Nishiyama, N. (1988). The optimal operation planning of kanban to minimize the total operation cost. *International Journal of Production Research* 26(10):1605–1611.

Monden, Y. (1981). Adaptable kanban system helps Toyota maintain just-in-time production. *Industrial Engineering* 13(5):29–46.

Monden, Y. (1983). *Toyota Production System.* Industrial Engineering and Management Press, Institute of Industrial Engineers, Norcross, Georgia.

O'Calahan, R. (1986). A system dynamics perspective on JIT–kanban. International Conference of the System Dynamics Society, Sevilla, Spain, pp. 961–1004.

Olhager, J., and Ostlund, B. (1990). An integrated push–pull manufacturing strategy. *European Journal of Operational Research* 45:135–142.

Papoulis, A. (1965). *Probability, Random Variables and Stochastic Processes.* McGraw-Hill Book Company, New York.

Payne, S., Slack, N., and Wild, R. (1972). Research note: A note on operating characteristics of balanced and unbalanced production flow lines. *International Journal of Production Research* 10(1):93–98.

Pegels, C. C. (1984). The Toyota production system—lessons for American management. *International Journal of Operations and Production Management* 4(1):3–11.

Philipoom, P. R., Rees, L. P., Taylor, B. W., III, and Huang, P. Y. (1987). An investigation of the factors influencing the number of kanbans required in the implementation of the JIT technique with kanbans. *International Journal of Production Research* 25(3):457–472.

Philipoom, P. R., Rees, L. P., Taylor, B. W., III and Huang, P. Y. (1990). A mathematical programming approach for determining workcentre lotsizes in a just-in-time system with signal kanbans. *International Journal of Production Research* 28(1):1–15.

Rees, L. P., Huang, P. Y., and Taylor, B. W., III. (1989). A comparative analysis of MRP lot-for-lot system and a kanban system for a multistage production operation. *International Journal of Production Research* 27(8):1427–1443.

Rees, P. R., Philipoom, P. R., Taylor, B. W., and Huang, P. Y. (1987). Dynamically adjusting the number of kanbans in a just-in-time production system using estimated values of leadtime. *IIE Transactions* 19(2):199–207.

Rice, J. W., and Yoshikawa, T. (1982). A comparison of kanban and misconcepts for the control of repetitive manufacturing systems. *Production and Inventory Management* 23(1):1–13.

Sarkar, B. R., and Fitzsimmons, J. A. (1989). The performance of push and pull systems: A simulation and comparative study. *International Journal of Production Research* 27(10):1715–1731.

Sarkar, B. R., and Harris, R. D. (1988). The effect of imbalance in a just-in-time production system: A simulation study. *International Journal of Production Research* 26(1):1–18.

Schonberger, R. J. (1982). *Japanese Manufacturing Techniques: Nine Hidden Lessons in Simplicity.* Free Press, New York.

Schonberger, R. J. (1983). Applications of single-card and dual-card kanban. *Interfaces* 13(4):56–67.

Seidmann, A. (1988). Regenerative pull (kanban) production control policies. *European Journal of Operations Research* 35:401–413.

Shanthikumar, J. G., and Stecke, K. E. (1986). Reducing work in process inventory in certain classes of flexible manufacturing systems. *European Journal of Operational Research* 26:266–271.

Singh, N., and Brar, J. K. (1992). Just-in-time manufacturing systems modelling and analysis: A review. *International Journal of Operations and Production Management* 12(2):3–14.

Singh, N., Shek, K. H., and Meloche, D. (1990). The development of a kanban system: A case study. *International Journal of Operations and Production Management* 10(7):27–35.

Sipper, D., and Shapira, R. (1989). JIT vs. WIP—a trade-off analysis. *International Journal of Production Research* 27(6):903–914.

Sohal, A. S., Keller, A. Z., and Fouad, R. H. (1988). A review of literature relating to JIT. *International Journal of Operations and Production Management* 9(3):15–25.
Spearman, M. L., Woodruff, D. L., and Hopp, W. J. (1990). CONWIP: A pull alternative to kanban. *International Journal of Production Research* 28(5):879–894.
Steudel, H. J. and Desruelle, P. (1992). Manufacturing in the Nineties: How to become a Mean, Lean, World-class competitor, Van Nostrand Reinhold, New York.
Sugimori, Y., Kussunoki, K., Cho, F., and Uchikawa, S. (1977). Toyota production system: Materialization of just-in-time and respect-for-human system. *International Journal of Production Research* 15(6):553–564.
Toni, A. D., Caputo, M., and Vinelli, A. (1987). Production management techniques: Push–pull classification and application conditions. *International Journal of Operations and Production Management* 8(2):35–51.
Uzsoy, R., and Martin-Vega, L. A. (1990). Modelling kanban-based demand-pull systems: A survey and critique. *Manufacturing Review* 3(3):155–160.
Westbrook, R. (1987). Time to forget just-in-time? Observations on a visit to Japan. *International Journal of Operations and Production Management* 8(4):5–21.

APPENDIX A

PROCEDURE FOR DETERMINING THE PMF FOR NUMBER OF KANBANS

We now present a procedure developed by Rees et al. (1987) for determining the pmf of the number of kanbans, n. First, the density function of lead time is estimated. Then it is combined with forecast demand value to produce the pmf for n. The preferred number of kanbans to use in the next period can then be determined by using the methodology developed in the previous section. The procedure consists of the following steps:

Step 1: *Start-up.* Permit the transient effects to die out before attempting step 2 if major changes have been made in the operation of the shop, perturbing the shop conditions.

Step 2: *Measuring period 1.* Compute autocorrelation at lag k using the following formula:

$$r_k = \frac{(1/N)\Sigma_{t=1}^{N-k}(x_{t+k} - \bar{x})(x_t - \bar{x})}{(1/N)\Sigma_{t=1}^{N}(x_t - \bar{x})^2}, \qquad k = 1, 2, \ldots, K \quad (11.A1)$$

where x_j is the jth observation of container lead time.

Autocorrelation gives an idea of the dependence of data. We require independently distributed data. For this lag k is determined. If observations are spaced more than k units, they may be treated as independent. Box and Jenkins (1976) suggest at least 50 observations. Rees et al. (1987) suggest between 50 and 100 observations. In practice, to obtain a useful estimate of auto-correlation, K may not be larger than $N/4$.

Step 3: *Measuring period 2.*

(a) Determine lag k in step 2 beyond which all autocorrelations are zero (or in practice below 0.05).

(b) Collect observations spaced k apart from each other to ensure that they are statistically independent.

(c) Estimate the probability density function of container lead times, $f_L(L)$, from at least 100 observations in step 3 (b) by developing a histogram.

Step 4: *Forecast demand.* For the item at the work center under consideration, determine an estimate of the next period demand, D, using company forecasting procedures.

Step 5: *Determine the pmf of the number of kanbans.* This requires a two-stage procedure as follows:

(a) Determine the probability density of random variable n' where $n' = DL$. Remember that D, once estimated, is considered a deterministic constant over the forecast period. In JIT it can be safely assumed that D_{t-1} will not differ from D_t will not differ from D_t so drastically as to change $f_L(L)$ appreciably. Accordingly, it can be shown (Papoulis, 1965) that

$$f_{n'}(n') = \frac{1}{|\hat{D}|} f_L\left(\frac{L}{|\hat{D}|}\right), \qquad \hat{D} \neq 0$$

or

$$f_{n'}(n') = \frac{1}{\hat{D}} f_L\left(\frac{L}{\hat{D}}\right), \qquad \hat{D} \geq 0 \tag{11.A2}$$

where $\hat{D}$ is the observed value of D. Notice that $f_{n'}(n')$ is a scaled-down and reshaped version of $f_L(L)$ obtained in step 3c.

(b) Determine $p_n(n)$ from $f_{n'}(n')$ with mass located at $n = 1, 2, 3, \ldots$ and density at each point k equal to $\int_{k-1}^{k} f_{n'}(n')\, dn'$.

EXAMPLE 11.A1

In this example we illustrate the methodology developed for determining the pmf of the number of kanbans from Rees et al. (1987). The approach can be similarly implemented in industries for dynamically updating the optimal number of kanbans.

Consider a product manufactured in a shop operating 8 h per shift, two shifts per day, and 5 days per week. The other data assumed are:

Unit cost = \$1000.00

Container processing time = 0.335 h

Coefficient of variation of processing times = 0.4

Demand for the product = 20 containers per shift

Solution

The illustration is based on a simulation (using the Q-GERT simulation language) output. However, any simulation language such as SLAM II or GPSS can be used.

Step 1: *Startup.* The startup period to allow transient effects to die down was observed to be 1 week.

Step 2: *Measuring period 1.* Generate correlograms using at least 100 observations at a certain utilization level and Equation (11.A1). The resulting correlogram is plotted for the 91 percent utilization rate in Figure 11.A1.

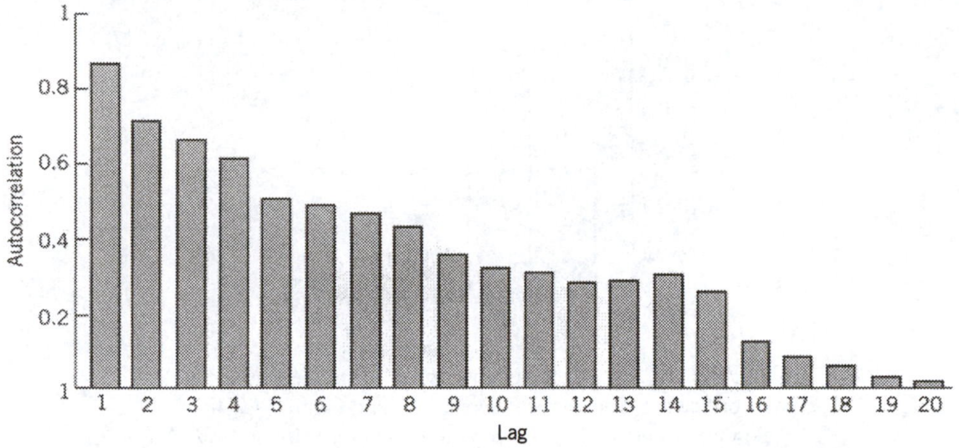

FIGURE 11.A1 Autocorrelation of lead time at the work center. Source for Figure 11.A1 and Figure 11.A2 (below): Rees et al. (1987). Reproduced with permission from the Institute of Industrial Engineers.

Step 3: *Measuring period 2.* Notice from Figure 11.A1 that no correlation exceeds 0.05 beyond lag 19. That means an observation spaced every 20 (actually 19 is rounded to 20) lead times (one per shift) constitutes an independent observation. Collect at least 100 such independent observations. Using these observations, the density function $f_L(L)$ is then constructed as shown in Figure 11.A2.

Step 4: *Forecasting demand.* The demand is constant at the work center for the product. Therefore, the demand for the next demand cycle period ($\hat{D}$) is 20 containers per shift.

Step 5: *Determining the pmf for the number of kanbans.* Using Equation (11.A2) the density function for n' is obtained as follows:

$$f_{n'}(n') = \frac{1}{20} f_L\left(\frac{L}{20}\right)$$

Notice that $f_{n'}(n')$ is scaled down vertically as well as enlarged horizontally by a factor of 20. The density function is shown in Figure 11.A3 and the pmf is shown in Figure 11.A4.

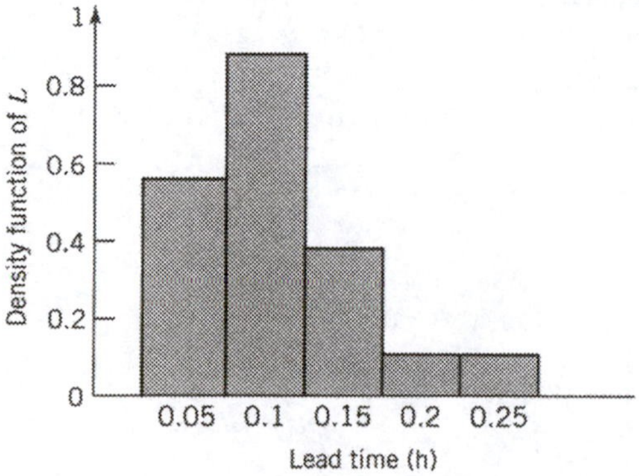

FIGURE 11.A2 Histogram estimates of $f_L(L)$ at the work center.

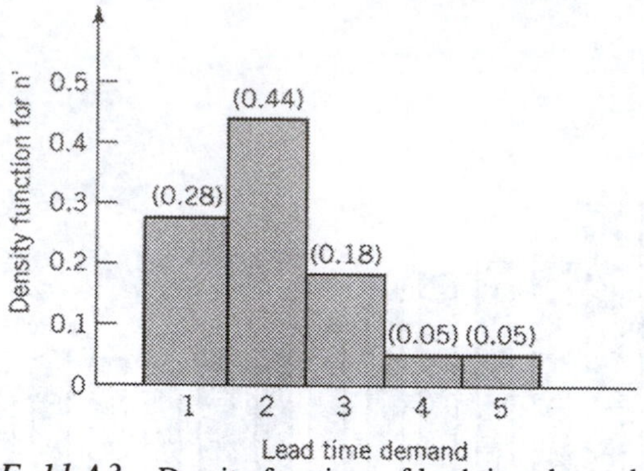

FIGURE 11.A3 Density functions of lead time demand at the work center. Source for Figure 11.A3 and Figure 11.A4 (below): Rees et al. (1987). Reproduced with permission from the Institute of Industrial Engineers.

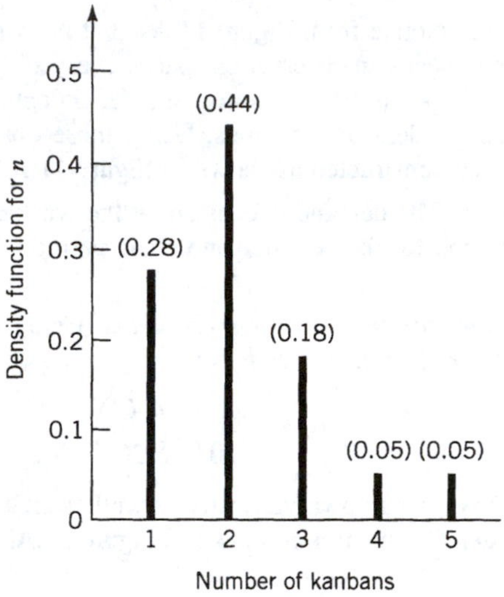

FIGURE 11.A4 The pmf of the number of kanbans at the work center.

APPENDIX B

THE SET OF CONSTRAINTS AND OBJECTIVE FUNCTION FOR EXAMPLE 11.5

Minimize

$$Z = Q_1 + Q_2 + Q_3$$

subject to:

$$0.1q_{11} + 0.1q_{12} + 0.2q_{13} + 0.5Y_{11} + 0.5Y_{12} + 0.3Y_{13} - t_1 \leq 0$$
$$0.1q_{21} + 0.1q_{22} + 0.2q_{23} + 0.5Y_{21} + 0.5Y_{22} + 0.3Y_{23} - t_2 \leq 0$$
$$Y_{11} + Y_{21} = 1$$
$$Y_{12} + Y_{22} = 1$$
$$Y_{13} + Y_{23} = 1$$
$$q_{11} - 10{,}000.00Y_{11} \leq 0.0$$
$$q_{12} - 10{,}000.00Y_{12} \leq 0.0$$
$$q_{13} - 10{,}000.00Y_{13} \leq 0.0$$
$$q_{21} - 10{,}000.00Y_{21} \leq 0.0$$
$$q_{22} - 10{,}000.00Y_{22} \leq 0.0$$
$$q_{23} - 10{,}000.00Y_{23} \leq 0.0$$
$$8Q_1 + 10{,}000.00Y_{11} - 40t_1 \leq 10{,}000.00$$
$$8Q_1 + 10{,}000.00Y_{21} - 40t_2 \leq 10{,}000.00$$
$$8Q_2 + 10{,}000.00Y_{12} - 30t_1 \leq 10{,}000.00$$
$$8Q_2 + 10{,}000.00Y_{22} - 30t_2 \leq 10{,}000.00$$
$$8Q_3 + 10{,}000.00Y_{13} - 30t_1 \leq 10{,}000.00$$
$$8Q_3 + 10{,}000.00Y_{23} - 30t_2 \leq 10{,}000.00$$
$$8Q_1 - 10{,}000.00Y_{11} - 40t_1 \geq -10{,}000.00$$
$$8Q_1 - 10{,}000.00Y_{21} - 40t_2 \geq -10{,}000.00$$
$$8Q_2 - 10{,}000.00Y_{12} - 30t_1 \geq -10{,}000.00$$
$$8Q_2 - 10{,}000.00Y_{22} - 30t_2 \geq -10{,}000.00$$
$$8Q_3 - 10{,}000.00Y_{13} - 30t_1 \geq -10{,}000.00$$
$$8Q_3 - 10{,}000.00Y_{23} - 30t_2 \geq -10{,}000.00$$
$$Q_1 - q_{11} - q_{21} = 0$$
$$Q_2 - q_{12} - q_{22} = 0$$
$$Q_3 - q_{13} - q_{23} = 0$$
$$q_{ij} \geq 0,\ Q_j \geq 0,\ Y_{ij} = \{0, 1\}\ \forall\ (i, j)$$

CHAPTER 12

GROUP TECHNOLOGY AND CELLULAR MANUFACTURING SYSTEMS

Batch manufacturing is a dominant manufacturing activity in the world, generating a great deal of industrial output. It accounts for 60 to 80 percent of all manufacturing activities. The major difficulties in batch manufacturing are due to the high level of product variety and small manufacturing lot sizes. The product variations present design engineers with the problem of designing many different parts. The decisions made at the design stage significantly affect manufacturing cost, quality, and delivery lead times. The impact of these product variations in manufacturing is high investment in equipment, high tooling costs, complex scheduling and loading, lengthy setup time and costs, excessive scrap, and high quality-control costs. However, to compete in a global market, it is essential to improve the productivity in batch manufacturing industries. For this purpose, some innovative methods are needed to reduce product cost and lead time and enhance product quality to help increase market share and profitability. What is also needed is a higher level of integration of the design and manufacturing activities in a company. Group technology provides such a link between design and manufacturing. The adoption of group technology concepts, which allow small batch production to gain economic advantages similar to those of mass production while retaining the flexibility of the job shop, will help address some of the problems. In this chapter we discuss general concepts of group technology and cellular manufacturing. These concepts are used in the design of flexible manufacturing systems. Issues related to flexible manufacturing systems are discussed in the next chapter.

12.1 WHAT IS GROUP TECHNOLOGY?

Group technology (GT) is a philosophy that implies the notion of recognizing and exploiting similarities in three different ways (Hyer and Wemmerlöv, 1985):

1. By performing like activities together
2. By standardizing similar tasks
3. By efficiently storing and retrieving information about recurring problems

The primary advantage of GT implementation is that a large manufacturing system to produce a set of parts can be decomposed into smaller subsystems of part families based on similarities in design attributes and manufacturing features. The decomposition based on similarities of design attributes, manufacturing features, and functions leads to improved productivity in various functional areas of an organization. For example, in product design, parts are classified and coded on the basis of their geometric similarities. The emphasis is on families of parts having similarities of function, shape, and size. To implement GT, formal classification and coding systems are incorporated into a computerized design retrieval system. When designing a new part, a design engineer can find a part in the database that has geometric and functionality features similar to those of the new part. In some cases, only minimal modifications may be necessary. This results in reduced time and cost of product development. In manufacturing, productivity and cost savings are realized by exploiting similarities in machining operations, tooling, setup procedures, and material handling. Parts having similar manufacturing requirements can be processed together in dedicated work cells, leading to reduced setups, tooling, and material handling. Cellular manufacturing, which is an application of GT in manufacturing, provides a strategy for obtaining economic advantages in an environment of high-variety, low-demand production that are normally associated with high-volume repetitive flow production.

In this chapter we study various aspects of GT and its application to manufacturing called *cellular manufacturing.*

12.2 DESIGN ATTRIBUTES AND MANUFACTURING FEATURES

Typical *design attributes* include part configuration (round or prismatic), dimensional envelope (length/diameter ratios), surface integrity (e.g., surface roughness, dimensional tolerances), material type, raw material state (e.g., casting, forging, bar stock), and so forth. The part *manufacturing features* include operations (such as turning, drilling, and milling) and their sequences, batch sizes, machine tools and cutting tools needed to perform operations, processing times, and so forth.

12.3 GT IMPLEMENTATION

A number of GT approaches have been developed to decompose a large manufacturing system into smaller, manageable systems based on similarities of design attributes and part features. These approaches can be broadly categorized into two classes: classification approaches using coding systems and cell formation approaches using production flow information. There are two variations of classification methods: the *visual inspection method* and the *coding method.*

12.3.1 Visual Inspection Method

The visual inspection method involves arranging a set of parts into groups known as part families by visually inspecting the physical characteristics of the parts or their photographs. For example, consider the set of parts in Figure 12.1*a*. These parts are arranged into two families by visual inspection as shown Figure 12.1*b*. This method is

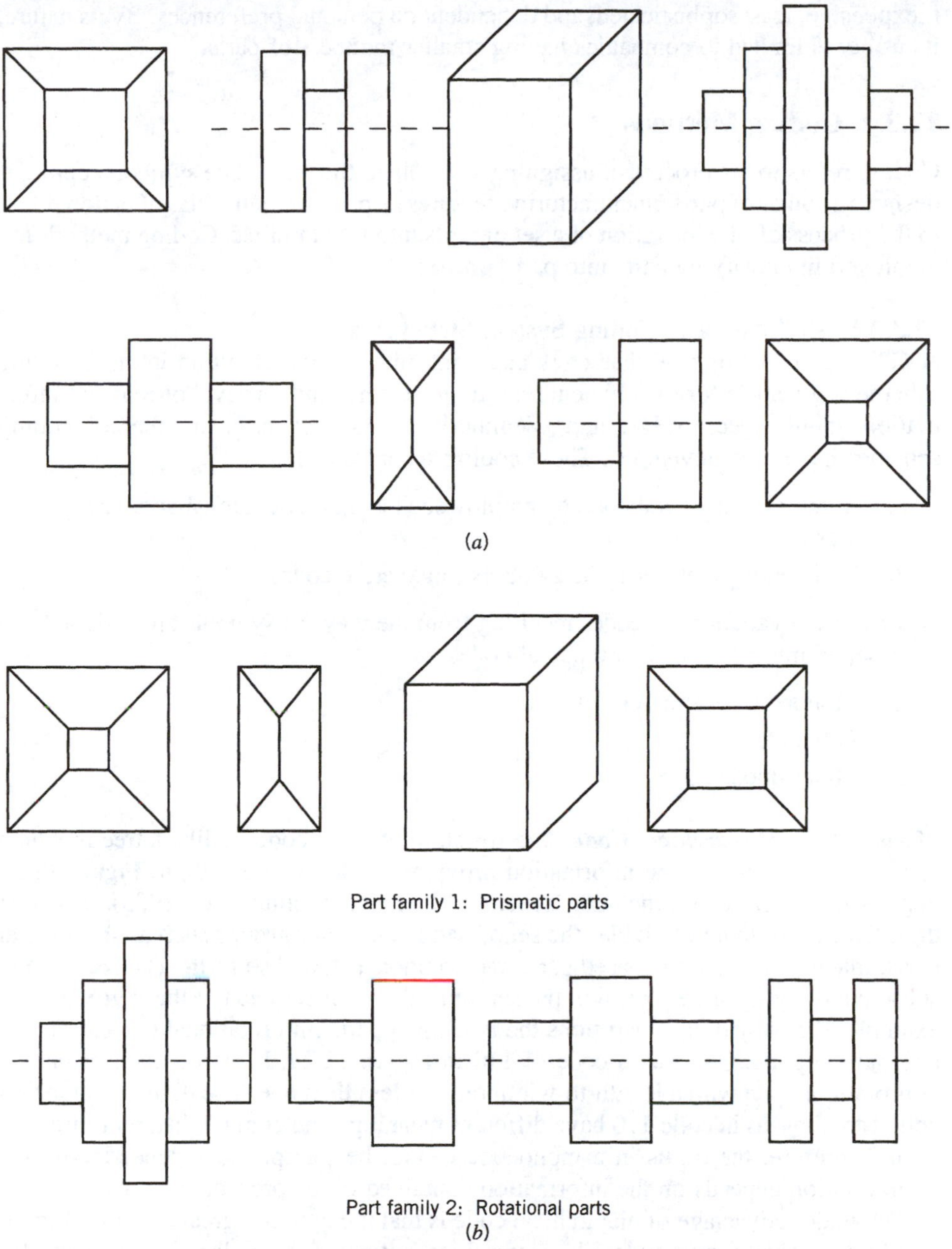

FIGURE 12.1 (*a*) A set of parts with dissimilar features. (*b*) Parts decomposed into part families by visual inspection.

inexpensive, least sophisticated, and dependent on personal preferences. By its nature, its utility is limited to companies having smaller numbers of parts.

12.3.2 Coding Methods

Coding refers to the process of assigning symbols to the parts. The symbols represent design attributes of parts, manufacturing features of parts, or both. Classification refers to the process of categorization of a set of parts into part families. Coding methods are employed in classifying parts into part families.

12.3.2.1 GT Codes and Coding System Structures

A GT code is a string of characters capturing information about an item. A coding scheme is a vehicle for the efficient recording, sorting, and retrieval of relevant information about objects (Hyer and Wemmerlöv, 1985). A large number of coding schemes have been developed. These coding schemes differ:

1. In terms of the symbols they employ such as numeric, alphabetic, or alphanumeric
2. In the assignment of these symbols to generate codes

However, the variations in codes resulting from the way the symbols are assigned can be grouped into three distinct types of codes:

1. Monocode or hierarchical code
2. Polycode
3. Mixed-mode code

Monocode or Hierarchical Code The structure of these codes is like a tree in which each symbol amplifies the information provided in the previous digit. Figure 12.2*a* depicts the monocode generation scheme (Hyer and Wemmerlöv, 1985). The first digit (from zero to nine) divides the set of parts into major groups such as sheet metal parts, machined parts, purchased parts and components, and so forth. The second and subsequent digits further partition the set into subgroups for each of these groups. For example, the second digit partitions the machined parts into rotational (0) and nonrotational (1) parts. Consider a code of 110 in Figure 12.2*a*. It represents a machined nonrotational part with a length-to-width ratio of less than one. The digits 1 in the first and second fields in code 110 have different meanings and contain different information. Therefore, the digits in a monocode cannot be interpreted independently; the interpretation depends on the information contained in the preceding symbol.

The major advantage of hierarchical code is that it captures a great deal of information in a relatively short code. The hierarchical nature of the code makes it useful for storage and retrieval of design-related information such as part geometry, material, and size as depicted in Figure 12.2*a*. The applicability of these codes in manufacturing is rather limited, as it is difficult to capture information on manufacturing sequences in a hierarchical manner. The disadvantage of this type of code is that it requires expertise to conceive such a coding system for a part spectrum. The polycode and monocode structures are often combined for use in practical manufacturing operations involving design information.

Polycode Polycode is also known by many other names, such as chain code, discrete code, and fixed-digit code. In polycode the code symbols are independent of each

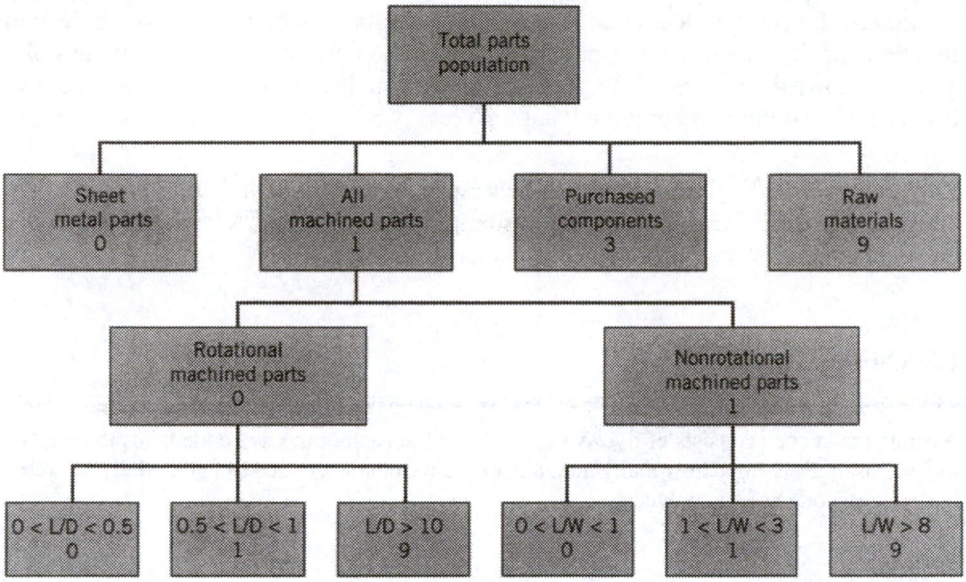

(a)

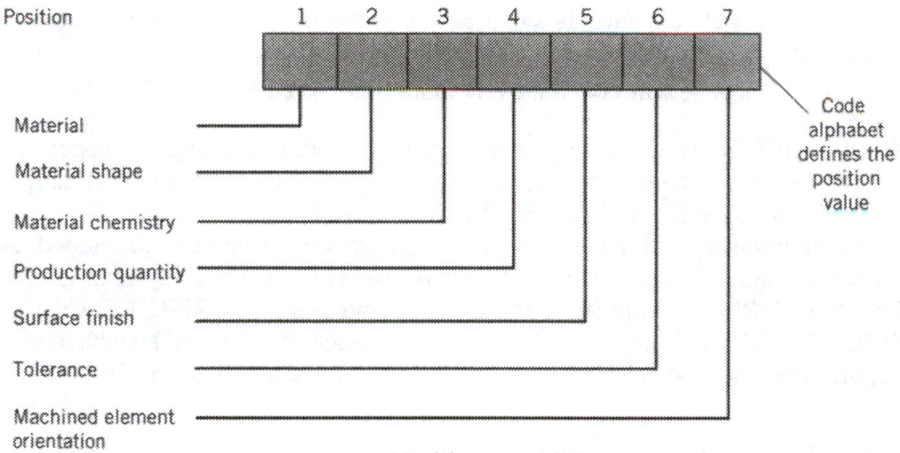

(b)

FIGURE 12.2 (*a*) Examples of a monocode (Reproduced with permission from Hyer and Wemmerlöv, 1985). (*b*) A polycode.

other. Each digit in a specific location of the code describes a unique property of the workpiece. It is easy to learn and useful in manufacturing situations in which the part functions or the manufacturing processes have to be described. An example of polycode is shown in Figure 12.2*b*. The length of a polycode may become excessive because of its unlimited combinational features.

Differences in Information Storage Capacity between Monocode and Polycode. We illustrate the differences in information storage capacity of monocodes and polycodes by an example.

EXAMPLE 12.1

Assume that a code consists of five symbols and that in each of the five code fields the digits 0 to 9 are used. Determine how many mutually exclusive characteristics can potentially be stored in the monocode and the polycode.

Solution

$$\text{Number of characteristics stored in a monocode} = 10^1 + 10^2 + 10^3 + 10^4 + 10^5 = 111110$$

$$\text{Number of characteristics stored in a polycode} = 10 + 10 + 10 + 10 + 10 = 50$$

As you will notice from this small example, the information storage capacity of monocodes grows exponentially, compared with the linear growth in the polycodes. However, monocode will take relatively more time to retrieve information.

Mixed Code Mixed code retains the advantages of both mono- and polycodes. Therefore, most coding systems use this code structure. For example, the Opitz classification system discussed in Section 12.3.3 is based on mixed code.

A large number of classification and coding systems have been developed, and a number of commercial codes are available. A brief summary of 44 systems is given in Ham et al. (1985). A comparative evaluation of four systems, BRISCH BIRN, CODE, MICLASS/MULTICLASS, and Opitz, based on usage, structure and length, computer support, and other special features, is given in Hyer and Wemmerlöv (1985).

12.3.3 The Opitz Classification System

In this section we describe Opitz classification and coding. We have selected the Opitz system for the following reasons:

1. It is nonproprietary (Optiz, 1970).
2. It is widely used.
3. It provides a basic framework for understanding the classification and coding process.
4. It can be applied to machined parts, non-machined parts (both formed and cast), and purchased parts.
5. It considers both design and manufacturing information.

The Opitz system was developed at the Technical University of Aachen under the auspices of the German Machine Tool Association. The following digit sequence is used in the Opitz system:

12345	6789	ABCD
↓	↓	↓
Form code	Supplementary code	Secondary code

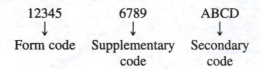

The basic structure consists of nine code fields divided into two parts as shown in Figure 12.3*a*. The five-digit mixed-mode primary code focuses on part geometry, dimensions and features relevant to part design. The supplementary code is a polycode consisting of four digits. This includes information relevant to manufacturing, such as raw material, tolerances, and surface roughness. To help identify the production processes and production sequences, a secondary code consisting of four alphabetic symbols can be defined by the user. The attributes of rotational parts are described by the first five digits as shown in Figure 12.3*b*.

EXAMPLE 12.2

A part design is shown in Figure 12.4. Develop a form code using the Opitz system.

Solution

Using information from Figure 12.3*b*, the form code with explanations is given below:

Form code	1	3	1	0	6

Part class:

- Rotational part, $L/D = 9.9/4.8 = 2.0$ (approximately) based on the pitch circle diameter of the gear. Therefore, the first digit would be 1.

External shape:

- The part is stepped on one side with a functional groove, so the second digit would be 3.

Internal shape:

- The third digit code is 1 because of the through hole.

Plain surface machining:

- The fourth digit is zero because there is no plain surface machining.

Auxiliary holes and gear teeth:

- The fifth digit is 6 because there are spur gear teeth on the part.

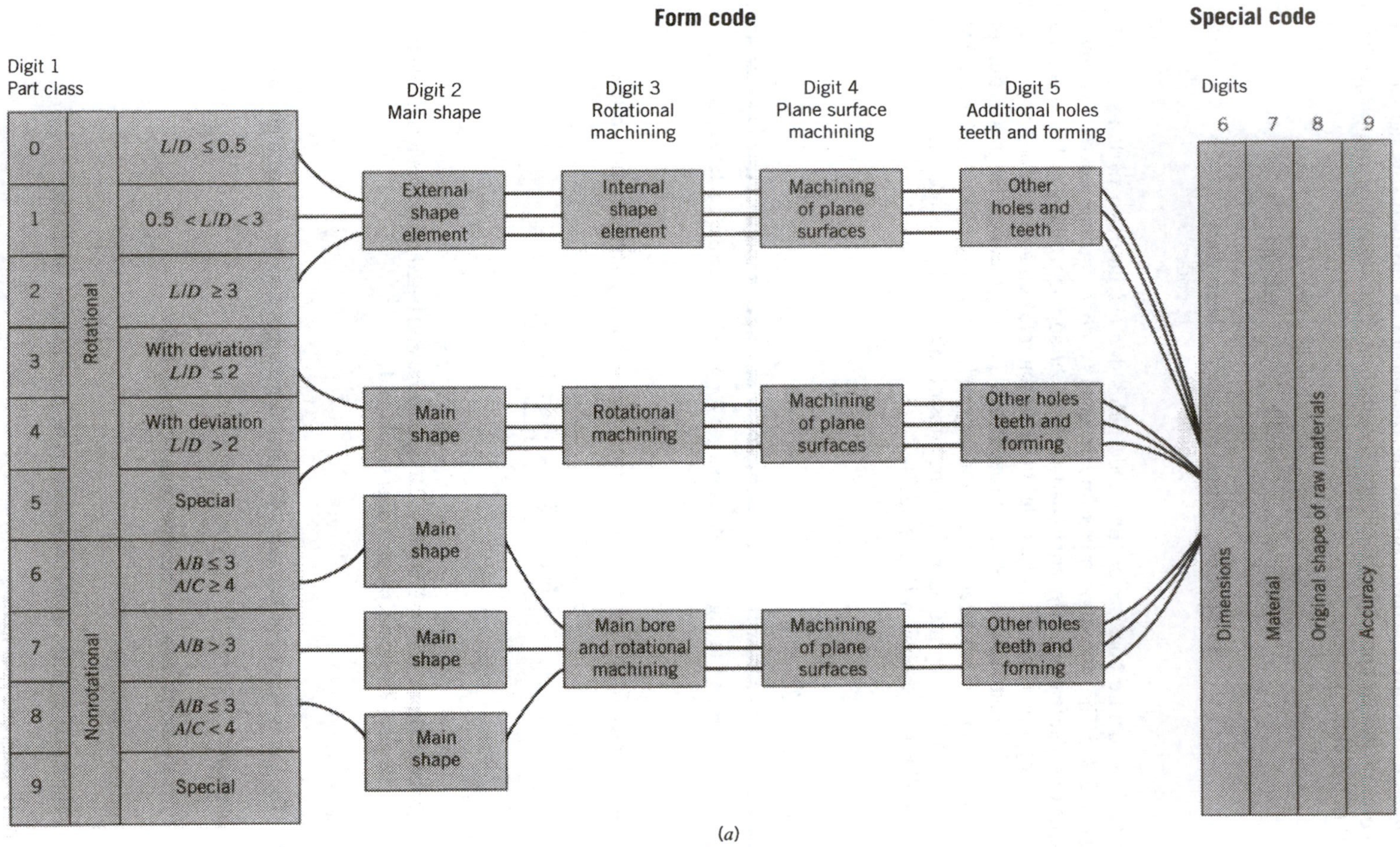

(a)

FIGURE 12.3 (*a*) Basic structure of Opitz code. (*b*) Attributes of rotational parts (Opitz code).

Digit 1			Digit 2			Digit 3			Digit 4		Digit 5		
Part class			External shape, external shape elements			Internal shape, internal shape elements			Plane surface machining		Auxiliary holes and gear teeth		
0	Rotational parts	$L/D \leq 0.5$	0		Smooth, no shape elements	0		No hole, no breakthrough	0	No surface machining	0	No gear teeth	No auxiliary hole
1		$0.5 < L/D < 3$	1	Stepped to one end	No shape elements	1	Smooth or stepped to one end	No shape elements	1	Surface plane and/or curved in one direction, external	1		Axial, not on pitch circle diameter
2		$L/D \geq 3$	2	Stepped to one end or smooth	Thread	2		Thread	2	External plane surface related by graduation around a circle	2		Axial on pitch circle diameter
3			3		Functional groove	3		Functional groove	3	External groove and/or slot	3		Radial, not on pitch circle diameter
4			4	Stepped to both ends	No shape elements	4	Stepped to both ends	No shape elements	4	External spline (polygon)	4		Axial and/or radial and/or other direction
5			5		Thread	5		Thread	5	External plane surface and/or slot, external spline	5		Axial and/or radial on pitch circle diameter (p.c.d.) and/or other directions
6			6		Functional groove	6		Functional groove	6	Internal plane surface and/or slot	6	With gear teeth	Spur gear teeth
7	Nonrotational parts		7		Functional cone	7		Functional cone	7	Internal spline (polygon)	7		Bevel gear teeth
8			8		Operating thread	8		Operating thread	8	Internal and external polygon, groove and/or slot	8		Other gear teeth
9			9		All others	9		All others	9	All others	9		All others

FIGURE 12.3 (continued)

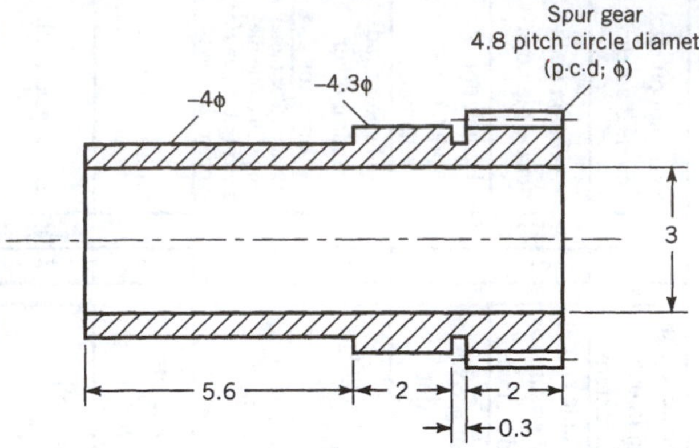

FIGURE 12.4 A simple part to illustrate Opitz form code.

12.4 PART FAMILY FORMATION: CLASSIFICATION AND CODING SYSTEMS

One of the primary uses of coding systems in manufacturing is to develop part families. For example, consider the family of ferrous parts formed by first three digits of Opitz form code 132. This implies that the attributes associated with the family members are length/diameter ratio in the range 0.5 to 3.0, all parts stepped to one end, and internal shape elements with threads.

A number of mathematical approaches have also been developed to form part families using classification and coding systems. For example, Kusiak (1983) proposed a hierarchical clustering algorithm to form part families and a p-median formulation (1985). Gongaware and Ham (1981) and Han and Ham (1986) used part codes in a multiobjective clustering algorithm to form part families.

12.5 SELECTION OF CLASSIFICATION AND CODING SYSTEMS

For the purpose of selecting or developing your own code, it is important to understand the attributes of classification and coding systems. Some of the important classification and coding system attributes include:

1. Flexibility for various applications such as part family formation, process planning, costing, and purchasing
2. Accuracy, to provide correct information on parts
3. Expendability, to accommodate information on more part attributes deemed important later on
4. Ease of learning
5. Ease of retrieval
6. Reliability and availability of software
7. Suitability for specific applications

Matching these attributes with the objectives of an organization would be helpful in selecting or developing a coding system to meet organizational needs.

12.6 BENEFITS OF GROUP TECHNOLOGY

Group technology is a management strategy to help eliminate waste caused by duplication of effort. It affects all areas of a company, including engineering, equipment specification, facilities planning, process planning, production control, quality control, tool design, purchasing, and service. Some of the well-known tangible and intangible benefits of implementing GT in companies in these functional areas are:

1. *Engineering design*
   - Reduction in new parts design
   - Reduction in the number of drawings through standardization
   - Reduction of drafting effort in new shop drawings
   - Reduction of number of similar parts, easy retrieval of similar functional parts, and identification of substitute parts
2. *Layout planning*
   - Reduction in production floor space required
   - Reduced material-handling effort
3. *Specification of equipment, tools, jigs, and fixtures*
   - Standardization of equipment
   - Implementation of cellular manufacturing systems
   - Reduced number of tools, pallets, jigs, and fixtures
   - Significant reduction in up-front costs incurred in the release of new parts for manufacture
4. *Manufacturing: process planning*
   - Reduction in setup time and production time
   - Alternative routing leading to improved part routing
   - Improved machine loading and shortened production cycles
   - Reduction in number of machining operations and numerical control (NC) programming time
5. *Manufacturing: production control*
   - Reduced work-in-process inventory
   - Easy identification of bottlenecks
   - Improved material flow and reduced warehousing costs
   - Faster response to schedule changes
   - Improved usage of jigs, fixtures, pallets, tools, material handling, and manufacturing equipment
6. *Manufacturing: quality control*
   - Reduction in number of defects leading to reduced inspection effort
   - Reduced scrap generation

- Better output quality
- Increased accountability of operators and supervisors responsible for quality production, making it easier to implement total quality control concepts.

7. *Purchasing*
   - Coding of purchased parts leading to standardized rules for purchasing
   - Economies in purchasing possible because of accurate knowledge of raw material requirements
   - Reduced number of parts and raw materials
   - Simplified vendor evaluation procedures leading to just-in-time purchasing
8. *Customer service*
   - Accurate and faster cost estimates
   - Efficient spare parts management, leading to better customer service

12.7 WHAT IS CELLULAR MANUFACTURING?

Cellular manufacturing is an application of group technology in manufacturing in which all or a portion of a firm's manufacturing system has been converted into cells. A manufacturing cell is a cluster of machines or processes located in close proximity and dedicated to the manufacture of a family of parts. The parts are similar in their processing requirements, such as operations, tolerances, and machine tool capacities (Wemmerlöv and Hyer, 1987).

The primary objectives in implementing a cellular manufacturing system are to reduce setup times (by using part family tooling and sequencing) and flow times (by reducing setup and move times and wait time for moves and using smaller batch sizes) and, therefore, reduce inventories and market response times. In addition, cells represent sociological units conducive to teamwork (Fazakerly, 1976; Huber and Hyer, 1985). This means that motivation for process improvements often arises naturally in manufacturing cells. Manufacturing cells are natural candidates for just-in-time (JIT) implementation.

12.7.1 Design of Cellular Manufacturing Systems

In this section we address some of the basic issues in the design of cellular manufacturing systems: What is cell design? What are the factors affecting cell design and what are the cell design criteria? (Approaches to cell design are given in Section 12.8.)

12.7.1.1 Cell Design

Design of cellular manufacturing systems is a complex exercise with broad implications for an organization. The cell design process involves issues related to both system structure and system operation (Wemmerlöv and Hyer, 1987).

Structural issues include:

1. Selection of part families and grouping of parts into families
2. Selection of machine and process populations and grouping of these into cells
3. Selection of tools, fixtures, and pallets

4. Selection of material-handling equipment
5. Choice of equipment layout

Issues related to procedures include:

1. Detailed design of jobs
2. Organization of supervisory and support personnel around the cellular structure
3. Formulation of maintenance and inspection policies
4. Design of procedures for production planning, scheduling, control, and acquisition of related software and hardware
5. Modification of cost control and reward systems
6. Outline of procedures for interfacing with the remaining manufacturing system (in terms of work flow and information, whether computer controlled or not)

It is not possible to delineate a strict sequence of decisions to be made in connection with cell design. One can, however, say that structure-oriented decisions tend to precede procedure-oriented ones. Furthermore, the system structure and the procedures can be changed as experience is derived during the operation of the cell system over time. For example, the part population, the machine routings, and even the machine population are subject to change during the implementation phase or later because of changing internal or external conditions. Within the group of structural decisions, identification of part families and machine groups takes on particular significance, since most subsequent decisions depend on these choices.

12.7.1.2 Evaluation of Cell Design Decisions

The evaluation of design decisions can be categorized as related to either the system structure or system operation (Wemmerlöv and Hyer, 1987). Typical considerations related to system structure include:

1. Equipment and tooling investment (low)
2. Equipment relocation cost (low)
3. Inter- and intracell material-handling costs (low)
4. Floor space requirements (low)
5. Extent to which parts are completed in a cell (high)
6. Flexibility (high)

Evaluations of cell system design are incomplete and not totally meaningful unless they relate to the operation of the system. A few typical performance variables related to system operation are:

1. Equipment utilization (high)
2. Work-in-process inventory (low)
3. Queue lengths at each workstation (short)
4. Job throughput time (short)
5. Job lateness (low)

A major problem throughout the cell design process is the necessity of trading off against each other objectives related to structural parameters and performance variables. For example, higher machine utilization can be achieved if several cells route their parts through the same machine. The drawbacks are increased queuing and control problems.

System cost and performance are affected by every decision related to system structure and system operation. It is, therefore, necessary to evaluate each important design and relate its performance to preestablished criteria. For example, structural variables such as number of machines must be balanced against operational variables such as machine utilization and throughput time using analytical and simulation approaches.

12.8 CELL FORMATION APPROACHES

A number of cell formation approaches have been developed. A comprehensive review of cell formation approaches is given in Singh (1993). In this section we present and illustrate a few of the cell formation approaches.

12.8.1 Machine–Component Group Analysis

Machine–component group analysis (MCGA) is based on production flow analysis (PFA) (Burbidge, 1971, 1977). In MCGA-based methods, machine–component groups are formed by permuting rows and columns of the machine–component chart in the form of a zero–one matrix.

12.8.1.1 Production Flow Analysis

PFA involves four stages, described briefly as follows:

Stage 1: *Machine classification.* Machines are classified on the basis of operations that can be performed on them. A machine type number is assigned to machines capable of performing similar operations.

Stage 2: *Checking parts list and production route information.* For each part, information on the operations to be undertaken and the machines required to perform each of these operations is checked thoroughly.

Stage 3: *Factory flow analysis.* This involves a micro-level examination of flow of components through machines. This, in turn, allows the problem to be decomposed into a number of machine–component groups.

Stage 4: *Machine–component group analysis.* An intuitive manual method is suggested to manipulate the matrix to form cells. However, as the problem size becomes large, the manual approach does not work. Therefore, there is a need to develop analytical approaches to handle large problems systematically.

EXAMPLE 12.3

Consider a small problem of four machines and six parts as shown in Table 12.1. Modify the matrix through row and column exchanges to form cells. The part operations to be performed on the machines are represented by 1 in the matrix; a blank means no operations.

Solution

The solution is obviously to group parts 1, 3, and 5 in one family and the rest of the parts in another family. The two cells thus formed are shown in Table 12.2.

TABLE 12.1 **Part–Machine Data for Production Flow Analysis**

	Components					
Machines	*1*	*2*	*3*	*4*	*5*	*6*
M1		1		1		1
M2		1		1		1
M3	1		1		1	
M4	1		1		1	

TABLE 12.2 **The Cells Formed after Matrix Manipulation Using PFA**

	Components					
Machines	*2*	*4*	*6*	*1*	*3*	*5*
M1	1	1	1			
M2	1	1	1			
M3				1	1	1
M4				1	1	1

12.8.1.2 Rank Order Clustering Algorithm

Rank order clustering (ROC) (King, 1980) is a simple algorithm used to form machine–part groups. The algorithm, which is based on sorting rows and columns of the machine–part incidence matrix, is given below:

Step 1: Assign binary weight and calculate a decimal weight for each row and column using the formulas

$$\text{Decimal weight for row } i = \sum_{p=1}^{m} b_{ip} 2^{m-p}$$

$$\text{Decimal weight for column } j = \sum_{p=1}^{n} b_{pj} 2^{n-p}$$

Step 2: Rank the rows in order of decreasing decimal weight values.

Step 3: Repeat steps 1 and 2 for each column.

Step 4: Continue preceding steps until there is no change in the position of each element in each row and column.

EXAMPLE 12.4

Consider the machine–component matrix in Table 12.3. Use the ROC algorithm to form machine cells.

TABLE 12.3 **Machine–Component Matrix**

	Components									
Machines	*1*	*2*	*3*	*4*	*5*	*6*	*7*	*8*	*9*	*10*
M1	1	1	1	1	1		1	1	1	1
M2		1	1	1					1	1
M3	1				1	1	1			
M4		1	1	1				1	1	1
M5	1	1	1	1	1	1	1	1		

Solution

Use the steps of the ROC algorithm:

Step 1: For each row of the machine–component matrix, assign binary weights and calculate decimal equivalents as given in the following matrix (Table 12.4).

Step 2: Arranging rows by sorting the decimal weights in decreasing order results in the matrix given in Table 12.5.

Step 3: Repeating steps 2 and 3 for columns results in the matrix given in Table 12.6.

Step 4: There is no change in the row and column positions with further iterations.

From the block diagonal matrix shown in Table 12.6, there are a few possible ways to identify the number of part families and machine groups. One such solution, given in Table 12.6, results in three cells. Other solutions may result in two or more cells. The question is which cell configuration is the best. Selection of the best configuration depends on the users and a number of factors such as part types, machine types, and intercell and intracell material-handling effort. Later, in Section 12.8.4, we provide some approaches to answering this question.

12.8.1.3 Other Sorting Algorithms

A number of sorting algorithms have been developed. A direct clustering algorithm (DCA) (Chan and Milner, 1982) sorts the total number of 1s in each row and column in increasing and decreasing order to form the clusters. Other algorithms that offer improvements over ROC include MODROC developed by Chandrasekaran and Rajagopalan (1986b).

TABLE 12.4 **Decimal Equivalents for Each Row**

	Components										
	1	*2*	*3*	*4*	*5*	*6*	*7*	*8*	*9*	*10*	
	Binary weight										*decimal*
Machines	2^9	2^8	2^7	2^6	2^5	2^4	2^3	2^2	2^1	2^0	*equivalent*
M_1	1	1	1	1	1		1	1	1	1	1007
M_2		1	1	1					1	1	451
M_3	1				1	1	1				568
M_4		1	1	1				1	1	1	455
M_5	1	1	1	1	1	1	1	1			1020

TABLE 12.5 **Row Arrangement in Decreasing Order of the Decimal Weights**

		Components									
		1	*2*	*3*	*4*	*5*	*6*	*7*	*8*	*9*	*10*
Machines	*Binary weight*	2^9	2^8	2^7	2^6	2^5	2^4	2^3	2^2	2^1	2^0
M_5	2^4	1	1	1	1	1	1	1	1		
M_1	2^3	1	1	1	1	1		1	1	1	1
M_3	2^2	1				1	1	1			
M_4	2^1		1	1	1				1	1	1
M_2	2^0		1	1	1					1	1
Column decimal equivalent		28	27	27	27	28	20	28	26	11	11

12.8.2 Similarity Coefficient–Based Approaches

In similarity coefficient methods, the basis is to define a measure(s) of similarity between machines, tools, design features, and so forth and then use it to form part families and machine groups. A number of methods have been developed, such as single-linkage cluster analysis (McAuley, 1972), average-linkage method (Seifoddini and Wolfe, 1986), complete linkage, centroid, and median methods (Mosier, 1989), MACE (Waghodekar and Sahu, 1984), cluster identification algorithm (Kusiak and Chow, 1987), and mathematical classification (Purchek, 1975). In this section we present the single-linkage cluster analysis algorithm.

12.8.2.1 Single-Linkage Cluster Analysis

McAuley (1972) used a hierarchical machine grouping method known as single-linkage cluster analysis (SLCA) using similarity coefficients between machines. SLCA was originally developed by Sneath (see Sneath and Sokal, 1973). The procedure is to construct a tree called a dendrogram. Similarity coeffieients between machines are used to construct the dendrogram. The similarity coefficient between two machines is

TABLE 12.6 **One Solution for the Example Using ROC Algorithm**

		Components										
		1	*5*	*7*	*2*	*3*	*4*	*8*	*6*	*9*	*10*	
Machines	*Binary weight*	2^9	2^8	2^7	2^6	2^5	2^4	2^3	2^2	2^1	2^0	*Row decimal equivalent*
M_5	2^4	1	1	1	1	1	1	1	1			1020
M_1	2^3	1	1	1	1	1	1	1		1	1	1019
M_3	2^2	1	1	1					1			900
M_4	2^1				1	1	1	1		1	1	123
M_2	2^0				1	1	1			1	1	115
Column decimal equivalent		28	28	28	27	27	27	26	20	11	11	

defined as the ratio of the number of parts visiting both machines and the number of parts visiting one of the two machines as follows:

$$S_{ij} = \frac{\sum_{k=1}^{N} X_{ijk}}{\sum_{k=1}^{N} (Y_{ik} + Z_{jk} - X_{ijk})} \qquad (12.1)$$

where X_{ijk} = operation on part k performed both on machine i and j,

Y_{ik} = operation on part k performed on machine i,

Z_{jk} = operation on part k performed on machine j.

12.8.2.2 SLCA Algorithm

This algorithm helps in constructing dendrograms. Essentially, a dendrogram is a pictorial representation of bonds of similarity between machines as measured by the similarity coefficients. It is used to present the clustering results. The branches represent machines in the machine cells and the horizontal lines connecting branches represent the threshold values at which machine cells are formed. The steps of the algorithm are as follows:

Step 1: Compute similarity coefficients for all possible pairs of machines.

Step 2: Select the two most similar machines to form the first machine cell.

Step 3: Lower the similarity level (threshold) and form new machine cells by including all the machines with similarity coefficients not less than the threshold value.

Step 4: Continue step 3 until all the machines are grouped into a single cell.

Let us illustrate the construction of a dendrogram and how it can be used to form machine groups.

EXAMPLE 12.5

Consider the matrix of 5 machines and 10 components given in Table 12.3 in Example 12.4. Develop a dendrogram and discuss the resulting cell structures.

Solution

Step 1: Determine similarity coefficients between all pairs of machines. The similarity coefficient between machine 1 and machine 2 is determined as follows:

$$SC_{12} = \frac{5}{9 + 5 - 5} = 0.556$$

Similarly, other similarity coefficients are calculated and are given in Table 12.7.

Step 2: Select machines M2 and M4, having the highest similarity coefficient of 0.83, to form the first cell.

TABLE 12.7 **Similarity Coefficients for the Problem Data Given in Table 12.3**

Machine pair:	M1 M2	M1 M3	M1 M4	M1 M5	M2 M3	M2 M4	M2 M5	M3 M4	M3 M5	M4 M5
Similarity coefficient:	0.55	0.30	0.67	0.70	0.00	0.83	0.30	0.00	0.50	0.40

Step 3: The next lower coefficient of similarity is between machines M1 and M5. Use these to form the second cell.

Step 4: The next lower coefficient of similarity is now 0.67 between machines M1 and M4. At this threshold value machines M1, M2, M4, and M5 will form one machine group. The next lower coefficient of similarity is 0.55 between machines M1 and M2, which is dominated by the similarity coefficient of 0.67 (for example, see Figure 12.5). The lowest nondominated similarity coefficient is 0.50 between machines M3 and M5, at which all the machines belong to one cell.

The dendrogram constructed using the similarity coefficient data given in Table 12.7 is shown in Figure 12.5. Cells can be identified at different threshold values by drawing a horizontal line at that value. For example, four cells {(M2, M4), (M5), (M1), (M3)} will be formed at a threshold value of 0.80, whereas only one cell is formed at a threshold value of 0.40.

12.8.2.3 Other Measures of Similarity Coefficients

A number of similarity coefficients have been defined in the literature that capture manufacturing information that is not available in a 0–1 matrix. We present one such similarity coefficient between machines due to Seifoddini and Wolfe (1986), which also considers the demand of each part. Here, the meanings of X_{ijk}, Y_{ik}, and Z_{jk} are the same as in Equation (12.1).

$$\mathrm{SV}_{ij} = \frac{\sum_{k=1}^{N} n_k X_{ijk}}{\sum_{k=1}^{N} n_k (Y_{ik} + Z_{jk} - X_{ijk})} \tag{12.2}$$

where n_k is the production volume for part k and SV is the similarity coefficient that considers production volume.

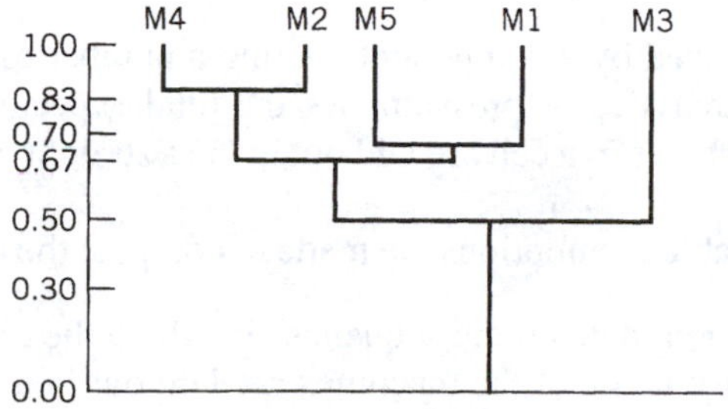

FIGURE 12.5 The dendrogram for the data of Example 12.5.

12.8.3 Exceptional Parts and Bottleneck Machines

The creation of mutually independent machine cells with no intercell movement is one of the important goals of cell design. However, it may not always be economical or practical to achieve mutually independent cells. In practice, therefore, some parts need to be processed in more than one cell. These are known as "exceptional" parts and the machines processing them are known as "bottleneck" machines. Bottleneck machines are the source of intercellular moves that can be eliminated by duplicating a sufficient number of bottleneck machines in the appropriate cells. The decision to duplicate machines should be traded off against long-term savings resulting from reduced intercell material-handling cost.

The problem of exceptional elements can possibly be eliminated by

- Generating alternative process plans
- Duplication of machines
- Subcontracting these operations

However, a solution will depend very much on the nature of the operations involved. A number of analytical methods have been suggested in the literature (Vannelli and Kumar, 1986; Seifoddini, 1989) to help resolve the problem of exceptional elements and bottleneck machines.

12.8.4 Evaluation of Cell Designs

In Example 12.5, we notice from the dendrogram that four, three, two, and one cells are formed at similarity coefficients of 0.83, 0.70, 0.67, and 0.50, respectively. Also, five cells will be formed if each machine is treated as an independent cell resulting in a similarity coefficient of 1. These cell configurations are shown in Table 12.8. The question now arises, which cell configuration is the best and what are the factors that influence such a cell design decision?

A number of criteria can be used to decide on the optimal cell configuration, as mentioned in Section 12.6. However, to choose a cell design from a set of alternatives, a criterion of minimizing the total material-handling cost of intercell (between cells) and intracell (within cell) movements of parts is particularly relevant if parts have a number of operations visiting a number of machines. However, the following factors influence these costs of inter- and intracell moves:

1. The layout of machines in a group
2. The layout of machine groups
3. The sequences of parts through machines and machine groups

The total distances moved by a component visiting a number of machines in a cell has to be determined. Analytical expressions for the total expected distances moved can be determined if machines in a cell are laid out in (1) a straight line, (2) a rectangle, or (3) a square.

The following reasonable assumptions are made to compute the expected distances:

1. In the absence of real data on the sequences in which the components visit the machines, it is assumed that the machines are laid out in a random manner.
2. There is one unit distance between each machine in a group of N machines.
3. A part has to visit two machines in a group of N machines.

TABLE 12.8 **Alternative Cell Configurations**

Similarity coefficient	*Number of cells formed*	*Cell configuration*
1.00	5	(M1), (M2)*, (M3), (M4), (M5)
0.83	4	(M2, M4), (M5), (M1), (M3)
0.70	3	(M2, M4), (M1, M5), (M3)
0.67	2	(M1, M2, M4, M5), (M3)
0.50	1	(M1, M2, M3, M4, M5)

* Each set of parentheses (,) designates a cell.

The expected distance a part moves between two machines in a cell having a group of N machines can be shown to be:

$$\text{Expected distance for a straight-line layout} = \frac{N+1}{3}$$

$$\text{Expected distance for a rectangle layout with } M \text{ rows of } L \text{ machines} = \frac{M+L}{3}$$

$$\text{Expected distance for a square layout} = 2\,\frac{\sqrt{N}}{3}$$

$$\text{Total distance moved in } j\text{th cell for the } i\text{th configuration} = \sum_{j}^{m} d_{ij}k_{ij}$$

where d_{ij} = expected distance moved between two machines for ith configuration in jth cell

k_{ij} = number of moves between two machines by all parts for ith configuration in jth cell

m = total number of cells

The total cost of inter- and intracellular movements (TC_i) for the ith configuration:

$$TC_i = C_1 N_i + C_2 \sum_{j}^{m} d_{ij}k_{ij}$$

where C_1 = cost of an intercell movement

C_2 = cost per unit distance of an intracell movement

N_i = number of intercell movements for ith configuration

The best configuration i is given by the minimum of TC_i over all i.

We now illustrate the calculation of intercell moves and intracell expected distance for the cell configuration $[(M_1, M_5), (M_2, M_4), (M_3)]$ as shown in Table 12.9. The cellular design with machine–component allocations for the third configuration is given in Table 12.9. It may be pointed out that the number of inter- and intracell moves does not depend on the assignment of parts to specific cells. It is, however, important to allocate parts to the machine groups to form complete cells. One of the approaches

TABLE 12.9 **Cell Design with Three Cell Configuration**

	Components									
Machines	*1*	*5*	*2*	*3*	*4*	*7*	*8*	*9*	*10*	*6*
M1	1	1	1	1	1	1	1	1	1	
M5	1	1	1	1	1	1	1			1
M2			1	1	1			1	1	
M4			1	1	1		1	1	1	
M3	1	1				1				1

could be to allocate parts to a machine group in which the maximum number of operations can be performed.

The number of moves passing through two machines by all the parts in a cell (M_1, M_5) is seven. In cell (M_2, M_4) there are five moves (two for parts 9 and 10 within the cell and three for parts 2, 3, and 4 outside the cell but processed within the cell). In cell (M_3), there are zero moves, since there is only one machine.

Total distance for all intracell moves assuming straight line layout

$$= \left(\frac{2+1}{3}\right)7 + \left(\frac{2+1}{3}\right)5 + 0 = 12$$

The number of intercell moves is 10 for this cell configuration. Assuming $C_1 = \$2.00$ and $C_2 = \$1.00$, the total cost of intercell and intracell moves for all the solutions is given in Table 12.10. The third configuration is the optimal solution as given in Table 12.9.

In this approach, the cell layout and the cost of inter- and intracell material handling are assumed to be known. There may, however, be situations in which such information is not available. Next, we present an evaluation approach for the cell configuration that does not require all this information.

12.8.5 An Alternative Approach to Evaluating Goodness of Heuristic Solutions

The heuristic algorithms used for forming part families and machine cells essentially try to rearrange the rows and columns of the matrix to get a block diagonal form. The

TABLE 12.10 **Cell Configurations and Their Analysis of Intercell Moves, Intracell Moves, and Total Cost Assuming Straight Line Layout**

	Cell Configuration	*Number of Intercell Moves*	*Total Distance of Intracell Moves*	*Total Cost of Intercell and Intracell Moves*
5-cells	(M1), (M2)*, (M3), (M4), (M5)	22	0	$2 \cdot 22 + 1 \cdot 0 = 44$
4-cells	(M2, M4), (M5), (M1), (M3)	17	5	$2 \cdot 17 + 1 \cdot 5 = 39$
3-cells	(M2, M4), (M1, M5), (M3)	10	12	$2 \cdot 10 + 1 \cdot 12 = 32$
2-cells	(M1, M2, M4, M5), (M3)	4	30	$2 \cdot 4 + 1 \cdot 30 = 38$
1-cell	(M1, M2, M3, M4, M5)	0	44	$2 \cdot 0 + 1 \cdot 44 = 44$

* Each set of parentheses (,) designates a cell.

ideal situation is to have all ones in the diagonal blocks and zeros in the off-diagonal blocks. However, the block diagonal form is usually far from ideal because of the properties of the data, the inadequacies of the algorithm, or both. It is therefore important to have some measure of goodness of the solution obtained by any algorithm. In the previous section we presented an evaluation of cell configuration based on the cost of inter- and intracellular material-handling cost. This approach depends on the assumed layout of the machines in the cell and cost estimates.

Kumar and Chandrasekharan (1990) have developed an alternative quantitative criterion for evaluating the goodness of block diagonal forms of binary matrices, called *grouping efficacy*. This measure is particularly useful in the absence of information on the physical layout of machines in the cell and the cost of inter- and intracellular material handling. The grouping efficacy (Γ) is defined as

$$\Gamma = \frac{1 - \psi}{1 + \phi} \tag{12.3}$$

where $\psi = \dfrac{\text{number of exceptional elements}}{\text{total number of operations}}$

$$\phi = \frac{\text{number of voids in the diagonal blocks}}{\text{total number of operations}}$$

An analysis of the grouping efficacy function (for details, see Kumar and Chandrasekharan, 1990) reveals the following:

- An increase in intercell movements or voids or both will lead to a reduction in grouping efficacy.
- Change in the number of exceptional elements has a greater influence than change in the number of voids in the diagonal blocks.
- At lower efficacies the voids in the diagonal blocks become less and less significant.

It is worth mentioning here that the grouping efficacy–based approach may yield a different cell configuration than that suggested by the cost model.

EXAMPLE 12.6

Consider the machine–component data of Table 12.3. Further, consider the three solutions with two-, three-, and four-cell configurations obtained using the single-linkage cluster analysis approach and given in Table 12.10. Calculate the grouping efficacy values for these cell configurations. Recommend a solution based on the grouping efficacy criterion.

Solution

Two-cell configuration:

$$\Gamma = \frac{1 - 11/32}{1 + 5/32} = 0.56756$$

Three-cell configuration:

$$\Gamma = \frac{1 - 13/32}{1 + 0/32} = 0.59375$$

Four-cell configuration:

$$\Gamma = \frac{1 - 17/32}{1 + 0/32} = 0.46875$$

The highest efficacy value is for the three-cell configuration. Therefore, the recommendation based on grouping efficacy is to have a cell design with three cells.

12.8.6 Mathematical Programming Models

In the previous sections, we have discussed a number of heuristics for forming part families and machine groups. In these procedures it was assumed that each part can be produced using one process plan. Also, if a machine was assigned to a cell, it was assumed that sufficient capacity was available in each cell to process all the parts assigned to the cell. Moreover, all copies of the same machine type were lumped and considered as one machine. Manufacturing aspects such as demand and processing cost are not considered in most of these approaches in an explicit manner.

In this section we are interested in designing new cells for the parts to be produced. Thus our objective is to identify part families and machine groups by selecting the appropriate process plans for each part and machine type so that the total investment in machines is minimized. There are two ways we can accomplish this: (1) by forming part families and then assigning machines to the part families to form cells or vice versa and (2) by forming cells by simultaneously forming part families and machine groups. The former is referred to as the sequential approach and the latter as the simultaneous approach. If there is only one process plan for each part, then the possibility of forming mutually exclusive cells is limited without duplicating machines. Duplication of machines obviously requires additional investment. It does not mean that the existence of alternative process plans guarantees the formation of mutually exclusive cells. However, if we permit alternative process plans, possibly for each part, and assign machines during cell formation, it may be possible to select process plans so that no additional investment is incurred. This may also lead to a reduction in intercell material-handling cost. Accordingly, in the following sections we present two mathematical models developed by Rajamani, Singh, and Aneja (1990) for optimal cell design. Because the number of machines of each type selected must be a non-negative integer, the models implicitly minimize underutilization of machines.

12.8.6.1 Cell Design with Known Part Families (Sequential Approach)

In this model, it is assumed that the part families are known through a classification and coding system. In a survey of 53 respondents in the United States (Wemmerlöv and Hyer, 1987), 62 percent of the respondents indicated the use of one or more classification and coding schemes in conjunction with GT applications. Furthermore, we assume that alternative process plans for the parts have been developed. As one of the major drawbacks of the cellular manufacturing systems is more investment in machines, we assign part families to machines and form manufacturing cells so that the total investment in machines is minimized.

Consider that there are K part types ($k = 1, 2, \ldots, K$) having demand d_k and M machine types ($m = 1, 2, \ldots, M$) each having a capacity of b_m. Assume that S_k

($s = 1, 2, \ldots, S_k$) operations are performed on part type k using plan $p(p = 1, 2, \ldots, P)$. The unit processing cost and unit processing time required to perform an operation on a part are defined as follows:

$$c_{mskp} = \begin{cases} \text{unit processing cost if operation } s \text{ is performed on machine } m \text{ for the } kp \\ \text{combination} \\ \infty \quad \text{if such an operation cannot be performed on machine } m. \end{cases}$$

$$t_{mskp} = \begin{cases} \text{unit processing time if operation } s \text{ is performed on machine } m \text{ for combina-} \\ \text{tion } kp \\ \infty \quad \text{if such an operation cannot be performed on machine } m. \end{cases}$$

Furthermore, we define

$$a_{skp} = \begin{cases} 1 & \text{if operation } s \text{ has to be performed for combination } kp \\ 0 & \text{otherwise} \end{cases}$$

$$\alpha_{mskp} = \begin{cases} 1 & \text{if operation } s \text{ is performed on machine } m \text{ for combination } kp \\ 0 & \text{otherwise} \end{cases}$$

$$\beta_{kf} = \begin{cases} 1 & \text{if part } k \text{ is a member of part family } f \\ 0 & \text{otherwise} \end{cases}$$

where C_m = cost per machine of type m

B = operating budget

Z_{mf} = number of machines of type m in part family f

Z_{mc} = number of machines of type m in cell c

Decision variables are:

$$Y_{kp} = \begin{cases} 1 & \text{if part } k \text{ is manufactured using plan } p \\ 0 & \text{otherwise} \end{cases}$$

$$X_{mskp} = \begin{cases} 1 & \text{if machine } m \text{ is used to perform operation } s \text{ for combination } kp \\ 0 & \text{otherwise} \end{cases}$$

Minimize

$$f_1 = \sum_{mf} C_m Z_{mf} \tag{12.4}$$

subject to:

$$\sum_{p} Y_{kp} = 1 \qquad \forall\, k \tag{12.5}$$

$$\sum_{m} \alpha_{mskp} X_{mskp} = a_{skp} Y_{kp} \qquad \forall\, s, k, p \tag{12.6}$$

$$\sum_{kps} (\beta_{kf} d_k) X_{mskp} t_{mskp} \leq b_m Z_{mf} \qquad \forall\ m, f \tag{12.7}$$

$$\sum_{kpms} d_k X_{mskp} c_{mskp} \leq B \tag{12.8}$$

where X_{mskp} and Y_{kp} are (0, 1), Z_{mf} are general integer variables, and $\forall$ means "for all."

The objective function (12.4) minimizes the total discounted investment on machines of different types assigned to all part families. Constraints (12.5) guarantee that only one process plan is selected for a given part. Constraints (12.6) ensure that all the operations in the selected process plan are performed on one of the available machines. Constraints (12.7) ensure that the capacity of each machine type is not violated. Constraints (12.8) restrict the operating cost of producing all parts to be within budget.

We now illustrate the model with a small example.

EXAMPLE 12.7

Consider a small company manufacturing four part types. Using a coding and classification system, the first two parts have been grouped into the first part family and the third and the fourth parts into the second family. The parts can be processed on three types of machines. Alternative process plans have been developed for all the parts. The discounted purchase costs for three machine types are \$100, \$250, and \$300, respectively, and the operating budget available is \$350. The unit processing costs and time data for all the parts and the alternative process plans are given in Table 12.11.

Determine the cell configuration and the number of machines of each type using the model developed to minimize the total discounted investment cost in machines.

Solution

The variables are defined as given in the model. For this problem, the detailed formulation and solution are given in Appendix A to this chapter. Once the data file is ready, it is easy to solve this model using any linear integer programming package. On solving the linear integer programming model developed, we obtain the following cell configuration:

Cell 1: Parts 1 and 2 produced on machine types 1 and 2 (two machines of type 1 and one machine of type 2 are required).

Cell 2: Parts 3 and 4 produced on machine types 1 and 2 (one machine of type 1 and one machine of type 2 are required).

Process plans selected for each part:

Plan 1 for part 1

Plan 2 for part 2

Plan 1 for part 3

Plan 1 for part 4

It is relevant to point out here that the model with known part families may lead to a suboptimal solution. This is due to the fact that by preassigning the parts to families, we restrict the parts to remain in a cell. Such a restriction during the cell formation process may lead to inferior results. We present a model in the next section to address this problem.

TABLE 12.11 **Data for Example 12.7**

		Machine Types									
		m = 1			*m = 2*			*m = 3*			
Part/Operations		*s = 1*	*s = 2*	*s = 3*	*s = 1*	*s = 2*	*s = 3*	*s = 1*	*s = 2*	*s = 3*	*Demand*
$k = 1$	$p = 1$	5, 3*				3, 5		7, 2	4, 3		10
	$p = 2$			8, 8		9, 8	7, 7		7, 9		
$k = 2$	$p = 1$	3, 4		10, 9		7, 8	8, 9	4, 3	7, 7		10
	$p = 2$			6, 5		3, 3	6, 6		2, 3		
$k = 3$	$p = 1$	2, 2				3, 3		2, 2	4, 4		10
	$p = 2$			11, 7		1, 2	8, 8		2, 4		
	$p = 3$	8, 1		7, 4		5, 9	9, 5	9, 2	3, 10		
$k = 4$	$p = 1$	1, 2		3, 5		2, 3	2, 6	2, 1	2, 4		10
	$p = 2$	9, 7				9, 8		8, 9	10, 9		
Capacity			100			100			100		

* First figure indicates unit processing time and the second figure unit processing cost.

12.8.6.2 Cell Design Model with Unknown Part Families (Simultaneous Approach)

We present a mathematical programming model to identify part families and machine groups simultaneously. This model is particularly suitable for situations in which the part families are not known. The cell design objective is to minimize the total investment in machines. The complete model is as follows:

Minimize

$$f_2 = \sum_{mc} C_m Z_{mc} \tag{12.9}$$

subject to:

$$\sum_{p} Y_{kp} = 1 \qquad \forall\, k \tag{12.10}$$

$$\sum_{m} \alpha_{mskp} X_{mskp} = a_{skp} Y_{kp} \qquad \forall\, s, k, p \tag{12.11}$$

$$\sum_{kps} (r_{kc} d_k) X_{mskp} t_{mskp} \leq b_m Z_{mc} \qquad \forall\, m, c \tag{12.12}$$

$$\sum_{kpms} d_k X_{mskp} c_{mskp} \leq B \tag{12.13}$$

$$\sum_{c} r_{kc} = 1 \qquad \forall\, k \tag{12.14}$$

$$\sum_{m} Z_{mc} \leq MAX_c \qquad \forall\, c \tag{12.15}$$

where $r_{kc} = 1$ if part k belongs to cell c, 0 otherwise. X_{ms} and Y_{kp} are (0, 1) and Z_{mc} are general integer variables. MAX_c defines the maximum number of machines permitted in cell c.

The product term $r_{kc} X_{mskp}$ renders the set of constraints (12.12) nonlinear. This can be linearized as follows. Replacing the product term by L_{cmspk}, we have

$$r_{kc} + X_{mskp} - 1 \leq L_{cmspk} \quad \text{for all } \{c, m, s, k, p\}$$

where L_{cmspk} are continuous variables but assume (0, 1) values because of the nature of the constraints. The other constraints have meanings similar to those of the model in the previous section except that the parameter f representing family f is replaced by parameter c representing cell c. Furthermore, the additional constraints (12.14) ensure that a part is manufactured in one cell only, and the constraints (12.15) specify the limit on the number of machines allowed in cells.

EXAMPLE 12.8

Consider the data given in the previous example. Furthermore, assume that a maximum of two cells can be formed and that in each cell no more than two machines are permitted. Now, using the simultaneous model presented in this section, determine the cell configuration, the number of machines of each type, and the process plans selected. Discuss why the results obtained with the simultaneous grouping model (which considers part families formation and machine grouping simultaneously) are superior to or at least as good as those obtained with the sequential model.

Solution

Using the model developed in this section, we obtain the following cell configuration and the number of machines of each type:

Cell 1: Part 2 is produced on machine type 2 (one machine of type 2 is required).

Cell 2: Parts 1, 3, and 4 are produced on machine types 1 and 2 (one machine of type 1 and one machine of type 2 are required).

Process plans selected for each part:

Plan 1 for part 1

Plan 2 for part 2

Plan 1 for part 3

Plan 1 for part 4

The simultaneous grouping model gives better results or at least as good results as the sequential model because the sequential model provides only a feasible solution for the simultaneous approach. In the simultaneous approach, there may be many such feasible solutions and the optimal solution selected may not be the feasible solution given by the sequential approach.

EXAMPLE 12.9

Influence of Alternative Process Plans on Cell Configuration

In this example, we illustrate the influence of alternative process plans on cell configuration. Suppose process plans ($p = 1$), ($p = 2$), ($p = 2$), and ($p = 1$) are prescribed for parts 1, 2, 3, and 4, respectively. Using the sequential and simultaneous models, discuss the impact of alternative process plans on cell formation.

Solution

First, we solve the sequential model with fixed process plans. The results are:

Cell 1: Parts 1 and 2 are produced on machine types 1 and 2 (two machines of type 1 and one machine of type 2 are required).

Cell 2: Parts 3 and 4 are produced on machine types 1 and 2 (two machines of type 1 and one machine of type 2 are required).

Then, the simultaneous model is solved. The results obtained are:

Cell 1: Parts 1 and 4 are produced on machine types 1 and 2 (one machine of type 1 and one machine of type 2 are required).

Cell 2: Parts 2 and 3 are produced on machine type 2 (two machines of type 2 are required).

Without alternative process plans, the objective function values for sequential and simultaneous models are 900 and 850. Now compare the results obtained in Examples 12.8 and 12.9 with respect to objective function values. With alternative process plans the objective function values are 800 and 600, respectively. Obviously, the alternative process plans result in efficient resource utilization.

12.9 ECONOMICS OF GROUP TOOLING IN CELLULAR MANUFACTURING

One of the objectives in cell formation is to group parts into part families requiring similar tooling. This helps reduce the setup time and costs. In processing a part family, a group fixture and a couple of adapters are required, which are much cheaper than the number of fixtures required in a conventional manufacturing situation. For the purpose of cost comparison we present the following analysis from Mitrofanov (1966) and Ham et al. (1985):

12.9.1 Conventional Tooling Method

The unit cost of conventional tooling (UCC) using p different jigs or fixtures can be written as

$$\mathrm{UCC} = \frac{1}{n}\left(\sum_{i=1}^{p} C_i\right) \tag{12.16}$$

where C_i is the cost of a jig or a fixture and p is the number of different fixtures used to produce n parts.

12.9.2 Group Tooling Method

The unit cost of group tooling (UCG) is given by

$$\mathrm{UCG} = \frac{1}{n}\left(\sum_{j=1}^{q} C_j + C_g\right) \tag{12.17}$$

where C_j is the cost of an adapter, q different types of adapters are required, and C_g is the cost of a group fixture.

Normally, the cost of an adapter is much less than that of a fixture in conventional tooling. It is therefore obvious from these relations that group tooling would become more economical with an increase in the number of parts in the family.

12.10 PRODUCTION PLANNING AND CONTROL IN CELLULAR MANUFACTURING SYSTEMS

In this section we discuss some issues related to production planning and control in cellular manufacturing systems. The basic framework proposed in Chapter 10 suggests a hierarchical decision process for manufacturing planning and control. This framework is also applicable to cellular manufacturing systems with suitable modifications. Cellular manufacturing systems have certain characteristics that make the production planning problems different from those in traditional production systems. For example:

1. Use of group tooling considerably reduces setup time.
2. Machines are more flexible in performing various operations.
3. Low demands and large variety of parts.
4. Fewer machines than part types.

These characteristics alter the nature of production planning problems in GT–cellular manufacturing systems and permit us to take advantage of similarities of setups and operations by integrating GT concepts with material requirements planning (MRP). A hierarchical approach to cell planning and control, integrating the concepts of GT and MRP, is given here. We discuss through suitable examples how the concepts of GT and MRP can be used together to provide an efficient tool for production planning and control in cellular manufacturing.

We know that GT is one of the useful approaches to small-lot, multiproduct production. We also know that MRP is an effective production planning and control system for a batch type of production system. In an MRP-based system, optimal lot sizes are determined for various parts required for products. However, similarities among the parts requiring similar setups and operations are not exploited. The grouping of the parts for loading and scheduling based on similar setups and operations will reduce setup time. On the other hand, the time-phased requirement planning aspect is not considered in GT. That is, all the parts in a group are assumed to be available at the beginning of the period. Obviously, integration of GT and MRP will lead to a better production planning and control system. We provide an integrated GT and MRP framework for production planning and control in cellular manufacturing systems.

12.10.1 An Integrated GT and MRP Framework

The objective of an integrated GT and MRP framework is to exploit the similarities of setups and operations from GT and time-phased requirements from MRP. This can be accomplished through a series of simple steps as follows (Ham et al., 1985):

Step 1: Collect the data normally required for both the group technology and MRP concepts (that is, parts and their description, machine capabilities, a breakdown of each final product into its individual components, a forecast of final product demand, and so forth).

Step 2: Use GT procedures discussed in the previous sections to determine part families. Designate each family as GI ($I = 1, 2, \ldots, N$).

Step 3: Use MRP to assign each component part to a specific time period.

Step 4: Arrange the component part–time period assignments of step 3 according to the part family groups of step 2.

Step 5: Use a suitable group scheduling algorithm to determine the optimal schedule for all the parts within a given group for each time period.

We now illustrate the integrated framework with a simple example.

TABLE 12.12 **Product Structure**

Product Name	*Part Name*	*Number of Units Required*
P1	A1	1
	A2	1
	A3	2
P2	A2	1
	A4	1
	A6	1
P3	A1	1
	A2	1
	A5	1
P4	A6	1
	A7	1
	A8	1
P5	A7	1
	A8	1
	A9	1

EXAMPLE 12.10

Johnson and Johnson (JJ) produces all the parts in a flexible manufacturing cell required to assemble five products designated as P1, . . . , P5. These products are assembled using parts A1, A2, . . . , A9. Product structure is given in Table 12.12. Using group technology, we are able to divide these nine parts into three part families, designated G1, G2, and G3. The number of units required for each product for the month of March has been determined to be P1 = 50, P2 = 100, P3 = 150, P4 = 100, and P5 = 100. Using GT and MRP concepts, determine weekly requirements for all three groups.

Solution

Product demand is exploded to parts level and the information is summarized in Table 12.13.

Using MRP, the precise number of each part on a short-term (e.g., weekly) basis can be determined. Suppose the weekly requirements for products P1, P2, . . . , P5 are obtained as shown in Table 12.14. This table gives the number of units of each product needed in each week of the month under consideration. However, we do not know the schedule within each week.

TABLE 12.13 **Monthly Requirement of Parts in Each Group**

Group	*Part Name*	*Monthly Requirement*
G1	A1	200
	A3	100
	A5	150
G2	A2	300
	A4	100
G3	A6	200
	A7	200
	A8	200
	A9	100

TABLE 12.14 **Weekly Requirements for the Products**

Part Name	*Week 1*	*Week 2*	*Week 3*	*Week 4*
P1	25	00	25	00
P2	25	25	25	25
P3	25	50	25	50
P4	50	00	00	50
P5	00	50	50	00

Thus, to take full advantage of the integrated GT–MRP system, Tables 12.12, 12.13, and 12.14 are combined into the integrated form as given in Table 12.15. This table provides weekly requirements for all the parts for all the groups.

Next, by applying an appropriate scheduling algorithm to these sets of parts within a common group and week, we may obtain an optimal schedule for each week of the entire month that takes advantage of the group technology–induced cellular manufacturing as well as the MRP-derived due-date considerations. However, if a group scheduling algorithm is used alone on the data given in Table 12.13, such a schedule could well violate specific due-date constraints. For example, one might schedule 50 units of product P1 for production in week 2, whereas 25 of these are actually needed in week 1 and 25 in week 3. We illustrate these concepts in the following example.

EXAMPLE 12.11

Three groups of parts discussed in Example 12.10 are to be manufactured on a machining center in a flexible manufacturing cell that has multiple spindles and a tool magazine with 150 slots for tools. Group set up time and unit processing time for all the parts are given in Table 12.16. The machining center is available for 1000 units of time per week. Using the data given in this and Example 12.10:

(a) Determine whether available capacity is sufficient for all the weeks.

(b) Determine the scheduling sequence for groups and parts within each group.

TABLE 12.15 **Combined GT/MRP Data**

		Weekly Requirements for the Parts			
Group	*Part Name*	*Week 1 Demand*	*Week 2 Demand*	*Week 3 Demand*	*Week 4 Demand*
G1	A1	50	50	50	50
	A3	50	00	50	00
	A5	25	50	25	50
G2	A2	75	75	75	75
	A4	25	25	25	25
G3	A6	75	25	25	75
	A7	50	50	50	50
	A8	50	50	50	50
	A9	00	50	50	00

TABLE 12.16 **Group Setup and Unit Processing Time for All Parts**

Group Name	*Group Setup Time*	*Parts Name*	*Unit Processing Time*
G1	15	A1	2
		A3	3
		A5	4
G2	10	A2	3
		A4	4
G3	20	A6	2
		A7	3
		A8	2
		A9	1

Solution

(a) Using the data of Tables 12.15 and 12.16, we can calculate the capacity required for processing parts in group 1 in the first week as follows:

Group setup time of G1 + 1st week demand × unit processing time of A1 + 1st week demand × unit processing time of A3 + 1st week demand × unit processing time of A5 = $15 + 50 \times 2 + 50 \times 3 + 25 \times 4 = 365$

Similarly, we can calculate capacity requirements for all other groups in all weeks. The results are summarized in Table 12.17.

We observe that the given capacity of 1000 units per week is sufficient only for the second week. For the remaining weeks we have to decide about overtime or subcontracting or some other policy for meeting capacity requirements. Models similar to those discussed in Chapter 10 may be helpful in making these decisions.

(b) Suppose the objective is to minimize the mean completion time of all the parts in the cell. One simple and efficient way to schedule is to use the shortest processing time (SPT) rule. For sequencing groups we will consider the total processing time required by all the jobs in a group plus the group setup time. These times are given in Table 12.17. Accordingly, using the SPT rule, we may schedule as follows:

Week	***Sequence***
First week	G2, G3, and G1
Second week	G1, G2, and G3
Third week	G2, G1, and G3
Fourth week	G1, G2, and G3.

TABLE 12.17 **Capacity Requirements for Part Groups**

Group Name	*Week 1 Capacity*	*Week 2 Capacity*	*Week 3 Capacity*	*Week 4 Capacity*
G1	365	315	365	315
G2	335	335	335	335
G3	345	345	445	445
Total capacity	1045	985	1145	1095

Parts within a group can be similarly sequenced using the SPT rule. For the first week, the parts in group G1 will be sequenced in the order A1, A5, and A3; the parts in groupG2 in the order A4 and A2; and the parts in group G3 in the order A9, A8, and A6. Notice that part A7 is not scheduled during week 1 (why?). Sequences for the second, third, and fourth weeks can be similarly decided.

12.10.2 Operations Allocation in a Cell with Negligible Setup Time

Cellular manufacturing systems permit machine flexibility. That is, an operation on a part can be performed on alternative machines. Consequently, it may take more processing time on a machine at less operating cost, compared with less processing time at higher operating cost on another machine. Therefore, the allocations of operations will be different for a minimum-cost production plan than for production plans for minimum processing time or balancing of workloads.

Production of parts with minimum processing cost and quick delivery of parts are the two important criteria from the manufacturing management point of view. The other consideration from the cell operation point of view is balancing of workloads on the machines. In this section we present simple mathematical programming models for operations allocations in a cell meeting these objectives when the setup times are negligible.

Consider that there are K part types ($k = 1, 2, \ldots, K$) having demand d_k and M machine types ($m = 1, 2, \ldots, M$) each having a capacity of b_m. Assume that $J_k(j = 1, 2, \ldots, J_k)$ operations are performed on part type k. The unit processing cost and unit processing time required to perform an operation on a part are defined as follows:

$$c_{kjm} = \begin{cases} \text{unit processing cost to perform } j\text{th operation on } k\text{th part on } m\text{th machine} \\ \infty \quad \text{otherwise} \end{cases}$$

$$t_{kjm} = \begin{cases} \text{unit processing time to perform } j\text{th operation on } k\text{th part on } m\text{th machine} \\ \infty \quad \text{otherwise} \end{cases}$$

Because the machines are flexible, an operation can be performed on alternative machines. Therefore, a part can be manufactured along a number of processing routes. For example, if a part has three operations and if the first, second, and third operations can be performed on two, three, and two alternative machines respectively, a set of alternate process plans, $l \varepsilon L$, would include, $2 \times 3 \times 2 = 12$ processing routes.

$$a_{kljm} = \begin{cases} 1 & \text{if in plan } l \text{ the } j\text{th operation on the } k\text{th part is performed on the } m\text{th machine} \\ 0 & \text{otherwise} \end{cases}$$

Let X_{kl} be the decision variable representing the number of units of part k to be processed using plan l. The objective of minimizing the total processing cost to manufacture all the parts is given by

$$\text{Minimize:} \quad Z_1 = \sum_{(kljm)} a_{kljm} c_{kjm} X_{kl} \tag{12.18}$$

Similarly, the objective of minimizing the total processing time to manufacture all the parts is given by

$$\text{Minimize:} \quad Z_2 = \sum_{(kljm)} a_{kljm} t_{kjm} X_{kl} \tag{12.19}$$

The objective of balancing workloads on machines can easily be considered by minimizing the maximum of the workloads (processing times) on the machines as follows:

$$\text{Minimize:} \quad Z_3 = \text{maximum}\left(\sum_{(kljm)} a_{kljm} t_{kjm} X_{kl} \right) \tag{12.20}$$

Mathematically, this is equivalent to:

Minimize Z_3 subject to:

$$\begin{aligned} & Z_3 - \sum_{(klj)} a_{kljm} t_{kjm} X_{kl} \geq 0 \qquad \forall\, m \\ & X_{kl} \geq 0 \qquad \forall\, k, l \end{aligned} \tag{12.21}$$

The demand for all the parts must be met. Accordingly,

$$\sum_{l} X_{kl} \geq d_k \qquad \forall\, k \tag{12.22}$$

Also, the total capacity available on machines must not be violated. The following constraints take care of the capacity of machines.

$$\sum_{(klj)} a_{kljm} t_{kjm} X_{kl} \leq b_m \qquad \forall\, m \tag{12.23}$$

$$X_{kl} \geq 0 \qquad \forall\, k, l \tag{12.24}$$

We now formally present three production planning models for a cell.

1. Minimum total processing cost model. The minimum total processing cost model is given by

   Minimize Z_1

   subject to: constraints given by Equations (12.22)–(12.24)

2. Minimum total processing time model. The minimum total processing time model is given by

   Minimize Z_2

   subject to: constraints given by Equations (12.22)–(12.24)

3. Balancing of workloads model. The model for balancing workloads on machines is given by

   Minimize Z_3

   subject to: constraints given by Equations (12.21)–(12.24)

These models are simple linear programming models and can easily be solved using any linear programming package. However, efficient solution schemes based on column generation have been developed by Singh et al. (1992) and Rajamani et al. (1992). It is important to note, however, that X_{kl} variables appearing in the models are integers. Treating these variables as linear enables us to obtain a lower bound on the optimal objective function value. The fact that most realistic cellular manufacturing systems have many more part types K than machines M allows us to claim the proximity of linear programming (LP) solutions to integer solutions. Since the problem has only $K + M$ constraints, the LP optimal solution has at most $K + M$ positive X_{kl} variables. Because at least one X_{kl} is positive for each k, at most M additional decision variables can be positive (that is, at most M parts can have more than one process plan). Thus, at least $K - M$ parts are completely processed using just one plan. For example, if $K = 500$ and $M = 20$, then at least 480 decision variables in the model would be integral (assuming, of course, that the demands are integral).

EXAMPLE 12.12

Consider the manufacture of five part types on four types of machines. Each part has a number of operations. The information on demand for each part, capacity available on machines, unit processing cost, and time for each operation on alternative machines are given in Table 12.18.

Develop a production plan using the following models:

1. Minimum processing cost model
2. Minimum processing time model
3. Balancing of workloads model

Discuss the insights obtained from these solutions.

TABLE 12.18 **Data for Production Planning for Example 12.12**

Parts/Operations		Machine Types m_1	m_2	m_3	m_4	Demands of Parts
1	Op 1	(10, 20)*		6.5, 30		100
	Op 2	†	9.5, 40	4.5, 70		
2	Op 1			6, 80	10, 60	80
	Op 2	7.5, 60		6.5, 70		
	Op 3				8.5, 20	
3	Op 1		13.5, 10	8.5, 25		70
	Op 2	9, 40		5, 25		
4	Op 1	7, 35		5.5, 60	9.5, 20	50
	Op 2		8.5, 40	4,80		
	Op 3		11, 10			
5	Op 1		9.5, 40	7, 60		40
	Op 2	10.5, 25				
Capacity of machines		2400	1960	960	1920	

* (Unit processing time, unit processing cost).

† Blank entries mean that an operation cannot be performed on that machine.

TABLE 12.19 **Results of Operations Allocation and Production Planning for Example**

Parts	*Process Routes*	*Minimum Cost Production Plan*	*Minimum Processing Time Production Plan*	*Production Plan with Balancing of Workloads*
Part 1	m_1-m_2	83		6
	m_1-m_3	17	100	94
Part 2	m_4-m_1-m_4	80	80	80
Part 3	m_3-m_3	31*		
	m_2-m_3		60	70
	m_2-m_1		10	
	m_3-m_1	39		
Part 4	m_1-m_2-m_2	4*	10	4
	m_1-m_3-m_2		32	
	m_4-m_2-m_2	46*		
	m_4-m_3-m_2		8	46
Part 5	m_2-m_1	21	40	40
	m_3-m_1	19		

* These figures have been rounded off to the nearest integer value.

TABLE 12.20 **Machine Loading for Various Operations Allocation Strategies**

Machine Types	*Minimum Cost Production Plan*	*Minimum Processing Time Production Plan*	*Production Plan with Balancing of Workloads*
m_1	2400.00	2400.00	2045.00
m_2	1960.00	1960.00	1960.00
m_3	960.00	960.00	960.00
m_4	1920.00	1557.00	1920.00

Solution

On solving the three models using the LINDO (a linear programming) package, the results shown in Table 12.19 are obtained. (For this problem, the detailed formulation and solution are given in Appendix B to this chapter.)

We notice that some of the parts are produced through a number of alternative process plans. Furthermore, look at the resource utilization of various operation allocation strategies in Table 12.20. We observe from the slack analysis that various allocation strategies result in different resource utilizations of machines. For example, consider machine m_1; its resource utilization for the minimum processing cost, minimum processing time, and balancing of workloads strategies are 2400, 2400, and 2045 units of time, respectively. All three strategies result in 100 percent utilization of machines m_2 and m_3, making these bottleneck machines. This information is helpful in scheduling production of parts as well as preventive maintenance of machines.

12.11 SUMMARY

The focus in this chapter was on understanding GT concepts and their application in cellular manufacturing systems. GT is important because it rationalizes discrete parts manufacturing by capitalizing on design and manufacturing similarities among parts. A survey of 53 U.S. companies showed that the use of GT and cellular manufacturing in U.S. industries has met with success (Wemmerlöv and Hyer, 1989). The benefits reported from these studies include:

- Reduction in throughput time by 45.6 percent
- Reduction in work-in-process inventory by 41.4 percent
- Reduction in material handling by 39.3 percent
- Reduction in setup time by 32.0 percent
- Improvement in quality by 29.6 percent

The surveyed companies enthusiastically supported the cellular manufacturing concept, indicating that benefits exceeded costs. Close to 70 percent indicated that more cells will be built at their plants in the future. It is not surprising. The reality is that cellular manufacturing coupled with just-in-time manufacturing in a concurrent engineering environment is the winning strategy for success in the twenty-first century. The twenty-first century marketplace will be dynamic because of global competition. Product variety will be very high and demands will be low. Customers will demand not only low-cost, high-quality products but also quick deliveries. Under these circumstances, GT and cellular manufacturing will play a key role in meeting the objectives of companies. In this chapter we provided a conceptual understanding of various issues such as classification and coding systems and design, planning, and control of cellular manufacturing systems.

PROBLEMS

12.1 What do you understand by the term, "group technology"? Discuss the uses of GT in various functional departments of an organization.

12.2 Discuss with examples the following: classification and coding systems, monocode, polycode, and mixed code.

12.3 Assume that a code consists of eight symbols and that in each of the eight code fields the digits 0 to 9 are used. Determine how many mutually exclusive characteristics can potentially be stored in a monocode and a polycode.

12.4 Based on the Opitz coding system, develop a form code for the parts in Figure P12.1.

12.5 What is production flow analysis? Discuss various steps involved in PFA.

12.6 What do you understand by cellular manufacturing systems? What do you understand by cell design? What are the criteria used for cell design? Why should you want to have a diagonalized matrix structure?

12.7 Consider the following matrix of eight parts and five machines:

	Components							
Machines	*1*	*2*	*3*	*4*	*5*	*6*	*7*	*8*
M1		1	1		1		1	1
M2	1	1		1	1			1
M3	1			1	1	1	1	1
M4		1		1		1		
M5	1		1	1		1	1	1

(a) Determine similarity coefficients between all pairs of machines.

(b) Use the single-linkage cluster analysis method and develop a dendrogram.

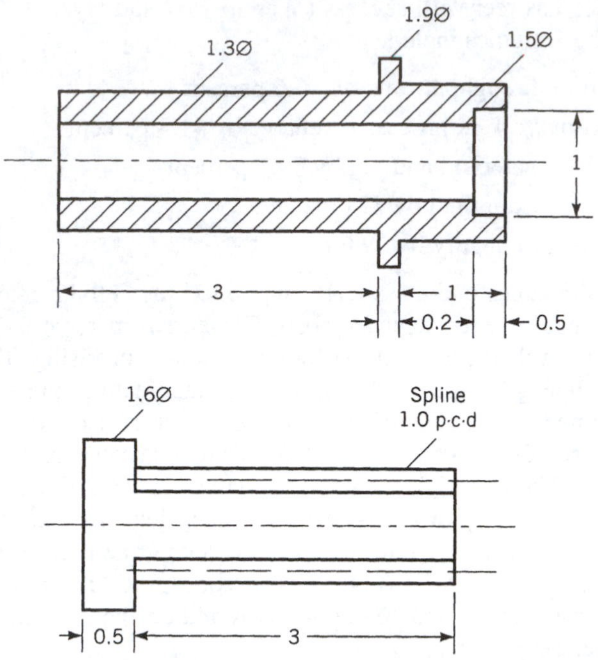

FIGURE P12.1 Parts for Opitz code.

(c) Analyze all the cell configurations in the similarity range 0.5 to 0.8.
(d) Assuming that intercell moves cost five times intracell moves, determine the optimal cell configuration to minimize the total cost of inter- and intracell material handling.
(e) Discuss the ways in which you can resolve the problem of exceptional elements and bottleneck machines.

12.8 For each of the cell configurations obtained in Problem 12.7, determine the value of the grouping efficacy. Discuss and analyze the values obtained for this example.

12.9 Use the rank order clustering algorithm for the cell design for the part machine matrix given in Problem 12.7. Discuss how you are going to resolve the issues of exceptional elements and bottleneck machines. Compare with the results obtained in Problem 12.7.

12.10 Consider the following similarity coefficient data developed from a machine-component matrix. Design a cell using the single-linkage cluster analysis algorithm.

Similarity coefficients between pair of machines	A	B	C	D	E
B	0.75				
C	0.50	0.10			
D	0.20	0.40	0.45		
E	0.10	0.20	0.45	0.50	
F	0.00	0.00	0.45	0.55	0.50

12.11 Johnson and Johnson manufacturing company manufactures four part types. Using a coding and classification system, two part families have been formed: the first two parts have been grouped into the first part family, the third and the fourth parts into the second family. The parts can be processed on three types of machines. Alternative process plans have been developed for some parts. The discounted purchase costs for the three machine types are \$500, \$750, and \$900. The unit processing cost and time data for all the parts and the alternative process plans are given in Table P12.1 on the next page.

Determine the cell configuration and the number of machines of each type using the sequential and simultaneous cell formation models to minimize the total discounted investment cost in machines. Compare the two solutions with respect to investment in machines and allocation of process plans. Assume that not more than eight machines are permitted in a cell. The operating budget is limited to \$600.00.

12.12 JJ company has designed a cellular manufacturing system. JJ is interested in maximizing the total production in the cell. Develop a production planning model for JJ company to maximize the output from the cell in which four types of parts are produced. Compare the results with the minimum cost and balanced workload production plans for the cell. There are two types of NC machines in the cell. Other relevant data is given in the following table.

Parts/Operations		Machine Types m_1	m_2	Demands of Parts
1	Op 1	(10, 20)*		50
	Op 2	†	9.5, 40	
2	Op 1	7.5, 60		60
3	Op 1		13.5, 10	70
	Op 2	9, 40		
4	Op 1	9.5, 30	8.5, 40	30
	Op 2	12, 15	11, 10	
5	Op 1		9.5, 40	80
Capacity of machines		1400	960	

* (Unit processing time, unit processing cost).

† Blank entries mean that an operation cannot be performed on that machine.

12.13 Discuss the following concepts as applied to cellular manufacturing using both suitable examples and the discussion in Appendix C to this chapter:

(a) Syntactic pattern recognition approach

(b) Levenshtein distance

(c) Consider that the JJ company has a cellular manufacturing system consisting of three cells. The company has identified the dominant strings of all the parts in each cell as given in the following table. JJ has now decided to manufacture a new part for an automobile company. The string identifying the sequence of operations for the part under consideration is dfikn. Determine the assignment of this part to a cell using the syntactic pattern recognition approach.

Cell	Dominant strings for the parts
1	acd, bde
2	cfh, fgh
3	ijkl, ilmn

12.14 The JJ company is interested in determining the economics of group tooling for the manufacture of a family of parts recently introduced in the company. Compute unit conventional and group tooling costs if the following data are available:

Cost of a conventional fixture is \$1500, and 25 types of fixtures are required.

Cost of a fixture for group tooling is \$2500.

Cost of an adapter is \$200, and 50 adapters are required.

Parts in a family: 100.

TABLE P12.1 **Unit processing costs and time data for Problem 12.11 on preceding page.**

Part/Operations		Machine Types									
		m = 1			*m = 2*			*m = 3*			
		$s = 1$	$s = 1$	$s = 3$	$s = 1$	$s = 2$	$s = 3$	$s = 1$	$s = 2$	$s = 3$	*Demand*
$k = 1$	$p = 1$	4, 2*				4, 5		7, 2	5, 3		20
	$p = 2$			7, 6		7, 8	9, 7		7, 10		
$k = 2$	$p = 1$	2, 3		8, 7		7, 8	8, 9	4, 3	7, 7		10
	$p = 2$			6, 5		8, 3	5, 6		3, 6		
$k = 3$	$p = 1$	3, 3				4, 9		2, 2	5, 4		40
$k = 4$	$p = 1$			11, 7		1, 2	7, 8		7, 4		50
	$p = 2$	9, 2		8, 5		2, 8	2, 5	9, 2	4, 9		
Capacity			400			300			350		

* The first figure indicates unit processing time and the second figure unit processing cost.

12.15 Develop a plan for implementing GT in a wood furniture manufacturing company.

12.16 Discuss the role of GT as a means of integrating design and manufacturing.

REFERENCES AND SUGGESTED READING

Askin, R. G., and Chiu, K. S. (1990). A graph partitioning procedure for machine assignment and cell formation in group technology. *International Journal of Production Research* 28:1555–1572.

Askin, R. G., and Subramanian, S. P. (1987). A cost based heuristic for GT configuration. *International Journal of Production Research* 25:101–113.

Ballakur, A., and Steudel, H. J. (1987). A within cell utilization based heuristic for designing cellular manufacturing systems. *International Journal of Production Research* 25:639–665.

Bedworth, D. D., Handerson, M. R., and Wolfe, P. M. (1991). *Computer Integrated Design and Manufacturing.* McGraw-Hill Book Company, New York.

Black, J. T. (1991). *The Design of the Factory with a Future.* McGraw-Hill Book Company, New York.

Black, J. T., and Schroer, B. J. (1988). Decouplers in integrated cellular manufacturing systems. *Trans. ASME: Journal of Engineering for Industry* 110(1):77–85.

Burbidge, J. L. (1971). Production flow analysis. *Production Engineer* 50:139.

Burbidge, J. L. (1977). A manual method for production flow analysis. *Production Engineer* 56:34.

Chan, H. M., and Milner, D. A. (1982). Direct clustering algorithm for group formation in cellular manufacture. *Journal of Manufacturing Systems* 1:64.

Chandrasekharan, M. P., and Rajagopalan, R. (1986a). An ideal seed non-hierarchical clustering algorithm for cellular manufacturing, *International Journal of Production Research* 24:451–464.

Chandrasekharan, M. P., and Rajagoplan, R. (1986b). MODROC: An extension of rank order clustering for group technology. *International Journal of Production Research* 24:1221–1233.

Chevalier, P. W. (1984). Group technology as a CAD/CAM integrator in batch manufacturing. *International Journal of Operations and Production Research* 3:3–12.

Choobineh, F. (1988). A framework for the design of cellular manufacturing systems. *International Journal of Production Research* 26:1161–1172.

Chu, C. H., and Pan, P. (1988). The use of clustering techniques in manufacturing cellular formation. *Proceedings: International Industrial Engineering Conference,* Orlando, Florida, p. 495–500.

Co, H. C., and Arrar, A. (1988). Configuring cellular manufacturing systems. *International Journal of Production Research* 26:1511–1522.

Damodaran, V., Singh, N., and Lashkari, R. S. (1993). Design of cellular manufacturing systems with refixturing and material handling considerations. *Applied Stochastic Models and Data Analysis,* 9, pp. 97–109.

De Witte, J. (1980). The use of similarity coefficients in production flow analysis. *International Journal of Production Research* 18:503–514.

Faber, Z., and Carter, M. W. (1986). A new graph theory approach for forming machine cells in cellular production systems. In *FMS: Methods and Studies* (A. Lisoal, ed. North-Holland, Amsterdam, p. 301.

Fazakerly, G. (1976). Research report on the human aspects of group technology and cellular manufacturing. *International Journal of Production Research* 14:123–135.

Fu, K. S. (1982). *Syntactic Pattern Recognition and Applications.* Prentice Hall, Englewood Cliffs, New Jersey.

Gongaware, T. A., and Ham, I. (1981). Cluster analysis applications for GT manufacturing systems. *Proceedings: IX North America Metal Working Research Conference.* SME, Dearborn, Michigan, p. 503.

Groover, M. P. (1987). *Automation, Production Systems and Computer-Integrated Manufacturing.* Prentice Hall, Englewood Cliffs, New Jersey.

Ham, I. (1978). Introduction of group technology. Technical Report, SME, Dearborn, Michigan.

Ham, I., Hitomi, K., and Yoshida, T. (1985). *Group Technology: Applications to Production Management.* Kluwer, Nijhoff Publishing, Boston, Massachusetts.

Han, C, and Ham, I. (1986). "Multi-objective cluster analysis for part family formations. *Journal of Manufacturing Systems* 5:223–230.

Harhalakis, G., Nagi, R., and Proth, J. M. (1990). An efficient heuristic in manufacturing cell formation for group technology applications. *International Journal of Production Research* 28:185–198.

Huber, V., and Hyer, N. (1985). The human impact of cellular manufacturing. *Journal of Operations Management* 4:183.

Hyer, N. L., and Wemmerlöv, U. (1982). MRP/GT: A framework for production planning and control of cellular manufacturing. *Decision Sciences* 13:681.

Hyer, N. L., and Wemmerlöv, U. (1985). Group technology oriented coding systems: Structures, applications and implementation. *Production and Inventory Management* 26:55–78.

Hyer, N. L., and Wemmerlöv, U. (1989). Group technology in the US manufacturing industry: A survey of current practices. *International Journal of Production Research* 27:1287–1304.

Kasilingam, R. G. (1989). Mathematical programming approach to cell formation problems in flexible manufacturing systems. Ph.D. dissertation, University of Windsor, Windsor, Ontario.

King, J. R. (1980). Machine-component grouping in production flow analysis: An approach using rank order clustering algorithm. *International Journal of Production Research* 18:213–232.

King, J. R., and Nakoranchai V. (1982). Machine-component group formation in group technology: Review and extension. *International Journal of Production Research* 20:117–133.

Kumar, C. S., and Chandrasekharan, M. P. (1990). Grouping efficacy: A quantitative criterion for goodness of block diagonal forms of binary matrices in group technology. *International Journal of Production Research* 28(2):233–243.

Kumar, K. R., Kusiak, A., and Vannelli, A. (1986). Grouping of parts and components in flexible manufacturing systems. *European Journal of Operational Research* 24:387–397.

Kusiak, A. (1983). Part families selection model for flexible manufacturing systems. *Proceedings: Annual Industrial Engineering Conference,* Louisville, Kentucky, p. 575–580.

Kusiak, A. (1985). The part families problem in FMSs. *Annals of Operations Research* 3:279–300.

Kusiak, A. (1987). The generalized group technology concept. *International Journal of Production Research* 25:561–569.

Kusiak, A. (1988). EXGT-S: A knowledge based system for group technology. *International Journal of Production Research* 26:887–904.

McAuley, J. (1972). Machine grouping for efficient production. *Production Engineer* 51:53–57.

McCormick, W. T., Schweitzer, R. J., and White, T. W. (1972). Problem decomposition and data reorganization by clustering techniques. *Operations Research* 20:993–1009.

Mitrofanov, S. P. (1966). *The Scientific Principles of Group Technology,* National Lending Library Translation, Boston, Spa, Yorks, UK.

Mosier, C. T. (1989). An experiment investigating the application of clustering procedures and similarity coefficient to the GT machine cell formation problem. *International Journal of Production Research* 27:1811–1835.

Oliva-Lopez, E., and Purcheck, G. (1979). Load balancing for group technology planning and control. *International Journal of Machine Tool Design and Research* 19:259.

Opitz, H. (1970). *A Classification System to Describe Work Pieces.* Pergamon Press, Oxford.

Purcheck, G. (1975). A mathematical classification as a basis for the design of group technology production cells. *Production Engineer* 54:35–48.

Rajagopalan, R., and Batra, J. L. (1975). Design of cellular production systems—a graph theoretic approach. *International Journal of Production Research* 13:567–579.

Rajamani, D., Singh, N., and Aneja, Y. P. (1990). Integrated design of cellular manufacturing systems in the presence of alternate process plans. *International Journal of Production Research* 28:1541–1554.

Rajamani, D., Singh, N., and Aneja, Y. P. (1992a). A model for cell formation in manufacturing systems with sequence dependence. *International Journal of Production Research* 30(6):1227–1235.

Rajamani, D., Singh N., and Aneja, Y. P. (1992b). Selection of parts and machines for cellularization: A mathematical programming approach. *European Journal of Operational Research* 62:47–54.

Rana, S. P., and Singh, N. (1994). Group scheduling of jobs on a single machine: A multi-objective approach with preemptive priority structure. *European Journal of Operational Research* 79(1):38–50.

Remold, U, Blume, C., and Dilmann, R. (1985). *Computer-Integrated Manufacturing Technology and Systems.* Marcel Dekker, New York.

Seifoddini, H. (1989). Duplication process in machine cells formation in group technology. *IIE Transactions* 21:382–388.

Seifoddini, H., and Wolfe, P. M. (1986). Application of similarity coefficient method in GT. *IIE Transactions* 18:271–277.

Shtub, A. (1989). Modelling group technology cell formation as a generalized assignment problem. *International Journal of Production Research* 27:775–782.

Singh, N. (1993). Design of cellular manufacturing systems: An invited review. *European Journal of Operational Research* (special issue on cellular manufacturing systems) 69:284–291.

Singh, N., and Mohanty, B. K. (1991). Fuzzy multi-objective routing problem with applications to process planning in manufacturing systems. *International Journal of Production Research* 29:1161–1170.

Singh, N., and Sushil (1990). A physical system theory framework for modelling manufacturing systems. *International Journal of Production Research,* 28:1067–1082.

Singh, N., Aneja, Y. P., and Rana, S. P. (1990). Multi-objective modelling and analysis of a process planning problem in a manufacturing. *International Journal of System Sciences* 24:621–630.

Singh, N., Aneja, Y. P., and Rana, S. P. (1992). A bicriterion framework for operations assignment and routing flexibility analysis in cellular manufacturing systems. *European Journal of Operational Research* (special issue on manufacturing flexibility), 60:200–210.

Sneath, S. H. A., and Sokal, R. R. (1973) *Numerical Taxonomy.* W. H. Freeman, San Francisco.

Srinivasan, G., Narendran, T. T., and Mahadevan, B. (1990). An assignment model for the part-families problem in group technology. *International Journal of Production Research* 28:145–152.

Vannelli, A., and Kumar, K. R. (1986). A method for finding minimal bottle neck cells for grouping part-machine families. *International Journal of Production Research* 24:387–400.

Waghodekar, P. H., and Sahu, H. (1984). Machine-component cell formation in GT: MACE. *International Journal of Production Research* 22:937–948.

Wemmerlöv, U., and Hyer, N. L. (1986). Procedures for the part family machine group identification problem in cellular manufacturing. *Journal of Operations Management* 6:125–147.

Wemmerlöv, U., and Hyer, N. L. (1987). Research issues in cellular manufacturing. *International Journal of Production Research* 25:413–431.

Wemmerlöv, U., and Hyer, N. L. (1989). Cellular manufacturing in the US industry: A survey of users. *International Journal of Production Research* 27(9):1511–1530.
Wu, H. L., Venugopal, R., and Barash, M. M. (1986). Design of cellular manufacturing systems: A syntactic pattern approach. *Journal of Manufacturing Systems* 5:81–88.
Xu, H., and Wang, H. P. (1989) Part family formation for GT applications based on fuzzy mathematics. *International Journal of Production Research* 27:1637–1651.

APPENDIX A

THE INTEGER PROGRAMMING FORMULATION FOR EXAMPLE 12.7 IN LINDO FORMAT

```
MIN 100Z11+100Z12+250Z21+250Z22+300Z31+300Z32
SUBJECT TO
! ONLY ONE PLAN IS CHOSEN
Y11+Y12=1
Y21+Y22=1
Y31+Y32+Y33=1
Y41+Y42=1
! ONLY ONE MACHINE IS CHOSEN
X1111+X3111-Y11=0
X1121+X3121-Y21=0
X1131+X3131-Y31=0
X1133+X3133-Y33=0
X1141+X3141-Y41=0
X1142+X3142-Y42=0
X2211+X3211-Y11=0
X2212+X3212-Y12=0
X2221+X3221-Y21=0
X2222+X3222-Y22=0
X2231+X3231-Y31=0
X2232+X3232-Y32=0
X2233+X3233-Y33=0
X2241+X3241-Y41=0
X2242+X3242-Y42=0
X1312+X2312-Y12=0
X1321+X2321-Y21=0
```

```
X1322+X2322-Y22=0
X1332+X2332-Y32=0
X1333+X2333-Y33=0
X1341+X2341-Y41=0
! MEET THE CAPACITY
50X1111+30X1121+80X1312+100X1321+60X1322
-100Z11<=0
30X2211+90X2212+70X2221+30X2222+70X2312+
80X2321+60X2322-100Z21<=0
70X3111+40X3121+40X3211+70X3212+70X3221+
20X3222-100Z31<=0
20X1131+80X1133+10X1141+90X1142+110X1332+
70X1333+30X1341-100Z12<=0
30X2231+10X2232+50X2233+20X2241+90X2242+
80X2332+90X2333+20X2341-100Z22<=0
20X3131+90X3133+20X3141+80X3142+40X3231+
20X3232+30X3233+20X3241+
100X3242-100Z32<=0
! MEET THE BUDGET
30X1111+40X1121+80X1312+90X1321+50X1322+
50X2211+80X2212+80X2221+30X2222+70X2312+90X2321+
60X2322+20X3111+30X3121+30X3211+90X3212+70X3221+
30X3222+20X1131+10X1133+20X1141+70X1142+70X1332+
40X1333+50X1341+30X2231+20X2232+90X2233+30X2241+
80X2242+80X2332+50X2333+60X2341+20X3131+20X3133+
10X3141+90X3142+40X3231+40X3232+100X3233+40X3241+
90X3242<=350
END
BAT
INT 51*
GIN Z11
GIN Z12
GIN Z21
GIN Z22
GIN Z31
GIN Z32
LEAVE
```

Running LINDO software will give the following result:
Objective function value
1) 800.000000

* There are 51 zero–one integer variables for this problem. Some systems may require typing all the integer variables, especially when the problem has both zero–one and general integers.

Variable	*Value*	*Reduced cost*
X1111	1.000000	.000000
X1131	1.000000	.000000
X1141	1.000000	.000000
X2211	1.000000	.000000
X2222	1.000000	.000000
X2231	1.000000	.000000
X2241	1.000000	.000000
X1322	1.000000	.000000
X2341	1.000000	.000000
Y11	1.000000	.000000
Y22	1.000000	.000000
Y31	1.000000	.000000
Y41	1.000000	.000000
Z11	2.000000	100.000000
Z12	1.000000	100.000000
Z21	1.000000	250.000000
Z22	1.000000	250.000000

APPENDIX B

LINEAR PROGRAMMING FORMULATION OF EXAMPLE 12.12

1. Minimum Processing Cost Objective

$$\text{Min } f = 60X_{11} + 90X_{12} + 100X_{13} + 70X_{14} + 140X_{21} + 170X_{22} + 160X_{23} + 150X_{24} + 50X_{31} + 35X_{32} + 50X_{33} + 65X_{34} + 85X_{41} + 125X_{42} + 110X_{43} + 150X_{44} + 70X_{45} + 110X_{46} + 65X_{51} + 85X_{52}$$

Subject to:
Demand satisfaction constraints

$$X_{11} + X_{12} + X_{13} + X_{14} \geq 100$$
$$X_{21} + X_{22} + X_{23} + X_{24} \geq 80$$
$$X_{31} + X_{32} + X_{33} + X_{34} \geq 70$$
$$X_{41} + X_{42} + X_{43} + X_{44} + X_{45} + X_{46} \geq 50$$
$$X_{51} + X_{52} \geq 40$$

Machine capacity constraints:

$$10X_{11} + 10X_{12} + 7.5X_{21} + 7.5X_{23} + 9X_{33} + 9X_{34} + 7X_{41} + 7X_{42} + 10.5X_{51} + 10.5X_{52} \leq 2400$$

$9.5X_{11} + 9.5X_{14} + 13.5X_{32} + 13.5X_{33} + 19.5X_{41} + 11X_{42} + 19.5X_{43} + 11X_{44} + 19.5X_{45} + 11X_{46} + 9.5X_{51} \leq 1960$

$4.5X_{12} + 11X_{13} + 6.5X_{14} + 12.5X_{22} + 6X_{23} + 6.5X_{24} + 13.5X_{31} + 5X_{32} + 8.5X_{34} + 5.5X_{42} + 5.5X_{43} + 9.5X_{44} + 4X_{46} + 7X_{52} \leq 960$

$18.5X_{21} + 8.5X_{22} + 8.5X_{23} + 18.5X_{24} + 9.5X_{45} + 9.5X_{46} \leq 1920$

2. Minimum Processing Time Objective

$$\text{Min}\, f = 19.5X_{11} + 14.5X_{12} + 11X_{13} + 16X_{14} + 26X_{21} + 21X_{22} + 22X_{23} + 25X_{24} + 13.5X_{31} + 18.5X_{32} + 22.5X_{33} + 17.5X_{34} + 26.5X_{41} + 22X_{42} + 25X_{43} + 20.5X_{44} + 29X_{45} + 24.5X_{46} + 20X_{51} + 17.5X_{52}$$

Subject to:
The same constraints as given for the minimum cost model.

3. Balancing Of Workloads Objective Function

$$\text{Min}\, f = Z_3$$

Subject to:
All the constraints given for the first model as well as the following extra constraints:

$Z_3 - (10X_{11} + 10X_{12} + 7.5X_{21} + 7.5X_{23} + 9X_{33} + 9X_{34} + 7X_{41} + 7X_{42} + 10.5X_{51} + 10.5X_{52}) \geq 0$

$Z_3 - (9.5X_{11} + 9.5X_{14} + 13.5X_{32} + 13.5X_{33} + 19.5X_{41} + 11X_{42} + 19.5X_{43} + 11X_{44} + 19.5X_{45} + 11X_{46} + 9.5X_{51}) \geq 0$

$Z_3 - (4.5X_{12} + 11X_{13} + 6.5X_{14} + 12.5X_{22} + 6X_{23} + 6.5X_{24} + 13.5X_{31} + 5X_{32} + 8.5X_{34} + 5.5X_{42} + 5.5X_{43} + 9.5X_{44} + 4X_{46} + 7X_{52}) \geq 0$

$Z_3 - (18.5X_{21} + 8.5X_{22} + 8.5X_{23} + 18.5X_{24} + 9.5X_{45} + 9.5X_{46}) \geq 0$

APPENDIX C

SYNTACTIC PATTERN RECOGNITION APPROACH TO ALLOCATION OF NEW PARTS TO EXISTING PART FAMILIES AND CELLS

The syntactic pattern recognition (SPR) approach has been applied in the design of cellular manufacturing systems (Wu et al., 1986). Over a period of time, design changes take place and many existing parts are replaced by new ones. To accommodate such changes in a cellular manufacturing environment, the most important question is, to which cell should these new parts be allocated so that the setup requirements are minimal as possible? SPRA considers the sequence of operations to determine the distances. It is therefore particularly useful in situations involving part operations with high setup times. In this section we illustrate the application of SPRA to assigning new parts to existing cells.

Syntactic pattern recognition is analogous to natural languages and borrows most of its analysis methods from formal language theory. A pattern is represented by a sentence in a language that is specified by grammar. The language, which provides the structural description of patterns in terms of a set of pattern primitives and their composition relations, is sometimes called the *pattern description language.* The rules that define valid composition of primitives into patterns are specified by *pattern grammar.* Formally, a grammar G is defined as a 4-tuple (Fu, 1982):

$$G = (V_t, V_n, P, S)$$

where $V_t = \{a, b\}$ is a set of terminal symbols (the primitives)

$V_n = \{\mathrm{S, A}\}$ is a set of nonterminal symbols (the primitives)

$P = \{S \rightarrow aA, A \rightarrow aA, A \rightarrow b\}$ is a set of production rules or rewrite rules and $\rightarrow$ represents "deduces"

S = a unique symbol called the start symbol

A sentence in the language $L(G)$ may be derived from the start symbol S by applying production rules from P. An example of generating a pattern of $L(G)$ is as follows:

1. From the start symbol S, applying the first rule of P, the subpattern aA is obtained.

$$S \rightarrow aA$$

2. Applying the third rule of P, a pattern ab is obtained.

$$aA \rightarrow ab$$

3. Since no further rules can be applied to *ab,* it is the final pattern. In general, the language $L(G)$ is the set of all strings of the form $a^n b$, $n = 1, 2, \ldots$.

In the context of manufacturing, the order in which the operations are performed can be written in the form of grammar.

Consider a part requiring five operations: turning (t), drilling (d), boring (b), milling (m), and grinding (g). The grammar G can be written as follows:

$$G = (V_t, V_n, P, S)$$

where $V_t = \{\mathrm{t, d, b, m, g}\}$ is a set of terminal symbols (the primitives)

$V_n = \{S, A, B, C, D\}$ is a set of nonterminal symbols (the primitives)

$P = \{S \rightarrow \mathrm{t}A, A \rightarrow dB, B \rightarrow bC, C \rightarrow \mathrm{md}, D \rightarrow \mathrm{g}\}$,

By applying the production rules, the sequence of operations to be performed on the part can be obtained.

THE CONCEPT OF LEVENSHTEIN DISTANCE

In a cellular manufacturing situation, a string essentially represents the sequences of operations of parts. The distance between two strings x and y is defined as the smallest number of transformations required to derive y from x. Such a measure is called *Levenshtein distance* (Fu, 1982). The types of transformations defined are deletions, insertions, and substitutions. Weights can be attached to these distances. Let us illustrate these transformations by an example from Wu et al. (1986). Consider the strings *abcd, ab, ade,* and *ef.* The distances between string *abcd* and the other three strings are:

Strings	***Distance***
abcd → *ab*	2 deletions
abcd → *ade*	2 deletions + 1 insertion
abcd → *ef*	2 substitutions + 2 deletions

EXAMPLE 12.A1

Assignment of New Parts to Existing Cells: The SPR Approach

Suppose two cells are being operated in a company. The first cell consists of five machines coded as *abcde.* The first cell has parts with dominant strings of *acd* and *bcde.* The second cell consists of four machines coded as *fghi.* The dominant strings of parts are *fh* and *fgi.* Now the company decides to manufacture a new part requiring operations on machines *a, c, d,* and *h.* The corresponding string is *acdh.* Determine the assignment of the new part to a cell.

Solution

The assignment of a new part to a cell is based on the minimum Levenshtein distance. The Levenshtein distances between the part and the first and second cell strings, respectively, are:

Cell	***Dominant Component Strings***	***Distance with* acdh**
1	*acd, bcde*	1 (1 insertion)
2	*fh, fgi*	3 (2 insertions + 1 substitution)

The distance of the part with cell 1 is 1, whereas with cell 2 it is 3. Therefore, the part is assigned to the first cell.

CHAPTER 13

FLEXIBLE MANUFACTURING SYSTEMS

The customers are changing, and so is the nature of their demand. Customer demand is becoming individualistic, leading to product variations. The multitude of product variations, the complexity and exacting nature of these products coupled with increased international competition, the need to reduce the manufacturing cycle time, and the pressure to cut production costs require the development of manufacturing technologies and methods that permit small-batch production to gain economic advantages similar to those of mass production while retaining the flexibility of discrete-product manufacturing. The development of computer-integrated manufacturing (CIM) systems for the manufacture of parts ranging from low-volume, high-variety to high-volume, low-variety parts, and particularly of flexible manufacturing systems (FMSs) for mid-volume, mid-variety parts, addresses many of these problems.

In the previous chapter we discussed issues related to group technology and cellular manufacturing. These concepts are a significant part of an FMS. In this chapter we provide a basic understanding of flexibility, volume–variety relationships, and their characteristics that distinguish between various CIM systems. The physical and control subsystems of FMS are discussed. Layout problems specific to FMS are detailed and a simple mathematical analysis for one case is presented. Some discussions of part type selection and tool management strategies are given. Sequencing in a robotic cell is discussed. Furthermore, basic concepts in discrete-event system simulation are covered, followed by a case study.

13.1 FLEXIBILITY

Flexibility is the cornerstone of and one of the key concepts used in the design of modern automated manufacturing systems such as flexible manufacturing systems. A number of papers have appeared in the literature on various aspects of flexibility. Gupta and Goyal (1990) provide a comprehensive review of the literature on flexibility. The facts are that flexibility has multiple dimensions and the concept of flexibility still remains vague. In this section we attempt to answer these questions: What is flexibility? What are the different types of flexibility? What are the implications of flexibility in manufacturing systems? How are manufacturing systems distinguished on the basis of flexibility?

Flexibility can be defined as a collection of properties of a manufacturing system that support changes in production activities or capabilities (Carter, 1986). Normally, the changes are due to both internal and external factors. Internal changes could be due to equipment breakdowns, software failures, worker absenteeism, variability in processing times, and so forth. Some degree of redundancy in the system is required to cope with internal changes. This, however, adds more capacity. Changes in product design, demand, and product mix typically represent external changes. To absorb uncertainties due to product design changes, the manufacturing system must be versatile and able to produce the intended variety of part types with minimal cost and lead time. Some degree of redundancy may, however, be required to cope with changes in the demand and product mix. We can therefore say that the flexibility refers to the ability of the manufacturing system to respond effectively to both internal and external changes by having built-in redundancy of versatile equipment. We will consider various types of manufacturing systems and implications of flexibility for their performance in Section 13.2.

A number of types of flexibility have been discussed. Gerwin (1982), Browne et al. (1984), Carter (1986), and Falkner (1986), among others, have defined a number of flexibility measures. In the following section we discuss various types of flexibility.

13.1.1 Machine Flexibility

Machine flexibility refers to the capability of a machine to perform a variety of operations on a variety of part types and sizes.

The other measure of machine flexibility is the universe of part types that a machine can produce. It implies ease with which the parts are changed over from one part type to another on a machine. The changeover time, which includes setup, tool changing, part-program transfer, and part move times, is an important measure of machine flexibility. Computer numerical control (CNC) machining centers are normally equipped with automatic tool changer, part buffer storage, part programs, and fixtured parts on pallets. The benefits resulting from such machine flexibility and quick part type changeovers are that the small lot sizes are economical and lead times are lower. Furthermore, machine flexibility provides routing and mix flexibility.

13.1.2 Routing Flexibility

Routing flexibility means that a part(s) can be manufactured or assembled along alternative routes. The alternative routes are possible if manufacturing or assembly operations can be performed on alternative machines, in alternative sequences, or with alternative resources. Because a wide variety of operations can be performed on flexible machines, they provide routing flexibility.

Routing flexibility is used primarily to manage internal changes resulting from equipment breakdowns, tool breakages, controller failures, and so on. Of course, the internal changes can be minimized by such measures as on-line monitoring of failures and preventive maintenance programs. Inventory has traditionally been employed to provide dependable production under conditions of equipment failures. Routing flexibility is yet another means of providing dependable production.

Routing flexibility can also help increase throughput in the presence of external changes such as product mix, engineering changes, or new product introductions.

These changes alter machine workloads and cause bottlenecks. The use of alternative routings helps provide relief, thereby resolving the bottleneck problem and permitting increased production. Therefore, routing flexibility is one way to achieve mix flexibility.

Routing flexibility is becoming a more acceptable means of improving the dependability of manufacturing systems. However, a balanced approach is required, employing a combination of small work-in-process buffers, machinery improvements, better repair and preventive maintenance practices, and routing flexibility.

13.1.3 Process Flexibility

Process flexibility, also known as mix flexibility, refers to the ability to absorb changes in the product mix by performing similar operations or producing similar products or parts on multipurpose, adaptable, CNC machining centers. Mix flexibility provides protection against market variability by accommodating changes in product mix due to the use of shared resources. However, extreme mix variations would result in requirements for a greater number of tools, fixtures, and other resources.

13.1.4 Product Flexibility

Product flexibility, also known as mix-change flexibility, refers to the ability to change over to a new set of products economically and quickly in response to markets or engineering changes or even to operate on a make-to-order basis. The changeover time includes time in all the activities of new product manufacture, such as design, process planning, tooling, and fixturing. This time can be minimized by using the principles of group technology in design and manufacturing as well as using flexible machines and software. The product flexibility of a manufacturing system in a company is a barometer of its competitiveness.

13.1.5 Production Flexibility

Production flexibility refers to the ability to produce a range of products without adding major capital equipment, even though new tooling or other resources may be required. The product envelope, that is, the range of products that can be produced by a manufacturing system at moderate cost and time, is determined by the process envelope. The process envelope in turn is determined by the hardware and software capabilities of a manufacturing system, such as variety of machines, their flexibility, the material-handling system, and the factory information and control system. If the process envelope is large, production flexibility enables quick introductions of new products or redesign of existing products without major equipment additions. However, the greater the production flexibility, the higher will be the investment in flexible capital equipment and software.

13.1.6 Expansion Flexibility

Expansion flexibility refers to the ability to change a manufacturing system with a view to accommodating a changed product envelope. In the case of production flexibility there is no change in the major capital equipment. In the case of expansion flexibility there are additions as well as replacements of equipment, but these changes are easy to make because such provisions are made in the original manufacturing system design. For example, automated guided vehicles can be more easily rerouted than conveyors; modular design of system software makes it possible to change a module rather than the whole system. The objectives are to reduce implementation time and cost of new products, variations in current products, and changes in designs.

13.2 VOLUME–VARIETY RELATIONSHIPS FOR UNDERSTANDING PRODUCTION SYSTEMS

Production systems can be classified based on the volume–variety considerations. A highly flexible system permits manufacture of a high variety of parts. Two extreme production situations are *high-volume, low-variety* (H–L) and *low-volume, high-variety* (L–H). Between these two extremes there is an important *mid-volume, mid-variety* (M–M) production situation. We discuss five types of manufacturing systems:

1. Transfer line
2. Stand-alone numerical control (NC) machine
3. Manufacturing cell
4. Special manufacturing system
5. Flexible manufacturing system

These systems cover H–L, L–H, and M–M production situations. There is an inverse relationship between variety (flexibility) and production volume as shown in Figure 13.1.

13.2.1 High-Volume, Low-Variety (H–L) Production System

A classical example of high-volume, low-variety manufacturing system is a transfer line. It is also referred to as a fixed automation manufacturing system in which dedi-

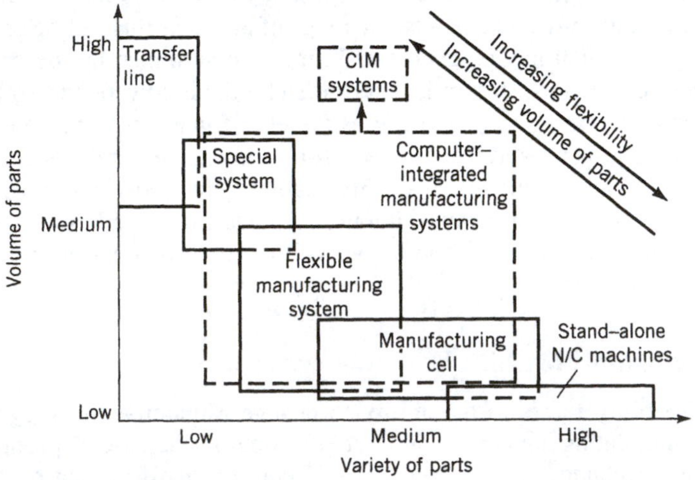

FIGURE 13.1 Volume–variety relationships categorizing production systems.

cated processing and material-handling equipment is used. The variety of parts is limited (one or two). Production rates are high because of dedicated equipment. However, the transfer lines are expensive and inflexible from the point of view of changing from one product to another.

13.2.2 Low-Volume, High-Variety (L–H) Production System

Stand-alone NC machines can produce any variety of parts. Of course, the processing requirements of parts should be within a machine's capability. A low-volume, high-variety production system normally consists of an NC machine augmented by a part buffer, a tool changer, a pallet changer, and so on. Such an augmented system is also known as a flexible manufacturing module (Kusiak, 1985). Sometimes the tool changer and the pallet changer can be replaced by a robot.

Remember, the variety in a parts population could be due to either changes in the design of existing parts, new parts entering the system, or to a job-shop production situation. Therefore, NC machines provide the highest level of flexibility to perform a wide range of operations on a family of parts but the production rate is relatively low. The unit costs of production are much higher than those for similar parts on a transfer line.

13.2.3 Mid-Volume, Mid-Variety (M–M) Production Systems

Between the extremes of one or two part types produced on a transfer line and a large variety of parts produced on a stand-alone NC machine, there is an important category of mid-volume, mid-variety parts, which constitutes approximately 75 percent of discrete-parts manufacturing. The manufacturing system requirements for the M–M production are different from those of the L–H and H–L production systems. For example, in an M–M system both flexibility and production volume are of prime importance, whereas flexibility to process a variety of parts is more important in an L–H system and production volume in an H–L system.

The simultaneous requirements of flexibility and production volume place more emphasis on system integration and automation. Depending on the degree of integration and level of automation, the M–M manufacturing systems popularly known as computer-integrated manufacturing systems can be further classified as

- Manufacturing cell
- Special manufacturing system
- Flexible manufacturing system

13.2.3.1 Manufacturing Cell

The design of manufacturing cells is based on the concepts of group technology. The objective is to process some families of parts on a group of NC machines within a cell so that the intercellular material-handling effort is minimized. The selection of parts for processing on machines may be both sequential and random. In a cell the NC machines are linked together by a direct numerical control (DNC) system. Also, the NC machines in a manufacturing cell are often equipped with part buffers, tool changers, and pallet changers. The machines may or may not be connected by a material-handling system. A material-handling system, if used in a cell, could be a handling robot, an automated guided vehicle, or a gantry robot. The type of material-handling equipment used decides the type of layout, that is, circular, single row, or double row, and the cluster machine layout. The details of these layouts are given in Section 13.8. The manufacturing cell is the most flexible category of computer-integrated manufacturing systems.

13.2.3.2 Special Manufacturing System

In a special manufacturing system the machines are laid out to manufacture a family of parts based on the sequence of operations. A fixed-path material-handling system links the machines. The parts move on the material-handling system in a sequence from machine to machine. The special manufacturing system has a high production rate because of dedication of machines based on sequence of operations and integration of machining and material-handling subsystems. The sequence-based dedication of machines, however, makes this one of the least flexible computer-integrated manufacturing systems.

13.2.3.3 Flexible Manufacturing System

A flexible manufacturing system lies between the two extremes of a manufacturing cell and a special manufacturing system. Accordingly, it is a true mid-volume, mid-variety manufacturing system, having a higher production rate than a manufacturing cell and much more flexibility than a special manufacturing system. There is some degree of overlap between these systems. In particular, an FMS is closer to a cell manufacturing system. An FMS is, however, characterized by a higher level of computer control and more non-machine entities such as coordinate measuring machines, and part washers. The key characteristics of various high- to low-volume manufacturing systems are summarized in the following section.

13.3 KEY CHARACTERISTICS OF VARIOUS MANUFACTURING SYSTEMS

Here we provide a summary of key characteristics of various systems.

Transfer Line

- Machines dedicated to manufacture of one or two product types; system permits no flexibility at all.
- Maximum utilization and very high production volume.
- Direct labor involvement is minimal.
- Low unit cost of production.

Flexible Manufacturing Module (Stand-Alone NC Machines)

- Highest level of flexibility; any job can be processed provided it is in the range of process capability of the NC machine.
- Low utilization and low production volume.
- Unit cost of production is much higher than for a similar product manufactured on a transfer line.

Manufacturing Cell

- Low to mid volume.
- A variety of parts are manufactured in batch mode.

- A manufacturing cell is an FMS without central control.
- More flexible than an FMS but lower production rate.

Special Manufacturing System

- A fixed-path material-handling system links the machines together.
- Least flexible category of CIM system.
- Uses multispindle heads and low-level controller.
- High production rate and low unit production cost.

Flexible Manufacturing System

- True mid-volume, mid-variety manufacturing system consisting of a series of flexible machines, automated material-handling system, automated tool changer, other equipment such as coordinate measuring machines, part washers, and so on, all under high-level centralized computer control.
- Permits both sequential and random routing of a wide variety of parts.
- Higher production rate than a manufacturing cell and much higher flexibility than a special manufacturing system.

Let us now formally understand what an FMS is and what its physical and control subsystem components are.

13.4 WHAT IS AN FMS?

An FMS is an automated, mid-volume, mid-variety, central computer–controlled manufacturing system. It covers a wide spectrum of manufacturing activities such as machining, sheet metal working, welding, fabricating, and assembly. In an FMS, families of parts with similar characteristics are processed. Therefore, group technology (GT) and consequently cellular manufacturing are significant parts of the system. The concepts of GT and cellular manufacturing are discussed in detail in Chapter 12. The essential physical components of the FMS are:

1. Potentially independent NC machine tools capable of performing multiple functions and having automated tool interchange capabilities.
2. Automated material-handling system to move parts between machine tools and fixturing stations.
3. All the components (machine tools, material-handling equipment, tool changers) are hierarchically computer controlled.
4. Equipment such as coordinate measuring machines and part-washing devices.

Before machining is started on the parts, they are mounted onto fixtures. Both the parts and the fixtures are then mounted onto special pallets. The material-handling system moves the pallets to the machining centers for processing. If a machining center is busy, the pallets are automatically transferred to an idle machining center, thereby ensuring effective utilization of the FMS.

In the following section we present a framework for understanding the components of an FMS. A flexible manufacturing system consists of two subsystems:

1. Physical subsystem
2. Control subsystem

Line diagrams and photographs of two typical flexible manufacturing systems with their major identifiable physical and control subsystems are shown in Figure 13.2. The physical subsystem includes the following:

(a) *Workstations* consisting of NC machine tools, inspection equipment, part-washing devices, load and unload area, and work area.

(b) *Storage–retrieval systems* consisting of pallet stands at each workstation and other devices such as carousels used to store parts temporarily between the workstations or operations. An automated storage and retrieval system can also be considered part of an FMS in a broader sense.

(c) *Material-handling systems* consisting of powered vehicles, towline carts, conveyors, automated guided vehicles (AGVs), and other systems to carry parts between workstations.

The control subsystem required to ensure optimum performance of the FMS includes the following:

(a) Control hardware, which includes mini- and microcomputers, programmable logic controllers, communication networks, sensors, switching devices and many other peripheral devices such as printers and mass storage memory equipment.

(b) Control software consisting of a set of files and programs used to control physical subsystems. It is important to have hardware and software compatibility for efficient control of the FMS.

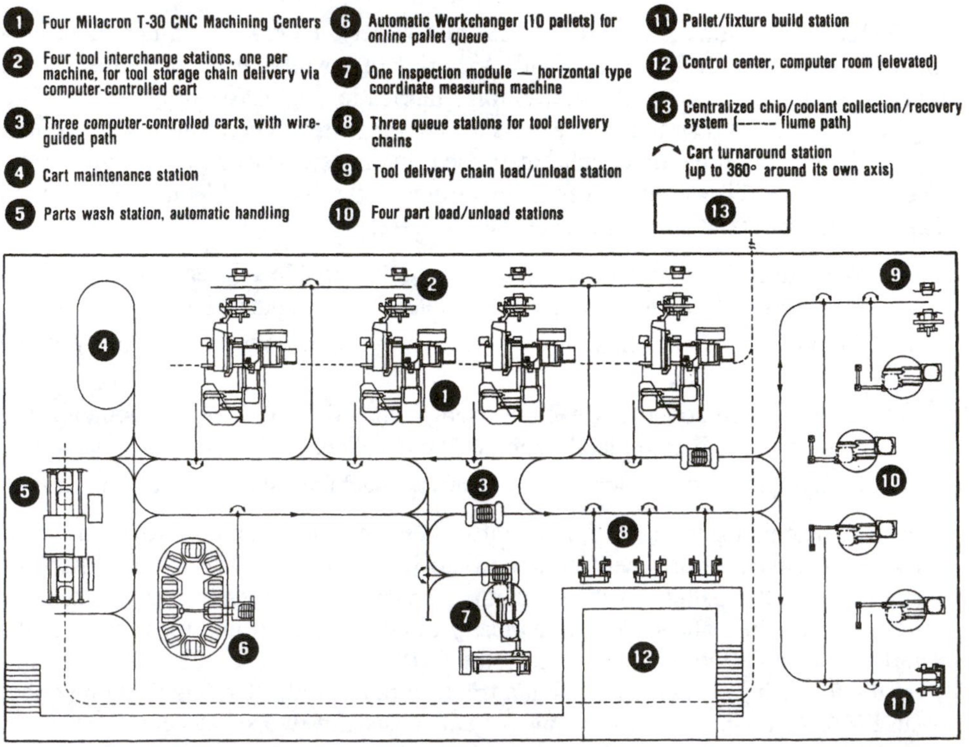

FIGURE 13.2 (*a*) Line diagram of an FMS used by Cincinnati Milacron Plastics Machinery Division; (*b*) photograph of FMS shown in (*a*); (*c*) line diagram of FMS used by FMC Corporation; (*d*) photograph of FMS shown in (*c*) (Courtesy of Cincinnati Milacron).

(b)

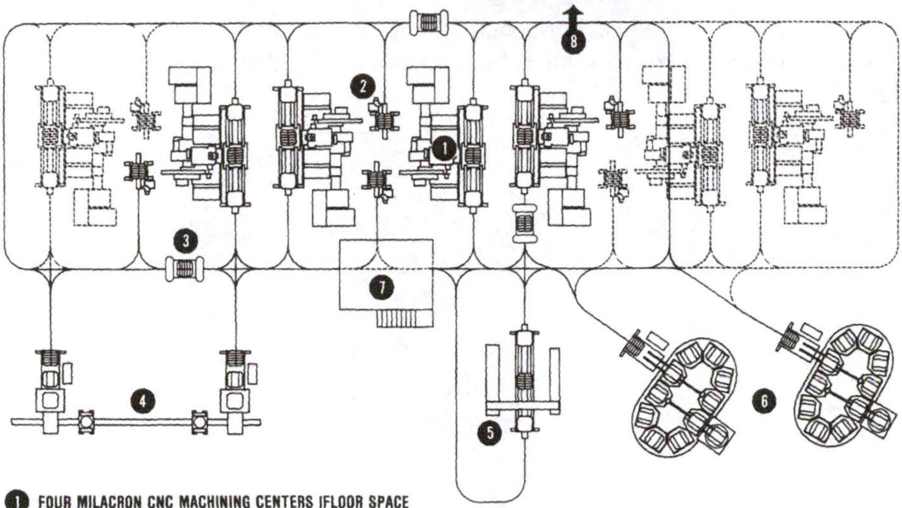
1 FOUR MILACRON CNC MACHINING CENTERS (FLOOR SPACE RESERVED FOR ADDING THREE MORE)
2 FOUR TOOL INTERCHANGE SYSTEMS (ONE PER MACHINE), COMPUTER-CONTROLLED TOOL DELIVERY VIA CART
3 THREE REMOTELY CONTROLLED CARTS WITH WIRE-GUIDED PATH
4 TWO LOAD/UNLOAD, CLEAN/ORIENT STATIONS WITH COOLANT/CHIP HANDLING
5 ONE INSPECTION MODULE (COORDINATE MEASURING MACHINE)
6 TWO AUTOMATIC WORKCHANGERS (10 PALLETS EACH) FOR PART OVERFLOW AND QUEUE
7 RAISED OFFICE (CART PATH UNDER)
8 CART MAINTENANCE STATION

(c)

(d)

FIGURE 13.2 (continued)

13.5 BASIC FEATURES OF PHYSICAL COMPONENTS OF AN FMS

A brief description of basic features of physical components of an FMS is given next.

13.5.1 Numerical Control Machine Tools

The major building blocks of an FMS are machine tools. They determine the degree of flexibility and capabilities of the FMS. We discuss some of the characteristics of machine tools used in an FMS.

1. The majority of FMSs use horizontal and vertical spindle machines. Machining centers with vertical spindle machines offer less flexibility than horizontal machining centers.

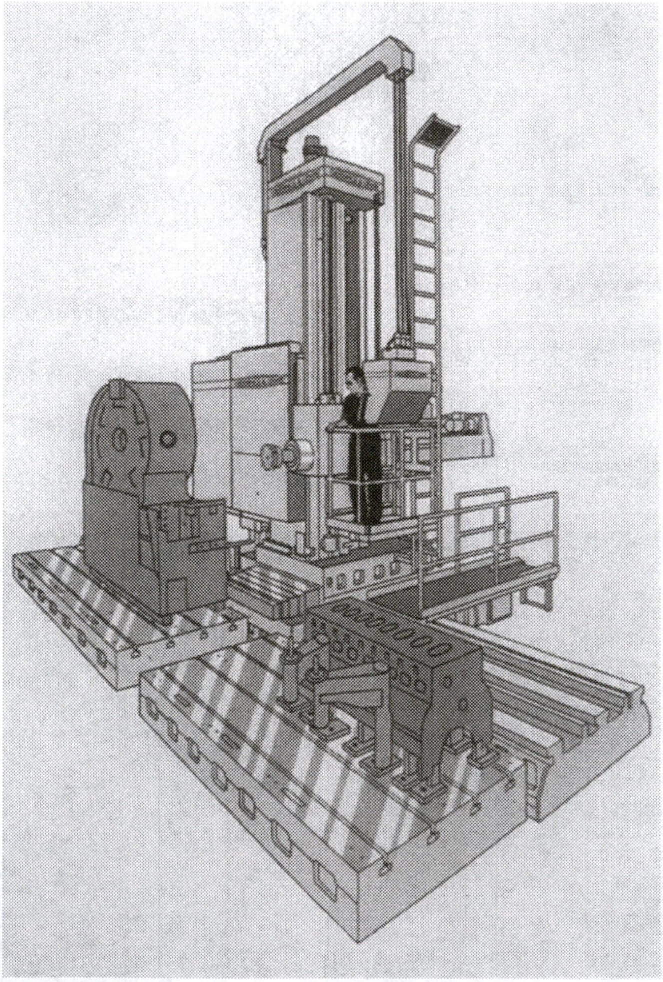

FIGURE 13.3 (a) Numerically controlled horizontal spindle machining centers: three axes. (Courtesy of Guiddings & Lewis.)

2. Machining centers with numerical control of movements in up to five axes (that is, spindle movements in *x*-, *y*-, and *z*-directions, rotation of table, and tilting of table toward the column) are available. Movements in more axes mean more flexibility but higher cost. NC machining centers with three, four, and five axes are shown in Figure 13.3.

3. The machining centers have the flexibility of performing a wide variety of operations, from simple turning to hole drilling to five-axis contouring. The shape (rotational and prismatic) of parts, accuracy requirements, weight, and so forth would determine the type of machining center suitable for an FMS. For example, the power and the work envelope are determined by the shape and weight of parts. Other factors affecting the choice of a machining center are its compatibility with the material-handling and storage systems. This is an important consideration in FMSs because the machining centers are equipped with pallet exchangers interfacing with material-handling devices that carry the pallets within and between machining centers as well as automated storage and retrieval systems.

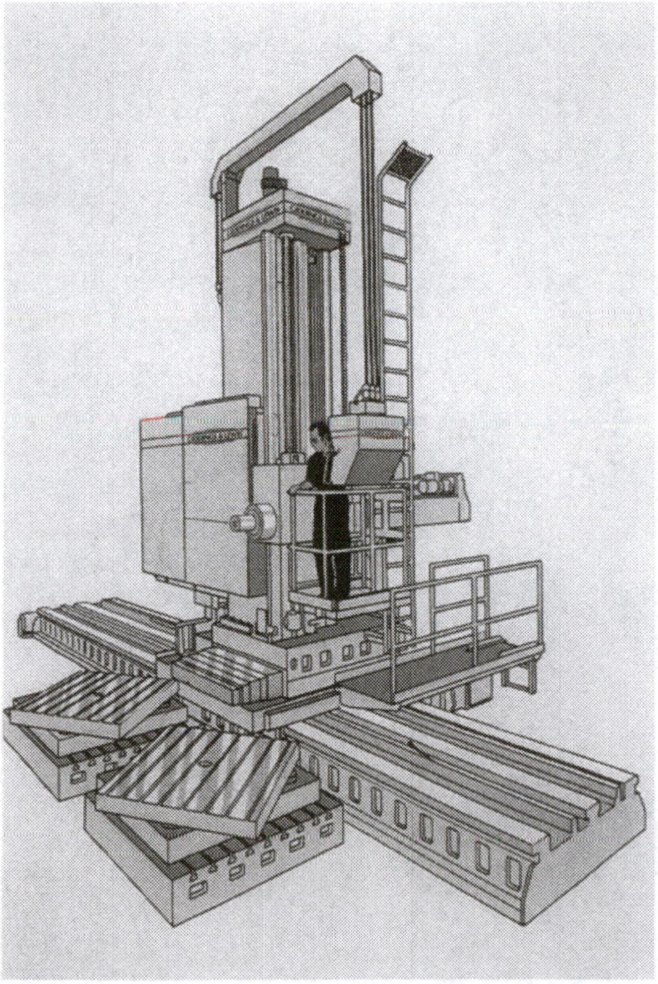

FIGURE 13.3 (b) Numerically controlled horizontal spindle machining centers: four axes. (Courtesy of Guiddings & Lewis.)

13.5.2 Workholding and Tooling Considerations

Effective utilization of a flexible manufacturing system depends on the workholding (fixtures and pallets), tooling, tool storage and tool changers, tool identification systems, coolant, and chip removal systems. FMS-specific fixturing considerations are:

1. Fixtures must be designed to minimize part-handling time. Modular fixturing is an attractive way to fixture a variety of parts quickly.

2. Before machining is started on the parts, they are mounted on fixtures. Both the parts and the fixtures are then mounted on special pallets. This may lead to error buildup in the part-to-fixture, fixture-to-pallet, and pallet-to-machining center steps and render some of the parts out of tolerance. To reduce the error buildup problem, some fixtures should be pinned to the pallets.

3. Part variety considerations in FMSs lead to high usage of fixtures. Management strategies must be evolved for identification, storage, and retrieval of fixtures and their integration with the automated storage and retrieval system (AS/RS) and material-handling systems such as AGVS.

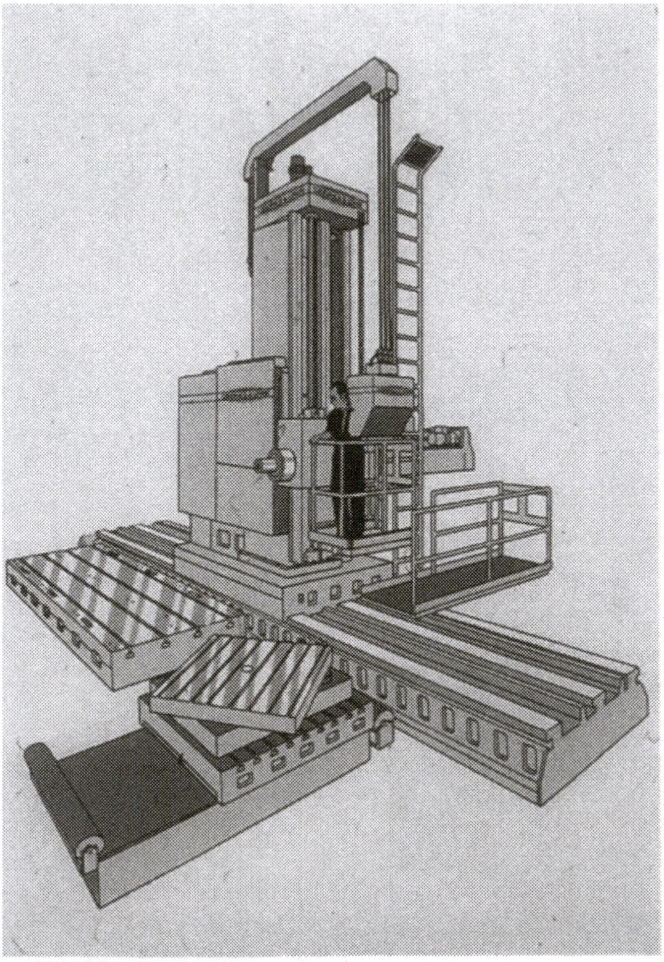

FIGURE 13.3 (c) Numerically controlled horizontal spindle machining centers: five axes. (Courtesy of Guiddings & Lewis.)

4. All the machining centers are equipped with tool storage systems known as tool magazines. Common types of tool magazines, as shown in Figure 13.4, are:

- Disk type
- Drum type
- Turret type
- Chain type

An optimal tool management strategy should include duplication of the most often used tools in the tool magazines, quick tool changers, tool regrinding, tool maintenance, and provision of spares. Types of tool management strategies are discussed in Section 13.7.1.5.

13.5.3 Material-Handling Equipment

Depending on the nature and variety of parts, the material-handling systems used in flexible manufacturing systems are robots, conveyors, automated guided vehicle systems, and many other specially designed systems for customized FMS. The most important consideration in selecting a material-handling system should be integration

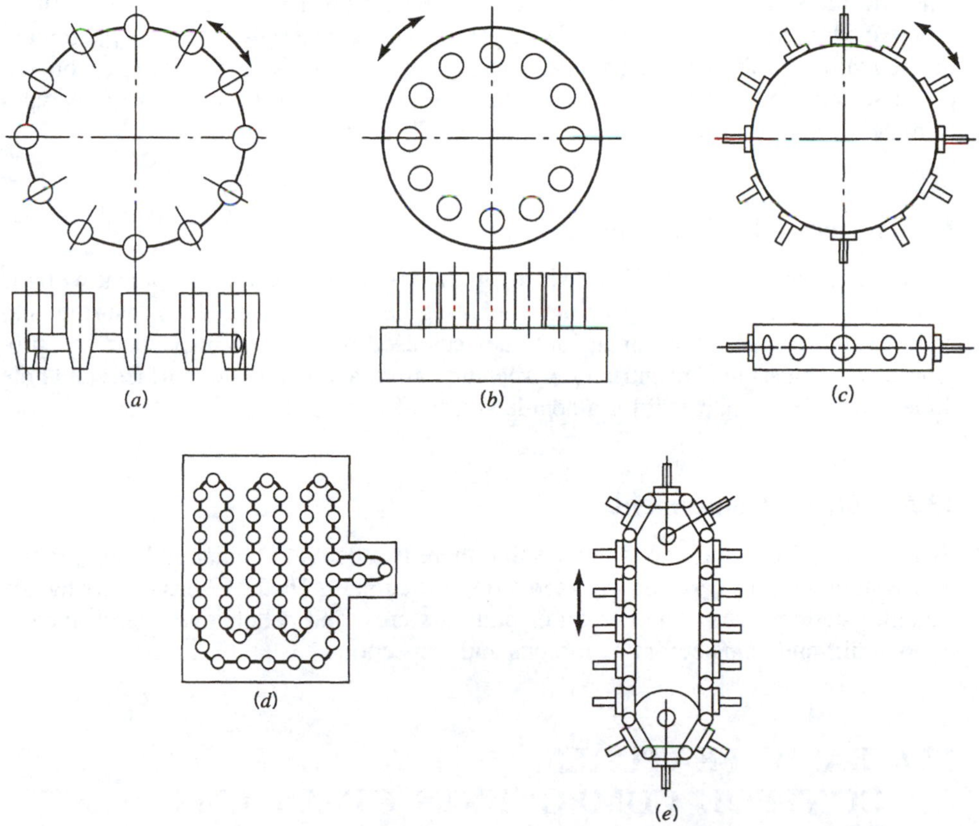

FIGURE 13.4 Various types of tool magazines: (*a*) disk type, (*b*) drum type, (*c*) turret type, (*d*) chain type, and (*e*) chain type. (Kusiak, Andrew: *Intelligent Manufacturing Systems,* ® 1990, Figure 2.23, p. 40, reprinted by permission of Prentice Hall Inc., Englewood Cliffs, NJ.)

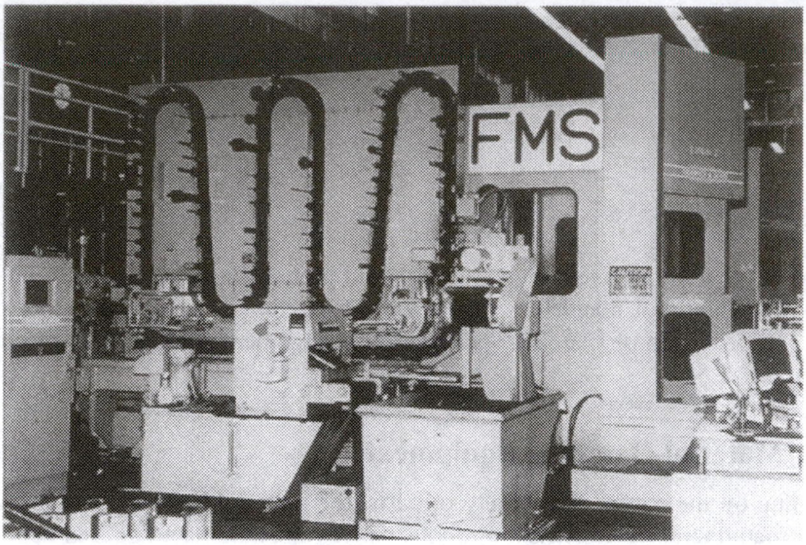

FIGURE 13.4 (f) Photograph of a chain-type tool magazine. (Courtesy of Guiddings & Lewis.)

with the machining centers and the storage and retrieval systems together with an efficient identification system. The full potential of a material-handling system cannot be realized without having a bar-coding system to identify raw materials, work-in-process, finished parts, tools, fixtures, and pallets in different locations. Various types of material-handling systems are discussed in Chapter 7.

13.5.4 Inspection Equipment

The distinguishing feature of FMSs is integration of the inspection equipment with the machining centers such as probing machining centers. Coordinate measuring machines (CMMs) are three-dimensional devices used for off-line inspection and programmed to measure concentricity, perpendicularity, and flatness of surfaces and hole dimensions. (See Chapter 9 for a detailed discussion of CMMs.)

13.5.5 Other Components

Environmental considerations require that there is a central coolant and chip separation system with the capability of recovering the coolant. The FMS has deburring and cleaning stations. The combination of parts, fixtures, and pallets must be cleaned to remove dirt and chips before operations and inspections.

13.6 BASIC FEATURES OF CONTROL COMPONENTS OF AN FMS

Flexible manufacturing systems are designed and developed to meet specific customer requirements. These requirements dictate that the system:

- Is flexible enough to produce the quantities and varieties of parts desired by the customer.
- Has the ability to transfer parts automatically to other machining centers in case of system failures or systems being busy.

Manufacturing a variety of parts involves real-time coordination of various subsystems such as parts, pallets, fixtures, machine tools, tools, material handling, and storage. There could be a number of variations in developing a control system for an FMS to organize, coordinate, and control these functions. In this section we provide a basic framework for developing a control system for a flexible manufacturing system (Dunlap, 1984; May, 1986; Maleki, 1991). Accordingly, we divide the total manufacturing control activity into the following control functions:

1. Work-order processing and part control system
2. Machine-tool control system including inspection machines
3. Tool management and control system
4. Traffic management control system
5. Quality control management system
6. Maintenance control system
7. Management control system
8. Interfacing of these subsystems with central computer

13.6.1 Work-Order Processing and Part Control System

The work-order processing and part control system is the system that essentially drives other control systems. The basic information used in the part control system is contained in a number of files. For example, a part identification file contains the information about the part name and the number of parts required. For each part, the part routing file contains information such as number of operations, alternate machining centers on which these operations can be done, names of part program files, machine identification files, tools required, operation time and operating cost, and sequence selection options. The manufacturing instruction file, also known as the part program file, contains ASCII (American Standard Code for Information Interchange) or EIA (Electronic Industries Association) program data in CNC format for each machining operation. The part setup file contains information on fixturing and palletizing of parts.

The part control system consists of a number of modules. For example, the part process planning module creates a process plan using information from the part identification, part routing, and program files. The process plan and the part routing modules are used to control the part movements in an FMS. The part setup module in conjunction with part identification controls the fixturing and palletization of parts.

13.6.2 Machine-Tool Control System

The machine-tool control system has a number of modules such as a DNC transmitter, NC editor, and machine monitor and control modules. The NC tape image of a part is transmitted to the machine tool by the DNC transmitter control module. The NC editor permits manual editing as well as creation of a new version of the tapes at the machine tool. Error monitoring and correction during the cutting process, including starting and stopping the machine tools, are controlled by the machine monitor and control module.

13.6.3 Tool Management and Control System

One of the distinguishing features of an FMS is the tool magazine, which holds a large number of tools. The tool magazine capacity is an influential factor in determining the flexibility of the system. A proper tool management and control system is needed to control the processing of parts and enhance the flexibility to manufacture variety of parts. Tool identification, tool setup, and tool routing are accomplished by the tool management and control system. Tool replacement strategies can also be part of such a control system. Details of various tool replacement strategies are given in later sections.

13.6.4 Traffic Management Control System

The material handling and storage control system coordinates part routing, fixtures, pallets, and tool modules with the objective of tracking the destination of parts for successive operations on machining centers. In addition, it records and controls the storage and retrieval of parts, tools, fixtures, and pallets for quick availability.

13.6.5 Quality Control Management System

The quality control management system is an important module of an FMS control system. The capabilities of the system include collection, storage, retrieval, and archiving of workpiece inspection data. The inspection programs for the workpieces are created at the coordinate measuring machines. These programs are then uploaded to the FMS computer for storage and retrieval of data.

13.6.6 Maintenance Control System

The maintenance control system, also known as the service control system, is a kind of help menu. In the event of alarms due to problems in the operation of the machining centers and other equipment and systems, on-line help is available through this system.

13.6.7 Management Control System

The management control system is designed to provide the management status of output performance. It consists of a number of modules that coordinate with various other systems, including a provision for manual scheduling and control, scheduling of parts based on their requirements available from the material requirements planning (MRP) system, and report generation on output statistics of parts. A number of control architectures are possible, depending on the complexity of an FMS. However, the management control system provides a direct link into the corporate system database. This helps provide management information on the status of the system on a real-time basis.

13.6.8 Interfacing of These Subsystems with the Central Computer

The complete FMS control system can be linked with the company's corporate computer. The objective is to integrate the FMS subsystem with other subsystems such as finance, marketing, and personnel.

13.7 OPERATIONAL PROBLEMS IN FMS

The operational problems in FMS concern detailed decision making on a short-term planning horizon. The following problems must be solved:

- Part selection and tool management
- Fixture and pallet selection
- Machine grouping and loading, considering part and tool assignments

13.7.1 Part Type Selection and Tool Management Problems

This problem concerns the determination of a subset of part types from a set of part types for processing. A number of criteria can be used for selecting a set of part types for immediate processing. For example, due date is an important consideration. Limited availability of tools on the tool magazine and different requirements of tools by part types complicate the process of part type selection in FMSs. A number of mathematical programming models and heuristics for part type selection have been developed (Hwang, 1986; Rajgopalan, 1986) considering tool magazine limitations. Two basic approaches (Stecke and Kim, 1988) for part type selection have been proposed: the *batching approach* and the *flexible approach.*

13.7.1.1 The Batching Approach

In the batching approach, part types are partitioned into separate sets called batches. The selected part types in a particular batch are manufactured continuously until all the production requirements are completed. Then for processing the next batch, the system setup and the tool changeover time consists of removing all the tools not required by the current batch and loading new tools required to perform all the operations for all the part types of the next scheduled batch. Most FMS users and researchers have followed a batching approach, because it results in lower frequency of tool changeovers and is easier to implement in real systems.

13.7.1.2 The Flexible Approach

The flexible approach, suggested by Stecke and Kim (1986), works as follows. When the production requirements of some part types are finished, space becomes available in the tool magazine. New part types may be introduced into the system for immediate and simultaneous processing if this input can help increase utilization of the system. This approach, however, requires more frequent tool changes. Stecke and Kim (1988) have reported a simulation study comparing a number of batching approaches and the flexible approach to part type selection. The major finding was that the flexible approach tends to make the system more highly utilized.

In the following section we present two simple mathematical programming models for maximizing the number of part types in a batch (that is, minimizing the number of batches for given part types).

13.7.1.3 Hwang's Integer Programming Model

The following notation is used:

$i = 1, 2, \ldots, N$ = part types

$c = 1, 2, \ldots, C$ = cutting tool types

t = tool magazine capacity

$$b_{ic} = \begin{cases} 1 \text{ if part type } i \text{ requires tool } c \\ 0 \text{ otherwise} \end{cases}$$

d_c = number of tool slots required to hold cutting tool c in a tool magazine of each machine

$$z_i = \begin{cases} 1 \text{ if part type } i \text{ is selected in the batch} \\ 0 \text{ otherwise} \end{cases}$$

$$y_c = \begin{cases} 1 \text{ if cutting tool } c \text{ is loaded on a machine} \\ 0 \text{ otherwise} \end{cases}$$

In this model, z_i and y_c are the decision variables. We consider a system of identical machines (all of the same type). In that case,

$$\text{Maximize} \sum_i z_i$$

$$\text{subject to: } \sum_c d_c y_c \le t \tag{13.1}$$

$$b_{ic} z_i \le y_c \qquad \text{all } i, c \tag{13.2}$$

$$z_i = 0 \text{ or } 1 \qquad \text{all } i \tag{13.3}$$

$$y_c = 0 \text{ or } 1 \qquad \text{all } c \tag{13.4}$$

The objective function maximizes the number of part types in a batch. Subsequent batches, if any, are formed by repeatedly solving the problem after deleting already selected part types from the model. Tool magazine capacity is considered for each machine type by constraint (13.1). Constraint (13.2) ensures that if a part type is selected, all cutting tools required for all operations of the selected part types are loaded into the tool magazine on each machine. Constraints (13.3) and (13.4) define zero–one variables.

EXAMPLE 13.1

Consider the simple example of eight part types and the corresponding required tools given in Table 13.1 for processing on a flexible manufacturing module. The number of slots required by each tool is given in Table 13.2. The tool magazine capacity is limited to 5 tool slots. Determine the batches of part types selected.

Solution

The detailed formulation of this example is given in Appendix A of this chapter. The solution of this integer programming model yields the following batches of part types selected:

Batch 1: P1, P2, P3, P4, P5, P6

Batch 2: P7

Batch 3: P8

TABLE 13.1 **Part Types and Required Tools**

Part types	*P1*	*P2*	*P3*	*P4*	*P5*	*P6*	*P7*	*P8*
Types of tools required	t1	t2	t3	t4	t1, t2	t3, t5	t6	t1, t2, t7

TABLE 13.2 **Tool Types and Required Slots**

Tool types	*t1*	*t2*	*t3*	*t4*	*t5*	*t6*	*t7*
Number of slots required	1	1	1	1	1	2	2

This model is myopic and ignores the potential for more tool sharing among parts. Although the first batch has more part types, this can lead to a larger than necessary total number of batches to produce all part types. For example, part type 8, which requires all the tools required by part types 1, 2, and 5, should be grouped with them.

13.7.1.4 Stecke and Kim Extension of Hwang's Model

Stecke and Kim (1988) modified the objective function of Hwang's model by incorporating the number of tool slots required for all operations for each part type as a coefficient. With this modification, the objective function aims to select early the part types with the largest number of required tools. This permits the consideration of more tool overlaps. The modified model is

$$\text{Maximize} \sum_i \left(\sum_c b_{ic} d_c \right) z_i$$

$$\text{subject to: } \sum_c d_c y_c \leq t \tag{13.5}$$

$$b_{ic} z_i \leq y_c \qquad \text{all } i, c \tag{13.6}$$

$$z_i = 0 \text{ or } 1 \qquad \text{all } i \tag{13.7}$$

$$y_{ck} = 0 \text{ or } 1 \qquad \text{all } c \tag{13.8}$$

EXAMPLE 13.2

Using the data in Example 13.1, solve the Stecke and Kim model and determine the optimal number of batches of part types selected.

Solution

This model differs from that of Hwang's model only in the objective function. The objective function for this problem is given in Appendix A of this chapter. The model yields two batches as follows:

Batch 1: P1, P2, P3, P5, P8

Batch 2: P4, P6, P7

The number of batches is now reduced to two, compared with three obtained with Hwang's model. This reduction in batches has a tremendous influence on the performance of an FMS, because it will lead to a considerable reduction in setup time.

13.7.1.5 Tool Allocation Policies

Tooling is estimated to account for about 20 percent of the cost of new manufacturing systems and it may be much higher in the case of an FMS (Tomek, 1986). Furthermore, increased numbers of tooling components and their application requirements hinder the productivity of FMSs. Therefore, it is important to design a tool management and control system so that the proper tools are available at the right machines at the desired times for processing of the scheduled parts. The tool magazine capacity, which is typically 30, 60, or 120 slots in commercial flexible manufacturing systems, constrains the number of tools mounted on a machine. This limits the number of parts that can be processed on a machine without reloading the tools. A number of tool allocation strategies have been investigated (Amoako-Gyampah et al., 1992) to improve FMS productivity, such as:

1. Bulk exchange policy
2. Tool migration policy
3. Resident tooling policy
4. Tool sharing policy

Bulk Exchange Policy In this tool allocation policy, for each planning period, a new set of tools is mounted on the tool magazine to process the parts in that planning period. Every tool allocation policy also determines the batch sizes of parts. For example, in the bulk exchange tooling policy, each time a part is assigned to a machine the tools required by that part are assigned to the tool magazine. The assignment of tools continues for other parts until the tool magazine is full. The assigned part types thus form the batch to be processed for that period. The number of tools should be sufficient to process the parts, as no replacement of tools occurs during the production window.

Tool Migration Policy In terms of part routing, this policy is quite similar to the bulk exchange policy. However, the tools are replaced once the parts are processed to make room for tools for processing other parts. In this system, tool changing and shuttling are accomplished by the material-handling robot that is used to remove and place parts within the machining centers.

Resident Tooling Policy The resident tooling policy aims at forming clusters of different combinations of tools representing similar processing requirements of parts with the objective of keeping these clusters permanently at various machines. Tool changes occur only when a particular tool reaches the end of its scheduled life. Ease of tool condition monitoring and easy identification of tools for replacements are some of the benefits of this policy.

EXAMPLE 13.3

Illustration of Tool Resident Policy

Consider the matrix of tools required to process parts as given in Table 13.3. Only two machining centers are available. Develop a resident tooling policy consisting of two groups of tools to be mounted on two machining centers. Use the concepts of production flow analysis.

TABLE 13.3 **Tool Type and Part Type Matrix**

	Part types														
Tools	*p1*	*p2*	*p3*	*p4*	*p5*	*p6*	*p7*	*p8*	*p9*	*p10*	*p11*	*p12*	*p13*	*p14*	*p15*
t1	1		1		1	1				1	1		1		1
t2	1		1		1	1				1	1		1		1
t3		1		1			1	1	1			1		1	
t4		1					1		1			1		1	
t5	1		1			1				1	1		1		1
t6	1		1		1	1				1	1		1		1
t7		1		1			1	1	1			1		1	
t8		1					1	1				1		1	
t9		1		1			1	1	1			1		1	

Solution

The solution process is similar to the part machine cell formation approach as given in Chapter 12. Using similarity coefficients between the tools and the single-linkage cluster analysis approach, we obtain two groups of tools that can be permanently mounted on two machining centers to process the parts as follows:

Machining Centers	*Tools*	*Parts*
First	(t1, t2, t5, t6)	(P1, P3, P5, P6, P10, P11, P13, P15)
Second	(t3, t4, t7, t8, t9)	(P2, P4, P7, P8, P9, P12, P14)

Tool-Sharing Policy The tool-sharing policy is a kind of hybrid of the bulk exchange and resident tooling policies. Tools are resident on machines based on tool clustering. Whenever a new part enters the system, it is identified with a part family and then, based on its routing and tooling requirements, the tool-sharing arrangement is made on the machines.

Assignment of parts to machines is done randomly in the bulk exchange and migration policies, whereas the specific parts are assigned to specific machines based on the availability of tooling on those groups.

Comparison of Various Tooling Strategies Amoako-Gyampah et al. (1992) compared four tooling strategies by simulating an FMS consisting of five machining centers each capable of processing every part and having a tool magazine capacity of 30 slots, a transporter to move parts from one station to another, and a robotic material-handling system to load and unload parts and change cutting tools. The FMS processes a total of 25 different part types, of which 14 have production requirements for every production window of 24 hours.

Five measures of performance were used in the study:

1. Mean flow time of parts representing the average time a part spends in the system
2. Mean tardiness of parts representing the average lateness of all late jobs
3. Percentage of jobs that are tardy
4. Average utilization of machines
5. Average utilization of the robotic system

The following three part-type selection heuristics were used:

1. *LNT heuristic.* This part-type selection rule, due to Rajgopalan (1986), is based on assigning higher priority to the part types requiring the largest number of tools (LNT) for processing. The rationale of the rule is that starting with the part that requires the largest number of tools ensures a minimum number of tool changes on the machine. Minimization of tool changes means improvements in machine utilization.

2. *SNT heuristic.* This part-type selection rule, due to Hwang (1986), is based on assigning higher priority to the parts requiring the smallest number of tools (SNT) for processing. This rule permits the selection of a large number of part types into one batch, thus minimizing the number of batches. Minimizing the number of batches reduces the idle time, leading to higher utilization of the machines.

3. *EDD rule.* This part-type selection rule is based on assigning higher priority to parts with the earliest due date. In a survey of 22 FMS users in the United States in 1985, Smith et al. (1986) observed that due date considerations in the selection of parts are important from the customer satisfaction point of view. The results are compared in Table 13.4.

It is observed from Table 13.4 that different strategies of tool management provide different results based on selection rules and performance criteria. Furthermore, the performance of the FMS depends not only on the availability of machines and the tool magazine capacity but also on the availability of the robotic tool-changing unit. Another interesting observation is that the migration and resident policies result in higher robot utilization than the bulk exchange and sharing policies because of higher frequency of tool changes with the former policies. The migration policy also provides better performance on flow times, tardiness, and the percentage of jobs tardy than the sharing policy. Therefore, minimization of the frequency of tool changes should not always be the overriding concern.

13.7.2 Fixture and Pallet Selection Problem

The use of palletized parts in FMSs is one of the most important factors in the integration of machines, material-handling equipment, and in-process storage facilities. A fixture provides a fixed orientation of the part and can be configured for a part or family of parts. The geometry of parts governs the type of fixture suitable for the part types. For example, rotational and prismatic parts would require different fixturing considerations. Because the pallets moving the fixtured parts interface with the machine tools, material-handling equipment, in-process storage facilities, and load–unload stations, the selection of fixtures and pallets must be compatible with these systems. The fixture and pallet selection problem can be considered as a subset of the part selection problem. The approximate number of pallets required can be estimated using the following equation:

$$\text{Number of pallets} = \frac{\begin{array}{c}(\text{parts required per shift}) \times \\ (\text{average pallet cycle time})\end{array}}{\begin{array}{c}(\text{planned production time per shift}) \times \\ (\text{number of parts per pallet})\end{array}}$$

TABLE 13.4 **Comparison of Four Tooling Strategies**

Measures of performance	*Part-type selection rules* Largest number of tools (LNT)	*Smallest number of tools (SNT)*	*Earliest due date (EDD)*
Mean flow time (MFT)	B-M-S-R*	B-M-S-R	B-M-S-R
Mean tardiness (TD)	B-M-S-R	B-M-S-R	B-M-S-R
Percent jobs tardy (PJT)	B-S-M-R	B-S-M-R	B-S-M-R
Average machine utilization (AMU)	M-B-R-S	M-B-S-R	M-B-R-S
Robot utilization (RU)	R-M-B-S	R-M-B-S	R-M-B-S

* B represents bulk, M migration, S sharing, and R resident tooling policies. The order B-M-S-R represents the order of decreasing performance.

The pallet cycle time is the time span from the entry of a part into a loading station until the part leaves an unloading station. This cycle time depends on a number of operational issues such as scheduling rules and processing times. If the number of pallets obtained from this equation is a fractional number, the next higher integer number may be selected.

EXAMPLE 13.4

Consider the following data available from a simulation study:

Parts required per shift = 20

Average pallet cycle time = 120 min

Planned production time per shift = 480 min

Number of parts per pallet = 1

Solution

Using the formula given in Section 13.7.2, the number of pallets required = $(20 \times 120)/480 = 5$.

13.7.3 Machine Grouping and Loading Problems

The machine grouping and loading problem refers to grouping of machines and allocation of operations and tools required for the selected part types among the machine groups subject to technological and capacity constraints of the machines in an FMS. There could be a number of allocation criteria for loading problems in an FMS (Stecke and Solberg, 1981), such as:

1. Balance the assigned machine processing times.
2. Minimize the number of movements from machine to machine.
3. Balance the workload per machine for a system of groups of pooled machines of equal sizes.
4. Unbalance the workload per machine for a system of groups of pooled machines of unequal sizes.
5. Fill the tool magazines as densely as possible.
6. Maximize the number of weighted operations assigned to the machines.

Treatment of these problems is mathematically involved and is beyond the scope of this book.

13.8 LAYOUT CONSIDERATIONS

One of the important design characteristics of manufacturing systems is layout. For example, a job shop is characterized by a large variety of parts, general-purpose machines, and a functional layout (also known as process layout). In functional layout the machines are collected by function—that is, all milling machines together, all grinding machines together, and so forth. A manufacturing system with large lots, less variety, special-purpose machines, and more mechanization is known as a flow shop. In a flow shop the machines are laid out in a line, so the layout is known as a product (or line) layout. A transfer line producing a gearbox is a typical example. The GT layout combines both product and process layouts.

In an FMS the principles of GT are used to form part families. An analysis of over 50 flexible manufacturing systems (Heragu and Kusiak, 1988) shows that the layout of machines to process part families in an FMS is determined by the type of material-handling equipment used. In this section, we discuss five types of layouts based on the use of material-handling equipment.

13.8.1 Linear Single- and Double-Row Machine Layout

Automated guided vehicle systems are becoming common material-handling systems. An AGV is most efficient when the movement is in a straight line. Accordingly, the machines are arranged in straight lines along the AGV path as shown in Figure 13.5*a* and *b*.

13.8.2 Circular Machine Layout

If a handling robot is used in an FMS cell, the machines are laid out in a circle. The robot envelope essentially determines the arrangement of machines (Browne et al., 1984), as shown in Figure 13.5*c*.

13.8.3 Cluster Machine Layout

The cluster type of layout, shown in Figure 13.5*d*, uses gantry robots to transfer parts among the machines. The layout considerations are the size of the machines, the working envelope of the gantry robot, and the access of the robot arm to the machines.

13.8.4 Loop Layout

The loop layout uses a conveyor system that allows only unidirectional flow of parts around the loop. A secondary material-handling system is provided at each workstation and permits the flow of parts without any obstruction. Many other variations of the loop layout are possible. For example, a ladder layout contains rungs on which workstations are located; an open-field layout consists of loops, ladders, and sidings.

13.8.5 A Model for the Single-Row Machine Layout Problem

In this section we present an analytical model for the single-row machine layout problem based on Neghabat (1974), Heragu and Kusiak (1988), and Kusiak (1990). The machines are arranged in a straight line. The objective is to determine the non-overlapping optimal sequence of machines such that total cost of making the required trips between machines is minimized. Consider the following notation:

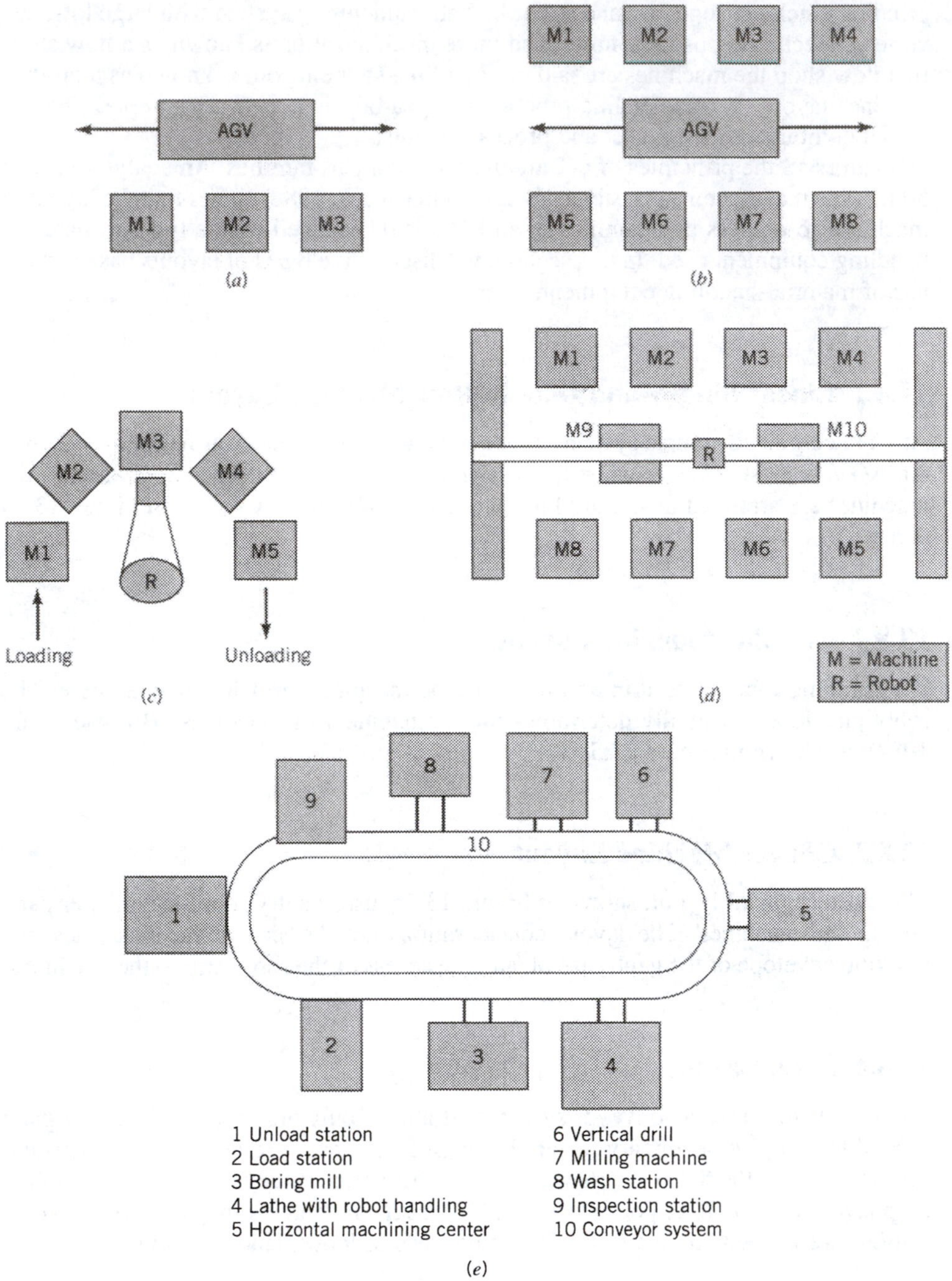

FIGURE 13.5 FMS layouts: (*a*) linear single-row machine layout; (*b*) double-row machine layout; (*c*) circular machine layout; (*d*) cluster machine layout; (*e*) loop machine layout.

m = number of machines
f_{ij} = frequency trips between all pairs of machines (frequency matrix) for all (i, j), $i \neq j$
c_{ij} = material-handling cost per unit distance between all pairs of machines for all (i, j), $i \neq j$
l_i = length of ith machine
d_{ij} = clearance between machines i and j
x_j = distance of jth machine from the vertical reference line as shown in the Figure 13.6.

$$\text{Minimize } Z = \sum_{i=1}^{m-1} \sum_{j=i+1}^{m} c_{ij} f_{ij} |x_i - x_j| \tag{13.9}$$

subject to:

$$|x_i - x_j| \geq \tfrac{1}{2}(l_i + l_j) + d_{ij} \quad \text{for all } i,\ i = 1, 2, \ldots, m-1, \text{ and } j = i+1, \ldots, m \tag{13.10}$$

$$x_i \geq 0 \quad \text{for all } i = 1, \ldots, m \tag{13.11}$$

Equation (13.9) represents the total cost of trips between machines. The constraint (13.10) ensures that there is no overlap between the machines. The non-negativity constraints are given by (13.11). The absolute terms in the model can easily be transformed, resulting in an equivalent linear integer programming model. Although the model can be solved using standard linear programming packages, we provide a simple heuristic algorithm in the following section.

13.8.6 Heuristic Algorithm for Circular and Linear Single-Row Machine Layouts

The following heuristic algorithm, due to Heragu and Kusiak (1988), provides the sequence in which machines are placed in the layout. The objective is to sequence the machines so that the material-handling effort is minimized. This is done by arranging the machines according to the product of frequency of trips and the cost of material handling per unit distance traveled per trip made by the material-handling equipment (robot or AGV).

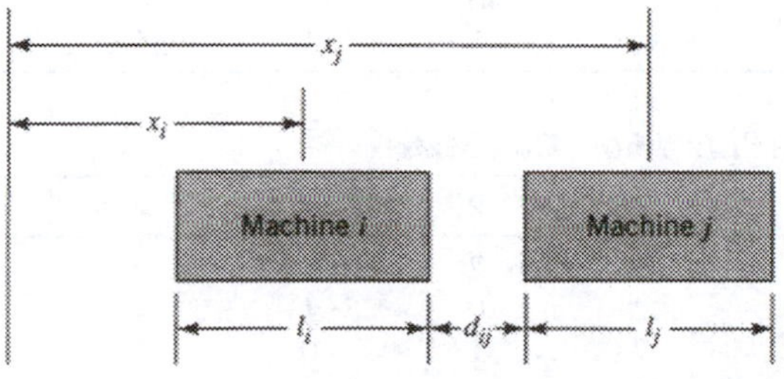

FIGURE 13.6 Machine location relative to reference line.

Data Required

- Number of machines, m
- Frequency of trips between all pairs of machines (frequency matrix), f_{ij}, for all $(i, j), i \neq j$
- Material-handling cost per unit distance between all pairs of machines, c_{ij} for all $(i, j), i \neq j$

Step 1: From the frequency and cost matrices, determine the adjusted flow matrix as follows:

$$\bar{F} = [\bar{f}_{ij}] = [f_{ij}c_{ij}]$$

Step 2: Determine $\bar{f}_{i'j'} = \max[\bar{f}_{ij}$, for all i and $j]$. Obtain the partial solution by connecting i' and j'. Set $\bar{f}_{i'j'} = \bar{f}_{j'i'} = -\infty$.

Step 3: Determine

$$\bar{f}_{p'q'} = \max[\bar{f}_{i'k}, \bar{f}_{j'l}: k = 1, 2, \ldots, m; l = 1, 2, \ldots, m]$$

Step 3.1: Connect q' to p' and add q' to the partial solution.

Step 3.2: Delete row p' and column p' from $[\bar{f}_{ij}]$.

Step 3.3: If $p' = i'$, set $i' = q'$; otherwise, set $j' = q'$.

Step 4: Repeat step 3 until all the machines are included in the solution.

EXAMPLE 13.5

Consider that there are five machines in a flexible manufacturing system to be served by an automated guided vehicle. A linear single-row layout is recommended because of the use of an AGV. The data on the frequency of AGV trips, material-handling costs per unit distance, and clearance between the machines are given in Tables 13.5, 13.6, 13.7, and 13.8. Suggest a suitable layout.

TABLE 13.5 **Frequency of Trips between Pairs of Machines**

	1	*2*	*3*	*4*	*5*
1	0	20	70	50	30
2	20	0	10	40	15
3	70	10	0	18	21
4	50	40	18	0	35
5	30	15	21	35	0

TABLE 13.6 **Cost Matrix**

	1	*2*	*3*	*4*	*5*
1	0	2	7	5	3
2	2	0	1	4	2
3	7	1	0	1	2
4	5	4	1	0	3
5	3	2	2	3	0

TABLE 13.7 **Clearance Matrix**

	1	*2*	*3*	*4*	*5*
1	0	2	1	1	1
2	2	0	1	2	2
3	1	1	0	1	2
4	1	2	1	0	1
5	1	2	2	1	0

TABLE 13.8 **The Machine Dimensions**

Machine	*M1*	*M2*	*M3*	*M4*	*M5*
Machine Sizes	10 × 10	15 × 15	20 × 30	20 × 20	25 × 15

Solution

Step 1: Determine the adjusted flow matrix as follows:

	1	*2*	*3*	*4*	*5*
1	0	40	490	250	90
2	40	0	10	160	30
3	490	10	0	18	42
4	250	160	18	0	105
5	90	30	42	105	0

Step 2: Include machines 1 and 3 in the partial solution, as they are connected.

Step 3: Add machine 4 to the partial solution, as it is connected to machine 1. Delete row 1 and column 1.

Step 3: Add machine 2 to the partial solution, as it is connected to machine 4. Delete row and column 4 from the matrix.

Step 3: Add machine 5 to the partial solution.

Step 4: Because all the machines are connected, stop. The final sequence is 5, 2, 4, 1, 3. It is obtained by arranging the adjusted flow weights in increasing order while retaining the connectivity of the machines. Accordingly, the final layout considering the clearances between the machines is as shown in Figure 13.7.

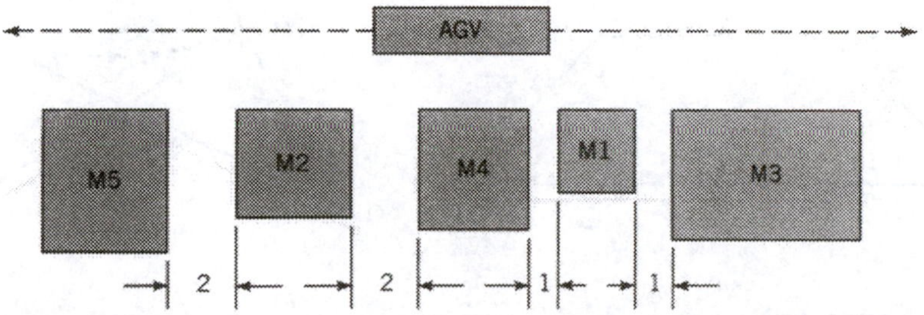

FIGURE 13.7 Final layout of the linear single-row machine problem.

13.9 SEQUENCING OF ROBOT MOVES IN ROBOTIC CELLS

In the previous section we studied a circular layout in which machines are served by a robot. Viswanadham and Narahari (1992) and Asfahl (1992) have given a procedure for determining the cycle time for a single alternative for two- and three-machine robotic cells, respectively. However, for a single robot cell with n machines, the number of possible alternative sequences of robot moves is n factorial ($n!$). To obtain the optimal cycle time and consequently the best sequence of robot moves, Sethi et al. (1992) completely characterized single robot cells with two and three machines. In this section we present a simplified algorithm based on their work for determining the optimal sequence of robot moves to minimize the cycle time in a two-machine robotic cell. The case of a three-machine robotic cell is given in Appendix B to this chapter.

13.9.1 Sequencing of Robot Moves in a Two-Machine Robotic Cell

The following are the two alternative robot sequences for the two-machine robotic cell as shown in Figure 13.8*a* and *b*. I and O represent the input pickup and output release points, respectively.

Alternative 1: The robot picks up a part at I, moves to machine M1, loads the part on machine M1, waits at M1 until the part has been processed, unloads the part from M1, moves to machine M2, loads the part on M2, waits at M2 until the part has been processed there, unloads the part from M2, moves to O, drops the part at O, and moves back to I.

Alternative 2: The robot picks up a part, say P1, at I, moves to M1, loads P1 on machine M1, waits at M1 until part P1 has been processed, unloads P1 from M1, moves to M2, loads P1 on M2, moves back to I, and picks up another part P2 at I, moves to M1, loads P2 on M1, moves to M2, if necessary waits at M2 until the earlier part P1 has been processed, unloads P1, moves to O, drops P1 at O, moves to M1, if necessary waits at M1 until part P2 has been processed, unloads P2, moves to M2, loads P2 on M2, and moves to I.

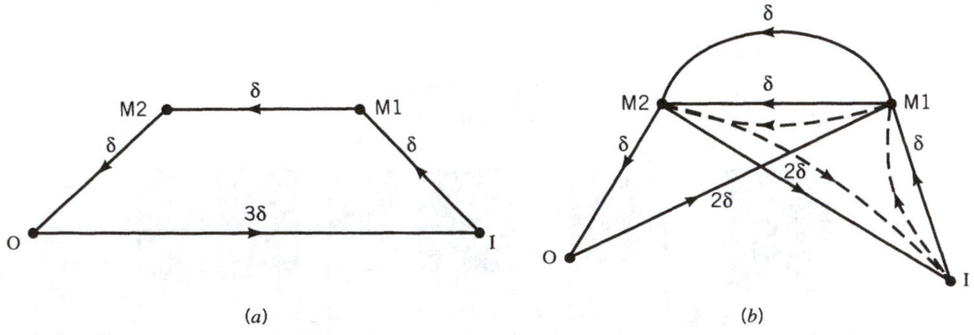

FIGURE 13.8 Alternative sequences of robot moves in a two-machine robot cell.

The cycle time (T1) for alternative 1 is

$$\begin{aligned} T1 &= \varepsilon + \delta + \varepsilon + 3\delta + \varepsilon + \delta + \varepsilon + a + \varepsilon + \delta + \varepsilon + b \\ T1 &= 6\varepsilon + 6\delta + a + b \end{aligned} \qquad (13.12)$$

where a and b are the processing times of machines M1 and M2, respectively; ε is the time for each pickup, load, unload, and drop operation; and δ is the robot travel time between any pair of adjacent locations.

In alternative 2, the cycle can be started at any instant. For ease of respresentation we start cycle 2 with unloading of machine M2 and write the cycle as follows: Unload M2, move and leave part at O, move to M1, wait if necessary, otherwise unload part at M1, move to M2, and leave part at M2, move to I and pick up part at I, move to M1 and release, move to M2 and wait if necessary, before picking up part at M2. These robot activities can easily be expressed as follows:

The cycle time (T2) for alternative 2 is

$$\begin{aligned} T2 &= \varepsilon + \delta + \varepsilon + 2\delta + w1 + \varepsilon + \delta + \varepsilon + 2\delta + \varepsilon + \delta + \varepsilon + \delta + w2 \\ T2 &= 6\varepsilon + 8\delta + w1 + w2 \end{aligned} \qquad (13.13)$$

where w1 and w2 are the robot waiting times at M1 and M2, respectively.

$$w1 = \max\{0, a - 4\delta - 2\varepsilon - w2\}$$

$$w2 = \max\{0, b - 4\delta - 2\varepsilon\}$$

Note that the component $6\varepsilon + 8\delta$ on the right-hand side of Equation (13.13) can be split into two components, α and μ, where $\alpha = 4\varepsilon + 4\delta$ and $\mu = 2\varepsilon + 4\delta$. Then (13.13) becomes

$$\begin{aligned} T2 &= \alpha + \mu + w2 + w1 \\ &= \alpha + \mu + \max\{0, b - \mu\} + \max\{0, a - \mu - \max\{0, b - \mu\}\} \\ &= \alpha + \max\{\mu, b\} + \max\{0, a - \max\{\mu, b\}\} \\ &= \alpha + \max\{\max\{\mu, b\}, a\} \\ &= \alpha + \max\{\mu, b, a\} = 4\varepsilon + 4\delta + \max\{2\varepsilon + 4\delta, a, b\} \end{aligned}$$

where $\alpha + \mu$ represents the total time of the robot activities (pickup, drop off, and move times) in a cycle. The α represents the total time of the robot activities associated with any directed triangle (M2-O-M1 or M1-M2-I in Figure 13.8*b*) in the cycle, and μ represents the total time of the remaining robot activities.

To determine the optimal cycle time, we must determine the conditions under which an alternative has the minimum cycle time, which means that one dominates the other. We consider these cases as follows:

1. For example, from the equation for cycle time T2, if $\mu \le \max\{a, b\}$, then T2 is either $\alpha + a$ or $\alpha + b$. In both cases, comparing T2 with T1, we find that T2 is less than T1.
2. Similarly, if $\mu > \max\{a, b\}$ and $2\delta \le a + b$, then T2 is less than T1.
3. However, if $\mu > \max\{a, b\}$ and $2\delta > a + b$, then T2 is more than T1.

We can conveniently represent these cases in algorithmic form as follows:

13.9.2 Algorithm

Step 0: Calculate $\mu = 2\varepsilon + 4\delta$.

Step 1: If $\mu \leq \max\{a, b\}$, then T2 is optimal. Calculate T2 and stop. Otherwise go to step 2.

Step 2: If $\mu > \max\{a, b\}$ and $2\delta \leq a + b$, then T2 is optimal. Calculate T2 and stop. Otherwise go to step 3.

Step 3: If $\mu > \max\{a, b\}$ and $2\delta > a + b$, then T1 is optimal. Calculate T1 and stop.

EXAMPLE 13.6

Determine the optimal cycle time and corresponding robot sequences in a two-machine robotic cell with the following data:

Processing time of machine M1	= 11.00 min
Processing time of machine M2	= 09.00 min
Robot gripper pickup	= 0.16 min
Robot gripper release time	= 0.16 min
Robot move time between the two machines	= 0.24 min

Solution

Step 0:

$$\mu = 2\varepsilon + 4\delta$$
$$\mu = 2(0.16) + 4(0.24) = 1.28 \text{ min}$$

Step 1:

$$\mu \leq \max\{a, b\}$$
$$1.28 \leq \max\{11, 9\}$$

1.28 is less than 11. Therefore, T2 is optimal.

$$\text{T2} = \alpha + \max\{\mu, a, b\}$$
$$\text{T2} = [4\varepsilon + 4\delta] + \max\{1.28, 11, 9\} = [4(0.16) + 4(0.24)] + 11$$
$$\text{T2} = 1.6 + 11 = 12.6 \text{ min}$$

The optimal cycle time is 12.6 min and the optimal robot sequence is given by Figure 13.8*b*.

13.10 SIMULATION MODELING

Simulation is a modeling and analysis tool widely used for the purpose of designing, planning, and control of manufacturing systems. In this section we provide a basic understanding of simulation modeling and later present a case study of improving the efficiency of a flexible manufacturing cell using a simulation model.

Simulation is synonymous with imitation. A simulation model may be defined as a concise framework for the analysis and understanding of a system. It is an abstract framework of a system that facilitates imitating the behavior of the system over a period of time. In contrast to mathematical models, simulation models do not need explicit mathematical functions to relate variables. Therefore, they are suitable for representing complex systems to get a feeling for the real system. One of the greatest advantages of a simulation model is that it can compress or expand time (Fishman, 1978). Compression of time refers to the ability of these models to simulate several years of activities within minutes or even a few seconds. Simulation models can also be used to observe a phenomenon that cannot be observed in real time by expanding time and taking observations at very small intervals of time. Simulation can also stop time for a detailed analysis of a system at a particular instant of time, without loss of continuity of the experiment. These advantages of using simulation models for manufacturing systems can be understood better with the help of some illustrations.

For example, in a manufacturing system we may be interested in seeing the long-term implications of a change in maintenance policy. A simulation model may provide information within a few minutes about the failure rate of equipment, including mean time between failures (MTBF), total time for which the equipment was down, average time taken in repair, and other similar statistics. Also, it can provide information about the effects of such a policy on other system parameters, such as job tardiness, throughput, and work-in-process inventories. Of course, when we say a few minutes we are not including the time taken in developing a model and analyzing the data provided by the model. Once a model is developed for any system, it provides an efficient tool for analyzing effects of various parameters and studying the implications of various policies.

A good example of expanding time is in observing the failure pattern of a cutting tool. A simulation model may be developed to see the pattern of cutting tool breakage. In real time, breaking takes place so quickly and abruptly that we cannot observe the stages through which the tool goes while breaking. A simulation model can help in this regard by showing the breaking phenomenon with visual animation stage by stage. Besides expanding and compressing time, we need to stop time for certain analyses at the moment some specific event happens. This is a type of "snapshot" taken at a particular time, but simulation snapshots provide great insight into what was happening in the system at that time. For example, a manufacturing system analyst may be interested in the state of queues of jobs, in-process inventory, and the number of rejected items at each machine on completion of every shift of work. Simulation models provide this information with great ease.

To summarize, simulation modeling techniques are powerful for manipulation of time, system inputs, and logic. They are cost effective for modeling a complex system, and with visual animation capabilities they provide an efficient means of learning, experimenting, and analyzing real-life complex systems such as flexible manufacturing systems. Simulation models are capable of taking care of stochastic variability without much complexity. They enable the behavior of the system as a whole to be predicted. This, in turn, helps in obtaining information about the different elements of the system with a controlled input. A simulation model may be the only choice for experimenting, as it is impossible or uneconomical to experiment with a real system.

Flexible manufacturing systems involve complex and costly subsystems. Simulation is a highly appropriate method for observing interactions among various elements of the FMS and their effects on the system as a whole. Most FMS phenomena are discrete and stochastic in nature. Therefore, discrete, Monte Carlo simulation is the technique to use for their modeling and analysis. Two basic elements of discrete simulation are the rules that determine the occurrence of the next event and rules for changing the state of the model when an event occurs.

13.10.1 The Elements of Discrete Simulation

We shall now discuss some of the common but important elements of discrete event simulation. These are entity, activity, events, queues, attributes, and states (Carrie, 1988).

1. *Entities.* Entities are the nouns of simulation language. They are the building blocks of a manufacturing system, for example, machines, workpieces, AGVs, and Robots. Entities are of two types: permanent and temporary. Permanent entities, as the name suggests, remain in the model for the duration of the simulation experiment. Temporary entities enter the model and pass through it for a limited time period. Permanent and temporary entities are sometimes also referred to as facilities and transactions, respectively. Examples of permanent entities in FMSs are machining centers and AGVs, and temporary entities are jobs in the system.

2. *Activities.* Functions performed by the entities in the system are termed activities. They are the verbs in simulation language. During any activity multiple entities interact for a definite period of time. One of the important aspects of activities in simulation is that their duration is either fixed or assumed to be fixed. Whenever an activity starts, its finish time is known. Transportation of material by AGVs and processing of jobs by CNC machines are good examples of activities of manufacturing systems.

3. *Events.* Events are the points on the time scale at which some change takes place in the model. They represent the beginning or end of one or more activities. Events are classified as endogenous (or internal) and exogenous (or external). Endogenous events are caused by some interaction of elements within the model, and exogenous events are caused from outside the model, for example, by the arrival of a job in a manufacturing system.

4. *Queues.* Queues are formed when an entity is waiting in the system for some activity. For example, in a manufacturing system a job waiting to be processed on a machine that is not yet available for this job will be a part of the queue for this machine.

5. *Attributes.* These are the adjectives of simulation language, qualifying nouns (i.e., entities). Attributes are the characteristics of entities and serve as identification for an entity in a simulation model.

6. *States.* States define the condition of various elements and of the model as a whole. The state of the model at a particular time gives information about entities and queues.

7. *Activity cycle diagram (ACD).* This is a diagram used in defining the logic of a simulation model. It is equivalent to a flowchart of a general-purpose computer program. In some of the literature these diagrams are also referred as entity cycle diagrams. The ACD shows the cycle for every entity in the model. Conventions for drawing ACDs are as follows (Carrie, 1988).

(a) Each type of entity has an activity cycle.
(b) The cycle consists of activities and queues.
(c) Activities and queues alternate in the cycle.
(d) The cycle is closed.
(e) Activities are depicted by rectangles and queues by circles or ellipses.

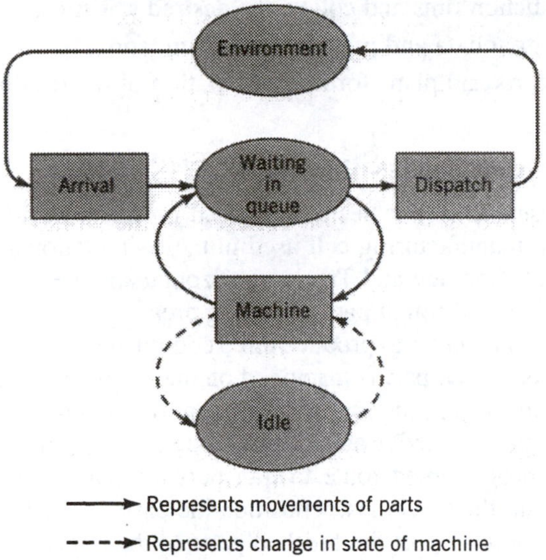

FIGURE 13.9 Activity cycle diagram.

Using these concepts and conventions, Figure 13.9 shows a simple ACD for a machine shop. Here jobs are arriving from the outside environment. Jobs are waiting in a queue for the machine. As soon as the machine is available, a job goes to the machine for processing. Once processing is over, the job again joins a queue waiting to be dispatched. Machines remain idle and wait for the next available job. In some cases flowcharts are used to define the logic instead of ACDs, but on the whole, activity cycle diagrams give a better understanding of a system for simulation modeling. Activity cycle diagrams are good for logical understanding, but much more is involved in simulation modeling. In the following section we discuss basic steps for developing and using a simulation model.

13.10.2 Basic Steps in Developing and Using a Simulation Model

1. Define the problem by specifying objectives and specific issues to be considered.
2. Collect data about entities and identify the attributes of each type of entity.
3. Develop an ACD using all the entities; also define the duration of each activity and queue disciplines.
4. Specify initial conditions and values of the variables; also specify the statistics to be collected.
5. Validate the preceding information by involving the people who are actually working on the system and have an in-depth understanding of it.
6. Construct a computer program for the simulation model using an appropriate software and hardware combination.
7. Make pilot runs to test the sensitivity of the output to variations in input parameters. This will help in validating the simulation model.
8. If necessary, make changes in the model based on the information gathered during pilot runs.

9. Make production runs and collect the desired statistics.
10. Analyze output data and prepare recommendations.
11. Present reports and plans for implementation of the results.

13.10.3 A Simulation Case Study of an FMS Cell

The case study presented in this section is based on the work of Musil and Akbay (1989). The flexible manufacturing cell used in their simulation study consists of an ASEA six-axis robot, Kearney and Trecker horizontal spindle mill, Mori Seiki lathe, gripper change station, and rough part unloading area.

In this case, the cell is set up to produce three components: base, jaw, and screw for the assembly of a vise. Each part is machined on one particular machine: the base on the Kearney and Trecker mill, the jaw on a Bridgeport mill, and the screw on the Mori Seiki lathe. The components arrive at the cell as rough castings in the loading area. The robot follows a preprogrammed route to transport the parts to their respective machines, load them onto the machines, reposition the parts for additional operations on the same machine, and transport the finished parts to the unloading area. The gripper change station is necessary because the base and jaw require that the robot use a straight gripper while the screw requires the use of a curved gripper.

Simulation Model The simulation model of the flexible manufacturing cell was developed in the Simulation Language for Alternative Modeling (SLAM II) and the Extended Simulation Support System (TESS). TESS adds a relational database management system and animation capabilities to the simulation.

13.10.3.2 Analysis of the Current System

The model of the flexible manufacturing cell was run over a simulated time span of 4800 min, or ten 8-hour shifts. Key data values or statistics, with regard to the intended objectives, were:

1. Time in the system for each component part
2. Number of observations (product output)
3. Average waiting time for each resource
4. Percentage of time that each resource was captured

The statistics for the simulation run of the current system as well as policies experimented with are summarized in Table 13.9. The absolute minimum time required to produce a particular part can be determined by summing all the necessary activities for that part throughout the system. This would result in minimum times of 5.19, 6.56, and 2.90 min for the base, jaw, and screw, respectively. These times could be achieved only if an entity never had to wait for a resource. With the help of this information and the statistics in Table 13.9, we can obtain the average waiting time and percentage of time that each resource was captured.

As seen from Table 13.9, the jaw spent the longest time in the system, 10.87 min per part. A key aim was to reduce this critical or system-dependent time, without increasing the processing time of the base or screw above the processing time of the jaw. After initial runs, it was checked that the output of the simulated model coincided with that of the actual system, validating the model. Experiments with the model could now be performed with the expectation of realistic results.

TABLE 13.9 **Results for the Case Study**

	Current system	*Policy 1*	*Policy 2*	*Policy 3*
Time in system for base (min)	9.62	8.66	8.51	6.49
Time in system for jaw (min)	10.87	9.91	9.76	7.43
Time in system for screw (min)	5.13	5.13	6.55	8.79
System output (cycle)	441.00	484.00	491.00	546.00
Percentage increase	—	9.75	11.33	23.81

The objective of this study was to increase the output of the cell by making only scheduling changes. The way to alter the scheduling order of the component parts in the model is to change the priorities associated with the resources. The only resource in the cell that requires prioritizing is the robot, because it is the only resource that is shared by more than one component part. In the model, the priorities of the parts requesting the robot resource can be changed, making it possible to "experiment with the programming" of the robot without affecting the cell itself.

A comparison of the order in which the parts are processed by the robot in the current system and in the three policies to be considered is as follows:

Current policy: B-J-S-B-J-W-J-B-J
Policy 1: B-J-S-J-B-J-B-J
Policy 2: B-J-S-J-B-S-J-B-J
Policy 3: S-J-B-J-W-B-W-J-B-J-S

where B stands for base, J for jaw, S for screw, and W for wait.

Policy 1 In this case the order of the base and jaw was switched after processing the screw. This change caused the order of the remaining processing for these two parts to be reversed and eliminated the time during which the robot was waiting for the second operation on the jaw to be finished. The results of this simulation run are summarized in Table 13.9. The results demonstrate that the changes made in this experiment provided an increase in output by 9.75 percent and that the time in the system for the jaw was reduced from 10.87 to 9.91 min per production cycle. This simple change in the processing order of the base and jaw made a significant impact on the productivity of the cell.

Policy 2 The next question to be considered was: What if the screw processing was split up into multiple steps? The intent of Policy 2 was to answer this question. The results of this simulation run are summarized in Table 13.9. The output was raised to 491 units, an increase of 50 units over the current system, which translates to an increase in productivity of 11.3 percent. It is apparent that dividing the processing of the screw into two steps decreased the waiting time of both the base and the jaw while raising the processing time of the screw only slightly. This increased time, however, is still less than the critical time for the cell, which is the time for the jaw.

Policy 3 The results thus far are acceptable, but could the output be improved even further without going beyond scheduling changes? Considering that the screw has the shortest processing time of the three parts, it would be best if the screw did most of the waiting, thereby reducing the waiting time of the jaw. In this experiment, the second step in the processing of the screw was moved all the way to the end, after completion of both the base and the screw. In order to do this, the robot was made to wait for a short time at two points in the processing of the other parts. This simulation run produced the data shown in Table 13.9. The critical time was no longer the time spent in the system by the jaw, because the time to process the screw had increased to a point above that of the jaw. However, this time was well below the critical time in the other cases, providing an output of 546 units, which is an increase in productivity of 23.8 percent over the current system.

13.10.3.3 Study Results

With simulation modeling, it is possible to create and test countless scenarios. In this study, among the scenarios considered, the processing order in Policy 3 provided the best scheduling to meet the intended objectives. Although Policy 3 may or may not be the best possible processing order, it provides an excellent improvement over the current system. With the help of this simulation model, it was shown that a 24 percent increase in productivity would be realized by modifying the processing order as shown in the third policy.

13.11 FMS BENEFITS

FMS offers manufacturers more than just a manufacturing system that is flexible. It offers a concept to improve productivity in mid-variety, mid-volume production situations, an entire strategy for changing company operations ranging from internal purchasing and ordering procedures to distribution and marketing. Benefits resulting from implementing FMS technology cut across all the functional boundaries in any organization. The principal benefits of FMS are associated with the *system flexibility,* that is, responsiveness to problems on a short- and long-term basis. Examples are responsiveness to short-term problems on the shop floor and responsiveness to long-term problems by accommodating alterations in the system.

13.11.1 Responsiveness to Short-Term Problems

Two major elements in an FMS are responsible for short term responsiveness: the NC machines and the control systems.

The use of NC machines permits flexibility in absorbing market fluctuations resulting in engineering and process changes. These changes result in different NC codes, process sequences, and, in some cases, workholding and tooling devices. Most of the changes can be taken care of concurrently by making changes in the NC codes, using modular fixturing and automated tool changing. Thus, these changes can be accommodated without affecting the output of existing parts.

The control system built in the FMS permits the effective use of high capital investment equipment. For example, if a machine is busy, then the parts are automatically transferred to an idle machine. Similarly, the control system tracks down the tool breakdowns and machine malfunctions through built-in sensor systems. In case of tool failures, they are automatically changed. The machine malfunctions are reported to the central control systems. If queuing up of jobs continues because of the non-availability of machines, then the central control system may even reschedule the arrival of parts into the system.

13.11.2 Responsiveness to Long-Term Problems

Let us first understand what long-term problems may necessitate changes in the system configuration. Over a period of time, some of the existing products are phased out and new products are added to the production stream. Furthermore, the product mixes and their volumes change. Therefore, the major long-term problems could be how to cope with new products and changing product mixes and volumes. The solutions to these problems lie in long-range planning to accommodate the new products in the existing part families and expanding capacity to accommodate increased volume.

These characteristics of short-term responsiveness and long-term accommodation essentially represent various types of flexibility in an FMS, such as in machines, routing, volume, and mix, and are primarily responsible for a number of benefits:

- Reduction in direct labor by removing the operators from the machine site
- Improved operational control through feedback control mechanisms and reduction in the number of uncontrollable variables
- Improved machine utilization through elimination and/or reduction of machine setup time, use of automated tool changers and fixtures to change tools and workpieces, and optimal tool replacement using tool wear monitoring
- Reduction in inventory through small lot sizes, improved inventory turnovers, and implementation of just-in-time principles

The benefits of installing FMS include reduced lead time, improved machine utilization, reduced unit cost, reduced labor requirements, reduced scrap levels, reduced work-in-process, and increased flexibility in responding to internal and external changes. These outweigh the problems of high investment. The automotive parts manufacturing industry is a leader in FMS applications for manufacture of prismatic parts, rotational parts, and sheet metal parts. The most exciting future application area is flexible assembly, which is the biggest user of manual labor. There is a tremendous growth potential for FMSs in America, Europe, and Japan.

13.12 SUMMARY

The flexible manufacturing system is a manufacturing concept for mid-volume, mid-variety parts production. There could be a number of FMS configurations, depending on the levels of flexibility and production rates. Furthermore, the degree of automation of the machine tools, material-handling system, and computer system, the three major components of a manufacturing system, may vary depending on the goals of an organization.

An FMS is capable of accommodating engineering and process changes that may occur during manufacturing. In this chapter various aspects of FMS, such as physical and control components, layout planning, and benefits, were discussed. Some analytical treatment of part selection problems, tool management problems, and layout problems was given because these problems characterize FMSs and are different from those in traditional manufacturing systems.

PROBLEMS

13.1 Classify production systems based on volume–variety considerations.

13.2 What do you understand by FMS? What are the components of an FMS?

13.3 Flexibility is not the only essential ingredient for a flexible manufacturing system. Explain.

13.4 All flexible manufacturing systems have common characteristics irrespective of their types. Identify and explain these characteristics.

13.5 Discuss important differences among the following:
(a) Transfer line
(b) Stand-alone NC machine
(c) Manufacturing cell
(d) Special manufacturing system
(e) Flexible manufacturing system

13.6 Describe the physical subsystems of an FMS.

13.7 Discuss the following control subsystems of an FMS:
(a) Part control system
(b) Machine-tool control system including inspection machines
(c) Tool control and tool management system
(d) Material handling and storage control system
(e) Maintenance control system
(f) Management control system
(g) Interfacing of these subsystems with central computer

13.8 Discuss various types of flexibility:
(a) Machine flexibility
(b) Routing flexibility
(c) Mix flexibility
(d) Mix-change flexibility
(e) Production flexibility
(f) Expansion flexibility

13.9 The data in Table P13.1 are available on the use of tools for various part types. Using the Hwang model and revised model due to Stecke and Kim, determine the batches of the parts selected. Discuss the differences between the results obtained. Assume that each tool requires one slot of a tool magazine.

13.10 What impact does tool magazine capacity have on FMS productivity? Discuss the following tooling policies:
(a) Bulk exchange policy
(b) Tool migration policy
(c) Resident tooling policy
(d) Tool-sharing policy

13.11 Layout considerations in FMS are different from those in other manufacturing systems. Discuss the following types of layouts in the design of flexible manufacturing systems:

TABLE P13.1 **Part-Tool Requirements**

Part types	*P1*	*P2*	*P3*	*P4*	*P5*	*P6*	*P7*	*P8*	*P9*
Tools required	t1	t2	t3	t1, t2	t2, t3	t4, t5	t6, t7, t8, t9	t6, t8, t10, t11	t12, t1, t2, t6, t5

(a) Linear single-row machine layout
(b) Double-row machine layout
(c) Circular machine layout
(d) Cluster machine layout
(e) Loop layout

13.12 Using a diagram, explain the structure of FMS software.

13.13 What is the relationship between group technology and a flexible manufacturing system? Discuss.

13.14 Data available on tool types and part types are given in Table P13.2. Develop a tool resident policy considering three machine tools.

13.15 Consider that there are five machines in a flexible manufacturing system to be served by an automated guided vehicle. A linear single-row layout is recommended because of the use of an AGV. Data on the frequency of AGV trips, material-handling costs per unit distance, and clearance between the machines are given in Tables P13.3–P13.6. Suggest the suitable layout.

TABLE P13.2 **Tool Type and Part Type Matrix**

	Part types														
Tools	*p1*	*p2*	*p3*	*p4*	*p5*	*p6*	*p7*	*p8*	*p9*	*p10*	*p11*	*p12*	*p13*	*p14*	*p15*
t1		1	1		1	1	1			1	1		1		1
t2		1	1		1	1	1			1	1		1		1
t3	1			1				1	1			1		1	
t4	1			1				1	1			1		1	
t5		1	1			1	1			1	1		1		1
t6		1	1		1	1				1	1		1		1
t7				1				1	1			1		1	
t8	1			1				1				1		1	
t9	1			1				1	1			1		1	

TABLE P13.3 **Frequency of AGV Trips**

	1	*2*	*3*	*4*	*5*
1	0	30	80	60	40
2	30	0	20	40	25
3	80	20	0	38	51
4	60	40	38	0	55
5	40	25	51	55	0

TABLE P13.4 **Material-Handling Cost per Unit**

	1	*2*	*3*	*4*	*5*
1	0	3	7	6	4
2	3	0	4	7	2
3	7	4	0	1	9
4	6	7	1	0	2
5	4	2	9	2	0

TABLE P13.5 **Clearance Between Machines**

	1	*2*	*3*	*4*	*5*
1	0	1	2	1	2
2	1	0	1	1	2
3	2	1	0	1	2
4	1	1	1	0	1
5	2	2	2	1	0

TABLE P13.6 **The Machine Dimensions**

Machines	*M1*	*M2*	*M3*	*M4*	*M5*
Machine sizes	20 × 10	25 × 15	20 × 30	20 × 10	15 × 25

13.16 Determine the optimal cycle time as well as robot sequences for a two-machine robotic cell with the following data:

Processing time of machine M1	= 20.00 min
Processing time of machine M2	= 10.00 min
Robot gripper pickup time	= 0.20 min
Robot gripper release time	= 0.20 min
Robot move time between the two machines	= 0.30 min

13.17 Determine the optimal cycle time and corresponding robot sequence for a three-machine robotic cell. The following data are given:

Processing time for machine M1	= 10.00 min
Processing time for machine M2	= 07.00 min
Processing time for machine M3	= 04.00 min
Robot gripper pickup time	= 0.20 min
Robot gripper release time	= 0.20 min
Robot move time between two consecutive machines	= 0.30 min

REFERENCES AND SUGGESTED READING

Amoako-Gyampah, K., Meredith, J. K., and Raturi, A. (1992). A comparison of tool management strategies and part selection rules for a flexible manufacturing system. *International Journal of Production Research* 30(4):733–748.

Anon. (1994). Simulation software buyers' guide. *IE Magazine* 26(5):58–71.

Asfahl, C. R. (1992). *Robots and Manufacturing Automation,* Second Edition. John Wiley & Sons, New York, pp. 272–281.

Browne, J., Dubois, D., Rathmil, K., Sethi, S. P., and Stecke, K. E. (1984). Classification of manufacturing systems. *FMS Magazine* 2(2):114–117.

Buzacott, J. A., and Shantikumar, J. G. (1980). Models for understanding flexible manufacturing systems. *AIIE Transactions* 12(4):339–349.

Carrie, C. (1988). *Simulation of Manufacturing.* John Wiley & Sons, New York.

Carter, M. F. (1986). Designing flexibility into automated manufacturing systems. In *Proceedings of the Second ORSA/TIMS Conference on Flexible Manufacturing Systems: Operations Research Models and Applications* (K. E. Stecke and R. Suri, eds.), Elsevier Science Publishers B. V., New York, pp. 107–118.

Denzler, D. R., and Boe, W. J. (1987). Experimental investigation of flexible manufacturing system scheduling rules. *International Journal of Production Research* 25(7):979–994.

Dunlap, J. (1984). *Flexible Manufacturing Systems.* Cincinnati Milacron, Cincinnati, Ohio.

Falkner, C. H. (1986). Flexibility in manufacturing plants. *Proceedings of the Second ORSA/TIMS Conference on Flexible Manufacturing Systems: Operations Research Models and Applications* (K. E. Stecke and R. Suri, eds.), Elsevier Science Publishers B. V., New York, pp. 95–106.

Fishman, G. S. (1978). *Principles of Discrete Event Simulation.* Wiley-Interscience, New York.

Gerwin, D. (1982). Do's and don't do's of computerized manufacturing. *Harvard Business Review* 60(2):107–116.

Groover, M. P. (1987). *Automation, Production Systems, and Computer-Integrated Manufacturing.* Prentice Hall, Englewood Cliffs, New Jersey.

Gupta, Y. P., and Goyal, S. (1989). Flexibility of manufacturing systems: Concepts and measurements. *European Journal of Operational Research* 43:119–135.

Heragu, S. S., and Kusiak, A. (1988). Machine layout problem in flexible manufacturing systems. *Operations Research* 36(2):258–268.

Hwang, S. (1986). A constraint-directed method to solve the part selection problem in flexible manufacturing systems planning stage. *Proceedings of the Second ORSA/TIMS Conference on Flexible Manufacturing Systems: Operations Research Models and Applications* (K. E. Stecke and R. Suri, eds.), Elsevier Science Publishers B. V., New York, pp. 297–309.

Kasilingam, R. G. (1989). Mathematical programming approach to cell formation problems in flexible manufacturing systems. Ph.D. Dissertation, University of Windsor, Windsor, Ontario, Canada.

Kumar, P., Tewari, N.K., and Singh, N. (1990). Joint consideration of grouping and loading problems in a flexible manufacturing system. *International Journal of Production Research* 28(7):1345–1356.

Kumar, P., Singh, N., and Tewari, N. K. (1991). A nonlinear goal programming model for multi-stage multi-objective decision problems with applications to grouping and loading in a flexible manufacturing systems. *European Journal of Operational Research* 53(2):166–171.

Kusiak, A. (1985). Flexible manufacturing systems: A structural approach. *International Journal of Production Research* 23(6):1057–1073.

Kusiak, A. (1990). *Intelligent Manufacturing Systems.* Prentice Hall, Englewood Cliffs, New Jersey.

Lenz, J. E. (1988). *Flexible Manufacturing: Benefits for the Low-Inventory Factory.* Marcel Dekker, New York.

Liang, M. (1991). The combined part selection and machine loading problems in flexible manufacturing systems. Ph.D. dissertation, University of Windsor, Windsor, Ontario, Canada.

Luggen, W. W. (1991). *Flexible Manufacturing Cells and Systems.* Prentice Hall, Englewood Cliffs, New Jersey.

Maleki, R. A. (1991). *Flexible Manufacturing Systems: The Technology and Management.* Prentice Hall, Englewood Cliffs, New Jersey.

May, B. (1986). FMS software basics. Technical paper no. MS86-172, Society of Manufacturing Systems, Dearborn, Michigan.

Musil, D. C., and Akbay, K. S. (1989). Improve efficiency of a FMS cell through use of a computer simulation model. *IE Magazine* 21(11):28–34.

Neghabat, F. (1974). An efficient equipment layout algorithm. *Operations Research* 22:622–628.

O'Grady, P. J., and Menon, P. (1986). A concise review of flexible manufacturing systems and FMS literature. *Computers in Industry* 7:155–167.

Rajgopalan, S. (1986). Formulation and heuristic solutions for parts grouping and tool loading in flexible manufacturing systems, *Proceedings of the Second ORSA/TIMS Conference on Flexible Manufacturing Systems: Operations Research Models and Applications* (K. E. Stecke and R. Suri, eds.), Elsevier Science Publishers B. V., New York, pp. 311–320.

Sethi, S. P., Srikandarajah, C., Blazewicz, J., and Kubiak, W. (1992). Sequencing of robot moves and multiple parts in a robotic cell. *International Journal of Flexible Manufacturing Systems* 4:331–358.

Shanker, K., and Tzen, Y. J. (1985). A loading and dispatching problem in a random flexible manufacturing system. *International Journal of Production Research* 23(3):579–595.

Smith, M. L., Ramesh, R., Dudek, R. A., and Blair, E. R. (1986). Characteristics of U.S. flexible manufacturing systems—a survey. *Proceedings of the Second ORSA/TIMS Conference on Flexible Manufacturing Systems: Operations Research Models and Applications* (K. E. Stecke and R. Suri, eds.), Elsevier Science Publishers B. V., New York, pp. 477–486.

Stecke, K. E. (1983). Formulations and solutions of nonlinear integer production planning problems for flexible manufacturing systems. *Management Science* 29(3):273.

Stecke, K. E., and Kim, I. (1986). A flexible approach to implementing the short term FMS planning function. *Proceedings of the Second ORSA/TIMS Conference on Flexible Manufacturing Systems: Operations Research Models and Applications* (K. E. Stecke and R. Suri, eds.), Elsevier Science Publishers B. V., New York, pp. 283–295.

Stecke, K. E., and Kim, I. (1988). A study of FMS part type selection approaches for short term production planning. *International Journal of Flexible Manufacturing Systems* 1(1):7–29.

Stecke, K. E., and Solberg, J. J. (1981). Loading and control policies for flexible manufacturing systems. *International Journal of Production Research* 19(5):481.

Tomek, P. (1986). Tooling strategies related to FMS management. *FMS Magazine* 4:102–107.

Viswanadham, N., and Narahari, Y. (1992). *Performance Modelling of Automated Manufacturing Systems.* Prentice Hall, Englewood Cliffs, New Jersey, pp. 82–84.

Young, C. and Greene, A. (1986). *Flexible Manufacturing Systems.* American Management Association, New York.

APPENDIX A

PROBLEM FORMULATION FOR EXAMPLES 13.1 AND 13.2

Example 13.1

Maximize $f = z_1 + z_2 + \cdots + z_8$
subject to:

$$y_1 + y_2 + y_3 + y_4 + y_5 + 2y_6 + 2y_7 \leq 5 \tag{13.A1}$$

$$z_1 - y_1 \leq 0 \tag{13.A2}$$

$$z_2 - y_2 \leq 0 \quad (13.A3)$$

$$z_3 - y_3 \leq 0 \quad (13.A4)$$

$$z_4 - y_4 \leq 0 \quad (13.A5)$$

$$z_5 - y_1 \leq 0 \quad (13.A6)$$

$$z_5 - y_2 \leq 0 \quad (13.A7)$$

$$z_6 - y_3 \leq 0 \quad (13.A8)$$

$$z_6 - y_5 \leq 0 \quad (13.A9)$$

$$z_7 - y_6 \leq 0 \quad (13.A10)$$

$$z_8 - y_1 \leq 0 \quad (13.A11)$$

$$z_8 - y_2 \leq 0 \quad (13.A12)$$

$$z_8 - y_7 \leq 0 \quad (13.A13)$$

Objective Function for Example 13.2

Maximize $f = z_1 + z_2 + z_3 + z_4 + 2z_5 + 2z_6 + 2z_7 + 4z_8$

subject to: constraints given by Equations (13.A1) to (13.A13).

APPENDIX B

SEQUENCING OF ROBOT MOVES IN A THREE-MACHINE ROBOTIC CELL

In this case, there are six alternatives as shown in Figure 13.B1*a–f*. The cycle time for each alternative can be determined as follows. For details, refer to Sethi, et al (1992).

Alternative 1

The cycle time (T1) for alternative 1 (see Figure 13.B1*a*) is

$$T1 = 8\varepsilon + 8\delta + a + b + c$$

or

$$T1 = \alpha + \beta - 4\delta + a + b + c$$

where $\alpha = 4\varepsilon + 4\delta$, $\beta = 4\varepsilon + 8\delta$, and a, b, and c are the processing times at machines M1, M2, and M3, respectively. ε and δ have the same meaning as for a two-machine cell.

Alternative 2

The cycle time (T2) for alternative 2 (see Figure 13.B1*b*) is

$$T2 = 8\varepsilon + 12\delta + wl + w2 + w3$$

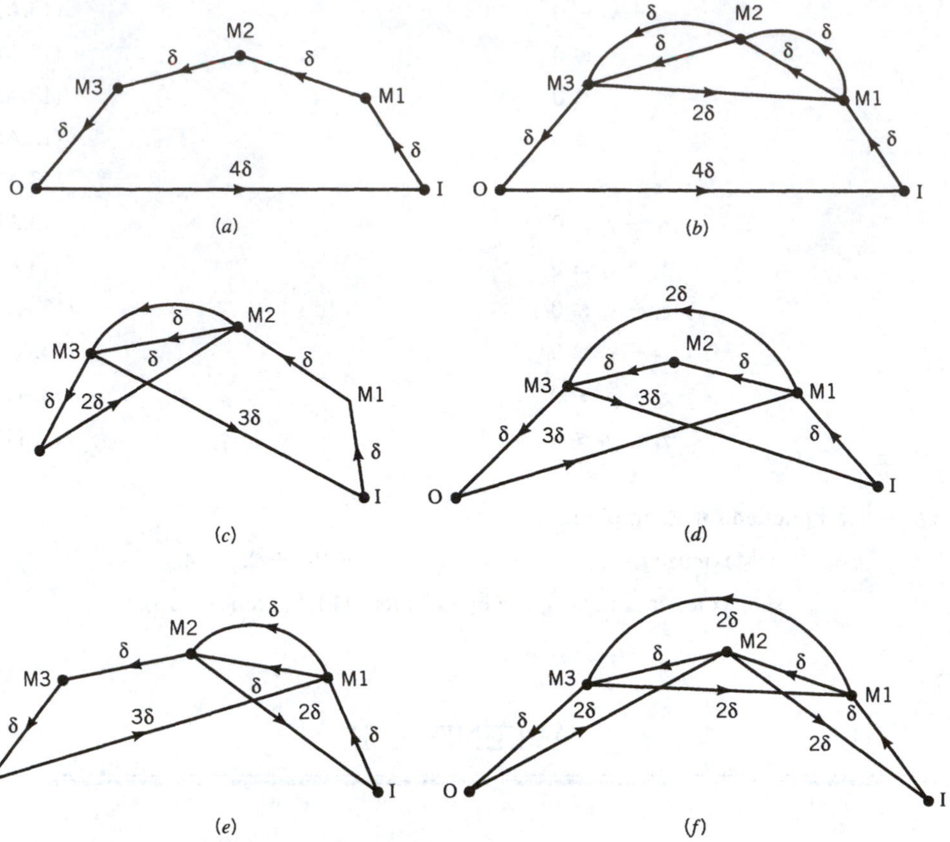

FIGURE 13.B1 Alternative sequences of robot moves in a machine cell robotic cell.

where w1, w2, and w3 are the robot waiting times at machines M1, M2, and M3, respectively.

$$\text{w1} = \max\{0, a - 2\varepsilon - 4\delta - \text{w2}\}$$

$$\text{w2} = \max\{0, b - 4\varepsilon - 8\delta - \text{w3}\}$$

$$\text{w3} = \max\{0, c - 2\varepsilon - 4\delta\}$$

or

$$\text{T2} = \alpha + \max\{\beta, b, \beta/2 + a, \beta/2 + c, (a + b + c)/2\}$$

Alternative 3

The cycle time (T3) for alternative 3 (see Figure 13.B1*c*) is

$$\text{T3} = 8\varepsilon + 10\delta + \text{w2} + \text{w3} + a$$

where

$$\text{w2} = \max\{0, b - 2\varepsilon - 4\delta - \text{w3}\}$$

$$\text{w3} = \max\{0, c - 4\varepsilon - 6\delta - a\}$$

or

$$\text{T3} = \alpha + \max\{\beta - 2\delta + a, c, a + b + \beta/2 - 2\delta\}$$

Alternative 4

The cycle time (T4) for alternative 4 (see Figure 13.B1*d*) is

$$T4 = 8\varepsilon + 12\delta + b + w1 + w3$$

where

$$w1 = \max\{0, a - 2\varepsilon - 6\delta - w3\}$$

$$w3 = \max\{0, c - 2\varepsilon - 6\delta\}$$

or

$$T4 = \alpha + \max\{\beta + b, \beta/2 + a + b - 2\delta, \beta/2 + b + c - 2\delta\}$$

Alternative 5

The cycle time (T5) for alternative 5 (see Figure 13.B1*e*) is

$$T5 = 8\varepsilon + 10\delta + w1 + w2 + c$$

where

$$w1 = \max\{0, a - 4\varepsilon - 6\delta - w2 - c\}$$

$$w2 = \max\{0, b - 2\varepsilon - 4\delta\}$$

or

$$T5 = \alpha + \max\{a, \beta + c - 2\delta, \beta/2 + b + c - 2\delta\}$$

Alternative 6

The cycle time (T6) for alternative 6 (see Figure 13.B1*f*) is

$$T6 = 8\varepsilon + 12\delta + w1 + w2 + w3$$

where

$$w1 = \max\{0, a - 4\varepsilon - 8\delta - w2 - w3\}$$

$$w2 = \max\{0, b - 4\varepsilon - 8\delta - w3\}$$

$$w3 = \max\{0, c - 4\varepsilon - 8\delta\}$$

or

$$T6 = \alpha + \max\{\beta, a, b, c\}$$

From the foregoing alternatives, it is easily seen that alternative 6 dominates alternative 2 and 4. We therefore ignore these two alternatives (i.e., alternatives 2 and 4). We can represent these results in an algorithmic form as in a two-machine case.

Algorithm

Step 0: Calculate $\beta = 4\varepsilon + 8\delta$

Step 1: If $\beta \leq \max\{a, b, c\}$, then T6 is optimal. Calculate T6 and stop. Otherwise go to step 2.

Step 2: If $\beta > \max\{a, b, c\}$ and one of the following conditions holds:

1. $a \geq 2\delta$ and $c \geq 2\delta$
2. $a \geq 2\delta$, $c < 2\delta$ and $b + c \geq \beta/2 + 2\delta$
3. $a < 2\delta$, $c \geq 2\delta$, and $a + b \geq \beta/2 + 2\delta$
4. $a < 2\delta$, $c < 2\delta$, $a + b \geq \beta/2 + 2\delta$, and $b + c \geq \beta/2 + 2\delta$, then T6 is optimal.

Calculate T6 and stop. Otherwise go to step 3.

Step 3: If $\beta > \max\{a, b, c\}$ and one of the following conditions holds:

1. $a \geq 2\delta$, $c < 2\delta$, and $b + c < \beta/2 + 2\delta$
2. $a < 2\delta$, $c < 2\delta$, $a + b \geq \beta/2 + 2\delta$, and $b + c < \beta/2 + 2\delta$, then T5 is optimal.

Calculate T5 and stop. Otherwise go to step 4.

Step 4: If $\beta > \max\{a, b, c\}$ and one of the following conditions holds:

1. $a < 2\delta$, $c \geq 2\delta$, and $a + b < \beta/2 + 2\delta$
2. $a < 2\delta$, $c < 2\delta$, $a + b < \beta/2 + 2\delta$, and $b + c \geq \beta/2 + 2\delta$, then T3 is optimal.

Calculate T3 and stop. Otherwise go to step 5.

Step 5: If $\beta > \max\{a, b, c\}$ and $b + c \leq 2\delta$ and $a + b \geq 2\delta$, then T1 is optimal. Calculate T1 and stop.

EXAMPLE 13.7

Determine the optimal cycle time and corresponding robot sequence for a three-machine robotic cell. The following data are given:

Processing time for machine M1	= 12.00 min
Processing time for machine M2	= 07.00 min
Processing time for machine M3	= 09.00 min
Robot gripper pickup time	= 0.19 min
Robot gripper release time	= 0.19 min
Robot move time between two consecutive machines	= 0.27 min

Solution

Step 0: $\beta = 4\varepsilon + 8\delta = 4(0.19) + 8(0.27) = 2.92$ min

Step 1:

$$\beta \leq \max\{a, b, c\}$$

$$2.92 \leq \max\ \{12, 7, 9\}$$

2.92 is less than 12, therefore T6 is optimal.

$$T6 = \alpha + \max\{\beta, a, b, c\} = [4\varepsilon + 4\delta] + \max\{2.92, 12, 7, 9\}$$

$$T6 = [4(0.19) + 4(0.27)] + 12 = 1.84 + 12 = 13.84 \text{ min}$$

$$T6 = 13.84 \text{ min}$$

The optimal cycle time is 13.84 min and the optimal robot sequence is given by Figure 13.B1*f*.

CHAPTER 14

ENTERPRISE INTEGRATION, CIM, AND FUTURE TRENDS

The twenty-first century market will be characterized by high variety and relatively low demand for individual products. This mass customization, managed through virtual organizations, will be the prevalent manufacturing environment. Enterprise-wide integration is necessary to coordinate the myriad activities and information needed for mass customization of products. The idea in enterprise-wide integration is to integrate people, technology, business processes, customers, and suppliers located at dispersed geographic locations. This integration is necessary for meeting enterprise goals. Tools of integration are required to empower people. Three tools for integration, needed to overcome the locational and structural peculiarities of enterprise data processing applications, are network communications, database management systems, and groupware. In this chapter we provide an understanding of basic concepts of integration and integration tools. A framework for enterprise-wide integration is given, followed by a case study.

14.1 INTRODUCTION TO CIM AND ENTERPRISE-WIDE INTEGRATION

The phrase *computer-integrated manufacturing* (CIM) was coined by Dr. J. Harrington, Jr. in 1973. He argued for an integrated approach to the enterprise and against highly fragmented manufacturing operations that lead to localized optimization. Considering the current and future market trends for customized products, the formation of virtual organizations is considered a strategic weapon to combat competition and stay in business over the long term. For virtual organizations to succeed in achieving corporate goals and objectives, there is a greater need for integrated solutions to the many problems across the enterprise, as well as for its customers and suppliers.

The goal of CIM is the integration of all enterprise operations and activities around a common corporate data repository, as seen from the following definition of CIM:

CIM is the integration of the total manufacturing enterprise through the use of integrated systems and data communications coupled with new managerial philosophies that im-

prove organizational and personnel efficiency. (The Computer and Automation Systems Association of the Society of Manufacturing Engineers)

The Society of Manufacturing Engineers (SME) CIM wheel provides a clear portrayal of relationships among all parts of an enterprise. It illustrates a three-layered integration structure of an enterprise as shown in Figure 14.1. The outer layer represents general management, which includes marketing, strategic planning, finance, manufacturing management, and human resources management. The middle layer has three process segments: product and process definition, manufacturing planning and control, and factory automation. These process segments represent all the activities in the design and manufacturing phases of a product life cycle taking the product from concept to assembly. The center of the wheel represents the third layer, which includes information resources management and the common database.

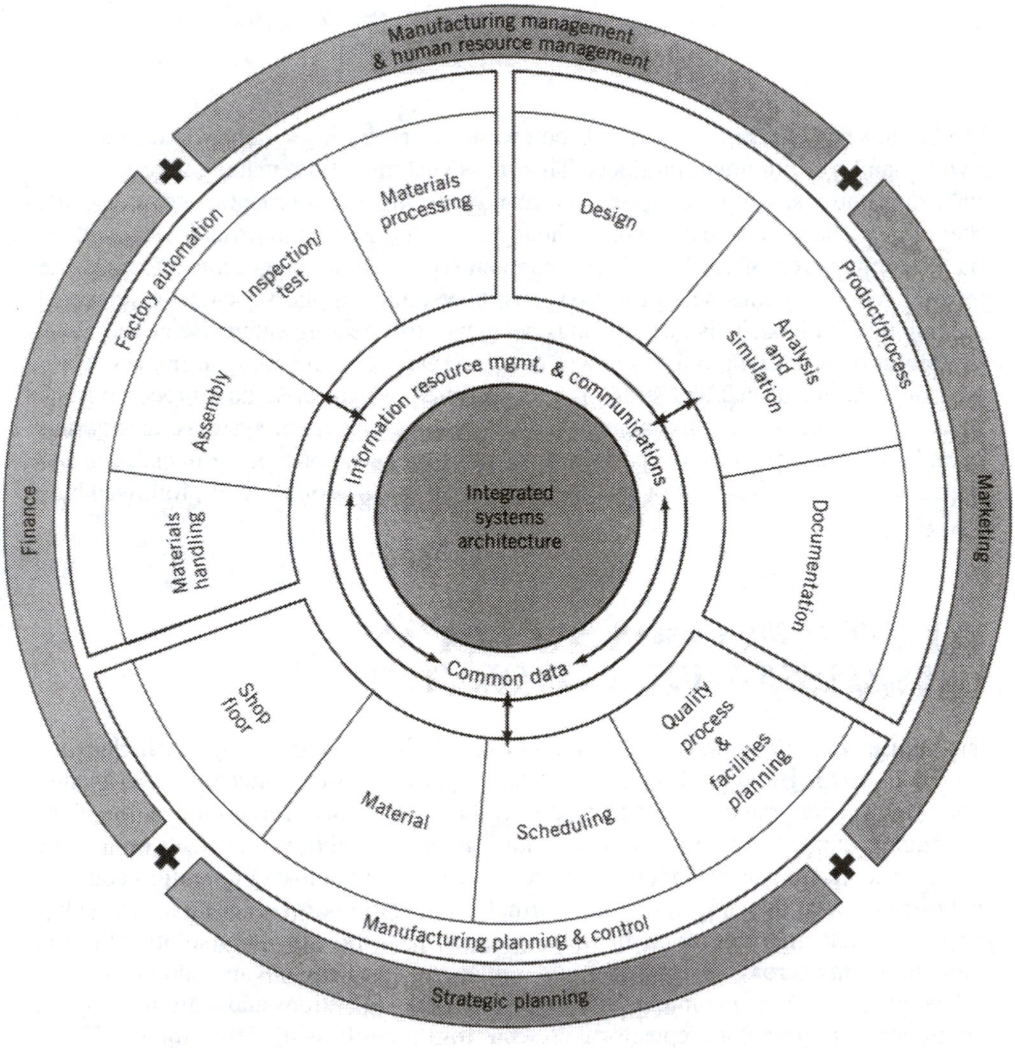

FIGURE 14.1 The SME CIM wheel. (© 1985, Society of Manufacturing Engineers, Dearborn, MI 48121. Note: The Computer and Automated Systems Association of SME (CASA/SME) has issued the *New Manufacturing Enterprise Wheel,* (© 1993, Third Edition, which focuses on the customer rather than the database).

In this book we have covered most of the issues in the middle layer in Chapters 2 through 13. In this chapter we briefly discuss the integration issues in the third layer, such as communication networks, database management systems, and groupware. It is important to understand that networks exist for the purpose of transporting data (design, manufacturing, service, distribution, process planning, costing, and so forth) between computers, terminals, and databases. Thus, databases form an integral part of data communications systems. Discussion of general management issues such as marketing, finance, and personnel management is beyond the scope of this book.

Traditionally, the concept of CIM activities has been confined to manufacturing operations. However, mass customization of products needs much more than manufacturing integration. It requires the formation of virtual organizations to tackle specific projects or market niches. Success of virtual organizations is predicated on empowerment of people within the enterprise with the aid of computer technology including communication networks, database management systems, and groupware. These facilitate team members of the virtual organization as they interact with customers and suppliers and make effective and faster group decisions. Such interaction lays the foundation for enterprise-wide integration (EWI), encompassing various plants and offices of an enterprise, possibly located in different countries and cities, as well as customers and suppliers worldwide. Therefore, EWI is much broader than factory automation integration, which is often the goal of CIM. It is the integration of people, technology, and the business processes throughout the enterprise. The major difference between EWI and CIM is that in EWI people in far-flung enterprises have the tools of integration to meet the needs of ever-changing organizational structures that can be reconfigured according to product and customer needs.

Enterprise-wide integration is required to ensure that all the technical and administrative units can work in unison. This, however, requires a great deal of information about a large number of activities, from product conception through manufacturing, customer delivery, and in-field support. All these life-cycle steps require a large volume of data. The transformation process from one stage to another yields volumes of new data. Furthermore, many of these design, manufacturing, distribution, and service activities, responsible for generating and using volumes of data, are scattered across a wide spectrum of physical locations. The information is generated by a diverse set of highly specialized software tools on heterogeneous computing hardware. Often, incompatible storage media with divergent data structures and formats are used for data storage. This is due to the peculiarities of the tools and systems that generate data without any regard to the needs of the tools or systems that would eventually use the data.

The main idea of enterprise-wide integration is the integration of all the processes necessary for meeting the enterprise goals. Three major tools for integration, required for overcoming the locational and structural peculiarities of an enterprise's data processing applications, are network communications, database management systems, and groupware. First we provide a basic treatment of these elements. Then we provide a framework for enterprise-wide integration.

Terminology used in Network Communications

Hertz (Hz):	Number of cycles per second
Baud:	Number of signals per second
Data rate:	Number of bits sent per second (bps). In general, data rate = baud rate × data bits per signal

Channel: A logical communication path

Bandwidth: Frequency used by a signal (measured in Hz)

Channel capacity: Number of bits that can be transmitted per second. This is the same as data rate.

Open system: A vendor-transparent environment in which users can mix and match hardware and software from various vendors on networks from different vendors.

Interoperability: The ability of two systems to work with each other through well-defined interfaces.

14.2 NETWORK COMMUNICATIONS

A communication network is the backbone of enterprise integration. Networks help to unify a company by linking together all the computerized devices irrespective of their physical location. Through networks we can integrate the whole enterprise, including suppliers and customers. For example, sales and marketing can send customer requirements for new products to design engineering. A computer-aided design (CAD)–generated bill of materials can then be transferred to material requirements planning (MRP) systems. Product design information can be transmitted to manufacturing for use in process planning. Operators can directly access these process plans as well as machine operation and inspection instruction sheets as they are needed on the shop floor. In this process, all kinds of data are being transferred between a variety of computer systems. For an enterprise to be successful, ready access to information (data) is needed across the company. This facilitates rapid interdepartmental responses to changes in design and production schedules that meet the customers' needs. To provide these facilities, well-developed enterprise networks are necessary. An organization can be mapped onto a communication hierarchy that includes an enterprise level, plant level, cell level, and equipment/device level.

The communication needs of these levels differ, and therefore their network requirements in terms of communication devices, distance, physical transmission media, bandwidth, and protocol functions will also be different. To unify the enterprise, three types of network technologies are required to interconnect these levels:

- Device-level subnetworks at the shop floor that connect individual devices such as robots and numerical control (NC) machines
- Plant-wide networks that connect cells and other departments
- Enterprise-wide networks that can globally link various plants/sites and interconnect corporations through electronic data interchange

First we provide a detailed discussion of network technology. Later, we will illustrate the enterprise network that unifies the company.

A communication network is a collection of equipment and physical media that interconnects two or more computers. Networks are generally classified into three categories based on the geographic area covered:

1. *Local area networks (LANs).* LANs are normally used to interconnect computers within the same building or organization and to transmit data at speeds up to 100 megabytes per second (Mbps).

2. *Metropolitan area networks (MANs).* MANs are essentially large LANs that cover a large city or a suburb. They are used to interconnect LANs within a metropolitan area.
3. *Wide area networks (WANs).* WANs use common carrier facilities over long distances with speeds in the range of 1.5 Mbps and are used to connect sites and equipment located long distances apart.

14.2.1 Selection of Network Technology

A number of factors should be considered in the selection of the network technology. These include:

- Communication medium
- Network topology
- Medium access control methods
- Signaling method

14.2.1.1 Communication Medium

Communication media are the physical materials that carry the electrical signal that encodes the data. The communication medium is used in a network to transmit data over short or long distances. Commonly used media include open-wire pairs, twisted-pair cables, coaxial cables, fiber-optic systems, and wireless media. Open-wire pairs are low-cost open copper wires, which are now becoming obsolete. Twisted-pair cables may include up to 3000 wire pairs, which give a bandwidth up to 250 kHz. These are often used in telephone circuits in buildings and are good for short-distance communications. Coaxial cables are used extensively in local area networks. They can deliver high data speeds, above 10 Mbps, and support many data, voice, and video channels. The undesirable feature of this technology is its high signal loss at high frequencies. For very high data transmission applications, optical fiber is becoming very popular. Reasons for its popularity are high bandwidth (frequency ranges higher than 20,000 MHz), data transmission at speeds over 400 Mbps, light weight, very low signal loss error rates, and very high security characteristics because of difficulty in tapping fiber-optic cables. However, the cost of optical fiber is relatively high. It is expected that cost will remain high until new technologies are developed to simplify the installation of these systems.

Factors to be considered in the selection of communication media include bandwidth, signal-to-noise ratio, reliability, and cost. It is desirable to have a communication medium with high bandwidth and good signal-to-noise ratio for its maximum data rate. Data rate is given by the following formula, proposed by Claude Shannon in 1948:

$$\text{Maximum data rate (bps)} = \text{Carrier bandwidth} \times \log_2\left(1 + \frac{\text{signal}}{\text{noise}}\right)$$

14.2.1.2 Network Topology

A network topology describes the relationship between the nodes in a communication system. The general physical layout for the four topologies; star, ring, bus, and tree, is shown in Figure 14.2.

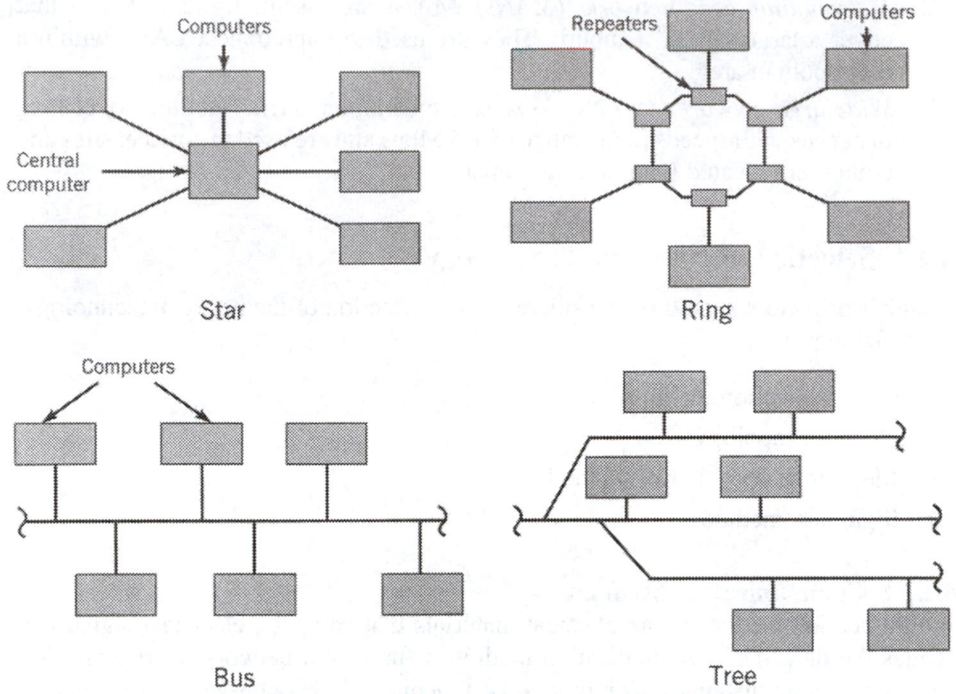

FIGURE 14.2 Various network topologies.

In the star topology, the central computer or host is located at the center. Each user is connected directly to the host. Because each connection does not support multiple users competing for access, high data transfer rates are possible. However, the central computer must be very fast. There are a number of disadvantages, also. For example, this topology requires a great deal of cable as all the users connect directly to the central host. Furthermore, if the central computer fails, the entire network fails.

In the ring topology, each device is connected to two others. In modern rings, the devices are attached to the ring cable. This means that if one device fails, the ring continues to function. An advantage of the ring topology is that the number of devices connected to the network is not limited by the number of slots in any device. At most two slots are required to connect a device to the ring.

The bus topology is one of the most commonly used network layouts. In the bus topology, the devices are connected to the cable, which is terminated at both ends. Advantages of this topology are that it requires less cable than the star topology and each device requires connection to one cable. The disadvantage is that all the devices have to share the cable (that is, all the devices compete for access).

In tree topologies, the devices are connected to a hub that passes the messages from one device to the other. An advantage of the tree topology is that it offers very flexible layouts. Another advantage is that a network can usually survive if a device or cable fails. Tree topologies are common in wide area networks because they are easy to monitor and diagnose or correct. A disadvantage of tree topologies is that if a hub fails, the subnet managed by the hub will fail. Another disadvantage is that the number of devices supported is limited by the number of communication slots in the hub. Thus, if a hub has only 11 slots, we have to buy another hub to connect a twelfth device.

14.2.1.3 Medium Access Control Methods for LANs

Consider the bus and ring topologies illustrated in Figure 14.2, in which several stations are connected to the network. In these cases, each node on the network has equal access to the network. When more than one station tries to send a message at the same time, contention for access occurs. Medium access control is concerned with controlling such access to the network. Medium access control techniques describe the rules for managing access to networks.

The two most commonly used techniques for medium access control are Carrier-Sense Multiple Access with Collision Detection (CSMA/CD) and token passing. There are two topologies that use token passing: token ring and token bus. We provide a brief discussion of how they function.

CSMA/CD (IEEE 802.3 Standard) Xerox Corporation developed the CSMA/CD network control technique in the 1970s in an implementation called Ethernet. Figure 14.3 shows a sample CSMA/CD packet. In this medium access control technique, the sender listens whether the line is busy or not. The sender transmits the message if the line is not busy. Collision may occur if two stations send data at the same time. If a collision is detected, the sender waits for a while before retransmitting the message. To avoid collisions, each computer waits a random amount of time before trying to repeat the transmission of messages.

Figure 14.4 shows a section of cabling of Ethernet having six computers connected to the network. Two Ethernet coaxial cables are connected together using a repeater. A repeater is an amplifier used to boost up signal levels that experience distance-related signal loss (for a discussion of repeaters, see the section on interconnection equipment and devices). A terminator is attached at each end of the cable to prevent the data from reaching the end of cable and being reflected back onto the network. Ethernet cards attached to the network through a tap are used to connect the computers to the network. An Ethernet card handles sending and receiving of packets. In CSMA/CD, any computer can transmit a message on the network when the network is not in use. Collision of data can occur when two computers start using the network at about the same time. If more computers are on the network, the probability of collision will be high.

The CSMA/CD LAN technique is widely used in engineering, manufacturing, and office environments. It provides good access at low workloads. Station interface cards for CSMA/CD and Ethernet are available for almost all computer systems at reason-

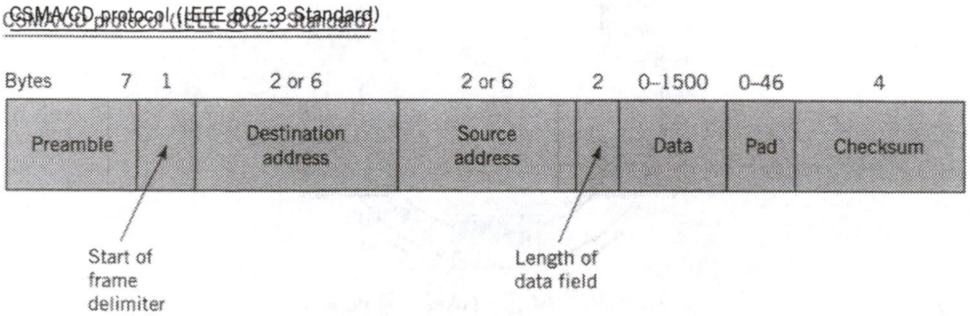

FIGURE 14.3 CSMA/CD frame format.

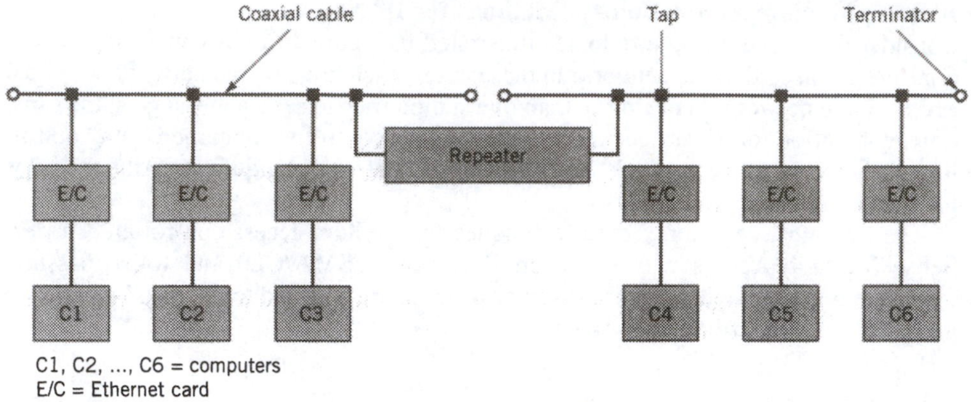

FIGURE 14.4 A section of Ethernet cable.

able prices. However, the chances of collision (and therefore degraded performance) increase as the traffic on the network increases.

Token Ring (IEEE 802.5 Standard) The problem of data collisions in CSMA/CD is completely solved in token ring networks. This is accomplished by having a token at the station to authorize transmission. A token is a packet that is used to send and receive messages. It moves in one direction around a ring to which LAN devices are attached as shown in Figure 14.5. A station ready to send the messages detects an empty token. The message and source and destination addresses are put on the token. The token is marked busy by turning on some flag bits and sent back into circulation. As the token passes through every station, it is checked for a match between the token destination address and the station address. If there is a match, the station retrieves the data and puts on the token an ACK for positive acknowledgment or NAK for negative acknowledgment of a garbled message and sends the token out to the network. The sender frees up the token after receiving the ACK or NAK acknowledgment. There is no limit on the number of computers that can be connected to the ring network compared to the Ethernet.

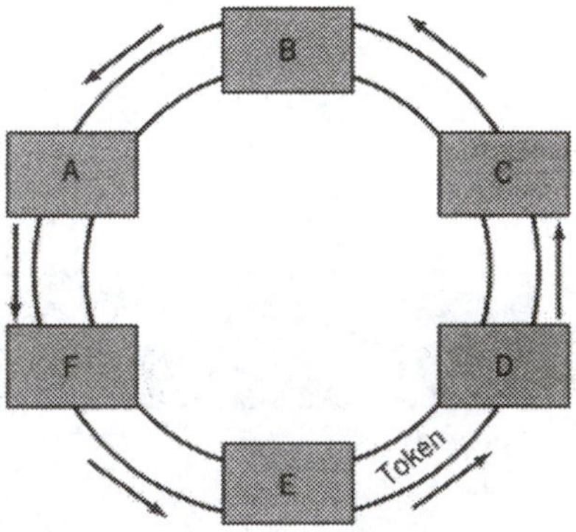

FIGURE 14.5 Token ring network.

Token Bus (IEEE 802.4 Standard) Conceptually, a token bus is similar to a token ring, as both use token passing for medium access control. The only difference is that the token bus operates on a bus instead of a ring topology. Also, a token bus is often a combination of token ring and Ethernet. Unlike a token ring, a token bus does not require repeaters at each station, because data are available to each computer at the same time. The use of a token avoids any possible collisions. The token bus is therefore suitable for use in real-time control applications that require collision-free operations, such as shop-floor control. Logically, the token bus protocol works just like a token ring because a station on a bus knows the addresses of its predecessor and successor stations as shown in Figure 14.6. Just as a baton authorizes runners to start off on their leg of a relay race, a token is the authorization to transmit, which is passed from station to station. The station with the highest address gets the token first, followed by the station with next lower address and so on. To pass the token on to a station, the address of the receiver station is inserted into the token header.

The token bus has excellent throughput performance. It is used in many manufacturing automation protocol (MAP) environments (for a discussion of MAP, refer to Section 14.2.2). Its major disadvantages are its complexity and high overhead in lightly loaded systems. For a detailed discussion of evaluation of LAN protocols, see Stallings (1992).

14.2.1.4 Signaling Methods

Data in a network are propagated from one point to another by means of signals. The signals are therefore the electromagnetic representation of transmitted data. Data or signal converters convert the data to signals for transmission on the sending end and back to data at the receiving end. A modem is a typical example of a converter. A modem converts data bits to continuous signals, which are transmitted across a network. LANs can be divided into various categories, including baseband, broadband, and carrierband, based on signaling methods.

LANs that use digital signals to transfer data between LAN devices are called *baseband* LANs. A baseband LAN uses the data itself as the signal by impressing the data directly onto the communication wire. Baseband LANs work well in small networks where there is no need for voice and video applications. They also use inexpensive cables.

In contrast, *broadband* LANs modulate (convert) data into signals before transmission, transmit signals, and then demodulate the signals into data at the receiving end. Broadband LANs need modems for modulation–demodulation and require more ex-

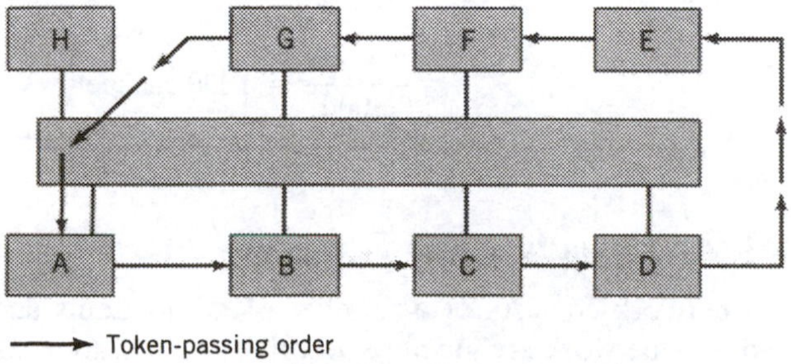

FIGURE 14.6 Token bus network.

pensive cables. Broadband systems serve well as backbones (highways) that support many channels. Each channel is assigned a frequency range. Different channels are assigned through frequency division multiplexing (FDM). FDM is the process of dividing up the bandwidth of a carrier (cable or telephone line) into data signal bandwidth. Let us illustrate this by an example. Suppose you want to transmit data on a network. Consider that the data signals are in the frequency range 400–3400. This gives a bandwidth of 3000 Hz. A carrier line that can carry between 26,000 and 41,000 Hz can support five channels as follows:

- Channel 1: 26,000 to 29,000 Hz
- Channel 2: 29,000 to 32,000 Hz
- Channel 3: 32,000 to 35,000 Hz
- Channel 4: 35,000 to 38,000 Hz
- Channel 5: 38,000 to 41,000 Hz

We can determine the number of users on a carrier by the simple formula:

$$\text{Number of channels (users on a carrier)} = \frac{\text{carrier bandwidth}}{\text{data bandwidth}}$$

When broadband systems are restricted to one channel, they are known as *carrierband* systems. In such cases, there is no need for FDM equipment. Accordingly, *carrierband* LANs can be used to satisfy long-distance requirements without the need for FDM equipment.

EXAMPLE 14.1

Determine the number of channels for a broadband system if the carrier bandwidth is 3 MHz and data bandwidth is 3000 Hz.

Solution

The number of channels is given by

$$\begin{aligned}\text{Number of channels} &= \frac{\text{carrier bandwidth}}{\text{data bandwidth}}\\ &= \frac{3 \times 10^6}{3000} = 1000 \text{ channels}\end{aligned}$$

14.2.2 Network Architectures and Protocols

A communication network consists of a number of components such as hardware, software, and media. A network architecture describes the components, the functions performed, and the interfaces and interactions between the components of a network. It encompasses hardware, software, standards, data link controls, topologies, and protocols. It defines the functions of, and interactions between, three types of components.

- Network hardware components such as cables, modems, communications controllers, and adapter cards
- Communication software modules, which establish and monitor sessions between remotely located processes and allow exchange of data and control messages
- Application programs (user processes) that use the networks

Protocols in network architecture define the set of rules of information exchange between two devices (peers). A protocol specifies the message format and the rules for interpreting and reacting to messages.

The open system interconnection (OSI) reference model proposed by the International Standards Organization (ISO) provides a framework for modeling communication protocols. This permits interoperability between dissimilar systems. The ISO/OSI model divides the communication process into seven layers as shown in Figure 14.7: the physical layer, the data link layer, the network layer, the transport layer, the session layer, the presentation layer, and the application layer.

The lower four layers are responsible for transport of information between the applications. The upper three layers support the applications. Standards are set for each layer to handle communications from one device to another. We provide a brief description of functions of these layers.

1. The *physical layer* consists of the hardware that drives the network and circuits. It specifies the type of cable that is used. It deals with mechanical, electrical, functional, and procedural characteristics to access the physical medium. This layer also covers the physical interface between devices and the rules by which bits are passed from one device to another. However, the physical layer is not concerned with the content of the message or how the message is organized into larger groups of data.

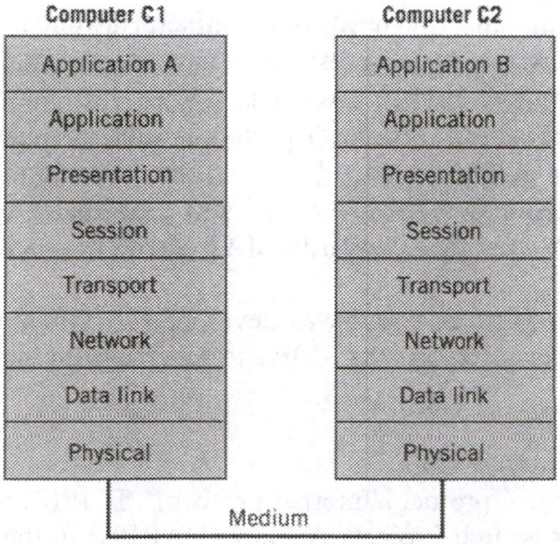

FIGURE 14.7 Architecture of OSI model.

2. The *data link layer* handles the task of transferring information across the physical link by sending blocks of data (frames) with necessary synchronization, error control, and flow control functions. For example, it recovers the data if the receiver is unable to accept the data at the time required by the sender. The reception, recognition, and transmission of tokens and Ethernet messages are handled by this layer.

3. The *network layer* decides which outgoing line will be used to send the message to a node. Because it knows about the physical connections and paths between the transport entities in a session, it relieves the transport layer of the need to know anything about the underlying network technologies used to connect end systems.

4. The *transport layer* provides transparent transfer of packets (data) to and from the session layer without disruption. It has three major functions: establishing a connection of the right type and quality (speed), initiating data transfer and managing the data to be sent, and releasing the connection.

5. The *session layer* controls communication between applications by establishing, managing, and terminating virtual connections between cooperating applications.

6. The *presentation layer* performs certain decoding and conversion operations on data to match the device and network requirements. It is therefore responsible for making the application processes independent of differences in data representation.

7. The *application layer* provides the user interface to the networking system. Therefore, in most cases the application layer is written by the user. The services provided by this layer include terminal emulation, file transfer, electronic mail, and distributed database managers.

A number of protocols have been developed based on the OSI reference model. Examples include MAP/TOP, TCP/IP, SNA from IBM, DECNET from DEC and many others. We provide brief discussions of MAP/TOP and TCP/IP. For details of these and other protocols, refer to Umar (1993).

14.2.2.1 MAP and TOP

The manufacturing automation protocol (MAP) was developed by General Motors to meet its manufacturing integration needs. It has now evolved into an open architecture to meet computer communication needs of manufacturing enterprises. To implement a computer-integrated system, it is necessary to have communication between factory devices such as numerical control machines, robots, cell controllers, and area controllers. MAP supports application-layer protocols such as manufacturing messaging specification (MMS) that are intended for real-time communication between these devices. MAP uses the ISO reference model and coordinates with the technical and office protocol (TOP) and other standards. MAP and TOP specifications are shown in Table 14.1.

The technical and office protocol was developed by Boeing Company for office communications and is based on OSI. TOP and MAP use the same protocols at layers 3, 4, 5, and 6.

14.2.2.2 TCP/IP Protocol Suite

The transmission control protocol/Internet protocol (TCP/IP) was developed by the Defense Advanced Research Projects Agency (DARPA) in the early 1970s to interconnect computers in the Advanced Research Projects Agency Network (ARPANET). The TCP/IP suite now consists of several major protocols, such as Internet protocol,

TABLE 14.1 **MAP and TOP Standards**

ISO Layers	*TOP Implementation*	*MAP Implementation*
Layer 7: Application	Association control service element File transfer, access, and management Message-handling system Virtual terminal protocol	Association control service element File transfer, access, and management Manufacturing message specification MAP directory services (X.50) MAP network management
Layer 6: Presentation	ISO presentation service	ISO presentation service
Layer 5: Session	ISO connection-oriented service	ISO connection-oriented service
Layer 4: Transport	ISO class 4 transport	ISO class 4 transport
Layer 3: Network	X.25 packet-switching protocol	X.25 packet-switching protocol
Layer 2: Data link	IEEE* 802.2 logical link control IEEE 802.3 CSMA/CD IEEE 802.4 token-passing bus	IEEE 802.2 logical link control IEEE 802.4 token passing bus
Layer 1: Physical	Broadband Baseband	10 Mbps broadband; 5 Mbps carrierband

* IEEE, Institute of Electrical and Electronics Engineers.

transmission control protocol, Telnet, file transfer protocol (FTP), and simple mail transfer protocol (SMTP). It is now available on a wide range of computing systems, such as mainframes, minicomputers, and microcomputers. It can be used to transfer files between heterogeneous systems such as SUN, DEC, IBM, Macintosh, and other computers. All Unix vendors support TCP/IP, and it is included in software packages by the SUN Microsystems Unix operating system.

A number of application protocols and user applications have been developed based on TCP/IP. These include Telnet, FTP, network file system (NFS), simple mail transfer protocol (SMTP), and simplified network management protocol (SNMP).

14.2.3 Network Interconnection and Devices

Many small networks are interconnected to form what we call internetworks. Each small constituent network of an internetwork is called a subnetwork. Connection between subnetworks is accomplished through the use of intermediate systems called relays. We discuss four types of relays for interconnecting subnetworks using the OSI model as a framework.

14.2.3.1 Repeaters

Repeaters are simple devices that interconnect segments of an extended network with identical protocols and speeds at the physical layer as shown in Figure 14.8*a*. They are used to regenerate fading digital signals operating at the physical layer. For example, DEC repeaters (DECREPs) are used to interconnect two DECnet subnetworks in two buildings.

14.2.3.2 Bridges

Bridges are simple devices that connect two similar or dissimilar LANs to form a large network at the data link layer. This means that they operate only at layers 1 and 2 as

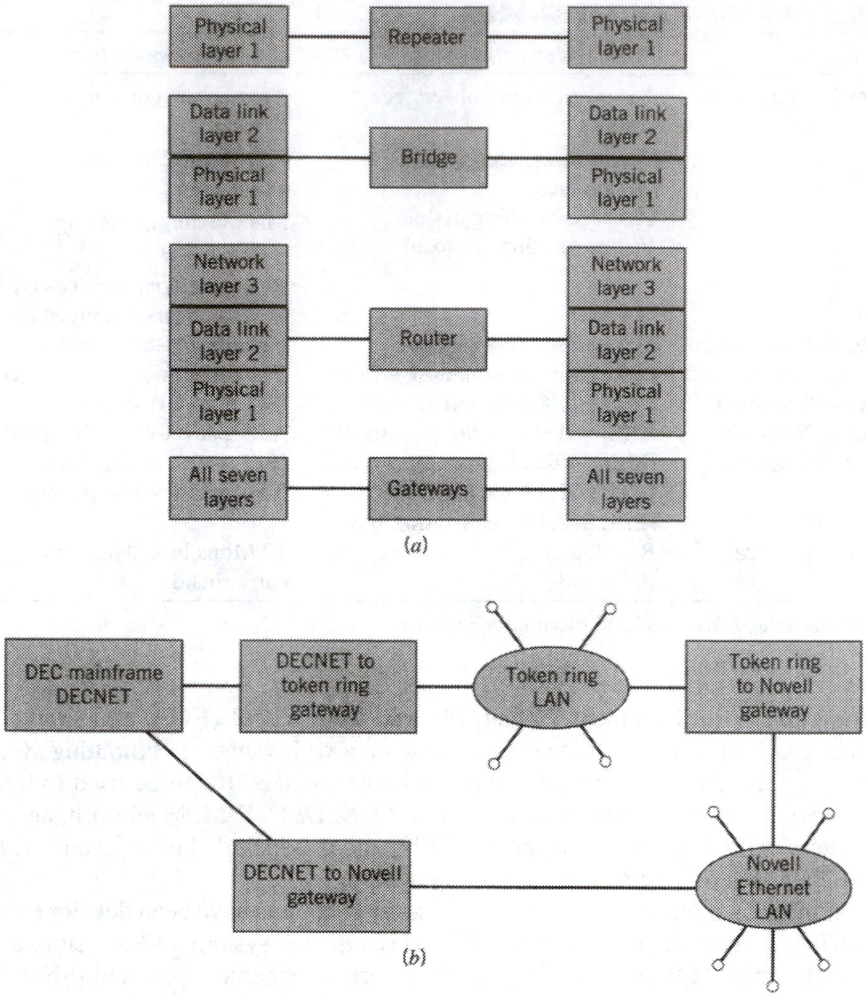

FIGURE 14.8 (*a*) Network interconnectivity devices. (*b*) Illustration of gateways in networks.

shown in Figure 14.8*a*. Since the bridges interconnect subnetworks at layer 1, they include all the functions of repeaters. An example of bridges forming a large network is DECLAN 100. It is used to interconnect small Ethernet LANS (a DEC Ethernet LAN is limited to 2.8 km) to form a super LAN. The super LAN can support up to 8000 stations over a distance of 22 km. Furthermore, bridges are used to interconnect LANs with different layer 1 technologies such as connecting broadband LANs to baseband and carrierband LANs. For example, bridges have been used to connect a 10-Mbps MAP broadband backbone with a 5-Mbps carrierband LANs in a MAP manufacturing environment.

14.2.3.3 Routers

Routers, as the name suggests, have functions of repeaters and bridges and also select a path from among several alternative routes. Therefore, routers have knowledge of the network topology. That means that routers operate at layers 1, 2, and 3 as shown in

Figure 14.8*a*. Multiple protocol routers are now available which permit different network protocols to share the same backbone network. For example, protocols such as DECnet, token ring, Appletalk, TCP/IP, and system network architecture (SNA) can share one corporate backbone with the help of routers. This solves the problem of isolation of different protocols. DEC, IBM, and many other vendors are supplying a variety of multiproduct routers.

14.2.3.4 Gateways

A gateway device is a special-purpose computer, a workstation with associated software, or a software module that runs as a task in a mainframe. It is essentially a protocol converter that facilitates the connection of two dissimilar network architectures. Gateways are integration tools to permit end-to-end communications. This means that they can be used to translate an application-layer protocol from one network architecture to a corresponding application-layer protocol of another architecture. Gateways operate at all seven OSI layers as shown in Figure 14.8*a*. Figure 14.8*b* shows gateways used to provide interoperability between a mainframe, workstations on token ring LAN, and an Ethernet LAN.

An example of interconnectivity of workstations, LANs, and other systems using devices such as bridges, routers, and gateways is shown in Figure 14.9. This is an enterprise network in which various divisional networks are connected to the corporate network through gateways. Interconnection between various divisions is accomplished through routers. Various plant subnetworks and cell controllers are connected through bridges.

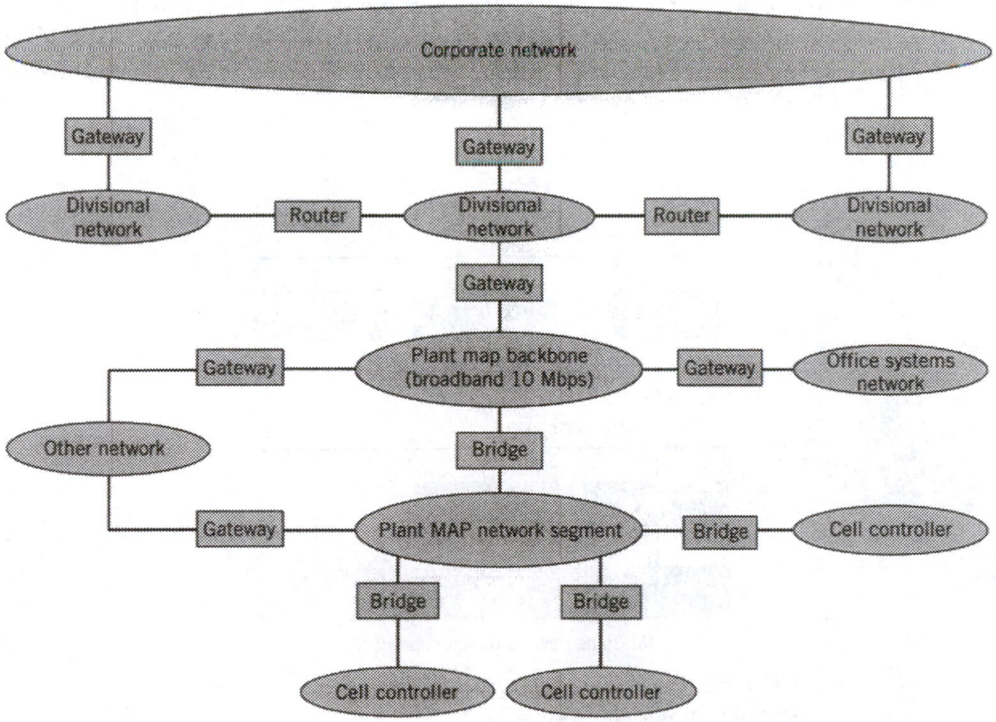

FIGURE 14.9 An enterprise network showing use of routers, gateways, and bridges.

EXAMPLE 14.2

Consider a company having four small plants in the Detroit area. Three plants produce a variety of parts involving various metal-cutting operations. The fourth plant is used for assembly purposes. All of these plants are located within 10 km of each other. The first plant is organized in three cells consisting of various manufacturing and control devices such as computer numerical control (CNC) machining centers, robots, and programmable logic controllers (PLCs). Implement a MAP network in the first plant under the following conditions:

(a) All the devices support MAP.
(b) All the devices do not support MAP.

Solution

(a) When all the devices support MAP, these devices can be directly connected to the MAP backbone as shown in Figure 14.10*a*.
(b) We need bridges to connect to the MAP backbone when the devices do not support MAP as shown in Figure 14.10*b*.

EXAMPLE 14.3

Develop an enterprise network for a company that is planning to manufacture computer products. The company has selected four sites. The corporate office is to be located in Los Angeles and the engineering office in Troy, a suburb of Detroit. The manufacturing and assembly plant is to be located in Detroit but in separate buildings. Suppose an IBM SNA network is to be used in the corporate office in Los Angeles, DECNET in the engineering office in Troy, and MAP in the manufacturing and assembly plant. There are over 200 retail stores for the company product lines located in major cities all over the United States.

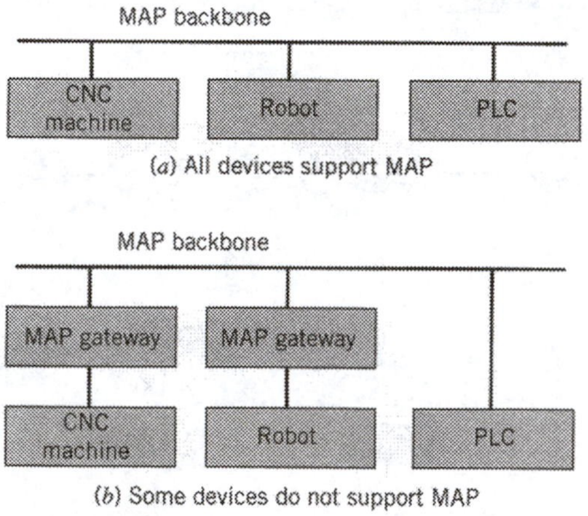

FIGURE 14.10 (*a*) All devices support MAP. (*b*) All devices do not support MAP.

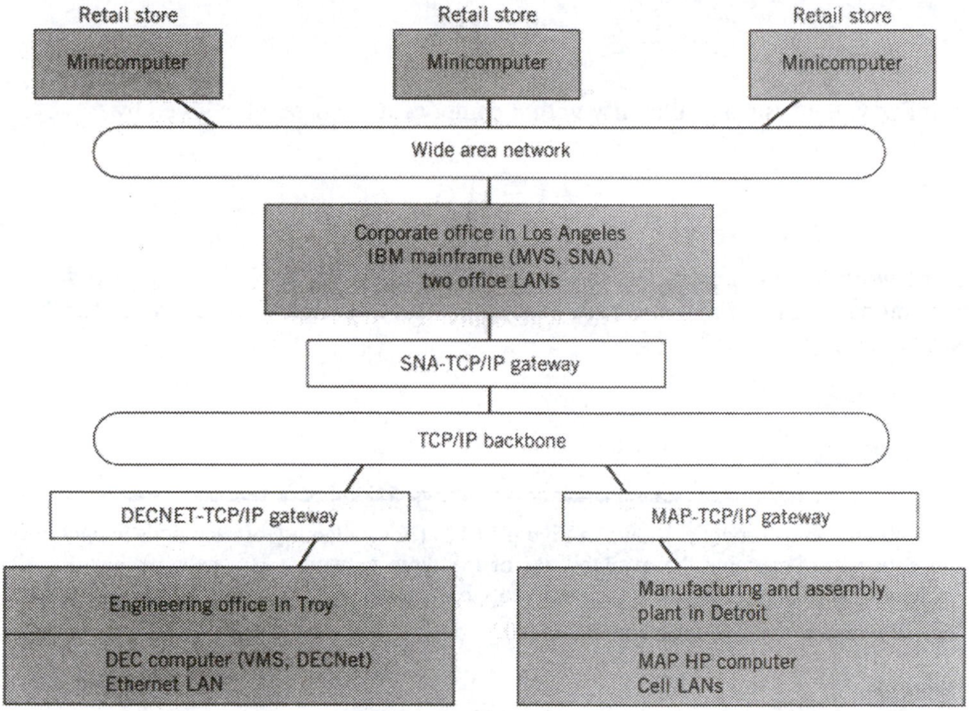

FIGURE 14.11 Interconnectivity through gateways from any to TCP/IP.

Solution

There could be a large number of possible options for the enterprise network. The technology is expanding rapidly. The options should be evaluated carefully. We can explore interconnectivity through gateways from any to any, gateways from any to TCP/IP, or selected gateways. The interconnectivity option with gateways from any to TCP/IP is shown in Figure 14.11.

14.2.4 Network Performance

As with any system, performance evaluation is an integral part of network system design and improvement. In the case of networks, a number of criteria are used for performance evaluation. These include availability, response time, throughput, and economic performance. Economic performance depends on a range of technological options. We discuss only the availability and response time performance criteria in this section. (For a detailed discussion of network performance evaluation and analysis, refer to Bertsekas and Gallager, 1992.)

14.2.4.1 Network Availability

Computations of network availability are similar to reliability calculations in serial, parallel, and mixed networks. If there are n components in series in a system and if a_i is the probability that the ith component is available, then the system availability, V, is given by

$$V = \prod_{i=1}^{n} a_i$$

Similarly, the system availability with n components in parallel is given by

$$V = 1 - \prod_{i=1}^{n} (1 - a_i)$$

A network having both series and parallel structures can be simplified by reducing several parallel paths into one path with equivalent availability. We illustrate this by a simple example.

EXAMPLE 14.4

Consider the three networks shown in Figure 14.12. The availability of each node is 0.99 in all the networks. Determine the availabilities of the three networks. If a network handles 10^7 packets a day and the owner makes 1.5 cents per packet, determine the loss if the average network unavailability during a month is 0.02.

Solution

(a) $V = a_1a_2a_3a_4 = (0.99)(0.99)(0.99)(0.99) = 0.96$

(b) $V = 1 - (1 - a_1)(1 - a_2)(1 - a_3)(1 - a_4)$
$= 1 - (1 - 0.99)(1 - 0.99)(1 - 0.99)(1 - 0.99) = 1 - 0.00000001$
$= 0.99999999$

(c) $V = a_1a_2a_3\{1 - (1 - a_4a_5)(1 - a_6a_7a_8)\}a_9$
$= (0.99)(0.99)(0.99)\{1 - (1 - 0.99 \times 0.99)(1 - 0.99 \times 0.99 \times 0.99)\}(0.99)$
$= 0.959$

Implications of network unavailability can be assessed in terms of potential business loss. The average availability of a large packet-switching network during a month is 0.98. Suppose

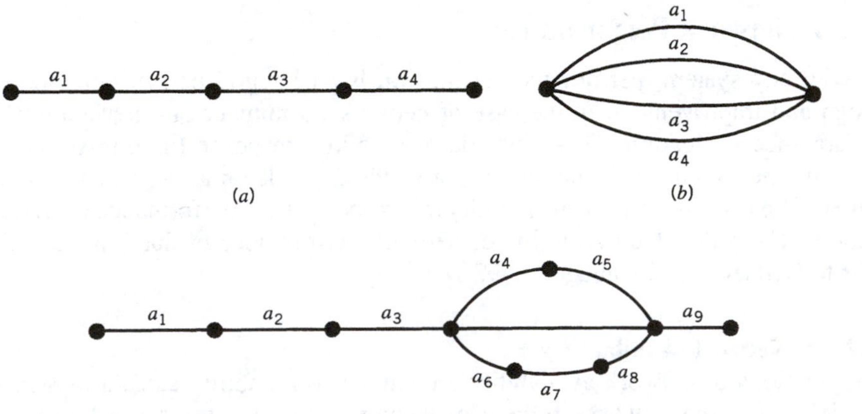

FIGURE 14.12 (*a*) A serial network. (*b*) A parallel network. (*c*) A mixed network.

the network operates 24 hours a day and every day of the month. Then the number of hours lost during the month equals 0.02 (unavailability) × 24 (hours per day) × 30 (days per month) = 14.4 hours. The network handles 10^7 packets a day, so the potential loss during a month = \$0.015 × (14.4/24) × 10^7 = \$90,000.

14.2.4.2 Response Time Performance

Response time is the average time it takes to complete a service, that is, the elapsed time between transaction request and completion. This includes time spent in processing as well as in queuing. Types of services include central processing unit (CPU) cycles, disk access, and communication transactions. We will illustrate response time using some of the simple results from queuing theory with the M/M/1 model (Markovian arrival, Markovian service, and one server). If arrival rate is $\lambda(i)$ and service rate is $\mu(i)$, then utilization of server i is

$$U(i) = \frac{\lambda(i)}{\mu(i)}$$

Queue length at server i is

$$Q(i) = \frac{\lambda(i)}{\mu(i) - \lambda(i)} = \frac{U(i)}{1 - U(i)}$$

$$\text{Waiting time} = \text{queue length} \times \text{service time} = Q(i) \times \frac{1}{\mu(i)}$$

$$\text{Response time of a transaction} = \Sigma(\text{service time} + \text{waiting time})$$

We illustrate the calculation of response time by a simple example.

EXAMPLE 14.5

Consider a user at a terminal accessing information about a customer account from a database. The information is in a database that is connected to the terminal through the network. The process of getting information works like this: A program P_a that runs on a computer C_a first reads a 30-byte user account number from a terminal T_a, locates the account number by reading the index and then reading the record, and then displays the customer information (150 bytes) on the terminal. What is the response time of a user sitting at terminal T_a if the computer can complete 30 input–outputs per second? Assume that each byte occupies 10 bits in the network (8 data bits + 2 start/stop bits).

Solution

The services required to complete the transaction are:

$$\text{Input to the program transmit time} = 30 \times \frac{10}{1500} = 0.20 \text{ s}$$

$$\text{Output to the program transmit time} = 150 \times \frac{10}{1500} = 1.00 \text{ s}$$

$$\text{Time per input/output service} = \frac{1}{30} = 0.0334 \text{ s}$$

Thus,

$$\text{Total response time} = 0.20 + 1.00 + 2 \times 0.0334 = 1.2668 \text{ s}$$

EXAMPLE 14.6

Performance Analysis of an Enterprise Network

The enterprise network of ABC Company has five Ethernet LANs with a 10 Mbps data transfer rate and one MAP network connected to an IBM mainframe through 100 kbps WAN lines as shown in Figure 14.13. Each LAN has about 50 workstations and the MAP network has about 50 devices (robots, CNC, PLC, and so on). Each workstation on a LAN generates one message of 1000 bytes per second (1 byte = 10 bits). Each device on the MAP generates two messages of 500 bytes per second. Most of the workstations and devices interact with each other through cell controllers. Only 10 percent of messages from devices and 10 percent from workstations are sent to the mainframe. Evaluate the impact of the workstations on LAN performance, the impact of devices on the MAP, and the impact of workstations and devices on the mainframe. The message sent to the mainframe causes access to a corporate database, which services requests at a rate of 100 input–outputs per second.

Solution

(a) Utilization of each LAN cable:

$$\text{Arrival rate at each LAN cable} = 50 \text{ messages/sec (50 workstations per LAN)}$$

$$\text{Service rate at each LAN cable} = \frac{\text{data rate}}{\text{average message length}}$$

$$= \frac{10{,}000{,}000}{1000 \times 10} = 1000 \text{ messages/sec}$$

$$\text{Utilization of each LAN} = \frac{\lambda(i)}{\mu(i)} = \frac{50}{1000} = 0.05$$

(b) Utilization of each WAN line:

$$\text{Arrival rate at WAN line} = 0.1 \times 50 = 5 \text{ messages/sec}$$

$$\text{Average message length from MAP} = 500 \times 2 \times \text{bytes} = 1000 \text{ bytes}$$

$$\text{Average message length from each LAN} = 1000 \text{ bytes}$$

$$\text{Service rate at WAN line} = \frac{\text{data rate}}{\text{average message length}}$$

$$= \frac{100{,}000}{1000 \times 10} = 10 \text{ messages/sec}$$

$$\text{Utilization of WAN} = \frac{\lambda(i)}{\mu(i)} = \frac{5}{10} = 0.2$$

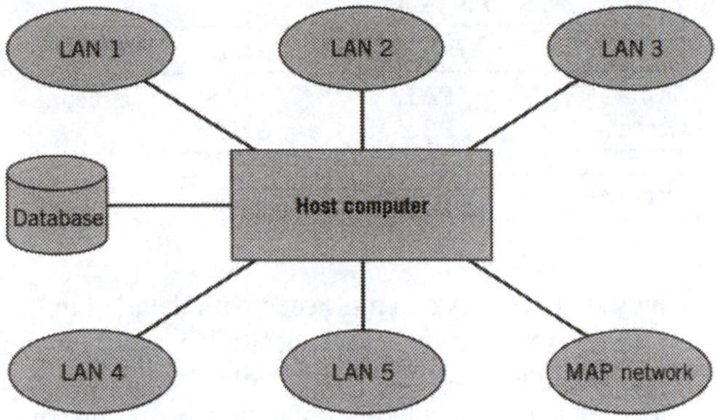

FIGURE 14.13 An enterprise network for ABC Company in Example 14.6.

(c) Utilization of the host server: There are 50 workstations per LAN, there are five LANs plus one MAP network, and 10 percent of the traffic goes to the database at the host computer. Accordingly,

$$\text{Arrival rate at the database} = 0.1 \times 50 \times 6 = 30 \text{ messages/sec}$$

$$\text{Service rate} = 100 \text{ input-outputs per second}$$

Therefore,

$$\text{Utilization of the server} = \frac{30}{100} = 0.30$$

Since the utilization of the LANs, the WAN, and the host is relatively low, they can handle the workloads.

14.3 DATABASE MANAGEMENT SYSTEMS

In the following section we discuss various data models and database management systems. Let us first define some basic terminology used in database management systems (DBMSs).

Basic Terminology used in Database Management Systems

Data item: Smallest unit of data that cannot be subdivided. Examples include part_no, part_name, and cost.

Data record: A collection of data items. A part record, which includes part information such as part_number, part_material, part_cost, and part_processes, is an example of a data record.

File: A collection of similar data records. Examples include customer files having data records on specific customers, part files having data records on parts, and machine files. The concepts of data item and data record are illustrated by the part file shown in Table 14.2

Database: A database is a collection of files as an organized assembly of information that users can access for various purposes; that is, adding, deleting, or modifying data. For example, a payroll database

TABLE 14.2 **Part File**

Part Name	*Part ID*	*Cost*	
Shaft	PA22	$12.88	} a record
Gear	PB25	$25.67	
← data item →	← data item →	← data item →	

may include files on employees with detailed information on their salaries, retirement benefits, health benefits, and so forth. A manufacturing database may include files having information on inventory of parts, machines, production plans, machining conditions, and so on.

Data model: A data model is a logical representation of a collection of data elements. Data models are the basic building blocks for designing all databases.

A great deal of information (contained in databases) is required for any task to be accomplished. For example, consider the simple case of manufacturing a simple shaft. We require design data such as the material, diameter, length, surface roughness, and tolerance. We also need manufacturing data, such as which machine tools, tools, and machining conditions to use to obtain the desired design dimensions at the minimum possible manufacturing cost and time and maximum quality. Suppose the shaft is to be assembled into a product consisting of several items. We then need design and manufacturing information on other items so that the shaft fits into the final product in order to meet its functional requirements. We need data on how many of these products to manufacture, how much inventory we have, how much inventory we should have, capacity information on machines, information on routing from one machine to another, and so forth. We can list hundreds of types of data that would be required to design, manufacture, distribute, and service such a product or family of products. Often, an application has to access data from different databases. For example, the data on weight of the shaft from the design database and data on surface roughness and tolerance from the manufacturing database are required to develop packaging for the shaft to be shipped. In real design and manufacturing situations, a vast amount of data is generated and manipulated using diverse computer programs. Furthermore, the data are often located on computer systems at different geographic locations. From the cost, time, and quality perspective, we need the right data to be rapidly accessible to many users so that the right design, manufacturing, distribution, and service decisions can be made faster. Given these complexities, what we need is a system that helps us control and manipulate data to suit our needs. A database management system (DBMS) is a software package that helps users control database access and manipulate the data.

An architectural view of a database management system is shown in Figure 14.14. A database dictionary/directory is used to store the data views, data relationships, data formats, and security restrictions. Database logs are used to keep a record of the transactions of the activities. For multiple users, lock tables permit synchronous concurrent access to the databases.

14.3.1 Data Models

An important element of a database management system is the data model. We consider only logical data models here as opposed to physical data models, where one is

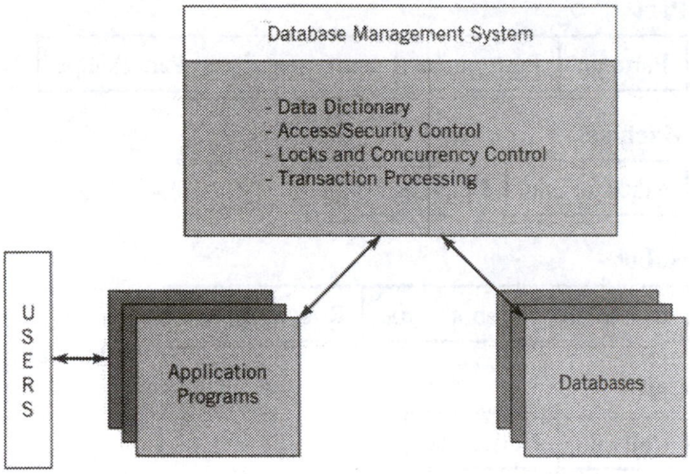

FIGURE 14.14 An architectural view of a database management system.

concerned with the organization of data on physical storage media such as a disk. Logical data models are broadly categorized into two groups: *record-based models* and *object-oriented models.* A number of data models have been proposed; a list of prominent data models is given below:

- Record-based data models
  - Network model
  - Hierarchical model
  - Relational model
- Object-oriented models

14.3.1.1 Record-Based Data Models: Basic Concepts

In these models, the database is described as a collection of records and the relationships among records are captured in terms of links. A record is simply a collection of fields or so-called attributes, each of which contains exactly one value. The records of part, machine, robot, and cell shown in Figure 14.15*a* are examples from a manufacturing database context.

A link describes an association between two records. The association can be one-to-one, one-to-many, or many-to-many, as shown in the following examples. Consider the records *cell* and *robot.* If each cell has only one robot associated with it which is dedicated to the cell, then the cell and robot have one-to-one association. This is shown in Figure 14.15*b* by a *bidirectional link* between two records. On the other hand, if multiple robots can belong to a cell but each robot is attached to a single cell, we have a one-to-many relationship from cell to robot. This is shown in Figure 14.15*c* by a *unidirectional link* from robot to cell. Another example of the one-to-many relationship is from cell to machine as shown in Figure 14.15*d.*

The association between part and machine is many-to-many since a part may require several machines during its processing and a machine in turn processes many parts. This is shown in Figure 14.15*e* by an *undirected link* between part and machine records.

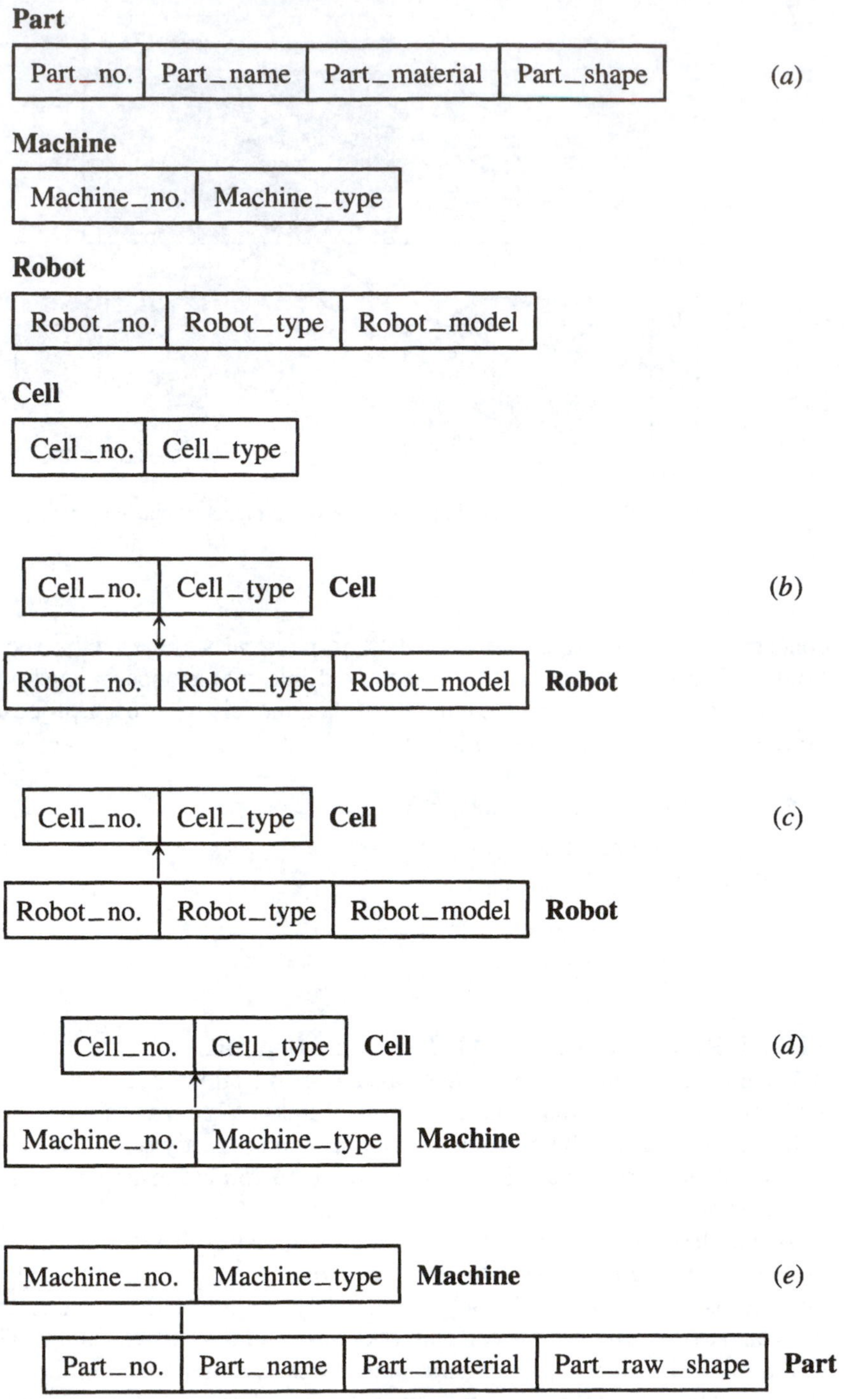

FIGURE 14.15 (*a*) Records of part, machine, robot, and cell. (*b*) One-to-one relationship between cell and robot. (*c*) One-to-many relationship between cell and robot. (*d*) One-to-many relationship between cell and machine. (*e*) Many-to-many relationship between machine and part.

Network Data Model A network data model is simply a graph wherein nodes represent unique records, and links between nodes represent association between the corresponding records. Figure 14.16*a* shows a partial model of a manufacturing database model. This example is comprised of five kinds of records: cell, machine, robot, part, and process. The relationships among records are:

- A cell is a collection of machines and robots.
- Each machine belongs to a unique cell.
- Each robot belongs to a unique cell and is dedicated to handle a group of distinct machines.
- A part is processed on one or more machines and each machine processes several parts.
- On each machine, many processes can be performed and different machines can perform similar processes.

Hierarchical Data Model The hierarchical data model is similar to the network data model except that the relationships among the records are represented in the form of tree structures. In order to represent arbitrary relationships as trees, the contents of a record may have to be replicated. Consider the example shown earlier in Figure 14.16*a*. Figures 14.16*b* and *c* show an equivalent hierarchical model for the example. The hierarchical model is a forest comprised of trees as shown in Figures 14.16*b*, *c*, and *d*. In this model, the contents of records 'machine' and 'robot' are duplicated. The hierarchical structure facilitates navigation of the database because of its top-down structure, as opposed to the network data model. On the other hand, the duplication of data introduces the problems of data inconsistency and incurs additional storage overhead. Data inconsistency occurs when the contents of a record are updated at one place while the update is not reflected in a copy of the above record.

Relational Data Model Hierarchical and network data models have been in use since the 1960s. The relational data model was introduced in the early 1970s. In the relational data model, the data is represented as a collection of tables. A table is closely related to the mathematical concept of a relation. Each table in the database has a unique name and is composed of rows and columns. A column (field) represents an attribute of a record. Each attribute takes values from a set of defined values, called the *domain of the attribute.* A row of a table is a collection of values, one for each attribute. A row is also referred to as a *tuple.*

Table 14.3 shows a simple relation called '*machine.*' The 'machine' relation has four attributes: 'machine_no.', 'machine_type', 'cell_no.', and 'robot_no.' and it has five tuples (rows). The data are added to the relational database by inserting rows in the tables. Also, the data are located by searching rows of tables. To speed up searches in a table, indexing schemes are used. The relationships between records are captured by providing common attributes in tables.

To uniquely identify a row in a table, the notion of a primary key is used. A primary key is a set of one or more attributes in a table which uniquely identifies a row and is used as the principal means of distinguishing among rows within a table. A foreign key is an attribute in a table which refers to a row in another table. The notion of foreign key is used to link two tables. In the 'machine' relation in Table 14.3, the attributes 'cell_no.' and 'robot_no.' are the foreign keys of relations 'cell' and 'robot', respectively (see Figure 14.17). Figure 14.17 shows the relational data model for the example previously described in the section on network and hierarchical data models.

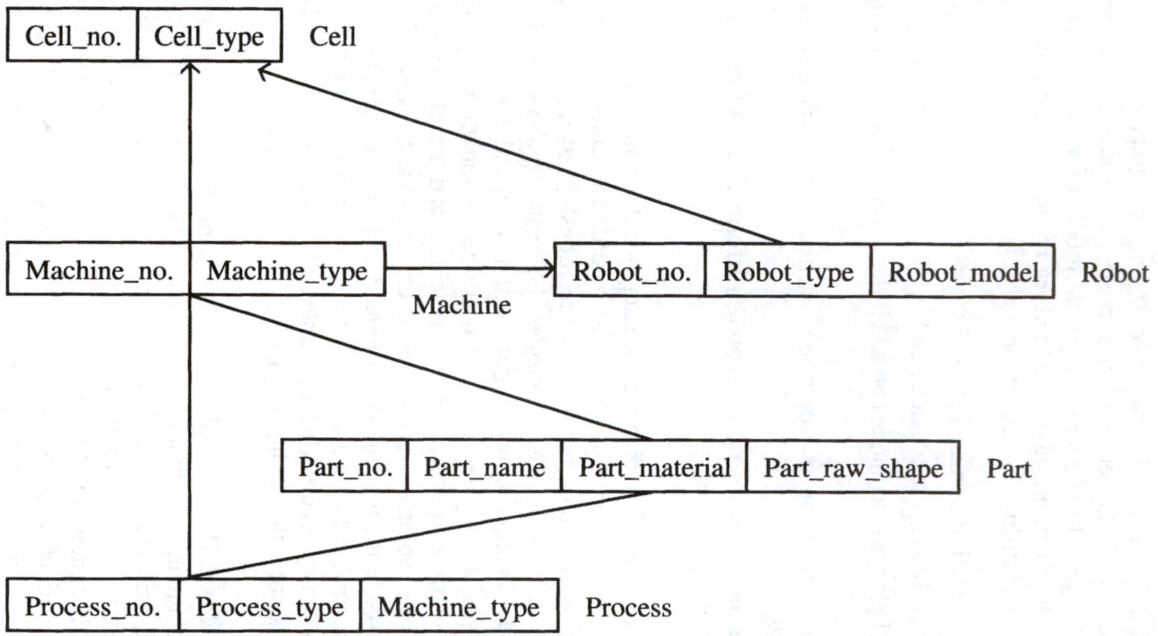

FIGURE 14.16 (*a*) Example of a network data model. (*b*) First hierarchical tree. (*c*) Second hierarchical tree. (*d*) Third hierarchical tree.

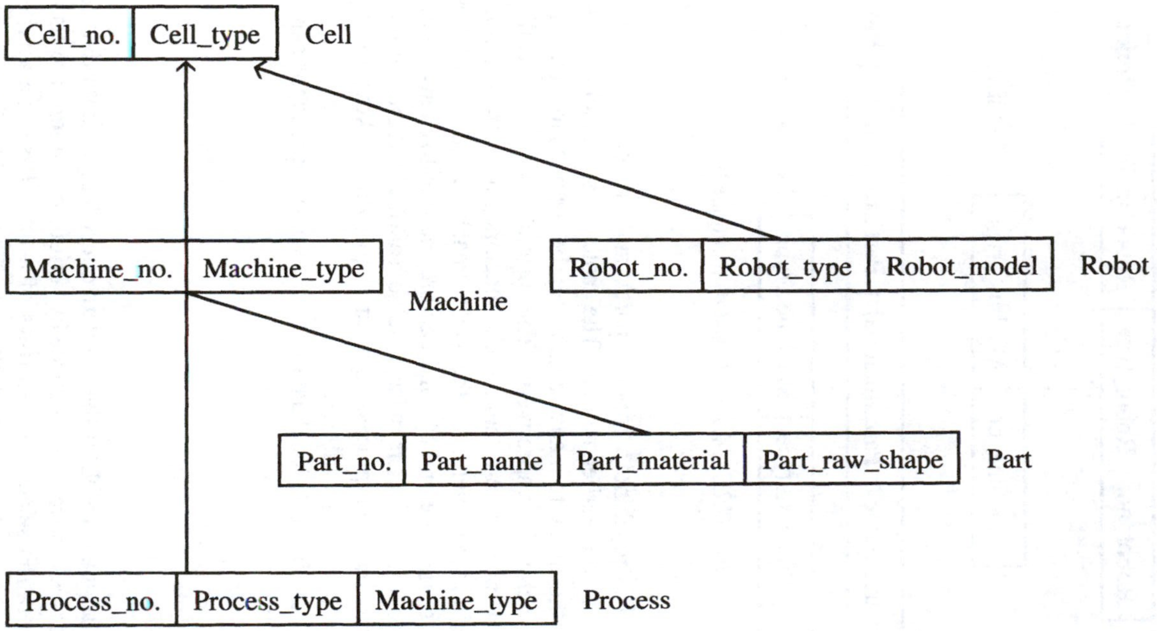

FIGURE 14.16 (*b*) (continued)

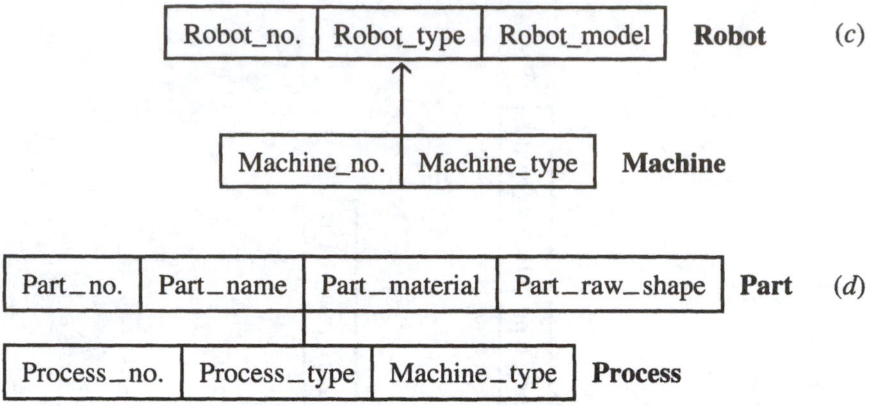

FIGURE 14.16 (*c* and *d*) (continued)

The tables 'cell', 'machine', 'robot', 'part', and 'process' each correspond to a record or entity in the earlier models. The tables 'part_machine' and 'process_machine' capture the many-to-many relationship between 'part' and 'machine', and 'process' and 'machine', respectively. The primary keys of 'cell', 'machine', 'robot', 'part', and 'process' are 'cell_no.', 'machine_no.', 'robot_no.', 'part_no.' and 'process_no.', respectively. In the table 'machine', the attributes 'cell_no.' and 'robot_no.' are the foreign keys and capture the one-to-many relationship from 'cell' and 'robot' to 'machine'. Likewise, in table 'robot', 'cell_no.' is the foreign key. In tables 'part_machine' and 'process_machine', the primary keys are represented by the entire combination of all attributes.

To manipulate data in a relational database, three basic operations can be applied to the tables. These are:

- Selection
- Projection
- Join

Structured query language (SQL) is the standard query language for data manipulation in relational databases. The results produced by various operations are also represented as tables. The operation **select** chooses rows of a table based on a criteria that is a condition expressed over the values of attributes in the table. Selection of machines belonging to cell number c101 in the 'machine' relation in Table 14.3 produces the table shown in Table 14.4.

TABLE 14.3 **The Machine Relation**

Machine_No.	*Machine_Type*	*Cell_No.*	*Robot_No.*
ml-10	Lathe machine	c-101	R-1
md-20	Drilling machine	c-102	R-2
ms-30	Slotting machine	c-101	R-1
mm-40	Milling machine	c-102	R-2
ml-50	Lathe machine	c-101	R-3

Cell

Cell_no.	Cell_type

Machine

Machine_no.	Machine_type	Robot_no.	Cell_no.

Robot

Machine_no.	Robot_type	Robot_model	Cell_no.

Part

Part_no.	Part_name	Part_material	Raw_shape

Process

Process_no.	Process_type	Machine_type

Part_machine

Part_no.	Machine_no.

Process_machine

Process_no.	Machine_no.

FIGURE 14.17 Example of a relational data model for a manufacturing cell.

The **projection** operation selects columns rather than rows of a table. For example, projection of a 'machine' relation in Table 14.3 on 'machine_no.' and 'machine_type' produces the table shown in Table 14.5.

The **join** operation combines data from two tables to form a composite table. To accomplish a join operation on two relations, there must be a common attribute among the above relations. Consider the table 'machine' given in Table 14.3 and the table 'cell' given in Table 14.6. The join of these two tables based on the attribute 'cell_no.' produces the following composite table as shown in Table 14.7. There are many types of join operations in relational databases. For details of these operations refer to any standard text book on database management systems.

TABLE 14.4 **The Relation as a Result of Operation Select**

Machine_No.	*Machine_Type*	*Cell_No.*	*Robot_No.*
ml-10	Lathe machine	c-101	R-1
ms-30	Slotting machine	c-101	R-1
ml-50	Lathe machine	c-101	R-3

TABLE 14.5 **The Relation as a Result of Operation Projection**

Machine_No.	*Machine_Type*
ml-10	Lathe machine
md-20	Drilling machine
ms-30	Slotting machine
mm-40	Milling machine
ml-50	Lathe machine

TABLE 14.6 **Cell Table**

Cell_No.	*Cell_type*
c-101	Shaft cell
c-102	Gear cell

TABLE 14.7 **Relation as a Result of Operation Join**

Machine_No.	*Machine_Type*	*Cell_No.*	*Robot_No.*	*Cell_type*
ml-10	Lathe machine	c-101	R-1	shaft cell
md-20	Drilling machine	c-102	R-2	gear cell
ms-30	Slotting machine	c-101	R-1	gear cell
mm-40	Milling machine	c-102	R-2	gear cell
ml-50	Lathe machine	c-101	R-3	shaft cell

The relational database model provides mathematically elegant approaches to maintaining data, relationships among data, and querying and processing of data. The shortcomings of the relational data model include its inability to capture complex data, since only simple values (numeric and character strings) are allowed in rows. Almost all applications in the design and manufacturing context involve manipulation of complex data. There have been extensions to the relational data model to capture complex data. However, the object-based models provide a more natural framework for complex data representation.

14.3.1.2 Object-Oriented Models

Database models have evolved in the past decade to deal with the need to manage a vast amount of information and the complexity of applications. New approaches have been influenced by the advances in object-oriented languages that provide the specification of entities at a logical level regardless of their implementation. Here, we describe the basic principles underlying object-oriented models. The object-oriented paradigm is based on the following key concepts:

- Object
- Attributes and methods
- Message
- Class
- Inheritance

Object The definition of object is very broad. It means something mental or physical toward which thought, feeling, or action is directed. Examples include a company, a car, an automated guided vehicle, a conveyor, a robot, and a process plan. An object is the basic modeling unit in object-oriented models.

Attributes and Methods An object is characterized by attributes that are either intrinsic properties of the object or describe its relationship with other objects. For example, consider a machine as an object. The characteristics of a machine such as machine name, machine type, and machine cost are examples of attributes of a machine. In addition to the attributes, an object description includes a list of methods. A method corresponds to an operation that can be invoked by users or clients of the object. Execution of methods may result in the change of value of one or more attributes and produce outputs. Examples of methods for the machine object include setup, start, stop, load, and unload. Table 14.8 shows further examples of objects and their attributes and methods. The attributes of an object capture its structural aspects whereas the methods specify the behavioral or dynamic aspects. This is in contrast to record-based models where the emphasis is purely on the structural aspects of the entity modeled.

Message A method (or operation) is invoked by a client by sending a message to the object. A client could be another object. A message is to be interpreted as a request to invoke an operation on an object. A message must include the unique identifier of the object, the name of the method invoked, and other arguments required by the method for its execution. An object responds to a message by invoking its corresponding method.

Class Objects can be categorized into classes. Objects of a class, also referred to as instances, exhibit common behavior by sharing methods and attribute types. A class is defined by providing a list of attributes, methods, and implementation of methods. In this respect, it provides a blueprint for creating instances (objects) of the class. A class is also frequently used to refer to the collection of instances of the class. A simple description of the class *robot* is as follows:

Class name: robot
Attributes: robot_id
robot_type
Methods: move
pickup
drop-off

Individual robots are instances of the class robot. Thus, all the robots will have a robot_id and robot_type and allow for the operations move, pickup, and drop-off.

TABLE 14.8 **Examples of Objects, Attributes, and Methods**

Object	*Attributes*	*Methods*
Robot	Name, robot_id, speed, degrees_of_freedom	Move, pickup, drop_off
Machine	Machine type, cost	Setup, load, unload, start, stop
CAD Workstation	Workstation type, vendor	Boot, login, logout

Inheritance A class can inherit attributes and methods from another class. The latter class is referred to as the *superclass* of the former. The inheriting class is called the *subclass* of the superclass. Inheritance allows one to create new classes as specialization of other classes. A superclass is considered to be a generalization of its subclasses. A subclass on the other hand is a specialization of its superclass. A subclass is generally obtained by adding or refining attributes and methods of its superclass. The specialization/generalization relationships among classes form an inheritance hierarchy. We illustrate the concept of inheritance in Figure 14.18 using the robot example discussed earlier in the context of a manufacturing cell database.

The classes rectangular robot and revolute robot are both subclasses of the superclass robot and represent specializations of the latter class. Both classes inherit the attribute robot_id, robot_type, robot_reach, and drive_system as well as the methods pick, drop, and move. In addition, the class rectangular robot as well as revolute robot have several attributes and methods of their own as shown in Figure 14.18. The move method in class robot requires a detailed path to be provided as an input argument. The move method in classes rectangular robot and revolute robot overrides the same method in their superclass. These methods add the capability to interpolate based on the robot configuration (rectangular or revolute) to develop a path for the robot to follow. Once the path has been computed, the same method in the superclass can then be used to actively move the robot. This illustrates the manner in which inheritance can be used to incrementally add functionality to the classes.

14.3.2 Designing a System Using the Object-Oriented Paradigm

In designing a system using the object-oriented paradigm, a systematic procedure can be used as follows:

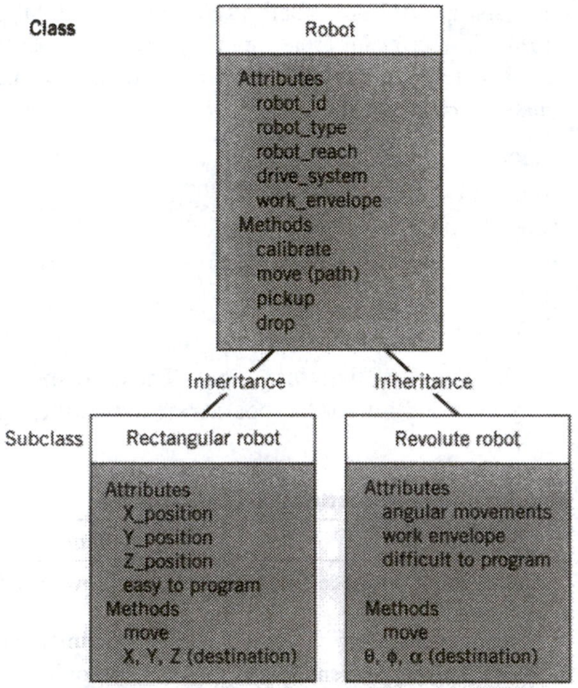

FIGURE 14.18 Illustration of Class and Inheritance.

1. Develop a conceptual model of the system by identifying key objects.
2. Associate attributes and methods with each object identified in step 1.
3. Arrange objects into a class inheritance hierarchy.
4. Refine the hierarchy by emphasizing reuse, specialization and generalization.
5. Identify client-server relationships and message exchanges among objects to capture system dynamics.
6. Develop a prototype implementation to validate requirements.
7. Refine the system design iteratively by modifying or adding objects, attributes, methods, or association.

14.3.3 Database Size Calculation

An important issue in the design of databases is determining the database size. We provide a simple model for determining the database storage requirements for relational databases (Mejabi, 1994). The following notation is defined:

J = number of databases required ($j = 1, 2, \ldots, J$)
r_j = number of records in the jth database
l_j = number of fields of the jth database
w_{ij} = field width of ith field of jth database ($i = 1, 2, \ldots, l_j$)
O = header overhead
F = header field descriptor size
D = database storage requirements (bytes)

We can determine the database storage requirements as follows:

$$D = (\text{Total data space} + \text{header space})$$
$$= \sum_{j=1}^{J} \left((r_j \sum_{i=1}^{l_j} w_{ij}) + Fl_j \right) + (O \times J)$$

The total storage requirement (bytes), T, can be determined as follows:

$$T = D + \text{index file requirements} + \text{miscellaneous requirements}$$

EXAMPLE 14.7

Determine the total storage requirements of a tool database for a flexible manufacturing system (FMS) database design. The following information is available:

Miscellaneous requirements = 750,000 bytes
Index file requirements = 500,000 bytes
Number of databases = 4

The database tables for part status, part sequences, tool life, and machine diagnostics are illustrated in Tables 14.9–14.12. Field widths for database tables are given in Table 14.13.

TABLE 14.9 **Part Status**

Part	*Current Operation*	*Current Location (Machine)*
X27	3	B
X28	—	A
X32	—	C

TABLE 14.10 **Part Sequences**

		Operation	
Part	*Machine*	*Start*	*Operation ID*
X27	A	2:21:1:21	PA2024321

TABLE 14.11 **Tool Life**

Tool	*Maximum Life*	*Remaining Life*	*Current Location*
T24	450	280.346	Machine SHOP-345
T54	348	150	NC center-233

TABLE 14.12 **Machine Diagnostics**

Machine	*Diagnostic File*
A	Diag-A
B	Diag-B

TABLE 14.13 **Field Widths for Database Tables**

	Field Width for Field Number (Bytes)			
Database	*1*	*2*	*3*	*4*
Part status	80	100	200	—
Part sequences	920	160	50	400
Tool life	600	280	1000	360
Machine diagnostics	320	540	—	—

Estimated numbers of records in the databases are:

Database Name	***Number of Records*** (r_j)
Part status	5000
Part sequences	10000
Tool life	500
Machine diagnostics	1250

Database Name	***Number of Fields*** (l_j)
Part status	3
Part sequences	4
Tool life	4
Machine diagnostics	2

O = 500 bytes
F = 420 bytes

Determine the total storage requirements.

Solution
We can obtain the total storage requirements using the formula given earlier:

$$D = 380 \times 5000 + 1530 \times 10000 + 2240 \times 500 + 860 \times 1250$$
$$+ 420\,(3 + 4 + 4 + 2) + 500 \times 4$$
$$= 1{,}900{,}000 + 15{,}300{,}000 + 1{,}120{,}000 + 1{,}075{,}000 + 5460 + 2000$$
$$= 19{,}397{,}000$$
$$T = 19{,}397{,}000 + 750{,}000 + 500{,}000 = 20{,}647{,}000 \text{ bytes}$$

EXAMPLE 14.8

A flexible manufacturing system produces a family of transmission components for large trucks. Outline a set of distributed databases to maintain the operating and process control data for managing the system.

Solution
The factory database system is grouped according to machine data, tool data, part data, and material-handling system (MHS) data as shown in Figure 14.19. Each data group includes several databases as shown in the figure. For example, three databases exist for tool data. They are the tool status database, the tool life database, and the tool classification database. Each database has a relational structure similar to that of the database represented in Example 14.7. Calculations of database size can be done by using the equation and the procedure outlined in Example 14.7.

14.4 DATABASE LINKAGES

We can distinguish different levels of database integration depending on the way the information is accessed between different applications (Kemper and Moerkotte, 1994; Wedekind, 1988) as follows:

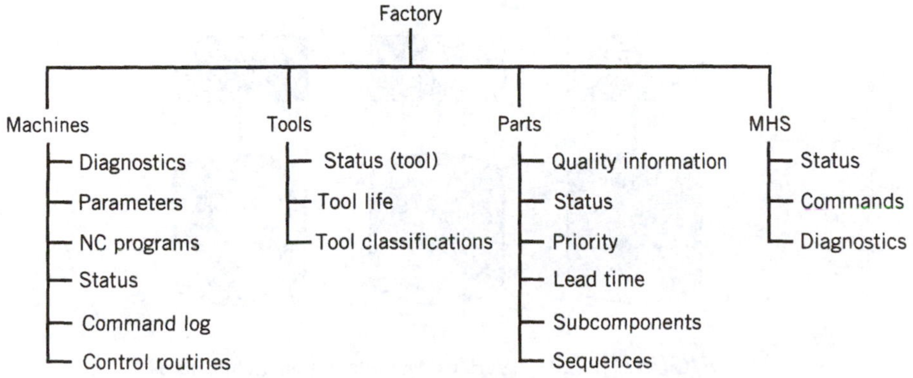

FIGURE 14.19 Sample data requirements at the shop floor.

- Level 0: Isolation
- Level 1: Converters
- Level 2: Neutral file format
- Level 3: A centralized database
- Level 4: Integration of stand-alone components

14.4.1 Level 0: Isolation

In this case, the diverse application modules manage their information independently in a highly customized database (DB) or file system (FS) as shown in Figure 14.20*a*. Information is exchanged between modules through human interaction. This is analogous to a situation in which CAD data are interpreted manually for developing process plans and so forth.

14.4.2 Level 1: Converters

In this system architecture, the interface of different modules is achieved with a converter program. Convertor programs are mostly used when both applications have different data structures or run at different times on different computers. For example, consider interfacing two application programs, A1 and A2, representing, say, CAD and computer-aided process planning (CAPP) as shown in Figure 14.20*b*. A converter program adapts the data structure of application A1 to the one used by application A2. There are numerous examples of convertor processors used in practice. For example, a CAD/PPC (production planning and control) processor called CADMIP developed by IBM is used to connect their CAD system CADAM with the PPC system COPICS. Another example is a CAD/NC processor called CADIS-NCS used by Siemans to connect their CAD system CADIS with the NC processor SIEAPT. The number of convertor programs needed to support N unique applications is $N(N-1)$, since two converter programs are required for information exchange between two applications A1 and A2 (one for A1 to A2 and one for A2 to A1).

14.4.3 Level 2: Neutral File Format

This architecture is based on the use of a neutral database or file system that is shared by all the applications as shown in Figure 14.20*c*. This permits a starlike structure, so

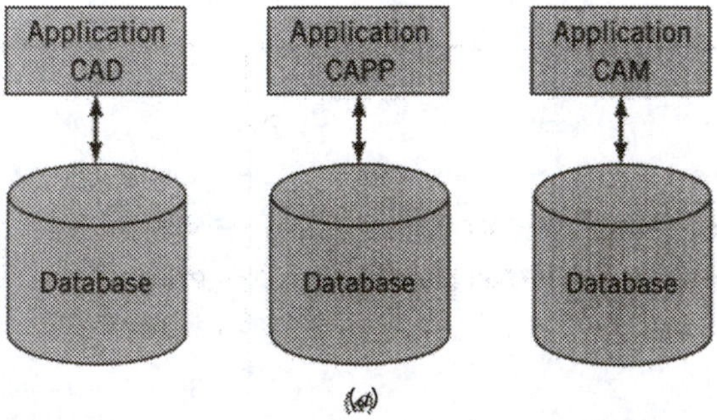

FIGURE 14.20 Various data integration architectures.

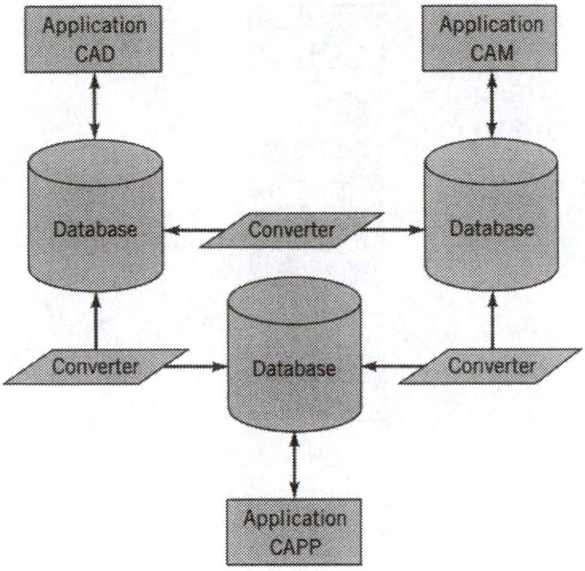

(b)

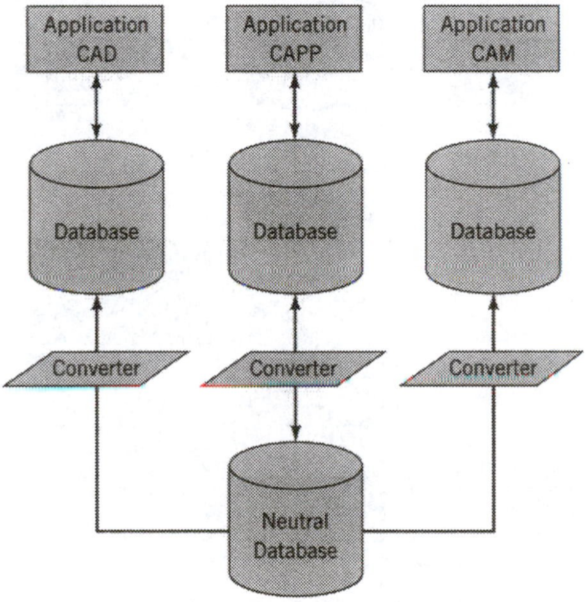

(c)

FIGURE 14.20 (continued)

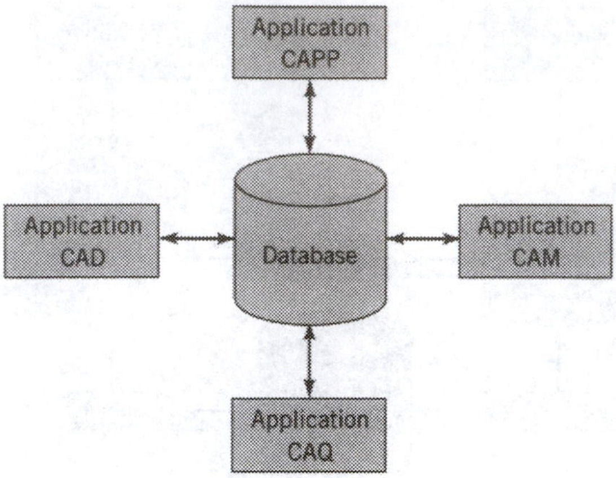

(d)

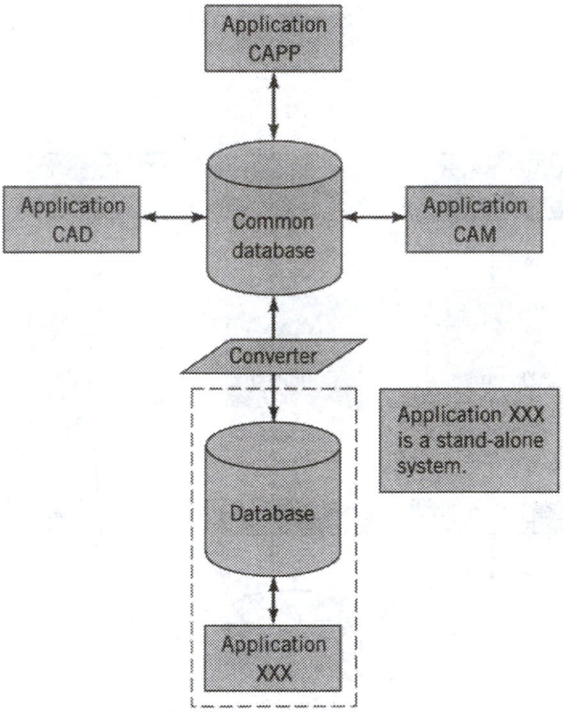

(e)

FIGURE 14.20 (continued)

the number of converters for *N* specification modules is reduced to 2*N*, compared with *N*(N − 1) in integration level 1. This structure does not change the data structure of application modules. In fact, all the application modules retain their customized data structure for local processing and data storage. Examples of neutral data exchange standards include the initial graphics exchange specification (IGES) discussed in Chapter 3 for mechanical engineering design data and the electronic design interchange format (EDIF) for very large scale integration (VLSI) design data.

14.4.4 Level 3: A Centralized Database

The idea is to have a common database with which all the application modules interface as a means of integration, as shown in Figure 14.20*d*. Although the common database appears to be centralized, centralization may be only at the logical level. This means that information may still be sitting at different locations or systems. However, such a distribution of information may be transparent to the user in well-designed distributed database systems. The concept of a common database appears to be the best strategy for achieving integration. Benefits of such a scheme include:

1. Complete elimination of data conversion; this considerably reduces cost.
2. Accessibility of data to all authorized users.
3. Efficient use of data because of retrieval of data objects and their reuse in similar (design, process planning, and manufacturing) activities.
4. Database consistency is easy to achieve because incompatible data structures, which are the primary sources of redundancy, can be avoided.

14.4.5 Level 4: Integration of Stand-Alone Components

The ultimate goal of integration is to have a common database architecture as given in integration level 3. Can we achieve such a goal? The reality is that application modules are diverse in terms of customized systems and data formats. It may be difficult to rewrite them to interface with a common database system. For such difficult cases we may have to use the strategy in integration level 2, whereby stand-alone components can be integrated through the use of customized converters in which the database system plays the role of the neutral data format. Such a scheme is shown in Figure 14.20*e*.

14.5 GROUP WORK IN ENTERPRISES

Group work in enterprises is needed for a variety of reasons. Prominent among drivers of work are (Holtham, 1993) *change management, coordination, collaboration,* and *control.*

1. *Change management.* Changes in enterprises result from strategic and operational decisions such as continuous improvement, changes in product designs, changes in product volumes, and evolving business processes. Decisions must be made about how to deal with each change. Such decision making may involve many individuals in an enterprise. Once decisions have been made, the impact of the change must be communicated to all those affected in the enterprise. Tools and technologies for group decision making and communication among employees, customers, and suppliers will be invaluable for achieving such group processes.

2. *Coordination.* A manufacturing enterprise requires a large number of activities to be performed. These activities must be coordinated to ensure that they are sufficiently synchronized. For example, manufacturing a lot of a particular product requires the coordination of activities in purchasing, shop-floor sheduling, and assembly. Coordination arises from the top-down needs of information exchange in an enterprise to ensure that its units are working together to achieve its objectives.

3. *Collaboration.* Collaboration reflects the bottom-up demands of an organization in the same way that coordination reflects the top-down needs. Collaboration reflects the needs of staff at all levels of the organization to exchange information and opinions. Collaboration may take place through formal or informal channels, such as teams, forums, and telephone exchanges. Suppliers and producers need to share information to utilize resources effectively and produce high-quality, low-cost products quickly.

4. *Control.* Control is central to all organizations to ensure that the cost, quality, lead time, and other goals are accomplished. This requires both top-down and bottom-up communication channels: top-down channels to communicate the set of directives to work and goals, bottom-up channels to report that the commands have been implemented and the goals have been achieved.

Tools and technology are required to manage change and to accomplish coordination, collaboration, and control. *Groupware* is the networked hardware and software that allows people to support each other in their efforts to achieve work goals regardless of where and when they want to do this. Collaborative computing means creation of systems in which sets of people use groupware in order to achieve the goals of their team, group, and organization. Strategic imperatives for deploying groupware include:

- "REs": reengineer, retool, resize, reinvent, remanufacture, restructure, rethink, redefine, reposition
- Teamwork, virtual teaming
- Focus on customer needs
- Focus on core competencies
- The network enterprise
- Flatter, leaner organizations
- Drive for efficiency and productivity gains

Two of the most important enabling technologies for groupware are networking and electronic mail. Electronic mail has emerged as an enabling technology as well as a category of groupware. Groupware products can be classified in the following categories (Held, 1993): *messaging, scheduling and coordination,* and *information sharing.*

1. *Messaging.* These products are primarily electronic mail systems. Messaging systems are groupware products that can easily be linked to other systems because several standard formats have already been defined for exchanging messages among dissimilar systems.

2. *Scheduling and coordination.* These products are designed for managing time of the users and coordinating with other users. The products include calender, personal information manager, and scheduling application.

3. *Information sharing.* These products are designed to allow users to manage and share information in an unstructured way on a network. They include Lotus Notes (from Lotus Development Corporation), PacerForum, and various bulletin board systems. Lotus Notes is an application development environment that can support communication, coordination, and collaboration within groups and organizations. Notes has some built-in features such as electronic mail. Other features such as discussion forums and customized view of shared databases can be built (for more details, see

TABLE 14.14 **Tools Grid**

	Interactivity		
Levels	*Low*	*Medium*	*High*
Top	Executive information system	Discussion conference scheduling	Group decision support
Middle	Project/status reports	Resource sharing, messaging/mail	Work flow monitoring Collaborative writing
Operational	Database access	Resource sharing Messaging/mail	Meetings/phone calls Time-critical applications

Source: Holtham (1993). Reproduced with permission from Morgan Kaufman Publishers, San Francisco, CA.

Marshak, 1990). Notes has an application programming interface (API) that allows developers to write applications that read and write data from other computer systems.

We can evaluate groupware technology needs by relating groupware functions to business processes (Holtham, 1993). The nine-box model shown in Table 14.14 can be used as one element in diagnosing for business processes and in evaluating groupware technology needs. For example, the low-interaction column includes access to large databases where the primary purpose is to input, retrieve, or analyze data. Similarly, the high-interaction column is related to functions that tend to be actively engaged in by virtually all members of the group. This grid is part of broader diagnostic framework against which businesses can review their long-term groupware requirements.

14.5.1 A Case Study of Groupware Systems

We provide an overview of the SHARE project (Toye et al., 1993), a joint venture of the Center for Design Research, Stanford University and Enterprise Integration Technologies, California. The SHARE project is concerned with how information technology can help engineers develop products. Most engineers in product design spend most of their time gathering and organizing information; communicating with clients, suppliers, and colleagues; negotiating trade-offs; and using each other's services. The SHARE system proposes an open heterogeneous, network-oriented collaborative environment for engineers to participate on a distributed team using their own tools and databases. Figure 14.21 provides an illustration of SHARE. The windows onto this world of networked resources and services will be multimedia "notebooks" in which to capture and organize information about a project: CAD drawings and solid models, audio notes, sketches, spreadsheets, pages from handbooks and catalogues, animated simulations, mail, excerpts from video conferences, and so forth.

Figure 14.22 shows the architecture of SHARE. At the top level is a set of agents interacting as peers over the Internet. Each agent may represent one or more of the following:

- A designer and his or her personal CAD tools
- A database or other information service
- A computational service that supports engineering or the engineering process

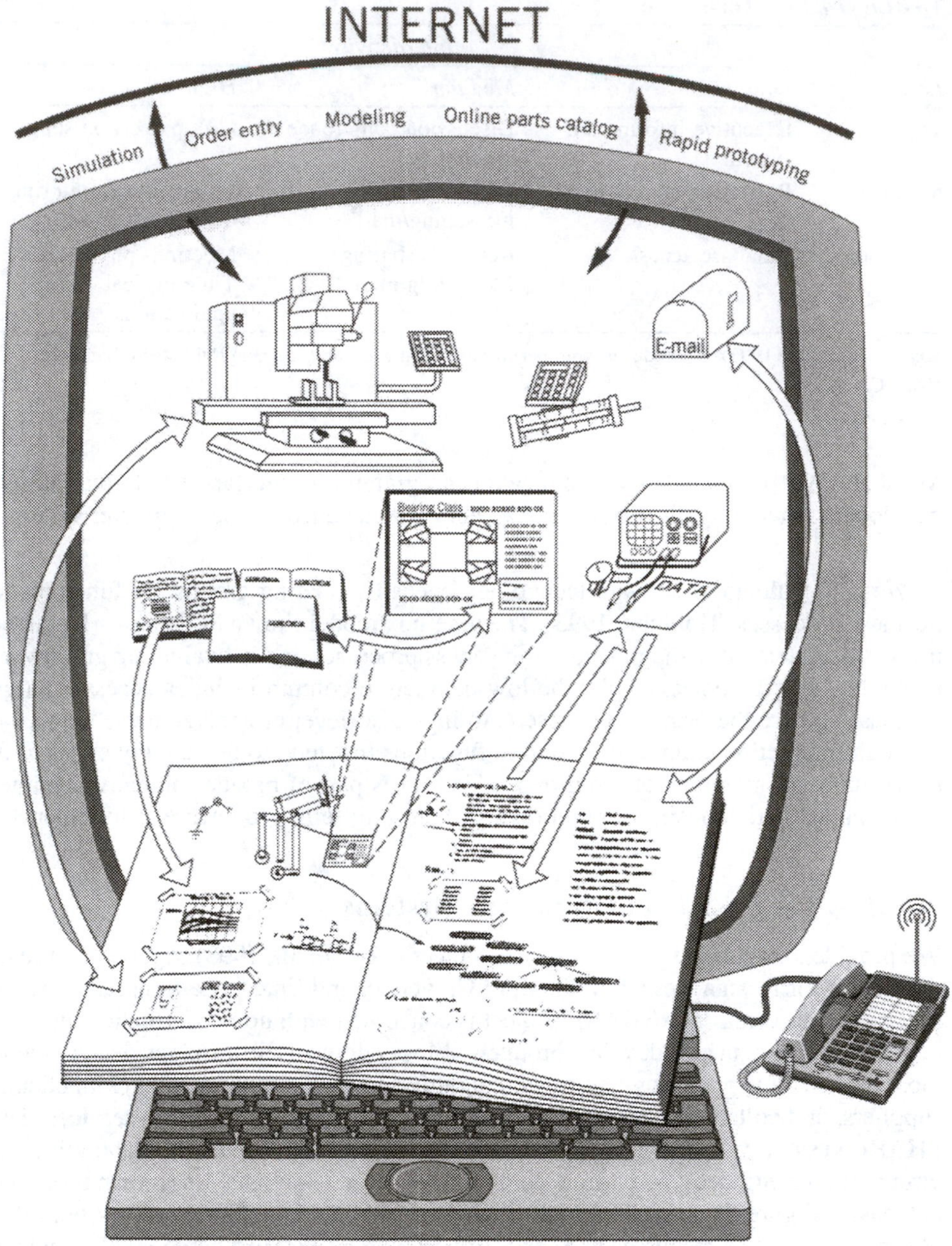

FIGURE 14.21 The SHARE vision. (Courtesy of G. Toye, Center for Design Research, Stanford University.)

Agents can exchange information and services using a simple command language and representation for multimedia information. Messages are sent using standard e-mail and TCP/IP transport services. E-mail is the primary medium for both human communication and tool integration. Standards in multimedia e-mail make it easy to exchange documents containing text, images, audio, video, and programs. Furthermore, to make design team collaboration successful, the SHARE environment has the following classes of groupware and other tools:

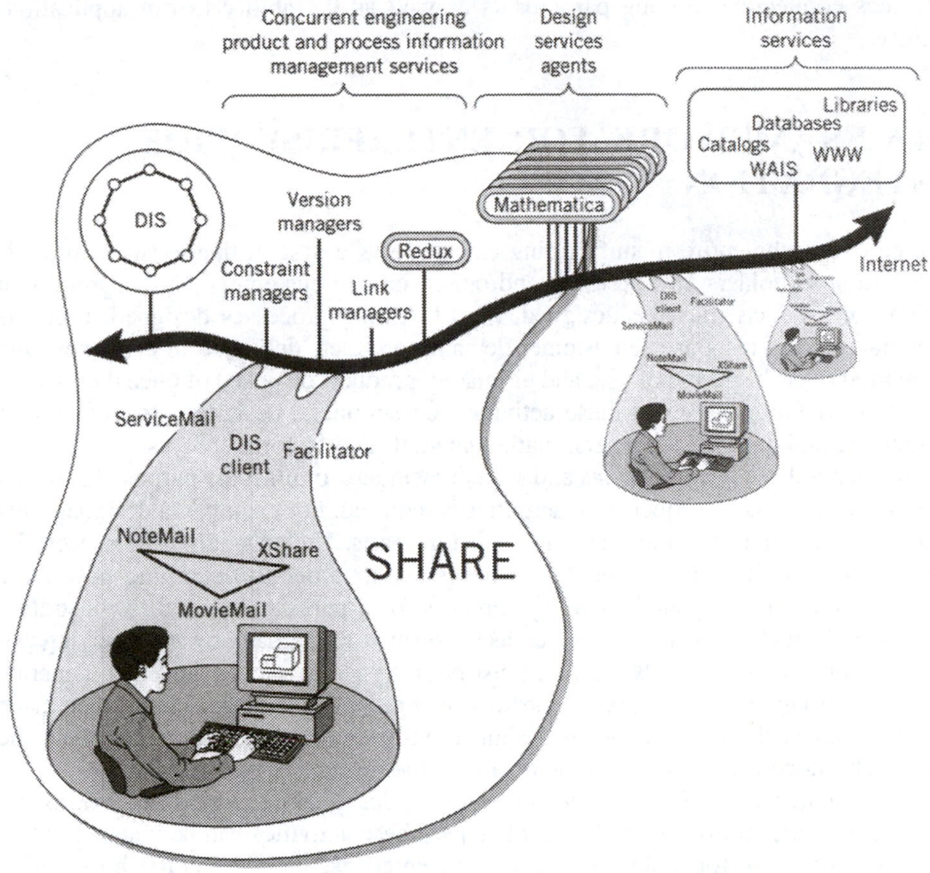

FIGURE 14.22 Application-oriented view of the SHARE architecture. (Courtesy of G. Toye, Center for Design Research, Stanford University.)

- NoteMail and Distributed Information Service to help engineers capture and manage product information
- MovieMail and X-Share, which help them collaborate with colleagues
- ServiceMail and Facilitators, which enable their tools to interoperate and invoke remote services

A brief discussion of these tools is provided next.

NoteMail is a tool for creating, viewing, and sharing multimedia engineering documents in a network environment. It combines the functions of an engineering notebook, hypermedia browser and authorizing environment, mail tool, and file application manager.

Distributed Information Service provides a centralized information and management service for all the data associated with a design: CAD files, e-mail messages, specifications, simulation results, and so forth.

MovieMail is a groupware tool that captures a workstation session as a series of screen dumps and video clips, narrated with mouse (cursor pointer) gestures and spoken commands.

X-share is a set of programs that provide real-time conferencing and application sharing over the Internet. Specifically, they provide interactive audio, video, text, and graphics connections among participants as well as the ability to run applications jointly.

14.6 FRAMEWORK FOR ENTERPRISE-WIDE INTEGRATION

We can view the entire manufacturing enterprise as a system that exists to provide profit to stockholders and products and/or services to customers. In the process of doing so, products must be designed, manufacturing processes designed, products manufactured in response to customer demand, products delivered to customers and supported over the period of use, and ultimately products disposed of once their useful life is over. Participating in these activities are suppliers, designers, manufacturing engineers, maintenance engineers, marketing staff, and so forth.

In a general sense, for systems and system elements to fulfill the purpose for which they were designed, a sequence of activities is required. For example, a designer must design parts and a machinist must manufacture parts. Understanding the process by which the activities are carried out is necessary in order to determine how these activities may be integrated. A design process for a part can be used to illustrate a system activity. The designer must collect information, perhaps by interviewing potential users, on what needs the part must be designed to satisfy, and then generate several alternative part design concepts to satisfy those needs. A decision is then made as to which is the best candidate design. Finally, the designer must complete the process by documenting the specific details of the design.

The system activity just described involves the design of a product. Other decision-making activities follow a similar set of steps. These activities can be mapped onto a generic framework for understanding generic enterprise activities. First information (I) must be obtained. The information is then used to determine requirements (R) for the activity. Next, additional information (I) must be obtained about different ways in which requirements may be met. Then, decision making (D) is used to select the best alternative, and actions (A) are used to implement or commit to the decision. This is known as the IRIDA framework for system activities and is a useful way of thinking about activities that go on in an enterprise (Mejabi and Singh, 1994).

14.6.1 Integration Concepts

Integration involves the coordination and harmonization of the activities that go on in a system. The ultimate goal of integration is to improve the overall performance of a system by linking local activities with its overall goals. In this sense, integration is nothing more than an attempt at global optimization.

A powerful analogy with integrated systems is the physiology of a human response to an external threat. As soon as the threat appears, information (I) must be collected by the senses (sight, smell, hearing, etc.) to suggest that a threat exists. That information must be processed to establish that a threat (a requirement, R, stating that all is not well at this time) exists. Based on the nature of the threat, more information (I) and analysis are used to determine alternative courses of action (run or fight). At this point a decision (D) must be made. Decisions must consider not only what kind of threat exists but also what state the leg muscles are in (in order to provide motion), how the lungs are (in order to provide the oxygen needed for energy), and how the heart is (in order to pump oxygenated blood to the muscles). If a decision is made to run, this must be carried out by a set of actions (A). For running to achieve the goal of survival, the muscles of both legs and both hands and the lungs and the heart must be properly synchronized. The heart must beat faster to pump more blood, the breathing rate must increase to obtain oxygen faster, and so on. For this whole process, a variety of signals (nerve signals and endocrine signals) and flows (oxygen and blood flow) must occur, otherwise integration will be compromised.

Following the analogy, the IRIDA framework will be used to describe how integrated manufacturing enterprises operate. We can use a life-cycle framework to view the activities that occur in the enterprise. Products must be designed, manufactured, distributed, supported, and finally disposed of. Each of these can be broken down into a set of lower-level activities. Each activity, however, involves to varying degrees different aspects of IRIDA. The need for integration comes about because decisions made and carried out within one activity have impacts on other activities. For example, a designer's material selection for a product affects the ease and cost of manufacture and, ultimately, the ease and cost of disposal. If material selection is made without regard to its effects on manufacturing and disposal costs, the costs will rise unnecessarily and stockholder profits will be jeopardized. Acting in an integrated manner, the designer will select the material only after some consideration of the life-cycle costs, which can be determined by obtaining input from manufacturing and environmental engineers.

Integration is much more than mere coupling of processes or information flow between them. Certainly, information flow contributes to integration, but it is just a subset of the overall integration paradigm. Consider a system with two processes, A and B, such that process A cannot make a decision without considering B's needs in relation to consequences of the decision (global). Information flow between the two processes, even if fast and smooth, does not provide complete integration. Rather, a marriage-like relationship must exist between them for integration to be minimally satisfactory. This means that each process can influence the decision making that the other process carries out, that there is good communication between them, and even that their actions are well synchronized.

Generalizing the concepts in the last paragraph, we observe that there are three prerequisites for achieving system integration:

- Integrated control and decision making
- Information flow and data integration
- Integrated action

14.6.1.1 Integrated Control and Decision Making

This involves the ability of each of the components of a system to arrive at decisions only after due consideration of the viewpoints and requirements of the other components in the system. If such a process works properly, it becomes possible for local decisions to reflect global optimization on a system-wide level. Although this connection has seldom been made, it is clear that concurrent engineering (as described in Chapter 4) is a method for achieving integrated control and decision making. One of the main tenets of concurrent engineering is the incorporation of different viewpoints into decisions that have to be made at each stage of the product life cycle. In this way design engineers must not myopically decide on the materials, dimensions, and tolerances of a product while considering only the functional requirements of the product. Rather, they must incorporate other issues—from manufacturing, such as one material is easier (and therefore cheaper) to machine than another, or from distribution, where one material might be more subject to damage in transit than another. By considering the different viewpoints, it becomes possible to arrive at decisions that contribute to minimizing the total life-cycle cost.

14.6.1.2 Information Flow and Data Integration

An immense amount of data is required for an enterprise to support a set of products and services over their entire life cycle. These include data pertaining to design, production, distribution, accounting, government regulations, and so on. For an enterprise to be properly integrated, all the information required for decision making and other processes must be instantly available in the form in which it is needed. Failure to do so introduces bottlenecks into the system and might preclude integrated control—for example, when certain decision-making activities cannot proceed because requirements and viewpoints have not been communicated from the other elements of the enterprise to the point where a decision is to be made. The link between design and manufacturing provides a good illustration of the need for timely flow of correctly formatted data between system components. On the one hand, communication must occur from manufacturing to design for manufacturing considerations to be included in the process of design decision making. On the other hand, once a design has been completed, it is highly desirable for the same data to be transmitted to the manufacturing activity to be used to produce the products. Indeed, the data integration system is the glue that holds an integrated system together. Inasmuch as each process requires a different view of the data, means must be provided to help present the data to each process in the form in which it is required. Integrated information flow requires a carefully designed linkage of sets of databases and computer networks that are managed to make data flow freely and transparently between system components.

14.6.1.3 Integrated Action

Integrated action is the third, but not least important, aspect of the systems integration concept. Even though integrated decision making and data integration may exist, a system cannot be considered well integrated without some means of synchronizing the actions carried out at different parts of the system. If actions occur in the system at random times, the physical synergy required to move the system toward achieving its goals may be lost completely. Effects of integrated action can be shown by using an analogy. If we consider that the goal of a system is to lift a load of 1000 lb and the system is designed with four lifting devices, each with a lifting capacity of 300 lb, we can see that the load will be lifted only if the times at which all four lifting devices actuate are well synchronized. Just-in-time (JIT) systems are another good example of integrated action. JIT recognizes that inventory costs money, but failure to meet customer demand in a timely fashion also costs money. JIT uses the kanban mechanism (described in Chapter 11) to provide the synchronizing signal that indicates the time at which production should start. In this way excess inventory is not produced and customer orders are not chronically late. Rather, production proceeds at various workstations so that products are shipped *just in time* to the customer.

14.6.2 Integration Architectures

To obtain a comprehensive view of the integration existing in any system, it is useful to understand the manner in which the system addresses certain elements of the integration scheme. These elements can be expressed in terms of architectures; therefore, we must understand the functional architecture, the control architecture, the data architecture, and finally the network architecture. These architectures, when understood as they relate to one another, will yield an understanding of how well integrated a system is. For example, we can see how easily data can flow from one part to another and how decision making in one area can address the requirements for other functions.

The most basic architecture of the four is the functional architecture, which is a plan of the functions provided by a system and indicates which system components are responsible for the functions, either individually or collectively. An example of a functional architecture is one in which the operations of an enterprise are distributed among divisions (maybe geographically, with a North American Division, Far East Division, and so on), and division responsibilities are further partitioned into department responsibilities (e.g., sales, marketing, engineering, manufacturing). It is important to emphasize that even though a functional architecture may suggest how the control, data, and network architectures look, it does not in any way imply a particular organization for the other architectures.

With a good understanding of the functional architecture, a control and management architecture may be developed next. A control architecture outlines the decision-making responsibilities of each of the system components. In one case a controller may be responsible for the decision making for several lower-level devices. On the other hand, decisions may be reached only after negotiation between a number of peers. A control architecture must specify which decisions can be made by particular components in a system. The control architecture provides an enterprise-wide decision support system (EWDSS) for an integrated system.

On top of the control and functional architectures lies the data architecture. Data are required in a system for the purposes of control and fulfilling functional obligations. For this reason, it may be possible to determine a preferred data architecture after the functional and control architectures have been established. The data architecture indicates where the data in a system are found and how they are organized. In a system in which databases are used for data management, the data architecture specifies which data are stored where and in what form. Relational and object-oriented database techniques were described in a previous section.

The final architecture for integration is the network architecture, which indicates the paths that exist for data to flow from one point in the system to another. Data must flow because not all functions in a system can be assumed to exist in the same place as the data required for the process. In the case of integrated decision making, for example, it is necessary for data to flow from various parts of the system to the point at which the decision is made so that the different viewpoints can be integrated into a final decision.

Together, the data architecture and the network architecture constitute the enterprise-wide information system (EWIS).

14.7 REALIZING CIM

So far integration has been discussed on an enterprise level. To make concrete many of the concepts presented, an illustration and a case study will be used to show how the more general issuses of integration can be used in computer integrated manufacturing (CIM). The illustration will demonstrate how action integration, data integration and decision making integration may be used in the design and manufacture of a complex product. The case study will show how an actual enterprise has used concepts of integration to improve its design and production operations.

14.7.1 An Illustration of Integration Concepts

Consider a company in the machine tool industry. The company produces a line of machining centers for small- to medium-sized parts. The most critical component of the machine tools is the spindle assembly which determines the precision of the machining centers. The company designs and manufactures its own spindles for use on the machine tools. The central requirement for the product includes high strength and stiffness, as well as low weight. Two main functions that are of interest are the processes of design and production. In designing the spindle, decisions must be made as to the best material to be used as well as to the values for main dimensions and tolerances on those dimensions. By recognizing that material costs are only part of the total life cycle cost and that manufacturing cost often turns out to be a major cost factor, an attempt is made to provide integrated decision-making by putting in place mechanisms that encourage input from manufacturing engineering before final design decisions are made. The integrating mechanism consists of a collection of software tools and a computer system for facilitating group design and decision making. The designer is able, for example, to run a design for assembly (DFA) simulator in order to determine the impact that different tolerance settings will have on assembly costs. Also, the group design software permits a manufacturing engineer to obtain access directly into the designer's workspace to suggest different materials that perform better from a machinability perspective. This is an example of *integrated control and decision making*. Links between the different computer and database systems involved are established by using *data integration*. Project management to ensure that the design process proceeds efficiently requires elements of *action integration* as the efforts of several engineers and managers are coordinated.

Once the design of the product has been completed, in order to get a finished item for use on its machining centers the components that make up the spindle must be machined and then assembled. Production facilities are in two locations separated by over 200 miles. The production planning process requires access to various types of data. Such data includes the real time status of different machines, the locations of tools required by each process, and the level of inventory of each component required for assembly. Database management systems help the company to organize the data and to provide means for rapid location and use. All users of data at production facilities, no matter where they are located relative to the physical data store, can obtain access to information that indicates how the data is organized. Since the databases exist at the different plants, a computer network is provided to move the data around. This is data integration. Since the two plants have some degree of overlap in capabilities, assignment of specific batches to one plant or the other requires *integrated control and decision making* as attempts are made to maximize overall throughput while equipment utilization is also kept as high as possible.

Before spindle assembly actually commences, all components required are delivered to the plant departments where assembly is carried out; any tools needed are also provided. By being able to properly synchronize the arrival of these items, the company is able to maximize its throughput, reduce lead-times, and keep inventory levels low. Central to this is the use of accurate scheduling to synchronize the times at which all important events, relative to production, occur. This is *action integration.* The actual design and process planning data is used as direct input to the assembly equipment. This data is obtained from the company's design database and from suppliers of the components that are out-sourced. This shows the *data integration* used in this process.

14.7.2 A Case Study of CIM

In this section we provide a case of CIM in the telecommunication equipment manufacturing industry as presented by Tateno and Matsui (1993), with few modifications. In this industry, the development and manufacturing of advanced, sophisticated products and ensuring their timely entry in highly competitive markets have made information processing and CIM systems indispensable.

A notable feature of telecommunications equipment is the rapid progress in its constituent technologies such as semiconductors and optical communications. Telecommunications growth is stimulated by the need for faster processing and transfer of ever larger amounts of information. Moreover, the increasingly diversified array of products required to meet customers' needs and the internationalization of manufacturing bases strongly affect production systems.

14.7.2.1 Unique Requirements for Telecommunication Equipment Manufacturing

The following are characteristics of telecommunications equipment manufacturing.

1. Telecommunications equipment is manufactured based on orders received and is designed to each customer's specifications. For this reason, production lines must often run several products in small lots at the same time.
2. As technology advances, the production line must adopt new assembly techniques, manufacturing technology, tooling, and equipment at an equal pace.
3. Production changes are common. Designs change frequently because of changes in customer specification, performance improvements, or vagaries in component supply. These factors can profoundly affect production.
4. Product quality and reliability must be guaranteed. Communications systems are vital, and failure can be catastrophic. Production systems figure greatly in the long-term reliability of strategically important products.

In developing manufacturing systems for telecommunications equipment, simply automating and improving the efficiency of such processes as design and manufacturing alone are insufficient. Instead, the system must integrate many of the functions of design, development, and manufacturing departments.

The enterprise in this case included thousands of employees on three continents. It could therefore be characterized as geographically distributed, culturally diverse, and large. This increases the need for integration while making it a more difficult goal to achieve.

14.7.2.2 The CIM System

The system configuration shown in Figure 14.25 enables production information integration and assures system reliability and expendability. The remotely located business information, computer-aided design, and manufacturing information systems areconnected via a wide area network. (WAN). Subsystems at the plant are part of the manufacturing information system and are connected via a local area network. Design activities are carried out in teams. However, members of each team are not at the same

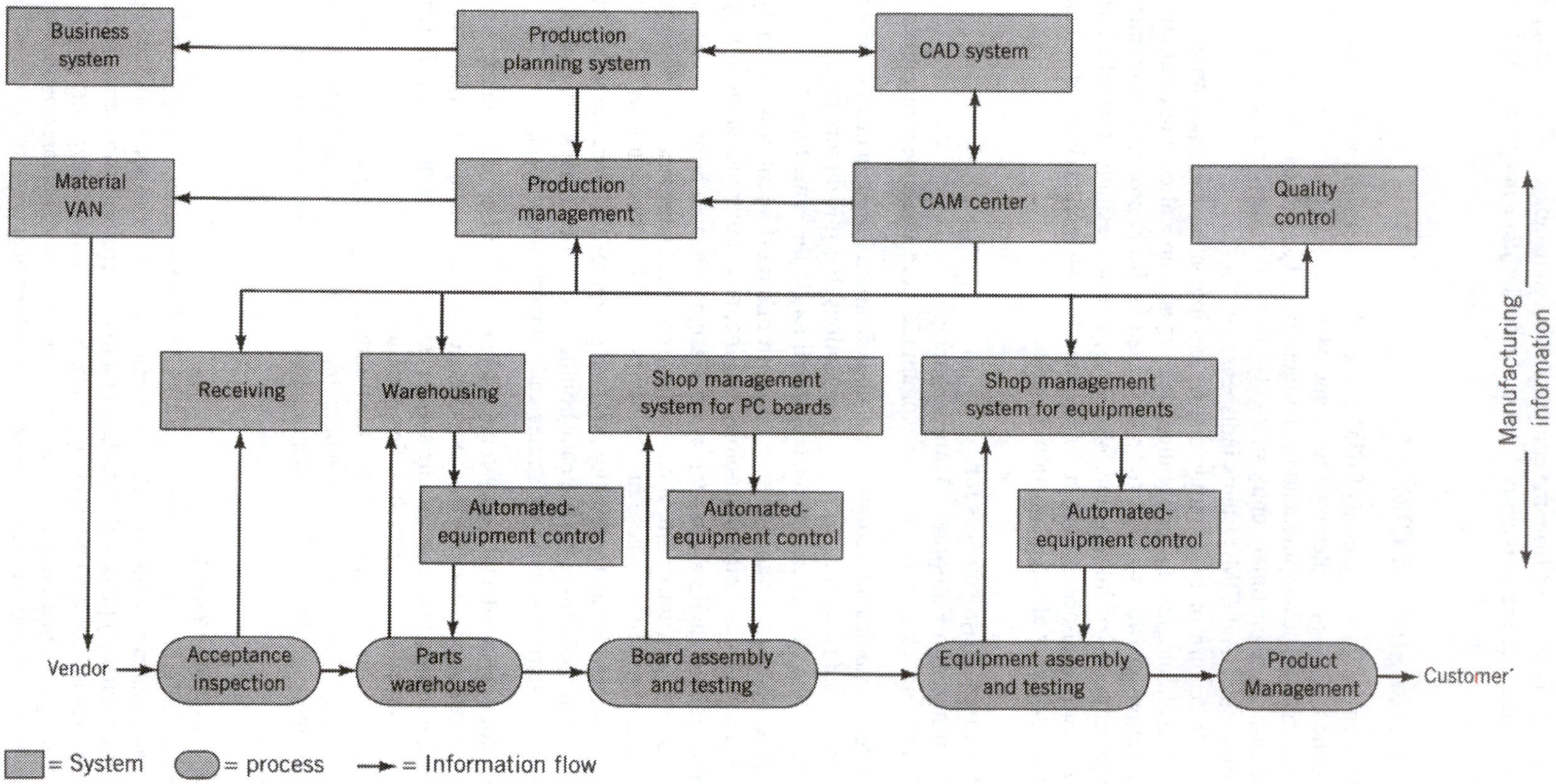

FIGURE 14.25 System configuration. (Reprinted from Tateno and Matsui 1993), with kind permission from Elsevier Science Ltd., U.K.)

physical location. A typical scenario involves a design team of three engineers, with two located in Japan and the third in Europe. Using a groupware software and the WAN, all the engineers can concurrently access the components and materials databases while interacting with one another on the design.

The information system automates the flow of design data, including geometric data from CAD systems and material specifications, directly into the CAM environment. In this way design data are instantly available for use in production.

The enterprise has a fully integrated business and production planning information system that collects and processes domestic and overseas order information, prepares production plans, and transmits them to affected plants and departments. This provides great flexibility in responding to unforseen events in the system. For example, two plants in separate parts of the world could be instructed to produce portions of a large order in the event that equipment failure occurs at the main production facility. The system is capable of coordinating the production of the end items as well as synchronizing their delivery just in time to the customer's warehouse.

The manufacturing information system consists of a computer-aided manufacturing center, production and plant management, and automated-equipment control systems. The CAM center system generates data such as part arrangement and automated-equipment programs based on design information and supplies the data to other systems downstream. The CAM center system also stores the data in a distributed database management system that is accessible to other subsystems such as production and management. The production management system oversees plant production management and operations such as:

- Customer order management based on orders received from the production planning system
- Parts data maintenance and management
- Total process management using a value-added network (VAN) for materials, for example, parts procurement from supplier plants, parts receiving, and products shipment

The shop management system receives automated-equipment data from the CAM center system and manufacturing orders from the production management system. It then sends this information on to the low-level automated-equipment control system. The shop management system also collects and manages information on the progress of each manufacturing process. Automated-equipment control supplies related data based on individual product identification labels, while also controlling automated conveyors and sending information on process progress to the plant management information system.

The production line starts at the parts warehouse and ends at the equipment test section. To manufacture small, short production runs of a wide variety of products, a material-handling line is added that feeds printed circuit (PC) boards, one by one, using conveyor belts, to assembly, testing, and storage stations.

I. CAM Center System The CAM center system improves work efficiency through

1. Interfacing between the design and manufacturing departments
2. CAD/CAM conversion promoting automated manufacturing
3. Preparation support for manufacturing data and facilities

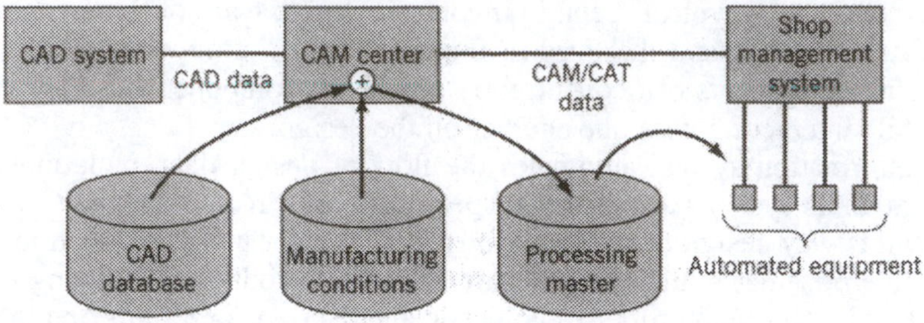

FIGURE 14.26 CAD, CAM, and CAT relationships. (Reprinted from Tateno and Matsui 1993), with kind permission from Elsevier Science Ltd., U.K.)

1. *Design data integration.* The following information from the design department is sent to the production or shop management systems after format conversion:

- Design change information
- Parts list data
- Parts and board assembly information
- Wiring information
- Firmware read-only memory (ROM) information.

Centralized management ensures the independence of the design and manufacturing departments and enables information to be shared.

2. *CAD/CAM conversion.* CAD data, for example, parts lists and assembly information received from the design department, are converted to automated-equipment processing data. Manufacturing conditions for individual equipment are stored in a master file (Figure 14.26). The parts assembly sequence heavily influences equipment efficiency. Rates are improved and time reduced by using artificial intelligence software.

3. *Preparatory support for manufacturing data and facilities.* ''As needed'' is the keyword for manufacturing data. Production facilities and parts must be ready as needed, while allowance is made for procurement periods that may take several months.

- *Preparation of manufacturing data.* To avoid stopping production because the needed data are unavailable, data availability is checked by using the CAM center system and daily schedule information in the production management system. The design department is prompted to supply required data when necessary.
- *Facilities installation plan.* Usually up to several months may be required to install production facilities, tune the automated-equipment operation, and procure parts. The materials quantity analysis system developed calculates monthly quantities by board and part type for six months into the future based on manufacturing plans or order data from the production management system (Figure 14.27). The number of parts scheduled for automated assembly is also determined and checked against equipment availability, and the result is reflected in

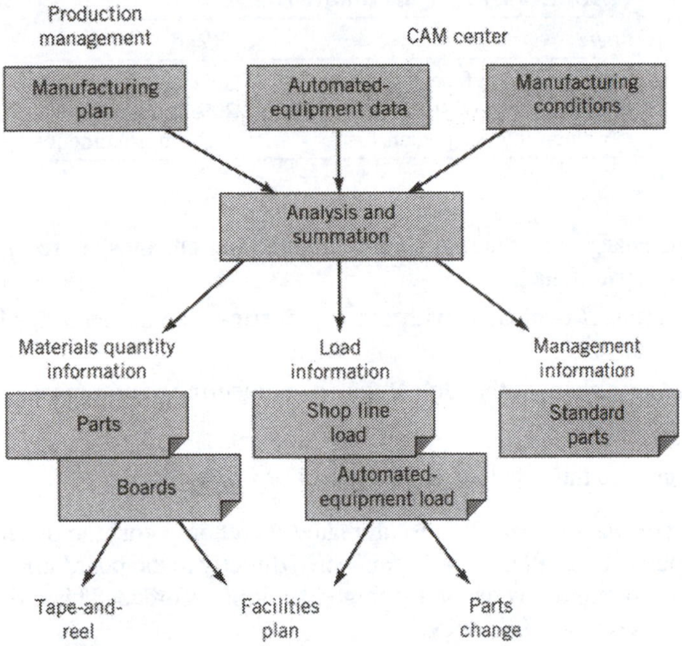

FIGURE 14.27 Manufacturing facilities preparation. (Reprinted from Tateno and Matsui 1993), with kind permission from Elsevier Science Ltd., U.K.)

facilities installation plans. Parts not produced in house are purchased and prepared. Setup required for parts in large quantities is planned on the basis of data from the materials quantity analysis system.

II. PC Board Line Feeding PC board line feeding involves

1. Grouping board types to optimize efficiency of manufacturing by the equipment operator
2. Assigning board priority based on customer delivery dates
3. Precisely and promptly processing design changes.
4. Storing completed boards.

1. *Grouping by product name.* Boards are grouped by type for individual operators based on bar codes to maximize operator efficiency. Bar code data are read by a personal computer and sent to the line control to ensure that boards of the same type arrive in the right order at each of the 10 line stations after soldering.

2. *Prioritizing types.* To avoid unbalanced loads in board assembly and testing, this system monitors the operation rate to reduce process time. This device sorts boards by type for testing, and sequences board types to determine priority in testing. Board sequencing is based on delivery dates.

3. *Instruction design changes.* Design changes are processed as follows:

TABLE 14.15 **Quantitative effects**

Item	*Effect*
Reduced manufacturing time	30% reduction
Improved use of stock	20% reduction
Productivity per person	25% improvement

- Design change information (board engineering changes) is received from the design department.
- Information is compared with the engineering requirements for boards being processed.
- Boards with changes that do not match engineering requirements are tagged for reconsideration.

Design changes are thus applied precisely and promptly.

4. *Storing completed boards.* An automated warehouse for completed boards has been developed and installed. This is connected directly to the board line. Based on the CAD data, boards are delivered and storage locations recorded. This reduces retrieval time and increases work efficiency.

The impact of CIM on the manufacturing process is given in Table 14.15, and is based on the information culled from three years of use. The benefits include:

1. *Quick response to market needs.* Production information on sales, design, and manufacturing is transmitted immediately to related departments. This improves the response to market needs and changes.
2. *Early problem detection.* Feedback due to the improved manufacturing improves relations between departments.
3. *Close linkage between departments.* The integrated information structure reduces the adverse effects of divisiveness among production groups.

14.8 FUTURE TRENDS IN MANUFACTURING SYSTEMS: AGILE MANUFACTURING

Globalization of markets has put tremendous pressure on manufacturing enterprises to be competitive. To cope with competitive pressures, a new paradigm in manufacturing known as *agile manufacturing* is emerging (Goldman, et al., 1995). The objective of agile manufacturing is to enable manufacturing enterprises to be competitive by dynamically reconfiguring software, equipment, and organization structures. There is, however, no universal prescription for becoming agile. Some of the characteristics of agile manufacturing, according to the Agile Manufacturing Enterprise Forum (AMEF), affiliated with the Iacocca Institute at Lehigh University, include:

- Greater product customization
- Rapid introduction of new or modified products
- Advanced interenterprise networking technology
- Upgradable products

- Increased emphasis on knowledgeable, highly trained, empowered workers
- Interactive customer relationships
- Dynamic reconfiguration of production processes
- Greater use of flexible production technologies
- Rapid prototyping
- An open systems information environment
- Innovative and flexible management structures
- Product pricing based on value to the customer
- Commitment to environmentally benign operations and product designs

14.8.1 Unlearning of Currently Held Truths

To implement an agile manufacturing system, we have to unlearn many of the currently held truths (Goldman and Preiss, 1991), which include:

- That cooperation is less desirable than succeeding on one's own;
- That labor–management relations must be adversarial;
- That information is power and can be shared only to one's detriment;
- That trust makes one vulnerable;
- That there are single technological solutions to complex problems;
- That breakthroughs are the only targets worth aiming at;
- That markets will appear by themselves once better mousetraps are invented;
- That infrastructure requirements will take care of themselves once pioneers have thrown up superstructures;
- That standards are constraining and their formulation dull work;
- That only parts can be invented, not whole systems.

14.9 SUMMARY

The development and manufacture of high-quality customized products at low cost with very little lead time have made enterprise-wide integration systems and CIM systems indispensable in any industry. We briefly discussed various aspects of enterprise-wide integration systems. Because the technology in enterprise-wide integration is emerging and the area of integration is so wide, it is difficult to cover all the issues in a chapter. There is, however, enough material in the chapter to provide an appreciation of the concepts. Details can be obtained from the accompanying references.

PROBLEMS

14.1 Discuss various elements of a manufacturing enterprise.

14.2 Discuss the following statement: Enterprise integration is a necessary strategy for survival in an era of mass customization.

14.3 What is meant by the term computer communication? Discuss various computer communication technologies available for a successful virtual corporation.

14.4 What is meant by the term database management system?

14.5 Consider requirements for manufacturing a simple product consisting of one or two components. Develop the following data models for this product considering design and manufacturing issues:
(a) Hierarchical
(b) Network
(c) Relational
(d) Object-oriented

14.6 Smith and Smith Company (SSC) is involved in designing and manufacturing a variety of transmission gears. The casting plant is located in Ohio. The machining of gears is carried out in a highly mechanized plant in Detroit. The machining system involves numerically controlled gear hobbing, gear shaving, slotting, and hole-finishing machines. The plant operates a fleet of AGVs interfaced with an AS/RS system. The gear production facility is organized as groups of cells based on group technology concepts. Production planning and control in the cells are based on just-in-time manufacturing concepts. Finished gears are shipped to various customers directly from the shipping warehouse in the Detroit plant. Develop a computer communication system for Smith and Smith Company.

14.7 What is meant by the term enterprise integration? Discuss the issues that should be considered in enterprise integration.

14.8 There are a number of emerging trends in business enterprise management. They include:
(a) Agile manufacturing
(b) Reengineering
(c) Virtual organization

Discuss these concepts with regard to a company currently producing a variety of personal computers.

Problems 14.9 through 14.13 refer to the enterprise described in the case study in the last section of this chapter.

14.9 For the case study described, show a sketch of the enterprise. Identify the enterprise activities occurring in the system. To what extent do the activities involve decision making?

14.10 Develop an IRIDA mapping for each activity in the enterprise.

14.11 Based on the description provided, develop a:
(a) Functional architecture for the enterprise
(b) Control architecture for the enterprise
(c) Data architecture for the enterprise
(d) Network architecture for the enterprise

14.12 In what ways are data integration, decision and control integration, and action integration provided in the enterprise? Critique the approach to integration. In what ways might integration be improved in the system?

14.13 Sketch out a comprehensive EWIS and EWDSS for the system.

14.14 Develop a detailed system design for enterprise-wide integration for a car manufacturing company called New Era Motor Company (NEMC). NEMC has over 10,000 distributors located in over 50 countries on five continents. The product variety includes over 100 types of vehicles, each with a variety of options provided on demand from customers. The head office is located in Detroit. The manufacturing plants are located in dozens of cities in the United States, Canada, Mexico, Germany, Italy, England, Nigeria, China, India, Malasia, and Thailand.

REFERENCES AND SUGGESTED READING

Bertsekas, D., and Gallager, R. (1992). *Data Networks,* 2nd ed. Prentice Hall, Englewood Cliffs, New Jersey.

Booch, G. (1991). *Object-Oriented Design with Applications.* Benjamins/Cummings, Redwood City, California.

Chorafus, D. N. (1993). *Manufacturing Databases and Computer Integrated Systems.* CRC Press, Ann Arbor, Michigan.

Dale, T. (1993). Groupware, the Macintosh, and collaboration environments. *Proceedings: Groupware 1993,* Morgan Kaufmann Publishers, Inc., San Mateo, California, pp. 316–332.

Davido, W. H., and Malone, M. S. (1992). *The Virtual Corporation: Structuring and Revitalizing the Corporation of the 21st Century.* Harper Business, New York.

Dransfield, J. (1994). Design for manufacturability at Northern Telecom. In *Successful Implementation of Concurrent Engineering Products and Processes* (S. G. Shina, ed.) Van Nostrand Reinhold, New York.

Duffie, N. A., and Piper, R. S. (1987). Non-hierarchical control of a flexible manufacturing cell. *Robotics and Computer-Integrated Manufacturing* 3(2):175–179.

Goldman, S., and Preiss, K., eds. (1991). 21st Century Manufacturing Enterprise Strategy: An Industry-Led View. Harold S. Mohler Laboratory, Iacocca Institute, Lehigh University, Bethlehem, Pennsylvania.

Goldman, G. L., Nagel, R. N. and Preiss, K. (1995). *Agile Competitors and Virtual organizations: Strategies for Enriching the Customer.* Van Nostrand Reinhold, New York.

Harrington, J. H. (1984). *Understanding the Manufacturing Process: Key to CAD/CAM Implementation.* Marcel Dekker, New York.

Held, J. (1993). Groupware in a multi-vendor environment. *Proceedings: Groupware 1993,* Morgan Kaufmann Publishers, Inc., San Mateo, California, pp. 305–310.

Holtham, C. (1993). Group communications, management processes and groupware tools. *Proceedings: Groupware 1993,* pp. 292–303. Morgan Kaufmann Publishers, Inc., San Mateo, California.

Jain, H. (1987). A comprehensive model for the design of distributed computing systems. *IEEE Transactions on Software Engineering,* October, pp. 1092–1104.

Jones, A. T., and McLean, C. R. (1986). A proposed hierarchical control model for automated manufacturing systems. *Journal of Manufacturing Systems* 5(1):15–25.

Kemper, A., and Moerkotte, G., (1994). *Object Oriented Database Management: Applications in Engineering and Computer Science.* Prentice Hall, Englewood Cliffs, New Jersey.

Lee, B. J., Ono, Y., and Lee, Y. (1993). Introduction to FANUC cell 60 and its application on MAP based large manufacturing FA system for 72 hour continuous unmanned operation: A case study. *Computers and Industrial Engineering* 24(4):593–605.

Marshak, D. S. (1990). Lotus notes: A platform for developing workgroup applications. Patricia Seyboard's Office Computing Report, July 1990.

Mejabi, O. O. (1994). Private Communication, Department of Industrial and Manufacturing Engineering, Wayne State University, Detroit, Michigan.

Mejabi, O. O., and Singh, N. (1994). A framework for enterprise-wide integration. Working paper, Department of Industrial and Manufacturing Engineering, Wayne State University, Detroit, Michigan.

Mize, J. H. (1994). *Guide to Systems Integration.* Institute of Industrial Engineers, Norcross, Georgia.

Moad, J. (1990). The new agenda for open systems. *Datamation,* April.

Nagata, T., Nagata, Y., and Koshimitsu, H. (1993). Building CIM system for compound plant: Utilization of distributed processing system. *Computers and Industrial Engineering* 24(4):561–569.

Nutt, G. (1992). *Open Systems.* Prentice Hall, Englewood Cliffs, New Jersey.

Orlikowski, W. J. (1993). Learning from notes: Organizational issues in groupware implementation. *Proceedings: Groupware 1993,* Morgan Kaufmann Publishers, Inc. San Mateo, California, pp. 356–363.

Ranky, P. G. (1986). *Computer Integrated Manufacturing: An Introduction with Case Studies.* Prentice Hall, Englewood Cliffs, New Jersey.

Rumbaugh, J., Blaha, M., Premerlani, W., Eddy, F., and Lorensen, W. (1991). *Object-Oriented Modelling and Design.* Prentice Hall, Englewood Cliffs, New Jersey.

Sata, T., and Ollings, G. (1989). *Software for Factory Automation.* North-Holland, Amsterdam.

Scholz-Reiter, B. (1992). *CIM Interfaces: Concepts, Standards and Problems of Interfaces in Computer-Integrated Manufacturing.* Chapman & Hall, London.

Sheridan, J. H. (1992). The CIM evolution: Bringing people back into the equation. *Industry Week,* April 20, pp. 29–51.

Sheridan, J. H. (1993). Agile manufacturing: Stepping beyond lean production. *Industry Week,* April 19, pp. 30–46.

Stallings, W. (1992). *Local and Metropolitan Area Networks.* Macmillan, New York.

Tateno, H., and Matsui, T. (1993). CIM system for telecommunications equipment. *Computers and Industrial Engineering* 24(4):571–578.

Teorey, T. J., and Umar, A. (1989). Distributed database design strategies. *Database Design and Programming,* April.

Toye, G. (1994). Private communication, Center for Design Research, Stanford University.

Toye, G., Cutkosky, M. R., Leifer, L. J., Tenebaum, J. M., and Glicksman, J. (1993). SHARE: A methodology and environment for collaborative product development, *Proceedings: Second Workshop on Enabling Technologies: Infrastructure for Collaborative Enterprises,* April 20–22, Morgantown, West Virginia, IEEE Computer Society Press.

Umar, A. (1993). *Distributed Computing: A Practical Synthesis.* PTR Prentice-Hall, Englewood Cliffs, New Jersey.

Umar, A., Krackenburg, R., and Lyons, T. (1991). Organizing for computer integrated manufacturing. *Information and Management Journal* 20:355–362.

Wedekind, H. (1988). Die Problematik des Computer Integrated Manufacturing (CIM)—Zu den Grundlagen eines ''strapazierten'' Begriffs. *Informatik*-Spektrum, 11:22–39.

APPENDIX

CUMULATIVE STANDARD NORMAL DISTRIBUTION

APPENDIX **Cumulative Standard Normal Distribution**

$$\Phi(z) = \int_{-\infty}^{\bar{v}} \frac{1}{\sqrt{2\pi}} e^{-\mu^2/2}\, du$$

z	0.00	0.01	0.02	0.03	0.04	z
0.0	0.50000	0.50399	0.50798	0.51197	0.51595	0.0
0.1	0.53983	0.54379	0.54776	0.55172	0.55567	0.1
0.2	0.57926	0.58317	0.58706	0.59095	0.59483	0.2
0.3	0.61791	0.62172	0.62551	0.62930	0.63307	0.3
0.4	0.65542	0.65910	0.62276	0.66640	0.67003	0.4
0.5	0.69146	0.69497	0.69847	0.70194	0.70540	0.5
0.6	0.72575	0.72907	0.73237	0.73565	0.73891	0.6
0.7	0.75803	0.76115	0.76424	0.76730	0.77035	0.7
0.8	0.78814	0.79103	0.79389	0.79673	0.79954	0.8
0.9	0.81594	0.81859	0.82121	0.82381	0.82639	0.9
1.0	0.84134	0.84375	0.84613	0.84849	0.85083	1.0
1.1	0.86433	0.86650	0.86864	0.87076	0.87285	1.1
1.2	0.88493	0.88686	0.88877	0.89065	0.89251	1.2
1.3	0.90320	0.90490	0.90658	0.90824	0.90988	1.3
1.4	0.91924	0.92073	0.92219	0.92364	0.92506	1.4
1.5	0.93319	0.93448	0.93574	0.93699	0.93822	1.5
1.6	0.94520	0.94630	0.94738	0.94845	0.94950	1.6
1.7	0.95543	0.95637	0.95728	0.95818	0.95907	1.7
1.8	0.96407	0.96485	0.96562	0.96637	0.96711	1.8
1.9	0.97128	0.97193	0.97257	0.97320	0.97381	1.9
2.0	0.97725	0.97778	0.97831	0.97882	0.97932	2.0
2.1	0.98214	0.98257	0.98300	0.98341	0.98382	2.1
2.2	0.98610	0.98645	0.98679	0.98713	0.98745	2.2
2.3	0.98928	0.98956	0.98983	0.99010	0.99036	2.3
2.4	0.99180	0.99202	0.99224	0.99245	0.99266	2.4
2.5	0.99379	0.99396	0.99413	0.99430	0.99446	2.5
2.6	0.99534	0.99547	0.99560	0.99573	0.99585	2.6
2.7	0.99653	0.99664	0.99674	0.99683	0.99693	2.7
2.8	0.99744	0.99752	0.99760	0.99767	0.99774	2.8
2.9	0.99813	0.99819	0.99825	0.99831	0.99836	2.9
3.0	0.99865	0.99869	0.99874	0.99878	0.99882	3.0
3.1	0.99903	0.99906	0.99910	0.99913	0.99916	3.1
3.2	0.99931	0.99934	0.99936	0.99938	0.99940	3.2
3.3	0.99952	0.99953	0.99955	0.99957	0.99958	3.3
3.4	0.99966	0.99968	0.99969	0.99970	0.99971	3.4
3.5	0.99977	0.99978	0.99978	0.99979	0.99980	3.5
3.6	0.99984	0.99985	0.99985	0.99986	0.99986	3.6
3.7	0.99989	0.99990	0.99990	0.99990	0.99991	3.7
3.8	0.99993	0.99993	0.99993	0.99994	0.99994	3.8
3.9	0.99995	0.99995	0.99996	0.99996	0.99996	3.9

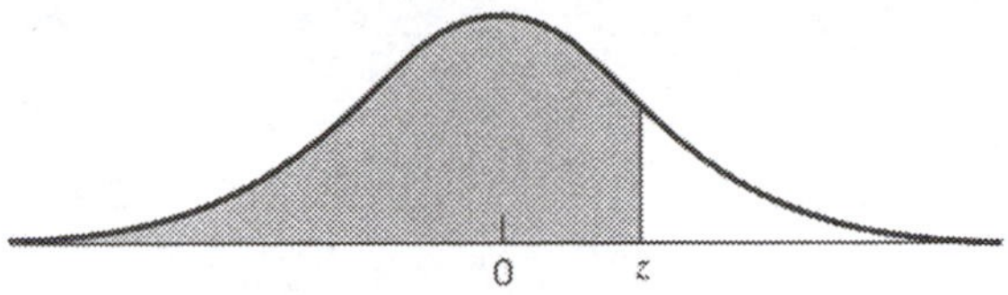

z	0.05	0.06	0.07	0.08	0.09	z
0.0	0.51994	0.52392	0.52790	0.53188	0.53586	0.0
0.1	0.55962	0.56356	0.56749	0.57142	0.57534	0.1
0.2	0.59871	0.60257	0.60642	0.61026	0.61409	0.2
0.3	0.63683	0.64058	0.64431	0.64803	0.65173	0.3
0.4	0.67364	0.67724	0.68082	0.68438	0.68793	0.4
0.5	0.70884	0.71226	0.71566	0.71904	0.72240	0.5
0.6	0.74215	0.74537	0.74857	0.75175	0.75490	0.6
0.7	0.77337	0.77637	0.77935	0.78230	0.78523	0.7
0.8	0.80234	0.80510	0.80785	0.81057	0.81327	0.8
0.9	0.82894	0.83147	0.83397	0.83646	0.83891	0.9
1.0	0.85314	0.85543	0.85769	0.85993	0.86214	1.0
1.1	0.87493	0.87697	0.87900	0.88100	0.88297	1.1
1.2	0.89435	0.89616	0.89796	0.89973	0.90147	1.2
1.3	0.91149	0.91308	0.91465	0.91621	0.91773	1.3
1.4	0.92647	0.92785	0.92922	0.93056	0.93189	1.4
1.5	0.93943	0.94062	0.94179	0.94295	0.94408	1.5
1.6	0.95053	0.95154	0.95254	0.95352	0.95448	1.6
1.7	0.95994	0.96080	0.96164	0.96246	0.96327	1.7
1.8	0.96784	0.96856	0.96926	0.96995	0.97062	1.8
1.9	0.97441	0.97500	0.97558	0.97615	0.97670	1.9
2.0	0.97982	0.98030	0.98077	0.98124	0.98169	2.0
2.1	0.98422	0.98461	0.98500	0.98537	0.98574	2.1
2.2	0.98778	0.98809	0.98840	0.98870	0.98899	2.2
2.3	0.99061	0.99086	0.99111	0.99134	0.99158	2.3
2.4	0.99286	0.99305	0.99324	0.99343	0.99361	2.4
2.5	0.99461	0.99477	0.99492	0.99506	0.99520	2.5
2.6	0.99598	0.99609	0.99621	0.99632	0.99643	2.6
2.7	0.99702	0.99711	0.99720	0.99728	0.99736	2.7
2.8	0.99781	0.99788	0.99795	0.99801	0.99807	2.8
2.9	0.99841	0.99846	0.99851	0.99856	0.99861	2.9
3.0	0.99886	0.99889	0.99893	0.99897	0.99900	3.0
3.1	0.99918	0.99921	0.99924	0.99926	0.99929	3.1
3.2	0.99942	0.99944	0.99946	0.99948	0.99950	3.2
3.3	0.99960	0.99961	0.99962	0.99964	0.99965	3.3
3.4	0.99972	0.99973	0.99974	0.99975	0.99976	3.4
3.5	0.99981	0.99981	0.99982	0.99983	0.99983	3.5
3.6	0.99987	0.99987	0.99988	0.99988	0.99989	3.6
3.7	0.99991	0.99992	0.99992	0.99992	0.99992	3.7
3.8	0.99994	0.99994	0.99995	0.99995	0.99995	3.8
3.9	0.99996	0.99996	0.99996	0.99997	0.99997	3.9

INDEX

Aggregate Production Plan, 403
  Mathematical Model, 405
Agile Manufacturing, 630
AMEF (Agile Manufacturing Enterprise Forum), 630
AGVS (Automated Guided Vehicle System), 259, 540
  Assembly Line Vehicles, 265
  Control Systems, 269
  Equipment, 259
  Forklift Trucks, 265
  Guidance System, 266
  Light Load Transporters, 265
  Load Transfer, 270
  Pallet Trucks, 253
  Principles, 258
  Steering Control, 267
  Towing Vehicles, 261
  Unit Load Transportation, 261
ANOVA (Analysis Of Variance), 363
ANSI (American National Standards Institute), 202
API (Application Programming Interface), 614
Appraisal Cost, 351
APT (Automatically Programmed Tools), 222
ASCII (American Standard Code for Information Interchange), 217
ASM (Analytical Solid Modeling), 83
ASQC (American Society Of Quality Control), 349
AS/RS (Automated Storage and Retrieval System), 277
  Cycle Time, 287
  Deep-lane, 282
  Dual Command Cycle, 288
  Lot Size, 282
  Miniload, 280
  P/D (Pick up and Deposit) Station, 279
  Person-on-board, 280
  S/R Machine, 278
  Single Command Cycle, 288
  Storage Space, 283
  Unit Load, 280
  Utilization, 289
Assembly, 341
Automated Inspection, 379
  On-line/in-process method, 379
  On-line/post-process method, 379
  Off-Line method, 379
Autonomation, 436
Average Lateness, 428
Average Tardiness, 428
Axiomatic Design, 132

Backward Kinematics Transformation, 321
B-Spline, 66, 69
  Non Uniform Rational, 69
  Rational, 45
Bandwidth, 579
Bar Code System, 418
Baud, 579
BCD (Binary Coded Decimal), 216
BCRU (Basic Control Resolution Unit), 309
BOM (Bill Of Material), 408

CAD (Computer Aided Design)
  Hardware, 20
  System Related, 24
  Geometric Modeling Related, 29
CAD/CAM, 3, 20
  Conversion, 628
  History, 20
  Input Devices, 24
  Output Devices, 27
CAD/CAM Systems, 20
  Mainframe-based, 21

CAD/CAM Systems, *(Continued)*
Microcomputer-based, 23
Minicomputer-based, 23
Selection of, 28
Workstation-based, 23
CAEA (Computer Aided Engineering Analysis), 79
FEA (Finite Element Analysis), 89, 66
Heat Transfer Analysis, 90
Motion Analysis, 93
Plastic Analysis, 91
Tolerance Analysis, 92
CAM-I (Computer Aided Manufacturing-International), 171
Capacity Planning, 407, 417
CAPP (Computer Aided Process Planning), 168
CE (Concurrent Engineering), 103
Benefits, 114
Characterization, 116
Difficulties, 130
Dimensions, 117
Elements, 119
Framework, 130
Mathematical Model, 108
Methodology, 124
Techniques, 132
Why CE?, 106
Cell Formation Approach, 490
Machine Component Group, 490
Math Programming Model, 500
Production Flow Analysis, 490
Rank Order Clustering Algorithm, 491
Similarity Coefficient, 493
Cellular Manufacturing, 488
Cell Design, 488
Cell Design Evaluation, 489
Cell Formation, 490
Design Attributes, 478
Economics, 506
Group Tooling, 506
Integration, 507
Operations allocation, 511
Production Planning and Control, 506
Channel Capacity, 580
Change Management, 615
CIM (Computer Integrated Manufacturing), 529, 577, 623
CMM (Coordinate Measuring Machine), 379, 543
Bridge type, 380
Cantilever type, 379
Column type, 380
Gantry type, 382
Horizontal Arm type, 382
CNC (Computer Numerical Control), 220
Coding Method, 480
Hierarchical Code, 480
Mixed Code, 480
Monocode, 480
Polycode, 480
Collaboration, 615
Computer-Aided Part Programming, 220
Computer Graphics, 29
Geometric Transformations, 30
Rotation, 33, 35
Scaling, 32, 35
Translation, 30, 35
Continuous Path Tool Motion, 222
Control, 616
Control Chart, 375
Attribute type, 377
np, p, c, and u charts, 377
Variable type, 376
$\bar{X}$, R and S charts, 376
Conveyor, 292
CONWIP (Constant-Work-In-Process), 460
Coordination, 615
CR (Critical Ratio), 425
Curves, 49
Bezier, 63
Hermite Cubic Spline, 59, 70
Nonparametric Representation, 52
Parametric Representation, 54
Synthetic, 56

Data Base, 609
Integration, 615
Linkage, 611
Size Calculation, 609
Data Communication, 247
Interrupts, 248
Parallel, 247
Polling, 248
Priorities, 248
Serial, 247
Data Models, 598
Hierarchical, 601
Network, 601
Object-Oriented, 606
Record Based, 599
Relational, 601
Data Rate, 579
DBMS (Data Base Management Systems), 597
Demand Forecasting, 400
Descriptive Approach, 400
Explanatory Approach, 400
Qualitative Approach, 400
Demand Management, 400
Dependent Demand, 409
Design Process, 17
Design Optimization, 93
DFA (Design For Assembly), 624
DFM (Design For Manufacturing), 132
Direct Clustering Algorithm, 492
Distributed Architecture, 291
Distributed Information Service, 619
DNC (Direct Numerical Control), 4, 219
DNC (Distributed Numerical Control), 221

Drilling Operation, 154
DXF (Drawing Exchange File Format), 96

EDD (Earliest Due Date), 425
EDIF (Electronic Design Interchange Format), 614
End-Effector (see robot), 307
Enterprise-Wide Decision Support System, 623
Ethernet, 583
EWI (Enterprise-Wide Integration), 577
Exponential Smoothing, 402
External Failure Cost, 351

FCFS (First Come First Serve), 425
Feature Recognition, 178
Fixture, 551
Flexibility, 529
  Expansion, 531
  Machine, 530
  Process, 530
  Product, 531
  Production, 531
  Routing, 530
FMEA (Failure Mode And Effect Analysis), 132, 368
FMS (Flexible Manufacturing System), 7, 529, 535, 566
  Benefits, 566
  Control Components, 542
  Layout, 552
  Part Type Selection, 545
  Physical Components, 538
  Tool Allocation Policy, 548
  Tool Management, 545
Forward Kinematics Transformation, 318

Geometric Modeling, 43
Geometric Transformations, 30
  2D Transformations, 30
  3D Transformations, 35
  Composition of Transformations, 37
  Homogenous Transformations, 36, 325
Grinding Operation, 156
Gross Requirement, 409
Grouping Efficiency, 499
Groupware, 615
GT (Group Technology), 132, 477, 486, 535
  Benefits, 487
  Coding, 480
  Group Tooling, 506
  Implementation, 477
  Part Family Formation, 486
  Visual Inspection, 478

Industrial Robot (see Robot), 303
IGES (Initial Graphics Exchange Specification), 94
Independent Demand, 409
Information Sharing, 615
Inspection Equipment, 542
Integration, 620
  Action, 624
  Architecture, 622
  Concepts, 624
  Data, 622
  Information Flow, 622
Internal Failure Cost, 351
IRIDA, 620
ISO (International Standard Organization), 95, 587

JIT (Just-In-Time), 435
  Barriers, 465
  Benefits, 465
  Cost, 449
  Integer Programming, 453
  Preconditions, 442
  Setup time, 449
  Muda, 436
  Mura, 437
  Muri, 438
  Jikoda, 436
  Yoidon, 436
Job Sequence, 425

Kanban, 436, 440
  Emergency, 455
  Express, 455
  Level Schedules, 456
  Number of, 443
  Production, 441
  Production Ordering, 451
  Raw Material Ordering, 451
  Signal, 450
  Through, 455
  Withdrawal, 440

LAN (Local Area Network), 249, 580
  Broad Band, 585
  Base Band, 585
  Carrier Band, 585
Lead Time, 411
Long Pull System, 460
LS (Least Slack), 425
LSPO (Least Slack Per Operation), 425

Machine Tool Control, 543
Machine Tools, 161
MAN (Metropolitan Area Network), 581
Manufacturing Cell, 533
Manufacturing Enterprise, 1
Manufacturing Throughout Time, 424
Manufacturing Process, 153
Manufacturing Systems, 532
  Flexible manufacturing system, 532
  Manufacturing Cell, 532
  Special manufacturing system, 532
  Stand alone NC machine, 532
  Transfer Line, 532

MAP (Manufacturing Automation Protocol), 588
Material Handling Equipment, 541
MCU (Machine Control Unit), 195
Mean Completion Time, 428
Messaging, 616
Milling Operation, 156
MMS (Manufacturing Message Specification), 588
Motion Analysis, 92
Moving Average, 401
MPCS (Manufacturing Planning and Control System), 397
  Framework, 397
MPS (Master Production System), 399, 407, 438
MRP Lot Sizing, 412
MRP (Material Requirements Planning), 507
  Algorithm, 413
Multiple Views, 46

NC, 6, 538
  Closed Loop Control, 196
  Motion And Coordinate, 197
  Open Loop Control, 196
NC Part Programming, 199
  Advanced Features, 216
  Axis Motion Command, 208
  CAD/CAM based, 232
  Feed and Speed Command, 209
  Fixed Sequential Format, 201
  G codes, 205
  Identification Command, 209
  Preparatory Functions, 204
  Special Characteristics, 211
  Structure, 200
  Tab Sequential Format, 201
  Types, 196
  Word Address Format, 202
Network, 580
  Architecture, 586
  Bus, 584
  Communication, 580
  Gateways, 591
  Performance, 593
  Repeaters, 589
  Ring, 584
  Routers, 590
  Star, 582
  Technology, 581
  Topology, 581
  Tree, 584
Network Interconnection and Devices, 589
  Repeaters, 589
  Bridges, 589
  Routers, 590
  Gateways, 591

Object, 606
  Attributes, 606
  Class, 606
  Inheritance, 606
  Message, 606
  Methods, 606
Off-Line Quality, 352
OIR (Organization For Industrial Research), 171
On-Line Quality, 352
OOM (Object-Oriented Models), 606
Open systems, 579
Operations Schedule, 423
Opitz Classification, 482
Order Release, 417
OSI (Open System Architecture), 587
  Application Layer, 588
  Data Link Layer, 588
  Network Layer, 588
  Physical Layer, 588
  Presentation Layer, 588
  Session Layer, 588
  Transport Layer, 588

Pallet, 551
Parameter Design, 353
Parametric Design, 84
Part Control System, 543
Part Family Formation, 486
Part Programming, 232
Parts Explosion, 409
Payback Period Method, 344
PDES (Product Data Exchange Standard), 95
Periodic Pull System, 460
Planned Order Release, 410
  Scheduled Receipts, 410
  Net Requirements, 410
PLC (Programmable Logic Controller), 7, 235
  Counters, 241
  Logical Control, 238
  Times, 241
Point To Point Tool Motion, 222
Prevention Cost, 351
Process Control, 246
Process Interface, 246
Process Planning, 158
  Analysis of Part Requirements, 159
  Manufacturing Operation And Sequence, 159
  Selection of Inspection Equipment, 163
  Selection of Raw Material, 159
  Selection of Tools, 161
  Steps, 159
Process Planning Approach, 168
  Generative CAPP, 172
  Knowledge Based, 174
  Manual, 168
  Variant CAPP, 169
Product Design Process, 17
Product Life Cycle, 578
Product Structure, 408
Protocol, 586

Pull System, 438
Purchasing, 461
Push System, 438

QFD (Quality Function Deployment), 133, 350
  Product Planning Phase, 133
  Part Deployment Phase, 138
  Process Deployment Phase, 139
  Production Deployment Phase, 140
Quality, 349
  Cost, 351
  Culture, 464
  Dimensions, 350
  Improvement Framework, 352
  Loss, 354
  Principle of, 463

Robot, 7, 315, 558
  Application, 338
  Classification, 315
  Continuous Path Control, 317
  Economic Justification, 344
  Hand, 307
  Joint Space, 318
  Motion Analysis, 317
  Multi Machine Cell, 340
  Point To Point Control, 316
  Reach, 317
  Repeatability, 310
  Sequencing, 558
  Single Machine Cell, 338
  World Space, 318
Robotic Joint, 310
  Revolving Joint, 311
  Rotational Joint, 311
  Rotational Movement, 310
  Twisting Joint, 311
  Vertical Movement, 310
RCA (Robot Industries Association), 303
Robot Programming, 329
Robust Design, 132, 358
  Between Product Noise, 360
  Controllable Factors, 360
  Inner Noise, 360
  Noise Factors, 360
  Outer Noise, 360
  Uncontrollable Factors, 360

Scanner, 421
Scheduling, 615
Sequential Engineering, 104, 111, 115
Serial Engineering, 104, 111, 115
Shop Floor Control, 418
Simulation, 560
  Activity Cycle Time, 562
  Entities, 562
Single Linkage Clustering Algorithm, 493
Solid Modeling, 75
  Analytical Solid, 81
  BREP, 75
  Cell Decomposition, 81
  CSG, 75
  Sweep, 81
SPC (Statistical Process Control), 349, 372
  Cause Effect Diagram, 374
  Check Sheet, 373
  Defect Concentration Diagram, 375
  Histogram, 373
  Pareto Chart, 374
  Scatter Diagram, 375
Spray Painting, 341
SPT (Shortest Processing Time), 425
SQL (Structured Query Language), 604
STEP, 95
Surface Modeling, 67
  Entities, 68
  Plane Surface, 68
  Representation, 69
  Ruled Surface, 68

Taguchi Method, 253
  Parameter Design, 353
  Signal-To-Noise Ratio, 361
  System Design, 353
  Tolerance Design, 353
Taguchi Loss Function, 354
  Larger-the-Better, 356
  Nominal-the-Best, 356
  Smaller-the-Better, 356
TCP/IP, 588
Tolerance Analysis, 92
Tool Allocation, 548
  EDD Rule, 551
  LNT Heuristic, 551
  SNT Heuristic, 550
Tool Management, 545
TOP (Technical and Office Protocol), 588
Toyota Production System, 435
TQC (Total Quality Control), 463
Turning Operation, 153

Value Engineering, 132
VAN (Value Added Network), 627
Variational Design, 86

WAN (Wide Area Network), 581
Welding, 340
Wire Frame Modeling, 46
  Modeling Analytic Curves, 49
  Modeling Entities, 47
  Modeling Limitations, 46

X-Share, 619

CPSIA information can be obtained
at www.ICGtesting.com
Printed in the USA
BVHW010402221121
622069BV00032B/215

9 780471 585176